MrExcel
LIBRARY

Excel® 2016 Formulas and Functions

Paul McFedries

800 East 96th Street
Indianapolis, Indiana 46240 USA

Contents at a Glance

Excel® 2016 Formulas and Functions

Copyright © 2016 by Pearson Education, Inc.

ISBN-13: 978-0-7897-5564-3
ISBN-10: 0-7897-5564-5

Library of Congress Control Number: 2015944776

Printed in the United States of America

First Printing: October 2015

Trademarks

All terms mentioned in this book that are known to be trademarks or service marks have been appropriately capitalized. Que Publishing cannot attest to the accuracy of this information. Use of a term in this book should not be regarded as affecting the validity of any trademark or service mark.

Cover design by Chuti Prasertsith
Cover graphic by ©foxie/ShutterStock

Warning and Disclaimer

Special Sales

For information about buying this title in bulk quantities, or for special sales opportunities (which may include electronic versions; custom cover designs; and content particular to your business, training goals, marketing focus, or branding interests), please contact our corporate sales department at corpsales@pearsoned.com or (800) 382-3419.

For government sales inquiries, please contact governmentsales@pearsoned.com.

For questions about sales outside the U.S., please contact international@pearsoned.com.

Editor-in-Chief
Greg Wiegand

Acquisitions Editor
Michelle Newcomb

Development Editor
Joyce Neilsen

Managing Editor
Kristy Hart

Senior Project Editor
Lori Lyons

Technical Editor
Bob Umlas

Copy Editor
Kitty Wilson

Indexer
Tim Wright

Proofreader
Gill Editorial Services

Editorial Assistant
Kristen Watterson

Compositor
Nonie Ratcliff

Cover Designer
Chuti Prasertsith

Contents

PART I: MASTERING EXCEL RANGES AND FORMULAS

PART II: HARNESSING THE POWER OF FUNCTIONS

PART III: BUILDING BUSINESS MODELS

PART IV: BUILDING FINANCIAL FORMULAS

About the Author

Paul McFedries is an Excel expert and full-time technical writer. Paul has been authoring computer books since 1991 and has more than 85 books to his credit, which combined have sold more than 4 million copies worldwide. His titles include the Que Publishing books *My Office 2016*, *Windows 10 In Depth* (with coauthor Brian Knittel), and *PCs for Grownups*, as well as the Sams Publishing book *Windows 7 Unleashed*. Paul is also the proprietor of Word Spy (www.wordspy.com), a website devoted to *lexpionage*, the sleuthing of new words and phrases that have entered the English language. Please drop by Paul's personal website at www.mcfedries.com or follow Paul on Twitter, at twitter.com/wordspy.

Dedication

To Karen

Acknowledgments

Substitute damn every time you're inclined to write very; your editor will delete it and the writing will be just as it should be.

—Mark Twain

I didn't follow Mark Twain's advice in this book (the word *very* appears throughout), but if my writing still appears "just as it should be," then it's because of the keen minds and sharp linguistic eyes of the editors at Que. Near the front of the book you'll find a long list of the hard-working professionals whose fingers made it into this particular paper pie. However, there are a few folks I worked with directly, so I'd like to single them out for extra credit. A big, heaping helping of thanks goes out to acquisitions editor Michelle Newcomb, development editors Todd Brakke and Joyce Nielsen, project editor Lori Lyons, copy editor Kitty Wilson, compositor Nonie Ratcliff, and technical editor Bob Umlas.

We Want to Hear from You!

As the reader of this book, *you* are our most important critic and commentator. We value your opinion and want to know what we're doing right, what we could do better, what areas you'd like to see us publish in, and any other words of wisdom you're willing to pass our way.

We welcome your comments. You can email or write to let us know what you did or didn't like about this book—as well as what we can do to make our books better.

Please note that we cannot help you with technical problems related to the topic of this book.

When you write, please be sure to include this book's title and author as well as your name and email address. We will carefully review your comments and share them with the author and editors who worked on the book.

Email: feedback@quepublishing.com

Mail: Que Publishing
            ATTN: Reader Feedback
            800 East 96th Street
            Indianapolis, IN 46240 USA

Reader Services

Visit our website and register this book at quepublishing.com/register for convenient access to any updates, downloads, or errata that might be available for this book.

INTRODUCTION

The old 80/20 rule for software—that 80% of a program's users use only 20% of a program's features—doesn't apply to Microsoft Excel. Instead, this program probably operates under what could be called the 95/5 rule: Ninety-five percent of Excel users use a mere 5% of the program's power. On the other hand, most people *know* that they could be getting more out of Excel if they could only get a leg up on building formulas and using functions. Unfortunately, this side of Excel appears complex and intimidating to the uninitiated, shrouded as it is in the mysteries of mathematics, finance, and impenetrable spreadsheet jargon.

If this sounds like the situation you find yourself in, and if you're a businessperson who *needs* to use Excel as an everyday part of your job, you've come to the right book. In *Excel 2016 Formulas and Functions*, I demystify the building of worksheet formulas and present the most useful of Excel's many functions in an accessible, jargon-free way. This book not only takes you through Excel's intermediate and advanced formula-building features but also tells you *why* these features are useful to you and shows you *how* to use them in everyday situations and real-world models. This book does all this with no-nonsense, step-by-step tutorials and lots of practical, useful examples aimed directly at business users.

Even if you've never been able to get Excel to do much beyond storing data and adding a couple of numbers, you'll find this book to your liking. I show you how to build useful, powerful formulas from the ground up, so no experience with Excel formulas and functions is necessary.

What's in the Book

This book isn't meant to be read from cover to cover, although you're certainly free to do just that if the mood strikes you. Instead, most of the chapters are set up as self-contained units that you can dip into at will to extract whatever nuggets of information you need. However, if you're a relatively new Excel user, I suggest starting with Chapters 1, "Getting the Most Out of Ranges," 2, "Using Range Names," 3, "Building Basic Formulas," and 6, "Understanding Functions," to ensure that you have a thorough grounding in the fundamentals of Excel ranges, formulas, and functions.

The book is divided into four main parts. To give you the big picture before diving in, here's a summary of what you'll find in each part:

- **Part I, "Mastering Excel Ranges and Formulas"**—The five chapters in Part I tell you just about everything you need to know about building formulas in Excel. Starting with a thorough look at ranges (crucial for mastering formulas), this part also discusses operators, expressions, advanced formula features, and formula-troubleshooting techniques.

- **Part II, "Harnessing the Power of Functions"**—Functions take your formulas to the next level, and you'll learn all about them in Part II. After you see how to use functions in your formulas, you'll examine the eight main function categories—text, logical, information, lookup, date, time, math, and statistical. In each case, I tell you how to use the functions and give you lots of practical examples that show you how you can use the functions in everyday business situations.

- **Part III, "Building Business Models"**—The five chapters in Part III are all business, as they examine various facets of building useful and robust business models. You'll learn how to analyze data with Excel tables and PivotTables, how to use what-if analysis and Excel's Goal Seek and scenarios features, how to use powerful regression-analysis techniques to track trends and make forecasts, and how to use the amazing Solver feature to solve complex problems.

- **Part IV, "Building Financial Formulas"**—The book finishes with more business goodies related to performing financial wizardry with Excel. You'll learn techniques and functions for amortizing loans, analyzing investments, and using discounting for business case and cash-flow analysis.

> **NOTE** You can download this chapter's sample workbooks at www.mcfedries. com/books/book.php?title=excel-2016-formulas-and-functions.

This Book's Special Features

Excel 2016 Formulas and Functions is designed to give you the information you need without making you wade through ponderous explanations and interminable technical background.

To make your life easier, this book includes various features and conventions that help you get the most out of the book and Excel itself:

- **Steps**—Throughout the book, each Excel task is summarized in step-by-step procedures.
- **Things you type**—Whenever I suggest that you type something, what you type appears in a **bold** font.
- **Commands**—I use the following style for Excel menu commands: File, Open. This means that you pull down the File menu and select the Open command.
- **Dialog box controls**—Dialog box controls have underlined accelerator keys: Close.
- **Functions**—Excel worksheet functions appear in capital letters and are followed by parentheses: SUM(). When I list the arguments you can use with a function, they appear in italics to indicate that they're placeholders you replace with actual values; also, optional arguments appear surrounded by square brackets: CELL(*info_type* [, *reference*]).
- **Code-continuation character (➡)**—When a formula is too long to fit on one line of this book, it's broken at a convenient place, and the code-continuation character appears at the beginning of the next line.

This book also uses the following boxes to draw your attention to important (or merely interesting) information.

> **NOTE**
> The Note box presents asides that give you more information about the topic under discussion. These tidbits provide extra insights that give you a better understanding of the task at hand.

> **TIP**
> The Tip box tells you about Excel methods that are easier, faster, or more efficient than the standard methods.

> **CAUTION**
> The all-important Caution box tells you about potential accidents waiting to happen. There are always ways to mess things up when you're working with computers. These boxes help you avoid at least some of the pitfalls.

→ These cross-reference elements point you to related material elsewhere in the book.

> You'll find these case studies throughout the book. They're designed to apply what you've learned to projects and real-world examples.

Getting the Most Out of Ranges

Other than performing data-entry chores, you probably spend most of your Excel life working with ranges in some way. Whether you're copying, moving, formatting, naming, or filling them, ranges are a big part of Excel's day-to-day operations. And why not? After all, working with a range of cells is a lot easier than working with each cell individually. For example, suppose that you want to know the average of a column of numbers running from B1 to B30. You *could* enter all 30 cells as arguments in the AVERAGE function, but I'm assuming that you have a life to lead away from your computer screen. Typing =AVERAGE(B1:B30) is decidedly quicker (and probably more accurate).

In other words, ranges save time, and they save wear and tear on your typing fingers. But there's more to ranges than that. Ranges are powerful tools that can unlock the hidden depths of Excel. So, the more you know about ranges, the more you'll get out of your Excel investment, particularly when it comes to building formulas. This chapter takes you beyond the range routine and shows you some techniques for taking full advantage of Excel's range capabilities.

Advanced Range-Selection Techniques

As you work with Excel, you'll come across three situations when you'll need to select a cell range:

- When a dialog box field requires a range input
- While entering a function argument
- Before selecting a command that uses a range input

In a dialog box field or function argument, the most straightforward way to select a range is to enter the range coordinates by hand. You do this by typing the address of the upper-left cell (called the *anchor cell*), followed by a colon and then the address of the lower-right cell. To use this method, either you must be able to see the range you want to select or you must know in advance the range coordinates you want. Because this is often not the case, most people don't type the range coordinates directly; instead, they select ranges using either the mouse or the keyboard.

This chapter assumes that you know the basic, garden-variety range-selection techniques. Therefore, the next few sections show you a few advanced techniques that can make your selection chores faster and easier.

Mouse Range-Selection Tricks

Keep these handy techniques in mind when using a mouse to select a range:

- When selecting a rectangular, contiguous range, if you select the wrong lower-right corner, your range will be either too big or too small. To fix it, hold down the Shift key and click the correct lower-right cell. The range adjusts automatically.

- After selecting a large range, you'll often no longer see the active cell because you may have scrolled it off the screen. If you need to see the active cell before continuing, you can either use the scroll bars to bring it into view or press Ctrl+Backspace.

- You can use Excel's Extend mode as an alternative method for using the mouse to select a rectangular, contiguous range. Click the upper-left cell of the range you want to select, press F8 to enter Extend mode (you see "Extend Selection" in the status bar), and then click the lower-right cell of the range. Excel selects the entire range. Press F8 again to turn off Extend mode.

- If the cells you want to work with are scattered willy-nilly throughout the sheet, you need to combine them into a noncontiguous range. The secret to defining a noncontiguous range is to hold down the Ctrl key while selecting the cells. That is, you first select a cell or range you want to include in the noncontiguous range, press and hold down the Ctrl key, and then select the other cells or rectangular ranges you want to include in the noncontiguous range.

> **CAUTION**
>
> When you're selecting a noncontiguous range, always press and hold down the Ctrl key after you've selected your first cell or range. Otherwise, Excel includes the currently selected cell or range as part of the noncontiguous range. This action could create a circular reference in a function if you are defining the range as one of the function's arguments.

→ If you're not sure what a "circular reference" is, **see** "Fixing Circular References," **p. 118**.

Keyboard Range-Selection Tricks

Excel comes with a couple of tricks to make selecting a range via the keyboard easier or more efficient:

■ If you want to select a contiguous range that contains data, there's an easy way to select the entire range: Select any cell within the range and then press Ctrl+* or Ctrl+A. (For the latter, if you then press Ctrl+A a second time, Excel selects the entire sheet.)

> **CAUTION**
>
> The Ctrl+A behavior in Excel 2013 and later is actually more bizarre than I've let on so far. Pressing Ctrl+A twice to select the entire sheet works only if the current cell is within a range that contains data *or* if the current cell is between two ranges that have only a single column or row between them. If the current cell is one row above or one column to the left of a range with data, pressing Ctrl+A selects the empty row or column and the range but pressing Ctrl+A again does nothing. If the current cell is not adjacent to a range or has no data to the right or below, then pressing Ctrl+A selects the entire sheet.

■ To select a contiguous range where the current cell becomes the upper-left corner of the selection, press Ctrl+Shift+End.

■ If the range you select is so large that all the cells don't fit on the screen, you can scroll through the selected cells by activating the Scroll Lock key, if your keyboard has one. ("Scroll Lock" appears in the status bar.) When Scroll Lock is on, pressing the arrow keys (or Page Up and Page Down) scrolls you through the cells while keeping the selection intact.

Working with 3D Ranges

A *3D range* is a range selected on multiple worksheets. This is a powerful concept because it means that you can select a range on two or more sheets and then enter data, apply formatting, or give a command, and the operation will affect all the ranges simultaneously. This is useful when you're working with a multisheet model where some or all the labels are the same on each sheet. For example, in a workbook of expense calculations where each sheet details the expenses from a different division or department, you might want the label "Expenses" to appear in cell A1 on each sheet.

To create a 3D range, first you need to group the worksheets you want to work with. To select multiple sheets, use any of the following techniques:

■ To select adjacent sheets, click the tab of the first sheet, hold down the Shift key, and click the tab of the last sheet.

■ To select nonadjacent sheets, click the tab of a sheet you want to include in the group, hold down the Ctrl key, and click the tab of each additional sheet you want to include in the group.

■ To select all the sheets in a workbook, right-click any sheet tab and click the Select All Sheets command.

When you've selected your sheets, each tab is highlighted, and "[Group]" appears in the workbook title bar. To ungroup the sheets, click a tab that isn't in the group. Alternatively, you can right-click one of the group's tabs and select the Ungroup Sheets command from the shortcut menu.

With the sheets now grouped, you create your 3D range by switching to any of the grouped sheets and then selecting a range. Excel selects the same cells in all the other sheets in the group.

You can also type in a 3D range by hand when, say, entering a formula. Here's the general format for a 3D reference:

```
FirstSheet:LastSheet!ULCorner:LRCorner
```

Here, FirstSheet is the name of the first sheet in the 3D range, LastSheet is the name of the last sheet, and ULCorner and LRCorner define the cell range you want to work with on each sheet. (Note that *UL* refers to *Upper Left* and *LR* refers to *Lower Right*.) For example, to specify the range A1:E10 on worksheets Sheet1, Sheet2, and Sheet3, use the following reference:

```
Sheet1:Sheet3!A1:E10
```

┌─ C A U T I O N ──┐

If one or both of the sheet names used in the 3D reference contain a space, be sure to enclose the sheet names in single quotation marks, as in this example:

```
'First Quarter:Fourth Quarter'!A1:F16
```

└──┘

┌─ C A U T I O N ──┐

After you're finished with the 3D range, be sure to ungroup the worksheets so that you don't accidentally overwrite data or make other inadvertent changes in the grouped sheets.

└──┘

You normally use 3D references in worksheet functions that accept them. These functions include AVERAGE(), COUNT(), COUNTA(), MAX(), MIN(), PRODUCT(), STDEV(), STDEVP(), SUM(), VAR(), and VARP(). (You'll learn about these and other functions in Part II, "Harnessing the Power of Functions.")

Selecting a Range Using Go To

For very large ranges, Excel's Go To command comes in handy. You normally use the Go To command to jump quickly to a specific cell address or range name. The following steps show you how to exploit this power to select a range:

1. Select the upper-left cell of the range.

2. Select Home, Find & Select, Go To (or press F5 or Ctrl+G). The Go To dialog box appears, as shown in Figure 1.1.

Figure 1.1
You can use the Go To dialog box to easily select a large range.

3. Use the Reference text box to enter the cell address of the lower-right corner of the range.

> **TIP** You also can select a range using Go To by entering the range coordinates in the Reference text box.

4. Hold down the Shift key and click OK. Excel selects the range.

> **TIP** Another way to select very large ranges is to select View, Zoom and click a reduced magnification in the Zoom dialog box (say, 50% or 25%; you can also click and drag the Zoom slider in the status bar or hold down Ctrl and scroll the mouse wheel). You can then use this "big picture" view to select your range.

Using the Go To Special Dialog Box

You normally select cells according to their position within a worksheet. However, Excel includes a powerful feature that enables you to select cells according to their contents or other special properties. If you select Home, Find & Select, Go To Special (or click the Special button in the Go To dialog box), the Go To Special dialog box appears, as shown in Figure 1.2.

Figure 1.2
Use the Go To Special dialog box to select cells according to their contents, formula relationships, and more.

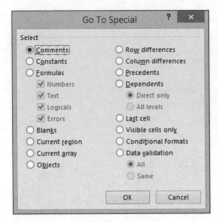

Selecting Cells by Type

The Go To Special dialog box contains many options, but only four of them enable you to select cells according to the type of contents they contain. Table 1.1 summarizes these four options. (The next few sections discuss the other Go To Special options.)

Table 1.1   Options for Selecting a Cell by Type

Option	Description
Comments	Selects all cells that contain a comment. (You can also select Home, Find & Select, Comments.)
Constants	Selects all cells that contain constants of the types specified in one or more of the check boxes listed under the Formulas option. (You can also select Home, Find & Select, Constants.)
Formulas	Selects all cells containing formulas that produce results of the types specified in one or more of the following four check boxes (you can also select Home, Find & Select, Formulas): **Numbers**—Selects all cells that contain numbers. **Text**—Selects all cells that contain text. **Logicals**—Selects all cells that contain logical values. **Errors**—Selects all cells that contain errors.
Blanks	Selects all cells that are blank.

Selecting Adjacent Cells

The Go To Special dialog box gives you two options for selecting cells adjacent to the active cell. Click the Current Region option to select a rectangular range that extends to the right from the active cell to (but not including) the next empty column and down from the active cell to (but not including) the next empty row.

If the active cell is part of an array, click the Current Array option to select all the cells in the array.

→ For an in-depth discussion of Excel arrays, **see** "Working with Arrays," **p. 87**.

Selecting Cells by Differences

Excel also enables you to select cells by comparing rows or columns of data and selecting only those cells that are different. The following steps show you how it's done:

1. Select the rows or columns you want to compare. (Make sure that the active cell is in the row or column with the comparison values you want to use.)

2. Display the Go To Special dialog box and click one of the following options:
    * **Row Differences**—This option uses the data in the active cell's column as the comparison values. Excel selects the cells in the corresponding rows that are different.
    * **Column Differences**—This option uses the data in the active cell's row as the comparison values. Excel selects the cells in the corresponding columns that are different.

3. Click OK.

For example, Figure 1.3 shows a selected range of numbers. The values in column B are the budget numbers assigned to all the company's divisions; the values in columns C and D are the actual numbers achieved by the East Division and the West Division, respectively. Suppose you want to know the items for which a division ended up either under or over the budget. In other words, you want to compare the numbers in columns C and D with those in column B, and then you want to select the ones in C and D that are different. Because you're comparing rows of data, you'd select the Row Differences option from the Go To Special dialog box. Figure 1.4 shows the results.

Figure 1.3
Before using the Go To Special feature that compares rows (or columns) of data, select the entire range of cells involved in the comparison.

⊿	A	B	C	D
1		Comparison Values	Cells to be Checked for Differences	
2				
3		Budget Values	Actual Values	
4	Code	All Divisions	East Division	West Division
5	EX01	45	44	45
6	EX02	67	67	70
7	EX03	34	30	34
8	EX04	87	87	87
9	EX05	41	41	45
10	EX06	37	37	37
11	EX07	98	98	98
12	EX08	56	55	56
13	EX09	43	40	46
14	EX10	22	22	22
15	EX11	14	14	15
16	EX12	76	72	76
17	EX13	61	61	61
18				

Sheet1 | Sheet2 | Sheet3 | ⊕

Figure 1.4
After running the Row Differences option, Excel shows those rows in columns C and D that are different from the value in column B.

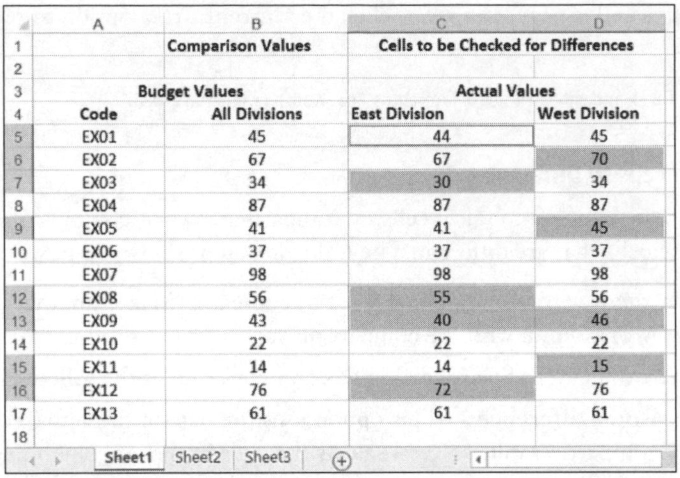

	A	B	C	D
1		Comparison Values	Cells to be Checked for Differences	
2				
3		Budget Values	Actual Values	
4	Code	All Divisions	East Division	West Division
5	EX01	45	44	45
6	EX02	67	67	70
7	EX03	34	30	34
8	EX04	87	87	87
9	EX05	41	41	45
10	EX06	37	37	37
11	EX07	98	98	98
12	EX08	56	55	56
13	EX09	43	40	46
14	EX10	22	22	22
15	EX11	14	14	15
16	EX12	76	72	76
17	EX13	61	61	61
18				

Sheet1 | Sheet2 | Sheet3 | (+)

> **NOTE** You can download this chapter's sample workbooks at www.mcfedries.com/books/book. php?title=excel-2016-formulas-and-functions.

Selecting Cells by Reference

If a cell contains a formula, Excel defines the cell's *precedents* as those cells that the formula refers to. For example, if cell A4 contains the formula =SUM(A1:A3), cells A1, A2, and A3 are the precedents of A4. A *direct* precedent is a cell referred to explicitly in the formula. In the preceding example, A1, A2, and A3 are direct precedents of A4. An *indirect* precedent is a cell referred to by a precedent. For example, if cell A1 contains the formula =B3*2, cell B3 is an indirect precedent of cell A4.

Excel also defines a cell's dependents as those cells with a formula that refers to the cell. In the preceding example, cell A4 would be a dependent of cell A1. Like precedents, dependents can be direct or indirect.

> **NOTE** Think of dependents this way: The value that appears in cell A4 *depends on* the value that's entered in cell A1.

The Go To Special dialog box enables you to select precedents and dependents as described in these steps:

1. Select the range you want to work with.
2. Display the Go To Special dialog box.
3. Click either the Precedents option or the Dependents option.

4. Click the Direct Only option to select only direct precedents or dependents. If you need to select both the direct and the indirect precedents or dependents, click the All Levels option.

5. Click OK.

Other Go To Special Options

The Go To Special dialog box includes a few more options to help you in your range-selection chores:

Option	Description
Last Cell	Selects the last cell in the worksheet (that is, the lower-right corner) that contains data or formatting.
Visible Cells Only	Selects only cells that are unhidden.
Conditional Formats	Selects only cells that contain conditional formatting. (You can also select Home, Find & Select, Conditional Formatting.)
Data Validation	Selects cells that contain data-validation rules. (You can also select Home, Find & Select, Data Validation.) If you click All, Excel selects every cell with a data-validation rule; if you click Same, Excel selects every cell that has the same validation rule as the current cell.

→ To learn about conditional formatting, **see** "Applying Conditional Formatting to a Range," **p. 25**.

→ To learn about data validation, **see** "Applying Data-Validation Rules to Cells," **p. 100**.

Shortcut Keys for Selecting via Go To

Table 1.2 lists the shortcut keys you can use to run many of the Go To Special operations.

Table 1.2 Shortcut Keys for Selecting Precedents and Dependents	
Shortcut Key	**Selects**
Ctrl+*	Current region (you can also press Ctrl+A)
Ctrl+/	Current array
Ctrl+\	Row differences
Ctrl+|	Column differences
Ctrl+[	Direct precedents
Ctrl+]	Direct dependents

Shortcut Key	Selects
Ctrl+{	All levels of precedents
Ctrl+}	All levels of dependents
Ctrl+End	The last cell
Alt+;	Visible cells

Data Entry in a Range

If you know in advance which range you'll use for data entry, you can save yourself some time and keystrokes by selecting the range before you begin. As you enter your data in each cell, use the keys listed in Table 1.3 to navigate the range.

Table 1.3   Navigation Keys for a Selected Range

Key	Result
Enter	Moves down one row.
Shift+Enter	Moves up one row.
Tab	Moves right one column.
Shift+Tab	Moves left one column.
Ctrl+. (period)	Moves from corner to corner in the range.
Ctrl+Alt+right arrow	Moves to the next range in a noncontiguous selection.
Ctrl+Alt+left arrow	Moves to the preceding range in a noncontiguous selection.

The advantage of this technique is that the active cell never leaves the range. For example, if you press Enter after adding data to a cell in the last row of the range, the active cell moves back to the top row and over one column.

Filling a Range

If you need to fill a range with a particular value or formula, Excel gives you two methods:

■ Select the range you want to fill, type the value or formula, and press Ctrl+Enter. Excel fills the entire range with whatever you entered in the formula bar. If you entered a formula with relative cell references, Excel adjusts those references as it fills the range.

■ Enter the initial value or formula, select the range you want to fill (including the initial cell), and select Home, Fill. Then select the appropriate command from the submenu that appears. For example, if you're filling a range down from the initial cell, select the

Down command. If you've selected multiple sheets, use Home, Fill, Across Worksheets to fill the range in each worksheet.

> **TIP** Press Ctrl+D to select Home, Fill, Down; press Ctrl+R to select Home, Fill, Right.

Using the Fill Handle

The *fill handle* is the small green square in the lower-right corner of the active cell or range. This versatile little tool can do many useful things, including create a series of text or numeric values and fill, clear, insert, and delete ranges. The next few sections show you how to use the fill handle to perform each of these operations.

Using AutoFill to Create Text and Numeric Series

Worksheets often use text series (such as January, February, March, or Sunday, Monday, Tuesday) and numeric series (such as 1, 3, 5, or 2014, 2015, 2016). Instead of entering these series by hand, you can use the fill handle to create them automatically. This handy feature is called AutoFill, and the following steps show you how it works:

1. For a text series, select the first cell of the range you want to use and enter the initial value. For a numeric series, enter the first two values and then select both cells.

2. Position the mouse pointer over the fill handle. The pointer changes to a plus sign (+).

3. Click and drag the mouse pointer until the gray border encompasses the range you want to fill. If you're not sure where to stop, keep your eye on the pop-up value that appears near the mouse pointer and shows you the series value of the last selected cell.

4. Release the mouse button. Excel fills in the range with the series.

When you release the mouse button after using AutoFill, Excel not only fills in the series but also displays the Auto Fill Options button. To see the options, move your mouse pointer over the button and then click the downward-pointing arrow to drop down the list. The options you see depend on the type of series you created. (See "Creating a Series," later in this chapter, for details on some of the options you might see.) However, you'll usually see at least the following five:

- **Copy Cells**—Choose this option to fill the range by copying the original cell or cells.
- **Fill Series**—Choose this option to get the default series fill.
- **Fill Formatting Only**—Choose this option to apply only the original cell's formatting to the selected range.
- **Fill Without Formatting**—Choose this option to fill the range with the series data but without the formatting of the original cell.
- **Flash Fill**—Choose this option to fill the range based on the pattern you specified in the original cell. See "Flash-Filling a Range," later in this chapter, for the details.

Figure 1.5 shows several series created with the fill handle. (The shaded cells are the initial fill values.) In particular, notice that Excel increments any text value that includes a numeric component, such as Quarter 1 (see column E) and Customer 1001 (see column F).

Figure 1.5

Some sample series created with the fill handle. Shaded entries are the initial fill values.

Auto Fill Options list

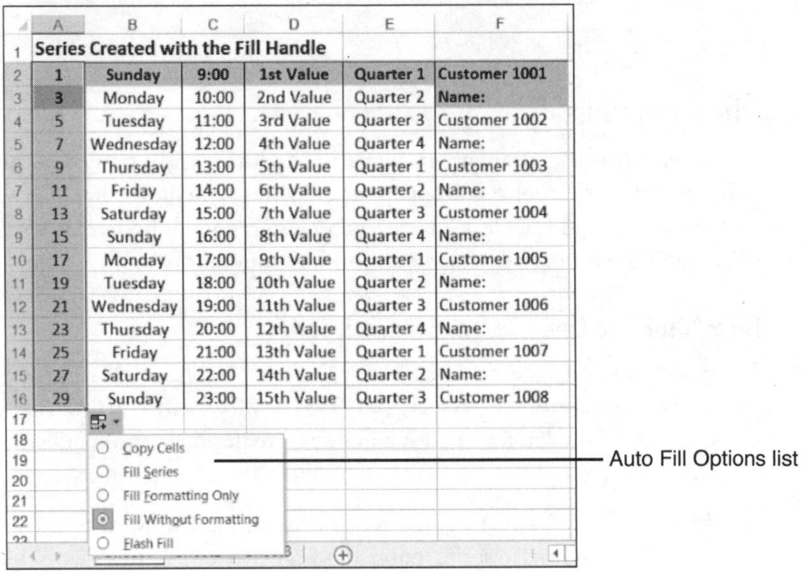

Keep the following guidelines in mind when using the fill handle to create a series:

- Clicking and dragging the handle down or to the right increments the values. Clicking and dragging up or to the left decrements the values.

- The fill handle recognizes standard abbreviations such as Jan (January) and Sun (Sunday).

- To vary the series interval for a text series, enter the first two values of the series and then select both of them before clicking and dragging. For example, entering **1st** and **3rd** produces the series 1st, 3rd, 5th, and so on.

- If you use three or more numbers as the initial values for the fill handle series, Excel creates a "best fit" or "trend" line.

→ To learn more about using Excel for trend analysis, **see** Chapter 16, "Using Regression to Track Trends and Make Forecasts," p. 371.

Creating a Custom AutoFill List

As you saw in the previous section, Excel recognizes certain values, such as January, Sunday, and Quarter 1, as parts of larger lists. When you drag the fill handle from a cell containing one of these values, Excel fills the cells with the appropriate series. However, you're not stuck with just the few lists that Excel recognized out of the box. Instead, you're free to define your own AutoFill lists, as described in the following steps:

1. Select File, Options to display the Excel Options dialog box.
2. Click Advanced and then click Edit Custom Lists to open the Custom Lists dialog box.
3. In the Custom Lists box, click New List. An insertion point appears in the List Entries box.
4. Type an item from your list into the List Entries box and press Enter. Repeat this step for each item. (Make sure you add the items in the order in which you want them to appear in the series.) Figure 1.6 shows an example.

> **TIP**
> If you already have the list in a worksheet range, don't bother entering each item by hand. Instead, activate the Import List from Cells edit box and enter a reference to the range (either by typing the reference or selecting the cells directly on the worksheet). Click the Import button to add the list to the Custom Lists box.

Figure 1.6
Use the Custom Lists tab to create your own lists that Excel can fill in automatically, using the AutoFill feature.

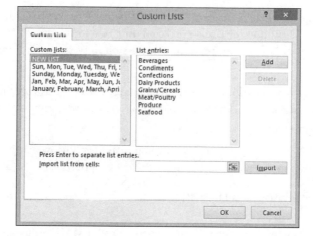

5. Click Add to add the list to the Custom Lists box.
6. Click OK and then click OK again to return to the worksheet.

> **NOTE**
> If you need to delete a custom list, select it in the Custom Lists box and then click Delete.

Using the Fill Handle to Fill a Range

You can use the fill handle to fill a range with a value or formula. To do this, enter your initial value or formula and then click and drag the fill handle over the destination range. When you release the mouse button, Excel fills the range.

Note that if the initial cell contains a formula with relative references, Excel adjusts the references accordingly. For example, suppose the initial cell contains the formula =A1. If you fill down, the next cell will contain the formula =A2, the next will contain =A3, and so on.

➔ For information on relative references, **see** "Understanding Relative Reference Format," **p. 62**.

Flash-Filling a Range

If you've inherited workbooks from someone else or if you've imported data from external data sources, you've probably come across your fair share of data that was either structured or formatted (or both) in such a way that it was either difficult to read or difficult to work with. It could be mainframe data that arrives as all-uppercase letters, dates that appear in non-date formats, phone numbers that don't have dashes or parentheses, or fields that combine multiple pieces of data (such as first names and last names).

One way to tackle such data is to simply reenter it by hand in the structure or format you prefer or require. That's fine for a few records, but it gets tedious and time-consuming for dozens of records, and it becomes pretty much mission impossible for hundreds or thousands of records.

The preferred way to tackle these large-scale changes is to forge a worksheet formula that does the heavy lifting for you. There are many examples of these types of formulas in this book. Here are just a few:

■ Converting names or other text from all-uppercase (or all-lowercase) to sentence case (where just the first letter of each name or word is uppercase)

➔ **See** "Converting Text to Sentence Case," **p. 153**.

■ Converting a date in a non-date format such as YYYYMMDD (for example, 20160823) to a date format such as M/D/YYYY (for example, 8/23/2016)

➔ **See** "A Date-Conversion Formula," **p. 154**.

■ Extracting just first names or just last names from a range where each cell contains a full name

➔ **See** "Extracting a First Name or Last Name," **p. 156**.

These formulas work great, but setting them up and getting them right can take a bit of work. Fortunately, creating such formulas may now be a thing of the past, thanks to a remarkable feature (found in Excel 2013 and later) called Flash Fill. Given a column of original data, if you use the first cell in the next column to enter the corrected data (which could be data extracted from the original cell or the same data formatted in a different way) and then begin the same data correction in the second cell, Flash Fill "recognizes" what you're doing and *automatically* fills in the rest of the column with the corrected data. This sounds like voodoo, I know, but it really works.

Here's the general procedure:

1. Make sure the column of original data has a heading.
2. Type a heading for the column of new data.
3. Type the first value you want in the first cell of the new column.
4. In the second cell of the new column, begin typing the second value. Flash Fill recognizes the pattern and displays suggestions for the rest of the column.
5. Press Enter. Excel flash-fills the column with the new data.

Let's look at a few examples. Figure 1.7 is a composite image that shows five flash-filled ranges:

- Column A contains a list of all-uppercase company names. In column B, I used cell B2 to type the sentence-case version of the text in cell A2 and then used cell B3 to begin typing the sentence-case version of the text in cell A3. After I typed **An**, Flash Fill recognized the pattern and displayed its suggestions—sentence-case versions of all the other cells in column A—which you see from cell B4 down.

- Column D contains a list of full names, where each cell contains the first name, middle initial, and last name. In cell E2, I typed just the first name from cell D2, and then in cell E3 I began typing the first name from cell D3. Again, Flash Fill recognized the pattern and displayed its suggestions: the first names from the rest of column D.

- In column F, I used cell F2 to type the middle initial from cell D2 (including the period). When I used cell F3 to begin typing the middle initial from cell D3, Flash Fill recognized the pattern and displayed its suggestions: the middle initials from the rest of column D.

- Column H contains a list of phone numbers without any parentheses or dashes. In cell I2, I typed the phone number from cell H2 and added the parentheses and dash. When I typed the opening parenthesis into cell I3, Flash Fill recognized the pattern and displayed its suggestions: the formatted phone numbers from the rest of column H.

- Column J contains a list of dates in YYYMMDD format. Notice, however, that you don't see any Flash Fill suggestions in column K. That's because Flash Fill works best with text or alphanumeric values, so it doesn't display its automatic suggestions for numbers, dates, or times. To make these work with Flash Fill, you have to invoke Flash Fill by hand. In this example, I first applied a custom date format (MM/DD/YYYY) to the cells in column K. I then used cells K2 and K3 to enter the first two dates in the format I wanted. Finally, I selected the range I wanted to fill (K2:K19) and selected the Data, Flash Fill command.

→ To learn how to apply a custom date format, **see** "Customizing Date and Time Formats," **p. 84.**

Figure 1.7
In this composite image, you can see that Excel's new Flash Fill feature can automatically extract or format data based on a pattern you set.

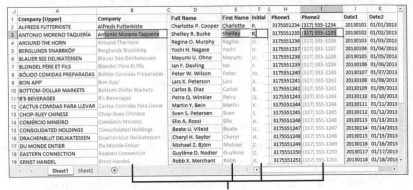

Flash Fill suggestions

> **NOTE**
> For Flash Fill's automatic suggestions to appear, you must have headings at the top of both the column of original data and the column you are using for the filled data. Also, there must not be any blank columns between the filled column and the original column, and the sample entries you make in the filled column must occur one after the other.

Creating a Series

Instead of using the fill handle to create a series, you can use Excel's Series command to gain a little more control over the whole process. Follow these steps:

1. Select the first cell you want to use for the series and then enter the starting value. If you want to create a series out of a particular pattern (such as 2, 4, 6, and so on), fill in enough cells to define the pattern.

2. Select the entire range you want to fill.

3. Select Home, Fill, Series. Excel displays the Series dialog box.

4. Either click Rows to create the series in rows, starting from the active cell, or click Columns to create the series in columns.

5. Use the Type group to click the type of series you want. You have the following options:

   - **Linear**—This option finds the next series value by adding the step value (see step 7) to the preceding value in the series.

- **Growth**—This option finds the next series value by multiplying the preceding value by the step value.
- **Date**—This option creates a series of dates based on the option you select in the Date Unit group (Day, Weekday, Month, or Year).
- **AutoFill**—This option works much like the fill handle. You can use it to extend a numeric pattern or a text series (for example, Qtr1, Qtr2, Qtr3).

6. If you want to extend a series trend, activate the Trend check box. You can use this option only with the Linear or Growth series types.

7. If you chose a Linear, Growth, or Date series type, enter a number in the Step Value box. This number is what Excel uses to increment each value in the series.

8. To place a limit on the series, enter the appropriate number in the Stop Value box.

9. Click OK. Excel fills in the series and returns you to the worksheet.

Figure 1.8 shows some sample column series. Note that the Growth series stops at cell C12 (value 128) because the next term in the series (256) is greater than the stop value of 250. The Day series fills the range with every second date (because the step value is 2). The Weekday series is slightly different: The dates are sequential, but weekends are skipped.

Figure 1.8
Some sample column series generated with the Series command.

	A	B	C	D	E	F
1	Series Type:	Linear	Growth	Date (Day)	Date (Weekday)	Date (Month)
2	Step Value:	5	2	2	1	6
3	Stop Value:	-	250			
4						
5		0	1	1/1/2016	1/1/2016	1/1/2016
6		5	2	1/3/2016	1/2/2016	7/1/2016
7		10	4	1/5/2016	1/3/2016	1/1/2017
8		15	8	1/7/2016	1/4/2016	7/1/2017
9		20	16	1/9/2016	1/7/2016	1/1/2018
10		25	32	1/11/2016	1/8/2016	7/1/2018
11		30	64	1/13/2016	1/9/2016	1/1/2019
12		35	128	1/15/2016	1/10/2016	7/1/2019
13		40		1/17/2016	1/11/2016	1/1/2020
14		45		1/19/2016	1/14/2016	7/1/2020
15						

Advanced Range Copying and Pasting

The standard Excel range-copying techniques—for example, choosing Home, Copy (or pressing Ctrl+C) and then choosing Home, Paste (or pressing Ctrl+V)—normally copy the entire contents of each cell in the range: the value or formula, the formatting, and any attached cell comments. If you like, you can tell Excel to paste only some of these attributes, you can transpose rows and columns, or you can combine the source and destination ranges arithmetically. All this is possible with Excel's Paste Special command. These techniques are outlined in the next three sections.

Pasting Selected Cell Attributes

When rearranging a worksheet, you can save time by combining cell attributes. For example, if you need to copy several formulas to a range but don't want to disturb the existing formatting, you can tell Excel to paste only the formulas.

If you want to paste only selected cell attributes, follow these steps:

1. Select and then copy the range you want to work with.
2. Select the destination range.
3. Select Home, pull down the Paste menu, and then select Paste Special. Excel displays the Paste Special dialog box, shown in Figure 1.9.

Figure 1.9
Use the Paste Special dialog box to select the cell attributes you want to paste.

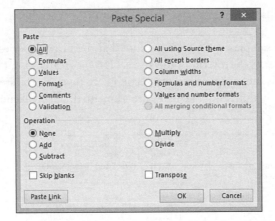

> **TIP**
> You also can display the Paste Special dialog box by pressing Ctrl+Alt+V or by right-clicking the destination range and choosing Paste Special from the shortcut menu.

4. In the Paste group, click the attribute you want to paste into the destination range:
   - **All**—Pastes all the source range's cell attributes.
   - **Formulas**—Pastes only the cell formulas. (You can also select Home, Paste, Formulas.)
   - **Values**—Converts the cell formulas to values and pastes only the values. (You can also select Home, Paste, Paste Values.)
   - **Formats**—Pastes only the cell formatting.
   - **Comments**—Pastes only the cell comments.
   - **Validation**—Pastes only the cell-validation rules.
   - **All Using Source Theme**—Pastes all the cell attributes and then formats the copied range using the theme that's applied to the copied range.

- **All Except Borders**—Pastes all the cell attributes except the cell's border formatting. (You can also select Home, Paste, No Borders.)

- **Column Widths**—Changes the widths of the destination columns to match the widths of the source columns. No data is pasted.

- **Formulas and Number Formats**—Pastes the cell formulas and numeric formatting.

- **Values and Number Formats**—Converts the cell formulas to values and pastes only the values and the numeric formats.

- **All Merging Conditional Formats**—Pastes all the cell attributes and merges the conditional formatting from the source and destination ranges.

5. If you don't want Excel to paste any blank cells included in the selection, activate the Skip Blanks check box.

6. If you want to paste only formulas that set the destination cells equal to the values of the source cells, click Paste Link. (For example, if the source cell is A1, the value of the destination cell is set to the formula =$A$1.) Otherwise, click OK to paste the range.

Combining Two Ranges Arithmetically

Excel enables you to combine two ranges arithmetically. For example, suppose you have a range of constants that you want to double. Instead of creating formulas that multiply each cell by 2 (or, even worse, doubling each cell by hand), you can place the number 2 in a cell, copy it, and then "paste" it to the range of constants using multiplication.

A more complex example would be a list of prices that you want to increase, but by varying amounts: some by $1, some by $2, some by $0.50, and so on. Again, instead of handling these increases by creating formulas or performing the arithmetic by hand, you can get Excel to do the work. In this case, you'd create a new range of values, each of which represents a price increase for the corresponding original price, so the resulting range would be the same size as the range of original prices. You then combine this new range with the old one and tell Excel to add the two ranges.

The following steps show you what to do:

1. Create the range of values you want to apply to the original range:
   - If you want to apply a single value to the original range (for example, multiplying the original values by 2), enter that value in a single cell.
   - If you want to apply multiple values to the original range, create a range of values that's the same size as the original range.

2. Select the range you created in step 1.

3. Select Home, Copy.

4. Select the range of original values.

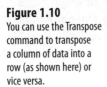

5. Select Home, click the bottom half of the Paste button, and then select Paste Special to display the Paste Special dialog box.

6. Use the following options in the Operation group to click the arithmetic operator you want to use:

   - **None**—Performs no operation.
   - **Add**—Adds the destination cells to the source cells.
   - **Subtract**—Subtracts the source cells from the destination cells.
   - **Multiply**—Multiplies the source cells by the destination cells.
   - **Divide**—Divides the destination cells by the source cells.

7. If you don't want Excel to include any blank cells in the operation, activate the Skip Blanks check box.

8. Click OK. Excel pastes the results of the operation into the destination range. Note that the results are the final values, not formulas.

Transposing Rows and Columns

If you have row data that you'd prefer to see in columns (or vice versa), you can use the Transpose command to transpose the data. Follow these steps:

1. Select and copy the source cells.

2. Select the upper-left corner of the destination range.

3. Select Home, pull down the Paste menu, and select Transpose. (If you already have the Paste Special dialog box open, activate the Transpose check box and then click OK.) Excel transposes the source range, as shown in Figure 1.10.

Figure 1.10
You can use the Transpose command to transpose a column of data into a row (as shown here) or vice versa.

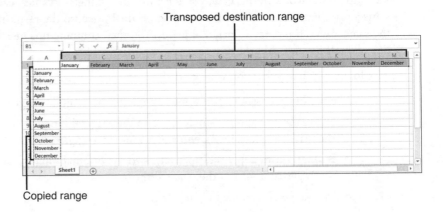

Transposed destination range

Copied range

Clearing a Range

Deleting a range actually removes the cells from the worksheet. However, if you want the cells to remain, but you want their contents or formats cleared, you can use Excel's Clear command, as described in the following steps:

1. Select the range you want to clear.

2. Select Home, Clear. Excel displays a submenu of Clear commands.

3. Select Clear All, Clear Formats, Clear Contents, Clear Comments, or Clear Hyperlinks, as appropriate.

To clear the values and formulas in a range with the fill handle, you can use either of the following two techniques:

- If you want to clear only the values and formulas in a range, select the range and then click and drag the fill handle into the range and over the cells you want to clear. Excel grays out the cells as you select them. When you release the mouse button, Excel clears the cells' values and formulas.

- If you want to scrub everything from the range (values, formulas, formats, and comments), select the range and then hold down the Ctrl key. Next, click and drag the fill handle into the range and over each cell you want to clear. Excel clears the cells when you release the mouse button.

Applying Conditional Formatting to a Range

Many Excel worksheets contain hundreds of data values. This book is designed to help you make sense of large sets of data by creating formulas, applying functions, and performing data analysis. However, there are plenty of times when you don't really want to analyze a worksheet per se. Instead, all you really want are answers to simple questions such as the following:

- Which cell values are less than 0?
- What are the top 10 values?
- Which cell values are above average, and which are below average?

These simple questions aren't easy to answer just by glancing at the worksheet, and the more numbers you're dealing with, the harder it gets. To help you "eyeball" your worksheets and answer these and similar questions, Excel lets you apply *conditional formatting* to the cells. This is a special format that Excel only applies to cells that satisfy some condition, which Excel calls a *rule*. For example, you could show all the negative values in a red font.

Creating Highlight Cells Rules

A *highlight cell* rule is one that applies a format to cells that meet specified criteria. To create a highlight cell rule, begin by choosing Home, Conditional Formatting, Highlight Cells Rules. Excel displays seven choices:

- **Greater Than**—Select this command to apply formatting to cells with values greater than the value you specify. For example, if you want to identify sales reps who increased their sales by more than 10% over last year, you'd create a column that calculates the percentage difference in yearly sales, and you'd then apply the Greater Than rule to that column to look for increases greater than 0.1.

- **Less Than**—Select this command to apply formatting to cells with values less than the value you specify. For example, if you want to recognize divisions, products, or reps whose sales fell from the previous year, you'd use this command to look for percentage or absolute differences that are less than 0.

- **Between**—Select this command to apply formatting to cells with values between the two values you specify. For example, if you have a series of fixed-income investment possibilities on a worksheet and you're only interested in medium-term investments, you'd apply this rule to highlight investments where the value in the Term column (expressed in years) is between 5 and 10.

- **Equal To**—Select this command to apply formatting to cells with values equal to the value you specify. For example, in a table of product inventory where you're interested in products that are currently out of stock, you'd apply this rule to highlight those products where the value in the On Hand column equals 0.

- **Text That Contains**—Select this command to apply formatting to cells with text values that contain the text value you specify (which is not case sensitive). For example, in a table of bonds that includes ratings where you're interested only in those bonds that are upper-medium quality or higher (A, AA, or AAA), you'd apply this rule to highlight ratings that include the letter A. (Note that this doesn't work for certain rating codes that include A in lower ratings, such as Baa and Ba.)

- **A Date Occurring**—Select this command to apply formatting to cells with date values that satisfy the condition you select: Yesterday, Today, Tomorrow, In the Last 7 Days, Next Week, and so on. For example, in a table of employee data that includes birthdays, you could apply this command to the birthdays to look for those that occur next week so you can plan celebrations ahead of time.

- **Duplicate Values**—Select this command to apply formatting to cells with values that appear more than once in the range. For example, if you have a table of account numbers, no two customers should have the same account number, so you can apply the Duplicate Values rule to those numbers to make sure they're unique. You can also format cells with unique values—values that appear only once in the range.

In each case, you see a dialog box that you use to specify the condition and the formatting that you want applied to cells that match the condition. For example, Figure 1.11 shows the

Less Than dialog box. In this case, I'm looking for cell values that are less than 0; Figure 1.12 shows the worksheet with the conditional formatting applied.

Figure 1.11
In the Highlight Cells Rules menu, select a command to display a dialog box for entering your condition, such as the Less Than dialog box shown here.

Figure 1.12
The conditional formatting rule shown in Figure 1.11 applied to the percentages in column D.

	A	B	C	D
1	**Sales Rep**	**2015**	**2016**	**% +/-**
2	Nancy Freehafer	$ 996,336	$ 960,492	-4%
3	Andrew Cencini	$ 606,731	$ 577,983	-5%
4	Jan Kotas	$ 622,781	$ 967,580	55%
5	Mariya Sergienko	$ 765,327	$ 771,399	1%
6	Steven Thorpe	$ 863,589	$ 827,213	-4%
7	Michael Neipper	$ 795,518	$ 669,394	-16%
8	Robert Zare	$ 722,740	$ 626,945	-13%
9	Laura Giussani	$ 992,059	$ 574,472	-42%
10	Anne Hellung-Larsen	$ 659,380	$ 827,932	26%
11	Kyra Harper	$ 509,623	$ 569,609	12%
12	David Ferry	$ 987,777	$ 558,601	43%
13	Paul Voyatzis	$ 685,091	$ 692,182	1%
14	Andrea Aster	$ 540,484	$ 693,762	28%
15	Charles Granek	$ 650,733	$ 823,034	26%
16	Karen Aliston	$ 509,863	$ 511,569	0%
17	Karen Hammond	$ 503,699	$ 975,455	94%
18	Vince Durbin	$ 630,263	$ 599,514	-5%
19	Paul Sellars	$ 779,722	$ 596,353	-24%
20	Gregg O'Donoghue	$ 592,802	$ 652,171	10%
21				

Highlight Cells   Top-Bottom   Data ...

Creating Top/Bottom Rules

A *top/bottom* rule is a rule that applies a format to cells that rank in the top or bottom (for numerical items, the highest or lowest) values in a range. You can select the top or bottom either as an absolute value (for example, the top 10 items) or as a percentage (for example, the bottom 25%). You can also apply formatting to cells that are above or below the average. To create a top/bottom rule, begin by choosing Home, Conditional Formatting, Top/Bottom Rules. Excel displays six choices:

- **Top 10 Items**—Select this command to apply formatting to cells with values that rank in the top X items in the range, where X is the number of items you want to see. (The default is 10.) For example, in a table of product sales, you could use this rule to see the top 50 products.

- **Top 10%**—Select this command to apply formatting to cells with values that rank in the top X percentage of items in the range, where X is the percentage you want to see. (The default is 10.) For example, in a table of sales by sales rep, you could recognize your elite performers by applying this rule to see those reps who are in the top 5%.

- **Bottom 10 Items**—Select this command to apply formatting to cells with values that rank in the bottom X items in the range, where X is the number of items you want to see. (The default is 10.) For example, if you have a table of unit sales by product, you could apply this rule to see the 20 products that sold the fewest units with an eye to either promoting those products or discontinuing them.

- **Bottom 10%**—Select this command to apply formatting to those cells with values that rank in the bottom X percentage of items in the range, where X is the percentage you want to see. (The default is 10.) For example, in a table that displays product manufacturing defects, you could apply this rule to see those products that rank in the bottom 10% and so are the most reliably produced.

- **Above Average**—Select this command to apply formatting to those cells with values that are above the average of all the values in the range. For example, in a table of investment returns, you could apply this rule to see those investments that are performing above the average for all your investments.

- **Below Average**—Select this command to apply formatting to those cells with values that are below the average of all the values in the range. For example, if you have a list of products and the margins they generate, you could apply this rule to see those that have below-average margins so that you can take steps to improve sales or reduce costs.

In each case, you see a dialog box that you use to set up the specifics of the rule. For the Top 10 Items, Top 10%, Bottom 10 Items, and Bottom 10% rules, you use the dialog box to specify the condition and the formatting you want applied to cells that match the condition. (For the Above Average and Below Average rules, you use the dialog box to specify the formatting only.) For example, Figure 1.13 shows the Top 10 Items dialog box. In this case, I'm looking for the top 10 values in the range; Figure 1.14 shows the worksheet with the conditional formatting applied.

Figure 1.13
In the Top/Bottom Rules menu, select a command to display a dialog box for entering your condition, such as the Top 10 Items dialog box shown here.

Figure 1.14
The conditional formatting rule shown in Figure 1.13 applied to the dollar values in column C.

	A	B	C
1	**Product Name**	**Units**	**$ Total**
2	Northwind Traders Almonds	20	$ 200
3	Northwind Traders Beer	487	$ 6,818
4	Northwind Traders Boysenberry Spread	100	$ 2,500
5	Northwind Traders Cajun Seasoning	40	$ 880
6	Northwind Traders Chai	40	$ 720
7	Northwind Traders Chocolate	200	$ 2,550
8	Northwind Traders Chocolate Biscuits Mix	85	$ 782
9	Northwind Traders Clam Chowder	290	$ 2,799
10	Northwind Traders Coffee	650	$ 29,900
11	Northwind Traders Crab Meat	120	$ 2,208
12	Northwind Traders Curry Sauce	65	$ 2,600
13	Northwind Traders Dried Apples	40	$ 2,120
14	Northwind Traders Dried Pears	40	$ 1,200
15	Northwind Traders Dried Plums	75	$ 263
16	Northwind Traders Fruit Cocktail	40	$ 1,560
17	Northwind Traders Gnocchi	10	$ 380
18	Northwind Traders Green Tea	275	$ 822
19	Northwind Traders Long Grain Rice	40	$ 280
20	Northwind Traders Marmalade	40	$ 3,240
21	Northwind Traders Mozzarella	90	$ 3,132
22	Northwind Traders Olive Oil	25	$ 534
23	Northwind Traders Ravioli	100	$ 1,950
24	Northwind Traders Scones	20	$ 200
25	Northwind Traders Syrup	50	$ 500

◀ ▶ ... Top-Bottom | Data Bars | Color Sca ... ⊕ ◀

CAUTION

Excel supports unlimited (within the confines of your system memory) conditional formatting rules for any range. Be careful, though: When you apply a rule, select the range, and then apply another rule, Excel does *not* replace the original rule. Instead, it adds the new rule to the existing one. If you want to change an existing rule, select Home, Conditional Formatting, Manage Rules, click the rule, and then click Edit Rule.

Adding Data Bars

Applying formatting to cells based on highlight cells rules or top/bottom rules is a great way to get particular values to stand out in a crowded worksheet. However, what if you're more interested in the *relationship* between similar values in a worksheet? For example, if you have a table of products that includes a column showing unit sales, how do you compare the relative sales of all the products? You could create a new column that calculates the percentage of unit sales for each product relative to the highest value. If the product with the highest sales sold 1,000 units, a product that sold 500 units will show 50% in the new column.

That would work, but all you're doing is adding more numbers to the worksheet, which might not make things any clearer. You really need some way to *visualize* the relative values in a range, and that's where Excel's *data bars* come in. Data bars are colored, horizontal bars that appear "behind" the values in a range. (They're reminiscent of a bar chart.) Their key feature is that the length of the data bar that appears in each cell depends on the value in that cell: The larger the value, the longer the data bar. The cell with the highest value has the longest data bar, and the data bars that appear in the other cells have lengths that reflect their values. (For example, a cell with a value that is half of the largest value would have a data bar that's half as long as the longest data bar.)

To apply data bars to the selected range, select Home, Conditional Formatting, Data Bars and then select the color you prefer. Figure 1.15 shows data bars applied to the values in the worksheet's Units column.

	A	B	C
1	**Product Name**	**Units**	**$ Total**
2	Northwind Traders Almonds	20	$ 200
3	Northwind Traders Beer	487	$ 6,818
4	Northwind Traders Boysenberry Spread	100	$ 2,500
5	Northwind Traders Cajun Seasoning	40	$ 880
6	Northwind Traders Chai	40	$ 720
7	Northwind Traders Chocolate	200	$ 2,550
8	Northwind Traders Chocolate Biscuits Mix	85	$ 782
9	Northwind Traders Clam Chowder	290	$ 2,799
10	Northwind Traders Coffee	650	$ 29,900
11	Northwind Traders Crab Meat	120	$ 2,208
12	Northwind Traders Curry Sauce	65	$ 2,600
13	Northwind Traders Dried Apples	40	$ 2,120
14	Northwind Traders Dried Pears	40	$ 1,200
15	Northwind Traders Dried Plums	75	$ 263
16	Northwind Traders Fruit Cocktail	40	$ 1,560
17	Northwind Traders Gnocchi	10	$ 380
18	Northwind Traders Green Tea	275	$ 822
19	Northwind Traders Long Grain Rice	40	$ 280
20	Northwind Traders Marmalade	40	$ 3,240
21	Northwind Traders Mozzarella	90	$ 3,132
22	Northwind Traders Olive Oil	25	$ 534
23	Northwind Traders Ravioli	100	$ 1,950
24	Northwind Traders Scones	20	$ 200
25	Northwind Traders Syrup	50	$ 500

◄ ► ... Data Bars | Color Scales | Icon Sets ... ⊕ | ◄

Figure 1.15 ·
Use data bars to visualize the relative values in a range.

Excel configures its default data bars with the longest data bar based on the highest value in the range, and the shortest data bar based on the lowest value in the range. However, what if you want to visualize your values based on different criteria? With test scores, for example, you might prefer to see the data bars based on values between 0 and 100 (so for a value of 50, the data bar always fills only half the cell, no matter what the top mark is).

To apply custom data bars, select the range and then select Home, Conditional Formatting, Data Bars, More Rules to display the New Formatting Rule dialog box, shown in Figure 1.16. In the Edit the Rule Description group, make sure Data Bar appears in the Format Style list. Notice that there's a Type list for both Minimum and Maximum. The type determines how Excel applies the data bars. You have six choices:

- **Automatic**—This is the default choice, and it means that Excel selects the type automatically, based on the data.

- **Lowest/Highest Value**—With this bar type, the lowest value in the range gets the shortest data bar, and the highest value in the range gets the longest data bar. This is the most common type, and it's the type Excel usually selects when you have the Type list values set to Automatic.

- **Number**—Use this type to base the data bar lengths on values that you specify in the two Value text boxes. For Shortest Bar, any cell in the range that has a value less than or equal to the value you specify will get the shortest data bar; similarly, for Longest Bar, any cell in the range that has a value greater than or equal to the value you specify will get the longest data bar.

- **Percent**—Use this type to base the data bar lengths on a percentage of the largest value in the range. For Shortest Bar, any cell in the range that has a relative value less than or equal to the percentage you specify will get the shortest data bar; for example, if you specify 10% and the largest value in the range is 1,000, any cell with a value of 100 or less will get the shortest data bar. For Longest Bar, any cell in the range that has a relative value greater than or equal to the percentage you specify will get the longest data bar; for example, if you specify 90% and the largest value in the range is 1,000, any cell with a value of 900 or more will get the longest data bar.

- **Formula**—Use this type to base the data bar lengths on a formula. I discuss this type in Chapter 8, "Working with Logical and Information Functions."

→ To learn how to use the Formula type, **see** "Applying Conditional Formatting with Formulas," **p. 171**.

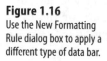

Figure 1.16
Use the New Formatting Rule dialog box to apply a different type of data bar.

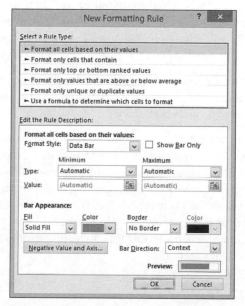

■ **Percentile**—Use this type to base the data bar lengths on the percentile within which each cell value falls, given the overall range of the values. In this case, Excel ranks all the values in the range and assigns each cell a position within the ranking. For Shortest Bar, any cell in the range that has a rank less than or equal to the percentile you specify will get the shortest data bar; for example, if you have 100 values and specify the 10th percentile, the cells ranked 10th or less will get the shortest data bar. For Longest Bar, any cell in the range that has a rank greater than or equal to the percentile you specify will get the longest data bar; for example, if you have 100 values and specify the 75th percentile, any cell ranked 75th or higher will get the longest data bar.

Adding Color Scales

When examining your data, it's often useful to get more of a "big picture" view. For example, you might want to know something about the overall distribution of the values. Are there lots of low values and just a few high values? Are most of the values clustered around the average? Are there any *outliers*, values that are much higher or lower than all or most of the other values? Similarly, you might want to make value judgments about your data. High sales and low numbers of product defects are "good," whereas low margins and high employee turnover rates are "bad."

You can analyze your worksheet data in these and similar ways by using Excel's color scales. A *color scale* is similar to a data bar in that it compares the relative values of cells in a range. Instead of bars in each cell, though, you see cell shading, where the shading color reflects the cell's value. For example, the lowest values might be shaded red, the higher values might be shaded light red, then orange, yellow, lime green, and finally deep green for the highest values. The distribution of the colors in the range gives you an immediate visualization of the distribution of the cell values, and outliers jump out because they have a completely different shading from the rest of the range. Value judgments are built in because (in this case) you can think of red as being "bad" (think of a red light) and green as being "good" (a green light).

To apply a color scale, select a range, select Home, Conditional Formatting, Color Scales, and then select the colors. Figure 1.17 shows color scales applied to a range of gross domestic product (GDP) growth rates for various countries.

Your configuration options for color scales are similar to those you learned about in the previous section for data bars. To apply a custom color scale, select the range and then select Home, Conditional Formatting, Color Scales, More Rules to display the New Formatting Rule dialog box. In the Edit the Rule Description group, you can select either 2-Color Scale or 3-Color Scale in the Format Style list. If you select 3-Color Scale, you can select Type, Value, and Color for three parameters Minimum, Midpoint, and Maximum, as shown in Figure 1.18. Note that the items in the Type lists are the same as the ones I discussed for data bars in the previous section.

Figure 1.17
Use color scales to visualize the distribution of values in a range.

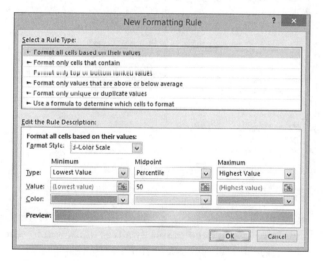

	A	B	C	D	E	F	G	H	I	J	K
1	GDP — % Annual Growth Rates (Source: The World Bank)										
2		2002	2003	2004	2005	2006	2007	2008	2009	2010	2011
3	World	2.0	2.7	4.0	3.5	4.0	3.9	1.3	-2.2	4.3	2.7
4	Albania	2.9	5.7	5.9	5.5	5.0	5.9	7.7	3.3	3.5	3.0
5	Algeria	4.7	6.9	5.2	5.1	2.0	3.0	2.4	2.4	3.3	2.5
6	Angola	14.5	3.3	11.2	18.3	20.7	22.6	13.8	2.4	3.4	3.4
7	Antigua and Barbuda	2.5	5.1	7.0	4.2	13.3	-9.6	1.5	-10.3	-8.9	-4.2
8	Argentina	-10.9	8.8	9.0	9.2	8.5	8.7	6.8	0.9	9.2	8.9
9	Armenia	13.2	14.0	10.5	13.9	13.2	13.7	6.9	-14.1	2.1	4.6
10	Australia	3.9	3.3	4.2	3.0	3.1	3.6	3.8	1.4	2.3	1.8
11	Austria	1.7	0.9	2.6	2.4	3.7	3.7	1.4	-3.8	2.3	3.1
12	Azerbaijan	10.6	11.2	10.2	26.4	34.5	25.0	10.8	9.3	5.0	1.0
13	Bahamas, The	2.7	-1.3	0.9	3.4	2.5	1.4	-2.3	-4.9	0.2	1.6
14	Belarus	5.0	7.0	11.4	9.4	10.0	8.6	10.2	0.2	7.7	5.3
15	Belgium	1.4	0.8	3.3	1.8	2.7	2.9	1.0	-2.8	2.2	1.9
16	Belize	5.1	9.3	4.6	3.0	4.7	1.3	3.5	0.0	2.9	2.0
17	Benin	4.5	3.9	3.1	2.9	4.1	4.6	5.1	3.8	3.0	3.1
18	Bhutan	8.9	8.6	8.0	8.8	6.8	17.9	4.7	6.7	7.4	8.4
19	Bolivia	2.5	2.7	4.2	4.4	4.8	4.6	6.1	3.4	4.1	5.1
20	Bosnia and Herzegovina	5.3	4.0	6.1	5.0	6.2	6.8	5.4	-2.9	0.8	1.7
21	Botswana	9.0	6.3	6.0	1.6	5.1	4.8	2.9	-4.8	7.0	5.1
22	Brazil	2.7	1.1	5.7	3.2	4.0	6.1	5.2	-0.3	7.5	2.7
23	Bulgaria	4.7	5.5	6.7	6.4	6.6	6.4	6.2	-5.5	0.4	1.7
24	Burkina Faso	4.7	8.0	4.6	8.7	6.8	3.6	5.8	3.0	7.9	4.2
25	Burundi	4.4	-1.2	4.8	0.9	5.4	4.8	5.0	3.5	3.8	4.2

Data Bars | Color Scales | Icon Sets

Figure 1.18
Select 3-Color Scale in the Format Style list to apply three colors to your cells.

New Formatting Rule

Select a Rule Type:
- Format all cells based on their values
- Format only cells that contain
- Format only top or bottom ranked values
- Format only values that are above or below average
- Format only unique or duplicate values
- Use a formula to determine which cells to format

Edit the Rule Description:

Format all cells based on their values:
Format Style: 3-Color Scale

	Minimum	Midpoint	Maximum
Type:	Lowest Value	Percentile	Highest Value
Value:	(Lowest value)	50	(Highest value)
Color:			

Preview:

OK   Cancel

Adding Icon Sets

When you're trying to make sense of a great deal of data, symbols are often a useful aid for cutting through the clutter. With movie reviews, for example, a simple thumbs-up (or thumbs-down) is immediately comprehensible and tells something useful about the movie. There are many such symbols that people have strong associations with. For example, a check mark means something is good or finished or acceptable, whereas an X means something is bad or unfinished or unacceptable; a green circle is positive, whereas a red circle is negative (think traffic lights); a smiley face is good, whereas a sad face is bad; an up arrow means things are progressing, a down arrow means things are going backward, and a horizontal arrow means things are remaining as they are.

Excel puts these and many other symbolic associations to good use with the *icon sets* feature. As with data bars and color scales, you use icon sets to visualize the relative values of cells in a range. In this case, however, Excel adds a particular icon to each cell in the range, and that icon tells you something about the cell's value relative to the rest of the range. For example, the highest values might get an upward-pointing arrow, the lowest values a downward-pointing arrow, and the values in between a horizontal arrow.

To apply an icon set to the selected range, select Home, Conditional Formatting, Icon Sets and then select the set you want. Figure 1.19 shows the 5 Arrows icon set applied to the percentage increases and decreases in employee sales.

Figure 1.19
Use icon sets to visualize relative values with meaningful symbols.

	A	B	C	D	E
1	Sales Rep	2015 Sales	2016 Sales	% +/-	
2	Nancy Freehafer	$ 996,336	$ 960,492	-4%	
3	Andrew Cencini	$ 606,731	$ 577,983	-5%	
4	Jan Kotas	$ 622,781	$ 967,580	55%	
5	Mariya Sergienko	$ 765,327	$ 771,399	1%	
6	Steven Thorpe	$ 863,589	$ 827,213	-4%	
7	Michael Neipper	$ 795,518	$ 669,394	-16%	
8	Robert Zare	$ 722,740	$ 626,945	-13%	
9	Laura Giussani	$ 992,059	$ 574,472	-42%	
10	Anne Hellung-Larsen	$ 659,380	$ 827,932	26%	
11	Kyra Harper	$ 509,623	$ 569,609	12%	
12	David Ferry	$ 987,777	$ 558,601	-43%	
13	Paul Voyatzis	$ 685,091	$ 692,182	1%	
14	Andrea Aster	$ 540,484	$ 693,762	28%	
15	Charles Granek	$ 650,733	$ 823,034	26%	
16	Karen Aliston	$ 509,863	$ 511,569	0%	
17	Karen Hammond	$ 503,699	$ 975,455	94%	
18	Vince Durbin	$ 630,263	$ 599,514	-5%	
19	Paul Richardson	$ 779,722	$ 596,353	-24%	
20	Gregg O'Donoghue	$ 592,802	$ 652,171	10%	
21					

Your configuration options for icon sets are similar to those you learned about for data bars and color scales. In this case, you need to specify a type and value for each icon (although the range for the lowest icon is always assumed to be less than the lower bound of the second-lowest icon range). To apply a custom icon set, select the range and then select Home, Conditional Formatting, Icon Sets, More Rules to display the New Formatting Rule dialog box, as shown in Figure 1.20. In the Edit the Rule Description group, select the icon set you want in the Icon Style list. Then select an operator, a value, and a type for each icon.

Figure 1.20
The New Formatting Rule dialog box for a custom icon set.

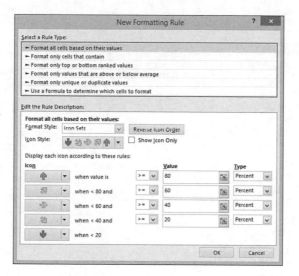

1

From Here

- For information on relative references, **see** "Understanding Relative Reference Format," **p. 62**.
- For an in-depth discussion of Excel arrays, **see** "Working with Arrays," **p. 87**.
- To learn about data validation, **see** "Applying Data-Validation Rules to Cells," **p. 100**.
- If you're not sure what a circular reference is, **see** "Fixing Circular References," **p. 118**.
- To learn how to create formula-based rules, **see** "Applying Conditional Formatting with Formulas," **p. 171**.
- To learn more about using Excel for trend analysis, **see** "Using Regression to Track Trends and Make Forecasts," **p. 371**.

Using Range Names

2

Although ranges enable you to work efficiently with large groups of cells, there are some disadvantages to using range coordinates:

- Each time you want to use a range, you must check to see whether it still has the same coordinates (for example, one or more cells might have been inserted or deleted) and, if not, redefine its coordinates.

- Range notation is not intuitive. To know what a formula such as =SUM(E6:E10) is adding, you have to look at the range itself.

- A slight mistake in defining the range coordinates can lead to disastrous results, especially when you're erasing a range.

You can overcome these problems by using *range names*, which are labels applied to a single cell or to a range of cells. You can use a defined name in place of the range coordinates. For example, to include the range in a formula or range command, you use the name instead of selecting the range or typing in its coordinates. You can create as many range names as you like, and you can even assign multiple names to the same range.

Range names also make your formulas intuitive and easy to read. For example, assigning the name AugustSales to a range such as E6:E10 immediately clarifies the purpose of a formula such as =SUM(AugustSales). Range names also increase the accuracy of your range operations because you don't have to specify range coordinates.

Besides overcoming these problems, range names bring several other advantages to the table:

- Names are easier to remember than range coordinates.
- Names don't change when you move a range to another part of the worksheet.
- Named ranges adjust automatically whenever you insert or delete rows or columns within the range.
- Names make it easier to navigate a worksheet. You can use the Go To command to jump to a named range quickly.
- You can use worksheet labels to create range names quickly.

In this chapter, I will show you how to define and work with range names, and I also hope to show you the power and flexibility that range names bring to your worksheet chores.

Defining a Range Name

Range names can be quite flexible, but you need to keep in mind a few restrictions and guidelines:

- The name can be a maximum of 255 characters.
- The name must begin with either a letter or the underscore character (_). For the rest of the name, you can use any combination of characters, numbers, or symbols (except spaces). For multiple-word names, separate the words by using the underscore character or by mixing case (for example, Cost_Of_Goods or CostOfGoods). Excel doesn't distinguish between uppercase and lowercase letters in range names.
- Don't use cell addresses (such as Q1) or any of the operator symbols (such as +, –, *, /, <, >, and &) because these can cause confusion if you use the name in a formula.
- Range names that begin with R or C followed by one or more numbers are illegal because of conflicts with Excel's R1C1 reference style, where each cell is referenced by its row number followed by its column number (such as R1C1 or R8C2).
- To make typing easier, try to keep names as short as possible while still keeping them meaningful. TotalProfit2016 is faster to type than Total_Profit_For_Fiscal_Year_2016, and it's certainly clearer than the more cryptic TotPft16.
- Don't use any of Excel's built-in names: Auto_Activate, Auto_Close, Auto_Deactivate, Auto_Open, Consolidate_Area, Criteria, Data_Form, Database, Extract, FilterDatabase, Print_Area, Print_Titles, Recorder, and Sheet_Title.

With these guidelines in mind, the next few sections show you various methods for defining range names.

Working with the Name Box

The Name box in Excel's formula bar usually shows just the address of the active cell. However, the Name box also comes with a couple extra features that make it easier to work with range names:

- After you've defined a name, it appears in the Name box whenever you select the range, as shown in Figure 2.1.

- The Name box doubles as a drop-down list. To select a named range quickly, drop the list down and select the name you want. Excel moves to the range and selects the cells.

2

Figure 2.1
When you select a range with a defined name, the name appears in Excel's Name box.

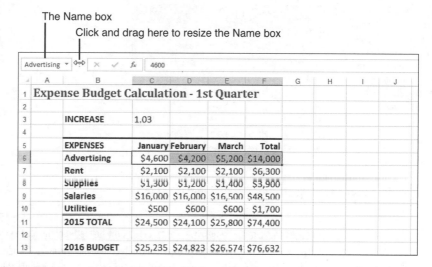

The Name box

Click and drag here to resize the Name box

> **NOTE** You can download this chapter's sample workbooks at www.mcfedries.com/books/ book.php?title=excel-2016-formulas-and-functions.

One handy feature of the Name box is that it's resizable. If you can't see all of the current name, move the mouse cursor to the right edge of the Name box. After it turns into a horizontal, two-headed arrow (see Figure 2.1), click and drag the edge to resize the box.

Using the Name box also happens to be the easiest way to define a range name. Here's what you do:

1. Select the range you want to name.

2. Click inside the Name box to display the insertion point.

3. Type the name you want to use and then press Enter. Excel defines the new name automatically. (If the range name you typed already exists, Excel selects the range instead of defining a new range name.)

Using the New Name Dialog Box

Using the Name box to define a range name is fast and intuitive, but Excel has other range-naming options available, such as defining the scope of the name and adding a comment for the name. To access these options, follow these steps to define a range name using the New Name dialog box:

1. Select the range you want to name.

2. Select Formulas, Define Name. (Alternatively, right-click the selection and then click Define Name.) The New Name dialog box appears, as shown in Figure 2.2.

Figure 2.2

When you display the New Name dialog box to define a range name, the coordinates of the selected range appear automatically in the Refers To box.

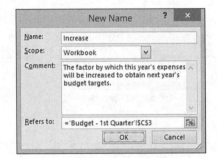

3. Enter the range name in the Name text box.

> **TIP**
>
> When defining a range name, always enter at least the first letter of the name in uppercase. Why? This will prove invaluable later, when you need to troubleshoot your formulas. The idea is that you type the range name entirely in lowercase letters when you insert it into a formula. When you accept the formula, Excel converts the name to the case you used when you first defined the range name. If the name remains in lowercase letters, you can tell that Excel doesn't recognize the name, so it's likely that you misspelled the name when typing it.

4. Use the Scope list to select where you want the name to be available. In most cases, you want to select Workbook, but in the next section I talk about the advantages of limiting the name to a worksheet (see "Changing the Scope to Define Sheet-Level Names").

5. Use the Comment text box to enter a description or other notes about the range name. This text appears when you use the name in a formula; see "Working with AutoComplete for Range Names," later in this chapter.

6. If the range displayed in the Refers To box is incorrect, you can use one of two methods to change it:
   - Type the correct range address (being sure to begin the address with an equal sign).

- Click inside the Refers To box and then use the mouse or keyboard to select a new range on the worksheet.

> **CAUTION**
>
> If you need to move around inside the Refers To box with the arrow keys (say, to edit the existing range address), first press F2 to put Excel into Edit mode. If you don't, Excel remains in Point mode, and the program assumes that you're trying to select a cell on the worksheet.

7. Click OK to return to the worksheet.

Changing the Scope to Define Sheet-Level Names

Excel enables you to define the scope of a range name. The *scope* tells you the extent to which the range name will be recognized in formulas. In the New Name dialog box, if you select Workbook from the Scope list (or if you create the name directly using the Name box), the range name is available to all the sheets in a workbook (and is called a *workbook-level* name). This means, for example, that a formula in Sheet1 can refer to a named range in Sheet3 by using the name directly. This can be a problem, however, if you need to use the same name in different worksheets. For example, say that you have four sheets—First Quarter, Second Quarter, Third Quarter, and Fourth Quarter—and you need to define an Expenses range name in each sheet.

If you need to use the same name in different sheets, you can create a name where the scope is defined for a specific worksheet (and so is called a *sheet-level* name). This means that the name will refer only to the range on the sheet in which it was defined.

You create a sheet-level name by displaying the New Name dialog box and then using the Scope list to select the worksheet you want to use.

Using Worksheet Text to Define Names

When you use the New Name dialog box, Excel sometimes suggests a name for the selected range. For example, Figure 2.3 shows that Excel has suggested the name Advertising for the range C6:F6. As you can see, Advertising is the row heading of the selected range, so Excel has used an adjacent text entry to make an educated guess about what you want to use as a name.

Instead of waiting for Excel to guess (particularly since Excel sometimes refuses to guess, for reasons unknown), you can tell the program explicitly to use adjacent text as a range name. The following procedure shows you the appropriate steps:

1. Select the range of cells you want to name, including the appropriate text cells you want to use as the range names (see Figure 2.4).

Figure 2.3
Excel often uses adjacent text to guess the range name you want to use.

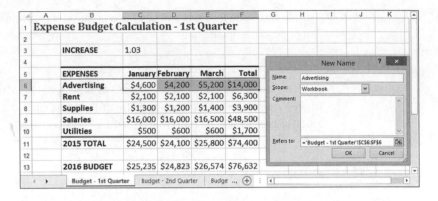

Figure 2.4
Include the text you want to use as the name when you select the range.

	A	B	C	D	E	F	G
1		**Expense Budget Calculation - 1st Quarter**					
2							
3		**INCREASE**	1.03				
4							
5		**EXPENSES**	**January**	**February**	**March**	**Total**	
6		**Advertising**	$4,600	$4,200	$5,200	$14,000	
7		**Rent**	$2,100	$2,100	$2,100	$6,300	
8		**Supplies**	$1,300	$1,200	$1,400	$3,900	
9		**Salaries**	$16,000	$16,000	$16,500	$48,500	
10		**Utilities**	$500	$600	$600	$1,700	
11		**2015 TOTAL**	$24,500	$24,100	$25,800	$74,400	
12							
13		**2016 BUDGET**	$25,235	$24,823	$26,574	$76,632	

Budget - 1st Quarter | Budget - 2nd Quarter | Budge ...

2. Select Formulas, Create from Selection or press Ctrl+Shift+F3. Excel displays the Create Names from Selection dialog box, shown in Figure 2.5. Excel guesses where the text for the range name is located and activates the appropriate check box (Left Column, in this example).

Figure 2.5
Use the Create Names from Selection dialog box to specify the location of the text to use as a range name.

Create Names from Selection

Create names from values in the:
- ☐ Top row
- ☑ Left column
- ☐ Bottom row
- ☐ Right column

OK | Cancel

3. If Excel hasn't correctly guessed about the check box you want, clear it and then activate the appropriate one.

4. Click OK.

> **NOTE** If the text you want to use as a range name contains any illegal characters (such as a space), Excel replaces those characters with an underscore (_).

When naming ranges from text, you're not restricted to working with just columns or rows. Instead, you can select ranges that include both row and column headings, and Excel will happily assign names to each row and column. For example, in Figure 2.6, the Create Names from Selection dialog box appears with both the Top Row and Left Column check boxes selected.

Figure 2.6
Excel can create names for rows and columns at the same time.

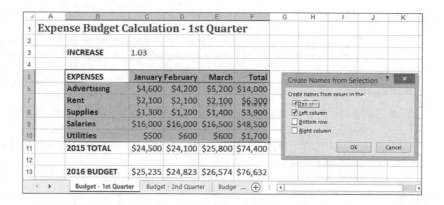

When you use this method to create names automatically, bear in mind that Excel gives special treatment to the top-left cell in the selected range. Specifically, it uses the text in that cell as the name for the range that includes the table data (that is, the table without the headings). In Figure 2.6, for example, the upper-left corner of the selected range is cell B5, which contains the label Expenses. After the names have been created, the table data—the range C6:F10—is given the name Expenses, as shown in Figure 2.7. If the top-left cell in the range is blank, Excel doesn't create a range name for the table.

Figure 2.7
When creating names from rows and columns at the same time, Excel uses the label in the top-left corner as the name of the range that includes the table data.

	A	B	C	D	E	F	G	H	I
1	**Expense Budget Calculation - 1st Quarter**								
2									
3	**INCREASE**	1.03							
4									
5	**EXPENSES**		**January**	**February**	**March**	**Total**			
6	**Advertising**		$4,600	$4,200	$5,200	$14,000			
7	**Rent**		$2,100	$2,100	$2,100	$6,300			
8	**Supplies**		$1,300	$1,200	$1,400	$3,900			
9	**Salaries**		$16,000	$16,000	$16,500	$48,500			
10	**Utilities**		$500	$600	$600	$1,700			
11	**2015 TOTAL**		$24,500	$24,100	$25,800	$74,400			
12									
13	**2016 BUDGET**		$25,235	$24,823	$26,574	$76,632			

Budget - 1st Quarter | Budget - 2nd Quarter | Budge ... (+)

Naming Constants

One of the best ways to make your worksheets comprehensible is to define names for every constant value. For example, if your worksheet uses an interest rate variable in several formulas, you can define a constant named Rate and use this name in your formulas to make them more readable. You can do this in two ways:

- Set aside an area of your worksheet for constants and name the individual cells. For example, Figure 2.8 shows a worksheet with three named constants: Rate (cell B5), Term (cell B6), and Amount (cell B7). Notice how the formula in cell E5 refers to each constant by name.

Figure 2.8
Grouping formula constants and naming them makes worksheets easy to read.

E5 ⊽ : × ✓ f_x =PMT(Rate / 12, Term * 12, Amount)

	A	B	C	D	E	F	G
2	**Loan Amortization**						
3							
4	**Constants:**			**Period**	**Payment**	**Interest**	**Principal**
5	Rate	5%		1	(299.71)	(41.67)	(258.04)
6	Term	3		2	(299.71)	(40.59)	(259.12)
7	Amount	10,000		3	(299.71)	(39.51)	(260.20)
8				4	(299.71)	(38.43)	(261.28)

- If you don't want to clutter a worksheet, you can name constants without entering them in the worksheet. Select Formulas, Define Name to display the New Name dialog box. Enter a name for the constant in the Name text box and the constant's value in the Refers To text box. Figure 2.9 shows an example.

Figure 2.9
You can create and name
constants in the New
Name dialog box.

2

When naming a constant, you're not restricted to the usual constant values of numbers and text
strings. Excel also allows you to assign a worksheet function to a name. For example, you could enter
`=YEAR(NOW())` in the Refers To text box to create a name that always returns the current year.
However, this feature is better suited to assigning a name to a long and complex formula that you
need to use in different places.

Working with Range Names

After you've defined a name, you can use it in formulas or functions, navigate with it, edit it,
and delete it. The next few sections take you through these techniques and more.

After you've defined several range names on a worksheet, it often becomes difficult to visualize the
location and dimensions of the ranges. Excel's Zoom feature can help. Select View, Zoom to display the
Zoom dialog box. In the Custom text box, enter a value of 39% or less and then click OK. Excel zooms
out and displays the named ranges by drawing a border around each one and displaying the range
name centered within the border.

Referring to a Range Name

Using a range name in a formula or as a function argument is straightforward: Just replace a
range's coordinates with the range's defined name. For example, suppose that a cell contains
the following formula:

```
=G1
```

This formula sets the cell's value to the current value of cell G1. However, if cell G1 is
named TotalExpenses, the following formula is equivalent:

```
=TotalExpenses
```

Similarly, consider the following function:

```
SUM(E3:E10)
```

If the range E3:E10 is named Sales, the following is equivalent:

```
SUM(Sales)
```

→ For more information on using names in your Excel formulas, **see** "Working with Range Names in Formulas," **p. 67**.

If you're not sure about a particular name, you can get Excel to paste it into the worksheet for you. Here are the steps required:

1. Start your formula or function and stop when you come to the spot where you need to insert the range name.

2. Select Formulas, Use in Formula. Excel displays a list of names whose scope includes the current worksheet, as shown in Figure 2.10.

Figure 2.10
Select the Use in Formula command to see a list of defined range names.

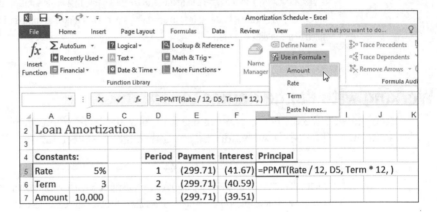

3. Click the name you want to use. Excel pastes the name.

If you're working with sheet-level names, how you use a name depends on where you use it:

- If you're using the sheet-level name on the sheet in which it was defined, you can just use the range name part. (That is, you don't need to specify the sheet name.)

- If you're using the sheet-level name on any other sheet, you must use the full name (SheetName!RangeName).

If the named range exists in a different workbook, you must precede the name with the name of the file in single quotation marks. For example, if the Mortgage Amortization workbook contains a range named Rate, you use the following in a different workbook to refer to this range:

```
'Mortgage Amortization.xlsx'!Rate
```

> **CAUTION**
>
> Excel doesn't mind if you create a sheet-level name that's the same as a workbook-level name. In all the other sheets, if you use the range name by itself, Excel assumes that you're talking about the workbook-level name. However, if you use only the range name on the sheet in which the sheet-level name was defined, Excel assumes that you're talking about the sheet-level name.
>
> So how do you refer to the workbook-level name from the sheet in which the sheet-level name was defined? You precede the range name with the workbook filename and an exclamation point. For example, in a workbook named Expenses.xlsx, suppose that the current worksheet has a sheet-level range named Total and that there's also a workbook-level range named Total. To refer to the latter in the current worksheet, you use the following:
>
> ```
> Expenses.xlsx!Total
> ```

Working with AutoComplete for Range Names

In Chapter 6, "Understanding Functions," you'll see that Excel has an AutoComplete feature that displays a list of function names that match what you've typed so far. If you see the function you want, you can select it from the list instead of typing the rest of the function name, which is usually faster and more accurate. Excel offers AutoComplete for range names as well. When you type the first few letters of a range name in a formula, Excel includes the range name as part of the AutoComplete list. As you can see in Figure 2.11, Excel also includes the comment text associated with a range name. To add the name to the formula, use the arrow keys to select it from the list and then press Tab.

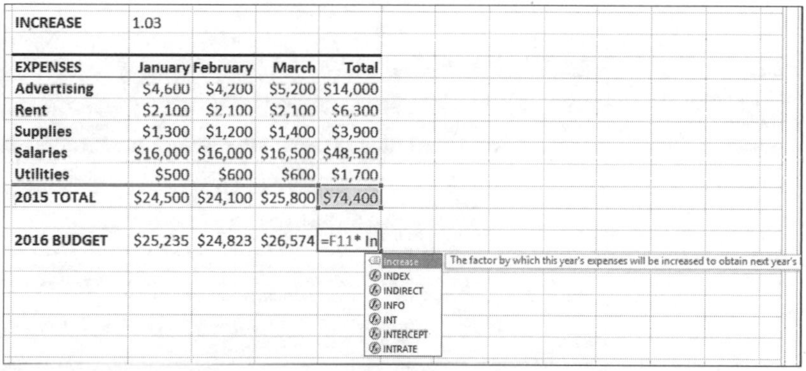

Figure 2.11
Excel offers AutoComplete for range names.

INCREASE	1.03			
EXPENSES	**January**	**February**	**March**	**Total**
Advertising	$4,600	$4,200	$5,200	$14,000
Rent	$2,100	$2,100	$2,100	$6,300
Supplies	$1,300	$1,200	$1,400	$3,900
Salaries	$16,000	$16,000	$16,500	$48,500
Utilities	$500	$600	$600	$1,700
2015 TOTAL	$24,500	$24,100	$25,800	$74,400
2016 BUDGET	$25,235	$24,823	$26,574	=F11* In

INCREASE — The factor by which this year's expenses will be increased to obtain next year's
INDEX
INDIRECT
INFO
INT
INTERCEPT
INTRATE

Navigating Using Range Names

Ranges that have defined names are easy to select. Excel gives you two methods:

■ The Name box doubles as a drop-down list. To select a named range quickly, drop the list down and select the name you want.

■ Select Home, Find & Select, Go To (or press F5 or Ctrl+G) to display the Go To dialog box. Click the range name in the Go To list and then click OK.

Pasting a List of Range Names in a Worksheet

If you need to document a worksheet for others to read (or figure out the worksheet yourself a few months from now), you can paste a list of the worksheet's range names. This list includes the name and the range it represents (or the value it represents, if the name refers to a constant). It's a static list (that is, it won't update if you make changes to the names or ranges), but it gives you a useful overview of the names you're using in the worksheet. Follow these steps to paste a list of range names:

1. Move to an empty area of the worksheet that's large enough to accept the list without overwriting any other data. (Note that the list uses up two columns: one for the names and one for the corresponding range coordinates.)

2. Select Formulas, Use in Formula, Paste Names or press F3. Excel displays the Paste Name dialog box.

3. Click Paste List. Excel pastes the worksheet's names and range coordinates.

Displaying the Name Manager

Excel comes with a Name Manager feature, which is a useful interface for working with range names. To display the Name Manager, select Formulas, Name Manager (or press Ctrl+F3). Figure 2.12 shows the Name Manager dialog box that appears. Note that the columns are resizable (click and drag the right edge of any column's header) and sortable (click a column's header to toggle between ascending and descending).

Figure 2.12
Use the Name Manager to modify, filter, or delete range names.

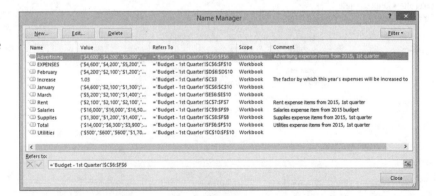

Filtering Names

If you have a workbook with a huge number of defined names, the Name Manager list can become quite unwieldy. To knock it down to size, Excel enables you to filter the display of range names. Click the Filter button and then click one of the following filters:

- **Clear Filter**—Click this item to deactivate all the filters.

- **Names Scoped to Worksheet**—Activate this filter to see only names that have the current worksheet as their scope.

- **Names Scoped to Workbook**—Activate this filter to see only names that have the current workbook as their scope.

- **Names with Errors**—Activate this filter to see only names that contain an error value, such as #NAME, #REF, or #VALUE.

- **Names without Errors**—Activate this filter to see only names that don't contain error values.

- **Defined Names**—Activate this filter to see only names that are built into Excel or that you've defined yourself (that is, you don't see names created automatically by Excel, such as table names).

- **Table Names**—Activate this filter to see only names that Excel has generated for tables.

Editing a Range Name's Coordinates

Sometimes you want an existing name to refer to a different set of range coordinates. Excel offers a couple of ways to edit the name:

- Move the range. When you do this, Excel moves the range name right along with it.

- If you want to adjust the existing coordinates or associate the name with a completely different range, display the Name Manager, click the name you want to change, and then edit the range coordinates using the Refers To text box.

Adjusting Range Name Coordinates Automatically

It's common in spreadsheet work to have a row or column of data that you add to constantly. For example, you might have to keep a list of ongoing expenses in a project, or you might want to track the number of units of a product that sell each day. From the perspective of range names, this isn't a problem if you always insert the new data within the existing range. In this case, Excel automatically adjusts the range coordinates to compensate for the new data. However, that doesn't happen if you always add the new data to the end of the range. In this case, you need to manually adjust the range coordinates to include the new data. The more data you enter, the bigger the pain this can be. To avoid this time-consuming drudgery, this section offers two solutions.

Solution 1: Including a Blank Cell at the End of the Range

The first solution is to define the range and include an extra blank cell at the end, if possible. For example, in the worksheet shown in Figure 2.13, the Amount name has been applied to the range C4:C12, where C12 is a blank cell.

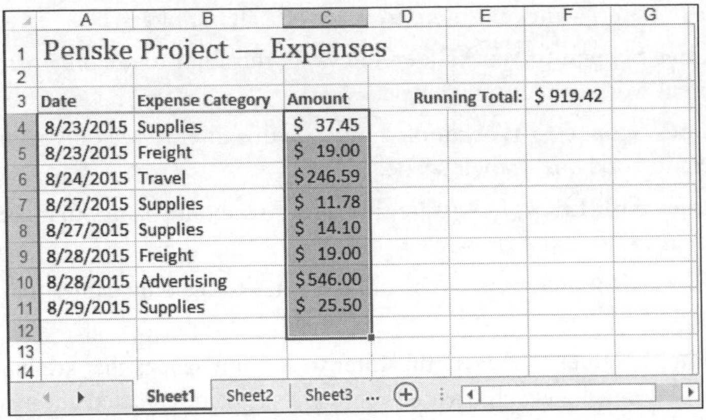

Figure 2.13
To get Excel to adjust a range name's coordinates automatically, include a blank cell at the end of the range, if possible.

The advantage here is that you can get Excel to adjust the Amount name's range coordinates automatically by inserting new data *above* (in this case) the blank row immediately below the table. Because you're inserting the new data within the existing range, Excel adjusts the name's range coordinates automatically, as shown in Figure 2.14.

Figure 2.14
The Amount name now refers to the range C4:C13.

Solution 2: Naming the Entire Row or Column

An even easier solution than the one I just showed is to name the entire row or column to which you're adding data. You do this by selecting the row or column, entering the name in the Name box, and pressing Enter. With this method, any data you add to the row or column automatically becomes part of the range name.

> **CAUTION**
>
> Use this method only if the row or column to which you're adding data contains no other conflict-ing data. For example, if you're adding numbers to a column and that column has other, unrelated numbers above or below, those numbers will be included in the range name you define for the entire column. This would prevent you from using the name in a formula because the formula would also include the extraneous data.

Changing a Range Name

If you need to change the name of one or more ranges, you can use one of two methods:

- If you've changed some row or column labels, redefine the range names based on the new text and then delete the old names (as described in the next section).

- Display the Name Manager, click the name you want to change, and then click Edit to display the Edit Name dialog box. Make your changes in the Name text box and then click OK.

Deleting a Range Name

If you no longer need a range name, you should delete the name from the worksheet to avoid cluttering the name list. The following procedure outlines the necessary steps:

1. Select Formulas, Name Manager.

2. Click the name you want to delete.

3. Click Delete. Excel asks you to confirm the deletion.

4. Click OK.

5. Click Close.

Using Names with the Intersection Operator

With ranges that overlap, you can use the *intersection* operator (a space) to refer to the over-lapping cells. For example, Figure 2.15 shows two ranges: C4:E9 and D8:G11. To refer to the overlapping cells (D8:E9), you use the following notation: C4:E9 D8:G11.

If you've named the ranges on your worksheet, the intersection operator can make things much easier to read because you can refer to individual cells by using the names of the cell's row and column. For example, in Figure 2.16, the range C6:C10 is named January, and the range C7:F7 is named Rent. This means that you can refer to cell C7 as January Rent (see cell I7).

Figure 2.15
The intersection operator returns the intersecting cells of two ranges.

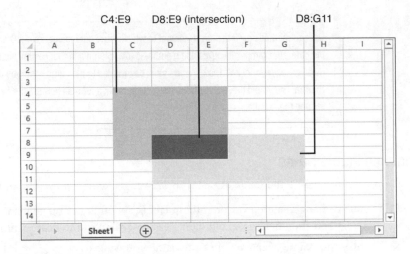

Figure 2.16
After you name ranges, you can combine row and column headings to create intersecting names for individual cells.

	A	B	C	D	E	F	G	H	I
1	**Expense Budget Calculation - 1st Quarter**								
2									
3		**INCREASE**	1.03						
4									
5		**EXPENSES**	**January**	**February**	**March**	**Total**			
6		**Advertising**	$4,600	$4,200	$5,200	$14,000			
7		**Rent**	$2,100	$2,100	$2,100	$6,300	**Rent for January:**		$2,100
8		**Supplies**	$1,300	$1,200	$1,400	$3,900			
9		**Salaries**	$16,000	$16,000	$16,500	$48,500			
10		**Utilities**	$500	$600	$600	$1,700			
11		**2015 TOTAL**	$24,500	$24,100	$25,800	$74,400			

I7 — fx =January Rent

CAUTION

If you try to define an intersection name and Excel displays #NULL! in the cell, it means that the two ranges don't have any overlapping cells.

From Here

■ To get the details of Excel's 3D ranges, **see** "Working with 3D Ranges," **p. 7.**

■ For more information on using names in your Excel formulas, **see** "Working with Range Names in Formulas," **p. 67.**

■ To learn about AutoComplete for functions, **see** "Typing a Function into a Formula," **p. 132.**

Building Basic Formulas

A worksheet is merely a lifeless collection of numbers and text until you define some kind of relationship among the various entries. You do this by creating *formulas* that perform calculations and produce results. This chapter takes you through some formula basics, including constructing simple arithmetic and text formulas, understanding the all-important topic of operator precedence, copying and moving worksheet formulas, and making formulas easier to build and read by taking advantage of range names.

Understanding Formula Basics

Most worksheets are created to provide answers to specific questions: What is the company's profit? Are expenses over or under budget, and by how much? What is the future value of an investment? How big will an employee's bonus be this year? You can answer these questions, and an infinite number of others, by using Excel formulas.

All Excel formulas have the same general structure: an equal sign (=) followed by one or more *operands*, which can be values, cell references, ranges, range names, or function names, separated by one or more *operators*, which are symbols that combine the operands in some way, such as the plus sign (+) and the greater-than sign (>).

Formula Limits in Excel 2016

It's a good idea to know the limits Excel sets on various aspects of formulas and worksheet models, even though it's unlikely that you'll ever bump up against these limits. Formula limits that were expanded in Excel 2007 remain the same in Excel 2016. So, in the unlikely event that you're coming to Excel 2016 from Excel 2003 or earlier, Table 3.1 shows you the updated limits.

Table 3.1 Formula-Related Limits in Excel 2016

Object	Excel 2016 Maximum	Excel 2003 Maximum
Columns	16,384	1,024
Rows	1,048,576	65,536
Formula length (characters)	8,192	1,024
Function arguments	255	30
Formula nesting levels	64	7
Array references (rows or columns)	Unlimited	65,335
PivotTable columns	16,384	255
PivotTable rows	1,048,576	65,536
PivotTable fields	16,384	255
Unique PivotField items	1,048,576	32,768

→ *Formula nesting levels* refers to the number of expressions that are nested within other expressions using parentheses; **see** "Controlling the Order of Precedence," **p. 58**.

Entering and Editing Formulas

Entering a new formula into a worksheet appears to be a straightforward process:

1. Select the cell in which you want to enter the formula.
2. Type an equal sign (=) to tell Excel that you're entering a formula.
3. Type the formula's operands and operators.
4. Press Enter to confirm the formula.

However, Excel has three different *input modes* that determine how it interprets certain keystrokes and mouse actions:

- When you type the equal sign to begin the formula, Excel goes into *Enter mode*, which is the mode you use to enter text (such as the formula's operands and operators).

- If you press any keyboard navigation key (such as Page Up, Page Down, or any arrow key), or if you click any other cell in the worksheet, Excel enters *Point mode*. This is the mode you use to select a cell or range as a formula operand. When you're in Point mode, you can use any of the standard range-selection techniques. Note that Excel returns to Enter mode as soon as you type an operator or any character.

- If you press F2, Excel enters *Edit mode*, which is the mode you use to make changes to the formula. For example, when you're in Edit mode, you can use the left and right arrow keys to move the cursor to another part of the formula for deleting or inserting characters. You can also enter Edit mode by clicking anywhere within the formula. Press F2 to return to Enter mode.

> **TIP**
> You can tell which mode Excel is currently in by looking at the status bar. On the left side, you'll see "Enter," "Point," or "Edit."

After you've entered a formula, you might need to return to it to make changes. Excel gives you three ways to enter Edit mode and make changes to a formula in the selected cell:

- Press F2.
- Double-click the cell.
- Use the formula bar to click anywhere inside the formula text.

Excel divides formulas into four groups: arithmetic, comparison, text, and reference. Each group has its own set of operators, and you use each group in different ways. In the next few sections, I show you how to use each type of formula.

Using Arithmetic Formulas

Arithmetic formulas are by far the most common type of formula. They combine numbers, cell addresses, and function results with mathematical operators to perform calculations. Table 3.2 summarizes the mathematical operators used in arithmetic formulas.

Table 3.2   The Arithmetic Operators

Operator	Name	Example	Result
+	Addition	=10+5	15
-	Subtraction	=10-5	5
-	Negation	=-10	–10
*	Multiplication	=10*5	50
/	Division	=10/5	2
%	Percentage	=10%	0.1
^	Exponentiation	=10^5	100000

Most of these operators are straightforward, but the exponentiation operator might require further explanation. The formula =x^y means that the value x is raised to the power y. For example, the formula =3^2 produces the result 9 (that is, 3*3=9). Similarly, the formula =2^4 produces 16 (that is, 2*2*2*2=16).

Using Comparison Formulas

A *comparison formula* is a statement that compares two or more numbers, text strings, cell contents, or function results. If the statement is true, the result of the formula is given the logical value TRUE (which is equivalent to any nonzero value). If the statement is false, the formula returns the logical value FALSE (which is equivalent to zero). Table 3.3 summarizes the operators you can use in comparison formulas.

Table 3.3   Comparison Formula Operators

Operator	Name	Example	Result
=	Equal to	=10=5	FALSE
>	Greater than	=10>5	TRUE
<	Less than	=10<5	FALSE
>=	Greater than or equal to	="a">="b"	FALSE
<=	Less than or equal to	="a"<="b"	TRUE
<>	Not equal to	="a"<>"b"	TRUE

Comparison formulas have many uses. For example, you can determine whether to pay a salesperson a bonus by using a comparison formula to compare actual sales with a predetermined quota. If the sales are greater than the quota, the rep is awarded the bonus. You also can monitor credit collection. For example, if the amount a customer owes is more than 150 days past due, you might send the invoice to a collection agency.

➔ Comparison formulas also make use of Excel's logical functions, so **see** "Adding Intelligence with Logical Functions," **p. 163**.

Using Text Formulas

The two types of formulas that I discussed in the previous sections, arithmetic formulas and comparison formulas, calculate or make comparisons and return values. A *text formula*, on the other hand, is a formula that returns text. Text formulas use the ampersand (&) operator to work with text cells, text strings enclosed in quotation marks, and text function results.

One way to use text formulas is to concatenate text strings. For example, if you enter the formula `="soft"&"ware"` into a cell, Excel displays `software`. Note that the quotation marks and the ampersand aren't shown in the result. You also can use & to combine cells that contain text. For example, if A1 contains the text `Ben` and A2 contains `Jerry`, entering the formula `=A1&" and "&A2` returns `Ben and Jerry`.

➔ For other uses of text formulas, **see** Chapter 7, "Working with Text Functions," **p. 139**.

Using Reference Formulas

The reference operators combine two cell references or ranges to create a single joint reference. Table 3.4 summarizes the operators you can use in reference formulas.

Table 3.4   Reference Formula Operators

Operator	Name	Description
: (colon)	Range	Produces a range from two cell references (for example, A1:C5).
(space)	Intersection	Produces a range that is the intersection of two ranges (for example, A1:C5 B2:E8).
, (comma)	Union	Produces a range that is the union of two ranges (for example, A1:C5,B2:E8).

Understanding Operator Precedence

You'll often use simple formulas that contain just two values and a single operator. In practice, however, most formulas you use will have a number of values and operators. In more complex expressions, the order in which the calculations are performed becomes crucial. For example, consider the formula `=3+5^2`. If you calculate from left to right, the answer you get is 64 (3+5 equals 8, and 8^2 equals 64). However, if you perform the exponentiation first and then the addition, the result is 28 (5^2 equals 25, and 3+25 equals 28). As this example shows, a single formula can produce multiple answers, depending on the order in which you perform the calculations.

To control this problem, Excel evaluates a formula according to a predefined *order of precedence*. This order of precedence enables Excel to calculate a formula unambiguously by determining which part of the formula it calculates first, which part second, and so on.

The Order of Precedence

Excel's order of precedence is determined by the various formula operators outlined earlier. Table 3.5 summarizes the complete order of precedence used by Excel.

Table 3.5   The Excel Order of Precedence

Operator	Operation	Order of Precedence
:	Range	1st
<space>	Intersection	2nd
,	Union	3rd
-	Negation	4th
%	Percentage	5th
^	Exponentiation	6th
* and /	Multiplication and division	7th
+ and -	Addition and subtraction	8th
&	Concatenation	9th
= < > <= >= <>	Comparison	10th

From this table, you can see that Excel performs exponentiation before addition. Therefore, the correct answer for the formula =3+5^2, given previously, is 28. Notice also that some operators in Table 3.5 have the same order of precedence (for example, multiplication and division). This means that it usually doesn't matter in which order these operators are evaluated. For example, consider the formula =5*10/2. If you perform the multiplication first, the answer you get is 25 (5*10 equals 50, and 50/2 equals 25). If you perform the division first, you also get an answer of 25 (10/2 equals 5, and 5*5 equals 25). By convention, Excel evaluates operators with the same order of precedence from left to right, so you should assume that's how your formulas will be evaluated.

Controlling the Order of Precedence

Sometimes you want to override the order of precedence. For example, suppose that you want to create a formula that calculates the pre-tax cost of an item. If you bought something for $10.65, including 7% sales tax, and you want to find the cost of the item minus the tax, you use the formula =10.65/1.07, which gives you the correct answer, $9.95. In general, the formula is the total cost divided by 1 plus the tax rate, as shown in Figure 3.1.

Figure 3.1
The general formula to
calculate the pre-tax cost
of an item.

$$Pre\text{-}tax\ Cost = \frac{Total\ Cost}{1 + Tax\ Rate}$$

Figure 3.2 shows how you might implement such a formula. Cell B5 displays the Total Cost variable, and cell B6 displays the Tax Rate variable. Given these parameters, your first instinct might be to use the formula =B5/1+B6 to calculate the original cost. This formula is shown (as text) in cell E9, and the result is given in cell D9. As you can see, this answer is incorrect. What happened? Well, according to the rules of precedence, Excel performs division before addition, so the value in B5 first is divided by 1 and then is added to the value in B6. To get the correct answer, you must override the order of precedence so that the addition 1+B6 is performed first. You do this by surrounding that part of the formula with parentheses, as shown in cell E10. When this is done, you get the correct answer (cell D10).

3

> **TIP**
> In Figure 3.2, how did I convince Excel to show the formulas in cells E9 and E10 as text? I used Excel's FORMULATEXT() function (see "Displaying a Cell's Formula by Using FORMULATEXT()," later in this chapter).

Figure 3.2
Use parentheses to con-
trol the order of prece-
dence in your formulas.

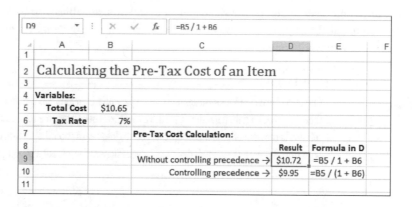

> **NOTE**
> You can download this chapter's sample workbooks at www.mcfedries.com/books/book. php?title=excel-2016-formulas-and-functions.

In general, you can use parentheses to control the order that Excel uses to calculate formulas. Terms inside parentheses are always calculated first; terms outside parentheses are calculated sequentially (according to the order of precedence).

TIP

Another good use for parentheses is raising a number to a fractional power. For example, if you want to take the *n*th root of a number, you use the following general formula:

```
=number ^ (1 / n)
```

For example, to take the cube root of the value in cell A1, use this:

```
=A1 ^ (1 / 3)
```

To gain even more control over your formulas, you can place parentheses inside one another; this is called *nesting* parentheses. Excel always evaluates the innermost set of parentheses first. Here are a few sample formulas:

Formula	1st Step	2nd Step	3rd Step	Result
3^(15/5)*2–5	3^3*2–5	27*2–5	54–5	49
3^((15/5)*2–5)	3^(3*2–5)	3^(6–5)	3^1	3
3^(15/(5*2–5))	3^(15/(10–5))	3^(15/5)	3^3	27

Notice that the order of precedence rules also hold within parentheses. For example, in the expression (5*2–5), the term 5*2 is calculated before 5 is subtracted.

Using parentheses to determine the order of calculations enables you to gain full control over your Excel formulas. This way, you can make sure that the answer given by a formula is the one you want.

CAUTION

One of the most common mistakes when using parentheses in formulas is to forget to close a parenthetic term with a right parenthesis. In such a case, Excel generates an error message (and offers a solution to the problem). To make sure that you've closed each parenthetic term, count all the left and right parentheses. If these totals don't match, you know you've left out a parenthesis.

Controlling Worksheet Calculation

Excel always calculates a formula when you confirm its entry, and the program normally recalculates existing formulas automatically whenever their data changes. This behavior is fine for small worksheets, but it can slow you down if you have a complex model that takes several seconds or even several minutes to recalculate. To turn off this automatic recalculation, Excel gives you two ways to get started:

- Select Formulas, Calculation Options.
- Select File, Options and then click Formulas.

Either way, you're presented with three calculation options:

- **Automatic**—This is the default calculation mode, and it means that Excel recalculates formulas as soon as you enter them and as soon as the data for a formula changes.

- **Automatic Except for Data Tables**—In this calculation mode, Excel recalculates all formulas automatically, except for those associated with data tables. This is a good choice if your worksheet includes one or more massive data tables that are slowing down the recalculation.

→ To learn how to set up data tables, **see** "Using What-If Analysis," **p. 349**.

- **Manual**—Select this mode to force Excel not to recalculate any formulas until either you manually recalculate or you save the workbook. If you're in the Excel Options dialog box, you can tell Excel not to recalculate when you save the workbook by clearing the Recalculate Workbook Before Saving check box.

With manual calculation turned on, you see "Calculate" in the status bar whenever your worksheet data changes and your formula results need to be updated. When you want to recalculate, first display the Formulas tab. In the Calculation group, you have two choices:

- Click Calculate Now (or press F9) to recalculate every open worksheet.
- Click Calculate Sheet (or press Shift+F9) to recalculate only the active worksheet.

> **TIP**
> If you want Excel to recalculate every formula—even those that are unchanged—in all open worksheets, press Ctrl+Alt+Shift+F9.

If you want to recalculate only part of your worksheet while manual calculation is turned on, you have two options:

- To recalculate a single formula, select the cell containing the formula, click in the formula bar, and then confirm the cell (by pressing Enter or clicking the Enter button).

- To recalculate a range, select the range; select Home, Find & Select, Replace (or press Ctrl+H); and enter an equal sign (=) in both the Find What and Replace With boxes. Click Replace All. Excel "replaces" the equal sign in each formula with another equal sign. This doesn't actually change any formula, but it forces Excel to recalculate each formula.

> **TIP**
> Excel supports multithreaded calculation on computers with either multiple processors or processors with multiple cores. For each processor (or core), Excel sets up a thread (a separate process of execution). Excel can then use each available thread to process multiple calculations concurrently. For a worksheet with multiple, independent formulas, this can dramatically speed up calculations. To make sure multi-threaded calculation is turned on, select File, Options, click Advanced, and then in the Formulas section ensure that the Enable Multi-Threaded Calculation check box is selected.

Copying and Moving Formulas

You copy and move ranges that contain formulas the same way you copy and move regular ranges, but the results aren't always straightforward.

For example, Figure 3.3 shows a list of expense data for a company. The formula in cell C11 uses the SUM() function to total the January expenses (range C6:C10). The idea behind this worksheet is to calculate a new expense budget number for 2016 as a percentage increase of the actual 2015 total. Cell C3 displays the INCREASE variable (in this case, the increase being used is 3%). The formula that calculates the 2016 BUDGET number (cell C13 for the month of January) multiplies the 2015 TOTAL by the INCREASE (that is, =C11*C3).

Figure 3.3
A budget expenses worksheet with two calculations for the January numbers: the total (cell C11) and a percentage increase for next year (cell C13).

	C11	▼ : × ✓ ƒx	=SUM(C6:C10)			
⊿	A	B	C	D	E	F	G
1	**Expense Budget Calculation**					
2						
3		**INCREASE**	1.03			
4						
5		**EXPENSES**	**January**	**February**	**March**	**Total**
6		Advertising	4,600	4,200	5,200	14,000
7		Rent	2,100	2,100	2,100	6,300
8		Supplies	1,300	1,200	1,400	3,900
9		Salaries	16,000	16,000	16,500	48,500
10		Utilities	500	600	600	1,700
11		**2015 TOTAL**	24,500			
12						
13		**2016 BUDGET**	25,235			
14						

The next step is to calculate the 2015 TOTAL expenses and the 2016 BUDGET figure for February. You could just type each new formula, but you can copy a cell much more quickly. Figure 3.4 shows the results when you copy the contents of cell C11 into cell D11. As you can see, Excel adjusts the range in the formula's SUM() function so that only the February expenses (D6:D10) are totaled. How did Excel know to do this? To answer this question, you need to know about Excel's relative reference format, which I discuss in the next section.

Understanding Relative Reference Format

When you use a cell reference in a formula, Excel looks at the cell address relative to the location of the formula. For example, suppose that you have the formula =A1*2 in cell A3. To Excel, this formula says, "Multiply the contents of the cell two rows above this one by 2." This is called the *relative reference format*, and it's the default format for Excel. This means that if you copy this formula to cell A4, the relative reference is still "Multiply the contents of the cell two rows above this one by 2," but the formula changes to =A2*2 because A2 is two rows above A4.

Figure 3.4
When you copy the January 2015 TOTAL formula to February, Excel automatically adjusts the range reference.

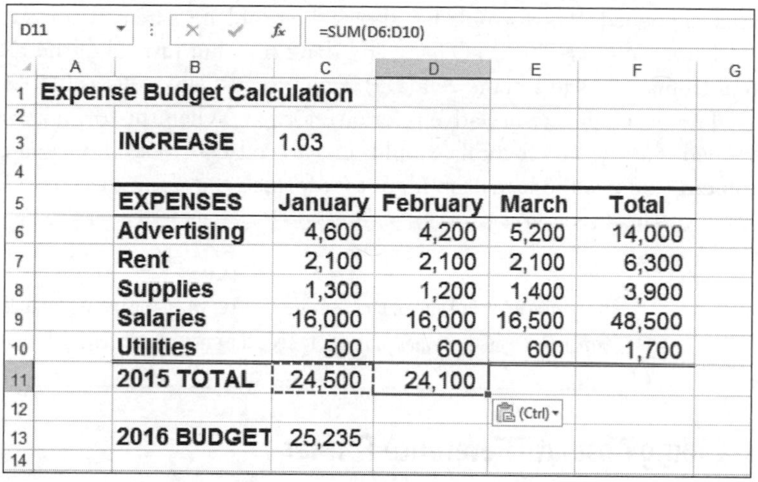

D11	▼	:	×	✓	fx	=SUM(D6:D10)		

	A	B	C	D	E	F	G
1	**Expense Budget Calculation**						
2							
3		**INCREASE**	1.03				
4							
5		**EXPENSES**	**January**	**February**	**March**	**Total**	
6		**Advertising**	4,600	4,200	5,200	14,000	
7		**Rent**	2,100	2,100	2,100	6,300	
8		**Supplies**	1,300	1,200	1,400	3,900	
9		**Salaries**	16,000	16,000	16,500	48,500	
10		**Utilities**	500	600	600	1,700	
11		**2015 TOTAL**	24,500	24,100			
12					(Ctrl) ▼		
13		**2016 BUDGET**	25,235				
14							

3

Figure 3.4 shows why this format is useful. You had only to copy the formula in cell C11 to cell D11 and, thanks to relative referencing, everything came out perfectly. To get the expense total for March, you would just have to paste the same formula into cell E11. You'll find that this way of handling copy operations will save you incredible amounts of time when you're building worksheet models.

However, you need to exercise some care when copying or moving formulas. Let's see what happens if you return to the budget expense worksheet and try copying the 2016 BUDGET formula in cell C13 to cell D13. Figure 3.5 shows that the result is 0!

Figure 3.5
Copying the January 2016 BUDGET formula to February creates a problem.

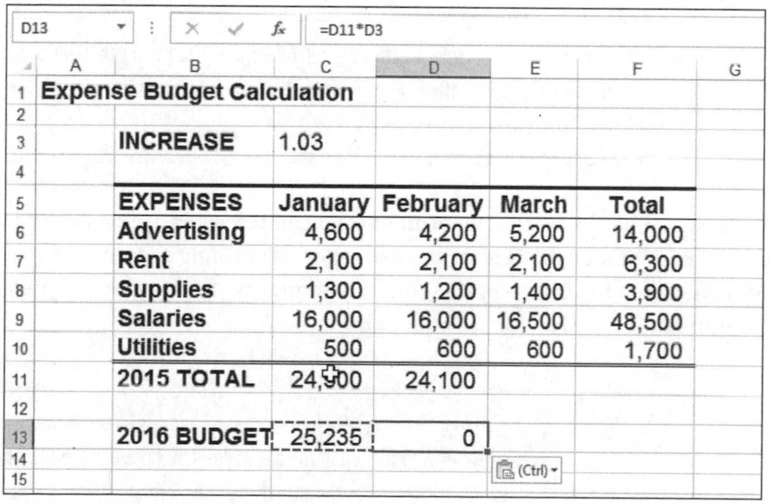

D13	▼	:	×	✓	fx	=D11*D3		

	A	B	C	D	E	F	G
1	**Expense Budget Calculation**						
2							
3		**INCREASE**	1.03				
4							
5		**EXPENSES**	**January**	**February**	**March**	**Total**	
6		**Advertising**	4,600	4,200	5,200	14,000	
7		**Rent**	2,100	2,100	2,100	6,300	
8		**Supplies**	1,300	1,200	1,400	3,900	
9		**Salaries**	16,000	16,000	16,500	48,500	
10		**Utilities**	500	600	600	1,700	
11		**2015 TOTAL**	24,500	24,100			
12							
13		**2016 BUDGET**	25,235	0			
14							
15					(Ctrl) ▼		

What happened? The formula bar shows the problem: The new formula is =D11*D3. Cell D11 is the February 2015 TOTAL, and that's fine, but instead of the INCREASE cell (C3), the formula refers to a blank cell (D3). Excel treats blank cells as 0, so the formula result is 0. The problem is the relative reference format. When the formula was copied, Excel assumed that the new formula should refer to cell D3. To see how you can correct this problem, you need to learn about another format, the *absolute reference format*, which I discuss in the next section.

> **NOTE**
> The relative reference format problem doesn't occur when you move a formula. When you move a formula, Excel assumes that you want to keep the same cell references.

Understanding Absolute Reference Format

When you refer to a cell in a formula using the absolute reference format, Excel uses the physical address of the cell. You tell the program that you want to use an absolute reference by placing dollar signs ($) before the row and column of the cell address. To return to the example in the preceding section, Excel interprets the formula =$A$1*2 as "Multiply the contents of cell A1 by 2." No matter where you copy or move this formula, the cell reference doesn't change. The cell address is said to be *anchored*.

To fix the budget expense worksheet, you need to anchor the INCREASE variable. To do this, you first change the January 2016 BUDGET formula in cell C13 to read =C11*$C$3. After making this change, copying the formula to the February 2016 BUDGET column gives the new formula =D11*$C$3, which produces the correct result.

> **CAUTION**
> Most range names refer to absolute cell references. This means that when you copy a formula that uses a range name, the copied formula will use the same range name as the original. This might produce errors in your worksheet.

You also should know that you can enter a cell reference using a mixed-reference format. In this format, you anchor either the cell's row (by placing the dollar sign in front of the row address only—for example, B$6) or its column (by placing the dollar sign in front of the column address only—for example, $B6).

> **TIP**
> You can quickly change the reference format of a cell address by using the F4 key. When editing a formula, place the cursor to the left of the cell address (or between the row and column values) and then keep pressing F4. Excel cycles through the various formats. When you see the format you want, press Enter. If you want to apply the new reference format to multiple cell addresses, highlight the addresses, press F4 until you get the format you want, and press Enter.

Copying a Formula Without Adjusting Relative References

If you need to copy a formula but don't want the formula's relative references to change, follow these steps:

1. Select the cell that contains the formula you want to copy.

2. Click inside the formula bar to activate it.

3. Use the mouse or keyboard to select the entire formula.

4. Copy the selected formula.

5. Press Esc to deactivate the formula bar.

6. Select the cell in which you want the copy of the formula to appear.

7. Paste the formula.

> **NOTE** Here are two other methods you can use to copy a formula without adjusting its relative cell references:
>
> ■ To copy a formula from the cell above, select the lower cell and press Ctrl+' (apostrophe).
>
> ■ Activate the formula bar and type an apostrophe (') at the beginning of the formula (that is, to the left of the equal sign) to convert it to text. Press Enter to confirm the edit, copy the cell, and then paste it in the desired location. Now, delete the apostrophe from both the source and destination cells to convert the text back to a formula.

3

Displaying Worksheet Formulas

By default, Excel displays in a cell the results of the cell's formula instead of the formula itself. If you need to see a formula, you can simply select the appropriate cell and look at the formula bar. However, sometimes you'll want to see all the formulas in a worksheet (such as when you're troubleshooting your work).

→ For more information about solving formula problems, **see** Chapter 5, "Troubleshooting Formulas," **p. 111**.

Displaying All Worksheet Formulas

To display all of a worksheet's formulas, select Formulas, Show Formulas.

> **TIP** You can also press Ctrl+` (backquote) to toggle a worksheet between values and formulas.

Displaying a Cell's Formula by Using FORMULATEXT()

In some cases, rather than showing all of a sheet's formulas, you might prefer to show the formulas in only a cell or two. For example, if you're presenting a worksheet to other people, that sheet might have some formulas you want to show, but it might also have one or more proprietary formulas that you don't want your audience to see. In such a case, you can display individual cell formulas by using the FORMULATEXT() function:

FORMULATEXT(*cell*)

cell   The address of the cell that contains the formula you want to show

For example, the following formula displays the formula text from cell D9:

=FORMULATEXT(D9)

Converting a Formula to a Value

If a cell contains a formula whose value will never change, you can convert the formula to that value. This speeds up large worksheet recalculations and frees up memory for your worksheet because values use much less memory than formulas do. For example, you might have formulas in part of your worksheet that use values from a previous fiscal year. Because these numbers aren't likely to change, you can safely convert the formulas to their values. To do this, follow these steps:

1. Select the cell containing the formula you want to convert.
2. Double-click the cell or press F2 to activate in-cell editing.
3. Press F9. The formula changes to its value.
4. Press Enter or click the Enter button. Excel changes the cell to the value.

You'll often need to use the result of a formula in several places. If a formula is in cell C5, for example, you can display its result in other cells by entering =C5 in each of the cells. This is the best method if you think the formula result might change because, if it does, Excel updates the other cells automatically. However, if you're sure that the result won't change, you can copy only the value of the formula into the other cells. Use the following procedure to do this:

1. Select the cell that contains the formula.
2. Copy the cell.
3. Select the cell or cells to which you want to copy the value.
4. Select Home, display the Paste list, and then select Paste Values. Excel pastes the cell's value to each cell you selected.

Another method is to copy the cell, paste it into the destination, drop down the Paste Options list, and then select Values Only.

> **CAUTION**
>
> If your worksheet is set to manual calculation, make sure that you update your formulas (by pressing F9) before copying the values of your formulas.

Working with Range Names in Formulas

In Chapter 2, "Using Range Names," you saw how to define and use range names in worksheets. You probably use range names often in your formulas. After all, a cell that contains the formula =Sales-Expenses is much more comprehensible than one that contains the more cryptic formula =F12-F3. The next few sections show you some techniques that make it easier to use range names in formulas.

Pasting a Name into a Formula

One way to enter a range name in a formula is to type the name in the formula bar. But what if you can't remember the name? Or what if the name is long, and you've got a deadline looming? For these kinds of situations, Excel has several features that enable you to select the name you want from a list and paste it right into the formula. Start your formula, and when you get to the spot where you want the name to appear, use any of the following techniques:

■ Select Formulas, Use in Formula and then click the name in the list that appears (see Figure 3.6).

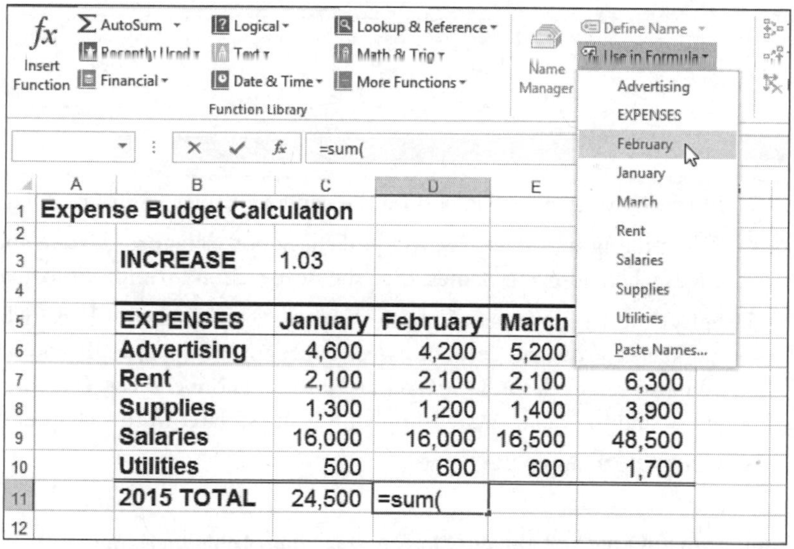

Figure 3.6
Drop down the Use in Formula list and then click the range name you want to insert into your formula.

■ Select Formulas, Use in Formula, Paste Names (or press F3) to display the Paste Name dialog box, click the range name you want to use, and then click OK.

■ Type the first letter or two of the range name to display a list of names and functions that start with those letters, select the name you want, and then press Tab.

Applying Names to Formulas

If you've been using ranges in your formulas and you name those ranges later, Excel doesn't automatically apply the new names to the formulas. Instead of substituting the appropriate names by hand, you can get Excel to do the hard work for you. Follow these steps to apply the new range names to your existing formulas:

1. Select the range in which you want to apply the names or select a single cell if you want to apply the names to the entire worksheet.

2. Select Formulas, Define Name, Apply Names. Excel displays the Apply Names dialog box, shown in Figure 3.7.

Figure 3.7
Use the Apply Names dialog box to select the names you want to apply to your formula ranges.

3. In the Apply Names list, choose the name or names you want applied from this list.

4. Select the Ignore Relative/Absolute check box to ignore relative and absolute references when applying names. (See the next section for more information on this option.)

5. Select the Use Row and Column Names check box to tell Excel whether to use the worksheet's row and column names when applying names. If you select this check box, you also can click the Options button to see more choices. (See the section "Using Row and Column Names When Applying Names," later in this chapter, for details.)

6. Click OK to apply the names.

Ignoring Relative and Absolute References When Applying Names

If you clear the Ignore Relative/Absolute option in the Apply Names dialog box, Excel replaces relative range references only with names that refer to relative references, and it replaces absolute range references only with names that refer to absolute references. If you leave this option selected, Excel ignores relative and absolute reference formats when applying names to a formula.

For example, suppose that you have a formula such as =SUM(A1:A10) and a range named Sales that refers to $A$1:$A$10. With the Ignore Relative/Absolute option turned off, Excel won't apply the name Sales to the range in the formula; Sales refers to an absolute range, and the formula contains a relative range. Unless you think you'll be moving your formulas around, you should leave the Ignore Relative/Absolute option selected.

Using Row and Column Names When Applying Names

For extra clarity in your formulas, leave the Use Row and Column Names check box selected in the Apply Names dialog box. This option tells Excel to rename all cell references that can be described as the intersection of a named row and a named column. In Figure 3.8, for example, the range C6:C10 is named January, and the range C7:E7 is named Rent. This means that cell C7—the intersection of these two ranges—can be referenced as January Rent.

As shown in Figure 3.8, the Total for the Rent row (cell F7) currently contains the formula =C7+D7+E7. If you applied range names to this worksheet and selected the Use Row and Column Names option, you'd think this formula would be changed to this:

```
=January Rent + February Rent + March Rent
```

Figure 3.8
Before range names are applied to the formulas, cell F7 (Total Rent) contains the formula =C7+D7+E7.

	A	B	C	D	E	F	G
	F7		fx	=C7+D7+E7			
1	**Expense Budget Calculation**						
2							
3		**INCREASE**	1.03				
4							
5		**EXPENSES**	**January**	**February**	**March**	**Total**	
6		Advertising	4,600	4,200	5,200	14,000	
7		Rent	2,100	2,100	2,100	6,300	
8		Supplies	1,300	1,200	1,400	3,900	
9		Salaries	16,000	16,000	16,500	48,500	
10		Utilities	500	600	600	1,700	
11		2015 TOTAL	24,500	24,100	25,800	74,400	
12							
13		2016 BUDGET	25,235	24,823	26,574	76,632	
14							

If you try this, however, you'll get a slightly different formula, as shown in Figure 3.9.

The reason for this is that when Excel is applying names, it omits the row name if the formula is in the same row. (It also omits the column name if the formula is in the same column.) In cell F7, for example, Excel omits Rent in each term because F7 is in the Rent row.

Figure 3.9
After range names are
applied, the Total Rent
cell contains the formula
`=January+`
`February+March.`

F7		⁞	✕ ✓	fx	=January+February+March		

	A	B	C	D	E	F	G
1		**Expense Budget Calculation**					
2							
3		**INCREASE**	1.03				
4							
5		**EXPENSES**	**January**	**February**	**March**	**Total**	
6		**Advertising**	4,600	4,200	5,200	14,000	
7		**Rent**	2,100	2,100	2,100	6,300	
8		**Supplies**	1,300	1,200	1,400	3,900	
9		**Salaries**	16,000	16,000	16,500	48,500	
10		**Utilities**	500	600	600	1,700	
11		**2015 TOTAL**	24,500	24,100	25,800	74,400	
12							
13		**2016 BUDGET**	25,235	24,823	26,574	76,632	
14							

Omitting row headings isn't a problem in a small model, but it can be confusing in a large worksheet, where you might not be able to see the names of the rows. Therefore, if you're applying names to a large worksheet, you'll probably prefer to include the row names when applying names.

Choosing the Options button in the Apply Names dialog box displays the expanded dialog box shown in Figure 3.10. This includes extra options that enable you to include column (and row) headings:

- **Omit Column Name if Same Column**—Clear this check box to include column names when applying names.
- **Omit Row Name if Same Row**—Clear this check box to include row names.
- **Name Order**—Use these options (Row Column or Column Row) to select the order of names in the reference.

Naming Formulas

In Chapter 2, you learned how to set up names for often-used constants. You can apply a similar naming concept for frequently used formulas. As with the constants, the formula doesn't physically have to appear in a cell. This not only saves memory but often makes your worksheets easier to read as well. Follow these steps to name a formula:

1. Select Formulas, Define Name to display the New Name dialog box.
2. Enter the name you want to use for the formula in the Name text box.
3. In the Refers To box, enter the formula exactly as you would if you were entering it in a worksheet.
4. Click OK.

Figure 3.10
The expanded Apply
Names dialog box.

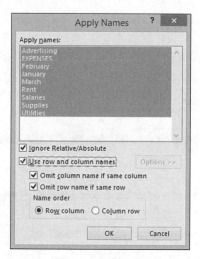

Now you can enter the formula name in your worksheet cells (instead of the formula itself). For example, the following is the formula for the volume of a sphere (r is the radius of the sphere):

$$4\pi r^3/3$$

So, assuming that you have a cell named Radius somewhere in the workbook, you could create a formula named, say, SphereVolume, and make the following entry in the Refers To box of the New Name dialog box (where PI() is the Excel worksheet function that returns the value of pi):

```
=(4 * PI() * Radius ^ 3) / 3
```

Working with Links in Formulas

If you have data in one workbook that you want to use in another, you can set up a link between the two workbooks. This action enables your formulas to use references to cells or ranges in the other workbook. When the other data changes, Excel automatically updates the link.

For example, Figure 3.11 shows two linked workbooks. The Budget Summary sheet in the 2017 Budget–Summary workbook includes data from the Details worksheet in the 2017 Budget workbook. Specifically, the formula shown for cell B2 in 2017 Budget–Summary contains an external reference to cell R7 in the Details worksheet of 2017 Budget. If the value in R7 changes, Excel immediately updates the 2017 Budget–Summary workbook.

> **NOTE** The workbook that contains the external reference is called the *dependent* workbook (or the *client* workbook). The workbook that contains the original data is called the *source* workbook (or the *server* workbook).

Figure 3.11
These two workbooks are linked because the formula in cell B2 of the 2017 Budget–Summary workbook references cell R7 in the 2017 Budget workbook.

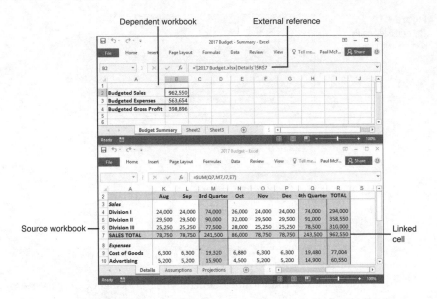

Understanding External References

There's no big mystery behind external reference links. You set up links by including an external reference to a cell or range in another workbook (or in another worksheet from the same workbook). In the example shown in Figure 3.11, all I did was enter an equal sign in cell B2 of the Budget Summary worksheet and then click cell R7 in the Details worksheet.

You just need to be comfortable with the structure of an external reference. Here's the syntax:

```
'path[workbookname]sheetname'!reference
```

path	The drive and directory in which the workbook is located, which can be a local path, a network path, or even an Internet address. You need to include the path only when the workbook is closed.
workbookname	The name of the workbook, including an extension. Always enclose the workbook name in square brackets ([ ]). You can omit *workbookname* if you're referencing a cell or range in another sheet of the same workbook.
sheetname	The name of the worksheet's tab. You can omit *sheetname* if *reference* is a defined name in the same workbook.
reference	A cell or range reference, or a defined name.

For example, if you close the 2017 Budget workbook, Excel automatically changes the external reference shown in Figure 3.11 to this (depending on the actual path of the file):

```
='C:\Users\Paul\Documents\[2017 Budget.xlsx]Details'!$R$7
```

You need the single quotation marks around the path, workbook name, and sheet name only if the workbook is closed or if the path, workbook, or sheet name contains spaces. If in doubt, include the single quotation marks anyway; Excel happily ignores them if they're not required.

Updating Links

The purpose of a link is to avoid duplicating formulas and data in multiple worksheets. If one workbook contains the information you need, you can use a link to reference the data without re-creating it in another workbook.

To be useful, however, the data in the dependent workbook should always reflect what actually is in the source workbook. You can make sure of this by updating the link, as explained here:

 If both the source and the dependent workbooks are open, Excel automatically updates the link whenever the data in the source file changes.

■ If the source workbook is open when you open the dependent workbook, Excel automatically updates the links again.

■ If the source workbook is closed when you open the dependent workbook, Excel displays a security warning in the information bar, which tells you that automatic updating of links has been disabled. In this case, click Enable Content.

TIP If you always trust the links in your workbooks (that is, if you never deal with third-party workbooks or any other workbooks from sources you don't completely trust), you can configure Excel to always update links automatically. To begin, select File, Options, click Trust Center, and then click Trust Center Settings. In the Trust Center dialog box, click External Content and then click to select the Enable Automatic Update for All Workbook Links option. Click OK and then click OK again.

■ If you didn't update a link when you opened the dependent document, you can update it any time by choosing Data, Edit Links. In the Edit Links dialog box that appears (see Figure 3.12), click the link and then click Update Values.

Changing the Link Source

If the name of the source document changes, you'll need to edit the link to keep the data up to date. You can edit the external reference directly, or you can change the source by following these steps:

1. With the dependent workbook active, select Data, Edit Links to display the Edit Links dialog box.
2. Click the link you want to work with.

3. Click Change Source. Excel displays the Change Source dialog box.

4. Find and then select the new source document and then click OK to return to the Edit Links dialog box.

5. Click Close to return to the workbook.

Figure 3.12
Use the Edit Links dialog box to update the linked data in the source workbook.

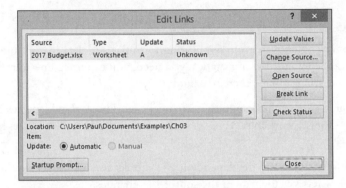

Formatting Numbers, Dates, and Times

One of the best ways to improve the readability of worksheets is to display your data in a format that is logical, consistent, and straightforward. Formatting currency amounts with leading dollar signs, percentages with trailing percent signs, and large numbers with commas are a few of the ways you can improve your spreadsheet style.

This section shows you how to format numbers, dates, and times using Excel's built-in formatting options. You'll also learn how to create your own formats to gain maximum control over the appearance of your data.

Numeric Display Formats

When you enter numbers in a worksheet, Excel removes any leading or trailing zeros. For example, if you enter 0123.4500, Excel displays 123.45. The exception to this rule occurs when you enter a number that is wider than the cell. In that case, Excel usually expands the width of the column to fit the number. However, in some cases, Excel tailors the number to fit the cell by rounding off some decimal places. For example, a number such as 123.45678 is displayed as 123.4568. Note that, in this case, the number is changed for display purposes only; Excel still retains the original number internally.

When you create a worksheet, each cell uses this format, known as the *General* number format, by default. If you want your numbers to appear differently, you can select from among Excel's seven categories of numeric formats:

- **Number**—The number formats have three components: the number of decimal places, whether the thousands separator (,) is used, and how negative numbers are displayed. For negative numbers, you can display the number with a leading minus sign, in red, surrounded by parentheses, or in red surrounded by parentheses.

N O T E Although you can select a number as high as 30 in the Decimal Places spin box, Excel will display only the first 14 decimal places. This applies to percentages as well (see below).

- **Currency**—The currency formats are similar to the number formats, except that the thousands separator is always used, and you have the option of displaying the numbers with a leading dollar sign ($) or some other currency symbol.

- **Accounting**—With the accounting formats, you can select the number of decimal places and whether to display a leading dollar sign (or other currency symbol). If you do use a dollar sign, Excel displays it flush left in the cell. All negative entries are displayed surrounded by parentheses.

- **Percentage**—The percentage formats display the number multiplied by 100 with a percent sign (%) to the right of the number. For example, .506 is displayed as 50.6%. You can display up to 14 decimal places.

- **Fraction**—The fraction formats enable you to express decimal quantities as fractions. There are nine fraction formats in all, including displaying the number as halves, quarters, eighths, sixteenths, tenths, and hundredths.

- **Scientific**—The scientific formats display the most significant number to the left of the decimal, 2–30 decimal places to the right of the decimal, and then the exponent. So, 123000 is displayed as 1.23E+05.

- **Special**—The special formats are a collection designed to take care of special cases. Here's a list of the special formats, with some examples:

Format	Enter This	It Displays as This
ZIP Code	1234	01234
ZIP Code + 4	123456789	12345-6789
Phone Number	1234567890	(123) 456-7890
Social Security Number	123456789	123-45-6789

Changing Numeric Formats

The quickest way to format numbers is to specify the format as you enter your data. For example, if you begin a dollar amount with a dollar sign ($), Excel automatically formats the number as currency. Similarly, if you type a percent sign (%) after a number, Excel automatically formats the number as a percentage. Here are a few more examples of this technique. Note that you can enter a negative value using either the negative sign (–) or parentheses.

Number Entered	Number Displayed	Format Used
$1234.567	$1,234.57	Currency
($1234.5)	($1,234.50)	Currency
10%	10%	Percentage
123E+02	1.23E+04	Scientific
5 3/4	5 3/4	Fraction
0 3/4	3/4	Fraction
3/4	4–Mar	Date

> **NOTE**
> Excel interprets a simple fraction such as 3/4 as a date (March 4, in this case). Always include a leading zero, followed by a space, if you want to enter a simple fraction in the formula bar.

Specifying the numeric format as you enter a number is fast and efficient because Excel guesses the format you want to use. Unfortunately, Excel sometimes guesses wrong (for example, interpreting a simple fraction as a date). In any case, you don't have access to all the available formats (for example, displaying negative dollar amounts in red). To overcome these limitations, you can select your numeric formats from a list. Here are the steps to follow:

1. Select the cell or range of cells to which you want to apply the new format.
2. Select the Home tab.
3. Pull down the Number Format list. Excel displays its built-in formats, as shown in Figure 3.13. Under the name of each format, Excel shows you how the current cell would be displayed if you chose that format.
4. Click the format you want to use.

For more numeric formatting options, use the Number tab of the Format Cells dialog box (or display the Number Format list and select More Number Formats). Select the cell or range and then select Home, Number Format, More Number Formats. (You can also click the Number group's dialog box launcher or press Ctrl+1.) As you can see in Figure 3.14, when you click a numeric format in the Category list, Excel displays more formatting options, such as the Decimal Places spin box. (The options you see depend on the category you select.) The Sample information box shows a sample of the format applied to the current cell's contents.

As an alternative to the Format Cells dialog box, Excel offers several keyboard shortcuts for setting the numeric format. Select the cell or range you want to format and use one of the key combinations listed in Table 3.6.

Figure 3.13
On the Home tab, pull
down the Number Format
list to see all of Excel's
built-in numeric formats.

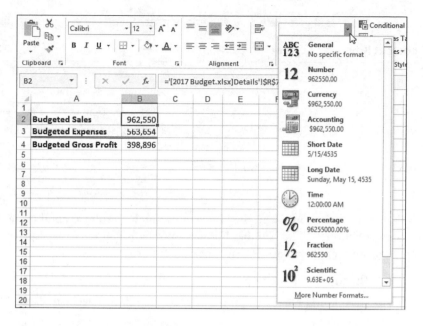

Figure 3.14
When you select a format
in the Category list, Excel
displays the format's
options.

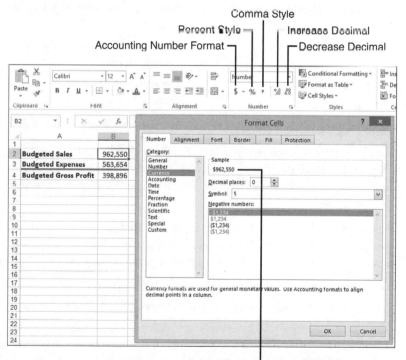

Table 3.6   Shortcut Keys for Selecting Numeric Formats

Shortcut Key	Format
Ctrl+~	General
Ctrl+!	Number (two decimal places; using thousands separator)
Ctrl+$	Currency (two decimal places; using dollar sign; negative numbers surrounded by parentheses)
Ctrl+%	Percentage (zero decimal places)
Ctrl+^	Scientific (two decimal places)

You can use the controls in the Home tab's Number group as another method of selecting numeric formats. The Number Format list (refer to Figure 3.13) displays all the formats. Here are the other controls that appear in this group:

Button	Format
Accounting Number Format	Accounting (two decimal places; using dollar sign)
Percent Style	Percentage (zero decimal places)
Comma Style	Number (two decimal places; using thousands separator)
Increase Decimal	Increases the number of decimal places in the current format
Decrease Decimal	Decreases the number of decimal places in the current format

Customizing Numeric Formats

Excel numeric formats give you lots of control over how your numbers are displayed, but they have their limitations. For example, no built-in format enables you to display a number such as 0.5 without the leading zero or to display temperatures using, for example, the degree symbol.

To overcome these and other limitations, you need to create your own custom numeric formats. You can do this either by editing an existing format or by entering your own from scratch. The formatting syntax and symbols are explained in detail later in this section.

Every Excel numeric format, whether built in or customized, has the following syntax:

```
positive format;negative format;zero format;text format
```

The four parts, separated by semicolons, determine how various numbers are presented. The first part defines how a positive number is displayed, the second part defines how a negative number is displayed, the third part defines how zero is displayed, and the fourth part defines how text is displayed. If you leave out one or more of these parts, numbers are controlled as shown here:

Number of Parts	Format Syntax Used
Three	*positive format;negative format;zero format*
Two	*positive and zero format; negative format*
One	*positive, negative, and zero format*

Table 3.7 lists the special symbols you use to define each of these parts.

Table 3.7 Numeric Formatting Symbols

Symbol	Description
General	Displays the number with the General format.
#	Holds a place for a digit and displays the digit exactly as typed. Displays nothing if no number is entered.
0	Holds a place for a digit and displays the digit exactly as typed. Displays 0 if no number is entered.
?	Holds a place for a digit and displays the digit exactly as typed. Displays a space if no number is entered.
. (period)	Sets the location of the decimal point.
, (comma)	Sets the location of the thousands separator. Marks only the location of the first thousand.
%	Multiplies the number by 100 (for display only) and adds the percent (%) character.
E+ e+ E- e-	Displays the number in scientific format. E- and e- place a minus sign in the exponent; E+ and e+ place a plus sign in the exponent.
/ (slash)	Sets the location of the fraction separator.
$ ( ) : - + <space>	Displays the character.
*	Repeats whatever character immediately follows the asterisk until the cell is full. Doesn't replace other symbols or numbers.
_ (underscore)	Inserts a blank space the width of whatever character follows the underscore.
\ (backslash)	Inserts the character that follows the backslash.
"text"	Inserts the text that appears within the quotation marks.
@	Holds a place for text.
[COLOR]	Displays the cell contents in the specified color.
[COLORn]	Displays the cell contents in the specified color value (where n is a number between 1 and 56).
[condition value]	Uses conditional statements to specify when the format is to be used.

3

Before looking at some examples, let's run through the basic procedure. To customize a numeric format, select the cell or range you want to format and then follow these steps:

1. Select Home, Number Format, More Number Formats (or press Ctrl+1) and select the Number tab, if it's not already displayed.

2. In the Category list, click Custom.

3. If you're editing an existing format, select it in the Type list box.

4. Edit or enter your format code.

5. Click OK. Excel returns you to the worksheet, where you see the custom format applied.

Excel stores each new format definition in the Custom category. If you edited an existing format, the original format is left intact, and the new format is added to the list. You can select the custom formats the same way you select the built-in formats. To use a custom format in other workbooks, you copy a cell containing the format to that workbook. Figure 3.15 shows a dozen examples of custom formats.

Figure 3.15
Sample custom numeric formats.

	Example	Custom Format	Cell Entry	Result
2				
3	1	0,.0	12500	12.5
4		0,,.0 "million"	12500000	12.5 million
5	2	#.##	.5	.5
6	3	#,##0;-#,##0;0;"Enter a number"	1234	1,234
7		#,##0;-#,##0;0;"Enter a number"	-1234	-1,234
8		#,##0;-#,##0;0;"Enter a number"	0	0
9		#,##0;-#,##0;0;"Enter a number"	text	Enter a number
10	4	0¢	25	25¢
11	5	#,##0 "Dollars"	1234	1,234 Dollars
12	6	#.##\M	1.44	1.44M
13	7	#,##0.0°F	98.6	98.6°F
14	8	;;;	1234	
15	9	"Acct"\# 00-0000;;;"Don't enter dash"	123456	Acct# 12-3456
16		"Acct"\# 00-0000;;;"Don't enter dash"	12-3456	Don't enter dash
17	10	#*.	1234	1234...:.................
18		;;;@*.	March	March.................
19	11	;;;*.@	March	................March
20	12	+?? ?/?;[Red]-?? /?	-12.75	-12 3/4

Here's a quick explanation of each example:

- **Example 1**—These formats show how you can reduce a large number to a smaller, more readable one by using the thousands separator. A format such as 0,000.0 would display, for example, 12500 as 12,500.0. If you remove the three zeros between the comma and the decimal (to get the format 0,.0), Excel displays the number as 12.5 (although it still uses the original number in calculations). In essence, you've told Excel to express the number in thousands. To express a larger number in millions, you just add a second thousands separator.

- **Example 2**—Use this format when you want to display no leading or trailing zeros.

- **Example 3**—These are examples of four-part formats. The first three parts define how Excel should display positive numbers, negative numbers, and zero. The fourth part displays the message "Enter a number" if the user enters text in the cell.

- **Example 4**—In this example, the cents sign (¢) is used after the value. To enter the cents sign, press Alt+0162 on your keyboard's numeric keypad. (This won't work if you use the numbers along the top of the keyboard.) Table 3.8 shows some common ANSI characters you can use.

Table 3.8   ANSI Character Key Combinations

Key Combination	ANSI Character
Alt+0162	¢
Alt+0163	£
Alt+0165	¥
Alt+0169	©
Alt+0174	®
Alt+0176	°

3

- **Example 5**—This example adds the thousands separator and the text string `"Dollars"` to the format.

- **Example 6**—In this example, an M is appended to any number, which is useful if your spreadsheet unit is megabytes.

- **Example 7**—This example uses the degree symbol (°) to display temperatures.

- **Example 8**—The three semicolons used in this example result in no number being displayed (which is useful as a basic method for hiding a sensitive value).

- **Example 9**—This example shows that you can get a number sign (#) to display in your formats by preceding # with a backslash (\).

- **Example 10**—In this example, you see a trick for creating dot trailers. Recall that the asterisk (*) symbol fills the cell with whatever character follows it. So, creating a dot trailer is a simple matter of adding `"*."` to the end of the format.

- **Example 11**—This example shows a similar technique that creates a dot leader. Here, the first three semicolons display nothing; then `"*."` runs dots from the beginning of the cell up to the text (represented by the @ sign).

- **Example 12**—This example shows a format that's useful for entering stock quotations.

3

Hiding Zeros

Worksheets look less cluttered and are easier to read if you hide unnecessary zeros. Excel enables you to hide zeros either throughout an entire worksheet or only in selected cells.

To hide all zeros, select File, Options, click the Advanced tab in the Excel Options dialog box, and scroll down to the Display Options for This Worksheet section. Clear the Show a Zero in Cells That Have Zero Value check box and then click OK.

To hide zeros in selected cells, create a custom format that uses the following format syntax:

```
positive format;negative format;
```

The extra semicolon at the end acts as a placeholder for the zero format. Because there's no definition for a zero value, nothing is displayed. For example, the format `$#,##0.00_);($#,##0.00);` displays standard dollar values, but it leaves the cell blank if it contains zero.

> **TIP**
>
> If your worksheet contains only integers (no fractions or decimal places), you can use the format `#,###` to hide zeros.

Using Condition Values

The actions of the formats you've seen so far have depended on whether the cell contents were positive, negative, zero, or text. Although this is fine for most applications, sometimes you need to format a cell based on different conditions. For example, you might want only specific numbers, or numbers within a certain range, to take on a particular format. You can achieve this effect by using the [condition value] format symbol. With this symbol, you set up conditional statements using the logical operators =, <, >, <=, >=, and <>, plus the appropriate numbers. You then assign these conditions to each part of your format definition.

For example, suppose you have a worksheet for which the data must be within the range –1,000 to 1,000. To flag numbers outside this range, you set up the following format definition:

```
[>=1000]"Error: Value >= 1,000";[<=-1000]"Error: Value <= -1,000";0.00
```

The first part defines the format for numbers greater than or equal to 1,000 (an error message). The second part defines the format for numbers less than or equal to –1,000 (also an error message). The third part defines the format for all other numbers (0.00).

→ To learn about using Excel's extensive conditional formatting features, **see** "Applying Conditional Formatting to a Range," **p. 25**.

Date and Time Display Formats

If you include dates or times in your worksheets, you need to make sure that they're presented in a readable, unambiguous format. For example, most Americans would interpret the date 8/5/16 as August 5, 2016. However, in some countries, this date would mean May 8, 2016. Similarly, if you use the time 2:45, do you mean a.m. or p.m.? To avoid these kinds of problems, you can use Excel's built-in date and time formats, listed in Table 3.9.

Table 3.9   Excel's Date and Time Formats

Format	Display
m/d	8/3
m/d/yy	8/3/16
mm/dd/yy	08/03/16
d-mmm	3-Aug
d-mmm-yy	3-Aug-16
dd-mmm-yy	03-Aug-16
mmm-yy	Aug-16
mmmm-yy	August-16
mmmm d, yyyy	August 3, 2016
h:mm AM/PM	3:10 PM
h:mm:ss AM/PM	3:10:45 PM
h:mm	15:10
h:mm:ss	15:10:45
mm:ss.0	10:45.7
[h]:[mm]:[ss]	25:61:61
m/d/yy h:mm AM/PM	8/23/16 3:10 PM
m/d/yy h:mm	8/23/16 15:10

The [h]:[mm]:[ss] format requires a bit of explanation. You use this format when you want to display hours greater than 24 or minutes and seconds greater than 60. For example, suppose that you have an application in which you need to sum several time values (such as the time you've spent working on a project). If you add, say, 10:00 and 15:00, Excel normally shows the total as 1:00 (because, by default, Excel restarts times at 0 when they hit 24:00). To display the result properly (that is, as 25:00), use the format [h]:00.

You use the same methods you used for numeric formats to select date and time formats. In particular, you can specify the date and time format as you input your data. For example, entering `Jan-16` automatically formats the cell with the mmm-yy format. Also, you can use the following shortcut keys:

Shortcut Key	Format
Ctrl+#	d—mmm—yy
Ctrl+@	h:mm AM/PM
Ctrl+;	Current date (m/d/yy)
Ctrl+:	Current time (h:mm AM/PM)

> **TIP**
>
> Excel for the Macintosh uses a different date system than Excel for Windows uses. If you share files between these environments, you need to use Macintosh dates in your Excel for Windows worksheets to maintain the correct dates when you move from one system to another. Select File, Options, click Advanced, scroll down to the When Calculating This Workbook section, and then select the Use 1904 Date System check box.

Customizing Date and Time Formats

Although the built-in date and time formats are fine for most applications, you might need to create your own custom formats. For example, you might want to display the day of the week (for example, `Friday`). Custom date and time formats generally are simpler to create than custom numeric formats. There are fewer formatting symbols, and you usually don't need to specify different formats for different conditions. Table 3.10 lists the date and time formatting symbols.

Table 3.10   Date and Time Formatting Symbols

Symbol	Description
Date Formats	
d	Day number without a leading zero (`1–31`)
dd	Day number with a leading zero (`01–31`)
ddd	Three-letter day abbreviation (`Mon`, for example)
dddd	Full day name (`Monday`, for example)
m	Month number without a leading zero (`1–12`)
mm	Month number with a leading zero (`01–12`)
mmm	Three-letter month abbreviation (`Aug`, for example)
mmmm	Full month name (`August`, for example)
yy	Two-digit year (`00–99`)
yyyy	Full year (`1900–2078`)

Symbol	Description
Time Formats	
h	Hour without a leading zero (0–24)
hh	Hour with a leading zero (00–24)
m	Minute without a leading zero (0–59)
mm	Minute with a leading zero (00–59)
s	Second without a leading zero (0–59)
ss	Second with a leading zero (00–59)
AM/PM, am/pm, A/P	12-hour clock time
/ : . -	Symbols used to separate parts of dates or times
[COLOR]	Date or time displayed in the color specified
[condition value]	Conditional statements specifying when the format is to be used

Figure 3.16 shows some examples of custom date and time formats.

Figure 3.16
Sample custom date and time formats.

	A	B	C	D
1				
2		Custom Format	Cell Entry	Result
3		dddd, mmmm d, yyyy	8/23/2016	Tuesday, August 23, 2016
4		mmmm, yyyy	8/23/2016	August, 2016
5		dddd	8/23/2016	Tuesday
6		mm.dd.yy	8/23/2016	08.23.16
7		mmddyy	8/23/2016	082316
8		yymmdd	8/23/2016	160823
9		[>8/15/16]"OVERDUE!";mm/dd/yy	8/23/2016	OVERDUE!
10				
11		hhmm "hours"	3:10 PM	1510 hours
12		hh"h" mm"m"	3:10 PM	15h 10m
13		[=.5]"12 Noon";[=0]"12 Midnight";h:mm AM/PM	0	12 Midnight
14		[=.5]"12 Noon";[=0]"12 Midnight";h:mm AM/PM	12:00	12 Noon
15		[=.5]"12 Noon";[=0]"12 Midnight";h:mm AM/PM	3:10 PM	3:10 PM

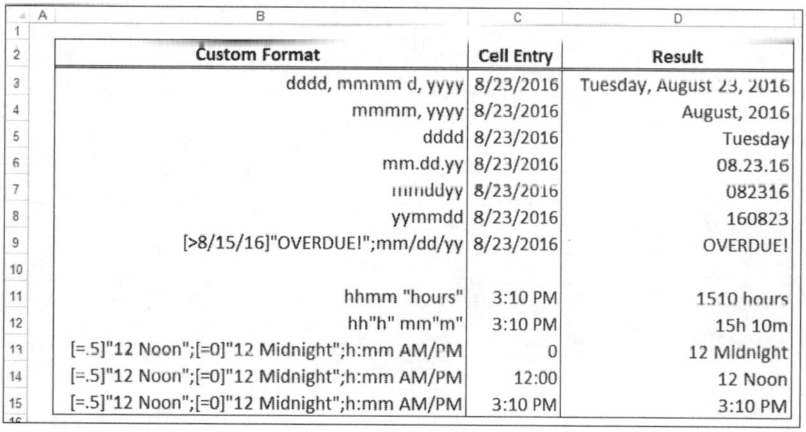

Deleting Custom Formats

The best way to become familiar with custom formats is to try your own experiments. Just remember that Excel stores each format you try. If you find that your list of custom formats is getting a bit unwieldy or that it's cluttered with unused formats, you can delete formats by following the steps outlined here:

1. Select Home, Number Format, More Number Formats.
2. Click the Custom category.

3. Click the format in the Type list box. (Note that you can delete only the formats that were added to Excel's standard list.)

4. Click Delete. Excel removes the format from the list.

5. To delete other formats, repeat steps 2 through 4.

6. Click OK. Excel returns you to the spreadsheet.

From Here

- To learn about conditional formatting, **see** "Applying Conditional Formatting to a Range," **p. 25**.

- To learn how to solve formula problems, **see** Chapter 5, "Troubleshooting Formulas," **p. 111**.

- To get details on text formulas and functions, **see** Chapter 7, "Working with Text Functions,"**p. 139**.

- If you want to use logical worksheet functions in your comparison formulas, **see** "Adding Intelligence with Logical Functions," **p. 163**.

- To learn how to create and use data tables, **see** "Using What-If Analysis," **p. 349**.

Creating Advanced Formulas

Excel is a versatile program with many uses, from acting as a checkbook to a flat-file database-management system, to an equation solver, to a glorified calculator. For most business users, however, Excel's forte is building models that enable quantification of particular aspects of the business. The skeleton of the business model is made up of the chunks of data entered, imported, or copied into the worksheets. But the lifeblood of the model and the animating force behind it is the collection of formulas for summarizing data, answering questions, and making predictions.

You saw in Chapter 3, "Building Basic Formulas," that, armed with the humble equal sign and Excel's operators and operands, you can cobble together useful, robust formulas. But Excel has many other tricks up its digital sleeve, and these techniques enable you to create muscular formulas that can take your business models to the next level.

Working with Arrays

When you work with a range of cells, it might appear as though you're working with a single thing. In reality, however, Excel treats the range as a number of discrete units.

This is in contrast with the subject of this section: the array. An *array* is a group of cells or values that Excel treats as a unit. In a range configured as an array, for example, Excel no longer treats the cells individually. Instead, it works with all the cells at once, which means you can apply a formula to every cell in the range by using just a single operation, for example.

You create arrays either by running a function that returns an array result (such as DOCUMENTS(); see the section "Functions That Use or Return Arrays," later in this chapter) or by entering an *array formula*, which is a single formula that either uses an array as an argument or enters its results in multiple cells.

Using Array Formulas

Here's a straightforward example that illustrates how array formulas work. In the Expenses workbook shown in Figure 4.1, the 2016 BUDGET totals are calculated using a separate formula for each month, as shown here:

Total	Formula
January 2016 BUDGET	=C11*$C$3
February 2016 BUDGET	=D11*$C$3
March 2016 BUDGET	=E11*$C$3

Figure 4.1
This worksheet uses three separate formulas to calculate the 2016 BUDGET figures.

	A	B	C	D	E	F
1		Expense Budget Calculation				
2						
3		INCREASE	1.03			
4						
5		EXPENSES	January	February	March	
6		Advertising	4,600	4,200	5,200	
7		Rent	2,100	2,100	2,100	
8		Supplies	1,300	1,200	1,400	
9		Salaries	16,000	16,000	16,500	
10		Utilities	500	600	600	
11		2015 TOTAL	24,500	24,100	25,800	
12						
13		2016 BUDGET	25,235	24,823	26,574	
14						

C13   fx   =C11*$C$3

You can replace all three formulas with a single array formula by following these steps:

1. Select the range you want to use for the array formula. In the 2016 BUDGET example, you'd select C13:E13.

2. Type the formula and, in the places where you would normally enter a cell reference, type a range reference that includes the cells you want to use. *Do not*—I repeat, *do not*—press Enter when you're done. In the example, you'd type `=C11:E11*$C$3`.

3. To enter the formula as an array, press Ctrl+Shift+Enter.

The 2016 BUDGET cells (C13, D13, and E13) now contain the same formula:

`{=C11:E11*$C$3}`

In other words, you were able to enter a formula into three different cells by using just a single operation. This saves you tremendous amounts of time when you would otherwise have to enter the same formula into many different cells.

Notice that the formula is surrounded by braces ({ }). This identifies the formula as an array formula. (When you enter array formulas, you never need to enter these braces yourself; Excel adds them automatically when you press Ctrl+Shift+Enter.)

> **NOTE**
>
> Because Excel treats an array as a unit, you can't move or delete part of an array. If you need to work with an array, you must select the whole thing. If you want to reduce the size of an array, select it, select the formula bar, and then press Ctrl+Enter to change the entry to a normal formula. You can then select the smaller range and reenter the array formula.
>
> Note that you can select an array quickly by selecting one of its cells and pressing Ctrl+/.

Understanding Array Formulas

To understand how Excel processes an array, you need to keep in mind that Excel always sets up a correspondence between the array cells and the cells of whatever range you entered into the array formula. In the 2016 BUDGET example, the array consists of cells C13, D13, and E13, and the range used in the formula consists of cells C11, D11, and E11. Excel sets up correspondences between array cell C13 and input cell C11, between D13 and D11, and between E13 and E11. To calculate the value of cell C13 (the January 2016 BUDGET), for example, Excel just grabs the input value from cell C11 and substitutes that in the formula. Figure 4.2 shows a diagram of this process.

Figure 4.2
When processing an array formula, Excel sets up a correspondence between the array cells and the range used in the formula.

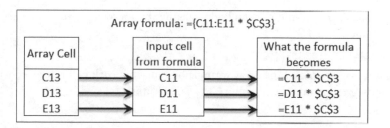

Array formula: =$\{$C11:E11 * C3$\}$

Array Cell	Input cell from formula	What the formula becomes
C13	C11	=C11 * $C$3
D13	D11	=D11 * $C$3
E13	E11	=E11 * $C$3

Array formulas can be confusing, but if you keep these correspondences in mind, you should have no trouble figuring out what's going on.

Array Formulas That Operate on Multiple Ranges

In the preceding example, the array formula operated on a single range, but array formulas also can operate on multiple ranges. For example, consider the Invoice Template worksheet shown in Figure 4.3. The totals in the Extension column (cells F12 through F16) are generated by a series of formulas that multiply the item's price by the quantity ordered:

Cell	Formula
F12	=B12*E12
F13	=B13*E13
F14	=B14*E14
F15	=B15*E15
F16	=B16*E16

Figure 4.3
This worksheet uses several formulas to calculate the extended totals for each line.

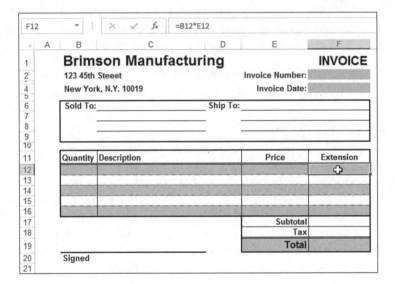

You can replace all these formulas by making the following entry as an array formula into the range F12:F16:

```
=B12:B16*E12:E16
```

Again, you've created the array formula by replacing each cell reference with the corresponding range (and by pressing Ctrl+Shift+Enter).

NOTE You don't have to enter array formulas in multiple cells. For example, if you don't need the Extended totals in the Invoice Template worksheet, you can still calculate the Subtotal by making the following entry an array formula in cell F17:

```
=SUM(B12:B16*E12:E16)
```

Using Array Constants

In the array formulas you've seen so far, the array arguments have been cell ranges. You also can use constant values as array arguments. This procedure enables you to input values into a formula without having them clutter your worksheet.

To enter an array constant in a formula, observe the following guidelines while entering the values right in the formula:

- Enclose the values in braces ({ }).
- If you want Excel to treat the values as a row, type a comma after each value (except the last value).
- If you want Excel to treat the values as a column, type a semicolon after each value (except the last value).

For example, the following array constant is the equivalent of entering the individual values in a column on your worksheet:

```
{1;2;3;4}
```

Similarly, the following array constant is equivalent to entering the values in a worksheet range of three columns and two rows:

```
{1,2,3;4,5,6}
```

As a practical example, Figure 4.4 shows two different array formulas. The one on the left (used in the range E4:E7) calculates various loan payments, given the different interest rates in the range C5:C8. The array formula on the right (used in the range F4:F7) does the same thing, but the interest rate values are entered as an array constant directly in the formula.

→ To learn how the PMT() function works, **see** "Calculating a Loan Payment," **p. 435**.

Functions That Use or Return Arrays

Many of Excel's worksheet functions either require an array argument or return an array result (or both). Table 4.1 lists several of these functions and explains how each one uses arrays. (See Part II, "Harnessing the Power of Functions," for explanations of these functions.)

Figure 4.4
Using array constants in your array formulas means you don't have to clutter your worksheet with the input values.

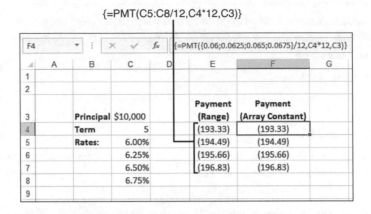

Table 4.1	Some Excel Functions That Use Arrays	
Function	**Uses Array Argument?**	**Returns Array Result?**
COLUMN()	No	Yes, if the argument is a range
COLUMNS()	Yes	No
GROWTH()	Yes	Yes
HLOOKUP()	Yes	No
INDEX()	Yes	Yes
LINEST()	No	Yes
LOGEST()	No	Yes
LOOKUP()	Yes	No
MATCH()	Yes	No
MDETERM()	Yes	No
MINVERSE()	No	Yes
MMULT()	No	Yes
ROW()	No	Yes, if the argument is a range
ROWS()	Yes	No
SUMPRODUCT()	Yes	No
TRANSPOSE()	Yes	Yes
TREND()	Yes	Yes
VLOOKUP()	Yes	No

NOTE
When you use functions that return arrays, be sure to select a range that's large enough to hold the resulting array and then enter the function as an array formula.

→ Arrays become truly powerful weapons in your Excel arsenal when you combine them with worksheet functions such as `IF()` and `SUM()`. I'll provide you with many examples of array formulas as I introduce you to Excel's worksheet functions throughout Part II. In particular, **see** "Combining Logical Functions with Arrays," **p. 173**.

Using Iteration and Circular References

A common business problem involves calculating a profit-sharing plan contribution as a percentage of a company's net profits. This isn't a simple multiplication problem because the net profit is determined partly by the profit-sharing figure. For example, suppose that a company has revenue of $1,000,000 and expenses of $900,000, which leaves gross profit of $100,000. The company also sets aside 10% of net profits for profit sharing. The net profit is calculated with the following formula:

```
Net Profit = Gross Profit - Profit Sharing Contribution
```

This is called a *circular reference formula* because there are terms on the left and right sides of the equal sign that depend on each other. Specifically, `Profit Sharing Contribution` is derived with the following formula:

```
Profit Sharing Contribution = (Net Profit) * 0.1
```

→ Circular references are usually a bad thing to have in a spreadsheet model. To learn how to combat the bad kind, **see** "Fixing Circular References," **p. 118**. (Chapter 5)

One way to solve such a formula is to guess at an answer and see how close you come. For example, because profit sharing should be 10% of net profits, a good first guess might be 10% of *gross* profits, or $10,000. If you plug this number into the formula, you end up with a net profit of $90,000. However, this isn't right because 10% of $90,000 is $9,000. Therefore, the profit-sharing guess is off by $1,000.

So, you can try again. This time, use $9,000 as the profit-sharing number. Plugging this new value into the formula gives a net profit of $91,000. This number translates into a profit-sharing contribution of $9,100—which is off by only $100.

If you continue this process, your profit-sharing guesses will get closer to (that is, it will converge on) the calculated value. When the guesses are close enough (for example, within $1), you can stop and pat yourself on the back for finding the solution. This technique is called *iteration*.

Of course, you didn't spend your (or your company's) hard-earned money on a computer so that you could do this sort of thing by hand. Excel makes iterative calculations a breeze, as you see in the following procedure:

1. Set up your worksheet and enter your circular reference formula. Figure 4.5 shows a worksheet for the profit-sharing example just discussed. If Excel displays a dialog box telling you that it can't resolve circular references, click OK and then select Formulas, Remove Arrows (see Chapter 5).

Figure 4.5
A worksheet with a circular reference formula.

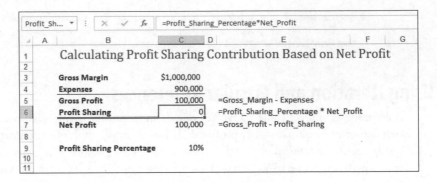

2. Select File, Options to display the Excel Options dialog box.

3. Click Formulas.

4. Activate the Enable Iterative Calculation check box.

5. Use the Maximum Iterations spin box to specify the number of iterations you need. In most cases, the default figure of 100 is more than enough.

6. Use the Maximum Change text box to tell Excel how accurate you want your results to be. The smaller the number, the longer the iteration takes and the more accurate the calculation will be. Again, the default value of 0.001 is a reasonable compromise in most situations.

7. Click OK. Excel begins the iteration and stops when it has found a solution (see Figure 4.6).

Figure 4.6
The solution to the iterative profit-sharing problem.

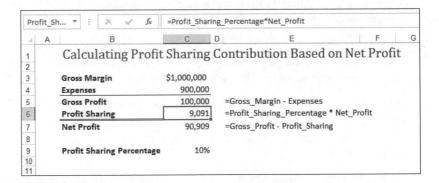

TIP

If you want to watch the progress of the iteration, select the Manual option button in the Calculation Options section of the Formulas tab and enter **1** in the Maximum Iterations spin box. When you return to your worksheet, each time you press F9, Excel performs a single pass of the iteration.

Consolidating Multisheet Data

Many businesses create worksheets for specific tasks and then distribute them to various departments. The most common example is budgeting. Accounting might create a generic "budget" template that each department or division in the company must fill out and return. Similarly, you often see worksheets distributed for inventory requirements, sales forecasting, survey data, experimental results, and more.

Creating these worksheets, distributing them, and filling them in are all straightforward operations. However, the tricky part comes when the sheets are returned to the originating department, and all the new data must be combined into a summary report showing companywide totals. This task is called *consolidating* the data, and it's often no picnic, especially for large worksheets. However, as you'll soon see, Excel has some powerful features that can take the drudgery out of consolidation.

Excel can consolidate your data using one of the following two methods:

- **Consolidating by position**—With this method, Excel consolidates the data from several worksheets, using the same range coordinates on each sheet. You can use this method if the worksheets you're consolidating have an identical layout.

- **Consolidating by category**—This method tells Excel to consolidate the data by looking for identical row and column labels in each sheet. For example, if one worksheet lists monthly Gizmo sales in row 1 and another lists monthly Gizmo sales in row 5, you can consolidate this information as long as both sheets have a "Gizmo" label at the beginning of these rows.

In both cases, you specify one or more *source ranges* (the ranges that contain the data you want to consolidate) and a *destination range* (the range where the consolidated data will appear). The next couple of sections take you through the details for both consolidation methods.

Consolidating by Position

If the sheets you're working with have the same layout, consolidating by position is the easiest way to go. For example, check out the three workbooks—Division I Budget, Division II Budget, and Division III Budget—shown in Figure 4.7. As you can see, each sheet uses the same row and column labels, so they're perfect candidates for consolidation by position.

Begin by creating a new worksheet that has the same layout as the sheets you're consolidating. Figure 4.8 shows a new Consolidation workbook that I'll use to consolidate the three budget sheets.

Let's look at how to go about consolidating the sales data in the three budget worksheets shown in Figure 4.7. We're dealing with three source ranges:

```
'[Division I Budget]Details'!B4:M6
'[Division II Budget]Details'!B4:M6
'[Division III Budget]Details'!B4:M6
```

Figure 4.7
When your worksheets are laid out identically, use consolidation by position.

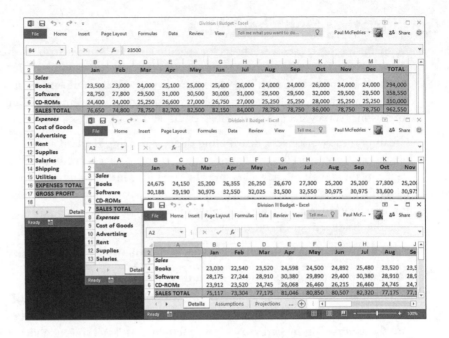

Figure 4.8
When consolidating by position, create a separate consolidation worksheet that uses the same layout as the sheets you're consolidating.

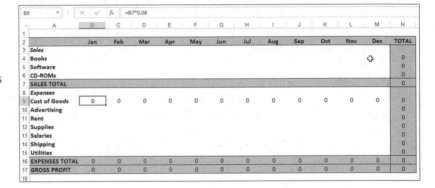

With the consolidation sheet active, follow these steps to consolidate by position:

1. Select the upper-left corner of the destination range. In the Consolidate By Position worksheet, the cell to select is B4.

2. Select Data, Consolidate. Excel displays the Consolidate dialog box.

3. In the Function drop-down list, click the operation to use during the consolidation. You'll use Sum most of the time, but Excel has 10 other operations to choose from, including Count, Average, Max, and Min.

4. In the Reference text box, enter a reference for one of the source ranges. Use one of the following methods:

- Type the range coordinates by hand. If the source range is in another workbook, be sure to include the workbook name enclosed in square brackets. If the workbook is in a different drive or folder, include the full path to the workbook as well.

- If the sheet is open, select it (either by clicking it or by clicking it in the View, Switch Windows menu), and then use your mouse to highlight the range.

- If the workbook isn't open, click Browse, select the file in the Browse dialog box, and then click OK. Excel adds the workbook path to the Reference box. Fill in the sheet name and the range coordinates.

5. Click Add. Excel adds the range to the All References box (see Figure 4.9).

6. Repeat steps 4 and 5 to add all the source ranges.

7. If you want the consolidated data to change whenever you make changes to the source data, leave the Create Links to Source Data check box selected.

8. Click OK. Excel gathers the data, consolidates it, and then adds it to the destination range (see Figure 4.10).

Figure 4.9
The Consolidate dialog box, with several source ranges added.

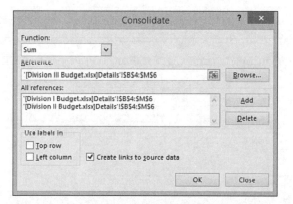

If you chose not to create links to the source data in step 7, Excel just fills the destination range with the consolidation totals. However, if you did create links, Excel does three things:

- Adds link formulas to the destination range for each cell in the source ranges you selected

  → To get the details on link formulas, **see** "Working with Links in Formulas," **p. 71**.

- Consolidates the data by adding SUM() functions (or whichever operation you selected in the Function list) that total the results of the link formulas

- Outlines the consolidation worksheet and hides the link formulas, as you can see in Figure 4.10

Figure 4.10
The consolidated sales budgets.

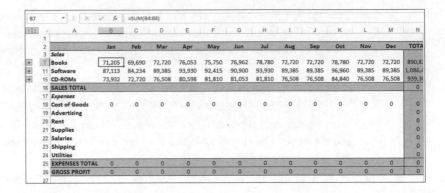

If you display the Level 1 data, you'll see the linked formulas. For example, Figure 4.11 shows the detail for the consolidated sales number for Books in January (cell B7). Cells B4, B5, and B6 contain formulas that link to the corresponding cells in the three budget worksheets (for example, `'[Division I Budget.xlsx]Details'!$B$4`).

Figure 4.11
The detail (linked formulas) for the consolidated data.

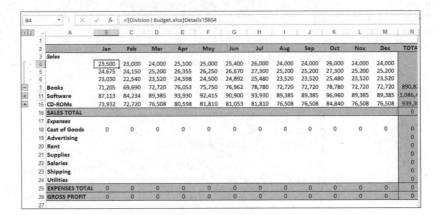

Consolidating by Category

If you want to consolidate date from worksheets that don't use the same layout, you need to tell Excel to consolidate the data *by category*. In this case, Excel examines each of your source ranges and consolidates data that uses the same row or column labels. For example, take a look at the Sales rows in the three worksheets shown in Figure 4.12.

Figure 4.12
Each division sells a different mix of products, so we need to consolidate by category.

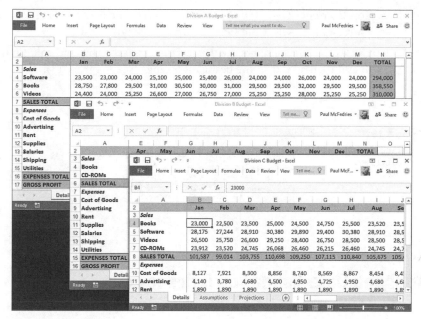

As you can see, Division C sells books, software, videos, and CD-ROMs; Division B sells books and CD-ROMs; and Division A sells software, books, and videos. Here's how you go about consolidating these numbers. (Note that I'm skipping over some of the details given in the preceding section.)

1. Create or select a new worksheet for the consolidation and select the upper-left corner of the destination range. It isn't necessary to enter labels for the consolidated data because Excel does it for you automatically. However, if you want to see the labels in a particular order, it's okay to enter them yourself.

CAUTION

If you enter the labels yourself, make sure that you spell the labels exactly as they're spelled in the source worksheets.

---

2. Select Data, Consolidate to display the Consolidate dialog box.
3. In the Function drop-down list, select the operation to use during the consolidation.
4. In the Reference text box, enter a reference for one of the source ranges. In this case, make sure you include in each range the row and column labels for the data.
5. Click Add to add the range to the All References box.
6. Repeat steps 4 and 5 to add all the source ranges.
7. If you want the consolidated data to change whenever you make changes to the source data, leave the Create Links to Source Data check box selected.
8. If you want Excel to use the data labels in the top row of the selected ranges, select the

Top Row check box. If you want Excel to use the data labels in the left column of the source ranges, select the Left Column check box.

9. Click OK. Excel gathers the data according to the row and column labels, consolidates it, and then adds it to the destination range (see Figure 4.13).

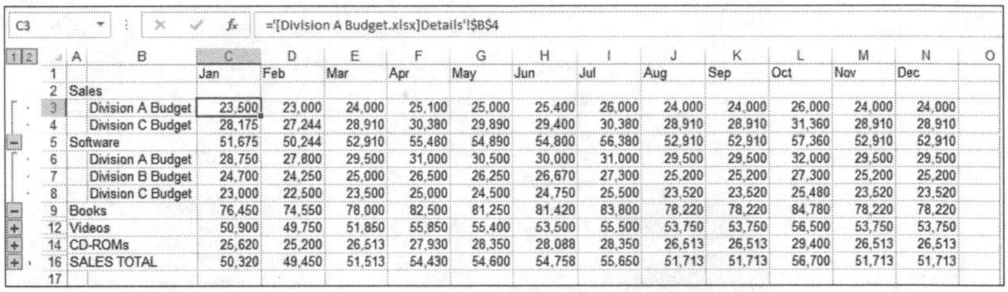
C3 ='[Division A Budget.xlsx]Details'!$B$4

	A	B	C	D	E	F	G	H	I	J	K	L	M	N	O
1			Jan	Feb	Mar	Apr	May	Jun	Jul	Aug	Sep	Oct	Nov	Dec	
2	Sales														
3		Division A Budget	23,500	23,000	24,000	25,100	25,000	25,400	26,000	24,000	24,000	26,000	24,000	24,000	
4		Division C Budget	28,175	27,244	28,910	30,380	29,890	29,400	30,380	28,910	28,910	31,360	28,910	28,910	
5	Software		51,675	50,244	52,910	55,480	54,890	54,800	56,380	52,910	52,910	57,360	52,910	52,910	
6		Division A Budget	28,750	27,800	29,500	31,000	30,500	30,000	31,000	29,500	29,500	32,000	29,500	29,500	
7		Division B Budget	24,700	24,250	25,000	26,500	26,250	26,670	27,300	25,200	25,200	27,300	25,200	25,200	
8		Division C Budget	23,000	22,500	23,500	25,000	24,500	24,750	25,500	23,520	23,520	25,480	23,520	23,520	
9	Books		76,450	74,550	78,000	82,500	81,250	81,420	83,800	78,220	78,220	84,780	78,220	78,220	
12	Videos		50,900	49,750	51,850	55,850	55,400	53,500	55,500	53,750	53,750	56,500	53,750	53,750	
14	CD-ROMs		25,620	25,200	26,513	27,930	28,350	28,088	28,350	26,513	26,513	29,400	26,513	26,513	
16	SALES TOTAL		50,320	49,450	51,513	54,430	54,600	54,758	55,650	51,713	51,713	56,700	51,713	51,713	
17															

Figure 4.13
The sales numbers consolidated by category.

Applying Data-Validation Rules to Cells

It's an unfortunate fact of spreadsheet life that formulas are only as good as the data they're given. It's the GIGO effect, as programmers say: garbage in, garbage out. In worksheet terms, *garbage in* means entering erroneous or improper data into a formula's input cells. For basic data entry errors (for example, entering the wrong date or transposing a number's digits), there's not a lot you can do other than exhort yourself or the people who use your worksheets to enter data carefully. Fortunately, you have a bit more control when it comes to preventing improper data entry. By *improper*, I mean data that falls in either of the following categories:

4

- **Data that is the wrong type**—For example, entering a text string in a cell that requires a number
- **Data that falls outside of an allowable range**—For example, entering **200** in a cell that requires a number between 1 and 100

You can prevent these kinds of improper entries, to a certain extent, by adding comments that provide details on what is allowable inside a particular cell. However, this requires other people to both read *and* act on the comment text. Another solution is to use custom numeric formatting to "format" a cell with an error message if the wrong type of data is entered. This is useful, but it works only for certain kinds of input errors.

→ To learn about custom numeric formats and see some examples of using them to display input error messages, **see** "Formatting Numbers, Dates, and Times," **p. 74**.

The best solution for preventing data entry errors is to use Excel's data-validation feature. With data validation, you create *rules* that specify exactly what kind of data can be entered and in what range that data can fall. You can also specify pop-up input messages that appear when a cell is selected, as well as error messages that appear when data is entered improperly.

> → You can also ask Excel to "circle" any cells that contain data-validation errors (which is handy when you import data into a list that contains data-validation rules). You do this by choosing Data, Data Validation, Circle Invalid Data. To learn more about this feature, **see** "Auditing a Worksheet," **p. 123**.

Follow these steps to define the settings for a data-validation rule:

1. Select the cell or range to which you want to apply the data-validation rule.
2. Select Data, Data Validation. Excel displays the Data Validation dialog box.
3. In the Settings tab, use the Allow list to click one of the following validation types:
    * **Any Value**—Allows any value in the range. (That is, it removes any previously applied validation rule. If you're removing an existing rule, be sure to also clear the input message if you created one, as shown in step 7.)
    * **Whole Number**—Allows only whole numbers (integers). Use the Data list to select a comparison operator (between, equal to, less than, and so on) and then enter the specific criteria. (For example, if you click the Between option, you must enter Minimum and Maximum values, as shown in Figure 4.14.)

Figure 4.14
Use the Data Validation dialog box to set up a data-validation rule for a cell or range.

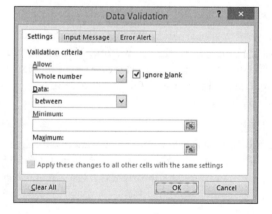

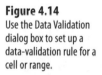

* **Decimal**—Allows decimal numbers or whole numbers. Use the Data list to select a comparison operator and then enter the specific numeric criteria.
* **List**—Allows only values specified in a list. Use the Source box to specify either a range on the same sheet or a range name on any sheet that contains the list of allowable values. (Precede the range or range name with an equal sign.) Alternatively, you can enter the allowable values directly into the Source box (separated by commas). If you want the user to be able to select from the allowable values using a drop-down list, leave the In-Cell Drop-Down check box selected.

- **Date**—Allows only dates. (If the user includes a time value, the entry is invalid.) Use the Data list to select a comparison operator and then enter the specific date criteria (such as a Start Date and an End Date).

- **Time**—Allows only times. (If the user includes a date value, the entry is invalid.) Use the Data list to select a comparison operator and then enter the specific time criteria (such as a Start Time and an End Time).

- **Text Length**—Allows only alphanumeric strings of a specified length. Use the Data list to select a comparison operator and then enter the specific length criteria (such as Minimum and Maximum lengths).

- **Custom**—Use this option to enter a formula that specifies the validation criteria. You can either enter the formula directly into the Formula box (be sure to precede the formula with an equal sign) or enter a reference to a cell that contains the formula. For example, if you're restricting cell A2 and you want to be sure the entered value is not the same as what's in cell A1, enter the formula =A2<>A1.

4. To allow blank entries, either in the cell itself or in other cells specified as part of the validation settings, leave the Ignore Blank check box selected. If you clear this check box, Excel treats blank entries as zero and applies the validation rule accordingly.

5. If the range had an existing validation rule that also applied to other cells, you can apply the new rule to those other cells by selecting the Apply These Changes to All Other Cells with the Same Settings check box.

6. Click the Input Message tab.

7. If you want a pop-up box to appear when the user selects the restricted cell or any cell within the restricted range, leave the Show Input Message When Cell Is Selected check box selected. Use the Title and Input Message boxes to specify the message that appears. For example, you could use the message to give the user information on the type and range of allowable values.

8. Click the Error Alert tab.

9. If you want a dialog box to appear when the user enters invalid data, leave the Show Error Alert After Invalid Data Is Entered check box selected. In the Style list, click the error style you want: Stop, Warning, or Information. Use the Title and Error Message boxes to specify the message that appears.

┌ **CAUTION** ─────────────────────────────────────
│ Only the Stop style can prevent the user from ignoring the error and entering the invalid data anyway.
└──

10. Click OK to apply the data-validation rule.

Using Dialog Box Controls on a Worksheet

In the previous section, you saw how using List for the type of validation enabled you to supply yourself or the user with an in-cell drop-down list of allowable choices. This is good data entry practice because it reduces the uncertainty about the allowable values.

One of Excel's slickest features is that it enables you to extend this idea and place not only lists but also other dialog box controls, such as spinners and check boxes, directly on a worksheet. You can then link the values returned by these controls to a cell to create an elegant method for entering data.

Displaying the Developer Tab

Before working with dialog box controls, you need to display the Ribbon's Developer tab:

1. Right-click any part of the Ribbon and then click Customize the Ribbon. The Excel Options dialog box appears, with the Customize Ribbon tab displayed.
2. In the Customize the Ribbon list, select the Developer check box.
3. Click OK.

Using the Form Controls

You add the dialog box controls by choosing Developer, Insert and then selecting tools from the Form Controls list, shown in Figure 4.15. Note that only some of the controls are available for worksheet duty. I discuss the controls in detail a bit later in this section.

Figure 4.15
Use the controls in the Form Controls list to draw dialog box controls on a worksheet.

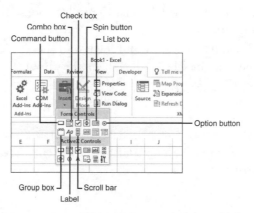

> **NOTE**
> You can add a command button to a worksheet, but you have to assign a Visual Basic for Applications (VBA) macro to it. To learn how to create macros, see the book *Excel 2016 VBA and Macros* (Que 2016; ISBN 9780789755858).

Adding a Control to a Worksheet

You add controls to a worksheet using the same steps you use to create any graphics object. Here's the basic procedure:

1. Select Developer, Insert and then click the form control you want to create. The mouse pointer changes to a crosshair.
2. Move the pointer onto the worksheet at the point where you want the control to appear.
3. Click and drag the mouse pointer to create the control.

Excel assigns a default caption to each group box, check box, and option button. To edit this caption, you have two ways to get started:

- Right-click the control and select Edit Text.
- Hold down Ctrl and click the control to select it. Then click inside the control.

Edit the text accordingly; when you're done, click outside the control. To reselect a control, hold down Ctrl and click the control.

Linking a Control to a Cell Value

To use the dialog box controls for inputting data, you need to associate each control with a worksheet cell. The following steps walk you through the procedure:

1. Select the control you want to work with. (Again, remember to hold down the Ctrl key before you click the control.)
2. Right-click the control and then click Format Control (or press Ctrl+1) to display the Format Control dialog box.
3. Click the Control tab and then use the Cell Link box to enter the cell's reference. You can either type the reference or select it directly on the worksheet.
4. Click OK to return to the worksheet.

> **TIP**
>
> Another way to link a control to a cell is to select the control and enter a formula in the formula bar in the form `=cell`. Here, `cell` is a reference to the cell you want to use. For example, to link a control to cell A1, you enter the formula `=A1`.

> **NOTE**
>
> When working with option buttons, you have to enter only the linked cell for one of the buttons in a group. Excel automatically adds the reference to the rest.

Understanding the Worksheet Controls

To get the most out of worksheet controls, you need to know the specifics of how each control works and how you can use each one for data entry. To that end, the next few sections take you through detailed accounts of various controls.

Group Boxes

Group boxes don't do much on their own. You use one to create a grouping of two or more option buttons. The user can then select only one option from the group. For this to work, you must proceed as follows:

1. Select Developer, Insert, Group Box in the Form Controls list.
2. Click and drag to draw the group box on the worksheet.
3. Select Developer, Insert, Option Button in the Form Controls list.
4. Click and drag within the group box to create an option button.
5. Repeat steps 3 and 4 as many times as needed to create the other option buttons.

Remember, it's important that you create the group box first and then draw option buttons within the group box.

> **NOTE** If you have one (and only one) option button outside a grouping, you can still include it in a group box. (If you have multiple option buttons outside a group box, this technique won't work.) To do this, first hold down Ctrl and click the option button to select it. Release Ctrl, click and drag an edge of the option button, and then drop it within the group box.

Option Buttons

Option buttons are controls that usually appear in groups of two or more, and the user can select only one of the options. As I said in the previous section, option buttons work in tandem with group boxes, in which the user can select only one of the option buttons within a group box.

> **NOTE** All of the option buttons that don't lie within a group box are treated as a de facto group. (That is, Excel allows you to select only one of these nongroup options at a time.) This means that a group box isn't strictly necessary when using option buttons on a worksheet. Most people do use them because they give the user visual clues about which options are related.

By default, Excel draws each option button in the unselected state. Therefore, you should specify in advance which of the option buttons is selected by default:

1. Hold down Ctrl and click the option button you want to display as selected.

2. Right-click the control and then click Format Control (or press Ctrl+1) to display the Format Control dialog box.

3. In the Control tab, select the Checked option.

4. Click OK.

On the worksheet, selecting a particular option button changes the value stored in the linked cell. The value stored depends on the option button, where the first button added to the group box has the value 1, the second button has the value 2, and so on. The advantage of this is that it enables you to translate a text option into a numeric value. For example, Figure 4.16 shows a worksheet in which the option buttons give the user three freight choices: Surface Mail, Air Mail, and Courier. The value of the chosen option is stored in the linked cell, which is E4. For example, if Air Mail is selected, the value 2 is stored in E4. In a production model, for example, the worksheet would use this value to look up the corresponding freight charges and adjust an invoice accordingly.

→ To learn how to look up values in a worksheet, **see** Chapter 9, "Working with Lookup Functions," **p. 191**.

Figure 4.16
For option buttons, the value stored in the linked cell is based on the order in which the buttons were added to the group box.

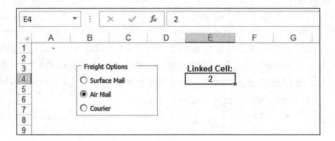

Check Boxes

Check boxes enable you to include options that the user can toggle on or off. As with option buttons, Excel draws each check box in the unchecked state. If you prefer that a particular check box start in the checked state, use the Format Control dialog box to select the control's Checked option, as described in the previous section.

On the worksheet, a selected check box stores the value TRUE in its linked cell; if the check box is cleared, it stores the value FALSE (see Figure 4.17). This is handy because it enables you to add a bit of logic to your formulas. That is, you can test whether a check box is selected and adjust a formula accordingly. Figure 4.17 shows a couple examples:

- **Use End-Of-Period Payments**—This check box could be used to specify whether a formula that determines the monthly payments on a loan assumes that those payments are made at the end of each period (TRUE) or at the beginning of each period (FALSE).

■ **Include Extra Monthly Payments**—This check box could be used to determine whether a model that builds a loan amortization schedule formula includes an extra principal repayment each month.

Figure 4.17
For check boxes, the value stored in the linked cell is TRUE when the check box is selected and FALSE when it is not selected.

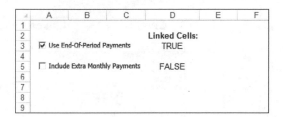

In both cases, and in most formulas that take into account check box results, you would use the IF() worksheet function to read the current value of the linked cell and branch accordingly.

→ To learn how to use the IF() worksheet function, **see** "Using the IF() Function," **p. 164**.

→ To learn how to build a loan amortization schedule, **see** "Building a Loan Amortization Schedule," **p. 440**.

List Boxes and Combo Boxes

A list box control creates a list box from which the user can select an item. The items in the list are defined by the values in a specified worksheet range, and the value returned to the linked cell is the number of the item chosen. A combo box is similar to a list box; however, the control shows only one item at a time until it's dropped down.

List boxes and combo boxes are different from other controls because you also have to specify a range that contains the items to appear in the list. The following steps show you how it's done:

1. Enter the list items in a range. (The items must be listed in a single row or a single column.)

2. Add the list box control to the sheet (if you haven't done so already) and then select it.

3. Right-click the control and then click Format Control (or press Ctrl+1) to display the Format Control dialog box.

4. Select the Control tab and then use the Input Range box to enter a reference to the range of items. You can either type in the reference or select it directly on the worksheet.

5. Click OK to return to the worksheet.

Figure 4.18 shows a worksheet with a list box and a drop-down list.

Figure 4.18
For list boxes and combo boxes, the value stored in the linked cell is the number of the selected list item. To get the item text, use the INDEX() function.

The list used by both controls in this example is in the range A3:A10. Notice that the linked cells display the number of the list selection, not the selection itself. To get the selected list item, you can use the INDEX() function with the following syntax:

```
INDEX(list_range, list_selection)
```

list_range   The range used in the list box or drop-down list.

list_selection The number of the item selected in the list.

For example, to find the item that's currently selected in the combo box in Figure 4.18, you use the following formula (as shown in cell E12):

```
=INDEX(A3:A10,E10)
```

➔ To learn more about the INDEX() function, **see** Chapter 9, "Working with Lookup Functions," **p. 191**.

Scroll Bars and Spin Boxes

The Scroll Bar tool creates a control that resembles a window scroll bar. You use this type of scroll bar to select a number from a range of values. Clicking the arrows or dragging the scroll box changes the value of the control. This value is what gets returned to the linked cell. Note that you can create either a horizontal scroll bar or a vertical scroll bar.

In the Format Control dialog box for a scroll bar, the Control tab includes the following options:

■ **Current Value**—The initial value of the scroll bar

■ **Minimum Value**—The value of the scroll bar when the scroll box is at its leftmost position (for a horizontal scroll bar) or its topmost position (for a vertical scroll bar)

- **Maximum Value**—The value of the scroll bar when the scroll box is at its rightmost position (for a horizontal scroll bar) or its bottommost position (for a vertical scroll bar)

- **Incremental Change**—The amount that the scroll bar's value changes when the user clicks on a scroll arrow

- **Page Change**—The amount that the scroll bar's value changes when the user clicks between the scroll box and a scroll arrow

The Spin Box tool creates a control that is similar to a scroll bar; that is, you can use a spin box to select a number between a maximum value and a minimum value by clicking the arrows. The number is returned to the linked cell. Spin box options are identical to those of scroll bars, except that you can't set a Page Change value.

Figure 4.19 shows an example of a scroll bar and an example of a spin box. Note that the numbers above the scroll bar giving the minimum and maximum values are extra labels I added by hand. Doing this is usually a good idea because it gives the user the numeric limits of the control.

Figure 4.19
For scroll bars and spin boxes, the value stored in the linked cell is the current numeric value of the control.

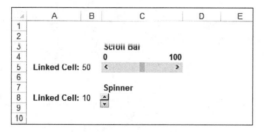

From Here

- To get the details on link formulas, **see** "Working with Links in Formulas," **p. 70**.

- To learn about custom numeric formats and to see some examples of using them to display input error messages, **see** "Formatting Numbers, Dates, and Times," **p. 74**.

- Circular references are usually a bad thing to have in a spreadsheet model. To learn how to combat the bad kind, **see** "Fixing Circular References," **p. 118**.

- To learn how to get Excel to "circle" cells that contain data-validation errors, **see** "Auditing a Worksheet," **p. 123**.

- To learn how to use the IF() worksheet function, **see** "Using the IF() Function," **p. 164**.

- To learn how to look up values in a worksheet, **see** Chapter 9, "Working with Lookup Functions," **p. 191**.

4

■ To learn more about the INDEX() function, **see** "The MATCH() and INDEX() Functions," **p. 202**.

■ To learn how the PMT() function works, **see** "Calculating a Loan Payment," **p. 435**.

■ To learn how to build a loan amortization schedule, see "Building a Loan Amortization Schedule," **p. 440**.

4

Troubleshooting Formulas

5

Despite your best efforts, the odd error might appear in your formulas from time to time. Such errors can be mathematical (for example, dividing by zero), or Excel might simply be incapable of interpreting the formula. In the latter case, problems can be caught while you're entering the formula. For example, if you try to enter a formula that has unbalanced parentheses, Excel won't accept the entry, and it displays an error message. Other errors are more insidious. For example, your formula might *appear* to be working—that is, it might return a value—but the result may be incorrect because the data is flawed or because your formula has referenced the wrong cell or range.

Whatever the error and whatever the cause, formula woes need to be worked out because you or someone else in your company is likely depending on your models to produce accurate results. Don't fall into the trap of thinking that *your* spreadsheets are problem free. A recent University of Hawaii study found that 50% of spreadsheets contained errors that led to "significant miscalculations." And the more complex the model, the greater the chance that errors can creep in. A KPMG study from a few years ago found that a staggering 90% of spreadsheets used for tax calculations contained errors.

The good news is that fixing formula flaws need not be drudgery. With a bit of know-how and Excel's top-notch troubleshooting tools, sniffing out and repairing model maladies isn't hard. This chapter tells you everything you need to know.

Understanding Excel's Error Values

When you enter or edit a formula or change one of the formula's input values, Excel might show an error value as the formula *result*. Excel has seven different error values: #DIV/0!, #N/A, #NAME?, #NULL!, #NUM!, #REF!, and #VALUE!. The next few sections give you a detailed look at these error values and offer suggestions for dealing with them.

#DIV/0!

The #DIV/0! error almost always means that the cell's formula is trying to divide by zero, a mathematical no-no. The cause is usually a reference to a cell that either is blank or contains the value 0. Check the cell's precedents (the cells that are directly or indirectly referenced in the formula) to look for possible culprits. You'll also see #DIV/0! if you enter an inappropriate argument in some functions. MOD(), for example, returns #DIV/0! if the second argument is 0.

→ To check items such as cell precedents and dependents, **see** "Auditing a Worksheet," **p. 123**.

That Excel treats blank cells as the value 0 can pose problems in a worksheet that requires the user to fill in the data. If your formula requires division by one of the temporarily blank cells, it will show #DIV/0! as the result, possibly causing confusion for the user. You can get around this by telling Excel not to perform the calculation if the cell used as the divisor is 0. This is done with the IF() worksheet function, which I discuss in detail in Chapter 8, "Working with Logical and Information Functions." For example, consider the following formula, which uses named cells to calculate gross margin:

```
=GrossProfit / Sales
```

→ For details on the IF() function, **see** "Using the IF() Function," **p. 164**.

→ An even better way to deal with potential formula errors is to use the IFERROR() function; **see** "Handling Formula Errors with IFERROR()," **p. 118**.

To prevent the #DIV/0! error from appearing if the Sales cell is blank (or 0), you'd modify the formula as follows:

```
=IF(Sales = 0, "", GrossProfit / Sales)
```

If the value of the Sales cell is 0, the formula returns the empty string; otherwise, it performs the calculation.

#N/A

The #N/A error value is short for *not available*, and it means that the formula couldn't return a legitimate result. You usually see #N/A when you use an inappropriate argument (or when you omit a required argument) in a function. HLOOKUP() and VLOOKUP(), for example, return #N/A if the lookup value is smaller than the first value in the lookup range.

To solve the problem, first check the formula's input cells to see whether any of them are displaying the #N/A error. If so, that's why your formula is returning the same error; the problem actually lies in the input cell. When you've found where the error originates, examine the formula's operands to look for inappropriate data types. In particular, check the arguments used in each function to ensure that they make sense for the function and that no required arguments are missing.

→ To learn about the HLOOKUP() and VLOOKUP() functions, **see** "Looking Up Values in Tables," **p. 196**.

> **NOTE**
> It's common in spreadsheet work to purposely generate an #N/A! error to show that a particular cell value isn't currently available. For example, you may be waiting for budget figures from one or more divisions or for the final numbers from month- or year-end. In such a case, you enter =NA() into the cell. You fix this "problem" by replacing the NA() function with the appropriate data when it arrives.

#NAME?

The #NAME? error appears when Excel doesn't recognize a name you used in a formula or when it interprets text within the formula as an undefined name. This means that the #NAME? error pops up in a wide variety of circumstances:

- You spelled a range name incorrectly.
- You used a range name that you haven't yet defined.
- You spelled a function name incorrectly.
- You used a function that's part of an uninstalled add-in.
- You used a string value without surrounding it with quotation marks.
- You entered a range reference and accidentally omitted the colon.
- You entered a reference to a range on another worksheet and didn't enclose the sheet name in single quotation marks.

> **TIP**
> When entering function names and defined names, use all lowercase letters. If Excel recognizes a name, it converts the function to all uppercase and the defined name to its original case. If no conversion occurs, you know that you misspelled the name, you haven't defined it yet, or you're using a function from an add-in that isn't loaded.
>
> Remember that you also can use these commands to enter functions and names safely: Formulas, Insert Function (or press Shift+F3); Formulas, Use in Formula list; or Formulas, Use In Formula, Paste Names (or press F3).

5

These are mostly syntax errors, so fixing them means double-checking your formula and correcting range name or function name misspellings, or inserting missing quotation marks or colons. Also, be sure to define any range names you use and to install the appropriate add-in modules for functions you use.

Case Study: Avoiding #NAME? Errors When Deleting Range Names

If you've used a range name in a formula and then you delete that name, Excel generates the #NAME? error. Wouldn't it be better if Excel just converted the name to its appropriate cell reference in each formula, the way Lotus 1-2-3 used to (if you can remember that far back)? Possibly, but there is an advantage to Excel's seemingly inconvenient approach. By generating an error, Excel enables you to catch range names that you delete by accident. Because Excel leaves the names in the formula, you can recover by redefining the original range name.

→ Redefining the original range name becomes problematic if you can't remember the appropriate range coordinates. This is why it's always a good idea to paste a list of range names and their references into each of your worksheets; **see** "Pasting a List of Range Names in a Worksheet," **p. 48**.

If you don't need this safety net, you can force Excel to convert deleted range names into their cell references. Here are the steps to follow:

1. Select File, Options to display the Excel Options dialog box.
2. Click Advanced.
3. In the Lotus Compatibility Settings For section, use the list to select the worksheet you want to use.
4. Click to select the Transition Formula Entry check box.
5. Click OK.

Excel now treats your formula entries the same way Lotus 1-2-3 did. Specifically, in formulas that use a deleted range name, the name automatically gets converted to its appropriate range reference. As an added bonus, Excel also performs the following automatic conversions:

■ If you enter a range reference in a formula, the reference gets converted to a range name (provided that a name exists, of course).

■ If you define a name for a range, Excel converts any existing range references into the new name. This enables you to avoid the Apply Names feature, discussed in Chapter 3, "Building Basic Formulas."

CAUTION
The treatment of formulas in the Lotus 1-2-3 manner only applies to formulas that you create *after* you select the Transition Formula Entry check box.

#NULL!

Excel displays the #NULL! error in a very specific case: when you use the intersection operator (a space) on two ranges that have no cells in common. For example, because the ranges A1:B2 and C3:D4 have no common cells, the following formula returns the #NULL! error:

```
=SUM(A1:B2 C3:D4)
```

Check your range coordinates to ensure that they're accurate. In addition, check to see if one of the ranges has been moved, causing the two ranges in your formula to no longer intersect.

#NUM!

The #NUM! error means there's a problem with a number in a formula. This almost always means that you entered an invalid argument in a math or trig function. For example, maybe you entered a negative number as the argument for the SQRT() or LOG() function. Check the formula's input cells—particularly those that are used as arguments for mathematical functions—to make sure the values are appropriate.

The #NUM! error also appears if you're using iteration (or a function that uses iteration) and Excel can't calculate a result. There could be no solution to the problem, or you might need to adjust the iteration parameters.

→ To learn more about iteration, **see** "Using Iteration and Circular References," **p. 93**.

#REF!

The #REF! error means that a formula contains an invalid cell reference, which is usually caused by one of the following actions:

■ You deleted a cell to which the formula refers. You need to add the cell back in or adjust the formula reference.

■ You cut a cell and then pasted it into a cell used by the formula. You need to undo the cut and then paste the cell elsewhere. (Note that it's okay to *copy* a cell and paste it onto a cell used by the formula.)

■ Your formula references a nonexistent cell address, such as B0. This can happen if you cut or copy a formula that uses relative references and paste it in such a way that the invalid cell address is created. For example, suppose that your formula references cell B1. If you cut or copy the cell containing the formula and paste it one row higher, the reference to B1 becomes invalid because Excel can't move the cell reference up one row.

#VALUE!

When Excel generates a #VALUE! error, it means you've used an inappropriate argument in a function. This is most often caused by using the wrong data type. For example, you might have entered or referenced a string value instead of a numeric value. Similarly, you might have used a range reference in a function argument that requires a single cell or value. Excel

5

also generates this error if you use a value that's larger or smaller than Excel can handle. In all these cases, you solve the problem by double-checking your function arguments to find and edit the inappropriate arguments.

> **NOTE**   Excel can work with values between $-1E-307$ and $1E+307$.

Fixing Other Formula Errors

Not all formula errors generate one of Excel's seven error values. Instead, you might see a warning dialog box from Excel (for example, if you try to enter a function without including a required argument). Or, you might not see any indication that something is wrong. To help you in these situations, the following sections cover some of the most common formula errors.

Missing or Mismatched Parentheses

If you miss a parenthesis when typing a formula, or if you place a parenthesis in the wrong location, Excel usually displays a dialog box like the one shown in Figure 5.1 when you attempt to confirm the formula. If the edited formula is what you want, click Yes to have Excel enter the corrected formula automatically; if the edited formula is not correct, click No and edit the formula by hand.

Figure 5.1
If you miss a parenthesis, Excel attempts to fix the problem and displays this dialog box to ask if you want to accept the correction.

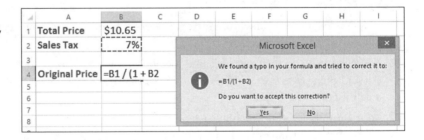

> **CAUTION**
> Excel doesn't always fix missing parentheses correctly. It tends to add the missing parenthesis to the end of the formula, which is often not what you want. Therefore, always check Excel's proposed solution carefully before accepting it.

To help you avoid missing or mismatched parentheses, Excel provides two visual clues in the formula itself when you're editing it:

- The first clue occurs when you type a right parenthesis. Excel highlights both the right parenthesis and its corresponding left parenthesis. If you type what you think is the last right parenthesis and Excel doesn't highlight the first left parenthesis, your parentheses are unbalanced.

- The second clue occurs when you use the left and right arrow keys to navigate a formula. When you cross over a parenthesis, Excel highlights the other parenthesis in the pair and formats both parentheses with the same color.

Erroneous Formula Results

If a formula produces no warnings or error values, the result might still be in error. If the result of a formula is incorrect, here are a few techniques that can help you understand and fix the problem:

- **Calculate complex formulas one term at a time.** In the formula bar, select the expression you want to calculate and then press F9. Excel converts the expression into its value. Make sure that you press the Esc key when you're done to avoid entering the formula with just the calculated values.

- **Evaluate the formula.** You can step through the various parts of a formula.

  → To learn how to evaluate formulas, **see** "Evaluating Formulas," **p. 126**.

- **Break up long or complex formulas.** One of the most problematic aspects of formula troubleshooting is making sense out of long formulas. The previous techniques can help (by enabling you to evaluate parts of the formula), but it's usually best to keep your formulas as short as you can at first. When you get things working properly, you often can combine formulas for a more efficient model.

- **Recalculate all formulas.** A particular formula might display the wrong result because other formulas on which it depends need to be recalculated. This is particularly true if one or more of those formulas use custom VBA functions. Press Ctrl+Alt+F9 to recalculate all worksheet formulas.

- **Pay attention to operator precedence.** As explained in Chapter 3, Excel's operator precedence means that certain operations are performed before others. An erroneous formula result could therefore be caused by Excel's precedence order. To control precedence, use parentheses.

- **Watch out for nonblank "blank" cells.** A cell might appear to be blank but actually contain data or even a formula. For example, some users "clear" a cell by pressing the spacebar, and Excel then treats the cell as nonblank. Similarly, some formulas return an empty string instead of a value. (For example, see the IF() function formula earlier in this chapter for avoiding the #DIV/0! error.)

- **Watch unseen values.** In a large model, your formula could be using cells that you can't see because they're offscreen or on another sheet. Excel's Watch Window enables you to keep an eye on the current value of one or more cells.

5

→ To learn about the Watch Window, **see** "Watching Cell Values," **p. 126**.

Fixing Circular References

A *circular reference* occurs when a formula refers to its own cell. This can happen in one of two ways:

- **Directly**—The formula explicitly references its own cell. For example, a circular reference would result if the following formula were entered into cell A1:

  `=A1+A2`

- **Indirectly**—The formula references a cell or function that, in turn, references the formula's cell. For example, suppose that cell A1 contains the following formula:

  `=A5*10`

- A circular reference would result if cell A5 referred to cell A1, as in this example:

  `=SUM(A1:D1)`

When Excel detects a circular reference, it displays the dialog box shown in Figure 5.2.

Figure 5.2
If you attempt to enter a formula that contains a circular reference, Excel displays this dialog box.

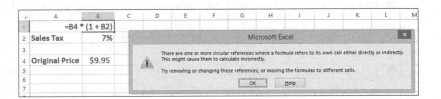

When you click OK, Excel displays *tracer* arrows that connect the cells involved in the circular reference. (Tracers are discussed in detail later in this chapter; see "Auditing a Worksheet.") Knowing which cells are involved enables you to correct the formula in one of them to solve the problem.

Handling Formula Errors with `IFERROR()`

Earlier you saw how to use the `IF()` function to avoid a `#DIV/0!` error by testing the value of the formula divisor to see if it equals 0. This works fine if you can anticipate the specific type of error the user may make. However, in many instances you can't know the exact nature of the error in advance. For example, the simple formula `=GrossProfit/Sales` would generate a `#DIV/0!` error if `Sales` equals 0. However, it would generate a `#NAME?` error if the name `GrossProfit` or the name `Sales` no longer exists, or it would generate a `#REF!` error if the cells associated with one or both of `GrossProfit` and `Sales` were deleted.

If you want to handle errors gracefully in your worksheets, it's often best to assume that *any* error can occur. Fortunately, that doesn't mean you have to construct complex tests using deeply nested `IF()` functions that check for every error type (`#DIV/0!`, `#N/A`, and so on). Instead, Excel enables you to use a simple test for *any* error.

In legacy versions of Excel, you'd use the ISERROR(`value`) function, where `value` is an expression. Here's what it does: If `value` generates any error, ISERROR() returns True; if `value` doesn't generate an error, ISERROR() returns False. You would then incorporate this into an IF() test, using the following general syntax:

```
=IF(ISERROR(expression), ErrorResult, expression)
```

If `expression` generates an error, this formula returns the ErrorResult value (such as the null string or an error message); otherwise, it returns the result of `expression`. Here's an example that uses the GrossProfit / Sales expression:

```
=IF(ISERROR(GrossProfit / Sales), "", GrossProfit / Sales)
```

The problem with using IF() and ISERROR() to handle errors is that you must input the expression twice: once in the ISERROR() function and again as the False result in the IF() function. This not only takes longer to input but also makes your formulas harder to maintain because if you make changes to the expression, you have to change both instances.

Excel makes handling formula errors much easier by offering the IFERROR() function, which essentially combines IF() and ISERROR() into a single function:

```
IFERROR(value, value_if_error)
```

`value`	The expression that may generate an error
`value_if_error`	The value to return if `value` returns an error

If the `value` expression doesn't generate an error, IFERROR() returns the expression result; otherwise, it returns `value_if_error` (which might be the null string or an error message). Here's an example:

```
=IFERROR((GrossProfit / Sales), "")
```

As you can see, this is much better than using IF() and ISERROR(). It's shorter, easier to read, and easier to maintain because you use your expression only once.

> **NOTE**
> If you want to handle the specific case of the #N/A error, use the IFNA(`value, value_if_na`) function. Here, `value` is the expression that you're testing for the #N/A error, and `value_if_na` is the value to return if `value` returns the #N/A error.

Using the Formula Error Checker

If you use Microsoft Word, you're probably familiar with the wavy green lines that appear under words and phrases that the grammar checker has flagged as being incorrect. The grammar checker operates by using a set of rules that determine correct grammar and syntax. As you type, the grammar checker operates in the background, constantly monitoring your writing. If something you write goes against one of the grammar checker's rules, the wavy line appears to let you know there's a problem.

5

Excel has a similar feature: the formula error checker. Like the grammar checker, the formula error checker uses a set of rules to determine correctness, and it operates in the background to monitor your formulas. If it detects something amiss, it displays an *error indicator*—a green triangle—in the upper-left corner of the cell containing the formula, as shown in Figure 5.3.

Figure 5.3
If Excel's formula error checker detects a problem, it displays a green triangle in the upper-left corner of the formula's cell.

Error indicator

| D4 | ▼ | : | ✕ | ✓ | *fx* | =D1 / (1 + D2) |

◢	A	B	C	D
1	**Total Price**	$10.65	$21.35	$32.05
2	**Sales Tax**	7%	7%	7%
3				
4	**Original Price**	$9.95	$22.96	$29.95
5				

Choosing an Error Action

When you select the cell with the formula error, Excel displays a formula error icon beside the cell. If you hover your mouse pointer over the icon, a pop-up message describes the error, as shown in Figure 5.4. The formula error icon drop-down list contains the following actions:

- *Corrective action*—This is a command (the name of which depends on the type of error) that Excel believes either will fix the problem or help you troubleshoot the error. In Figure 5.4, for example, Excel is reporting that the formula in cell C3 differs from its neighboring formulas. (In the formula bar, the expression in the parentheses should be 1+C2 instead of 1-C2.) In this case, the corrective action command in the formula error icon is Copy Formula from Left. Or, if Excel can't suggest a solution, it might show the command Show Calculation Steps, which runs the Evaluate Formula feature. See "Evaluating Formulas," later in this chapter.

- **Help on This Error**—Select this option to get information on the error via the Excel Help system.

- **Ignore Error**—Select this option to leave the formula as is.

- **Edit in Formula Bar**—Select this option to display the formula in Edit mode in the formula bar. You can then fix the problem by editing the formula.

- **Error-Checking Options**—Select this option to display the Formulas tab of the Excel Options dialog box (discussed next).

Figure 5.4
Select the cell containing the error and then move the mouse pointer over the formula error icon to see a description of the error.

C4		:	×	✓	f_x	=C1 / (1 - C2)			
	A	B	C	D	E	F	G	H
1	Total Price	$10.65	$21.35	$32.05				
2	Sales Tax	7%	7%	7%				
3								
4	Original Price	$9 ! ▾	$22.96	$29.95				
5			The formula in this cell differs from the formulas in this area of the spreadsheet.					
6								

Setting Error Checker Options

Like Word's grammar checker, Excel's formula error checker has a number of options that control how it works and which errors it flags. To see these options, you have two choices:

■ Select File, Options to display the Excel Options dialog box and then click Formulas.

■ Select Error-Checking Options in the formula error icon's drop-down list (as described in the previous section).

Either way, the options appear in the Error Checking and Error Checking Rules sections in the Formulas tab, as shown in Figure 5.5.

Figure 5.5
In the Formulas tab, the Error Checking and Error Checking Rules sections contain the options that govern the workings of the formula error checker.

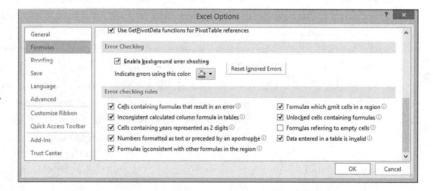

Here's a rundown of the available options:

■ **Enable Background Error Checking**—This check box toggles the formula error checker's background operation on and off. If you turn off the background checking, you can run a check at any time by choosing Formulas, Error Checking.

■ **Indicate Errors Using This Color**—Use this color palette to click the color of the error indicator.

■ **Reset Ignored Errors**—If you've ignored one or more errors, you can redisplay the error indicators by clicking this button.

- **Cells Containing Formulas That Result in an Error**—When this check box is selected, the formula error checker flags formulas that evaluate to #DIV/0!, #NAME?, or any of the other error values discussed earlier.

- **Inconsistent Calculated Column Formula in Tables**—When this check box is selected, Excel examines the formulas in a table's calculated column and flags any cell that contains a formula with a different structure than the other cells in the column. The formula error icon for this error includes the command Restore to Calculated Column Formula, which enables you to update the formula so that it's consistent with the rest of the column.

- **Cells Containing Years Represented as 2 Digits**—When this check box is selected, the formula error checker flags formulas that contain date text strings in which the year contains only two digits (a possibly ambiguous situation because the string could refer to a date in either the 1900s or the 2000s). In such a case, the list of options supplied in the formula error icon contains two commands—Convert XX to 19XX and Convert XX to 20XX—that enable you to convert the two-digit year to a four-digit year.

- **Numbers Formatted as Text or Preceded by an Apostrophe**—When this check box is selected, the formula error checker flags cells that contain a number that is either formatted as text or preceded by an apostrophe. In such a case, the list of options supplied in the formula error icon contains the Convert to Number command to convert the text to its numeric equivalent.

- **Formulas Inconsistent with Other Formulas in the Region**—When this check box is selected, the formula error checker flags formulas that are structured differently from similar formulas in the surrounding area. In such a case, the list of options supplied in the formula error icon contains a command such as Copy Formula from Left to bring the formula into consistency with the surrounding cells.

- **Formulas Which Omit Cells in a Region**—When this check box is selected, the formula error checker flags formulas that omit cells that are adjacent to a range referenced in the formula. For example, suppose that the formula is =AVERAGE(C4:C21), where C4:C21 is a range of numeric values. If cell C3 also contains a numeric value, the formula error checker flags the formula to alert you to the possibility that you missed including cell C3 in the formula. Figure 5.6 shows this example. In such a case, the list of options supplied in the formula error icon will contain the command Update Formula to Include Cells to adjust the formula automatically.

- **Unlocked Cells Containing Formulas**—When this check box is selected, the formula error checker flags formulas that reside in unlocked cells. This isn't an error so much as a warning that other people could tamper with the formula even after you have protected the sheet. In such a case, the list of options supplied in the formula error icon will contain the command Lock Cell to lock the cell and prevent users from changing the formula after you protect the sheet.

Figure 5.6
The formula error checker can flag formulas that omit cells that are adjacent to a range referenced by the formula. In this case, the formula in C23 should include cell C3.

| ▼ | : | ✕ | ✓ | *fx* | =AVERAGE(C4:C21) | | | |

	B	C	D	E	F
	Sales Rep	**2015 Sales**	**2016 Sales**		
	Nancy Freehafer	$996,336	$960,492		
	Andrew Cencini	$606,731	$577,983		
	Jan Kotas	$622,781	$967,580		
	Mariya Sergienko	$765,327	$771,399		
	Steven Thorpe	$863,589	$827,213		
	Michael Neipper	$795,518	$669,394		
	Robert Zare	$722,740	$626,945		
	Laura Giussani	$992,059	$574,472		
	Anne Hellung-Larsen	$659,380	$827,932		
	Kyra Harper	$509,623	$569,609		
	David Ferry	$987,777	$558,601		
	Paul Voyatzis	$685,091	$692,182		
	Andrea Aster	$540,484	$693,762		
	Charles Granek	$650,733	$823,034		
	Karen Aliston	$509,863	$511,569		
	Karen Hammond	$503,699	$975,455		
	Vince Durbin	$630,263	$599,514		
	Paul Sellars	$779,722	$596,353		
	Gregg O'Donoghue	$592,802	$652,171		
	TOTAL	$13,414,518	$13,414,518		
	AVERAGE	$689,899			

The formula in this cell refers to a range that has additional numbers adjacent to it.

- **Formulas Referring to Empty Cells**—When this check box is selected, the formula error checker flags formulas that reference empty cells. In such a case, the list of options supplied in the formula error icon will contain the command Trace Empty Cell to enable you to find the empty cell. (At this point, you can either enter data into the cell or adjust the formula so that it doesn't reference the cell.)

- **Data Entered in a Table Is Invalid**—When this check box is selected, the formula error checker flags cells that violate a table's data-validation rules. This can happen if you set up a data-validation rule with only a Warning or Information style, in which case the user can still opt to enter the invalid data. In such cases, the formula error checker will flag the cells that contain invalid data. The formula error icon list includes the Display Type Information command, which shows the data-validation rule that the cell data violates.

→ For a detailed look at data validation, **see** "Applying Data-Validation Rules to Cells," **p. 100**.

Auditing a Worksheet

As you've seen, some formula errors result from referencing other cells that contain errors or inappropriate values. The first step in troubleshooting these kinds of formula problems is to determine which cell (or group of cells) is causing an error. This is straightforward if the formula references only a single cell, but it gets progressively more difficult as the number of references increases. (Another complicating factor is the use of range names because it won't be obvious which range each name is referencing.)

To determine which cells are wreaking havoc on your formulas, you can use Excel's auditing features to visualize and trace a formula's input values and error sources.

Understanding Auditing

Excel's formula-auditing features operate by creating *tracers*—arrows that literally point out the cells involved in a formula. You can use tracers to find three kinds of cells:

- **Precedents**—These are cells that are directly or indirectly referenced in a formula. For example, suppose that cell B4 contains the formula =B2; then B2 is a direct precedent of B4. Now suppose that cell B2 contains the formula =A2/2; this makes A2 a direct precedent of B2, but it's also an *indirect* precedent of cell B4.

- **Dependents**—These are cells that are directly or indirectly referenced by a formula in another cell. In the preceding example, cell B2 is a direct dependent of A2, and B4 is an indirect dependent of A2.

- **Errors**—These are cells that contain an error value and are directly or indirectly referenced in a formula (and therefore cause the same error to appear in the formula).

Figure 5.7 shows a worksheet with three examples of tracer arrows:

- Cell B4 contains the formula =B2, and B2 contains =A2/2. The arrows (they're blue onscreen) point out the precedents (direct and indirect) of B4.

- Cell D4 contains the formula =D2, and D2 contains =D1/0. The latter produces the #DIV/0! error. Therefore, the same error appears in cell D4. The arrow (it's red onscreen) is pointing out the source of the error.

- Cell G4 contains the formula =Sheet2!A1. Excel displays the dashed arrow with the worksheet icon whenever the precedent or dependent exists on a different worksheet.

Figure 5.7
The three types of tracer arrows.

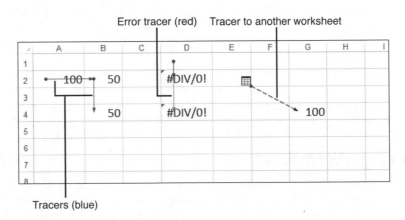

Error tracer (red)   Tracer to another worksheet

Tracers (blue)

N O T E
You can download this chapter's sample workbook at www.mcfedries.com/books/ book.php?title=excel-2016-formulas-and-functions.

Tracing Cell Precedents

To trace cell precedents, follow these steps:

1. Select the cell that contains the formula whose precedents you want to trace.

2. Select Formulas, Trace Precedents. Excel adds a tracer arrow to each direct precedent.

3. Keep repeating step 2 to see more levels of precedents.

> T I P
> You also can trace precedents by double-clicking the cell, provided that you turn off in-cell editing. You do this by choosing File, Options to display the Excel Options dialog box, clicking Advanced, and then deselecting the Allow Editing Directly in Cells check box. Now when you double-click a cell, Excel selects the formula's precedents.

Tracing Cell Dependents

Here are the steps to follow to trace cell dependents:

1. Select the cell whose dependents you want to trace.

2. Select Formulas, Trace Dependents. Excel adds a tracer arrow to each direct dependent.

3. Keep repeating step 2 to see more levels of dependents.

Tracing Cell Errors

To trace cell errors, follow these steps:

1. Select the cell that contains the error you want to trace.

2. Select Formulas, Error Checking, Trace Error. Excel adds a tracer arrow to each cell that produced the error.

Removing Tracer Arrows

To remove the tracer arrows, you have three choices:

- To remove all the tracer arrows, select Formulas, Remove Arrows.

- To remove precedent arrows one level at a time, select Formulas, drop down the Remove Arrows list, and select Remove Precedent Arrows.

- To remove dependent arrows one level at a time, select Formulas, drop down the Remove Arrows list, and select Remove Dependent Arrows.

5

Evaluating Formulas

Earlier, you learned that you can troubleshoot a wonky formula by evaluating parts of it. You do this by selecting the part of the formula you want to evaluate and then pressing F9. This works fine, but it can be tedious in a long or complex formula, and there's always a danger that you might accidentally confirm a partially evaluated formula and lose your work.

A better solution is to use Excel's Evaluate Formula feature. It does the same thing as the F9 technique, but it's easier and safer. Here's how it works:

1. Select the cell that contains the formula you want to evaluate.

2. Select Formulas, Evaluate Formula. Excel displays the Evaluate Formula dialog box.

3. The current term in the formula is underlined in the Evaluation box. At each step, you select from one or more of the following buttons:

   - **Evaluate**—Click this button to display the current value of the underlined term.

   - **Step In**—Click this button to display the first dependent of the underlined term. If that dependent also has a dependent, click this button again to see it (see Figure 5.8).

   - **Step Out**—Click this button to hide a dependent and evaluate its precedent.

4. Repeat step 3 until you've completed your evaluation.

5. Click Close.

Figure 5.8
With the Evaluate Formula feature, you can "step into" the formula to display its dependent cells.

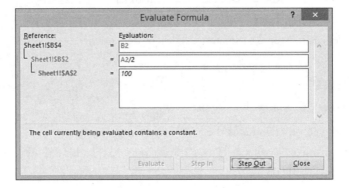

Watching Cell Values

In the precedent tracer example shown in Figure 5.7, the formula in cell G4 refers to a cell in another worksheet, which is represented in the trace by a worksheet icon. In other words, you can't see the formula cell and the precedent cell at the same time. This could also happen if the precedent existed on another workbook or even elsewhere on the same sheet if you're working with a large model.

This is a problem because there's no easy way to determine the current contents or value of the unseen precedent. If you're having a problem, troubleshooting requires that you track down the far-off precedent to see if it might be the culprit. That's bad enough with a single unseen cell, but what if your formula refers to 5 or 10 such cells? And what if those cells are scattered in different worksheets and workbooks?

This level of hassle—not at all uncommon in the spreadsheet world—was no doubt the inspiration behind an elegant solution: the Watch Window. This window enables you to keep tabs on both the value and the formula in any cell in any worksheet in any open workbook. Here's how you set up a watch:

1. Switch to the workbook that contains the cell or cells you want to watch.

2. Select Formulas, Watch Window. Excel displays the Watch Window.

3. Click Add Watch. Excel displays the Add Watch dialog box.

4. Either select the cell you want to watch or type in a reference formula for the cell (for example, =A1). Note that you can select a range to add multiple cells to the Watch Window.

5. Click Add. Excel adds the cell or cells to the Watch Window, as shown in Figure 5.9.

Figure 5.9
Use the Watch Window to keep an eye on the values and formulas of unseen cells that reside in other worksheets or workbooks.

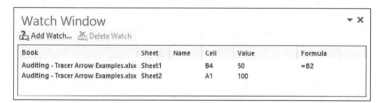

When you no longer need a watch, you should remove it to avoid cluttering the Watch Window. To remove a watch, select Formulas, Watch Window to open the Watch Window, click the watch, and then click Delete Watch.

From Here

- To learn how to paste range names, **see** "Pasting a List of Range Names in a Worksheet," **p. 48**.

- For the details of Excel's operator precedence rules, **see** "Understanding Operator Precedence," **p. 57**.

- To learn more about iteration, **see** "Using Iteration and Circular References," **p. 93**.

- For a detailed look at data validation, **see** "Applying Data-Validation Rules to Cells," **p. 100**.

- To learn about the IF() worksheet function, **see** "Using the IF() Function," **p. 164**.

- For the details of Excel's table features, **see** Chapter 13, "Analyzing Data with Tables," **p. 291**.

Understanding Functions

6

The formulas that you can construct based on the information presented in Part I, "Mastering Excel Ranges and Formulas," can range from simple additions and subtractions to powerful iteration-based solutions for otherwise difficult problems. Formulas that combine Excel's operators with basic operands such as numeric and string values are the bread and butter of any spreadsheet.

But to get to the real meat of a spreadsheet model, you need to expand your formula repertoire to include Excel's worksheet functions. Dozens of these functions exist, and they're essential to making your worksheet easier to work with and more powerful. Excel has various function categories, including the following:

- Text
- Logical
- Information
- Lookup and reference
- Date and time
- Math and trigonometry
- Statistical
- Financial
- Database and table

This chapter gives you a short introduction to Excel's built-in worksheet functions. You'll find out what the functions are, what they can do, and how to use them. The next six chapters give you detailed descriptions of the functions in the preceding list of categories. (The exceptions are the database and table category, which I cover in Chapter 13, "Analyzing Data with Tables," and the financial category, which I cover in Part IV, "Building Financial Formulas.")

> **NOTE**
> You can even create your own custom functions when Excel's built-in functions aren't up to the task you need to complete. You build these functions by using the Visual Basic for Applications (VBA) macro language, and it's easier than you think. See the book *Excel 2016 VBA and Macros* (Que, 2016).

About Excel's Functions

Functions are formulas that Excel has predefined. They're designed to take you beyond the basic arithmetic and text formulas you've seen so far. They do this in three ways:

- Functions make simple but cumbersome formulas easier to use. For example, suppose that you want to add a list of 100 numbers in a column, starting at cell A1 and finishing at cell A100. It's unlikely that you have the time or patience to enter 100 separate additions in a cell (that is, the formula =A1+A2+...+A100). Luckily, there's an alternative: the SUM() function. With this function, you would simply enter =SUM(A1:A100).

- Functions enable you to include in your worksheets complex mathematical expressions that otherwise would be difficult or impossible to construct using simple arithmetic operators. For example, determining a mortgage payment given the principal, interest, and term is a complicated matter at best, but you can do it with Excel's PMT() function just by entering a few arguments.

- Functions enable you to include data in your applications that you couldn't access otherwise. For example, the INFO() function can tell you how much memory is available on your system, what operating system you're using, what version number it is, and more. Similarly, the powerful IF() function enables you to test the contents of a cell—for example, to see whether it contains a particular value or an error—and then perform an action accordingly, depending on the result.

As you can see, functions are a powerful addition to your worksheet-building arsenal. With proper use of these tools, there is no practical limit to the kinds of models you can create.

The Structure of a Function

Every function has the same basic form:

```
FUNCTION(argument1, argument2, ...)
```

The FUNCTION part is the name of the function, which always appears in uppercase letters (such as SUM or PMT). Note, however, that you don't need to type in the function name using uppercase letters. Whatever case you use, Excel automatically converts the name to all uppercase. In fact, it's good practice to enter function names using only lowercase letters. That way, if Excel doesn't convert the function name to uppercase, you know that it doesn't recognize the name, which means you probably misspelled it.

The items that appear within the parentheses and separated by commas are the function *arguments*. The arguments are the function's inputs—the data the function uses to perform its calculations. With respect to arguments, functions come in two flavors:

■ **No arguments**—Many functions don't require any arguments. For example, the NOW() function returns the current date and time, and it doesn't require arguments.

■ **One or more arguments**—Most functions accept at least one argument, and some accept as many as nine or ten arguments. These arguments fall into two categories: required and optional. Required arguments are the arguments you *must* include when you use the function; otherwise, the formula will generate an error. You use the optional arguments only if your formula needs them.

Let's look at an example. The FV() function determines the future value of a regular investment, based on three required arguments and two optional ones:

```
FV(rate, nper, pmt[, pv][, type])
```

rate	The fixed rate of interest over the term of the investment.
nper	The number of deposits over the term of the investment.
pmt	The amount deposited each period.
pv	The present value of the investment. The default value is 0.
type	When the deposits are due (0 for the beginning of the period; 1 for the end of the period, which is the default).

This is called the function *syntax*. Three conventions are at work here and throughout the rest of this book:

■ *Italic type* indicates a placeholder. That is, when you use the function, you replace the placeholder with an actual value.

■ Arguments surrounded by square brackets are optional.

■ All other arguments are required.

> **CAUTION**
>
> Be careful how you use commas in functions that have optional arguments. If you omit the last optional argument, you must leave out the comma that precedes the argument. For example, if you omit just the *type* argument from FV(), you write the function like so:
>
> ```
> FV(rate, nper, pmt, pv)
> ```
>
> However, if you omit an optional argument within the syntax, you need to include all the commas so that there is no ambiguity about which value refers to which argument. For example, if you omit the *pv* argument from FV(), you write the function like this:
>
> ```
> FV(rate, nper, pmt, , type)
> ```

6

For each argument placeholder, you substitute an appropriate value. For example, in the FV() function, you substitute *rate* with a decimal value between 0 and 1, *nper* with an integer, and *pmt* with a dollar amount. Arguments can take any of the following forms:

- Literal alphanumeric values
- Expressions
- Cell or range references
- Range names
- Arrays
- The result of another function

The function operates by processing the inputs and then returning a result. For example, the FV() function returns the total value of the investment at the end of the term. Figure 6.1 shows a simple future-value calculator that uses this function. (In case you're wondering, I entered the Payment value in cell B4 as negative because Excel always treats any money you have to pay as a negative number.)

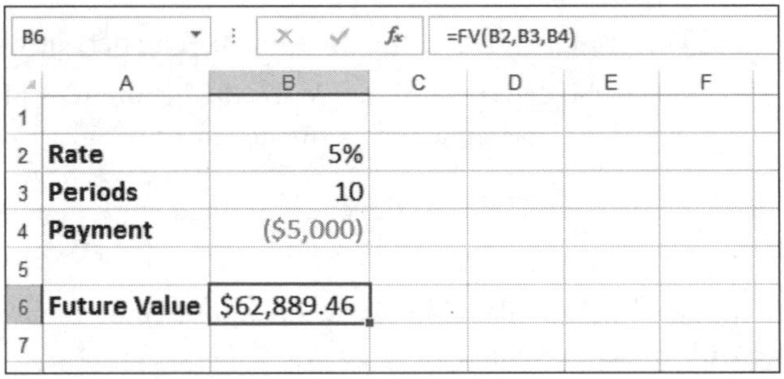

Figure 6.1
This example of the FV() function uses the values in cells B2, B3, and B4 as inputs for calculating the future value of an investment.

NOTE You can download this chapter's sample workbook at www.mcfedries.com/books/ book.php?title=excel-2016-formulas-and-functions.

6

Typing a Function into a Formula

You always use a function as part of a cell formula. So, even if you're using the function by itself, you still need to precede it with an equal sign. Whether you use a function on its own or as part of a larger formula, here are a few rules and guidelines to follow:

- You can enter the function name in either uppercase or lowercase letters. Excel always converts function names to uppercase.
- Always enclose function arguments in parentheses.

- Always separate multiple arguments with commas. (You might want to add a space after each comma to make a function more readable. Excel ignores the extra spaces.)

- You can use a function as an argument for another function. This is called *nesting* functions. For example, the function AVERAGE(SUM(A1:A10), SUM(B1:B15)) sums two columns of numbers and returns the average of the two sums.

In Chapter 2, "Using Range Names," I introduced you to Excel's AutoComplete feature for range names that shows you a list of named ranges that begin with the characters you've typed in a formula. That feature also applies to functions. As you can see in Figure 6.2, when you begin typing a name in Excel, the program displays a list of the functions that start with the letters you've typed and displays a description of the currently selected function. Select the function you want to use and then press Tab to include it in the formula (or double-click the function).

→ For the details on AutoComplete for named ranges, **see** "Working with AutoComplete for Range Names," **p. 47**.

Figure 6.2
When you begin typing a name in Excel, the program displays a list of functions with names that begin with the typed characters.

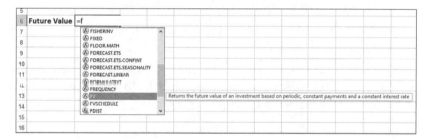

After you select the function from the AutoComplete list (or when you type a function name followed by the left parenthesis), Excel displays a pop-up banner that shows the function syntax. The current argument is displayed in bold type. In the example shown in Figure 6.3, the nper argument is shown in bold, so the next value (or cell reference, or whatever) entered will apply to that argument. When you type a comma, Excel bolds the next argument in the list.

6

Figure 6.3
After you type the function name and the left parenthesis, Excel displays the function syntax, with the current argument shown in bold type.

	A	B	C	D	E
1					
2	**Rate**	5%			
3	**Periods**	10			
4	**Payment**	($5,000)			
5					
6	**Future Value**	=FV(B2,			
7		FV(rate, **nper**, pmt, [pv], [type])			
8					

The current argument appears in bold type

Using the Insert Function Feature

Although you'll usually type your functions by hand, sometimes you might prefer to get a helping hand from Excel, such as in these circumstances:

■ You're not sure which function to use.

■ You want to see the syntax of a function before you use it.

■ You want to examine similar functions in a particular category before you choose the function that best suits your needs.

■ You want to see the effect that different argument values have on the function result.

For these situations, Excel offers two tools: the Insert Function feature and the Function Wizard.

You use the Insert Function feature to select the function you want from a dialog box. Here's how it works:

1. Select the cell in which you want to use the function.

2. Enter the formula up to the point where you want to insert the function.

3. Choose one of the following:

  • If the function you want is one you inserted recently, it might appear on the list of recent functions in the Name box. Drop down the Name box list (see Figure 6.4); if you see the name of the function you want, click it and skip to step 7.

Figure 6.4
Select Formulas, Insert Function or click the Insert Function button to display the Insert Function dialog box.

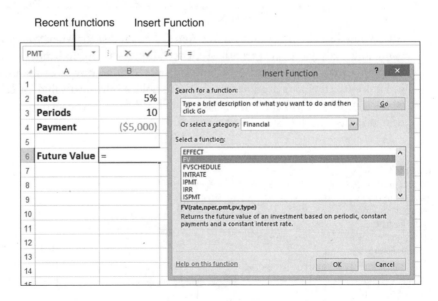

- To pick any function, select Formulas, Insert Function. (You can also click the Insert Function button in the formula bar—see Figure 6.4—or press Shift+F3.) In this case, the Insert Function dialog box appears, as shown in Figure 6.4.

4. (Optional) In the Or Select a Category list in the Insert Function dialog box, click the type of function you need. If you're not sure, click All.

5. In the Select a Function list, click the function you want to use. (Note that after you click inside the Select a Function list, pressing a letter moves the selection down to the first function that begins with that letter.)

6. Click OK. Excel displays the Function Arguments dialog box.

> **TIP**
>
> To skip the first six steps and go directly to the Function Arguments dialog box, enter the name of the function and the left parenthesis and then either click the Insert Function button or press Ctrl+A. Alternatively, press the equal sign (=) key and then select the function from the list of recent functions in the Name box. To skip the Function Arguments dialog box altogether, enter the name of the function in the cell and then press Ctrl+Shift+A.

7. For each required argument and each optional argument you want to use, enter a value, an expression, or a cell reference in the appropriate text box. Here are some notes to bear in mind when you're working in this dialog box (see Figure 6.5):

   - The names of the required arguments are shown in bold type.
   - When you move the cursor to an argument text box, Excel displays a description of the argument.
   - After you fill in an argument text box, Excel shows the current value of the argument to the right of the box.
   - After you fill in the text boxes for all the required arguments, Excel displays the current value of the function.

8. When you're finished, click OK. Excel pastes the function and its arguments into the cell.

6

Figure 6.5
Use the Function Arguments dialog box to enter values for a function's arguments.

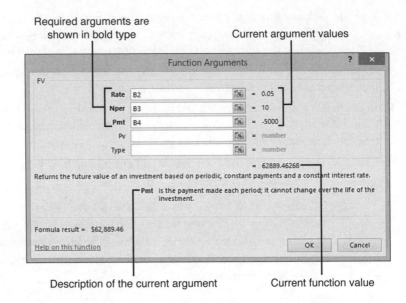

Required arguments are shown in bold type

Current argument values

Description of the current argument

Current function value

Loading the Analysis ToolPak

Excel's Analysis ToolPak is a large collection of powerful statistical tools. Some of these tools use advanced statistical techniques and were designed with only a limited number of technical users in mind. However, many of them have general applications and can be amazingly useful. I go through these tools in several chapters later in the book.

In early versions of Excel (that is, prior to Excel 2007), the Analysis ToolPak included dozens of powerful functions. In Excel 2007 and later, however, all those functions are now part of the Excel function library, so you can use them without loading the Analysis ToolPak.

If you need to use the Analysis ToolPak features, you must load the add-in that makes them available to Excel. The following procedure takes you through the steps:

1. Select File, Options to open the Excel Options dialog box.
2. Click Add-Ins.
3. In the Manage list, click Excel Add-ins and then click Go. Excel displays the Add-Ins dialog box.
4. Select the Analysis ToolPak check box, as shown in Figure 6.6.
5. Click OK.

Figure 6.6
Select the Analysis
ToolPak check box to load
these add-ins into Excel.

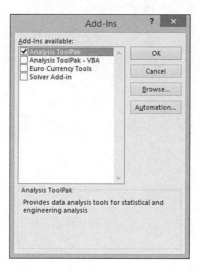

From Here

- For details on Excel's text-related functions, **see** Chapter 7, "Working with Text Functions."

- To learn about the logical and information functions, **see** Chapter 8, "Working with Logical and Information Functions."

- To get the specifics on Excel's powerful lookup functions, **see** Chapter 9, "Working with Lookup Functions."

- If you want to work with functions related to dates and times, **see** Chapter 10, "Working with Date and Time Functions."

- Excel has a huge library of mathematical functions; **see** Chapter 11, "Working with Math Functions."

- Excel's many statistical functions are a powerful tool for data analysis; **see** Chapter 12, "Working with Statistical Functions."

- To get the details on functions related to tables, **see** "Excel's Table Functions," **p. 313**. (Chapter 13)

- For information on using powerful regression functions such as TREND(), LINEST(), and GROWTH(), **see** Chapter 16, "Using Regression to Track Trends and Make Forecasts."

- Excel has many financial functions related to loans; **see** Chapter 18, "Building Loan Formulas."

- For information on functions related to investments, **see** Chapter 19, "Building Investment Formulas."

- To get details on Excel's discounting functions, **see** Chapter 20, "Building Discount Formulas."

Working with Text Functions

7

In Excel, *text* is any collection of alphanumeric characters that isn't a numeric value, a date or time value, or a formula. Words, names, and labels are all obviously text values, but so are cell values preceded by an apostrophe (') or formatted as Text. *Text values* are also called *strings*, and I use both terms interchangeably in this chapter.

In Chapter 3, "Building Basic Formulas," you learned about building text formulas in Excel—not that there was much to learn. Text formulas consist only of the concatenation operator (&) used to combine two or more strings into a larger string.

Excel's text functions enable you to take text formulas to a more useful level by giving you numerous ways to manipulate strings. With these functions, you can convert numbers to strings, change lowercase letters to uppercase (and vice versa), compare two strings, and more.

Excel's Text Functions

Table 7.1 summarizes Excel's text functions, and the rest of this chapter gives you details about and examples of how to use most of them.

Table 7.1 Excel's Text Functions

Function	Description
BAHTTEXT(number)	Converts number to baht (Thai) text.
CHAR(number)	Returns the character that corresponds to the ANSI code given by number.
CLEAN(text)	Removes all nonprintable characters from text.
CODE(text)	Returns the ANSI code for the first character in text.
CONCATENATE(text1[, text2],...)	Joins the specified strings into a single string.
DOLLAR(number[, decimals])	Converts number to a string that uses the Currency format.
EXACT(text1, text2)	Compares two strings to see whether they are identical.
FIND(find, within[, start])	Returns the character position of the text find within the text within. FIND() is case sensitive.
FIXED(number[, decimals][, no_commas])	Converts number to a string that uses the Number format.
LEFT(text[, number])	Returns the leftmost number characters from text.
LEN(text)	Returns the length of text.
LOWER(text)	Converts text to lowercase.
MID(text, start, number)	Returns number characters from text, starting at start.
NUMBERVALUE(text, decimal, group)	Converts text to a number by interpreting the decimal symbol within text as the decimal separator and the group symbol as the group separator.
PROPER(text)	Converts text to proper case (first letter of each word capitalized).
REPLACE(old, start, chars, new)	Replaces the old string with the new string.
REPT(text, number)	Repeats the text string number times.
RIGHT(text[, number])	Returns the rightmost number characters from text.
SEARCH(find, within[, start_num])	Returns the character position of the text find within the text within. SEARCH() is not case sensitive.
SUBSTITUTE(text, old, new[, num])	In text, substitutes the new string for the old string; optionally substitutes only the instance specified by num.
T(value)	Converts value to text.
TEXT(value, format)	Formats value and converts it to text.
TRIM(text)	Removes excess spaces from text.
UNICHAR(number)	Returns the character that corresponds to the UNICODE value given by number.
UNICODE(text)	Returns the UNICODE value for the first character in text.
UPPER(text)	Converts text to uppercase.
VALUE(text)	Converts text to a number.

7

Working with Characters and Codes

Every character you can display on your screen has its own underlying numeric code. For example, the code for the uppercase letter *A* is 65, whereas the code for the ampersand (&) is 38. These codes apply not only to the alphanumeric characters accessible via your keyboard but also to extra characters. The collection of these characters is called the *ANSI character set*, and the numbers assigned to each character are called the *ANSI codes*.

For example, the ANSI code for the copyright character (©) is 169. To display this character, press Alt+0169, where you use your keyboard's numeric keypad to enter the digits.

> **NOTE** When entering digits, remember to always include the leading zero for codes higher than 127.

The ANSI codes run from 1 to 255, although the first 31 codes are nonprinting codes that define *characters* such as carriage returns and line feeds.

The CHAR() Function

Excel enables you to determine the character represented by an ANSI code using the CHAR() function:

```
CHAR(number)
```

> *number*   The ANSI code, which must be a number between 1 and 255

For example, the following formula displays the copyright symbol (ANSI code 169):

```
=CHAR(169)
```

> **NOTE** If you are working with UNICODE values instead of ANSI values, use the UNICHAR() function instead of the CHAR() function.

Generating the ANSI Character Set

Figure 7.1 shows a worksheet that displays the entire ANSI character set, excluding the first 31 nonprinting characters (and note that ANSI code 32 represents the space character). In each case, the character is displayed by applying the CHAR() function to the value in the cell to the left.

7

> **NOTE** The actual character displayed by an ANSI code depends on the font applied to the cell. The characters shown in Figure 7.1 are the ones you see with normal text fonts, such as Arial. However, if you apply a font such as Symbol or Wingdings to the worksheet, you see a different set of characters.

Figure 7.1
This worksheet uses the CHAR() function to display each printing member of the ANSI character set.

L14   =CHAR(K14)

Code	CHAR()	Code	CHAR()	Code	CHAR()	Code	CHAR()	Code	CHAR()	Code	CHAR()	Code	CHAR()	Code	CHAR()	Code	CHAR()
32		57	9	82	R	107	k	132	„	157		182	¶	207	Ï	232	è
33	!	58	:	83	S	108	l	133	…	158	ž	183	·	208	Ð	233	é
34	"	59	;	84	T	109	m	134	†	159	Ÿ	184	¸	209	Ñ	234	ê
35	#	60	<	85	U	110	n	135	‡	160		185	¹	210	Ò	235	ë
36	$	61	=	86	V	111	o	136	ˆ	161	¡	186	º	211	Ó	236	ì
37	%	62	>	87	W	112	p	137	‰	162	¢	187	»	212	Ô	237	í
38	&	63	?	88	X	113	q	138	Š	163	£	188	¼	213	Õ	238	î
39	'	64	@	89	Y	114	r	139	‹	164	¤	189	½	214	Ö	239	ï
40	(	65	A	90	Z	115	s	140	Œ	165	¥	190	¾	215	×	240	ð
41	)	66	B	91	[	116	t	141		166	¦	191	¿	216	Ø	241	ñ
42	*	67	C	92	\	117	u	142	ž	167	§	192	À	217	Ù	242	ò
43	+	68	D	93	]	118	v	143		168	¨	193	Á	218	Ú	243	ó
44	,	69	E	94	^	119	w	144		169	©	194	Â	219	Û	244	ô
45	-	70	F	95	_	120	x	145	'	170	ª	195	Ã	220	Ü	245	õ
46	.	71	G	96	`	121	y	146	'	171	«	196	Ä	221	Ý	246	ö
47	/	72	H	97	a	122	z	147	"	172	¬	197	Å	222	Þ	247	÷
48	0	73	I	98	b	123	{	148	"	173		198	Æ	223	ß	248	ø
49	1	74	J	99	c	124			149	•	174	®	199	Ç	224	à	249	ù
50	2	75	K	100	d	125	}	150	–	175	¯	200	È	225	á	250	ú
51	3	76	L	101	e	126	~	151	—	176	°	201	É	226	â	251	û
52	4	77	M	102	f	127		152	˜	177	±	202	Ê	227	ã	252	ü
53	5	78	N	103	g	128	€	153	™	178	²	203	Ë	228	ä	253	ý
54	6	79	O	104	h	129		154	š	179	³	204	Ì	229	å	254	þ
55	7	80	P	105	i	130	‚	155	›	180	´	205	Í	230	æ	255	ÿ
56	8	81	Q	106	j	131	ƒ	156	œ	181	µ	206	Î	231	ç		

> **NOTE** You can download this chapter's sample workbooks at www.mcfedries.com/books/book.php?title=excel-2016-formulas-and-functions.

To build the character set shown in Figure 7.1, I entered the ANSI code and CHAR() function at the top of each column, and then I filled down to generate the rest of the column. A less tedious method (albeit one with a less useful display) is to take advantage of the ROW() function, which returns the row number of the current cell. Assuming that you want to start your table in row 2, you can generate any ANSI character by using the following formula:

```
=CHAR(ROW() + 30)
```

Figure 7.2 shows the results. (The values in column A are generated using the formula =ROW() + 30.)

Generating a Series of Letters

Excel's fill handle and Home, Fill, Series command are great for generating a series of numbers or dates, but they don't do the job when you need a series of letters (such as *a*, *b*, *c*, and so on). However, you can use the CHAR() function in an array formula to generate such a series.

B2 =CHAR(ROW() + 30)

	A	B	C	D	E	F	G	H	I
1	Code	CHAR()							
2	32								
3	33	!							
4	34	"							
5	35	#							
6	36	$							
7	37	%							
8	38	&							
9	39	'							
10	40	(							
11	41	)							
12	42	*							

Figure 7.2
This worksheet uses `=CHAR(ROW() + 30)` to generate the ANSI character set automatically.

To generate a column of the letters beginning with *a* (which corresponds to ANSI code 97), enter the following formula where you want the series to begin:

```
=CHAR(ROW(A97))
```

To generate a row of the letters beginning with *a*, enter the following formula where you want the series to begin:

```
=CHAR(COLUMN(CS1))
```

Now extend the series by dragging the fill handle down (for a column) or right (for a row).

For uppercase letters (where A corresponds to ANSI 65), begin with the following formulas and use the fill handle to extend the series:

```
=CHAR(ROW(A65))
=CHAR(COLUMN(BM1))
```

Figure 7.3 shows these formulas in action.

A1 =CHAR(ROW(A97))

	A	B	C	D	E	F	G	H	I	J	K
1	a	a	b	c	d	e	f	g	h	i	
2	b										
3	c										
4	d										
5	e										
6	f										
7	g										
8	h										
9	i										
10	j										
11											
12	A	A	B	C	D	E	F	G	H	I	
13	B										
14	C										

Figure 7.3
Combining the `CHAR()` and `ROW()` functions to produce a series of letters.

The CODE() Function

The CODE() function is the opposite of CHAR(). That is, given a text character, CODE() returns its ANSI code value:

```
CODE(text)
```

> *text*   A character or text string. Note that if you enter a multicharacter string, CODE() returns the ANSI code of the first character in the string.

For example, the following formulas both return 83, the ANSI code of the uppercase letter *S*:

```
=CODE("S")
=CODE("Spacely Sprockets")
```

> **NOTE** If you need to determine a character's UNICODE value instead of its ANSI value, use the UNICODE() function instead of the CODE() function.

Generating a Series of Letters Starting from Any Letter

Earlier in this section, you learned how to combine CHAR() and ROW() in an array formula to generate a series of letters beginning with the letter *a* or *A*. What if you prefer a different starting letter? You can do that by changing the initial value that's plugged in to the CHAR() function before the offsets are calculated. I used 97 in the previous example to begin the series with the letter *a*, but you could use 98 to start with *b*, 99 to start with *c*, and so on.

Instead of looking up the ANSI code of the character you prefer, however, use the CODE() function to have Excel do it for you:

```
=CHAR(CODE("letter") + ROW(range) - ROW(first_cell))
```

Here, replace *letter* with the letter you want to start the series with. For example, the following formula begins the series with uppercase *N*:

```
=CHAR(CODE("N") + ROW(A1:A13) - ROW(A1))
```

> **TIP** When working with the formulas in this section, remember to enter them as array formulas in the specified range.

Converting Text

Excel's forte is number crunching, and it often seems to give short shrift to strings, particularly when it comes to displaying strings in a worksheet. For example, appending a numeric value to a string results in the number being displayed without any formatting, even if the original cell had a numeric format applied to it. Similarly, strings imported from a database or text file can have the wrong case or no formatting. However, as you'll see in the next few sections, Excel offers a number of worksheet functions that enable you to convert strings to a more suitable text format or to convert between text and numeric values.

The LOWER() Function

The LOWER() function converts a specified string to all-lowercase letters:

```
LOWER(text)
```

   text   The string you want to convert to lowercase

For example, the following formula converts the text in cell B10 to lowercase:

```
=LOWER(B10)
```

The LOWER() function is often used to convert imported data, particularly data imported from a mainframe computer, which often arrives in all-uppercase characters.

The UPPER() Function

The UPPER() function converts a specified string to all-uppercase letters:

```
UPPER(text)
```

   text   The string you want to convert to uppercase

For example, the following formula converts the text in cells A5 and B5 to uppercase and concatenates the results with a space between them:

```
=UPPER(A5) & " " & UPPER(B5)
```

The PROPER() Function

The PROPER() function converts a specified string to proper case, which means the first letter of each word appears in uppercase and the rest of the letters appear in lowercase:

```
PROPER(text)
```

   text   The string you want to convert to proper case

For example, the following formula, entered as an array, converts the text in the range A1:A10 to proper case:

```
=PROPER(A1:A10)
```

The NUMBERVALUE() Function

The NUMBERVALUE() function, which was introduced in Excel 2013, converts a text value to a number by specifying the symbol used for the decimal and groups:

7

```
NUMBERVALUE(text[, decimal_separator][, group_separator])
```

text	The text representation of the number
decimal_separator	The symbol used within *text* to separate the integer portion from the fractional portion
group_separator	The symbol used within *text* to separate the numeric groupings, such as thousands and millions

This function is useful if you're faced with a worksheet that contains numbers that use non-standard symbols for the decimal and group separators. For example, suppose cell C6 contains 12,34, where the comma (,) is being used as a decimal separator (which is common in many European locales). To convert this value to a number that uses a period (assuming that's your local decimal separator symbol), you'd use the following formula:

```
=NUMBERVALUE(C6, ",")
```

As another example, suppose cell E5 contains the value 2~345'67, where tilde (~) is the group (thousands, in this case) separator and apostrophe (') is the decimal separator. Then the following formula converts this value to a number:

```
=NUMBERVALUE(E5, "'", "~")
```

Formatting Text

You learned in Chapter 3 that you can enhance the results of your formulas by using built-in or custom numeric formats to control things such as commas, decimal places, currency symbols, and more. That's fine for cell results, but what if you want to incorporate a result within a string? For example, consider the following text formula:

```
="The expense total for this quarter in 2015 is " & F11
```

No matter how you've formatted the result in F11, the number appears in the string using Excel's General number format. For example, if cell F11 contains $74,400, the previous formula will appear in the cell as follows:

```
The expense total for this quarter in 2015 is 74400
```

You need some way to format the number within the string. The next three sections show you some Excel functions that let you do just that.

The DOLLAR() Function

The DOLLAR() function converts a numeric value into a string value that uses the Currency format:

```
DOLLAR(number [,decimals])
```

number	The number you want to convert
decimals	The number of decimals to display (the default is 2)

To fix the string example from the previous section, you need to apply the `DOLLAR()` function to cell F11:

```
="The expense total for this quarter in 2015 is " & DOLLAR(F11, 0)
```

In this case, the number is formatted with no decimal places. Figure 7.4 shows a variation of this formula in action in cell B16. (The original formula is shown in cell B15.)

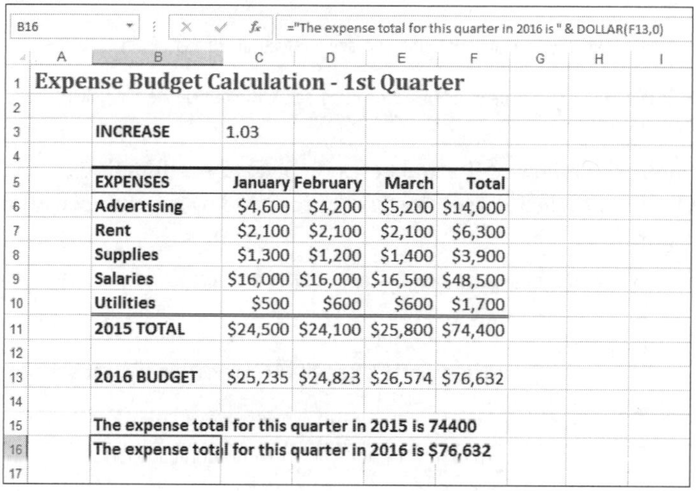

B16 =" The expense total for this quarter in 2016 is " & DOLLAR(F13,0)

	A	B	C	D	E	F
1	Expense Budget Calculation - 1st Quarter					
2						
3		INCREASE	1.03			
4						
5		EXPENSES	January	February	March	Total
6		Advertising	$4,600	$4,200	$5,200	$14,000
7		Rent	$2,100	$2,100	$2,100	$6,300
8		Supplies	$1,300	$1,200	$1,400	$3,900
9		Salaries	$16,000	$16,000	$16,500	$48,500
10		Utilities	$500	$600	$600	$1,700
11		2015 TOTAL	$24,500	$24,100	$25,800	$74,400
12						
13		2016 BUDGET	$25,235	$24,823	$26,574	$76,632
14						
15		The expense total for this quarter in 2015 is 74400				
16		The expense total for this quarter in 2016 is $76,632				
17						

Figure 7.4 Use the `DOLLAR()` function to display a number as a string with the Currency format.

The `FIXED()` Function

For some kinds of numbers, you can control the number of decimals and whether commas are inserted as the thousands separator by using the `FIXED()` function:

```
FIXED(number [,decimals] [,no_commas])
```

number	The number you want to convert to a string.
decimals	The number of decimals to display. (The default is `2`.)
no_commas	A logical value that determines whether commas are inserted into the string. Use `TRUE` to suppress commas; use `FALSE` to include commas. (This is the default.)

For example, the following formula uses the `SUM()` function to take a sum over a range and applies the `FIXED()` function to the result so that it is displayed as a string with commas and no decimal places:

```
="Total show attendance: " & FIXED(SUM(A1:A8), 0, FALSE) & " people."
```

The `TEXT()` Function

`DOLLAR()` and `FIXED()` are useful functions in specific circumstances. However, if you want total control over the way a number is formatted within a string, or if you want to include dates and times within strings, the powerful `TEXT()` function is what you need:

```
TEXT(number, format)
```

    number   The number, date, or time you want to convert

    format   The numeric or date/time format you want to apply to *number*

The power of the TEXT() function lies in its *format* argument, which is a custom format that specifies exactly how you want the number to appear. You learned about building custom numeric, date, and time formats back in Chapter 3.

→ To learn about custom numeric formatting, **see** "Customizing Numeric Formats," **p. 78.**

→ To learn about custom date and time formatting, **see** "Customizing Date and Time Formats," **p. 84.**

For example, the following formula uses the AVERAGE() function to take an average over the range A1:A31, and then it uses the TEXT() function to apply the custom format #,##0.00°F to the result:

```
="The average temperature was " & TEXT(AVERAGE(A1:A31), "#,##0.00°F")
```

> **NOTE**
>
> To insert the degree symbol (°), type Alt+0176 using your keyboard's numeric keypad.

Displaying When a Workbook Was Last Updated

Many people like to annotate their workbooks by setting Excel in manual calculation mode and entering a NOW() function into a cell (which returns the current date and time). The NOW() function doesn't update unless you save or recalculate the sheet, so you always know when the sheet was last updated.

Instead of just entering NOW() by itself, you might find it better to preface the date with an explanatory string, such as This workbook last updated:. To do this, you can enter the following formula:

```
="This workbook last updated: " & NOW()
```

Unfortunately, your output will look something like this:

```
This workbook last updated: 42238.51001
```

The number 42238.51001 is Excel's internal representation of a date and time. (The number to the left of the decimal is the date, and the number to the right of the decimal is the time.) To get a properly formatted date and time, use the TEXT() function. For example, to format the results of the NOW() function in the MM/DD/YY HH:MM format, use the following formula:

```
="This workbook last updated: " & TEXT(NOW(), "mm/dd/yy hh:mm")
```

Manipulating Text

The rest of this chapter takes you into the real heart of Excel's text-manipulation tricks. All the functions you'll learn about over the next few pages will be useful, but you'll see that by combining two or more of these functions into a single formula, you can bring out the amazing versatility of Excel's text-manipulation prowess.

Removing Unwanted Characters from a String

Characters imported from databases and text files often come with all kinds of string baggage in the form of extra characters that you don't need. These could be extra spaces in the string, or they could be line feeds, carriage returns, and other nonprintable characters embedded in the string. To fix these problems, Excel offers a couple functions: TRIM() and CLEAN().

The TRIM() Function

You use the TRIM() function to remove excess spaces within a string:

    TRIM(text)

> text   The string from which you want the excess spaces removed

Here, *excess* means all spaces before and after the string, as well as two or more consecutive spaces within the string. In the latter case, TRIM() removes all but one of the consecutive spaces.

Figure 7.5 shows the TRIM() function at work. Each string in the range A2:A7 contains a number of excess spaces before, within, or after the name. The TRIM() functions appear in column C. To help confirm the TRIM() function's operation, I use the LEN() text function in columns B and D. LEN() returns the number of characters in a specified string, using the following syntax:

    LEN(text)

> text   The string for which you want to know the number of characters

Figure 7.5
Use the TRIM() function to remove extra spaces from a string.

	A	B	C	D	E	F
	C2		fx	=TRIM(A2)		
1	**Original String**	**Length**	**Trimmed String**	**Length**		
2	Maria Anders	16	Maria Anders	12		
3	Ana Trujillo	17	Ana Trujillo	12		
4	Antonio Moreno	23	Antonio Moreno	14		
5	Thomas Hardy	17	Thomas Hardy	12		
6	Angus Glen Dunlop	26	Angus Glen Dunlop	17		
7	Christina Berglund	22	Christina Berglund	18		

7

The CLEAN() Function

You use the CLEAN() function to remove nonprintable characters from a string:

CLEAN(*text*)

   text   The string from which you want the nonprintable characters removed

Recall that the nonprintable characters are the codes 1 through 31 of the ANSI character set. The CLEAN() function is most often used to remove line feeds (ANSI 10) or carriage returns (ANSI 13) from multiline data. Figure 7.6 shows an example.

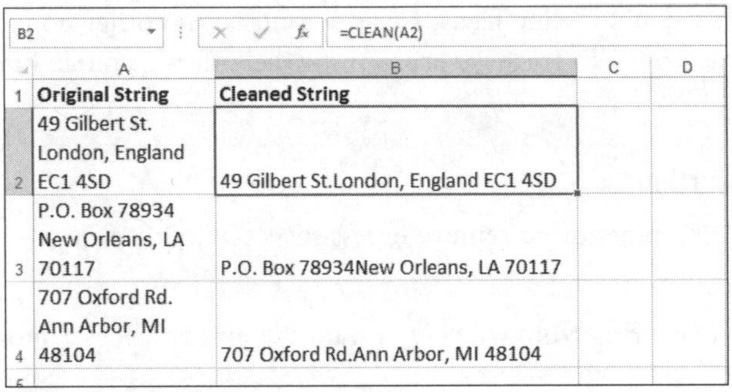

Figure 7.6
Use the CLEAN() function to remove nonprintable characters such as line feeds from a string.

The REPT() Function: Repeating a Character or String

The REPT() function repeats a character or string a specified number of times:

REPT(*text*, *number*)

   text   The character or string you want to repeat

   number   The number of times to repeat *text*

Padding a Cell

The REPT() function is sometimes used to pad a cell with characters. For example, you can use it to add leading or trailing dots in a cell. Here's a formula that creates trailing dots after a string:

="Advertising" & REPT(".", 20 - LEN("Advertising"))

This formula writes the string *Advertising* and then uses REPT() to repeat the dot character according to the following expression: 20 - LEN("Advertising"). This expression ensures that characters are written to the cell. Because *Advertising* is 11 characters, the expression result is 9, which means that nine dots are added to the right of the string. If the string were *Rent* (four characters) instead, 16 dots would be added as padding. Figure 7.7 shows how this technique creates a *dot follower* effect.

TIP For best results, the cells need to be formatted in a monotype font, such as Courier New. This ensures that all characters are the same width, which gives you consistent results in all the cells.

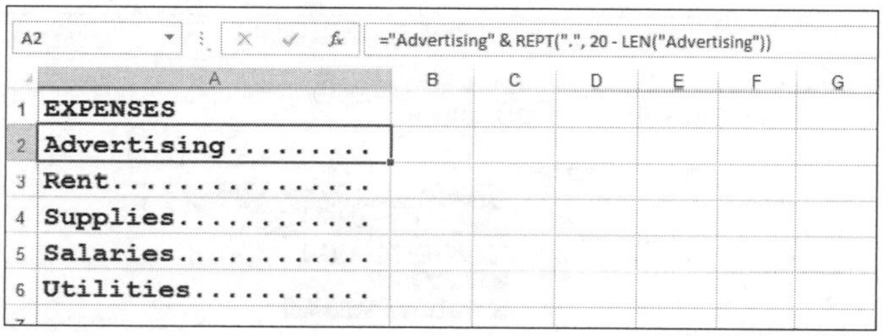

Figure 7.7
Use the `REPT()` function to pad a cell with characters, such as the dot followers shown here.

Building Text Charts

A more common use for the `REPT()` function is to build text-based charts. In this case, you use a numeric result in a cell as the `REPT()` function's `number` argument, and the repeated character then charts the result.

A simple example is a basic histogram, which shows the frequency of a sample over an interval. Figure 7.8 shows a text histogram in which the intervals are listed in column A and the frequencies are listed in column B. The `REPT()` function creates the histogram in column C by repeating the vertical bar (|) according to each frequency, as in this sample formula:

```
=REPT("|", B4)
```

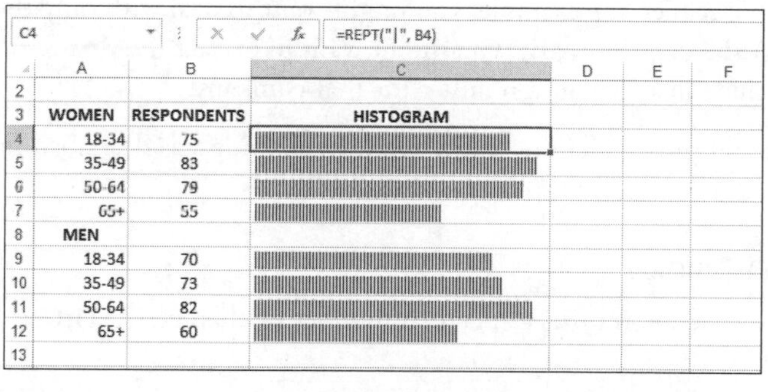

Figure 7.8
Use the `REPT()` function to create a text-based histogram.

With a simple trick, you can turn the histogram into a text-based bar chart, as shown in Figure 7.9. The trick here is to format the chart cells with the Webdings font. In this font, the letter *g* is represented by a block character, and repeating that character produces a solid bar.

To get the repeat value, I multiplied the percentages in column B by 100 to get a whole number. To keep the bars relatively short, I divided the result by 5.

Figure 7.9
Use the REPT() function to create a text-based bar chart.

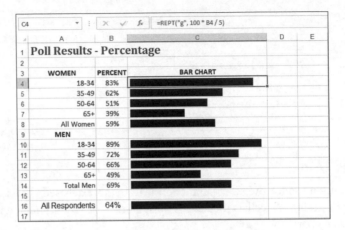

→ Excel offers a feature called data bars that enables you to easily add histogram-like analysis to your worksheets without formulas. **See** "Adding Data Bars," **p. 29.**

Extracting a Substring

String values often contain smaller strings, or *substrings*, that you need to work with. In a column of full names, for example, you might want to deal with only the last names so that you can sort the data. Similarly, you might want to extract the first few letters of a company name to include in an account number for that company.

Excel gives you three functions for extracting substrings, as described in the next three sections.

The LEFT() Function

The LEFT() function returns a specified number of characters, starting from the left of a string:

```
LEFT(text [,num_chars])
```

text	The string from which you want to extract the substring
num_chars	The number of characters you want to extract from the left (the default is 1)

For example, the following formula returns the substring Karen:

```
=LEFT("Karen Elizabeth McHammond", 5)
```

The `RIGHT()` Function

The `RIGHT()` function returns a specified number of characters, starting from the right of a string:

```
RIGHT(text [,num_chars])
```

| `text` | The string from which you want to extract the substring |
| `num_chars` | The number of characters you want to extract from the right (the default is 1) |

For example, the following formula returns the substring McHammond:

```
=RIGHT("Karen Elizabeth McHammond", 9)
```

The `MID()` Function

The `MID()` function returns a specified number of characters starting from any point within a string:

```
MID(text, start_num, num_chars)
```

`text`	The string from which you want to extract the substring
`start_num`	The character position at which you want to start extracting the substring
`num_chars`	The number of characters you want to extract

For example, the following formula returns the substring Elizabeth:

```
=MID("Karen Elizabeth McHammond", 7, 9)
```

Converting Text to Sentence Case

Microsoft Word's Change Case command has a *sentence case* option that converts a string to all-lowercase letters, except for the first letter, which is converted to uppercase (just as the letters would appear in a normal sentence). You saw earlier that Excel has LOWER(), UPPER(), and PROPER() functions, but it has nothing that can produce sentence case directly. However, it's possible to construct a formula that does this, by using the LOWER() and UPPER() functions combined with the LEFT() and RIGHT() functions.

You begin by extracting the leftmost letter and converting it to uppercase (assuming here that the string is in cell A1):

```
UPPER(LEFT(A1))
```

Then you extract everything to the right of the first letter and convert it to lowercase:

```
LOWER(RIGHT(A1, LEN(A1) - 1))
```

Finally, you concatenate these two expressions into the complete formula:

```
=UPPER(LEFT(A1)) & LOWER(RIGHT(A1, LEN(A1) - 1))
```

7

Figure 7.10 shows a worksheet that puts this formula through its paces.

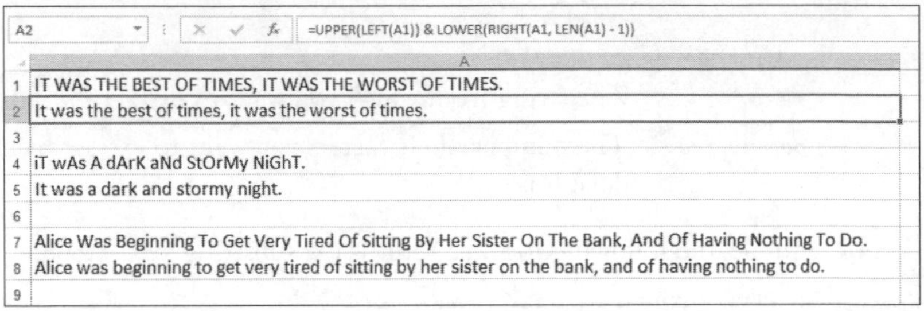

Figure 7.10

The LEFT() and RIGHT() functions combine with the UPPER() and LOWER() functions to produce a formula that converts text to sentence case.

A2	▾ : × ✓ fx	=UPPER(LEFT(A1)) & LOWER(RIGHT(A1, LEN(A1) - 1))

	A
1	IT WAS THE BEST OF TIMES, IT WAS THE WORST OF TIMES.
2	It was the best of times, it was the worst of times.
3	
4	iT wAs A dArK aNd StOrMy NiGhT.
5	It was a dark and stormy night.
6	
7	Alice Was Beginning To Get Very Tired Of Sitting By Her Sister On The Bank, And Of Having Nothing To Do.
8	Alice was beginning to get very tired of sitting by her sister on the bank, and of having nothing to do.
9	

A Date-Conversion Formula

If you import mainframe or server data into your worksheets, or if you import online service data such as stock market quotes, you'll often end up with date formats that Excel can't handle. One common example is the YYYYMMDD format (for example, 20160823).

To convert this value into a date that Excel can work with, you can use the LEFT(), MID(), and RIGHT() functions. If the unrecognized date is in cell A1, LEFT(A1, 4) extracts the year, MID(A1,5,2) extracts the month, and RIGHT(A1,2) extracts the day. Plugging these functions into a DATE() function gives Excel a date it can handle:

```
=DATE(LEFT(A1, 4), MID(A1, 5, 2), RIGHT(A1, 2))
```

→ To learn more about the DATE() function, **see** "DATE(): Returning Any Date," **p. 212**.

Case Study: Generating Account Numbers, Part I

Many companies generate supplier or customer account numbers by combining part of an account's name with a numeric value. Excel's text functions make it easy to generate such account numbers automatically.

To begin, let's extract the first three letters of the company name and convert them to uppercase for easier reading (assuming here that the name is in cell A2):

```
UPPER(LEFT(A2, 3))
```

Next, generate the numeric portion of the account number by grabbing the row number: ROW(A2). However, it's best to keep all account numbers a uniform length, so use the TEXT() function to pad the row number with zeros:

```
TEXT(ROW(A2), "0000")
```

Here's the complete formula, and Figure 7.11 shows some examples:

```
=UPPER(LEFT(A2, 3)) & TEXT(ROW(A2), "0000")
```

7

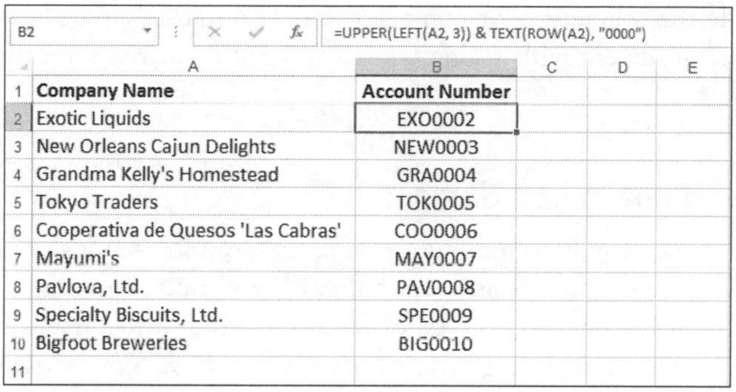

Figure 7.11
This worksheet uses the
UPPER(), LEFT(),
and TEXT() functions
to automatically generate
account numbers from
company names.

	A	B	C	D	E
		fx	=UPPER(LEFT(A2, 3)) & TEXT(ROW(A2), "0000")		
1	**Company Name**	**Account Number**			
2	Exotic Liquids	EXO0002			
3	New Orleans Cajun Delights	NEW0003			
4	Grandma Kelly's Homestead	GRA0004			
5	Tokyo Traders	TOK0005			
6	Cooperativa de Quesos 'Las Cabras'	COO0006			
7	Mayumi's	MAY0007			
8	Pavlova, Ltd.	PAV0008			
9	Specialty Biscuits, Ltd.	SPE0009			
10	Bigfoot Breweries	BIG0010			
11					

Searching for Substrings

You can take Excel's text functions up a notch or two by searching for substrings within some given text. For example, in a string that includes a person's first and last names, you can find out where the space falls between the names and then use that fact to extract either the first name or the last name.

The FIND() and SEARCH() Functions

Searching for substrings is handled by the FIND() and SEARCH() functions:

```
FIND(find_text, within_text [,start_num])
SEARCH(find_text, within_text [,start_num])
```

find_text	The substring you want to look for
within_text	The string in which you want to look
start_num	The character position at which you want to start looking (the default is 1)

Here are some notes to bear in mind when using these functions:

- These functions return the character position of the first instance (after the *start_num* character position) of *find_text* in *within_text*.
- Use SEARCH() for non-case-sensitive searches. For example, SEARCH("e", "Expenses") returns 1.
- Use FIND() for case-sensitive searches. For example, FIND("e", "Expenses") returns 4.
- These functions return the #VALUE! error if *find_text* is not in *within_text*.
- In the *find_text* argument of SEARCH(), use a question mark (?) to match any single character.
- In the *find_text* argument of SEARCH(), use an asterisk (*) to match any number of characters.

7

■ To include the character ? or * in a SEARCH() operation, precede each instance in the *find_text* argument with a tilde (~). If you want to search for a tilde character, use two tildes (~~).

Extracting a First Name or Last Name

If you have a range of cells containing people's first and last names, it can often be advantageous to extract these names from each string. For example, you might want to store the first and last names in separate ranges for later importing into a database table. Or perhaps you need to construct a new range using a *Last Name, First Name* structure for sorting the names.

The solution is to use the FIND() function to find the space that separates the first and last names and then use either the LEFT() function to extract the first name or the RIGHT() function to extract the last name.

→ Remember that Excel 2016 offers the Flash Fill feature, which is usually easier for tasks such as extracting names. **See** "Flash-Filling a Range," **p. 18**.

For the first name, you use the following formula (assuming that the full name is in cell A2):

```
=LEFT(A2, FIND(" ", A2) - 1)
```

Notice that the formula subtracts 1 from the FIND(" ", A2) result to avoid including the space in the extracted substring. You can use this formula in more general circumstances to extract the first word of any multiword string.

For the last name, you need to build a similar formula using the RIGHT() function:

```
=RIGHT(A2, LEN(A2) - FIND(" ", A2))
```

To extract the correct number of letters, the formula takes the length of the original string and subtracts the position of the space. You can use this formula in more general circumstances to extract the second word in any two-word string.

Figure 7.12 shows a worksheet that puts both formulas to work.

> **CAUTION**
>
> These formulas cause an error in any string that contains only a single word. To allow for this, use the IFERROR() function:
>
> ```
> =IFERROR(LEFT(A2, FIND(" ", A2) - 1), A2)
> ```
>
> This way, if the cell contains a space, all is well, and the formula runs normally. If the cell does not contain a space, the FIND() function returns an error. Therefore, instead of returning the formula result, the IFERROR() function returns just the cell text (A2).

Figure 7.12
Use the LEFT() and
FIND() functions to
extract the first name;
use the RIGHT() and
FIND() functions to
extract the last name.

D2		▼	:	×	✓	fx	=RIGHT(A2, LEN(A2) - FIND(" ", A2)) & ", " & LEFT(A2, FIND(" ", A2) - 1)			
▲	A		B	C		D		E	F	G
1	**Full Name**		**First Name**	**Last Name**		**Last Name, First Name**				
2	Charlotte Cooper		Charlotte	Cooper		Cooper, Charlotte				
3	Shelley Burke		Shelley	Burke		Burke, Shelley				
4	Regina Murphy		Regina	Murphy		Murphy, Regina				
5	Yoshi Nagase		Yoshi	Nagase		Nagase, Yoshi				
6	Mayumi Ohno		Mayumi	Ohno		Ohno, Mayumi				
7	Ian Devling		Ian	Devling		Devling, Ian				
8	Peter Wilson		Peter	Wilson		Wilson, Peter				
9	Lars Peterson		Lars	Peterson		Peterson, Lars				
10	Carlos Diaz		Carlos	Diaz		Diaz, Carlos				
11	Petra Winkler		Petra	Winkler		Winkler, Petra				
12	Martin Bein		Martin	Bein		Bein, Martin				

Extracting First Name, Last Name, and Middle Initial

If the full name you have to work with includes the person's middle initial, the formula for extracting the first name remains the same. However, you need to adjust the formula for finding the last name. There are a couple ways to go about this, but the method I'm showing you utilizes a useful FIND() and SEARCH() trick. Specifically, if you want to find the *second* instance of a substring, start the search one character position after the *first* instance of the substring. Here's an example of a string:

```
Karen D. McHammond
```

Assuming that this string is in A2, the formula =FIND(" ", A2) returns 6, the position of the first space. If you want to find the position of the second space, instead set the FIND() function's start_num argument to 7—or, more generally, to the location of the first space, plus 1:

```
=FIND(" ", A2, FIND(" ",A2) + 1)
```

You can then apply this result within the RIGHT() function to extract the last name:

```
=RIGHT(A2, LEN(A2) - FIND(" ", A2, FIND(" ", A2) +1))
```

To extract the middle initial, search for the period (.) and use MID() to extract the letter before it:

```
=MID(A2, FIND(".", A2) - 1, 1)
```

Figure 7.13 shows a worksheet that demonstrates these techniques.

Determining the Column Letter

Excel's COLUMN() function returns the column number of a specified cell. For example, for a cell in column A, COLUMN() returns 1. This is handy, as you saw earlier in this chapter ("Generating a Series of Letters"), but in some cases you might prefer to know the actual column letter.

Figure 7.13
Apply FIND() after the first instance of a substring to find the second instance of the substring.

	A	B	C	D	E
	Full Name	First Name	Middle Initial	Last Name	
1					
2	Charlotte P. Cooper	Charlotte	P	Cooper	
3	Shelley R. Burke	Shelley	R	Burke	
4	Regina O. Murphy	Regina	O	Murphy	
5	Yoshi H. Nagase	Yoshi	H	Nagase	
6	Mayumi U. Ohno	Mayumi	U	Ohno	
7	Ian F. Devling	Ian	F	Devling	
8	Peter W. Wilson	Peter	W	Wilson	
9	Lars X. Peterson	Lars	X	Peterson	
10	Carlos B. Diaz	Carlos	B	Diaz	
11	Petra Q. Winkler	Petra	Q	Winkler	

D2 ▾ : × ✓ fx =RIGHT(A2, LEN(A2) - FIND(" ", A2, FIND(" ", A2) +1))

This is a tricky proposition because the letters run from *A* to *Z*, then *AA* to *AZ*, and so on. However, Excel's CELL() function can return (among other things) the address of a specified cell in absolute format—for example, $A$2 or $AB$10. To get the column letter, you need to extract the substring between the two dollar signs. It's clear to begin with that the substring will always start at the second character position, so we can begin with the following formula:

```
=MID(CELL("Address", A2), 2, num_chars)
```

→ To learn more about the CELL() function, **see** "The CELL() Function," **p. 182.**

The *num_chars* value will be either 1, 2, or 3, depending on the column. Notice, however, that the position of the second dollar sign will either be 3, 4, or 5, depending on the column. In other words, the length of the substring will always be two less than the position of the second dollar sign. So, the following expression will give the *num_chars* value:

```
FIND("$", CELL("address",A2), 3) - 2
```

Here, then, is the full formula:

```
=MID(CELL("Address", A2), 2, FIND("$", CELL("address", A2), 3) - 2)
```

Getting the column letter of the current cell requires a slightly shorter formula:

```
=MID(CELL("Address"), 2, FIND("$", CELL("address"), 3) - 2)
```

Substituting One Substring for Another

The Office programs (and indeed most Windows programs) come with a Replace command that enables you to search for some text and then replace it with some other string. Excel's collection of worksheet functions also comes with such a feature, in the guise of the REPLACE() and SUBSTITUTE() functions.

The `REPLACE()` Function

Here's the syntax of the `REPLACE()` function:

```
REPLACE(old_text, start_num, num_chars, new_text)
```

`old_text`	The original string that contains the substring you want to replace
`start_num`	The character position at which you want to start replacing
`num_chars`	The number of characters to replace
`new_text`	The substring you want to use as the replacement

The tricky parts of this function are the `start_num` and `num_chars` arguments. How do you know where to start and how much to replace? This isn't hard if you know the original string in which the replacement is going to take place and if you know the replacement string. For example, consider the following string:

```
Expense Budget for 2015
```

To replace 2015 with 2016, and assuming that the string is in cell A1, the following formula does the job:

```
=REPLACE(A1, 20, 4, "2016")
```

However, it's a pain to have to calculate by hand the `start_num` and `num_chars` arguments. And in more general situations, you might not even know these values. Therefore, you need to calculate them:

- To determine the `start_num` value, use the `FIND()` or `SEARCH()` function to locate the substring you want to replace.

- To determine the `num_chars` value, use the `LEN()` function to get the length of the replacement text.

The revised formula then looks something like this (assuming that the original string is in A1 and the replacement string is in A2):

```
=REPLACE(A1, FIND("2015", A1), LEN("2015"), A2)
```

The `SUBSTITUTE()` Function

The extra steps required make the `REPLACE()` function unwieldy, so most people use the more straightforward `SUBSTITUTE()` function:

```
SUBSTITUTE(text, old_text, new_text [,instance_num])
```

`text`	The original string that contains the substring you want to replace
`old_text`	The substring you want to replace
`new_text`	The substring you want to use as the replacement
`instance_num`	The instance you want replaced (the default is all instances)

7

The following simpler formula does the same thing as the example in the previous section:

```
=SUBSTITUTE(A1, "2015", "2016")
```

Removing a Character from a String

Earlier, you learned about the CLEAN() function, which removes nonprintable characters from a string, as well as the TRIM() function, which removes excess spaces from a string. A common text scenario involves removing all instances of a particular character from a string. For example, you might want to remove spaces from a string or an apostrophe from a name.

Here's a generic formula that does this:

```
=SUBSTITUTE(text, character, "")
```

Here, replace *text* with the original string and *character* with the character you want to remove. For example, the following formula removes all the spaces from the string in cell A1:

```
=SUBSTITUTE(A1, " ", "")
```

> **NOTE**
>
> One surprising use of the SUBSTITUTE() function is to count the number of characters that appear in a string. The trick here is that if you remove a particular character from a string, the difference in length between the original string and the resulting string is the same as the number of times the character appeared in the original string. For example, the string expenses has eight characters. If you remove all the *e*'s, the resulting string is xpnss, which has five characters. The difference is 3, which is how many *e*'s there were in the original string.
>
> To calculate this in a formula, use the LEN() function and subtract the length of a string with the character removed from the length of the original string. Here's the formula that counts the number of *e*'s for a string in cell A1:
>
> ```
> =LEN(A1) - LEN(SUBSTITUTE(A1, "e", ""))
> ```

Removing Two Different Characters from a String

It's possible to nest one SUBSTITUTE() function inside another to remove two different characters from a string. For example, first consider the following expression, which uses SUBSTITUTE() to remove periods from a string:

```
SUBSTITUTE(A1, ".", "")
```

Because this expression returns a string, you can use that result as the text argument in another SUBSTITUTE() function. Here, then, is a formula that removes both periods and spaces from a string in cell A1:

```
=SUBSTITUTE(SUBSTITUTE(A1, ".", ""), " ", "")
```

Case Study: Generating Account Numbers, Part II

The formula I showed you earlier for automatically generating account numbers from an account name produces valid numbers only if the first three letters of the name are letters. If you have names that contain characters other than letters, you need to remove those characters before generating the account number. For example, if you have an account name such as J. D. BigBelly, you need to remove periods and spaces before generating the account name. You can do this by adding the expression from the previous section to the formula for generating an account name from earlier in this chapter. Specifically, you replace the cell address in LEFT() with the nested SUBSTITUTE() functions, as shown in Figure 7.14. Notice that the formula still works on account names that begin with three letters.

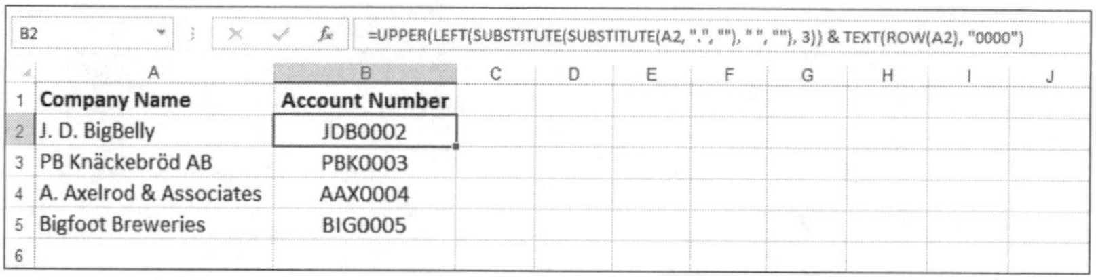

Figure 7.14
This worksheet uses nested SUBSTITUTE() functions to remove periods and spaces from account names before generating the account numbers.

	A	B	C	D	E	F	G	H	I	J
	Company Name	**Account Number**								
1										
2	J. D. BigBelly	JDB0002								
3	PB Knäckebröd AB	PBK0003								
4	A. Axelrod & Associates	AAX0004								
5	Bigfoot Breweries	BIG0005								
6										

B2 fx =UPPER(LEFT(SUBSTITUTE(SUBSTITUTE(A2, ".", ""), " ", ""), 3)) & TEXT(ROW(A2), "0000")

Removing Line Feeds

Earlier in this chapter, you learned about the CLEAN() function, which removes nonprintable characters from a string. In the example, I used CLEAN() to remove the line feeds from a multiline cell entry. However, you might have noticed a small problem with the result: There was no space between the end of one line and the beginning of the next line (refer to Figure 7.6).

If all you're worried about is line feeds, use the following SUBSTITUTE() formula instead of the CLEAN() function:

```
=SUBSTITUTE(A2, CHAR(10), " ")
```

This formula replaces the line feed character (ANSI code 10) with a space, resulting in a proper string, as shown in Figure 7.15.

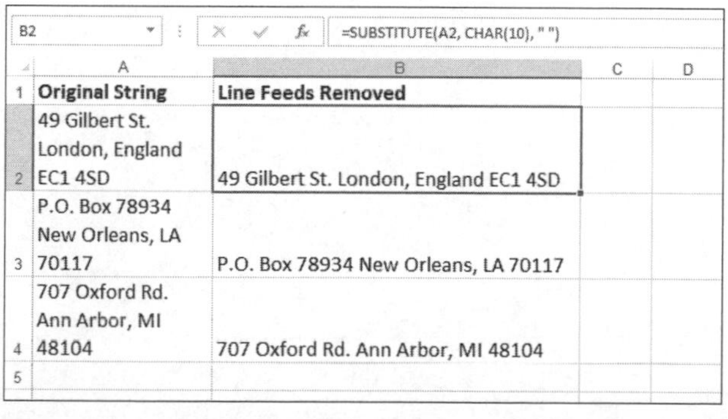

Figure 7.15
This worksheet uses SUBSTITUTE() to replace each line feed character with a space.

	A	B	C	D
1	**Original String**	**Line Feeds Removed**		
2	49 Gilbert St. London, England EC1 4SD	49 Gilbert St. London, England EC1 4SD		
3	P.O. Box 78934 New Orleans, LA 70117	P.O. Box 78934 New Orleans, LA 70117		
4	707 Oxford Rd. Ann Arbor, MI 48104	707 Oxford Rd. Ann Arbor, MI 48104		
5				

B2 fx =SUBSTITUTE(A2, CHAR(10), " ")

7

From Here

- For details on custom formatting, **see** "Formatting Numbers, Dates, and Times," **p. 74**.

- For a general discussion of function syntax, **see** "The Structure of a Function," **p. 130**.

- To learn more about the CELL() function, **see** "The CELL() Function," **p. 182**.

- To learn more about the DATE() function, **see** "DATE(): Returning Any Date," **p. 212**.

Working with Logical and Information Functions

I mentioned in Chapter 6, "Understanding Functions," that one of the advantages of using Excel's worksheet functions is that they enable you to build formulas that perform actions that are simply not possible with the standard operators and operands.

This idea becomes readily apparent when you learn about functions that can add intelligence and knowledge—the two cornerstones of good business analysis—to your worksheet models. You get these via Excel's logical and information functions, which I describe in detail in this chapter.

Adding Intelligence with Logical Functions

In the computer world, we *very* loosely define something as *intelligent* if it can perform tests on its environment and act in accordance with the results of those tests. However, computers are binary beasts, so "acting in accordance with the results of a test" means that the machine can do only one of two things. Still, even with this limited range of options, you'll be amazed at how much intelligence you can bring to your worksheets. Your formulas will actually be able to test the values in cells and ranges and then return results based on those tests.

This is all done with Excel's logical functions, which are designed to create decision-making formulas. For example, you can test cell contents to see whether they're numbers or labels, or you can test formula results for errors. Table 8.1 summarizes Excel's logical functions.

Table 8.1   Excel's Logical Functions

Function	Description
AND(*logical1*[,*logical2*],...)	Returns TRUE if all the arguments are true.
FALSE()	Returns FALSE.
IF(*logical_test*,*value_if_true* [,*value_if_false*])	Performs a logical test and returns a value based on the result.
IFERROR(*value, value_if_error*)	Returns *value_if_error* if *value* is an error.
IFNA(*value, value_if_na*)	Returns *value_if_na* if *value* returns the #N/A error.
NOT(*logical*)	Reverses the logical value of the argument.
OR(*logical1*[,*logical2*],...)	Returns TRUE if any argument is true.
TRUE()	Returns TRUE.
XOR(*logical1*[,*logical2*],...)	Returns TRUE if one and only one of the arguments is true.

→ To learn about the IFERROR() and IFNA() functions, **see** "Handling Formula Errors with IFERROR()," **p. 118**.

Using the IF() Function

I'm not exaggerating even the slightest when I tell you that the royal road to becoming an accomplished Excel formula builder involves mastering the IF() function. If you become comfortable wielding this function, a whole new world of formula prowess and convenience opens up to you. Yes, IF() is *that* powerful.

To help you master this crucial Excel feature, I'm going to spend a lot of time on it in this chapter. You'll get copious examples that show you how to use it in real-world situations.

IF(): The Simplest Case

Let's start with the simplest version of the IF() function:

```
IF(logical_test, value_if_true)
```

logical_test   A logical expression—that is, an expression that returns TRUE or FALSE (or their equivalent numeric values: 0 for FALSE and any other number for TRUE)

value_if_true   The value returned by the function if *logical_test* evaluates to TRUE

For example, consider the following formula:

```
=IF(A1 >= 1000, "It's big!")
```

The logical expression `A1 >= 1000` is used as the test. Let's say you enter this formula in cell B1. If the logical expression proves to be true (that is, if the value in cell A1 is greater than or equal to 1,000), the function returns the string `It's big!`, and that's the value you see in cell B1. (If A1 is less than 1,000, you see the value `FALSE` in cell B1 instead.)

Another common use for the simple `IF()` test is to flag values that meet a specific condition. For example, suppose you have a worksheet that shows the percentage increase or decrease in the sales of a long list of products. It would be useful to be able to flag just those products that had a sales decrease. A basic formula for doing this would look something like this:

```
=IF(cell < 0, flag)
```

Here, `cell` is the cell you want to test, and `flag` is some text that you use to point out a negative value. Here's an example:

```
=IF(B2 < 0, "<<<<<")
```

A slightly more sophisticated version of this formula would vary the flag, depending on the negative value. That is, the larger the negative number, the more less-than signs (in this case) the formula would display. This can be done using the `REPT()` function, discussed in Chapter 7, "Working with Text Functions":

```
REPT("<", B2 * -100)
```

→ For the details on the `REPT()` function, **see** "The `REPT()` Function: Repeating a Character or String," **p. 150**.

This expression multiplies the percentage value by –100 and then uses the result as the number of times the less-than sign is repeated. Here's the revised `IF()` formula:

```
=IF(B2 < 0, REPT("<", B2 * -100))
```

Figure 8.1 shows how it works in practice.

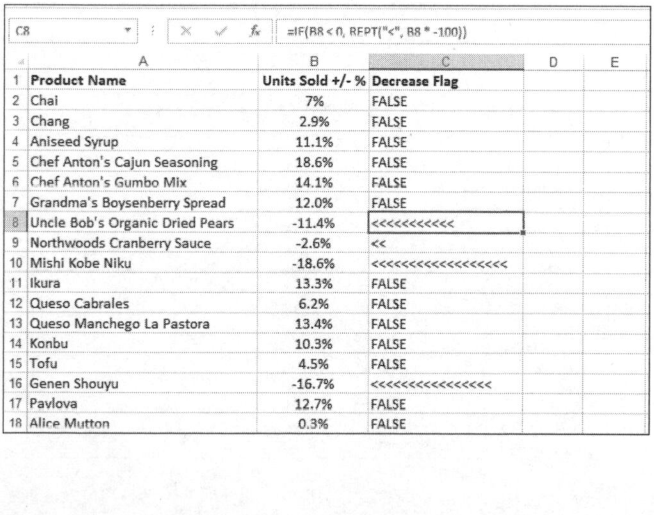

Figure 8.1

This worksheet uses the `IF()` function to test for negative values and then uses `REPT()` to display a flag for those values.

C8	▼ : × ✓ ƒx	=IF(B8 < 0, REPT("<", B8 * -100))			
	A	B	C	D	E
1	**Product Name**	**Units Sold +/- %**	**Decrease Flag**		
2	Chai	7%	FALSE		
3	Chang	2.9%	FALSE		
4	Aniseed Syrup	11.1%	FALSE		
5	Chef Anton's Cajun Seasoning	18.6%	FALSE		
6	Chef Anton's Gumbo Mix	14.1%	FALSE		
7	Grandma's Boysenberry Spread	12.0%	FALSE		
8	Uncle Bob's Organic Dried Pears	-11.4%	<<<<<<<<<<<		
9	Northwoods Cranberry Sauce	-2.6%	<<		
10	Mishi Kobe Niku	-18.6%	<<<<<<<<<<<<<<<<<<		
11	Ikura	13.3%	FALSE		
12	Queso Cabrales	6.2%	FALSE		
13	Queso Manchego La Pastora	13.4%	FALSE		
14	Konbu	10.3%	FALSE		
15	Tofu	4.5%	FALSE		
16	Genen Shouyu	-16.7%	<<<<<<<<<<<<<<<<		
17	Pavlova	12.7%	FALSE		
18	Alice Mutton	0.3%	FALSE		

8

NOTE You can download this chapter's sample workbooks at www.mcfedries.com/books/ book.php?title=excel-2016-formulas-and-functions.

Handling a FALSE Result

As you can see in Figure 8.1, if the result of the IF() condition calculates to FALSE, the function returns FALSE as its result. That's not inherently bad, but the worksheet would look tidier (and, hence, be more useful) if the formula returned, say, the null string ("") instead.

To do this, you need to use the full IF() function syntax:

IF(*logical_test*, *value_if_true*, *value_if_false*)

logical_test	A logical expression
value_if_true	The value returned by the function if *logical_test* evaluates to TRUE
value_if_false	The value returned by the function if *logical_test* evaluates to FALSE

For example, consider the following formula:

=IF(A1 >= 1000, "It's big!", "It's not big!")

This time, if cell A1 contains a value that's less than 1,000, the formula returns the string It's not big!.

For the negative value flag example, use the following revised version of the formula to return no value if the cell contains a nonnegative number:

=IF(B2 < 0, REPT("<", B2 * -100), "")

As you can see in Figure 8.2, the resulting worksheet looks much tidier than the first version.

Figure 8.2
This worksheet uses the full IF() syntax to return no value if the cell being tested contains a nonnegative number.

	A	B	C	D	E	F
1	**Product Name**	**Units Sold +/- %**	**Decrease Flag**			
2	Chai	7%				
3	Chang	2.9%				
4	Aniseed Syrup	11.1%				
5	Chef Anton's Cajun Seasoning	18.6%				
6	Chef Anton's Gumbo Mix	14.1%				
7	Grandma's Boysenberry Spread	12.0%				
8	Uncle Bob's Organic Dried Pears	-11.4%	<<<<<<<<<<<			
9	Northwoods Cranberry Sauce	-2.6%	<<			
10	Mishi Kobe Niku	-18.6%	<<<<<<<<<<<<<<<<<<			
11	Ikura	13.3%				
12	Queso Cabrales	6.2%				
13	Queso Manchego La Pastora	13.4%				
14	Konbu	10.3%				
15	Tofu	4.5%				
16	Genen Shouyu	-16.7%	<<<<<<<<<<<<<<<			
17	Pavlova	12.7%				
18	Alice Mutton	0.3%				

C2   fx   =IF(B2 < 0, REPT("<", B2 * -100), "")

Avoiding Division by Zero

As you saw in Chapter 5, "Troubleshooting Formulas," Excel displays the #DIV/0! error if a formula tries to divide a quantity by zero. To avoid this error, you can use IF() to test the divisor and ensure that it's nonzero before performing division.

→ To learn about the #DIV/0! error, **see** "#DIV/0!," **p. 112**.

For example, the basic equation for calculating gross margin is (Sales − Expenses)/Sales. To make sure that Sales isn't zero, use the following formula (assuming that you have cells named Sales and Expenses that contain the appropriate values):

```
=IF(Sales <> 0, (Sales - Expenses)/Sales, "Sales are zero!")
```

If the logical expression Sales <> 0 is true, that means Sales is nonzero, so the gross margin calculation can proceed. If Sales <> 0 is false, the Sales value is 0, so the message Sales are zero! is displayed instead.

Performing Multiple Logical Tests

The capability to perform a logical test on a cell is a powerful weapon indeed. You'll find endless uses for the basic IF() function in your everyday worksheets. The problem, however, is that the everyday world often presents us with situations that are more complicated than can be handled in a basic IF() function's logical expression. It's often the case that you have to test two or more conditions before you can make a decision.

To handle these more complex scenarios, Excel offers several techniques for performing two or more logical tests: nested IF() functions, the AND() function, and the OR() function. You'll learn about these techniques over the next few sections.

Nested IF() Functions

When building models using IF(), it's common to come upon a *second* fork in the road when evaluating either the *value_if_true* or *value_if_false* argument.

For example, consider the variation of our formula that outputs a description based on the value in cell A1:

```
=IF(A1 > 1000, "Big!", "Not big")
```

What if you want to return a different string for values greater than, say, 10,000? In other words, if the condition A1 > 1000 proves to be true, you want to run another test that checks to see whether A1 > 10000. You can handle this scenario by nesting a *second* IF() function inside the first as the *value_if_true* argument:

```
=IF(A1 > 1000, IF(A1 > 10000, "Really big!!", "Big!"), "Not big")
```

If A1 > 1000 returns TRUE, the formula evaluates the nested IF(), which returns Really big!! if A1 > 10000 is TRUE and returns Big! if it's FALSE; if A1 > 1000 returns FALSE, the formula returns Not big.

Note, too, that you can nest the `IF()` function in the *value_if_false* argument. For example, if you want to return the description `Small` for a cell value less than 100, you use this version of the formula:

```
=IF(A1 > 1000, "Big!", IF(A1 < 100, "Small", "Not big"))
```

Calculating Tiered Bonuses

A good time to use nested `IF()` functions arises when you need to calculate a *tiered* payment or charge. That is, if a certain value is X, you want one result; if the value is Y, you want a second result; and if the value is Z, you want a third result.

For example, suppose you want to calculate tiered bonuses for a sales team as follows:

- If the salesperson did not meet the sales target, no bonus is given.
- If the salesperson exceeded the sales target by less than 10%, a bonus of $1,000 is awarded.
- If the salesperson exceeded the sales target by 10% or more, a bonus of $10,000 is awarded.

Assuming that cell D2 contains the percentage that each salesperson's actual sales were above or below his target sales, here's a formula that handles these rules:

```
=IF(D2 < 0, "", IF(D2 < 0.1, 1000, 10000))
```

If the value in D2 is negative, nothing is returned; if the value in D2 is less than 10%, the formula returns `1000`; if the value in D2 is greater than or equal to 10%, the formula returns `10000`. Figure 8.3 shows this formula in action.

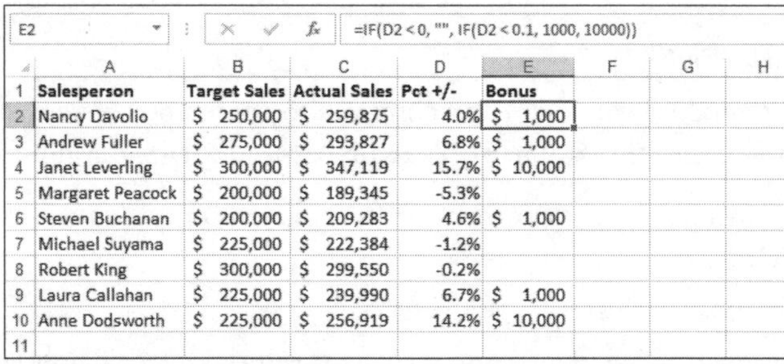

Figure 8.3
This worksheet uses nested `IF()` functions to calculate a tiered bonus payment.

	A	B	C	D	E	F	G	H
1	Salesperson	Target Sales	Actual Sales	Pct +/-	Bonus			
2	Nancy Davolio	$ 250,000	$ 259,875	4.0%	$ 1,000			
3	Andrew Fuller	$ 275,000	$ 293,827	6.8%	$ 1,000			
4	Janet Leverling	$ 300,000	$ 347,119	15.7%	$ 10,000			
5	Margaret Peacock	$ 200,000	$ 189,345	-5.3%				
6	Steven Buchanan	$ 200,000	$ 209,283	4.6%	$ 1,000			
7	Michael Suyama	$ 225,000	$ 222,384	-1.2%				
8	Robert King	$ 300,000	$ 299,550	-0.2%				
9	Laura Callahan	$ 225,000	$ 239,990	6.7%	$ 1,000			
10	Anne Dodsworth	$ 225,000	$ 256,919	14.2%	$ 10,000			
11								

Formula bar: E2 — `=IF(D2<0, "", IF(D2<0.1, 1000, 10000))`

The AND() Function

It's often necessary to perform an action if and only if two conditions are true. For example, you might want to pay a salesperson a bonus if and only if dollar sales exceeded the budget *and* unit sales also exceeded the budget. If either the dollar sales or the unit sales fell below budget (or if they both fell below budget), no bonus is paid. In Boolean logic, this is called an *And* condition because one expression *and* another must be true for a positive result.

In Excel, And conditions are handled, appropriately enough, by the AND() logical function:

```
AND(logical1 [,logical2,...])
    logical1            The first logical condition to test
    logical2,...        The second logical condition to test
```

You can enter up to 255 logical conditions.

The AND() result is calculated as follows:

- If *all* the arguments return TRUE (or any nonzero number), AND() returns TRUE.
- If one or more of the arguments return FALSE (or 0), AND() returns FALSE.

You can use the AND() function anywhere you would use a logical formula, but it's most often pressed into service as the logical condition in an IF() function. In other words, if all the logical conditions in the AND() function are TRUE, IF() returns its *value_if_true* result; if one or more of the logical conditions in the AND() function are FALSE, IF() returns its *value_if_false* result.

For example, suppose you want to pay out a bonus only if a salesperson exceeds his budget for both dollar sales and unit sales. Assuming that the difference between the actual and budgeted dollar amounts is in cell B2 and the difference between the actual and budgeted unit amounts is in cell C2, here's an example of a formula that determines whether a bonus is paid:

```
=IF(AND(B2 > 0, C2 > 0), "1000", "No bonus")
```

If the value in B2 is greater than 0 and the value in C2 is greater than 0, the formula returns 1000; otherwise, it returns No bonus.

Slotting Values into Categories

A good use for the AND() function is to slot items into categories that consist of a range of values. For example, suppose you have a set of poll or survey results, and you want to categorize these results based on the following age ranges: 18–34, 35–49, 50–64, and 65+. Assuming that each respondent's age is in cell B9, the following AND() function can serve as the logical test for entry into the 18–34 category:

```
AND(B9 >= 18, B9 <= 34)
```

If the response is in C9, the following formula will display it if the respondent is in the 18–34 age group:

```
=IF(AND(B9 >= 18, B9 <= 34), C9, "")
```

Figure 8.4 tries this on some data. Here are the formulas used for the other age groups:

```
35-49: =IF(AND(B9 >= 35, B9 <= 49), C9, "")
50-64: =IF(AND(B9 >= 50, B9 <= 64), C9, "")
65+:   =IF(B9 >= 65, C9, "")
```

8

Figure 8.4
This worksheet uses the AND() function as the logical condition for an IF() function to slot poll results into age groups.

	A	B	C	D	E	F	G	H	I
	D9	▾ : × ✓ fx	=IF(AND(B9 >= 18, B9 <= 34), C9, "")						
1	Poll Results — Question #1								
2		Key: 1 = Strongly Disagree							
3		2 = Disagree							
4		3 = Neutral							
5		4 = Agree							
6		5 = Strongly Agree							
7									
8	Subject ID	Age	Response	18-34	35-49	50-64	65+		
9	1	19	4	4					
10	2	23	5	5					
11	3	38	3		3				
12	4	44	4		4				
13	5	51	2			2			
14	6	20	4	4					
15	7	65	1				1		
16	8	49	4		4				
17	9	60	3			3			
18	10	69	2				2		
19									

The OR() Function

Similar to an And condition is the situation when you need to take an action if one thing *or* another is true. For example, you might want to pay a salesperson a bonus if she exceeded the dollar sales budget *or* if she exceeded the unit sales budget. In Boolean logic, this is called an *Or* condition.

You won't be surprised to hear that Or conditions are handled in Excel by the OR() function:

```
OR(logical1 [,logical2,...])
```

logical1	The first logical condition to test
logical2,...	The second logical condition to test

You can enter up to 255 logical conditions.

The OR() result is calculated as follows:

- If one or more of the arguments return TRUE (or any nonzero number), OR() returns TRUE.
- If *all* of the arguments return FALSE (or 0), OR() returns FALSE.

As with AND(), you use OR() wherever a logical expression is called for, most often within an IF() function. This means that if one or more of the logical conditions in the OR() function are TRUE, IF() returns its *value_if_true* result; if all the logical conditions in the OR() function are FALSE, IF() returns its *value_if_false* result.

For example, suppose you want to pay out a bonus only if a salesperson exceeds her budget for either dollar sales or unit sales (or both). Assuming that the difference between the actual and budgeted dollar amounts is in cell B2 and the difference between the actual and budgeted unit amounts is in cell C2, here's an example of a formula that determines whether a bonus is paid:

```
=IF(OR(B2 > 0, C2 > 0), "1000", "No bonus")
```

If the value in B2 is greater than 0 or the value in C2 is greater than 0, the formula returns 1000; otherwise, it returns No bonus.

> **NOTE** The OR() function returns TRUE when one or more of its arguments are TRUE. However, in some cases, you want an expression to return TRUE only when just *one* of the arguments is TRUE. In that case, use the XOR() function, which returns TRUE when one and only one of its arguments evaluates to TRUE.

Applying Conditional Formatting with Formulas

In Chapter 1, "Getting the Most Out of Ranges," you learned about the powerful conditional formatting features available in Excel. These features enable you to highlight cells, create top and bottom rules, and apply three types of formatting: data bars, color scales, and icon sets.

→ For the details on conditional formatting, **see** "Applying Conditional Formatting to a Range," **p. 25**.

Excel comes with another conditional formatting component that makes this feature even more powerful: You can apply conditional formatting based on the results of a formula. In particular, you can set up a logical formula as the conditional formatting criteria. If that formula returns TRUE, Excel applies the formatting to the cells; if the formula returns FALSE, instead, Excel doesn't apply the formatting. In most cases, you use an IF() function, often combined with another logical function such as AND() or OR().

Before we get to an example, here are the basic steps to follow to set up formula-based conditional formatting:

1. Select the cells to which you want the conditional formatting applied.
2. Select Home, Conditional Formatting, New Rule. Excel displays the New Formatting Rule dialog box.
3. Click Use a Formula to Determine Which Cells to Format.
4. In the Format Values Where This Formula Is True range box, type your logical formula.
5. Click Format to open the Format Cells dialog box.
6. Use the Number, Font, Border, and Fill tabs to specify the formatting you want to apply and then click OK.
7. Click OK.

For example, suppose you have a range or table of items and you want to highlight those items that have the maximum and minimum values in a particular column. You could set up separate top and bottom rules, but you can make things easier and more flexible by instead using a logical formula.

How you go about this in a conditional formatting rule is a bit tricky, but it can be extremely powerful when you know the trick. First, you can use the MAX() worksheet function to determine the maximum value in a range. For example, if the range is D2:D10, then the following function returns the maximum:

```
MAX($D$2:$D$10)
```

However, a conditional formatting formula works only if it returns TRUE or FALSE, so you need to create a comparison formula:

```
=MAX($D$2:$D$10)=$D2
```

There are two things to note here: First, you compare the range to the first value in the range; second, the cell address uses the mixed-reference format $D2, which tells Excel to keep the column (D) fixed, while varying the row number.

Next, you can use the MIN() function to determine the minimum, so you create a similar comparison formula:

```
=MIN($D$2:$D$10)=$D2
```

Finally, you want to check each cell in the column to see if it's the maximum or the minimum, so you need to combine these expressions by using the OR() function, like so:

```
=OR(MAX($D$2:$D$10)=$D2, MIN($D$2:$D$10)=$D2)
```

Figure 8.5 shows a range of sales results (A2:E10) that are conditionally formatted using the preceding formula. This shows which reps had the maximum and minimum percentage differences between target sales and actual sales (column D).

Figure 8.5
A range of sales rep data conditionally formatted using a logical formula.

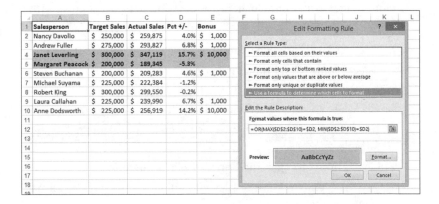

Combining Logical Functions with Arrays

When you combine the array formulas you learned about in Chapter 4, "Creating Advanced Formulas," with IF(), you can perform some remarkably sophisticated operations. Arrays enable you to do things such as apply the IF() logical condition across a range as well as sum only those cells in a range that meet the IF() condition.

→ To learn about array formulas, **see** "Working with Arrays," **p. 87**.

Applying a Condition Across a Range

Using AND() as the logical condition in an IF() function is useful for perhaps three or four expressions. After that, it just gets too unwieldy to enter all those logical expressions. If you're essentially running the same logical test on a number of different cells, a better solution is to apply AND() to a range and enter the formula as an array.

For example, suppose that you want to sum the cells in the range B3:B7 but only if all those cells contain values greater than 0. Here's an array formula to do this:

```
{=IF(AND(B3:B7 > 0), SUM(B3.B7), "")}
```

> **NOTE**
> Recall from Chapter 4 that you don't include the braces ({ }) when you enter an array formula. Type the formula without the braces and then press Ctrl+Shift+Enter.

This is useful in a worksheet in which you might not have all the numbers yet, and you don't want a total entered until the data is complete. Figure 8.6 shows an example. The array formula in B8 is the same as the previous one. The array formula in B16 returns nothing because cell B14 is blank.

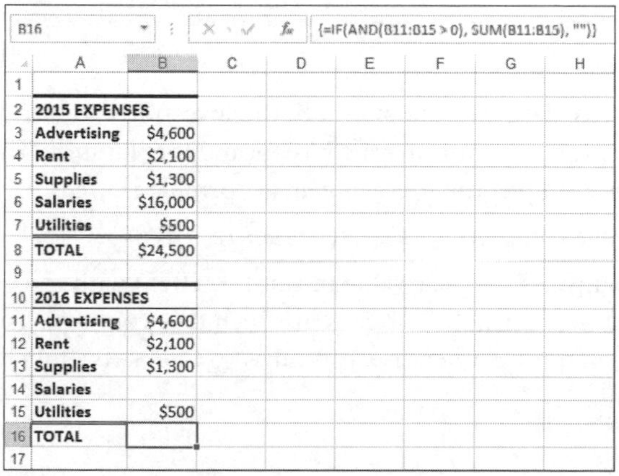

Figure 8.6
This worksheet uses IF(), AND(), and SUM() in two array formulas (B8 and B16) to total a range only if all the cells have nonzero values.

	A	B
2	2015 EXPENSES	
3	Advertising	$4,600
4	Rent	$2,100
5	Supplies	$1,300
6	Salaries	$16,000
7	Utilities	$500
8	TOTAL	$24,500
9		
10	2016 EXPENSES	
11	Advertising	$4,600
12	Rent	$2,100
13	Supplies	$1,300
14	Salaries	
15	Utilities	$500
16	TOTAL	

B16 formula: {=IF(AND(B11:B15 > 0), SUM(B11.B15), "")}

Operating Only on Cells That Meet a Condition

In the previous section, you saw how to use an array formula to perform an action only if a certain condition is met across a range of cells. A related scenario arises when you want to perform an action on a range, but only on cells that meet a certain condition. For example, you might want to sum only values that are positive.

To do this, you need to move the operation outside the IF() function. For example, here's an array formula that sums only values in the range B3:B7 that contain positive values:

    {=SUM(IF(B3:B7 > 0, B3:B7, 0))}

The IF() function returns an array of values based on the condition (the cell value if it's positive; 0 otherwise), and the SUM() function adds those returned values.

For example, suppose you have a series of investments that mature in various years. It would be nice to set up a table that lists these years and tells you the total value of the investments that mature in each year. Figure 8.7 shows a worksheet set up to do just that.

Figure 8.7
This worksheet uses array formulas to sum the yearly maturity values of various investments.

| F3 | | ▼ | : | × | ✓ | *fx* | {=SUM(IF(YEAR($B$3:$B$18) = E3, $C$3:$C$18, 0))} |

▲	A	B	C	D	E	F	G	H
1	Investment Maturity Dates and Future Values				Maturity Table			
2	Bond Code	Maturity Date	Maturity Value		Year	Total Value		
3	563469EM3	Sep 01, 2015	$ 14,000		2015	$ 36,000		
4	642866EX1	Jun 15, 2016	$ 16,000		2016	$ 46,000		
5	683234NX2	Nov 19, 2016	$ 20,000		2017	$ 45,000		
6	78009ZAE9	Apr 12, 2017	$ 20,000		2018	$ 45,000		
7	683234PQ5	Dec 02, 2015	$ 10,000		2019	$ 37,000		
8	07813ZAN4	Apr 12, 2015	$ 12,000		2020	$ 35,000		
9	135110AA2	Jun 30, 2018	$ 15,000		Total	$ 244,000		
10	40975TAA1	May 31, 2017	$ 10,000					
11	013014BS3	Jun 01, 2018	$ 15,000					
12	683234NX2	Nov 19, 2016	$ 10,000					
13	626209GC8	Jun 01, 2017	$ 15,000					
14	683234RX8	Dec 02, 2020	$ 20,000					
15	110709DG4	Aug 23, 2019	$ 17,000					
16	110709DF6	Jun 09, 2020	$ 15,000					
17	642866FB8	Dec 12, 2018	$ 15,000					
18	110709DG4	Aug 23, 2019	$ 20,000					
19								

The investment maturity dates are in column B, the investment values at maturity are shown in column C, and the various maturity years are in column E. To calculate the maturity total for 2015, for example, the following array formula is used:

    {=SUM(IF(YEAR($B$3:$B$18) = E3, $C$3:$C$18, 0))}

The IF() function compares the year value in cell E3 (2015) with the year component of the maturity dates in range B3:B18. For cells in which these are equal, IF() returns the corresponding value in column C; otherwise, it returns 0. The SUM() function then adds these returned values.

NOTE In Figure 8.7, notice that, with the exception of the reference to cell E3, I used absolute references so the formula can be filled down to the other years.

Determining Whether a Value Appears in a List

Many spreadsheet applications require you to look up a value in a list. For example, you might have a table of customer discounts in which the percentage discount is based on the number of units ordered. For each customer order, you need to look up the appropriate discount, based on the total units in the order. Similarly, a teacher might convert a raw test score into a letter grade by referring to a table of conversions.

You'll see some sophisticated tools for looking up values in Chapter 9, "Working with Lookup Functions." However, array formulas combined with logical functions also offer some tricks for looking up values.

For example, suppose that you want to know whether a certain value exists in an array. You can use the following general formula, entered into a single cell as an array:

$$\{=\text{OR}(value = range)\}$$

Here, *value* is the value you want to search for, and *range* is the range of cells in which to search. For example, Figure 8.8 shows a list of customers with overdue accounts. You enter the account number of the customer in cell B1, and cell B2 tells you whether the number appears in the list.

Figure 8.8

This worksheet uses the OR () function in an array formula to determine whether a value appears in a list.

	A	B	C	D	E	F	G	H
		B2		fx {=OR(B1 = B6:B29)}				
1	Account Number:	09-2111						
2	In the List?	TRUE	First Row:	14				
3	How Many Times?	2	Last Row:	22				
4								
5	Account Name	Account Number	Invoice Number	Invoice Amount	Due Date	Date Paid	Days Overdue	
6	Emily's Sports Palace	08-2255	117316	$ 1,584.20	26-Apr-13		55	
7	Refco Office Solutions	14-5741	117317	$ 303.65	27-Apr-13		54	
8	Brimson Furniture	10-0009	117321	$ 2,144.55	3-May-13		48	
9	Katy's Paper Products	12-1212	117322	$ 234.69	4-May-13		47	
10	Door Stoppers Ltd.	01-0045	117324	$ 101.01	10-May-13		41	
11	Voyatzis Designs	14-1882	117325	$ 1,985.25	10-May-13		41	
12	Brimson Furniture	10-0009	117327	$ 1,847.25	16-May-13		35	
13	Door Stoppers Ltd.	01-0045	117328	$ 58.50	17-May-13		34	
14	O'Donoghue Inc.	09-2111	117329	$ 1,234.56	18-May-13		33	
15	Refco Office Solutions	14-5741	117330	$ 456.78	18-May-13		33	
16	Renaud & Son	07-0025	117331	$ 565.77	23-May-13		30	
17	Simpson's Ltd.	16-6658	117332	$ 898.54	22-May-13		31	
18	Door Stoppers Ltd.	01-0045	117333	$ 1,685.74	26-May-13		27	
19	Renaud & Son	07-0025	117335	$ 3,005.14	28-May-13		25	
20	Rooter Office Solvents	07-4441	117336	$ 78.85	30-May-13		23	
21	Emily's Sports Palace	08-2255	117337	$ 4,347.21	2-Jun-13		20	
22	O'Donoghue Inc.	09-2111	117338	$ 2,144.55	2-Jun-13		20	
23	Brimson Furniture	10-0009	117339	$ 1,234.69	3-Jun-13		19	

Here's the array formula in cell B2:

```
{=OR(B1 = B6:B29)}
```

The array formula checks each value in the range B6:B29 to see whether it equals the value in cell B1. If any one of those comparisons is true, OR() returns TRUE, which means the value is in the list.

> **TIP**
>
> As a similar example, here's an array formula that returns TRUE if a particular account number is *not* in the list:
>
> ```
> {=AND(B1 <> B6:B29)}
> ```
>
> The formula checks each value in B6:B29 to see whether it does not equal the value in B1. If all those comparisons are true, AND() returns TRUE, which means the value is not in the list.

Counting Occurrences in a Range

Now you know how to find out whether a value appears in a list, but what if you need to know how many times the value appears? The following formula does the job:

```
{=SUM(IF(value = range, 1, 0))}
```

Again, *value* is the value you want to look up, and *range* is the range for searching. In this array formula, the IF() function compares *value* with every cell in *range*. The values that match return 1, and those that don't return 0. The SUM() function adds these returned values, and the final total is the number of occurrences of *value*. Here's a formula that does this for our list of overdue invoices:

```
{=SUM(IF(B1 = B6:B29, 1, 0))}
```

Figure 8.9 shows this formula in action (see cell B3).

> **NOTE**
>
> The generic array formula {=SUM(IF(*condition*, 1, 0))} is useful in any context where you need to count the number of occurrences in which *condition* returns TRUE. The *condition* argument is normally a logical formula that compares a single value with each cell in a range of values. However, it's also possible to compare two ranges, as long as they're the same shape (that is, they have the same number of rows and columns). For example, suppose that you want to compare the values in two ranges named Range1 and Range2 to see if any of the values are different. Here's an array formula that does this:
>
> ```
> {=SUM(IF(Range1 <> Range2, 1, 0))}
> ```
>
> This formula compares the first cell in Range1 with the first cell in Range2, the second cell in Range1 with the second cell in Range2, and so on. Each time the values don't match, the comparison returns 1; otherwise, it returns 0. The sum of these comparisons is the number of different values between the two ranges.

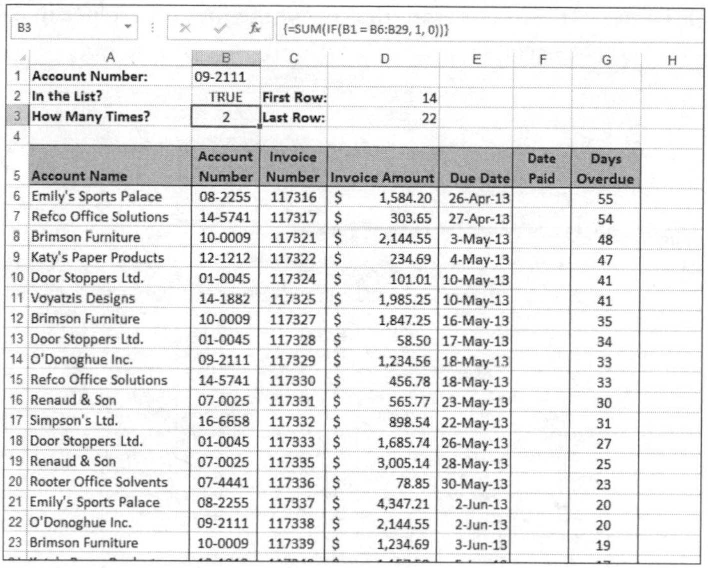

Figure 8.9
This worksheet uses
SUM() and IF() in
an array formula to count
the number of occur-
rences of a value in a list.

	Account Name	Account Number	Invoice Number	Invoice Amount	Due Date	Date Paid	Days Overdue
	B3		f_x	{=SUM(IF(B1 = B6:B29, 1, 0))}			
1	Account Number:	09-2111					
2	In the List?	TRUE	First Row:	14			
3	How Many Times?	2	Last Row:	22			
5	Account Name	Account Number	Invoice Number	Invoice Amount	Due Date	Date Paid	Days Overdue
6	Emily's Sports Palace	08-2255	117316	$ 1,584.20	26-Apr-13		55
7	Refco Office Solutions	14-5741	117317	$ 303.65	27-Apr-13		54
8	Brimson Furniture	10-0009	117321	$ 2,144.55	3-May-13		48
9	Katy's Paper Products	12-1212	117322	$ 234.69	4-May-13		47
10	Door Stoppers Ltd.	01-0045	117324	$ 101.01	10-May-13		41
11	Voyatzis Designs	14-1882	117325	$ 1,985.25	10-May-13		41
12	Brimson Furniture	10-0009	117327	$ 1,847.25	16-May-13		35
13	Door Stoppers Ltd.	01-0045	117328	$ 58.50	17-May-13		34
14	O'Donoghue Inc.	09-2111	117329	$ 1,234.56	18-May-13		33
15	Refco Office Solutions	14-5741	117330	$ 456.78	18-May-13		33
16	Renaud & Son	07-0025	117331	$ 565.77	23-May-13		30
17	Simpson's Ltd.	16-6658	117332	$ 898.54	22-May-13		31
18	Door Stoppers Ltd.	01-0045	117333	$ 1,685.74	26-May-13		27
19	Renaud & Son	07-0025	117335	$ 3,005.14	28-May-13		25
20	Rooter Office Solvents	07-4441	117336	$ 78.85	30-May-13		23
21	Emily's Sports Palace	08-2255	117337	$ 4,347.21	2-Jun-13		20
22	O'Donoghue Inc.	09-2111	117338	$ 2,144.55	2-Jun-13		20
23	Brimson Furniture	10-0009	117339	$ 1,234.69	3-Jun-13		19

Determining Where a Value Appears in a List

What if you want to know not just whether a value appears in a list but *where* it appears in the list? You can do this by getting the IF() function to return the row number for a positive result:

```
IF(value = range, ROW(range), "")
```

Whenever *value* equals one of the cells in *range*, the IF() function uses ROW() to return the row number; otherwise, it returns the empty string.

To return that row number, use either the MIN() function or the MAX() function, which returns the minimum or maximum, respectively, in a collection of values. The trick here is that both functions ignore null values, so applying this to the array that results from the previous IF() expression tells where the matching values are:

■ To get the first instance of the value, use the MIN() function in an array formula, like so:
```
{=MIN(IF(value = range, ROW(range), ""))}
```

■ To get the last instance of the value, use the MAX() function in an array formula, as shown here:
```
{=MAX(IF(value = range, ROW(range), ""))}
```

Here are the formulas you would use to find the first and last occurrences in the previous list of overdue invoices:

```
{=MIN(IF(B1 = B6:B29, ROW(B6:B29), ""))}
{=MAX(IF(B1 = B6:B29, ROW(B6:B29), ""))}
```

Figure 8.10 shows the results (with the row of the first occurrence in cell D2 and the row of the last occurrence in cell D3).

Figure 8.10
This worksheet uses MIN(), MAX(), ROW(), and IF() in array formulas to return the row numbers of the first (cell D2) and last (cell D3) occurrences of a value in a list.

	A	B	C	D	E	F	G	H
	D2		f_x {=MIN(IF(B1 = B6:B29, ROW(B6:B29), ""))}					
1	Account Number:	09-2111						
2	In the List?	TRUE	First Row:	14				
3	How Many Times?	2	Last Row:	22				
4								
5	Account Name	Account Number	Invoice Number	Invoice Amount	Due Date	Date Paid	Days Overdue	
6	Emily's Sports Palace	08-2255	117316	$ 1,584.20	26-Apr-13		55	
7	Refco Office Solutions	14-5741	117317	$ 303.65	27-Apr-13		54	
8	Brimson Furniture	10-0009	117321	$ 2,144.55	3-May-13		48	
9	Katy's Paper Products	12-1212	117322	$ 234.69	4-May-13		47	
10	Door Stoppers Ltd.	01-0045	117324	$ 101.01	10-May-13		41	
11	Voyatzis Designs	14-1882	117325	$ 1,985.25	10-May-13		41	
12	Brimson Furniture	10-0009	117327	$ 1,847.25	16-May-13		35	
13	Door Stoppers Ltd.	01-0045	117328	$ 58.50	17-May-13		34	
14	O'Donoghue Inc.	09-2111	117329	$ 1,234.56	18-May-13		33	
15	Refco Office Solutions	14-5741	117330	$ 456.78	18-May-13		33	
16	Renaud & Son	07-0025	117331	$ 565.77	23-May-13		30	
17	Simpson's Ltd.	16-6658	117332	$ 898.54	22-May-13		31	
18	Door Stoppers Ltd.	01-0045	117333	$ 1,685.74	26-May-13		27	
19	Renaud & Son	07-0025	117335	$ 3,005.14	28-May-13		25	
20	Rooter Office Solvents	07-4441	117336	$ 78.85	30-May-13		23	
21	Emily's Sports Palace	08-2255	117337	$ 4,347.21	2-Jun-13		20	
22	O'Donoghue Inc.	09-2111	117338	$ 2,144.55	2-Jun-13		20	
23	Brimson Furniture	10-0009	117339	$ 1,234.69	3-Jun-13		19	

TIP

It's also possible to determine the address of the cell that contains the first or last occurrence of a value in a list. To do this, use the ADDRESS() function, which returns an absolute address, given a row and column number:

```
{=ADDRESS(MIN(IF(B1 = B6:B29, ROW(B6:B29), "")),
COLUMN(B6:B29))}
{=ADDRESS(MAX(IF(B1 = B6:B29, ROW(B6:B29), "")),
COLUMN(B6:B29))}
```

Case Study: Building an Accounts Receivable Aging Worksheet

If you use Excel to store accounts receivable data, it's a good idea to set up an aging worksheet that shows past-due invoices, calculates the number of days past due, and groups the invoices into past-due categories (1–30 days, 31–60 days, and so on).

Figure 8.11 shows a simple implementation of an accounts receivable database. For each invoice, the due date (column D) is calculated by adding 30 to the invoice date (column C). Column E subtracts the due date (column D) from the current date (in cell B1) to calculate the number of days each invoice is past due.

D7 =C7 + 30

	A	B	C	D	E	F	G	H	I	J	K
1	Date:	21-Jun-16									
2							Past Due (Days):				
3	Account Number	Invoice Number	Invoice Date	Due Date	Past Due	Amount Due	1-30	31-60	61-90	91-120	Over 120
4	07-0001	1000	21-Apr-16	Saturday May 21, 2016	31	$2,433.25		$2,433.25			
5	07-0001	1025	10-May-16	Thursday Jun 9, 2016	12	$2,151.20	$ 2,151.20				
6	07-0001	1031	17-May-16	Thursday Jun 16, 2016	5	$1,758.54	$ 1,758.54				
7	07-0002	1006	3-Mar-16	Saturday Apr 2, 2016	80	$ 898.47			$ 898.47		
8	07-0002	1035	17-May-16	Thursday Jun 16, 2016	5	$1,021.02	$ 1,021.02				
9	07-0004	1002	21-Apr-16	Saturday May 21, 2016	31	$3,558.94		$3,558.94			
10	07-0005	1008	22-Feb-16	Wednesday Mar 23, 2016	90	$1,177.53			$1,177.53		
11	07-0005	1018	7-May-16	Monday Jun 6, 2016	15	$1,568.31	$ 1,568.31				
12	08-0001	1039	19-Jan-16	Thursday Feb 18, 2016	124	$2,958.73					$2,958.73
13	08-0001	1001	21-Apr-16	Saturday May 21, 2016	31	$3,659.85		$3,659.85			
14	08-0001	1024	10-May-16	Thursday Jun 9, 2016	12	$ 565.00	$ 565.00				

Figure 8.11
A simple accounts receivable database.

8

Calculating a Smarter Due Date

You might have noticed a problem with the due dates in Figure 8.11: Several of the dates, including the date in cell D7, fall on weekends. The problem here is that the due date calculation just adds 30 to the invoice date. To avoid weekend due dates, you need to test whether the invoice date plus 30 falls on a Saturday or Sunday. The `WEEKDAY()` function helps because it returns `7` if the date is a Saturday, and `1` if the date is a Sunday.

So, to check for a Saturday, you could use the following formula:

```
=IF(WEEKDAY(C4 + 30) = 7, C4 + 32, C4 + 30)
```

Here, I'm assuming that the invoice date resides in cell C4. If `WEEKDAY(C4 + 30)` returns `7`, the date is a Saturday, so you add 32 to C4 instead (to make the due date the following Monday). Otherwise, you just add 30 days as usual.

Checking for a Sunday is similar:

```
=IF(WEEKDAY(C4 + 30) = 1, C4 + 31, C4 + 30)
```

The problem, though, is that you need to combine these two tests into a single formula. To do that, you can nest one `IF()` function inside another. Here's how it works:

```
=IF(WEEKDAY(C4+30) = 7, C4+32, IF(WEEKDAY(C4+30) = 1, C4+31, C4+30))
```

The main `IF()` checks whether the date is a Saturday. If it is, you add 32 days to C4; otherwise, the formula runs the second `IF()`, which checks for Sunday. Figure 8.12 shows the revised aging sheet with the nonweekend due dates in column D.

➔ For calculating due dates based on workdays (that is, excluding weekends and holidays), Excel has a function named `WORKDAY()` that handles this calculation with ease; **see** "A Workday Alternative: The `WORKDAY()` Function," **p. 216**.

Figure 8.12
The revised worksheet uses the `IF()` and `WEEKDAY()` functions to ensure that due dates don't fall on weekends.

D7 =IF(WEEKDAY(C7 + 30) = 7, C7 + 32, IF(WEEKDAY(C7 + 30) = 1, C7 + 31, C7 + 30))

	A	B	C	D	E	F	G	H	I	J	K
1	Date:	21-Jun-16									
2							Past Due (Days):				
3	Account Number	Invoice Number	Invoice Date	Due Date	Past Due	Amount Due	1-30	31-60	61-90	91-120	Over 120
4	07-0001	1000	21-Apr-16	Monday May 23, 2016	29	$2,433.25	$ 2,433.25				
5	07-0001	1025	10-May-16	Thursday Jun 9, 2016	12	$2,151.20	$ 2,151.20				
6	07-0001	1031	17-May-16	Thursday Jun 16, 2016	5	$1,758.54	$ 1,758.54				
7	07-0002	1006	3-Mar-16	Monday Apr 4, 2016	78	$ 898.47			$ 898.47		
8	07-0002	1035	17-May-16	Thursday Jun 16, 2016	5	$1,021.02	$ 1,021.02				
9	07-0004	1002	21-Apr-16	Monday May 23, 2016	29	$3,558.94	$ 3,558.94				
10	07-0005	1008	22-Feb-16	Wednesday Mar 23, 2016	90	$1,177.53			$1,177.53		
11	07-0005	1018	7-May-16	Monday Jun 6, 2016	15	$1,568.31	$ 1,568.31				
12	08-0001	1039	19-Jan-16	Thursday Feb 18, 2016	124	$2,958.73					$2,958.73
13	08-0001	1001	21-Apr-16	Monday May 23, 2016	29	$3,659.85	$ 3,659.85				
14	08-0001	1024	10-May-16	Thursday Jun 9, 2016	12	$ 565.00	$ 565.00				
15											

Aging Overdue Invoices

For cash-flow purposes, you also need to correlate the invoice amounts with the number of days past due. Ideally, you'd like to see a list of invoice amounts that are between 1 and 30 days past due, between 31 and 60 days past due, and so on. Figure 8.13 shows one way to set up accounts receivable aging.

➔ The worksheet in Figures 8.11 through 8.13 uses ledger shading for easier reading. To learn how to apply ledger shading automatically, **see** "Creating Ledger Shading," **p. 251**.

Figure 8.13
Using `IF()` and `AND()` to categorize past-due invoices for aging purposes.

I7 =IF(AND(E7 >= 61, E7 <= 90), F7, "")

	A	B	C	D	E	F	G	H	I	J	K
1	Date:	21-Jun-16									
2							Past Due (Days):				
3	Account Number	Invoice Number	Invoice Date	Due Date	Past Due	Amount Due	1-30	31-60	61-90	91-120	Over 120
4	07-0001	1000	21-Apr-16	Monday May 23, 2016	29	$2,433.25	$ 2,433.25				
5	07-0001	1025	10-May-16	Thursday Jun 9, 2016	12	$2,151.20	$ 2,151.20				
6	07-0001	1031	17-May-16	Thursday Jun 16, 2016	5	$1,758.54	$ 1,758.54				
7	07-0002	1006	3-Mar-16	Monday Apr 4, 2016	78	$ 898.47			$ 898.47		
8	07-0002	1035	17-May-16	Thursday Jun 16, 2016	5	$1,021.02	$ 1,021.02				
9	07-0004	1002	21-Apr-16	Monday May 23, 2016	29	$3,558.94	$ 3,558.94				
10	07-0005	1008	22-Feb-16	Wednesday Mar 23, 2016	90	$1,177.53			$1,177.53		
11	07-0005	1018	7-May-16	Monday Jun 6, 2016	15	$1,568.31	$ 1,568.31				
12	08-0001	1039	19-Jan-16	Thursday Feb 18, 2016	124	$2,958.73					$2,958.73
13	08-0001	1001	21-Apr-16	Monday May 23, 2016	29	$3,659.85	$ 3,659.85				
14	08-0001	1024	10-May-16	Thursday Jun 9, 2016	12	$ 565.00	$ 565.00				
15											

The aging worksheet calculates the number of days past due by subtracting the due date from the date shown in cell B1. If you calculate days past due using only workdays (weekends and holidays excluded), a better choice is the `NETWORKDAYS()` function, covered in Chapter 10, "Working with Date and Time Functions."

➔ To learn more about the `NETWORKDAYS()` function, **see** "`NETWORKDAYS()`: Calculating the Number of Workdays Between Two Dates," **p. 225**.

For the invoice amounts shown in column G (1–30 days), the sheet uses the following formula (which appears in G4):

```
=IF(E4 <= 30, F4, "")
```

If the number of days the invoice is past due (cell E4) is less than or equal to 30, the formula displays the amount (from cell F4); otherwise, it displays a blank.

The amounts in column H (31–60 days) are a little trickier. Here, you need to check whether the number of days past due is greater than or equal to 31 days *and* less than or equal to 60 days. To accomplish this, you can press the AND() function into service:

```
=IF(AND(E4 >= 31, E4 <= 60), F4, "")
```

The AND() function checks two logical expressions: E4> = 31 and E4 <= 60. If both are true, AND() returns TRUE, and the IF() function displays the invoice amount. If one of the logical expressions isn't true (or if they're both not true), AND() returns FALSE, and the IF() function displays a blank. Similar formulas appear in column I (61–90 days) and column J (91–120 days). Column K (Over 120) looks for past-due values that are greater than 120.

Getting Data with Information Functions

Excel's information functions return data concerning cells, worksheets, and formula results. Table 8.2 lists all the information functions.

Table 8.2   Excel's Information Functions

Function	Description
CELL(*info_type*[,*reference*])	Returns information about various cell attributes, including formatting, contents, and location.
ERROR.TYPE(*error_val*)	Returns a number corresponding to an error type.
INFO(*type_text*)	Returns information about the operating system and environment.
ISBLANK(*value*)	Returns TRUE if *value* is blank.
ISERR(*value*)	Returns TRUE if *value* is any error value except #N/A.
ISERROR(*value*)	Returns TRUE if *value* is any error value.
ISEVEN(*number*)	Returns TRUE if *number* is even.
ISFORMULA(*reference*)	Returns TRUE if the cell specified by *reference* contains a formula.
ISLOGICAL(*value*)	Returns TRUE if *value* is a logical value.
ISNA(*value*)	Returns TRUE if *value* is the #N/A error value.
ISNONTEXT(*value*)	Returns TRUE if *value* is not text.
ISNUMBER(*value*)	Returns TRUE if *value* is a number.
ISODD(*number*)	Returns TRUE if *number* is odd.
ISREF(*value*)	Returns TRUE if *value* is a reference.
ISTEXT(*value*)	Returns TRUE if *value* is text.

Function	Description
N(*value*)	Returns *value* converted to a number (a serial number if *value* is a date, 1 if *value* is TRUE, 0 if *value* is any other non-numeric). Note that N() exists only for compatibility with other spreadsheets and is rarely used in Excel.
NA()	Returns the error value #N/A.
SHEET(*value*)	Returns the sheet number of the sheet referenced by *value*.
SHEETS(*reference*)	Returns the number of sheets in *reference*.
TYPE(*value*)	Returns a number that indicates the data type of *value*: 1 for a number, 2 for text, 4 for a logical value, 8 for a formula, 16 for an error, or 64 for an array.

The rest of this chapter takes you through the details of several of these functions.

The CELL() Function

CELL() is *one* of the most useful information functions. Its job is to return information about a particular cell:

```
CELL(info_type, [reference])
```

    info_type   A string that specifies the type of information you want.

    reference   The cell you want to use. (The default is the cell that contains the CELL() function.) If *reference* is a range, CELL() applies to the cell in the upper-left corner of the range.

Table 8.3 lists the various possibilities for the *info_type* argument.

Table 8.3 The CELL() Function's info_type Argument

INFO_TYPE Value	What CELL() Returns
address	The absolute address, as text, of the *reference* cell.
col	The column number of *reference*.
color	Returns 1 if *reference* has a custom cell format that displays negative values in a color; returns 0 otherwise.
contents	The contents of *reference*.
filename	The full path and filename of the file that contains *reference*, as text. Returns the null string ("") if the workbook that contains *reference* hasn't been saved for the first time.
format	A string that corresponds to the built-in Excel numeric format applied to *reference*. Here are the possible return values:

INFO_TYPE **Value**	What CELL() **Returns**
	Built-In Format CELL() **Returns**
	General G
	0 F0
	#,##0 ,0
	0.00 F2
	#,##0.00 ,2
	$#,##0_);($#,##0) C0
	$#,##0_);[Red]($#,##0) C0-
	$#,##0.00_);($#,##0.00) C2
	$#,##0.00_);[Red] ($#,##0.00) C2-
	0% P0
	0.00% P2
	0.00E+00 S2
	# ?/? or # ??/?? G
	d-mmm-yy or dd-mmm-yy D1
	d-mmm or dd-mmm D2
	mmm-yy D3
	m/d/yy or m/d/yy h:mm or mm/dd/yy D4
	mm/dd D5
	h:mm:ss AM/PM D6
	h:mm AM/PM D7
	h:mm:ss D8
	h:mm D9
parentheses	Returns 1 if *reference* has a custom cell format that uses parentheses for positive or all values; returns 0 otherwise.
prefix	A character that represents the text alignment used by *reference*. Here are the possible return values:

Alignment	CELL() **Returns**
Left	'
Center	^
Right	"

`INFO_TYPE` Value	What `CELL()` Returns	
	Fill	\
`protect`	Returns `0` if *`reference`* isn't locked; `1` otherwise.	
`row`	The row number of *`reference`*.	
`type`	A letter that represents the type of data in the *`reference`*. Here are the possible return values:	
	Data Type	`CELL()` **Returns**
	Text	`l`
	Blank	`b`
	All others	`v`
`width`	The column width of *`reference`*, rounded to the nearest integer, where one unit equals the width of one character in the default font size.	

Figure 8.14 shows how the `CELL()` function works.

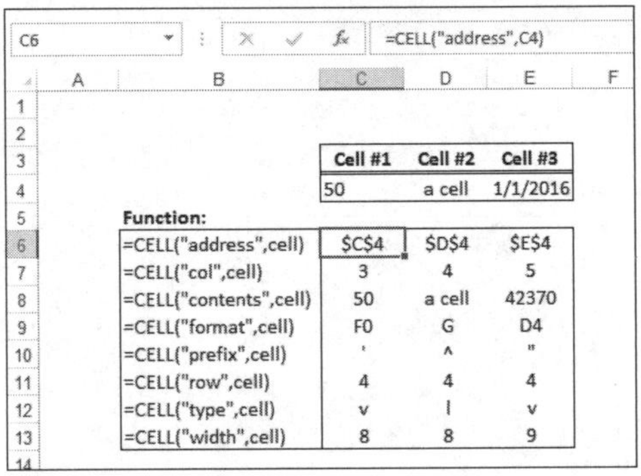

C6 | =CELL("address",C4)

	A	B	C	D	E	F
1						
2						
3			Cell #1	Cell #2	Cell #3	
4			50	a cell	1/1/2016	
5		Function:				
6		=CELL("address",cell)	$C$4	$D$4	$E$4	
7		=CELL("col",cell)	3	4	5	
8		=CELL("contents",cell)	50	a cell	42370	
9		=CELL("format",cell)	F0	G	D4	
10		=CELL("prefix",cell)	'	^	"	
11		=CELL("row",cell)	4	4	4	
12		=CELL("type",cell)	v	l	v	
13		=CELL("width",cell)	8	8	9	

Figure 8.14
Some examples of the `CELL()` function.

The ERROR.TYPE() Function

The `ERROR.TYPE()` function returns a value that corresponds to a specific Excel error value:

`ERROR.TYPE(`*`error_val`*`)`

`error_val` A reference to a cell containing a formula that you want to check for the error value. Here are the possible return values:

`error_val` **Value**	`ERROR.TYPE()` **Returns**
`#NULL!`	`1`
`#DIV/0!`	`2`
`#VALUE!`	`3`

#REF!	4
#NAME?	5
#NUM!	6
#N/A!	7
#GETTING_DATA	8
All others	#N/A

You most often use the ERROR.TYPE() function to intercept an error and then display a more useful or friendly message. You do this by using the IF() function to see if ERROR.TYPE() returns a value less than or equal to 7; if so, the cell in question contains an error value. Because the ERROR.TYPE() returns value ranges from 1 to 8, you can apply the return value to the CHOOSE() function to display the error message.

→ For the details of the CHOOSE() function, **see** "The CHOOSE() Function," **p. 193**.

Here's a formula that does all that. (I've split the formula so that different parts appear on different lines to make it easier for you to see what's going on.)

```
=IF(ERROR.TYPE(D8) <= 8,
➥"***ERROR IN " & CELL("address",D8) & ": " &
➥CHOOSE(ERROR.TYPE(D8),"The ranges do not intersect",
➥"The divisor is 0",
➥"Wrong data type in function argument",
➥"Invalid cell reference",
➥"Unrecognized range or function name",
➥"Number error in formula",
➥"Inappropriate function argument"
➥"Waiting for query data"))
```

Figure 8.15 shows this formula in an example. (Note that the formula displays #N/A when there is no error; this is the return value of ERROR.TYPE() when there is no error.)

Figure 8.15
A formula that uses IF() and ERROR_TYPE() to return a more descriptive error message to the user.

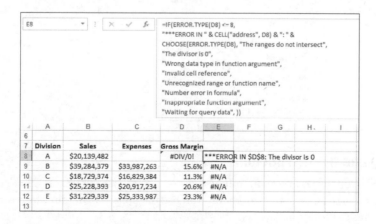

The INFO() Function

The INFO() function is seldom used, but it's handy when you do need it because it gives you information about the current operating environment:

INFO(*type_text*)

    type_text   A string that specifies the type of information you want.

Table 8.4 lists the possible values for the *type_text* argument.

Table 8.4   The INFO() Function's type_text Argument

TYPE_TEXT Value	What INFO() Returns
directory	The full pathname of the current folder. (That is, the folder that will appear the next time you display the Open or Save As dialog box.)
numfile	The number of worksheets in all the open workbooks.
origin	The address of the upper-left cell that is visible in the current worksheet. In Figure 8.16, for example, cell A2 is the visible cell in the upper-left corner. The absolute address begins with $A: for Lotus 1-2-3 release 3.*x* compatibility.
osversion	A string containing the current operating system version.
recalc	A string containing the current recalculation mode: Automatic or Manual.
release	A string containing the version of Microsoft Excel.
system	A string containing a code representing the current operating environment: pcdos for Windows or mac for Macintosh.

Figure 8.16 shows the INFO() function at work.

Figure 8.16
The INFO() function
in action.

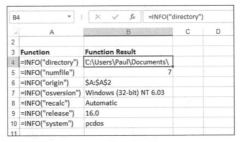

The SHEET() and SHEETS() Functions

Excel includes two information functions—SHEET() and SHEETS()—that return information about the worksheets in a workbook. You use the SHEET() function to return a sheet number using the following syntax:

```
SHEET([value])
```

    value   An optional value that specifies a sheet. If you omit *value*, Excel references the current sheet.

For example, the formula =SHEET() returns the number of the sheet that contains the formula, where 1 is the first sheet in the workbook, 2 is the second sheet, and so on. Note that Excel counts all sheet types, including worksheets and chart sheets.

If a worksheet has the name Budget, then the formula =SHEET("Budget") returns its sheet number. Alternatively, you can use a cell reference within that sheet, such as SHEET(Budget!A1).

You use the SHEETS() function (which takes no arguments) to return the total number of worksheets in the current workbook.

The IS Functions

Excel's so-called IS functions are Boolean functions that return either TRUE or FALSE, depending on the argument they're evaluating:

```
ISBLANK(value)
ISERR(value)
ISERROR(value)
ISEVEN(number)
ISFORMULA(reference)
ISLOGICAL(value)
ISNA(value)
ISNONTEXT(value)
ISNUMBER(value)
ISODD(number)
ISREF(value)
ISTEXT(value)
```

    value   A cell reference, function return value, or formula result

    reference   A cell reference

    number   A numeric value

The operation of these functions is straightforward, so rather than run through the specifics of all 11 functions, the next few sections show you some interesting and useful techniques that make use of these functions.

Counting the Number of Blanks in a Range

When putting together the data for a worksheet model, it's common to pull the data from various sources. Unfortunately, this often means that the data arrives at different times, and you end up with an incomplete model. If you're working with a big list, you might want to keep a running total of the number of pieces of data you're still missing.

This is the perfect opportunity to break out the ISBLANK() function and plug it into the array formula for counting that you learned earlier:

    {=SUM(IF(ISBLANK(*range*), 1, 0))}

The IF() function runs through the *range*, looking for blank cells. Each time it comes across a blank cell, it returns 1; otherwise, it returns 0. The SUM() function adds the results to give the total number of blank cells. Figure 8.17 shows an example (see cell G1).

Figure 8.17
As shown in cell G1, you can plug ISBLANK() into the array counting formula to count the number of blank cells in a range.

	A	B	C	D	E	F	G
1					Missing Values for 'Units In Stock':		10
2	Product ID	Product Name	Supplier	Category	Quantity Per Unit	Unit Price	Units In Stock
3	1	Chai	Exotic Liquids	Beverages	10 boxes x 20 bags	$18.00	39
4	2	Chang	Exotic Liquids	Beverages	24 - 12 oz bottles	$19.00	17
5	3	Aniseed Syrup	Exotic Liquids	Condiments	12 - 550 ml bottles	$10.00	13
6	4	Chef Anton's Cajun Seasoning	New Orleans Cajun Delights	Condiments	48 - 6 oz jars	$22.00	
7	5	Chef Anton's Gumbo Mix	New Orleans Cajun Delights	Condiments	36 boxes	$21.35	
8	6	Grandma's Boysenberry Spread	Grandma Kelly's Homestead	Condiments	12 - 8 oz jars	$25.00	120
9	7	Uncle Bob's Organic Dried Pears	Grandma Kelly's Homestead	Produce	12 - 1 lb pkgs.	$30.00	15
10	8	Northwoods Cranberry Sauce	Grandma Kelly's Homestead	Condiments	12 - 12 oz jars	$40.00	6
11	9	Mishi Kobe Niku	Tokyo Traders	Meat/Poultry	18 - 500 g pkgs.	$97.00	29
12	10	Ikura	Tokyo Traders	Seafood	12 - 200 ml jars	$31.00	31
13	11	Queso Cabrales	Cooperativa de Quesos 'Las Cabras'	Dairy Products	1 kg pkg.	$21.00	22
14	12	Queso Manchego La Pastora	Cooperativa de Quesos 'Las Cabras'	Dairy Products	10 - 500 g pkgs.	$38.00	
15	13	Konbu	Mayumi's	Seafood	2 kg box	$6.00	24
16	14	Tofu	Mayumi's	Produce	40 - 100 g pkgs.	$23.25	35
17	15	Genen Shouyu	Mayumi's	Condiments	24 - 250 ml bottles	$15.50	

> **TIP**
> Using an array formula to count blank cells is fine, but it's not the easiest way to go about it. In most cases, you're better off just using the COUNTBLANK(*range*) function, which counts the number of blank cells that occur in the range specified by the *range* argument.

Checking a Range for Non-Numeric Values

A similar idea is to check a range on which you'll be performing a mathematical operation to see if it holds any cells that contain non-numeric values. In this case, you plug the ISNUMBER() function into the array counting formula and then return 0 for each TRUE result and 1 for each FALSE result. Here's the general formula:

    {=SUM(IF(ISNUMBER(*range*), 0, 1))}

Counting the Number of Errors in a Range

For the final counting example, it's often nice to know not only whether a range contains an error value but also how many such values it contains. This is easily done using the ISERROR() function and the array counting formula:

    {=SUM(IF(ISERROR(*range*), 1, 0))}

Ignoring Errors When Working with a Range

Sometimes, you have to work with ranges that contain error values. For example, suppose that you have a column of gross margin results (which require division), but one or more of the cells are showing the #DIV/0! error because you're missing data. You could wait until the missing data is added to the model, but it's often necessary to perform preliminary calculations. For example, you might want to take the average of the results that you *do* have.

To do this efficiently, you need some way of bypassing the error values. Again, this is possible by using the ISERROR() function plugged into an array formula. For example, here's a general formula for taking an average across a range while ignoring any error values:

```
{=AVERAGE(IF(ISERROR(range), "", range))}
```

Figure 8.18 provides an example.

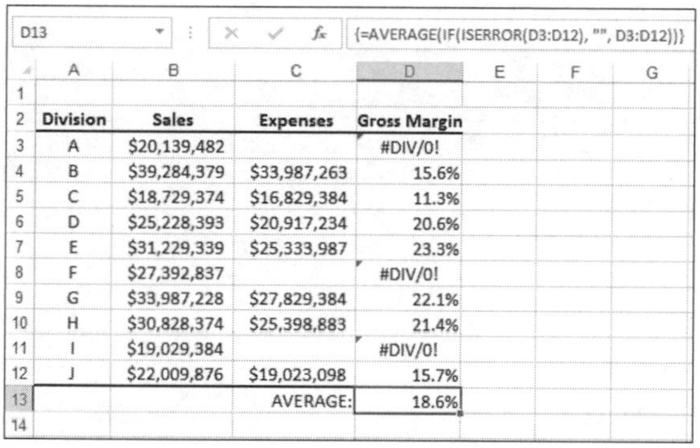

Figure 8.18
As shown in cell D13, you can use ISERROR() in an array formula to run an operation on a range while ignoring any errors in the range.

	A	B	C	D	E	F	G
				fx {=AVERAGE(IF(ISERROR(D3:D12), "", D3:D12))}			
2	Division	Sales	Expenses	Gross Margin			
3	A	$20,139,482		#DIV/0!			
4	B	$39,284,379	$33,987,263	15.6%			
5	C	$18,729,374	$16,829,384	11.3%			
6	D	$25,228,393	$20,917,234	20.6%			
7	E	$31,229,339	$25,333,987	23.3%			
8	F	$27,392,837		#DIV/0!			
9	G	$33,987,228	$27,829,384	22.1%			
10	H	$30,828,374	$25,398,883	21.4%			
11	I	$19,029,384		#DIV/0!			
12	J	$22,009,876	$19,023,098	15.7%			
13			AVERAGE:	18.6%			

From Here

- For the details on conditional formatting, **see** "Applying Conditional Formatting to a Range," **p. 25.**
- To learn about array formulas, **see** "Working with Arrays," **p. 87.**
- To learn about the #DIV/0! error, **see** "#DIV/0!," **p. 112.**
- To learn about the IFERROR() and IFNA() functions, **see** "Handling Formula Errors with IFERROR()," **p. 118.**
- For a general discussion of function syntax, **see** "The Structure of a Function," **p. 130.**
- For the details on the REPT() function, **see** "The REPT() Function: Repeating a Character or String," **p. 150.**
- To learn about extracting a name from a string, **see** "Extracting a First Name or Last Name," **p. 156.**
- For the details of the CHOOSE() function, **see** "The CHOOSE() Function," **p. 193.**
- To learn how to use the WORKDAY() function, **see** "A Workday Alternative: The WORKDAY() Function," **p. 216.**

- To learn how to apply ledger shading automatically, **see** "Creating Ledger Shading," **p. 251**.
- For information on referencing tables in formulas, **see** "Referencing Tables in Formulas," **p. 309**.

Working with Lookup Functions

9

Getting the meaning of a word in the dictionary is always a two-step process: First you look up the word itself, and then you read its definition. Same with an encyclopedia: First look up the concept, and then you read the article.

This idea of looking something up to retrieve some related information is at the heart of many spreadsheet operations. For example, you saw in Chapter 4, "Creating Advanced Formulas," that you can add option buttons and list boxes to a worksheet. Unfortunately, these controls return only the number of the item the user has chosen. To find out the actual value of the item, you need to use the returned number to look up the value in a table.

→ For the specifics of adding option buttons and list boxes to a worksheet, **see** "Understanding the Worksheet Controls," **p. 105.**

Excel's Lookup Functions

In many worksheet formulas, the value of one argument often depends on the value of another. Here are some examples:

■ In a formula that calculates an invoice total, the customer's discount might depend on the number of units purchased.

■ In a formula that charges interest on overdue accounts, the interest percentage might depend on the number of days each invoice is overdue.

■ In a formula that calculates employee bonuses as a percentage of salary, the percentage might depend on how much the employee improved on the given budget.

The usual way to handle these kinds of problems is to look up the appropriate value. This chapter introduces you to a number of functions that enable you to perform lookup operations in your worksheet models. Table 9.1 lists Excel's lookup functions.

Table 9.1   Excel's Lookup Functions

Function	Description
CHOOSE(*num*, *value1*[, *value2*, ...])	Uses *num* to select one of the list of arguments given by *value1*, *value2*, and so on.
GETPIVOTDATA(*data*, *table*, *field1*, *item1*, ...)	Extracts data from a PivotTable. (See Chapter 14, "Analyzing Data with PivotTables.")
HLOOKUP(*value*, *table*, *row*[, *range*])	Searches for *value* in *table* and returns the value in the specified *row*.
INDEX(*ref*, *row*[, *col*] [, *area*])	Looks in *ref* and returns the value of the cell at the intersection of *row* and, optionally, *col*.
LOOKUP(*lookup_value*, *array*)	Looks up a value in a range or array.
MATCH(*value*, *range*[, *match_type*])	Searches *range* for *value* and, if found, returns the relative position of *value* in *range*.
RTD(*progID*, *server*, *topic1*[, *topic2*, ...])	Retrieves data in real time from an automation server (not covered in this book).
VLOOKUP(*value*, *table*, *col*[, *range*])	Searches for *value* in *table* and returns the value in the specified *col*.

Understanding Lookup Tables

The table—more properly referred to as a *lookup table*—is the key to performing lookup operations in Excel. The most straightforward lookup table structure is one that consists of two columns (or two rows):

- **Lookup column**—This column contains the values that you look up. For example, if you were constructing a lookup table for a dictionary, this column would contain the words.

- **Data column**—This column contains the data associated with each lookup value. In the dictionary example, this column would contain the definitions.

In most lookup operations, you supply a value that the function locates in the designated lookup column. It then retrieves the corresponding value in the data column.

As you'll see in this chapter, there are many variations on the lookup table theme. The lookup table can be one of these:

- **A single column (or a single row)**—In this case, the lookup operation consists of finding the *n*th value in the column.

■ **A range with multiple data columns**—For instance, in the dictionary example, you might have a second column for each word's part of speech (noun, verb, and so on), and perhaps a third column for its pronunciation. In this case, the lookup operation must also specify which of the data columns contains the value required.

■ **An array**—In this case, the table doesn't exist on a worksheet but is either an array of literal values or the result of a function that returns an array. The lookup operation finds a particular position within the array and returns the data value at that position.

The CHOOSE() Function

The simplest of the lookup functions is CHOOSE(), which enables you to select a value from a list. Specifically, given an integer *n*, CHOOSE() returns the *n*th item from the list. Here's the function's syntax:

```
CHOOSE(num, value1[, value2,...])
```

num	Determines which of the values in the list is returned. If *num* is 1, *value1* is returned; if *num* is 2, *value2* is returned, and so on. *num* must be an integer (or a formula or function that returns an integer) between 1 and 254.
value1, value2...	The list of up to 254 values from which CHOOSE() selects the return value. The values can be numbers, strings, references, names, formulas, or functions.

For example, consider the following formula:

```
=CHOOSE(2,"Surface Mail", "Air Mail", "Courier")
```

The *num* argument is 2, so CHOOSE() returns the second value in the list, which is the string value Air Mail.

NOTE

If you use range references as the list of values, CHOOSE() returns the entire range as the result. For example, consider the following:

```
CHOOSE(1, A1:D1, A2:D2, A3:D3)
```

This function returns the range A1:D1. This enables you to perform conditional operations on a set of ranges, where the *condition* is the lookup value used by CHOOSE(). For example, the following formula returns the sum of the range A1:D1:

```
=SUM(CHOOSE(1, A1:D1, A2:D2, A3:D3))
```

Determining the Name of the Day of the Week

As you'll see in Chapter 10, "Working with Date and Time Functions," Excel's WEEKDAY() function returns a number that corresponds to the day of the week, where Sunday is 1, Monday is 2, and so on.

→ To learn about the WEEKDAY() function, **see** "The WEEKDAY() Function," **p. 214.**

What if you want to know the actual day (not the number) of the week? If you need only to display the day of the week, you can format the cell as dddd. If you need to use the day of the week as a string value in a formula, you need a way to convert the WEEKDAY() result into the appropriate string. Fortunately, the CHOOSE() function makes this process easy. For example, suppose that cell B5 contains a date. You can find the day of the week it represents with the following formula:

```
=CHOOSE(WEEKDAY(B5), "Sun", "Mon", "Tue", "Wed", "Thu", "Fri", "Sat")
```

I've used abbreviated day names to save space, but you're free to use any form of the day names that suits your purposes.

> **NOTE**
>
> Here's a similar formula for returning the name of the month, given the integer month number returned by the MONTH() function:
>
> ```
> =CHOOSE(MONTH(date), "Jan", "Feb", "Mar", "Apr", "May",
> "Jun", "Jul", "Aug", "Sep", "Oct", "Nov", "Dec")
> ```

Determining the Month of the Fiscal Year

For many businesses, the fiscal year does not coincide with the calendar year. For example, the fiscal year might run from April 1 to March 31. In this case, month 1 of the fiscal year is April, month 2 is May, and so on. It's often handy to be able to determine the fiscal month, given the calendar month.

To see how you'd set this up, first consider the following table, which compares the calendar month and the fiscal month for a fiscal year beginning April 1:

Month	Calendar Month	Fiscal Month
January	1	10
February	2	11
March	3	12
April	4	1
May	5	2
June	6	3
July	7	4

Month	Calendar Month	Fiscal Month
August	8	5
September	9	6
October	10	7
November	11	8
December	12	9

You need to use the calendar month as the lookup value and the fiscal months as the data values. Here's the result:

```
=CHOOSE(CalendarMonth, 10, 11, 12, 1, 2, 3, 4, 5, 6, 7, 8, 9)
```

Figure 9.1 shows an example.

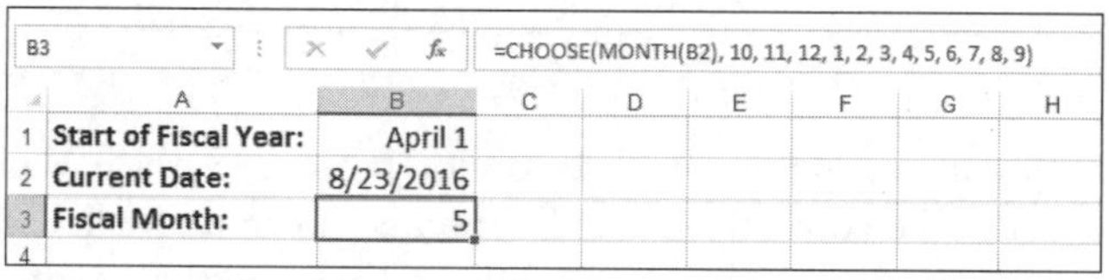

Figure 9.1
This worksheet uses the CHOOSE() function to determine the fiscal month (B3), given the start of the fiscal year (shown in B1) and the current date (B2).

> **NOTE** You can download this chapter's sample workbook at www.mcfedries.com/books/book.php?title=excel-2016-formulas-and-functions.

Calculating Weighted Questionnaire Results

One common use for CHOOSE() is to calculate weighted questionnaire responses. For example, suppose that you just completed creating a survey in which the respondents have to enter a value between 1 and 5 for each question. Some questions and answers are more important than others, so each question is assigned a set of weights. You use these weighted responses for your data. How do you assign the weights? The easiest way is to set up a CHOOSE() function for each question. For instance, suppose that question 1 uses the following weights for answers 1 through 5: 1.5, 2.3, 1.0, 1.8, and 0.5. If so, the following formula can be used to derive the weighted response:

```
=CHOOSE(Answer1, 1.5, 2.3, 1.0, 1.8, 0.5)
```

Assume that the answer for question 1 is in a cell named Answer1.

Integrating CHOOSE() and Worksheet Option Buttons

The CHOOSE() function is ideal for lookup situations in which you have a small number of data values and you have a formula or function that generates sequential integer values beginning with 1. A good example of this is the use of the worksheet option buttons

I mentioned at the beginning of this chapter. The option buttons in a group return integer values in the linked cell: 1 if the first option is clicked, 2 if the second option is clicked, and so on. Therefore, you can use the value in the linked cell as the lookup value in the CHOOSE() function. Figure 9.2 shows a worksheet that does this.

Figure 9.2
This worksheet uses the CHOOSE() function to calculate the shipping cost based on the option clicked in the Freight Options group.

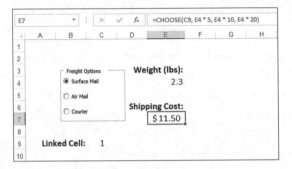

The Freight Options group presents three option buttons: Surface Mail, Air Mail, and Courier. The number of the currently selected option is shown in the linked cell, C9. A weight, in pounds, is entered into cell E4. Given the linked cell and the weight, cell E7 calculates the shipping cost by using CHOOSE() to select a formula that multiplies the weight by a constant:

```
=CHOOSE(C9, E4 * 5, E4 * 10, E4 * 20)
```

Looking Up Values in Tables

As you've seen, the CHOOSE() function is a handy and useful addition to your formula toolkit, and it's a function you'll turn to quite often if you build a lot of worksheet models. However, CHOOSE() does have its drawbacks:

■ The lookup values must be positive integers.

■ The maximum number of data values is 254.

■ Only one set of data values is allowed per function.

You'll trip over these limitations eventually, and you'll wonder if Excel has more flexible lookup capabilities. Can it use a wider variety of lookup values (negative or real numbers, strings, and so on)? Can it accommodate multiple data sets that each can have any number of values (subject, of course, to the worksheet's inherent size limitations)? The answer to both questions is "yes"; in fact, Excel has two functions that meet these criteria: VLOOKUP() and HLOOKUP().

The VLOOKUP() Function

The VLOOKUP() function works by looking in the first column of a table for the value you specify. (The *V* in VLOOKUP() stands for *vertical*.) It then looks across the appropriate number of columns (which you specify) and returns whatever value it finds there.

Here's the full syntax for VLOOKUP():

```
VLOOKUP(lookup_value, table_array, col_index_num[, range_lookup])
```

lookup_value	This is the value you want to find in the first column of table_array. You can enter a number, string, or reference.
table_array	This is the table to use for the lookup. You can use a range reference or a name.
col_index_num	If VLOOKUP() finds a match, col_index_num is the column number in the table that contains the data you want returned (the first column—that is, the lookup column—is 1, the second column is 2, and so on).
range_lookup	This is a Boolean value that determines how Excel searches for lookup_value in the first column.
	TRUE—VLOOKUP() searches for the first exact match for lookup_value. If no exact match is found, the function looks for the largest value that is less than lookup_value (this is the default).
	FALSE—VLOOKUP() searches only for the first exact match for lookup_value.

Here are some notes to keep in mind when you work with VLOOKUP():

- If range_lookup is TRUE or omitted, you must sort the values in the first column in ascending order.

- If the first column of the table is text, you can use the standard wildcard characters in the lookup_value argument. (Use ? to substitute for individual characters; use * to substitute for multiple characters.)

- If lookup_value is less than any value in the lookup column, VLOOKUP() returns the #N/A error value.

- If VLOOKUP() doesn't find a match in the lookup column, it returns #N/A.

- If col_index_num is less than 1, VLOOKUP() returns #VALUE!; if col_index_num is greater than the number of columns in table_array, VLOOKUP() returns #REF!.

The HLOOKUP() Function

The HLOOKUP() function is similar to VLOOKUP() except that it searches for the lookup value in the first row of a table. (The *H* in HLOOKUP() stands for *horizontal*.) If successful, this function then looks down the specified number of rows and returns the value it finds there. Here's the syntax for HLOOKUP():

9

```
HLOOKUP(lookup_value, table_array, row_index_num[, range_lookup])
```

`lookup_value`	This is the value you want to find in the first row of `table_array`. You can enter a number, string, or reference.
`table_array`	This is the table to use for the lookup. You can use a range reference or a name.
`row_index_num`	If `HLOOKUP()` finds a match, `row_index_num` is the row number in the table that contains the data you want returned. (The first row—that is, the lookup row—is 1, the second row is 2, and so on.)
`range_lookup`	This is a Boolean value that determines how Excel searches for `lookup_value` in the first row.
	`TRUE`—`VLOOKUP()` searches for the first exact match for `lookup_value`. If no exact match is found, the function looks for the largest value that is less than `lookup_value`. (This is the default.)
	`FALSE`—`VLOOKUP()` searches only for the first exact match for `lookup_value`.

Returning a Customer Discount Rate with a Range Lookup

The most common use for `VLOOKUP()` and `HLOOKUP()` is to look for a match that falls within a range of values. This section and the next one take you through a few of examples of this range-lookup technique.

In business-to-business transactions, the cost of an item is often calculated as a percentage of the retail price. For example, a publisher might sell books to a bookstore at half the suggested list price. The percentage that the seller takes off the list price for the buyer is called the *discount*. Often, the size of the discount depends on the number of units ordered. For example, ordering 1–3 items might result in a 20% discount, ordering 4–24 items might result in a 40% discount, and so on.

Figure 9.3 shows a worksheet that uses `VLOOKUP()` to determine the discount a customer gets on an order, based on the number of units purchased.

For example, cell D4 uses the following formula:

```
=VLOOKUP(A4, $H$5:$I$11, 2)
```

The `range_lookup` argument is omitted, which means `VLOOKUP()` searches for the largest value that is less than or equal to the lookup value; in this case, this is the value in cell A4. Cell A4 contains the number of units purchased (20, in this case), and the range $H$5:$I$11 is the discount schedule table. `VLOOKUP()` searches down the first column (H5:H11) for the largest value that is less than or equal to 20. The first such cell is H6, because the value in H7 (24) is larger than 20. `VLOOKUP()` therefore moves to the second column (because you specified `col_index_num` to be 2) of the table (cell I6) and grabs the value there (40%).

Figure 9.3
A worksheet that uses
VLOOKUP() to look up
a customer's discount in a
discount schedule.

| D4 | ▼ | : | × | ✓ | fx | =VLOOKUP(A4, $H$5:$I$11, 2) |

	A	B	C	D	E	F	G	H	I	J
1										
2										
3	Units Ordered	Part	List Price	Discount	Net Price	Total		Discount Schedule		
4	20	D-178	$17.95	40%	$10.77	$215.40		Units	Discount	
5	10	B-047	$6.95	40%	$4.17	$41.70		0	20%	
6	1000	C-098	$2.95	50%	$1.48	$1,475.00		4	40%	
7	50	B-111	$19.95	44%	$11.17	$558.60		24	42%	
8	2	D-017	$27.95	20%	$22.36	$44.72		49	44%	
9	25	D-178	$17.95	42%	$10.41	$260.28		99	46%	
10	100	A-182	$9.95	46%	$5.37	$537.30		249	48%	
11	250	B-047	$6.95	48%	$3.61	$903.50		499	50%	
12										

9

TIP

As I mentioned earlier in this section, both VLOOKUP() and HLOOKUP() return #N/A if no match is found in the lookup range. If you would prefer to return a friendlier or more useful message, use the IFNA() function to test whether the lookup will fail. Here's the general idea:

```
=IFNA(LookupExpression, "LookupValue not found")
```

Here, `LookupExpression` is the VLOOKUP() or HLOOKUP() function, and `LookupValue` is the same as the `lookup_value` argument used in VLOOKUP() or HLOOKUP(). If IFNA() detects an #N/A error, the formula returns the "`LookupValue not found`" string; otherwise, it runs the lookup normally.

Returning a Tax Rate with a Range Lookup

Tax rates are perfect candidates for a range lookup because a given rate always applies to any income that is greater than some minimum amount and less than or equal to some maximum amount. For example, a rate of 25% might be applied to annual incomes over $37,450 and less than or equal to $90,750. Figure 9.4 shows a worksheet that uses VLOOKUP() to return the marginal tax rate, given a specified income.

The lookup table is C9:F15, and the lookup value is cell B17, which contains the annual income. VLOOKUP() finds in column C the largest income that is less than or equal to the value in B17, which is $50,000. In this case, the matching value is $37,450 in cell C11. VLOOKUP() then looks in the fourth column to get the marginal rate in column F, which, in this case, is 25%.

TIP

You might find that you have multiple lookup tables in your model. For example, you might have multiple tax rate tables that apply to different types of taxpayers (single versus married, for example). If the tables use the same structure, you can use the IF() function to choose which lookup table is used in a lookup formula. Here's the general formula:

```
=VLOOKUP(lookup_value, IF(condition, table1, table2), col_index_num)
```

If `condition` returns TRUE, a reference to `table1` is returned, and that table is used as the lookup table; otherwise, `table2` is used.

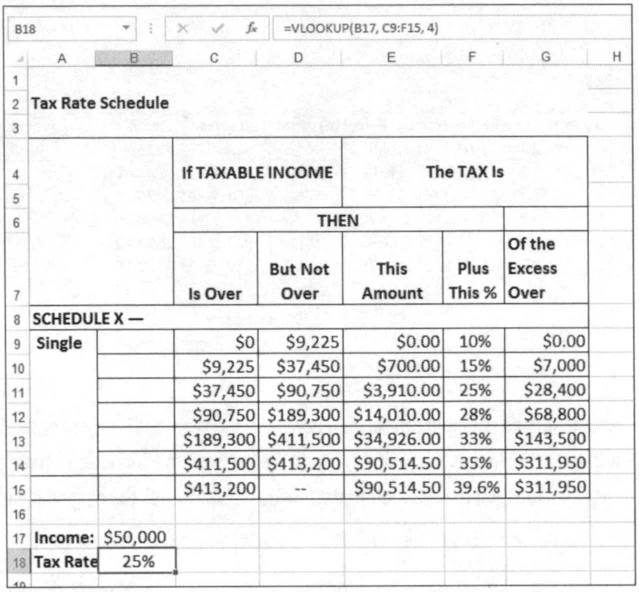

Figure 9.4
A worksheet that uses
VLOOKUP() to look
up a marginal income
tax rate.

B18		▼ : × ✓ fx	=VLOOKUP(B17, C9:F15, 4)				

	A	B	C	D	E	F	G	H
1								
2	**Tax Rate Schedule**							
3								
4			**If TAXABLE INCOME**		**The TAX Is**			
5								
6			**THEN**					
7			**Is Over**	**But Not Over**	**This Amount**	**Plus This %**	**Of the Excess Over**	
8	**SCHEDULE X —**							
9	**Single**		$0	$9,225	$0.00	10%	$0.00	
10			$9,225	$37,450	$700.00	15%	$7,000	
11			$37,450	$90,750	$3,910.00	25%	$28,400	
12			$90,750	$189,300	$14,010.00	28%	$68,800	
13			$189,300	$411,500	$34,926.00	33%	$143,500	
14			$411,500	$413,200	$90,514.50	35%	$311,950	
15			$413,200	--	$90,514.50	39.6%	$311,950	
16								
17	**Income:**	$50,000						
18	**Tax Rate**	25%						

Finding Exact Matches

In many situations, a range lookup isn't what you want. This is particularly true in lookup tables that contain a set of unique lookup values that represent discrete values instead of ranges. For example, if you need to look up a customer account number, a part code, or an employee ID, you want to be sure that your formula matches the value exactly. You can perform exact-match lookups with VLOOKUP() and HLOOKUP() by including the *range_lookup* argument with the value FALSE. The next couple sections demonstrate this technique.

Looking Up a Customer Account Number

A table of customer account numbers and names is a good example of a lookup table that contains discrete lookup values. In such a case, you want to use VLOOKUP() or HLOOKUP() to find an exact match for an account number you specify and then return the corresponding account name. Figure 9.5 shows a simple data-entry screen that automatically adds a customer name after the user enters the account number in cell B2.

The function that accomplishes this is in cell B4:

```
=VLOOKUP(B2, D3:E15, 2, FALSE)
```

The value in B2 is looked up in column D, and because the *range_lookup* argument is set to FALSE, VLOOKUP() searches for an exact match. If it finds one, it returns the text from column E.

Figure 9.5
A simple data-entry worksheet that uses the exact-match version of VLOOKUP() to look up a customer's name based on the entered account number.

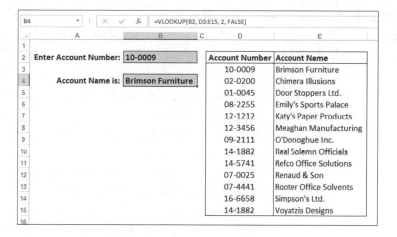

Combining Exact-Match Lookups with In-Cell Drop-Down Lists

In Chapter 4, you learned how to use data validation to set up an in-cell drop-down list. Whatever value the user selects from the list is the value that's stored in the cell. This technique becomes even more powerful when you combine it with exact-match lookups that use the current list selection as the lookup value.

→ To learn how to use data validation to set up an in-cell drop-down list, **see** "Applying Data-Validation Rules to Cells," **p. 100**.

Figure 9.6 shows an example. Cell C9 contains a drop-down list that uses as its source the header values in row 1 (C1:N1). The formula in cell C10 uses HLOOKUP() to perform an exact-match lookup using the currently selected list value from C9:

```
=HLOOKUP(C9, C1:N7, 7, FALSE)
```

Figure 9.6
An HLOOKUP() formula in C10 performs an exact-match lookup in row 1 based on the current selection in C9's in-cell drop-down list.

EXPENSES	January	February	March	April	May	June	July	August	September	October	November
Advertising	$4,600	$4,200	$5,200	$4,600	$4,200	$5,200	$4,600	$4,200	$5,200	$4,600	$4,200
Rent	$2,100	$2,100	$2,100	$2,100	$2,100	$2,100	$2,100	$2,100	$2,100	$2,100	$2,100
Supplies	$1,300	$1,200	$1,400	$1,300	$1,200	$1,400	$1,300	$1,200	$1,400	$1,300	$1,200
Salaries	$16,000	$16,000	$16,500	$16,000	$16,000	$16,500	$16,000	$16,000	$16,500	$16,000	$16,000
Utilities	$500	$600	$600	$500	$600	$600	$500	$600	$600	$500	$600
TOTAL	$24,500	$24,100	$25,800	$24,500	$24,100	$25,800	$24,500	$24,100	$25,800	$24,500	$24,100
Month	May										
Total	$24,100										

Advanced Lookup Operations

The basic lookup procedure—looking up a value in a column or row and then returning an offset value—will satisfy most of your needs. However, a few operations require a more sophisticated approach. The rest of this chapter examines these more advanced lookups, most of which make use of two more lookup functions: MATCH() and INDEX().

Chapter 9

The MATCH() and INDEX() Functions

The MATCH() function looks through a row or column of cells for a value. If MATCH() finds a match, it returns the relative position of the match in the row or column. Here's the syntax:

MATCH(*lookup_value, lookup_array*[, *match_type*])

lookup_value	The value you want to find. You can use a number, string, reference, or logical value.
lookup_array	The row or column of cells you want to use for the lookup.
match_type	How you want Excel to match the *lookup_value* with the entries in the *lookup_array*. You have three choices:

0 finds the first value that exactly matches *lookup_value*. The *lookup_array* can be in any order.

1 finds the largest value that's less than or equal to *lookup_value*. (This is the default value.) The *lookup_array* must be in ascending order.

-1 finds the smallest value that is greater than or equal to *lookup_value*. The *lookup_array* must be in descending order.

> **TIP**
> You can use the usual wildcard characters within the *lookup_value* argument (provided that *match_type* is 0 and *lookup_value* is text). You can use the question mark (?) for single characters and the asterisk (*) for multiple characters.

Normally, you don't use the MATCH() function by itself; you combine it with the INDEX() function. INDEX() returns the value of a cell at the intersection of a row and column inside a reference. Here's the syntax for INDEX():

INDEX(*reference, row_num*[, *column_num*] [, *area_num*])

reference	A reference to one or more cell ranges.
row_num	The number of the row in *reference* from which to return a value.
column_num	The number of the column in *reference* from which to return a value. You can omit *column_num* if *reference* is a single column.
area_num	If you entered more than one range for *reference, area_num* is the range you want to use. The first range you entered is 1 (this is the default), the second is 2, and so on.

The idea is that you use MATCH() to get *row_num* or *column_num* (depending on how your table is laid out) and then use INDEX() to return the value you need.

To give you the flavor of using these two functions, let's duplicate our earlier effort of looking up a customer name, given the account number. Figure 9.7 shows the result.

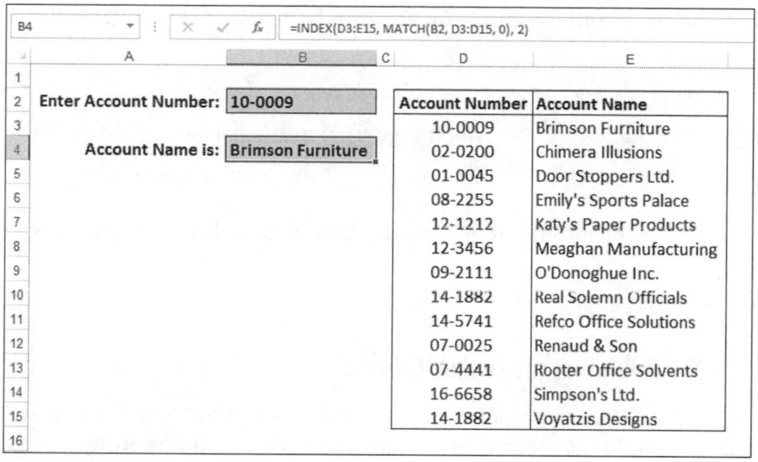
B4
=INDEX(D3:E15, MATCH(B2, D3:D15, 0), 2)
Enter Account Number: 10-0009
Account Name is: Brimson Furniture
Account Number | Account Name
10-0009 Brimson Furniture
02-0200 Chimera Illusions
01-0045 Door Stoppers Ltd.
08-2255 Emily's Sports Palace
12-1212 Katy's Paper Products
12-3456 Meaghan Manufacturing
09-2111 O'Donoghue Inc.
14-1882 Real Solemn Officials
14-5741 Refco Office Solutions
07-0025 Renaud & Son
07-4441 Rooter Office Solvents
16-6658 Simpson's Ltd.
14-1882 Voyatzis Designs

Figure 9.7
A worksheet that uses `INDEX()` and `MATCH()` to look up a customer's name, based on the entered account number.

In particular, notice the new formula in cell B4:

```
=INDEX(D3:E15, MATCH(B2, D3:D15, 0), 2)
```

The `MATCH()` function looks up the value in cell B2 in the range D3:D15. That value is then used as the *`row_num`* argument for the `INDEX()` function. That value is `1` in the example, so the `INDEX()` function reduces to this:

```
=INDEX(D3:E15, 1, 2)
```

This returns the value in the first row and the second column of the range D3:E15.

Looking Up a Value Using Worksheet List Boxes

If you use a worksheet list box or combo box as explained in Chapter 4, the linked cell contains the number of the selected item, not the item itself. Figure 9.8 shows a worksheet with a list box and a drop-down list. The list used by both controls is the range A3:A10. Notice that the linked cells (E3 and E10) display the number of the list selection, not the selection itself.

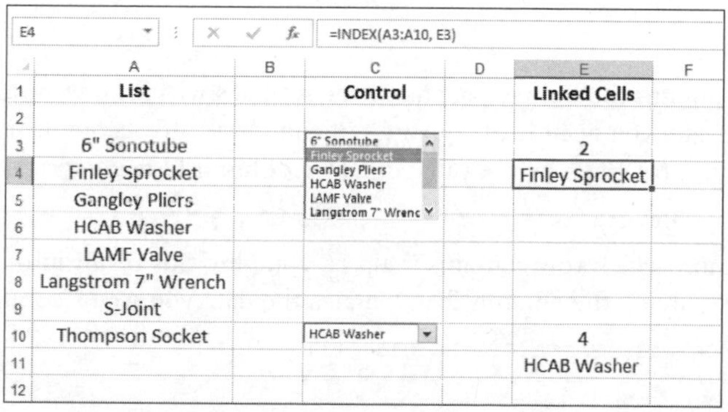
E4
=INDEX(A3:A10, E3)
List
Control
Linked Cells
6" Sonotube
Finley Sprocket
Gangley Pliers
HCAB Washer
LAMF Valve
Langstrom 7" Wrench
S-Joint
Thompson Socket
2
Finley Sprocket
HCAB Washer
4
HCAB Washer

Figure 9.8
This worksheet uses `INDEX()` to get the selected item from a list box and a combo box.

To get the selected list item, you can use the INDEX() function with the following modified syntax:

```
INDEX(list_range, list_selection)
```

list_range   The range used in the list box or drop-down list

list_selection   The number of the item selected in the list

For example, to find the item selected from the list box in Figure 9.8, you use the following formula:

```
=INDEX(A3:A10, E3)
```

Using Any Column as the Lookup Column

One of the major disadvantages of the VLOOKUP() function is that you must use the table's leftmost column as the lookup column. (HLOOKUP() suffers from a similar problem: It must use the table's topmost row as the lookup row.) This isn't a problem if you remember to structure your lookup table accordingly, but that might not be possible in some cases, particularly if you inherit the data from someone else.

Fortunately, you can use the MATCH() and INDEX() combination to use *any* table column as the lookup column. For example, consider the parts database shown in Figure 9.9.

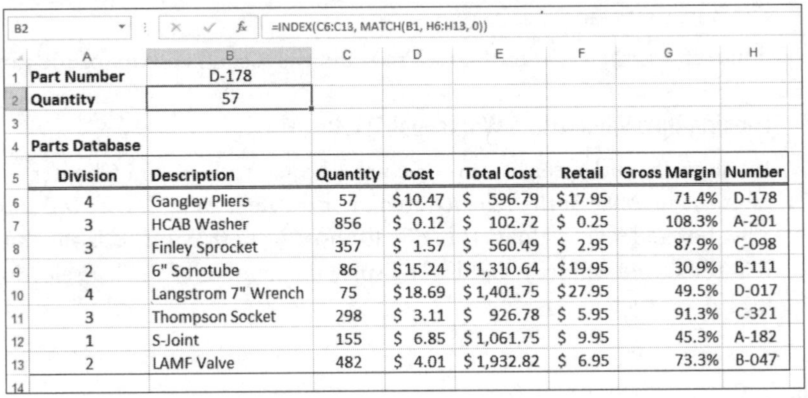

Figure 9.9

In this lookup table, the lookup values are in column H, and the value you want to find is in column C.

	B2	▾	:	×	✓	fx	=INDEX(C6:C13, MATCH(B1, H6:H13, 0))			
	A	B	C	D	E	F	G	H
1	Part Number	D-178						
2	Quantity	57						
3								
4	Parts Database							
5	Division	Description	Quantity	Cost	Total Cost	Retail	Gross Margin	Number
6	4	Gangley Pliers	57	$10.47	$ 596.79	$17.95	71.4%	D-178
7	3	HCAB Washer	856	$ 0.12	$ 102.72	$ 0.25	108.3%	A-201
8	3	Finley Sprocket	357	$ 1.57	$ 560.49	$ 2.95	87.9%	C-098
9	2	6" Sonotube	86	$15.24	$1,310.64	$19.95	30.9%	B-111
10	4	Langstrom 7" Wrench	75	$18.69	$1,401.75	$27.95	49.5%	D-017
11	3	Thompson Socket	298	$ 3.11	$ 926.78	$ 5.95	91.3%	C-321
12	1	S-Joint	155	$ 6.85	$1,061.75	$ 9.95	45.3%	A-182
13	2	LAMF Valve	482	$ 4.01	$1,932.82	$ 6.95	73.3%	B-047
14								

Column H contains the unique part numbers, so that's what you want to use as the lookup column. The data you need is the quantity in column C. To accomplish this, you first find the part number (as given by the value in B1) in column H using MATCH():

```
MATCH(B1, H6:H13, 0)
```

When you know which row contains the part, you plug this result into an INDEX() function that operates only on the column that contains the data you want (column C):

```
=INDEX(C6:C13, MATCH(B1, H6:H13, 0))
```

Creating Row-and-Column Lookups

So far, all the lookups you've seen have been one dimensional, meaning that they searched for a lookup value in a single column or row. However, in many situations, you need a two-dimensional approach. This means that you need to look up a value in a column *and* a value in a row and then return the data value at the intersection of the two. I call this a *row-and-column lookup*.

You do this by using *two* MATCH() functions: one to calculate the INDEX() function's `row_num` argument, and the other to calculate the INDEX() function's `column_num` argument. Figure 9.10 shows an example.

9

Figure 9.10
To perform a two-dimensional row-and-column lookup, use MATCH() functions to calculate both the row and the column values for the INDEX() function.

	A	B	C	D	E	F	G	H
	B3		✕ ✓ *fx*	=INDEX(A7:H14, MATCH(B1, H7:H14, 0), MATCH(B2, A6:H6, 0))				
1	Part Number	D-178						
2	Field Name	Cost						
3	Value	10.47						
4								
5	Parts Database							
6	Division	Description	Quantity	Cost	Total Cost	Retail	Gross Margin	Number
7	4	Gangley Pliers	57	$10.47	$ 596.79	$17.95	71.4%	D-178
8	3	HCAB Washer	856	$ 0.12	$ 102.72	$ 0.25	108.3%	A-201
9	3	Finley Sprocket	357	$ 1.57	$ 560.49	$ 2.95	87.9%	C-098
10	2	6" Sonotube	86	$15.24	$1,310.64	$19.95	30.9%	B-111
11	4	Langstrom 7" Wrench	75	$18.69	$1,401.75	$27.95	49.5%	D-017
12	3	Thompson Socket	298	$ 3.11	$ 926.78	$ 5.95	91.3%	C-321
13	1	S-Joint	155	$ 6.85	$1,061.75	$ 9.95	45.3%	A-182
14	2	LAMF Valve	482	$ 4.01	$1,932.82	$ 6.95	73.3%	B-047
15								

The idea here is to use both the part numbers (column H) and the field names (row 6) to return specific values from the parts database.

The part number is entered into cell B1, and getting the corresponding row in the parts table is no different from what you did in the previous section:

```
MATCH(B1, H7:H14, 0)
```

The field name is entered into cell B2. Getting the corresponding column number requires the following MATCH() expression:

```
MATCH(B2, A6:H6, 0)
```

These provide the INDEX() function's `row_num` and `column_num` arguments (see cell B3):

```
=INDEX(A7:H14, MATCH(B1, H7:H14, 0), MATCH(B2, A6:H6, 0))
```

Creating Multiple-Column Lookups

Sometimes it's not enough to look up a value in a single column. For example, in a list of employee names, you might need to look up both the first name and the last name if they're in separate fields. One way to handle this is to create a new field that concatenates all the lookup values into a single item. However, it's possible to do this without going to the trouble of creating a new concatenated field.

The secret is to perform the concatenation within the MATCH() function, as in this generic expression:

```
MATCH(value1 & value2, array1 & array2, match_type)
```

Here, *value1* and *value2* are the lookup values you want to work with, and *array1* and *array2* are the lookup columns. You can then plug the results into an array formula that uses INDEX() to get the needed data:

```
{=INDEX(reference, MATCH(value1 & value2, array1 & array2, match_type))}
```

For example, Figure 9.11 shows a database of employees, with separate fields for the first name, last name, title, and more.

Figure 9.11
To perform a two-column lookup, use MATCH() to find a row based on the concatenated values of two or more columns.

	A	B	C	D	E	F
	B3		fx	{=INDEX(C6:C14, MATCH(B1 & B2, A6:A14 & B6:B14, 0))}		
1	First Name	Nancy				
2	Last Name	Davolio				
3	Title	Account Manager				
4						
5	First Name	Last Name	Title	Title Of Courtesy	Birth Date	Hire Date
6	Nancy	Davolio	Account Manager	Ms.	8-Dec-48	1-May-02
7	Andrew	Fuller	Vice President, Sales	Dr.	19-Feb-52	14-Aug-02
8	Janet	Leverling	Account Manager	Ms.	30-Aug-63	1-Apr-02
9	Margaret	Peacock	Account Manager	Mrs.	19-Sep-37	3-May-03
10	Steven	Buchanan	Sales Manager	Mr.	4-Mar-55	17-Oct-03
11	Michael	Suyama	Account Manager	Mr.	2-Jul-63	17-Oct-03
12	Robert	King	Account Manager	Mr.	29-May-60	2-Jan-04
13	Laura	Callahan	Inside Sales Coordinator	Ms.	9-Jan-58	5-Mar-04
14	Anne	Dodsworth	Account Manager	Ms.	27-Jan-66	15-Nov-04

The lookup values are in B1 (first name) and B2 (last name), and the lookup columns are A6:A14 (the First Name field) and B6:B14 (the Last Name field). Here's the MATCH() function that looks up the required column:

```
MATCH(B1 & B2, A6:A14 & B6:B14, 0)
```

We want the specified employee's title, so the INDEX() function looks in C6:C14 (the Title field). Here's the array formula in cell B3:

```
{=INDEX(C6:C14, MATCH(B1 & B2, A6:A14 & B6:B14, 0))}
```

From Here

- To learn how to use data validation to set up an in-cell drop-down list, **see** "Applying Data-Validation Rules to Cells," **p. 100**.

- For the specifics of adding option buttons and list boxes to a worksheet, **see** "Understanding the Worksheet Controls," **p. 105**.

- For a general discussion of function syntax, **see** "The Structure of a Function," **p. 130**.

- To learn about the WEEKDAY() function, **see** "The WEEKDAY() Function," **p. 214**.

Working with Date and Time Functions

The date and time functions enable you to convert dates and times to serial numbers and perform operations on those numbers. This capability is useful for such things as accounts receivable aging, project scheduling, time-management applications, and much more. This chapter introduces you to Excel's date and time functions and puts them through their paces with many practical examples.

How Excel Deals with Dates and Times

Excel uses *serial numbers* to represent specific dates and times. To get a date serial number, Excel uses December 31, 1899, as an arbitrary starting point and then counts the number of days that have passed since then. For example, the date serial number for January 1, 1900, is 1; for January 2, 1900, it's 2; and so on. Table 10.1 displays some examples of date serial numbers.

Table 10.1   Examples of Date Serial Numbers

Serial Number	Date
366	December 31, 1900
16229	June 6, 1944
42735	December 31, 2016

To get a time serial number, Excel expresses time as a decimal fraction of the 24-hour day to get a number between 0 and 1. The starting point, midnight, is given the value 0, so noon—halfway through the day—has a serial number of 0.5. Table 10.2 displays some examples of time serial numbers.

Table 10.2   Examples of Time Serial Numbers

Serial Number	Time
0.25	6:00:00 a.m.
0.375	9:00:00 a.m.
0.70833	5:00:00 p.m.
.99999	11:59:59 p.m.

You can combine the two types of serial numbers. For example, 42735.5 represents noon on December 31, 2016.

The advantage of using serial numbers in this way is that it makes calculations involving dates and times very easy. A date or time is really just a number, so any mathematical operation you can perform on a number can also be performed on a date. This is invaluable for worksheets that track delivery times, monitor accounts receivable or accounts payable aging, calculate invoice discount dates, and so on.

Entering Dates and Times

Although it's true that serial numbers make it easier for the computer to manipulate dates and times, it's not the best format for humans to comprehend. For example, the number 25404.95555 is meaningless, but the moment it represents (July 20, 1969, at 10:56 p.m. EDT) is one of the great moments in history (the *Apollo 11* moon landing). Fortunately, Excel takes care of the conversion between these formats so that you never have to worry about it. To enter a date or time, use any of the formats shown in Table 10.3.

Table 10.3   Excel Date and Time Formats

Format	Example
m/d/yyyy	8/23/2016
d-mmm-yy	23-Aug-16
d-mmm	23-Aug (Excel assumes the current year)
mmm-yy	Aug-16 (Excel assumes the first day of the month)
h:mm:ss AM/PM	10:35:10 p.m.
h:mm AM/PM	10:35 p.m.
h:mm:ss	22:35:10
h:mm	22:35
m/d/y h:mm	8/23/16 22:35

Here are a couple shortcuts that will let you enter dates and times quickly. To enter the current date in a cell, press Ctrl+; (semicolon). To enter the current time, press Ctrl+: (colon).

Table 10.3 shows Excel's built-in formats, but these are not set in stone. You're free to mix and match these formats, as long as you observe the following rules:

- You can use either the forward slash (/) or the hyphen (-) as a date separator. Always use a colon (:) as a time separator.
- You can combine any date and time formats, as long as you separate them with a space.
- You can enter date and time values using either uppercase or lowercase letters. Excel automatically adjusts the capitalization to its standard format.
- To display times using the 12-hour clock, include either am (or just a) or pm (or just p). If you leave these off, Excel uses the 24-hour clock.

For more information on formatting dates and times, **see** "Formatting Numbers, Dates, and Times," **p. 74**.

10

Excel and Two-Digit Years

Entering two-digit years (such as 16 for 2016 and 99 for 1999) is problematic in Excel because various versions of the program treat them differently. In versions since Excel 97, the two-digit years 00 through 29 are interpreted as the years 2000 through 2029, whereas 30 through 99 are interpreted as the years 1930 through 1999. Earlier versions treated the two-digit years 00 through 19 as 2000 through 2019 and 20 through 99 as 1920 through 1999.

Two problems arise here: One is that using a two-digit year such as 25 will cause havoc if the worksheet is loaded into Excel 95 or some earlier version. The second is that you could throw a monkey wrench into your calculations by using a date such as 8/23/30 to mean August 23, 2030 because Excel treats it as August 23, 1930.

The easiest solution to both problems is to always use four-digit years to avoid ambiguity. Alternatively, you can put off the second problem by changing how Excel and Windows interpret two-digit years. Here are the steps to follow in Windows 8, Windows 7, and Windows Vista. (Windows XP and earlier have similar options.)

1. Open Control Panel:
   - **Windows 8 or later**—Press Windows Logo+X and then select Control Panel.
   - **Windows 7 and Windows Vista**—Select Start, Control Panel.
2. Select the Clock, Language, and Region link.
3. Select the Change Date, Time, or Number Formats link. The Region dialog box appears.

4. In the Formats tab, click Additional Settings. (In Vista, click Customize This Format instead.) The Customize Format dialog box appears.

5. Select the Date tab.

6. Use the When a Two-Digit Year Is Entered, Interpret It As a Year Between spinner to adjust the maximum year in which a two-digit year is interpreted as a twenty-first-century date. For example, if you never use dates prior to 1960, you could change the spin box value to 2059, which means Excel interprets two-digit years as dates between 1960 and 2059 (see Figure 10.1).

Figure 10.1
Use the Date tab to adjust how Windows (and, therefore, Excel) interprets two-digit years.

7. Click OK to return to the Region dialog box.

8. Click OK to put the new setting into effect.

Using Excel's Date Functions

Excel's date functions work with or return date serial numbers. All of Excel's date-related functions are listed in Table 10.4. (For the `serial_number` arguments, you can use any valid Excel date.)

Table 10.4   Excel's Date Functions

Function	Description
`DATE(year, month, day)`	Returns the serial number of a date, in which `year` is a number from 1900 to 2078, `month` is a number representing the month of the year, and `day` is a number representing the day of the month.
`DATEDIF(start_date, end_date[, unit])`	Returns the difference between `start_date` and `end_date`, based on the specified `unit`.
`DATEVALUE(date_text)`	Converts a date from text to a serial number.
`DAY(serial_number)`	Extracts the day component from the date given by `serial_number`.
`DAYS(end_date, start_date)`	Returns the number of days between `start_date` and `end_date`.
`DAYS360(start_date, end_date[, method])`	Returns the number of days between `start_date` and `end_date`, based on a 360-day year.
`EDATE(start_date, months)`	Returns the serial number of a date that is the specified number of `months` before or after `start_date`.
`EOMONTH(start_date, months)`	Returns the serial number of the last day of the month that is the specified number of `months` before or after `start_date`.
`ISOWEEKNUM(date)`	Returns a number that corresponds to the ISO week number for `date`.
`MONTH(serial_number)`	Extracts the month component from the date given by `serial_number` (January = 1).
`NETWORKDAYS(start_date, end_date[, holidays])`	Returns the number of working days between `start_date` and `end_date`; doesn't include weekends and any dates specified by `holidays`.
`TODAY()`	Returns the serial number of the current date.
`WEEKDAY(serial_number[, return_type])`	Converts a serial number to a day of the week (Sunday = 1).
`WEEKNUM(serial_number[, return_type])`	Returns a number that corresponds to where the week that includes `serial_number` falls numerically during the year.
`WORKDAY(start_date, days[, holidays])`	Returns the serial number of the day that is `days` working days from `start_date`; weekends and `holidays` are excluded.
`YEAR(serial_number)`	Extracts the year component from the date given by `serial_number`.
`YEARFRAC(start_date, end_date, basis)`	Converts the number of days between `start_date` and `end_date` into a fraction of a year.

10

Returning a Date

If you need a date for an expression operand or a function argument, you can enter it by hand if you have a specific date in mind. Much of the time, however, you need more flexibility, such as always entering the current date or building a date from day, month, and year components. Excel offers three functions that can help: TODAY(), DATE(), and DATEVALUE().

TODAY(): Returning the Current Date

When you need to use the current date in a formula, a function, or an expression, use the TODAY() function, which doesn't take any arguments:

```
TODAY()
```

This function returns the serial number of the current date, with midnight as the assumed time. For example, if today's date is December 31, 2016, the TODAY() function returns the following serial number (although by default, what you see in the cell is the date in m/d/yyyy format):

```
42735
```

Note that TODAY() is a dynamic function that doesn't always return the same value. Each time you edit the formula, enter another formula, recalculate the worksheet, or reopen the workbook, TODAY() updates its value to return the current system date.

DATE(): Returning Any Date

A date consists of three components: the year, month, and day. It often happens that a worksheet generates one or more of these components, and you need some way of building a proper date out of them. You can do that by using Excel's DATE() function:

```
DATE(year, month, day)
```

year	The year component of the date (a number between 1900 and 9999)
month	The month component of the date
day	The day component of the date

> **CAUTION**
>
> Excel's date inconsistencies rear up again with the DATE() function. That's because, if you enter a two-digit year (or even a three-digit year), Excel converts the number into a year value by adding 1900. So, entering 16 as the *year* argument gives you 1916, not 2016. To avoid problems, *always* use a four-digit year when entering the DATE() function's *year* argument.

For example, the following expression returns Christmas Day in 2016:

```
DATE(2016, 12, 25)
```

Note, too, that DATE() adjusts for wrong month and day values. For example, the following expression returns January 1, 2017:

```
DATE(2016, 12, 32)
```

Here, DATE() adds the extra day (there are 31 days in December) to return the date of the next day. Similarly, the following expression returns January 25, 2017:

```
DATE(2016, 13, 25)
```

DATEVALUE(): Converting a String to a Date

If you have a date value in string form, you can convert it to a date serial number by using the DATEVALUE() function:

```
DATEVALUE(date_text)
```

    date_text   The string containing the date

For example, the following expression returns the date serial number for the string August 23, 2016:

```
DATEVALUE("August 23, 2016")
```

→ To learn how to convert nonstandard date strings to dates, **see** "A Date-Conversion Formula," **p. 154**.

10

Returning Parts of a Date

The three components of a date—year, month, and day—can also be extracted individually from a given date. This might not seem all that interesting at first, but actually many useful techniques arise out of working with a date's component parts. A date's components are extracted using Excel's YEAR(), MONTH(), and DAY() functions.

The YEAR() Function

The YEAR() function returns a four-digit number that corresponds to the year component of a specified date:

```
YEAR(serial_number)
```

    serial_number   The date (or a string representation of the date) you want to
                          work with

For example, if today is August 23, 2016, the following expression will return 2016:

```
YEAR(TODAY())
```

The MONTH() Function

The MONTH() function returns a number between 1 and 12 that corresponds to the month component of a specified date:

```
MONTH(serial_number)
```

    serial_number   The date (or a string representation of the date) you want to
                          work with

For example, the following expression returns 8:

```
MONTH("August 23, 2016")
```

The DAY() Function

The DAY() function returns a number between 1 and 31 that corresponds to the day component of a specified date:

```
DAY(serial_number)
```

    serial_number   The date (or a string representation of the date) you want to work with

For example, the following expression returns 23:

```
DAY("8/23/2016")
```

The WEEKDAY() Function

The WEEKDAY() function returns a number that corresponds to the day of the week upon which a specified date falls:

```
WEEKDAY(serial_number[, return_type])
```

    serial_number   The date (or a string representation of the date) you want to work with.

    return_type   An integer that determines how the value returned by WEEKDAY() corresponds to the days of the week:
1—The return values are 1 (Sunday) through 7 (Saturday); this is the default.
2—The return values are 1 (Monday) through 7 (Sunday).
3—The return values are 0 (Monday) through 6 (Sunday).

For example, the following expression returns 3 because August 23, 2016, is a Tuesday:

```
WEEKDAY("8/23/2016")
```

→ To learn how to use CHOOSE() to convert the WEEKDAY() return value into a day name, **see** "Determining the Name of the Day of the Week," **p. 194**.

The WEEKNUM() Function

The WEEKNUM() function returns a number that corresponds to where the week that includes a specified date falls numerically during the year:

```
WEEKNUM(serial_number[, return_type])
```

    serial_number   The date (or a string representation of the date) you want to work with.

`return_type`	An integer that determines how `WEEKNUM()` interprets the start of the week:
	1—The week begins on Sunday; this is the default.
	2—The week begins on Monday.

For example, the following expression returns 35 because August 23, 2016, falls in the 35th week of 2016:

```
WEEKNUM("August 23, 2016")
```

> **TIP**
>
> You might need to return a week number that corresponds to ISO (International Standards Organization) 8601, which is the international standard for the representation of dates and times. The ISO 8601 week-numbering year always begins on the week with the year's first Thursday, so there will be dates at the beginning of the year and the end of the year where the ISO week number differs from the calendar week number. To always return the ISO week number, use Excel's `ISOWEEKNUM(date)` function (where `date` is the date you want to work with).

Returning a Date *X* Years, Months, or Days from Now

You can take advantage of the fact that, as I mentioned earlier, `DATE()` automatically adjusts wrong month and day values by applying formulas to one or more of the `DATE()` function's arguments. The most common use for this is returning a date that occurs *X* number of years, months, or days from now (or from any date).

For example, suppose that you want to know which day of the week the 4th of July falls on next year. Here's a formula that figures it out:

```
=WEEKDAY(DATE(YEAR(TODAY())) + 1, 7, 4)
```

As another example, if you want to work with whatever date is 6 months from today, you would use the following expression:

```
DATE(YEAR(TODAY()), MONTH(TODAY()) + 6, DAY(TODAY()))
```

Given this technique, you've probably figured out that you can return a date that is *X* days from now (or whenever) by adding to the day component of the `DATE()` function. For example, here's an expression that returns a date 30 days from now:

```
DATE(YEAR(TODAY()), MONTH(TODAY()), DAY(TODAY() + 30))
```

This is overkill, however, because date addition and subtraction works at the day level in Excel. That is, if you simply add or subtract a number to or from a date, Excel adds or subtracts that number of days. For example, to return a date 30 days from now, you need only use the following expression:

```
TODAY() + 30
```

10

A Workday Alternative: The WORKDAY() Function

Adding days to or subtracting days from a date is straightforward, but the basic calculation includes *all* days: workdays, weekends, and holidays. In many cases, you might need to ignore weekends and holidays and return a date that is a specified number of workdays from some original date.

You can do this by using the WORKDAY() function, which returns a date that is a specified number of working days from some starting date:

```
WORKDAY(start_date, days[, holidays])
```

start_date	The original date (or a string representation of the date).
days	The number of workdays before or after start_date. Use a positive number to return a later date; use a negative number to return an earlier date. Noninteger values are truncated (that is, the decimal part is ignored).
holidays	A list of dates to exclude from the calculation. This can be a range of dates or an array constant—that is, a series of date serial numbers or date strings, separated by commas and surrounded by braces ({}).

For example, the following expression returns a date that is 30 workdays from today:

```
WORKDAY(TODAY(), 30)
```

Here's another expression that returns the date that is 30 workdays from December 1, 2016, excluding December 25, 2016, and January 1, 2017:

```
=WORKDAY("12/1/2016", 30, {"12/25/2016","1/1/2017"})
```

→ It's possible to calculate the various holidays that occur within a year and place the dates within a range for use as the WORKDAY() function's holidays argument. **See** "Calculating Holiday Dates", **p. 221**.

Adding *X* Months: A Problem

You should be aware that simply adding *X* months to a specified date's month component won't always return the result you expect. The problem is that the months have a varying number of days. So, if you add a certain number of months to a date that falls on or near the end of a month, and the future month does not have the same number of days, Excel adjusts the day component accordingly.

For example, suppose that A1 contains the date 1/31/2017, and consider the following formula:

```
=DATE(YEAR(A1), MONTH(A1) + 3, DAY(A1))
```

You might expect this formula to return the last date in April as the result. Unfortunately, adding three months returns the wrong date, 4/31/2017 (there are only 30 days in April), which Excel automatically converts to 5/1/2017.

You can avoid this problem by using two functions: EDATE() and EOMONTH().

The EDATE() Function

The EDATE() function returns a date that is the specified number of months before or after a starting date:

```
EDATE(start_date, months)
```

start_date	The original date (or a string representation of the date).
months	The number of months before or after start_date. Use a positive number to return a later date; use a negative number to return an earlier date. Noninteger values are truncated. (That is, the decimal part is ignored.)

The nice thing about the EDATE() function is that it performs a "smart" calculation when working with dates at or near the end of the month: If the day component of the returned date doesn't exist (for example, April 31), EDATE() returns the last day of the month (April 30).

The EDATE() function is useful for calculating the coupon payment dates for bond issues. Given the bond's maturity date, you calculate the bond's first payment as follows (assuming that the bond was issued this year and that the maturity date is in a cell named MaturityDate):

```
=DATE(YEAR(TODAY()), MONTH(MaturityDate), DAY(MaturityDate))
```

If this result is in cell A1, the following formula will return the date of the next coupon payment:

```
=EDATE(A1, 6)
```

The EOMONTH() Function

The EOMONTH() function returns the date of the last day of the month that is the specified number of months before or after a starting date:

```
EOMONTH(start_date, months)
```

start_date	The original date (or a string representation of the date).
months	The number of months before or after start_date. Use a positive number to return a later date; use a negative number to return an earlier date. Noninteger values are truncated. (That is, the decimal part is ignored.)

For example, the following formula returns the last day of the month three months from now:

```
=EOMONTH(TODAY(), 3)
```

Returning the Last Day of Any Month

The EOMONTH() function returns the last date of some month in the future or the past. However, what if you have a date, and you want to know the last day of the month in which that date appears?

You can calculate this by using yet another trick involving the DATE() function's capability to adjust wrong values for date components. You want a formula that returns the last day of a particular month. You can't specify the day argument in the DATE() function directly because the months can have 28, 29, 30, or 31 days. Instead, you can take advantage of an apparently trivial fact: The last day of any month is always the day *before* the first day of the next month. The number before 1 is 0, so you can plug in 0 to the DATE() function as the day argument:

```
=DATE(YEAR(MyDate), MONTH(MyDate) + 1, 0)
```

Here, assume that MyDate is the date you want to work with.

Determining a Person's Birthday, Given the Birth Date

If you know a person's birth date, determining that person's birthday is easy: Just keep the month and day the same and substitute the current year for the year of birth. To accomplish this in a formula, you could use the following:

```
=DATE(YEAR(NOW()), MONTH(Birthdate), DAY(Birthdate))
```

Here, I'm assuming that the person's date of birth is in a cell named Birthdate. The YEAR(NOW()) component extracts the current year, and MONTH(Birthdate) and DAY(Birthdate) extract the month and day, respectively, from the person's date of birth. Combine these into the DATE() function, and you have the birthday.

Returning the Date of the *n*th Occurrence of a Weekday in a Month

It's a common date task to have to figure out the *n*th weekday in a given month. For example, you might need to schedule a budget meeting for the first Monday in each month, or you might want to plan the annual company picnic for the third Sunday in June. These are tricky calculations, to be sure, but Excel's date functions are up to the task.

As with many other complex formulas, the best place to start is with what you know for sure. In this case, you always know for sure the date of the first day of whatever month you're dealing with. For example, Labor Day always occurs on the first Monday in September, so you could begin with September 1 and know that the date you seek is some number of days after that. The formula begins like this:

```
=DATE(Year, Month, 1) + days
```

Here, `Year` is the year in which you want the date to fall, and `Month` is the number of the month you want to work with. The `days` value is what you need to calculate.

To simplify things for now, let's assume that you're trying to find a date that is the first occurrence of a particular weekday in a month (such as Labor Day, the first Monday in September).

Using the first of the month as your starting point, you need to ask whether the weekday you're working with is less than the weekday of the first of the month. (By "less than," I mean that the WEEKDAY() value of the day of the week you're working with is numerically smaller than the WEEKDAY() value the first of the month.) In the Labor Day example, September 1, 2016, falls on a Thursday (WEEKDAY() equals 5), which is greater than Monday (WEEKDAY() equals 2). The result of this comparison determines how many days you add to the 1st to get the date you seek:

10

- If the day of the week you're working with is less than the first of the month, the date you seek is the first plus the result of the following expression:

```
7 - WEEKDAY(DATE(Year, Month, 1)) + Weekday
```

Here, `Weekday` is the WEEKDAY() value of the day of the week you're working with. Here's the expression for the Labor Day example:

```
7 - WEEKDAY(DATE(2016, 9, 1)) + 2
```

- If the day of the week you're working with is greater than or equal to the first of the month, the date you seek is the first plus the result of the following expression:

```
Weekday - WEEKDAY(DATE(Year, Month, 1))
```

Again, `Weekday` is the WEEKDAY() value of the day of the week you're working with. Here's the expression for the Labor Day example:

```
2 - WEEKDAY(DATE(2016, 9, 1))
```

These conditions can be handled by a basic IF() function. Here, then, is the generic formula for calculating the first occurrence of a `Weekday` in a given `Year` and `Month`:

```
=DATE(Year, Month, 1) +
➡IF(Weekday < WEEKDAY(DATE(Year, Month, 1)),
➡7 - WEEKDAY(DATE(Year, Month, 1)) + Weekday,
➡Weekday - WEEKDAY(DATE(Year, Month, 1)))
```

Here's the formula for calculating the date of Labor Day in 2016:

```
=DATE(2016, 9, 1) +
➡IF(2 < WEEKDAY(DATE(2016, 9, 1)),
➡7 - WEEKDAY(DATE(2016, 9, 1)) + 2,
➡2 - WEEKDAY(DATE(2016, 9, 1)))
```

Generalizing this formula for the nth occurrence of a weekday is straightforward: The second occurrence comes one week after the first, the third occurrence comes two weeks after the first, and so on. Here's a generic expression to calculate the extra number of days to add (where n is an integer that represents the nth occurrence):

```
(n - 1) * 7
```

Here, then, in generic form, is the final formula for calculating the *n*th occurrence of a *Weekday* in a given *Year* and *Month*:

```
=DATE(Year, Month, 1) +
➡IF(Weekday < WEEKDAY(DATE(Year, Month, 1)),
➡7 - WEEKDAY(DATE(Year, Month, 1)) + Weekday,
➡Weekday - WEEKDAY(DATE(Year, Month, 1))) +
➡(n - 1) * 7
```

For example, the following formula calculates the date of the third Sunday (WEEKDAY() equals 1) in June for 2016:

```
=DATE(2016, 6, 1) +
➡IF(1 < WEEKDAY(DATE(2016, 6, 1)),
➡7 - WEEKDAY(DATE(2016, 6, 1)) + 1,
[ic:ccc]1 - WEEKDAY(DATE(2016, 6, 1))) +
[ic:ccc](3 - 1) * 7
```

Figure 10.2 shows a worksheet used for calculating the *n*th occurrence of a weekday.

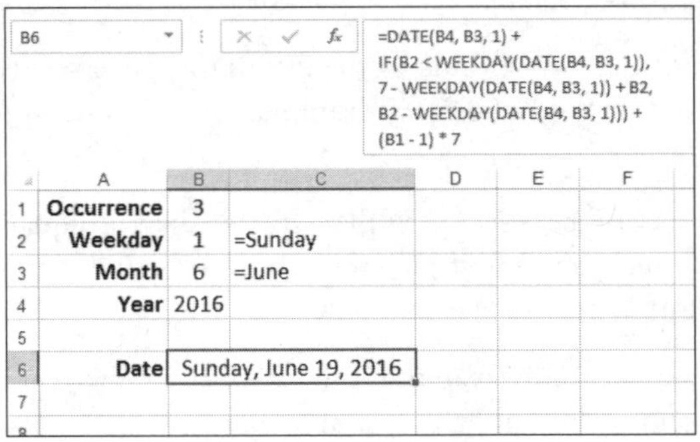

Figure 10.2
This worksheet calculates the *n*th occurrence of a specified weekday in a given year and month.

NOTE You can download this chapter's sample workbook at www.mcfedries.com/books/ book.php?title=excel-2016-formulas-and-functions.

The input cells are as follows:

■ **B1**—The number of the occurrence.

■ **B2**—The number of the weekday. (The formula in C2 shows the name of the entered weekday.)

■ **B3**—The number of the month. (The formula in C3 shows the name of the entered month.)

■ **B4**—The year.

The date calculation appears in cell B6. Here's the formula:

```
=DATE(B4, B3, 1) +
➡IF(B2 < WEEKDAY(DATE(B4, B3, 1)),
➡7 - WEEKDAY(DATE(B4, B3, 1)) + B2,
➡B2 - WEEKDAY(DATE(B4, B3, 1))) +
➡(B1 - 1) * 7
```

Calculating Holiday Dates

Given the formula from the previous section, it becomes a relative breeze to calculate the dates for most floating holidays (that is, holidays that occur on the *n*th weekday of a month instead of on a specific date each year, as do holidays such as Christmas, Independence Day, and Canada Day).

Here are the standard statutory floating holidays in the United States:

- **Martin Luther King Jr. Day**—Third Monday in January
- **Presidents Day**—Third Monday in February
- **Memorial Day**—Last Monday in May
- **Labor Day**—First Monday in September
- **Columbus Day**—Second Monday in October
- **Thanksgiving Day**—Fourth Thursday in November

Here's the list for Canada:

- **Victoria Day**—Monday on or before May 24
- **Good Friday**—Friday before Easter Sunday
- **Labor Day**—First Monday in September
- **Thanksgiving Day**—Second Monday in October

Figure 10.3 shows a worksheet used to calculate the holiday dates in a specified year.

Column A holds the name of the holiday; column B holds the occurrence within the month or, for fixed holidays, the actual date within the month; column C holds the days of the week; and column D holds the number of the month.

Most of the values in column E are calculated. For the floating holidays, for example, several CHOOSE() functions are used to construct the description. Here's an example for Martin Luther King, Jr., Day:

```
=B5 & CHOOSE(B5, "st", "nd", "rd", "th", "th") & " " & CHOOSE(C5,
➡"Sunday", "Monday", "Tuesday", "Wednesday", "Thursday", "Friday",
➡"Saturday") & " in " & CHOOSE(D5, "January", "February", "March",
➡"April", "May", "June", "July", "August", "September", "October",
➡"November", "December")
```

Finally, column F contains the formulas for calculating the date of each holiday based on the year entered in cell B1.

10

Figure 10.3
This worksheet calculates the dates of numerous holidays in a given year.

F4 =DATE($B$1, D4, 1) + IF(C4 < WEEKDAY(DATE($B$1, D4, 1)), 7 - WEEKDAY(DATE($B$1, D4, 1)) + C4, C4 - WEEKDAY(DATE($B$1, D4, 1))) + (B4 - 1) * 7

	A	B	C	D	E	F
1	Year:	2016				
2	**Holidays (U.S.)**	**Occurrence or Day**	**Weekday**	**Month**	**When It Occurs**	**Date**
3	New Year's Day	1		1	January 1	Fri Jan 1, 2016
4	Martin Luther King, Jr. Day	3	2	1	3rd Monday in January	Mon Jan 18, 2016
5	President's Day	3	2	2	3rd Monday in February	Mon Feb 15, 2016
6	Memorial Day	1	2	6	Last Monday in May (subtract 7 days from 1st Monday in June)	Mon May 30, 2016
7	Independence Day	4		7	July 4	Mon Jul 4, 2016
8	Labor Day	1	2	9	1st Monday in September	Mon Sep 5, 2016
9	Columbus Day	2	2	10	2nd Monday in October	Mon Oct 10, 2016
10	Veterans Day	11		11	November 11	Fri Nov 11, 2016
11	Thanksgiving Day	4	5	11	4th Thursday in November	Thu Nov 24, 2016
12	Christmas Day	25		12	December 25	Sun Dec 25, 2016
13						
14	**Holidays (Canada)**	**Occurrence or Day**	**Weekday**	**Month**	**When It Occurs**	**Date**
15	New Year's Day	1		1	January 1	Fri Jan 1, 2016
16	Good Friday				Friday before Easter Sunday	Fri Mar 25, 2016
17	Victoria Day	2	2	5	2nd Monday in May	Mon May 9, 2016
18	Canada Day	1		7	July 1	Fri Jul 1, 2016
19	Civic Holiday	1		8	August 1	Mon Aug 1, 2016
20	Labor Day	1	2	9	1st Monday in September	Mon Sep 5, 2016
21	Thanksgiving Day	2	2	10	2nd Monday in October	Mon Oct 10, 2016
22	Remembrance Day	11		11	November 11	Fri Nov 11, 2016
23	Christmas Day	25		12	December 25	Sun Dec 25, 2016

10

NOTE

Two exceptions exist in column F. The first is the formula for Memorial Day (cell F6), which occurs on the last Monday in May. To derive this date, you first calculate the first Monday in June and then subtract 7 days.

The second exception is the formula for Good Friday (cell F16). This occurs two days before Easter Sunday, which is a floating holiday, but its date is based on the phase of the moon, of all things. (Officially, Easter Sunday falls on the first Sunday after the first ecclesiastical full moon after the spring equinox.) There are no simple formulas for calculating when Easter Sunday occurs in a given year. The formula in the Holidays worksheet is a complex bit of business that uses the `FLOOR()` function, so I discuss it when I discuss that function in Chapter 11, "Working with Math Functions."

Calculating the Julian Date

Excel has built-in functions that convert a given date into a numerical day of the week (the `WEEKDAY()` function) and that return the numerical ranking of the week in which a given date falls (the `WEEKNUM()` function). However, Excel doesn't have a function that calculates the Julian date for a given date—the numerical ranking of the date for the year in which it falls. For example, the Julian date of January 1 is 1, January 2 is 2, and February 1 is 32.

If you need to use Julian dates in your business, here's a formula that will do the job:

```
=MyDate - DATE(YEAR(MyDate) - 1, 12, 31)
```

This formula assumes that the date you want to work with is in a cell named `MyDate`. The expression `DATE(YEAR(MyDate) - 1, 12, 31)` returns the date serial number for December 31 of the preceding year. Subtracting this number from `MyDate` gives you the Julian number.

Calculating the Difference Between Two Dates

In the previous section, you saw that Excel enables you to subtract one date from another. Here's an example:

```
=Date1 - Date2
```

Here, `Date1` and `Date2` can be date values or date strings. When you create such a formula, Excel returns a value equal to the number of days between the two dates. This date-difference formula returns a positive number if `Date1` is larger than `Date2`; it returns a negative number if `Date1` is less than `Date2`. Calculating the difference between two dates is useful in many business scenarios, including receivables aging, interest calculations, benefits payments, and more.

10

Besides the basic date-difference formula, you can use the date functions from earlier in this chapter to perform date-difference calculations. Also, Excel boasts a number of worksheet functions that enable you to perform more sophisticated operations to determine the difference between two dates. The rest of this section runs through a number of these date-difference formulas and functions.

Calculating a Person's Age, Part I

If you have a person's birth date entered into a cell named Birthdate and you need to calculate how old the person is, you might think that the following formula would do the job:

```
=YEAR(TODAY()) - YEAR(Birthdate)
```

This works, but only if the person's birthday has already passed this year. If he hasn't had a birthday yet, this formula reports the age as being one year greater than it really is.

To solve this problem, you need to take into account whether the person's birthday has passed. To see how to do this, check out the following logical expression:

```
-DATE(YEAR(NOW()), MONTH(Birthdate), DAY(Birthdate)) > TODAY()
```

This expression asks whether the person's birthday for this year (which uses the formula from earlier in this chapter—see "Determining a Person's Birthday, Given the Birth Date") is greater than today's date. If it is, the expression returns logical TRUE, which is equivalent to 1; if it isn't, the expression returns logical FALSE, which is equivalent to 0. In other words, you can get the person's true age by subtracting the result of the logical expression from the original formula, like so:

```
=YEAR(NOW()) - YEAR(Birthdate) - (DATE(YEAR(NOW()), MONTH(Birthdate),
➥DAY(Birthdate)) > NOW())
```

DAYS(): Returning the Number of Days Between Two Dates

If all you're interested in is the number of days between two dates, then the easiest way to perform such a calculation is to use Excel's DAYS() function:

```
DAYS(end_date, start_date)
```

end_date	The ending date
start_date	The starting date

For example, the following formula returns the number of days that have elapsed since the start of the current year:

```
=DAYS(TODAY(), DATE(YEAR(TODAY()), 1, 1))
```

The DATEDIF() Function

If you need to perform date-difference calculations based on a date unit other than days, then you need to use the DATEDIF() function, which returns the difference between two specified dates, based on a specified unit:

```
DATEDIF(start_date, end_date[, unit])
```

start_date	The starting date
end_date	The ending date
unit	The date unit used in the result:
	y—Returns the number of years between start_date and end_date
	m—Returns the number of months between start_date and end_date
	d—Returns the number of days between start_date and end_date
	md—Returns the difference in the day components between start_date and end_date (that is, the years and months are not included in the calculation)
	ym—Returns the difference in the month components between start_date and end_date (that is, the years and days are not included in the calculation)
	yd—Returns the number of days between start_date and end_date (with the year components excluded from the calculation)

You can use the DATEDIF() function to perform a Julian date calculation, as explained earlier in this chapter (see "Calculating the Julian Date"). If the date you want to work with is in a cell named MyDate, the following formula calculates its Julian date using DATEDIF():

```
=DATEDIF(DATE(YEAR(MyDate) - 1, 12, 31), MyDate, "d")
```

CAUTION

DATEDIF() is an undocumented Excel function because it was plagued with errors in earlier versions of Excel. Use this function with caution, and avoid using it altogether on very important worksheets.

Calculating a Person's Age, Part II

The DATEDIF() function can greatly simplify the formula for calculating a person's age. (See "Calculating a Person's Age, Part I," earlier in this chapter.) If the person's date of birth is in a cell named Birthdate, the following formula calculates his current age:

```
=DATEDIF(Birthdate, TODAY(), "y")
```

NETWORKDAYS(): Calculating the Number of Workdays Between Two Dates

If you calculate the difference in days between two days, Excel includes weekends and holidays. In many business situations, you need to know the number of workdays between two dates. For example, when calculating the number of days an invoice is past due, it's often best to exclude weekends and holidays.

This is easily done using the NETWORKDAYS() function (read the name as *net workdays*), which returns the number of working days between two dates:

```
NETWORKDAYS(start_date, end_date[, holidays])
```

start_date	The starting date (or a string representation of the date).
end_date	The ending date (or a string representation of the date).
holidays	A list of dates to exclude from the calculation. This can be a range of dates or an array constant—that is, a series of date serial numbers or date strings, separated by commas and surrounded by braces ({}).

For example, here's an expression that returns the number of workdays between December 1, 2016, and January 10, 2017, excluding December 25, 2016, and January 1, 2017:

```
=NETWORKDAYS("12/1/2016", "1/10/2017", {"12/25/2016","1/1/2017"})
```

Figure 10.4 shows an update to the accounts receivable worksheet that uses NETWORKDAYS() to calculate the number of workdays that each invoice is past due.

Figure 10.4
This worksheet calculates the number of workdays that each invoice is past due by using the `NETWORKDAYS()` function.

							Past Due (Days):		
Account Number	Invoice Number	Invoice Date	Due Date	Past Due	Amount Due	1-30	31-60	61-90	
07-0001	1000	January 11, 2016	Wednesday Feb 10, 2016	48	$2,433.25		$2,433.25		
07-0001	1025	January 29, 2016	Monday Feb 29, 2016	35	$2,151.20		$2,151.20		
07-0001	1031	February 5, 2016	Monday Mar 7, 2016	30	$1,758.54	$1,758.54			
07-0002	1006	November 23, 2012	Monday Dec 24, 2012	865	$898.47				
07-0002	1035	February 5, 2016	Monday Mar 7, 2016	30	$1,021.02	$1,021.02			
07-0004	1002	January 11, 2016	Wednesday Feb 10, 2016	48	$3,558.94		$3,558.94		
07-0005	1008	November 13, 2012	Thursday Dec 13, 2012	872	$1,177.53				
07-0005	1018	January 28, 2016	Monday Feb 29, 2016	35	$1,568.31		$1,568.31		
08-0001	1039	October 12, 2012	Monday Nov 12, 2012	895	$2,958.73				
08-0001	1001	January 11, 2016	Wednesday Feb 10, 2016	48	$3,659.85		$3,659.85		
08-0001	1024	January 29, 2016	Monday Feb 29, 2016	35	$565.00		$565.00		

(Cell E4 formula: `=NETWORKDAYS(D4,$B$1)`   Date: 15-Apr-16)

`DAYS360()`: Calculating Date Differences Using a 360-Day Year

Many accounting systems operate using the principle of a 360-day year, which divides the year into 12 periods of uniform (30-day) lengths. Finding the number of days between dates in such a system isn't possible with the standard addition and subtraction of dates. However, Excel makes such calculations easy with its `DAYS360()` function, which returns the number of days between a starting date and an ending date, based on a 360-day year:

```
DAYS360(start_date, end_date[, method])
```

start_date	The starting date (or a string representation of the date).
end_date	The ending date (or a string representation of the date).
method	A Boolean value that determines how `DAYS360()` performs certain calculations:

FALSE—If *start_date* is the 31st of the month, it is changed to the 30th of the same month. If *end_date* is the 31st of the month and *start_date* is less than the 30th of any month, the *end_date* is changed to the 1st of the next month. This is the North American method, and it's the default.

TRUE—Any *start_date* or *end_date* value that falls on the 31st of a month is changed to the 30th of the same month. This is the European method.

For example, the following expression returns the value 1:

```
DAYS360("3/30/2016", "4/1/2016")
```

`YEARFRAC()`: Returning the Fraction of a Year Between Two Dates

Business worksheet models often need to know the fraction of a year that has elapsed between one date and another. For example, if an employee leaves after 3 months, you might need to pay out a quarter of a year's worth of benefits. This calculation can be complicated by the fact that your company might use a 360-day accounting year. However, the `YEARFRAC()` function can help you. This function converts the number of days between a start date and an end date into a fraction of a year:

YEARFRAC(*start_date*, *end_date*[, *basis*])

start_date	The starting date (or a string representation of the date).
end_date	The ending date (or a string representation of the date).
basis	An integer that determines how YEARFRAC() performs certain calculations:

0—Uses a 360-day year divided into 12 30-day months. This is the North American method, and it's the default.

1—Uses the actual number of days in the year and the actual number of days in each month.

2—Uses a 360-day year and the actual number of days in each month.

3—Uses a 365-day year and the actual number of days in each month.

4—Any *start_date* or *end_date* value that falls on the 31st of a month is changed to the 30th of the same month. This is the European method.

For example, the following expression returns the value 0.25:

YEARFRAC("3/15/2016", "6/15/2016")

Using Excel's Time Functions

Working with time values in Excel is not greatly different from working with date values, although there are some exceptions, as you'll see in this section. Here you'll work mostly with Excel's time functions, which work with or return time serial numbers. All of Excel's time-related functions are listed in Table 10.5. (For the *serial_number* arguments, you can use any valid Excel time.)

Table 10.5 Excel's Time Functions

Function	Description
HOUR(*serial_number*)	Extracts the hour component from the time given by *serial_number*.
MINUTE(*serial_number*)	Extracts the minute component from the time given by *serial_number*.
NOW()	Returns the serial number of the current date and time.
SECOND(*serial_number*)	Extracts the seconds component from the time given by *serial_number*.
TIME(*hour*, *minute*, *second*)	Returns the serial number of a time, in which *hour* is a number between 0 and 23, and *minute* and *second* are numbers between 0 and 59.
TIMEVALUE(*time_text*)	Converts a time from text to a serial number.

10

Returning a Time

If you need a time value to use in an expression or a function, either you can enter it by hand if you have a specific date that you want to work with, or you can take advantage of the flexibility of three Excel functions: NOW(), TIME(), and TIMEVALUE().

NOW(): Returning the Current Time

When you need to use the current time in a formula, a function, or an expression, use the NOW() function, which doesn't take any arguments:

```
NOW()
```

This function returns the serial number of the current time, with the current date as the assumed date. For example, if it's noon and today's date is December 31, 2016, the NOW() function returns the following serial number (although in the cell you see this displayed using the m/d/yyyy h:mm format):

```
42735.5
```

If you just want the time component of the serial number, subtract TODAY() from NOW():

```
NOW() - TODAY()
```

Just like the TODAY() function, remember that NOW() is a dynamic function that doesn't keep its initial value (that is, the time at which you entered the function). Each time you edit the formula, enter another formula, recalculate the worksheet, or reopen the workbook, NOW() uptimes its value to return the current system time.

TIME(): Returning Any Time

A time consists of three components: the hour, minute, and second. It often happens that a worksheet generates one or more of these components, and you need some way of building a proper time out of them. You can do that by using Excel's TIME() function:

```
TIME(hour, minute, second)
```

hour	The hour component of the time (a number between 0 and 23)
minute	The minute component of the time (a number between 0 and 59)
second	The second component of the time (a number between 0 and 59)

For example, the following expression returns the time 2:45:30 p.m.:

```
TIME(14, 45, 30)
```

Like the DATE() function, TIME() adjusts for wrong hour, month, and second values. For example, the following expression returns 3:00:30 p.m.:

```
TIME(14, 60, 30)
```

Here, TIME() takes the extra minute and adds 1 to the hour value.

TIMEVALUE(): Converting a String to a Time

If you have a time value in string form, you can convert it to a time serial number by using the TIMEVALUE() function:

```
TIMEVALUE(time_text)
```

> time_text   The string containing the time

For example, the following expression returns the time serial number for the string `2:45:00 PM`:

```
TIMEVALUE("2:45:00 PM")
```

Returning Parts of a Time

The three components of a time—hour, minute, and second—can also be extracted individually from a given time, using Excel's HOUR(), MINUTE(), and SECOND() functions.

The HOUR() Function

The HOUR() function returns a number between 0 and 23 that corresponds to the hour component of a specified time:

```
HOUR(serial_number)
```

> serial_number   The time (or a string representation of the time) you want to work with

For example, the following expression returns 12:

```
HOUR(0.5)
```

The MINUTE() Function

The MINUTE() function returns a number between 0 and 59 that corresponds to the minute component of a specified time:

```
MINUTE(serial_number)
```

> serial_number   The time (or a string representation of the time) you want to work with

For example, if it's currently 3:15 p.m., the following expression returns 15:

```
MINUTE(NOW())
```

The SECOND() Function

The SECOND() function returns a number between 0 and 59 that corresponds to the second component of a specified time:

```
SECOND(serial_number)
```

> serial_number   The time (or a string representation of the time) you want to work with

For example, the following expression returns 30:

```
SECOND("2:45:30 PM")
```

10

Returning a Time *X* Hours, Minutes, or Seconds from Now

As I mentioned earlier, TIME() automatically adjusts wrong hour, minute, and second values. You can take advantage of this by applying formulas to one or more of the TIME() function's arguments. The most common use for this is to return a time that occurs *X* number of hours, minutes, or seconds from now (or from any time).

For example, the following expression returns the time 12 hours from now:

```
TIME(HOUR(NOW()) + 12, MINUTE(NOW()), SECOND(NOW()))
```

Unlike the DATE() function, the TIME() function doesn't enable you to simply add an hour, a minute, or a second to a specified time. For example, consider the following expression:

```
NOW() + 1
```

All this does is add 1 day to the current date and time.

If you want to add hours, minutes, and seconds to a time, you need to express the added time as a fraction of a day. For example, because there are 24 hours in a day, 1 hour is represented by the expression 1/24. Similarly, because there are 60 minutes in an hour, 1 minute is represented by the expression 1/24/60. Finally, because there are 60 seconds in a minute, 1 second is represented by the expression 1/24/60/60. Table 10.6 shows you how to use these expressions to add *n* hours, minutes, and seconds.

Table 10.6   Adding Hours, Minutes, and Seconds

Operation	Expression	Example	Example Expression
Add *n* hours	n*(1/24)	Add 6 hours	NOW()+6*(1/24)
Add *n* minutes	n*(1/24/60)	Add 15 minutes	NOW()+15*(1/24/60)
Add *n* seconds	n*(1/24/60/60)	Add 30 seconds	NOW()+30*(1/24/60/60)

Summing Time Values

When working with time values in Excel, you need to be aware that there are two subtly different interpretations for the phrase "adding one time to another":

■ **Adding time values to get a future time**—As you saw in the previous section, adding hours, minutes, or seconds to a time returns a value that represents a future time. For example, if the current time is 11:00 p.m. (23:00), adding 2 hours returns the time 1:00 a.m.

■ **Adding time values to get a total time**—In this interpretation, time values are summed to get a total number of hours, minutes, and seconds. This is useful if you want to know how many hours an employee worked in a week or how many hours to bill a client. In this case, for example, if the current total is 23 hours, adding 2 hours brings the total to 25 hours.

The problem is that adding time values to get a future time is Excel's default interpretation for added time values. So, if cell A1 contains 23:00 and cell A2 contains 2:00, the following formula returns `1:00:00 AM`:

```
=A1 + A2
```

The time value 25:00:00 is stored internally, but Excel adjusts the display so that you see the "correct" value `1:00:00 AM`. If you want to see 25:00:00 instead, apply the following custom format to the cell:

```
[h]:mm:ss
```

Calculating the Difference Between Two Times

Excel treats time serial numbers as decimal expansions (numbers between 0 and 1) that represent fractions of a day. Because they're just numbers, there's nothing to stop you from subtracting one from another to determine the difference between them:

```
EndTime - StartTime
```

This expression works just fine, as long as *EndTime* is greater than *StartTime*. (I used the names *EndTime* and *StartTime* purposefully so you'd remember to always subtract the later time from the earlier time.)

However, there's one scenario in which this expression fails: If *EndTime* occurs after midnight the next day, there's a good chance that it will be less than *StartTime*. For example, if a person works from 11:00 p.m. to 7:00 a.m., the expression `7:00 AM - 11:00 PM` results in an illegal negative time value. (Excel displays the result as a series of # symbols that fill the cell.)

To ensure that you get the correct positive result in this situation, use the following generic expression:

```
IF(EndTime < StartTime, 1 + EndTime - StartTime, EndTime - StartTime)
```

The `IF()` function checks to see whether *EndTime* is less than *StartTime*. If it is, 1 is added to the value *EndTime - StartTime* to get the correct result; otherwise, just *EndTime - StartTime* is returned.

Case Study: Building an Employee Time Sheet

In this case study, you'll put your new knowledge of time functions and calculations to good use building a time sheet that tracks the number of hours an employee works each week, takes into account hours worked on weekends and holidays, and calculates the total number of hours and the weekly pay. Figure 10.5 shows the completed time sheet.

Before starting, you need to understand three terms used in this case study:

- **Regular hours**—These are hours worked for regular pay.
- **Overtime hours**—These are hours worked beyond the maximum number of regular hours, as well as any hours worked on the weekend.
- **Holiday hours**—These are hours worked on a statutory holiday.

10

Figure 10.5
This employee time sheet tracks the daily hours, takes weekends and holidays into account, and calculates the employee's total working hours and pay.

| | H9 | | ▼ | : | × | ✓ | *fx* | =IF(OR(WEEKDAY(A9) = 7, WEEKDAY(A9) = 1), F9, 0) | |

	A	B	C	D	E	F	G	H	I
2	Employee Name:			Kyra Harper					
3	Maximum Hours Before Overtime:			40:00					
4	Hourly Wage:			$10.50					
5	Overtime Pay Rate:			1.5					
6	Holiday Pay Rate:			2					
7									
8	Date	Work Start Time	Lunch Start Time	Lunch End Time	Work End Time	Total Hours Worked	Non-Weekend, Non-Holiday Hours	Overtime Hours	Holiday Hours
9	Monday Sep 5, 2016	9:00 AM	12:00 PM	1:00 PM	6:00 PM	8:00	0:00	0:00	8:00
10	Tuesday Sep 6, 2016	8:00 AM	12:30 PM	1:45 PM	6:00 PM	8:45	8:45	0:00	0:00
11	Wednesday Sep 7, 2016	11:00 PM	3:00 AM	4:00 AM	9:00 AM	9:00	9:00	0:00	0:00
12	Thursday Sep 8, 2016	10:30 PM	2:00 AM	3:00 AM	5:00 AM	17:30	17:30	0:00	0:00
13	Friday Sep 9, 2016	7:00 PM	11:30 PM	12:30 AM	4:00 AM	8:00	8:00	0:00	0:00
14	Saturday Sep 10, 2016	12:00 PM	3:00 PM	3:30 PM	6:00 PM	5:30	0:00	5:30	0:00
15	Sunday Sep 11, 2016	12:00 PM			4:00 PM	4:00	0:00	4:00	0:00

Entering the Time Sheet Data

Let's begin at the top of the time sheet, where the following data is required:

■ **Employee Name**—You'll create a separate sheet for each employee, so enter the person's name here. You might also want to augment this with the date the person started or other data about the employee.

■ **Maximum Hours Before Overtime**—This is the number of regular hours an employee has to work in a week before overtime hours take effect. Enter the number using the hh:mm format. Cell D3 uses the [h]:mm custom format, to ensure that Excel displays the actual value.

■ **Hourly Wage**—This is the amount the employee earns per regular hour of work.

■ **Overtime Pay Rate**—This is the factor by which the employee's hourly rate is increased for overtime hours. For example, enter **1.5** if the employee earns time and a half for overtime.

■ **Holiday Pay Rate**—This is the factor by which the employee's hourly rate is increased for holiday hours. For example, enter **2** if the employee earns double time for holidays.

Calculating the Daily Hours Worked

Figure 10.6 shows the portion of the time sheet used to record the employee's daily hours worked. For each day, you enter five items:

■ **Date**—Enter the date the employee worked. This is formatted to show the day of the week, which is useful for confirming overtime hours worked on weekends.

■ **Work Start Time**—Enter the time of day the employee began working.

■ **Lunch Start Time**—Enter the time of day the employee stopped for lunch.

■ **Lunch End Time**—Enter the time of day the employee resumed working after lunch.

■ **Work End Time**—Enter the time of day the employee stopped working.

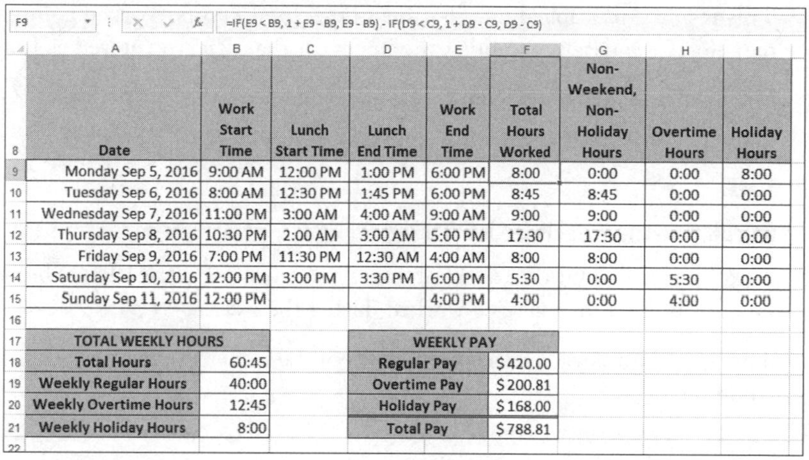

Figure 10.6
The section of the employee time sheet in which you enter the hours worked and in which the total daily hours are calculated.

F9		× ✓ fx	=IF(E9 < B9, 1 + E9 - B9, E9 - B9) - IF(D9 < C9, 1 + D9 - C9, D9 - C9)						

	A	B	C	D	E	F	G	H	I
8	Date	Work Start Time	Lunch Start Time	Lunch End Time	Work End Time	Total Hours Worked	Non-Weekend, Non-Holiday Hours	Overtime Hours	Holiday Hours
9	Monday Sep 5, 2016	9:00 AM	12:00 PM	1:00 PM	6:00 PM	8:00	0:00	0:00	8:00
10	Tuesday Sep 6, 2016	8:00 AM	12:30 PM	1:45 PM	6:00 PM	8:45	8:45	0:00	0:00
11	Wednesday Sep 7, 2016	11:00 PM	3:00 AM	4:00 AM	9:00 AM	9:00	9:00	0:00	0:00
12	Thursday Sep 8, 2016	10:30 PM	2:00 AM	3:00 AM	5:00 PM	17:30	17:30	0:00	0:00
13	Friday Sep 9, 2016	7:00 PM	11:30 PM	12:30 AM	4:00 AM	8:00	8:00	0:00	0:00
14	Saturday Sep 10, 2016	12:00 PM	3:00 PM	3:30 PM	6:00 PM	5:30	0:00	5:30	0:00
15	Sunday Sep 11, 2016	12:00 PM			4:00 PM	4:00	0:00	4:00	0:00
16									
17	**TOTAL WEEKLY HOURS**				**WEEKLY PAY**				
18	Total Hours	60:45			Regular Pay	$420.00			
19	Weekly Regular Hours	40:00			Overtime Pay	$200.81			
20	Weekly Overtime Hours	12:45			Holiday Pay	$168.00			
21	Weekly Holiday Hours	8:00			Total Pay	$788.81			
22									

The first calculation occurs in Total Hours Worked (column F). The idea here is to sum the number of hours the employee worked in a given day. The first part of the calculation uses the time-difference formula from the previous section to derive the number of hours between the Work Start Time (column B) and the Work End Time (column E). Here's the expression for the first entry (row 9):

```
IF(E9 < B9, 1 + E9 - B9, E9 - B9)
```

However, you also have to subtract the time the employee took for lunch, which is the difference between Lunch Start Time (column C) and Lunch End Time (column D). Here's the expression for the first entry (row 9):

```
IF(D9 < C9, 1 + D9 - C9, D9 - C9)
```

Let's skip over to the Weekend Hours calculation (column H). The idea behind this column is that if the employee worked on the weekend, all of the hours worked should be booked as overtime hours. So, the formula checks to see whether the date is a Saturday or Sunday:

```
=IF(OR(WEEKDAY(A9) = 7, WEEKDAY(A9) = 1), F9, 0)
```

If the OR() function returns TRUE, the date is on the weekend, so the value from the Total Hours Worked column (F9, in the example) is entered into the Weekend Hours column; otherwise, 0 is returned.

Next up is the Holiday Hours calculation (column I). Here, you want to see if the date is a statutory holiday. If it is, all of the hours worked that day should be booked as holiday hours. To that end, the formula checks to see if the date is part of the range of holiday dates calculated earlier in this chapter:

```
{=SUM(IF(A9 = Holidays!F4:F13, 1, 0)) * F9}
```

This is an array formula that compares the date with the dates in the holiday range (Holidays!F4:F13). If a match occurs, the SUM() function returns 1; otherwise, it returns 0.

This result is multiplied by the value in the Total Hours Worked column (F9, in the example). So, if the date is a holiday, the hours for that day are entered as holiday hours.

Finally, the value in the Non-Weekend, Non-Holiday Hours column (G) is calculated by subtracting Weekend Hours and Holiday Hours from Total Hours Worked:

```
=F9 - H9 - I9
```

Calculating the Weekly Hours Worked

Next up is the Total Weekly Hours section (refer to Figure 10.5), which adds the various types of hours the employee worked during the week.

The Total Hours value is a straight sum of the values in the Total Hours Worked column (F):

```
=SUM(F9:F15)
```

To derive the Weekly Regular Hours value, the calculation has to check to see if the total in the Non-Weekend, Non-Holiday Hours column (G) exceeds the number in the Maximum Hours Before Overtime cell (D3):

```
=IF(SUM(G9:G15) > D3, D3, SUM(G9:G15))
```

If this is true, the value in D3 is entered as the Regular Hours value; otherwise, the sum is entered.

Calculating the Weekly Overtime Hours value is a two-step process: First, you have to check to see if the sum in the Non-Weekend, Non-Holiday Hours column (G) exceeds the number in the Maximum Hours Before Overtime cell (D3). If so, the number of overtime hours is the difference between them; otherwise, it's 0:

```
IF(SUM(G9:G15) > D3, SUM(G9:G15) - D3, "0:00")
```

Second, you need to add the sum of the Overtime Hours column (H):

```
=IF(SUM(G9:G15) > D3, SUM(G9:G15) - D3, "0:00") + SUM(H9:H15)
```

Finally, the Weekly Holiday Hours value is a straight sum of the values in the Holiday Hours column (I):

```
=SUM(I9:I15)
```

Calculating the Weekly Pay

The final section of the time sheet is the Weekly Pay calculation. The dollar amounts for Regular Pay, Overtime Pay, and Holiday Pay are calculated as follows:

```
Regular Pay = Weekly Regular Hours * Hourly Wage * 24
Overtime Pay = Weekly Overtime Hours * Hourly Wage * Overtime Pay Rate * 24
Holiday Pay = Weekly Holiday Hours * Hourly Wage * Holiday Pay Rate * 24
```

Note that you need to multiply by 24 to convert the time value to a real number. Finally, the Total Pay is the sum of these values.

From Here

- For more information on formatting dates and times, **see** "Formatting Numbers, Dates, and Times," **p. 74**.

- For a general discuss of function syntax, **see** "The Structure of a Function," **p. 130**.

- To learn how to convert nonstandard date strings to dates, **see** "A Date-Conversion Formula," **p. 154**.

- To learn how to use CHOOSE() to convert the WEEKDAY() return value into a day name, **see** "Determining the Name of the Day of the Week," **p. 194**.

10

Working with Math Functions

11

Excel's mathematical underpinnings are revealed in the long list of math-related functions that come with the program. Functions exist for basic mathematical operations such as absolute values, lowest and greatest common denominators, square roots, and sums. Plenty of high-end operations also are available for things such as matrix multiplication, multinomials, and sums of squares. Not all of Excel's math functions are useful in a business context, but a surprising number of them are. For example, operations such as rounding and generating random numbers have business uses.

Excel's Math and Trig Functions

Table 11.1 lists the Excel math functions, but this chapter doesn't cover the entire list. Instead, I just focus on those functions that I think you'll find useful for your business formulas. Remember, too, that Excel comes with many statistical functions, covered in Chapter 12, "Working with Statistical Functions."

Table 11.1 Excel's Math Functions

Function	Description
ABS(*number*)	Returns the absolute value of *number*.
ARABIC(*string*)	Converts the roman numeral specified by *string* into its Arabic equivalent.
AGGREGATE(*function_num,options, ref1[,ref2,...]*)	Applies the function given by *function_num* (such as 1 for AVERAGE) to the specified range or table.
BASE(*number,radix [,min_length]*)	Converts *number* to the base given by *radix* (for example, set *radix* to 2 for binary).
CEILING.MATH(*number [,significance,mode]*)	Rounds *number* up to the nearest integer.
COMBIN(*number,number_chosen*)	Returns the number of unique ways that *number* objects can be combined in groups of *number_chosen*.
COMBINA(*number,number_chosen*)	Returns the number of non-unique ways that *number* objects can be combined in groups of *number_chosen*.
DECIMAL(*number,radix*)	Converts *number* to decimal from the base given by *radix*.
EVEN(*number*)	Rounds *number* up to the nearest even integer.
EXP(*number*)	Returns *e* raised to the power of *number*.
FACT(*number*)	Returns the factorial of *number*.
FACTDOUBLE(*number*)	Returns the double factorial of *number*.
FLOOR.MATH(*number[, significance, mode]*)	Rounds *number* down to the nearest integer.
GCD(*number1[,number2,...]*)	Returns the greatest common divisor of the specified numbers.
INT(*number*)	Rounds *number* down to the nearest integer.
LCM(*number1[,number2,...]*)	Returns the least common multiple of the specified numbers.
LN(*number*)	Returns the natural logarithm of *number*.
LOG(*number[,base]*)	Returns the logarithm of *number* in the specified *base*.
LOG10(*number*)	Returns the base-10 logarithm of *number*.
MDETERM(*array*)	Returns the matrix determinant of *array*.
MINVERSE(*array*)	Returns the matrix inverse of *array*.
MMULT(*array1,array2*)	Returns the matrix product of *array1* and *array2*.
MOD(*number,divisor*)	Returns the remainder of *number* after dividing by *divisor*.
MROUND(*number,multiple*)	Rounds *number* to the desired *multiple*.
MULTINOMIAL(*number1[,number2]*)	Returns the multinomial of the specified numbers.
MUNIT(*dimension*)	Returns the unit matrix for the specified *dimension* (for example, dimension 3 returns a 3×3-unit matrix).

11

Function	Description
ODD(*number*)	Rounds *number* up to the nearest odd integer.
PI()	Returns the value pi.
POWER(*number*,*power*)	Raises *number* to the specified *power*.
PRODUCT(*number1*[,*number2*,...])	Multiplies the specified numbers.
QUOTIENT(*numerator*,*denominator*)	Returns the integer portion of the result obtained by dividing *numerator* by *denominator* (that is, the remainder is discarded from the result).
RAND()	Returns a random number between 0 and 1.
RANDBETWEEN(*bottom*,*top*)	Returns a random number between *bottom* and *top*.
ROMAN(*number*[,*form*])	Converts the Arabic *number* to its Roman numeral equivalent (as text).
ROUND(*number*,*num_digits*)	Rounds *number* to a specified number of digits.
ROUNDDOWN(*number*,*num_digits*)	Rounds *number* down, toward 0.
ROUNDUP(*number*,*num_digits*)	Rounds *number* up, away from 0.
SERIESSUM(*x*,*n*,*m*,*coefficients*)	Returns the sum of a power series.
SIGN(*number*)	Returns the sign of *number* (1 = positive, 0 = zero, -1 = negative).
SQRT(*number*)	Returns the positive square root of *number*.
SQRTPI(*number*)	Returns the positive square root of the result of the expression *number* * *pi*.
SUBTOTAL(*function_num*,*ref1*[,*ref2*,...])	Returns a subtotal from a list.
SUM(*number1*[,*number2*,...])	Adds the arguments.
SUMIF(*range*,*criteria*[,*sum_range*])	Adds only those cells in *range* that meet the *criteria*.
SUMIFS(*sum_range*,*criteria_range*,*criteria*,...)	Adds only those cells in each *sum_range* that correspond to the items in each *criteria_range* that satisfy each *criteria*.
SUMPRODUCT(*array1*,*array2*[,*array3*,...])	Multiplies the corresponding elements in the specified arrays and then sums the resulting products.
SUMSQ(*number1*[,*number2*,...])	Returns the sum of the squares of the arguments.
SUMX2MY2(*array_x*,*array_y*)	Squares the elements in the specified arrays and then sums the differences between the corresponding squares.
SUMX2PY2(*array_x*,*array_y*)	Squares the elements in the specified arrays and then sums the corresponding squares.
SUMXMY2(*array_x*,*array_y*)	Squares the differences between the corresponding elements in the specified arrays and then sums the squares.
TRUNC(*number*[,*num_digits*])	Truncates *number* to an integer.

11

Although I don't discuss the details of Excel's trig functions in this book, Table 11.2 lists all of them. Here are some notes to keep in mind when you use these functions:

- In each function syntax, *number* is an angle expressed in radians.
- If you have an angle in degrees, convert it to radians by multiplying it by PI()/180. Alternatively, use the RADIANS(*angle*) function to convert *angle* from degrees to radians.
- A trig function returns a value in radians. If you need to convert a result to degrees, multiply it by 180/PI(). Alternatively, use the DEGREES(*angle*) function, which converts *angle* from radians to degrees.

Table 11.2   Excel's Trigonometric Functions

Function	Description
ACOS(*number*)	Returns a value in radians between 0 and pi that represents the arccosine of *number* (which must be between –1 and 1).
ACOSH(number)	Returns a value in radians that represents the inverse hyperbolic cosine of *number* (which must be greater than or equal to 1).
ACOT(*number*)	Returns a value in radians between 0 and pi that represents the arccotangent of *number*.
ACOTH(*number*)	Returns a value in radians that represents the inverse hyperbolic arccotangent of *number*.
ASIN(*number*)	Returns a value in radians between –pi/2 and pi/2 that represents the arcsine of *number* (which must be between –1 and 1).
ASINH(*number*)	Returns a value in radians that represents the inverse hyperbolic sine of *number*.
ATAN(*number*)	Returns a value in radians between –pi/2 and pi/2 that represents the arctangent of *number*.
ATAN2(*x_num*, *y_num*)	Returns a value in radians between (but not including) –pi and pi that represents the arctangent of the coordinates given by *x_num* and *y_num*.
ATANH(*number*)	Returns a value in radians that represents the inverse hyperbolic tangent of *number* (which must be between –1 and 1).
COS(*number*)	Returns a value in radians that represents the cosine of *number*.
COSH(*number*)	Returns a value in radians that represents the hyperbolic cosine of *number*.
COT(*number*)	Returns a value in radians that represents the cotangent of *number*.
COTH(*number*)	Returns a value in radians that represents the hyperbolic cotangent of *number*.
CSC(*number*)	Returns a value in radians that represents the cosecant of *number*.
CSCH(*number*)	Returns a value in radians that represents the hyperbolic cosecant of *number*.
DEGREES(*angle*)	Converts *angle* from radians to degrees.

11

Function	Description
RADIANS(*angle*)	Converts *angle* from degrees to radians.
SEC(*number*)	Returns a value in radians that represents the secant of *number*.
SECH(*number*)	Returns a value in radians that represents the hyperbolic secant of *number*.
SIN(*number*)	Returns a value in radians that represents the sine of *number*.
SINH(*number*)	Returns a value in radians that represents the hyperbolic sine of *number*.
TAN(*number*)	Returns a value in radians that represents the tangent of *number*.
TANH(*number*)	Returns a value in radians that represents the hyperbolic tangent of *number*.

Understanding Excel's Rounding Functions

Excel's rounding functions are useful in many situations, such as setting price points, adjusting billable time to the nearest 15 minutes, and ensuring that you're dealing with integer values for discrete numbers, such as inventory counts.

The problem is that Excel has so many rounding functions that it's difficult to know which one to use in a given situation. To help you, this section looks at the details of—and differences between—Excel's 10 rounding functions: ROUND(), MROUND(), ROUNDUP(), ROUNDDOWN(), CEILING.MATH(), FLOOR.MATH(), EVEN(), ODD(), INT(), and TRUNC().

The ROUND() Function

The rounding function you'll use most often is ROUND():

```
ROUND(number, num_digits)
```

number	The number you want to round
num_digits	An integer that specifies the number of digits you want *number* rounded to, as explained here:

num_digits	Description
> 0	Rounds *number* to *num_digits* decimal places
0	Rounds *number* to the nearest integer
< 0	Rounds *number* to *num_digits* to the left of the decimal point

Table 11.3 demonstrates the effect of the *num_digits* argument on the results of the ROUND() function. Here, *number* is 1234.5678.

Table 11.3 Effect of the `num_digits` Argument on the ROUND() Function Result

num_digits	Result of ROUND(1234.5678, num_digits)
3	1234.568
2	1234.57
1	1234.6
0	1235
-1	1230
-2	1200
-3	1000

The MROUND() Function

MROUND() is a function that rounds a number to a specified multiple:

MROUND(*number*, *multiple*)

number	The number you want to round
multiple	The multiple to which you want *number* rounded

Table 11.4 demonstrates MROUND() with a few examples. Note that if *number* and *multiple* have different signs, MROUND() produces the #NUM! error.

Table 11.4 Examples of the MROUND() Function

number	multiple	MROUND() Result
5	2	6
11	5	10
13	5	15
5	5	5
7.31	0.5	7.5
-11	-5	-10
-11	5	#NUM!

The ROUNDDOWN() and ROUNDUP() Functions

The ROUNDDOWN() and ROUNDUP() functions are similar to ROUND(), except that they always round in a single direction: ROUNDDOWN() always rounds a number toward 0, and ROUNDUP() always rounds away from 0. Here is the syntax for each of these functions:

```
ROUNDDOWN(number, num_digits)
ROUNDUP(number, num_digits)
```

number	The number you want to round
num_digits	An integer that specifies the number of digits you want *number* rounded to, as explained here:

num_digits	Description
> 0	Rounds *number* down or up to *num_digits* decimal places
0	Rounds *number* down or up to the nearest integer
< 0	Rounds *number* down or up to *num_digits* to the left of the decimal point

Table 11.5 tries out ROUNDDOWN() and ROUNDUP() with a few examples.

Table 11.5   Examples of the ROUNDDOWN() and ROUNDUP() Functions

number	num_digits	ROUNDDOWN()	ROUNDUP()
1.1	0	1	2
1.678	2	1.67	1.68
1234	-2	1200	1300
-1.1	0	-1	-2
-1234	-2	-1200	-1300

The CEILING.MATH() and FLOOR.MATH() Functions

The CEILING.MATH() and FLOOR.MATH() functions are an amalgam of the features found in MROUND(), ROUNDDOWN(), and ROUNDUP(). Here is the syntax of each one:

```
CEILING.MATH(number[, significance, mode])
FLOOR.MATH(number[, significance, mode])
```

number	The number you want to round
significance	The multiple to which you want *number* rounded; the default value is 1
mode	Determines whether Excel rounds negative numbers toward or away from zero.

Both functions round the value given by *number* to a multiple of the value given by *significance*, but they differ in how they perform this rounding:

- CEILING.MATH() rounds positive numbers *away from* 0 and negative numbers *toward* 0. For example, CEILING.MATH(1.56, 0.1) returns 1.6, and CEILING.MATH(-2.33, 0.5) returns -2. If you prefer to round negative numbers *away* from 0, add the *mode* parameter with any nonzero value.

■ FLOOR.MATH() rounds positive numbers *toward* 0 and negative numbers *away from* 0. For example, FLOOR.MATH(1.56, 0.1) returns 1.5, and FLOOR.MATH(-2.33, -.5) returns -2.35. If you prefer to round negative numbers *toward* 0, add the *mode* parameter with any nonzero value.

Determining the Fiscal Quarter in Which a Date Falls

When working with budget-related or other financial worksheets, you often need to know the fiscal quarter in which a particular date falls. For example, a budget increase formula might need to alter the increase depending on the quarter.

You can use the CEILING.MATH() function combined with the DATEDIF() function from Chapter 10, "Working with Date and Time Functions," to calculate the quarter for a given date:

```
=CEILING.MATH((DATEDIF(FiscalStart, MyDate, "m") + 1) / 3, 1)
```

→ To learn about DATEDIF(), **see** "The DATEDIF() Function," **p. 224**.

Here, *FiscalStart* is the date on which the fiscal year begins, and *MyDate* is the date you want to work with. This formula uses DATEDIF() with the *m* parameter to return the number of months between the two dates. The formula adds 1 to the result (to avoid getting a 0th quarter) and then divides by 3. Applying CEILING.MATH() to the result gives the quarter in which *MyDate* occurs.

Calculating Easter Dates

If you live or work in the United States, you'll rarely have to calculate for business purposes when Easter Sunday falls because there's no statutory holiday associated with Easter. However, if Good Friday or Easter Monday is a statutory holiday where you live (as Good Friday is in Canada and Easter Monday is in Britain), or if you're responsible for businesses in such jurisdictions, it can be handy to calculate when Easter falls in a given year.

Unfortunately, there's no straightforward way of calculating Easter. The official formula is that Easter falls on the first Sunday after the first ecclesiastical full moon after the spring equinox. Mathematicians have tried for centuries to come up with a formula, and although some have succeeded (most notably the famous mathematician Carl Friedrich Gauss), the resulting algorithms have been hideously complex.

Here's a relatively simple worksheet formula that employs the FLOOR.MATH() function and that works for the years 1900 to 2078:

```
=FLOOR.MATH(DATE(B1, 5, DAY(MINUTE(B1 / 38) / 2 + 56)), 7) - 36
```

This formula assumes that the current year is in cell B1.

→ To learn how to calculate when Good Friday and Easter Monday fall, **see** "Calculating Holiday Dates," **p. 221**.

The EVEN() and ODD() Functions

The EVEN() and ODD() functions round a single numeric argument:

```
EVEN(number)
ODD(number)
```

    number   The number you want to round

Both functions round the value given by *number* away from 0, as follows:

- EVEN() rounds to the next even number. For example, EVEN(14.2) returns 16, and EVEN(-23) returns -24.

- ODD() rounds to the next odd number. For example, ODD(58.1) returns 59 and ODD(-6) returns -7.

The INT() and TRUNC() Functions

The INT() and TRUNC() functions are similar in that you can use both of them to convert a value to its integer portion:

```
INT(number)
TRUNC(number[, num_digits])
```

    number   The *number* you want to round

    num_digits   An integer that specifies the number of digits you want *number* rounded to, as explained here:

num_digits	Description
> 0	Truncates all but *num_digits* decimal places
0	Truncates all decimal places (the default)
< 0	Converts *num_digits* to the left of the decimal point into zeros

For example, INT(6.75) returns 6, and TRUNC(3.6) returns 3. However, these functions have two major differences that you should keep in mind:

- For negative values, INT() returns the next number away from 0. For example, INT(-3.42) returns -4. If you just want to lop off the decimal part, you need to use TRUNC() instead.

- You can use the TRUNC() function's second argument (*num_digits*) to specify the number of decimal places to leave on. For example, TRUNC(123.456, 2) returns 123.45, and TRUNC(123.456, -2) returns 100.

Using Rounding to Prevent Calculation Errors

Most of us are comfortable dealing with numbers in decimal—or base-10—format (the odd hexadecimal-loving computer geek notwithstanding). Computers, however, prefer to work in the simpler confines of the binary—or base-2—system. So when you plug a value into a cell or formula, Excel converts it from decimal to its binary equivalent, makes its calculations, and then converts the binary result back into decimal format.

This procedure is fine for integers because every decimal integer value has an exact binary equivalent. However, many noninteger values don't have exact equivalents in the binary world. Excel can only approximate such numbers, and that approximation can lead to errors in formulas. For example, try entering the following formula into any worksheet cell:

```
=0.01 = (2.02 - 2.01)
```

This formula compares the value 0.01 with the expression 2.02 - 2.01. These should be equal, of course, but when you enter the formula, Excel returns a FALSE result. What gives?

The problem is that, in converting the expression 2.02 - 2.01 into binary and back again, Excel picks up a stray digit in its travels. To see it, enter the formula =2.02 - 2.01 in a cell and then format it to show 16 decimal places. You should see the following surprising result:

```
0.0100000000000002
```

That wanton 2 in the 16th decimal place is what threw off the original calculation. To fix the problem, use the TRUNC() function (or possibly the ROUND() function, depending on the situation) to lop off the extra digits to the right of the decimal point. For example, the following formula produces a TRUE result:

```
=0.01 = TRUNC(2.02 - 2.01, 2)
```

Setting Price Points

One common worksheet task is to calculate a list price for a product based on the result of a formula that factors in production costs and profit margin. If the product will be sold at retail, you'll likely want the decimal (cents) portion of the price to be .95, .99, or some other standard value. You can use the INT() function to help with this "rounding."

For example, the simplest case is to always round up the decimal part to .95. Here's a formula that does this:

```
=INT(RawPrice) + 0.95
```

Assuming that *RawPrice* is the result of the formula that factors in costs and profit, the formula simply adds 0.95 to the integer portion. (Note, too, that if the decimal portion of *RawPrice* is greater than .95, the formula rounds down to .95.)

Another case is to round up to .50 for decimal portions less than or equal to 0.5 and to round up to .95 for decimal portions greater than 0.5. Here's a formula that handles this scenario:

```
=INT(RawPrice) + IF(RawPrice - INT(RawPrice) <= 0.5, .50, .95)
```

Again, the integer portion is stripped from the *RawPrice*. Also, the IF() function checks to see whether the decimal portion is less than or equal to 0.5. If it is, the value .50 is returned; otherwise, the value .95 is returned. This result is added to the integer portion.

Case Study: Rounding Billable Time

An ideal use of MROUND() is to round billable time to some multiple number of minutes. For example, it's common to round billable time to the nearest 15 minutes. You can do this with MROUND() by using the following generic form of the function:

```
MROUND(BillableTime, 0:15)
```

Here, `BillableTime` is the time value you want to round. For example, the following expression returns the time value 2:15:

```
MROUND(2:10, 0:15)
```

Using MROUND() to round billable time has one significant flaw: Many (perhaps even most) people who bill their time prefer to round up to the nearest 15 minutes (or whatever). If the minute component of the MROUND() function's *number* argument is less than half the *multiple* argument, MROUND() rounds *down* to the nearest multiple.

To fix this problem, use the CEILING.MATH() function instead because it always rounds away from 0. Note, however, that CEILING.MATH() will only work in this scenario if you express your times using the TIME() function. Here's the generic expression to use for rounding up to the next 15-minute multiple:

```
CEILING.MATH(TIME(BillableHours,BillableMinutes,BillableSeconds,)
TIME(0,15,0))
```

Here, `BillableHours`, `BillableMinutes`, and `BillableSeconds` are the components of the time value you want to round. For example, the following expression rounds the time value 2:05 up to the time value 2:15:

```
CEILING.MATH(TIME(2, 5, 0), TIME(0, 15, 0))
```

Summing Values

Summing values—whether it's a range of cells, function results, literal numeric values, or expression results—is perhaps the most common spreadsheet operation. Excel enables you to add values by using the addition operator (+), but it's often more convenient to sum a number of values by using the SUM() function, which you'll learn more about in the next section.

The SUM() Function

Here's the syntax of the SUM() function:

```
SUM(number1[, number2, ...])
```

> *number1, number2,...* The values you want to add

In Excel 2007 and later, you can enter up to 255 arguments into the SUM() function. (In previous versions of Excel, the maximum number of arguments is 30.) Note, too, that you can enter the SUM() quickly by clicking the AutoSum command that appears in both the Home tab and the Formulas tab (or by pressing Alt+=).

11

For example, the following formula returns the sum of the values in three separate ranges:

```
=SUM(A2:A13, C2:C13, E2:E13)
```

> **TIP** If you need more than 255 arguments for the SUM() function, group multiple arguments together using parentheses. For example, SUM(A1, B1, C1, D1) uses four arguments, but Excel sees SUM((A1, B1), (C1, D1)) as using just two arguments.

Calculating Cumulative Totals

Many worksheets need to calculate cumulative totals. Most budget worksheets, for example, show cumulative totals for sales and expenses over the course of the fiscal year. Similarly, loan amortizations often show the cumulative interest and principal paid over the life of the loan.

Calculating these cumulative totals is straightforward. For example, see the worksheet shown in Figure 11.1. Column F tracks the cumulative interest on the loan, and cell F7 contains the following SUM() formula:

```
=SUM($D$7:D7)
```

Figure 11.1
The SUM() formulas in column F calculate the cumulative interest paid on a loan.

	A	B	C	D	E	F	G	H
						F7 =SUM($D$7:D7)		
1	Constants:							
2	Rate	6%						
3	Term	4						
4	Amount	$10,000						
5								
6	Period	Month	Payment	Interest	Principal	Total Interest	% Principal Paid	
7	1	Jun-16	$234.85	$50.00	$184.85	$50.00	1.85%	
8	2	Jul-16	$234.85	$49.08	$185.77	$99.08	3.71%	
9	3	Aug-16	$234.85	$48.15	$186.70	$147.22	5.57%	
10	4	Sep-16	$234.85	$47.21	$187.64	$194.44	7.45%	
11	5	Oct-16	$234.85	$46.28	$188.58	$240.71	9.34%	
12	6	Nov-16	$234.85	$45.33	$189.52	$286.04	11.23%	
13	7	Dec-16	$234.85	$44.38	$190.47	$330.43	13.14%	
14	8	Jan-17	$234.85	$43.43	$191.42	$373.86	15.05%	
15	9	Feb-17	$234.85	$42.48	$192.37	$416.34	16.97%	

> **NOTE** You can download this chapter's sample workbook at www.mcfedries.com/books/book.php?title=excel-2016-formulas-and-functions.

This formula just sums cell D7, which is no great feat. However, when you fill the range F7:F54 with this formula, the left part of the SUM() range ($D$7) remains anchored; the right side (D7) is relative and, therefore, changes. So, for example, the corresponding formula in cell F10 would be this:

```
=SUM($D$7:D10)
```

In case you're wondering, column G tracks the percentage of the total principal that has been paid off so far. Here's the formula used in cell G7:

```
=SUM($E$7:E7) / $B$4 * -1
```

The SUM($E$7:E7) part calculates the cumulative principal paid. To get the percentage, divide by the total principal (cell B4). The whole thing is multiplied by –1 to return a positive percentage.

Summing Only the Positive or Negative Values in a Range

If you have a range of numbers that contains both positive and negative values, what do you do if you need a total of only the negative values? Or only the positive ones? You could enter the individual cells into a SUM() function, but there's an easier way: use arrays.

To sum the negative values in a range, you use the following array formula:

```
{=SUM((range < 0) * range)}
```

Here, range is a range reference or named range. The range < 0 test returns TRUE (the equivalent of 1) for those range values that are less than 0; otherwise, it returns FALSE (the equivalent of 0). Therefore, only negative values get included in the SUM().

Similarly, you use the following array formula to sum only the positive values in range:

```
{=SUM((range > 0) * range)}
```

→You can apply much more sophisticated criteria to your sums by using the SUMIF() function. **See** "Using SUMIF()," **p. 314**.

The MOD() Function

The MOD() function calculates the remainder (or *modulus*) that results after dividing one number into another. Here's the syntax for this more-useful-than-you-think function:

```
MOD(number, divisor)
```

number	The dividend (that is, the number to be divided)
divisor	The number by which you want to divide number

For example, MOD(24, 10) equals 4 (that is, 24÷10 = 2, with remainder 4).

The MOD() function is well suited to values that are both sequential and cyclical. For example, the days of the week (as given by the WEEKDAY() function) run from 1 (Sunday) through

11

7 (Saturday) and then start over (the next Sunday is back to 1). So, the following formula always returns an integer that corresponds to a day of the week:

```
=MOD(number, 7) + 1
```

If `number` is any integer, the `MOD()` function returns integer values from 0 to 6, so adding 1 gives values from 1 to 7.

You can set up similar formulas using months (1 to 12), seconds or minutes (0 to 59), fiscal quarters (1 to 4), and more.

A Better Formula for Time Differences

In Chapter 10, I told you that subtracting an earlier time from a later time is problematic if the earlier time is before midnight and the later time is after midnight. Here's the expression I showed you to overcome this problem:

```
IF(EndTime < StartTime, 1 + EndTime - StartTime, EndTime - StartTime)
```

→ For the details on the time-difference formula, **see** "Calculating the Difference Between Two Times," **p. 231**.

However, time values are sequential and cyclical: They're real numbers that run from 0 to 1 and then start over at midnight. Therefore, you can use `MOD()` to greatly simplify the formula for calculating the difference between two times:

```
=MOD(EndTime - StartTime, 1)
```

This works for any value of `EndTime` and `StartTime`, as long as `EndTime` is later than `StartTime`.

Summing Every *n*th Row

Depending on the structure of your worksheet, you might need to sum only every *n*th row, where *n* is some integer. For example, you might want to sum only every 5th or 10th cell to get a sampling of the data.

You can accomplish this by applying the `MOD()` function to the result of the `ROW()` function, as in this array formula:

```
{=SUM(IF(MOD(ROW(Range), n) = 1, Range, 0))}
```

For each cell in `Range`, `MOD(ROW(Range), n)` returns 1 for every *n*th value. In that case, the value of the cell is added to the sum; otherwise, 0 is added. In other words, this sums the values in the first row of `Range`, the *n* + first row of `Range`, and so on. If instead you want the second row of `Range`, the *n* + second row of `Range`, and so on, compare the `MOD()` result with 2, like so:

```
{=SUM(IF(MOD(ROW(Range), n) = 2, Range, 0))}
```

Special Case No. 1: Summing Only Odd Rows

If you want to sum only the odd rows in a worksheet, use this straightforward variation on the formula:

```
{=SUM(IF(MOD(ROW(Range), 2) = 1, Range, 0))}
```

Special Case No. 2: Summing Only Even Rows

To sum only the even rows, you need to sum those cells where MOD(ROW(Range), 2) returns 0:

```
{=SUM(IF(MOD(ROW(Range), 2) = 0, Range, 0))}
```

Determining Whether a Year Is a Leap Year

If you need to determine whether a given year is a leap year, the MOD() function can help. Leap years (with some exceptions) are years divisible by 4. So, a year is (usually) a leap year if the following formula returns 0:

```
=MOD(year, 4)
```

In this case, *year* is a four-digit year number. This formula works for the years 1901 to 2099, which should take care of most people's needs. The formula doesn't work for 1900 and 2100 because, despite being divisible by 4, these years aren't leap years. The general rule is that a year is a leap year if it's divisible by 4 and it's not divisible by 100, *unless* it's also divisible by 400. Therefore, because 1900 and 2100 are divisible by 100 and not by 400, they aren't leap years. The year 2000, however, is a leap year. If you want a formula that takes the full rule into account, use the following one:

```
=(MOD(year, 4) = 0) - (MOD(year, 100) = 0) + (MOD(year, 400) = 0)
```

The three parts of the formula that compare a MOD() result to 0 return 1 or 0. Therefore, the result of this formula always is 0 for leap years and nonzero for all other years.

Creating Ledger Shading

Ledger shading is formatting in which rows alternate cell shading between a light color and a slightly darker color (for example, white and light gray). This type of shading is often seen in checkbook registers and account ledgers, but it's also useful in any worksheet that presents data in rows because it makes differentiating each row from its neighbors easier. Figure 11.2 shows an example.

11

Figure 11.2
This worksheet uses ledger shading for a checkbook register.

	A	B	C	D	E	F	G	H	I
1	Rec	Date	Num	Payee/Description	Category	Debit	Credit	✓	Balance
2	1	4/1/2016		Starting Balance			5,000.00	✓	5,000.00
3	2	4/3/2016		Withdrawal	Auto - Fuel	(20.00)			4,980.00
4	3	4/10/2016		Al's Auto Repair	Auto - Repair	(1,245.00)			3,735.00
5	4	4/13/2016			Salary		1,834.69		5,569.69
6									

However, ledger shading isn't easy to work with by hand:

- ■ If you have a large range to format, applying shading can take some time.
- ■ If you insert or delete a row, you have to reapply the formatting.

To avoid these headaches, you can use a trick that combines the MOD() function and Excel's conditional formatting. Here's how it's done:

1. Select the area you want to format with ledger shading.

2. Select Home, Conditional Formatting, New Rule to display the New Formatting Rule dialog box.

3. Click Use a Formula to Determine Which Cells to Format.

4. In the text box, enter the following formula:
   =MOD(ROW(), 2)

5. Click Format to display the Format Cells dialog box.

6. Select the Fill tab, click the color you want to use for the nonwhite ledger cells, and then click OK to return to the New Formatting Rule dialog box (see Figure 11.3).

7. Click OK.

Figure 11.3
This MOD() formula applies the cell shading to every second row (1, 3, 5, and so on).

The formula =MOD(ROW(), 2) returns 1 for odd-numbered rows and 0 for even-numbered rows. Because 1 is equivalent to TRUE, Excel applies the conditional formatting to the odd-numbered rows and leaves the even-numbered rows as they are.

T I P If you prefer to alternate shading on columns instead of on rows, use the following formula in the New Formatting Rule dialog box:

```
=MOD(COLUMN(), 2)
```

If you prefer to have the even rows shaded and the odd rows unshaded, use the following formula in the New Formatting Rule dialog box:

```
=MOD(ROW() + 1, 2)
```

Generating Random Numbers

If you're using a worksheet to set up a simulation, you need realistic data on which to do your testing. You could make up the numbers, but it's possible that you might unintentionally skew the data. A better approach is to generate the numbers randomly, using the worksheet functions RAND() and RANDBETWEEN().

→ Excel's Analysis ToolPak also comes with a tool for generating random numbers; **see** "Using the Random Number Generation Tool," **p. 285.**

11

The RAND() Function

The RAND() function returns a random number that is greater than or equal to 0 and less than 1. RAND() is often useful by itself. (For example, it's perfect for generating random time values.) However, you'll most often use it in an expression to generate random numbers between two values.

In the simplest case, if you want to generate random numbers greater than or equal to 0 and less than n, use the following expression:

```
RAND() * n
```

For example, the following formula generates a random number between 0 and 30:

```
=RAND() * 30
```

The more complex case is when you want random numbers greater than or equal to some number m and less than some number n. Here's the expression to use for this case:

```
RAND() * (n - m) + m
```

For example, the following formula produces a random number greater than or equal to 100 and less than 200:

```
=RAND() * (200 - 100) + 100
```

> ┌─ C A U T I O N ──
> RAND() is a volatile function, meaning that its value changes each time you recalculate or reopen
> the worksheet or edit any cell on the worksheet. To enter a static random number in a cell, type
> =RAND(), press F9 to evaluate the function and return a random number, and then press Enter to
> place the random number into the cell as a numeric literal.

Generating Random *n*-Digit Numbers

It's often useful to create random numbers with a specific number of digits. For example, you might want to generate a random six-digit account number for new customers, or you might need a random eight-digit number for a temporary filename.

The procedure for this is to start with the general formula from the previous section and apply the INT() function to ensure an integer result:

```
INT(RAND() * (n - m) + m)
```

In this case, however, you set *n* equal to 10^n, and you set *m* equal to 10^{n-1}:

```
INT(RAND() * (10ⁿ - 10ⁿ⁻¹) + 10ⁿ⁻¹)
```

For example, if you need a random eight-digit number, use this formula:

```
INT(RAND() * (100000000 - 10000000) + 10000000)
```

This generates random numbers greater than or equal to 10,000,000 and less than or equal to 99,999,999.

Generating a Random Letter

You normally use RAND() to generate a random number, but it's also useful for text values. For example, suppose that you need to generate a random letter of the alphabet. There are 26 letters in the alphabet, so you start with an expression that generates random integers greater than or equal to 1 and less than or equal to 26:

```
INT(RAND() * 26 + 1)
```

If you want a random uppercase letter (A to Z), note that these letters have character codes that run from ANSI 65 to ANSI 90, so you take the preceding formula, add 64, and plug in the result to the CHAR() function:

```
=CHAR(INT(RAND() * 26) + 65)
```

If you want a random lowercase letter (a to z) instead, note that these letters have character codes that run from ANSI 97 to ANSI 122, so you take the preceding formula, add 96, and plug the result into the CHAR() function:

```
=CHAR(INT(RAND() * 26) + 97)
```

Sorting Values Randomly

If you have a set of values on a worksheet, you might need to sort them in random order. For example, if you want to perform an operation on a subset of data, sorting the table randomly removes any numeric biases that might be inherent if the data was sorted in any way.

Follow these steps to randomly sort a data table:

1. Assuming that the data is arranged in rows, select a range in the column immediately to the left or right of the table. Make sure that the selected range has the same number of rows as the table.

2. Enter =RAND() and then press Ctrl+Enter to add the RAND() formula to every selected cell.

3. Select Formulas, Calculation Options, Manual.

4. Select the range that includes the data and the column of RAND() values.

5. Select Data, Sort to display the Sort dialog box.

6. In the Sort By list, select the column that contains the RAND() values.

7. Click OK.

8. Select Formulas, Calculation Options, Automatic and delete the RAND() formulas from the table.

This procedure tells Excel to sort the selected range according to the random values, thus sorting the data table randomly. Figure 11.4 shows an example. The data values are in column A, the RAND() values are in column B, and the range A2:B26 was sorted on column B.

The RANDBETWEEN() Function

Excel's RANDBETWEEN() function can simplify working with certain sets of random numbers. RANDBETWEEN() lets you specify a lower bound and an upper bound, and it returns a random integer between them:

```
RANDBETWEEN(bottom, top)
```

bottom   The smallest possible random integer. (That is, Excel generates a random number that is greater than or equal to *bottom*.)

top   The largest possible random integer. (That is, Excel generates a random number that is less than or equal to *top*.)

For example, the following formula returns a random integer between 0 and 59:

```
=RANDBETWEEN(0, 59)
```

Figure 11.4
To randomly sort data values, add a column of =RAND() formulas and then sort the entire range on the random values.

	A	B	C	D	E
1	Data Values	RAND() Values			
2	11	0.761440927			
3	6	0.31457355			
4	1	0.77868803			
5	18	0.126819265			
6	5	0.850611804			
7	10	0.225297755			
8	19	0.786535236			
9	3	0.01995069			
10	21	0.372743981			
11	13	0.452315554			
12	8	0.078090798			
13	9	0.367524739			
14	22	0.988395167			
15	16	0.134118234			
16	2	0.213973097			
17	7	0.650533735			
18	20	0.001210614			
19	12	0.932983948			
20	17	0.876957166			
21	25	0.724863909			
22	23	0.232539129			
23	14	0.812761069			
24	24	0.152750449			
25	15	0.534045045			
26	4	0.379005434			

B2 ▼ : × ✓ fx =RAND()

From Here

■ Excel comes with a large collection of statistical functions for calculating averages, maximums and minimums, standard deviations, and more. **See** Chapter 12, "Working with Statistical Functions," **p. 257**.

■ To learn how to create sophisticated distributions of random numbers, **see** "Using the Random Number Generation Tool," **p. 285**.

■ The SUMIF() function enables you to apply sophisticated criteria to sum operations. **See** "Using SUMIF()," **p. 314**.

Working with Statistical Functions

12

Excel's statistical functions calculate all the standard statistical measures, such as average, maximum, minimum, and standard deviation. For most of the statistical functions, you supply a list of values (which could be an entire *population* or just a *sample* from a population). You can enter individual values or cells, or you can specify a range.

Excel's Statistical Functions

Excel has dozens of statistical functions, many of which are rarely, if ever, used in business. Table 12.1 lists those statistical functions that have some utility in the business world.

Table 12.1   Statistical Functions of Use in the Business World

Function	Description
AVEDEV(number1[,number2,...])	Returns the average of the absolute deviations of the numeric arguments from their mean value.
AVERAGE(number1[,number2,...])	Returns the average of the numeric arguments.
AVERAGEA(value1[,value2,...])	Returns the average of the arguments, which can be non-numeric.
AVERAGEIF(range[,criteria, average_range])	Returns the average for those cells in range that satisfy the criteria.
AVERAGEIFS(range1,criteria1 [,range2,criteria2,...])	Returns the average for those cells in multiple ranges that satisfy their corresponding criteria.
CORREL(array1,array2)	Returns the correlation coefficient.
COUNT(value1[,value2,...])	Counts the numbers in the argument list.
COUNTA(value1[,value2,...])	Counts the values (numeric and non-numeric) in the argument list.
COUNTBLANK(range)	Counts the empty cells in range.
COUNTIF(range[,criteria])	Returns the count of those cells in range that satisfy the criteria.
COUNTIFS(range1,criteria1 [,range2,criteria2,...])	Returns the count of those cells in multiple ranges that satisfy their corresponding criteria.
COVAR(array1,array2)	The legacy version of the covariance calculation. Use this function if you need to maintain compatibility with Excel 2007 and earlier.
COVARIANCE.P(array1,array2)	Returns the population covariance, which is the average of the products of deviations for each data point pair.
F.TEST(array1, array2)	Returns an F-test result, the one-tailed probability that the variances in the two sets are not significantly different.
FORECAST.LINEAR(x,known_y's, known_x's)	Returns a forecast value for x based on a linear regression of the arrays known_y's and known_x's.
FREQUENCY(data_array,bins_array)	Returns a frequency distribution.
GROWTH(known_y's[,known_x's, new_x's,const])	Returns values along an exponential trend.
INTERCEPT(known_y's,known_x's)	Returns the y-intercept of the linear regression trend line generated by the known_y's and known_x's.
KURT(number1[,number2,...])	Returns the kurtosis of a frequency distribution.
LARGE(array,k)	Returns the kth largest value in array.
LINEST(known_y's[,known_x's, const,stats])	Uses the least squares method to calculate a straight-line regression fit through the known_y's and known_x's.
LOGEST(known_y's[,known_x's, const,stats])	Uses the least squares method to calculate an exponential regression fit through the known_y's and known_x's.

12

Function	Description
MAX(*number1*[,*number2*,...])	Returns the maximum value.
MAXA(*value1*[,*value2*,...])	Returns the maximum value, including text and Boolean values.
MEDIAN(*number1*[,*number2*,...])	Returns the median value.
MIN(*number1*[,*number2*,...])	Returns the minimum value.
MINA(*value1*[,*value2*,...])	Returns the minimum value, including text and Boolean values.
MODE.MULT(*number1*[,*number2*,...])	Returns an array of the most common values.
MODE.SNGL(*number1*[,*number2*,...])	Returns the most common value.
MODE(*number1*[,*number2*,...])	The legacy version of the mode calculation. Use this function if you need to maintain compatibility with Excel 2007 and earlier.
NORM.DIST(*x*, *mean*, *standard_dev*, *cumulative*)	Generates the normal distribution by returning the probability that x exists within a population.
PERCENTILE(*array*,*k*)	The legacy version of the percentile calculation. Use this function if you need to maintain compatibility with Excel 2007 and earlier.
PERCENTILE.EXC(*array*,*k*)	Returns the kth percentile of the values in *array*, where k is between 0 and 1, exclusive.
PERCENTILE.INC(*array*,*k*)	Returns the kth percentile of the values in *array*, where k is between 0 and 1, inclusive.
PERMUT(*number*,*number_chosen*)	Returns the total possible permutations, given *number* items and *number_chosen* items in each permutation.
RANK(*number*,*ref*[,*order*])	The legacy version of the rank calculation. Use this function if you need to maintain compatibility with Excel 2007 and earlier.
RANK.AVG(*number*,*ref*[,*order*])	Returns the rank of a number in a list or the average rank if more than one value has the same rank.
RANK.EQ(*number*,*ref*[,*order*])	Returns the rank of a number in a list or the first rank if more than one value has the same rank.
RSQ(*known_y's*,*known_x's*)	Returns the coefficient of determination that indicates how much of the variance in the *known_y's* is due to the *known_x's*.
SKEW(*number1*[,*number2*,...])	Returns the skewness of a frequency distribution.
SLOPE(*known_y's*,*known_x's*)	Returns the slope of the linear regression trend generated by the *known_y's* and *known_x's*.
SMALL(*array*,*k*)	Returns the kth smallest value in *array*.
STDEV(*number1*[,*number2*,...])	The legacy version of the standard deviation calculation. Use this function if you need to maintain compatibility with Excel 2007 and earlier.

12

Function	Description
STDEV.P(*number1*[,*number2*,...])	Returns the standard deviation based on an entire population.
STDEV.S(*number1*[,*number2*,...])	Returns the standard deviation based on a sample.
STDEVA(*value1*[,*value2*,...])	Returns the standard deviation based on a sample, which can include non-numeric values.
STDEVPA(*value1*[,*value2*,...])	Returns the standard deviation based on an entire population, which can include non-numeric values.
T.TEST(*array1*,*array2*,*tails*,*type*)	Returns the probability associated with a Student's t-test.
TREND(*known_y's*[,*known_x's*, *new_x's*,*const*])	Returns values along a linear trend.
VAR(*number1*[,*number2*,...])	The legacy version of the variance calculation. Use this function if you need to maintain compatibility with Excel 2007 and earlier.
VAR.P(*number1*[,*number2*,...])	Returns the variance based on an entire population.
VAR.S(*number1*[,*number2*,...])	Returns the variance based on a sample.
VARA(*value1*[,*value3*,...])	Returns the variance based on a sample, which can include non-numeric values.
VARPA(*value1*[,*value3*,...])	Returns the variance based on an entire population, which can include non-numeric values.
Z.TEST(*array*,*x*[,*sigma*])	Returns the p-value of a two-sample z-test for means with known variances.

→ For the details of the regression functions—FORECAST(), GROWTH(), INTERCEPT(), LINEST(), LOGEST(), RSQ(), SLOPE(), and TREND()—**see** Chapter 16, "Using Regression to Track Trends and Make Forecasts," **p. 371**.

Understanding Descriptive Statistics

One of the goals of this book is to show you how to use formulas and functions to turn a jumble of numbers and values into results and summaries that give you useful information about the data. Excel's statistical functions are particularly useful for extracting analytical sense out of data nonsense. Many of these functions might seem strange and obscure, but they reward a bit of patience and effort with striking new views of your data.

This is particularly true of the branch of statistics known casually as *descriptive statistics* (or *summary statistics*). As the name implies, descriptive statistics are used to describe various aspects of a data set, to give you a better overall picture of the phenomenon underlying the numbers. In Excel's statistical repertoire, 16 measures make up its descriptive statistics package: sum, count, mean, median, mode, maximum, minimum, range, *k*th largest, *k*th smallest, standard deviation, variance, standard error of the mean, confidence level, kurtosis, and skewness.

In this chapter, you'll learn how to wield all of these statistical measures (except sum, which you've already seen earlier in this book). The context is the worksheet database of product defects shown in Figure 12.1.

Figure 12.1
To demonstrate Excel's descriptive statistics capabilities, this chapter uses the data shown here in a database of product defects.

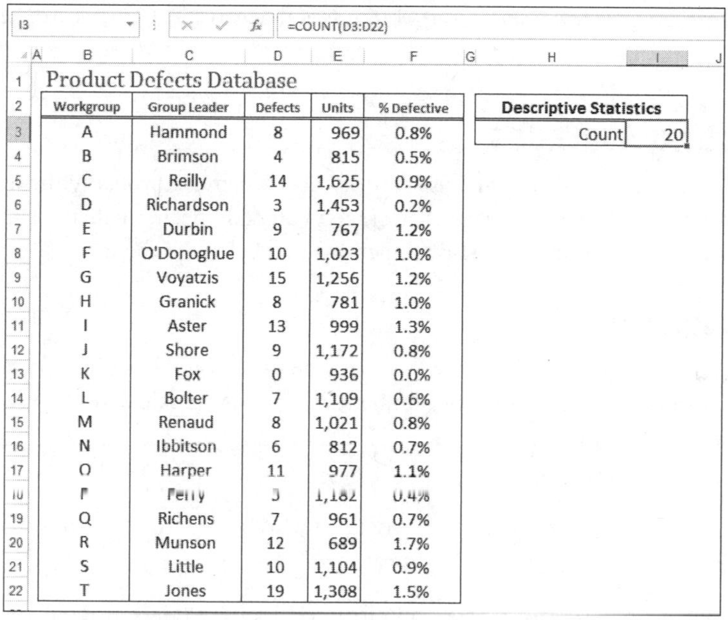

	B	C	D	E	F	G	H	I
1	Product Defects Database							
2	Workgroup	Group Leader	Defects	Units	% Defective		Descriptive Statistics	
3	A	Hammond	8	969	0.8%		Count	20
4	B	Brimson	4	815	0.5%			
5	C	Reilly	14	1,625	0.9%			
6	D	Richardson	3	1,453	0.2%			
7	E	Durbin	9	767	1.2%			
8	F	O'Donoghue	10	1,023	1.0%			
9	G	Voyatzis	15	1,256	1.2%			
10	H	Granick	8	781	1.0%			
11	I	Aster	13	999	1.3%			
12	J	Shore	9	1,172	0.8%			
13	K	Fox	0	936	0.0%			
14	L	Bolter	7	1,109	0.6%			
15	M	Renaud	8	1,021	0.8%			
16	N	Ibbitson	6	812	0.7%			
17	O	Harper	11	977	1.1%			
18	P	Perry	5	1,182	0.4%			
19	Q	Richens	7	961	0.7%			
20	R	Munson	12	689	1.7%			
21	S	Little	10	1,104	0.9%			
22	T	Jones	19	1,308	1.5%			

Cell I3 formula: =COUNT(D3:D22)

NOTE
You can download this chapter's sample workbook at www.mcfedries.com/books/book.php?title=excel-2016-formulas-and-functions.

12

Counting Items with the COUNT() Function

The simplest of the descriptive statistics is the total number of values, which is given by the COUNT() function:

```
COUNT(value1[,value2,...])
```

value1, value2,...   One or more ranges, arrays, function results, expressions, or literal values of which you want the count

The COUNT() function counts only the numeric values that appear in the list of arguments. Text values, dates, logical values, and errors are ignored. (If you want to include these non-numeric values, use the COUNTA() function instead.) In the worksheet shown in Figure 12.1, the following formula is used to count the number of defect values in the database:

```
=COUNT(D3:D22)
```

>
> **TIP**
>
> To get a quick look at the count, select the range or, if you're working with data in a table, select a single column in the table. Excel displays the count in the status bar. If you want to know how many numeric values are in the selection, right-click the status bar and then click the Numerical Count value.

Calculating Averages

The most basic statistical analysis worthy of the name is probably the average, although you always need to ask yourself *which* average you need: mean, median, or mode. The next few sections show you the worksheet functions that calculate them.

The AVERAGE() Function

The *mean* is what you probably think of when someone uses the term *average*. That is, it's the arithmetic mean of a set of numbers. In Excel, you calculate the mean by using the AVERAGE() function:

```
AVERAGE(number1[,number2,...])
```

> *number1, number2,...*   A range, an array, or a list of values of which you want the mean

For example, to calculate the mean of the values in the defects database, you use the following formula:

```
=AVERAGE(D3:D22)
```

> **TIP**
>
> If you need just a quick glance at the mean value, select the range. Excel displays the average in the status bar.

> **CAUTION**
>
> The AVERAGE() function (as well as the MEDIAN() and MODE() functions, discussed in the next two sections) ignores text and logical values. It also ignores blank cells, but it does *not* ignore cells that contain the value 0. If you want to include non-numeric values, use the AVERAGEA() function, which treats text values as 0 and the Boolean values TRUE and FALSE as 1 and 0, respectively.

The MEDIAN() Function

The *median* is the value in a data set that falls in the middle when all the values are sorted in numeric order. That is, 50% of the values fall below the median, and 50% fall above it.

The median is useful in data sets that have one or two extreme values that can throw off the mean result because the median isn't affected by extremes.

You calculate the median by using the MEDIAN() function:

```
MEDIAN(number1[,number2,...])
```

> *number1, number2, . . .* A range, an array, or a list of values of which you want the median

For example, to calculate the median of the values in the defects database, you use the following formula:

```
=MEDIAN(D3:D22)
```

The MODE() Function

The *mode* is the value in a data set that occurs most frequently. The mode is most useful when you're dealing with data that doesn't lend itself to being either added (necessary for calculating the mean) or sorted (necessary for calculating the median). For example, you might be tabulating the result of a poll that included a question about the respondent's favorite color. The mean and median don't make sense with such a question, but the mode will tell you which color was chosen the most.

You calculate the mode using one of the following functions:

```
MODE.MULT(number1[,number2,...])
MODE.SNGL(number1[,number2,...])
MODE(number1[,number2,...])
```

> *number1, number2, . . .*   A range, an array, or a list of values of which you want the mode

The MODE.SNGL() function returns the most common value in the list, so it's the function you'll use most often in Excel 2010 and later. If your list has multiple common values, use MODE.MULT() in Excel 2010 and later to return those values as an array. If you need to maintain compatibility with Excel 2007 and earlier versions, use the MODE() function.

For example, to calculate the mode of the values in the defects database, you use the following formula:

```
=MODE.SNGL(D3:D22)
```

Calculating the Weighted Mean

In some data sets, one value might be more important than another. For example, suppose that your company has several divisions, the biggest of which generates $100 million in annual sales and the smallest of which generates only $1 million in sales. If you want to calculate the average profit margin for the divisions, it doesn't make sense to treat the divisions equally because the largest is two orders of magnitude bigger than the smallest. You need some way of factoring the size of each division into your average profit margin calculation.

12

You can do this by calculating the *weighted mean*. This is an arithmetic mean in which each value is weighted according to its importance in the data set. Here's the procedure to follow to calculate the weighted mean:

1. For each value, multiply the value by its weight.
2. Sum the results from step 1.
3. Sum the weights.
4. Divide the sum from step 2 by the sum from step 3.

I'll make this more concrete by tying this into our database of product defects. Suppose you want to know the average percentage of product defects (the values in column F). Simply applying the AVERAGE() function to the range F3:F22 doesn't give an accurate answer because the number of units produced by each division is different. (The maximum is 1,625 in division C, and the minimum is 689 in division R.) To get an accurate result, you must give more weight to those divisions that produced more units. In other words, you need to calculate the weighted mean for the percentage of defective products.

In this case, the weights are the units produced by each division, so the weighted mean is calculated as follows:

1. Multiply the percentage defective values by the units. (The sharp-eyed reader will note that this just gives the number of defects. I'll ignore this for now for illustration purposes.)
2. Sum the results from step 1.
3. Sum the units.
4. Divide the sum from step 2 by the sum from step 3.

You can combine all of these steps into the following array formula, as shown in Figure 12.2:

```
{=SUM(F3:F22 * E3:E22) / SUM(E3:E22)}
```

Calculating Extreme Values

The average calculations tell you things about the "middle" of the data, but it can also be useful to know something about the "edges" of the data. For example, what's the biggest value, and what's the smallest? The next two sections take you through the worksheet functions that return the extreme values of a sample or population.

The MAX() and MIN() Functions

If you want to know the largest value in a data set, use the MAX() function:

```
MAX(number1[,number2,...])
```

> *number1, number2,...* A range, an array, or a list of values of which you want the maximum

Figure 12.2
This worksheet calculates
the weighted mean of the
percentage of defective
products.

I7		fx	{=SUM(F3:F22 * E3:E22) / SUM(E3:E22)}				

A	B	C	D	E	F	G	H	I
1		Product Defects Database						
2	Workgroup	Group Leader	Defects	Units	% Defective		Descriptive Statistics	
3	A	Hammond	8	969	0.8%		Count	20
4	B	Brimson	4	815	0.5%		Mean	8.9
5	C	Reilly	14	1,625	0.9%		Median	8.5
6	D	Richardson	3	1,453	0.2%		Mode	8
7	E	Durbin	9	767	1.2%		Weighted Mean %	0.8%
8	F	O'Donoghue	10	1,023	1.0%			
9	G	Voyatzis	15	1,256	1.2%			
10	H	Granick	8	781	1.0%			
11	I	Aster	13	999	1.3%			
12	J	Shore	9	1,172	0.8%			
13	K	Fox	0	936	0.0%			
14	L	Bolter	7	1,109	0.6%			
15	M	Renaud	8	1,021	0.8%			
16	N	Ibbitson	6	812	0.7%			
17	O	Harper	11	977	1.1%			
18	P	Ferry	5	1,182	0.4%			
19	Q	Richens	7	961	0.7%			
20	R	Munson	12	689	1.7%			
21	S	Little	10	1,104	0.9%			
22	T	Jones	19	1,308	1.5%			

For example, to calculate the maximum value in the defects database, you use the following formula:

```
=MAX(D3:D22)
```

To get the smallest value in a data set, use the MIN() function:

```
MIN(number1[,number2,...])
```

    number1, number2, . . .   A range, an array, or a list of values of which you want the minimum

For example, to calculate the minimum value in the defects database, you use the following formula:

```
=MIN(D3:D22)
```

> **TIP**
> If you need just a quick glance at the maximum or minimum value, select the range, right-click the status bar, and then click the Maximum or Minimum value.

> **NOTE**
> If you need to determine the maximum or minimum over a range or an array that includes text values or logical values, use the MAXA() or MINA() functions instead. These functions ignore text values and treat logical values as either 1 (for TRUE) or 0 (for FALSE).

12

The LARGE() and SMALL() Functions

Instead of knowing just the largest value, you might need to know the *k*th largest value, where *k* is some integer. You can calculate this by using Excel's LARGE() function:

```
LARGE(array, k)
```

array   A range, an array, or a list of values.

k   The position (beginning at the largest) within *array* that you want to return. (When *k* equals 1, this function returns the same value as MAX().)

For example, the following formula returns 15, the second-largest defects value in the product defects database:

```
=LARGE(D3:D22, 2)
```

Similarly, instead of knowing just the smallest value, you might need to know the *k*th smallest value, where *k* is some integer. You can determine this value by using the SMALL() function:

```
SMALL(array, k)
```

array   A range, an array, or a list of values.

k   The position (beginning at the smallest) within *array* that you want to return. (When *k* equals 1, this function returns the same value as MIN().)

For example, the following formula returns 4, the third-smallest defects value in the product defects database (see Figure 12.3):

```
=SMALL(D3:D22, 3)
```

Performing Calculations on the Top *k* Values

Sometimes, you might need to sum only the top three values in a data set or take the average of the top 10 values. You can do this by combining the LARGE() function and the appropriate arithmetic function (such as SUM()) in an array formula. Here's the general formula:

```
{=FUNCTION(LARGE(range, {1,2,3,...,k}))}
```

Here, FUNCTION() is the arithmetic function, *range* is the array or range containing the data, and *k* is the number of values you want to work with. In other words, LARGE() applies the top *k* values from *range* to the FUNCTION().

For example, suppose you want to find the mean of the top five values in the defects database. Here's an array formula that does this:

```
{=AVERAGE(LARGE(D3:D22,{1,2,3,4,5}))}
```

Figure 12.3
The product defects database with calculations derived using the MAX(), MIN(), LARGE(), and SMALL() functions.

				fx	=SMALL(D3:D22, 3)			

I11

A	B	C	D	E	F	G	H	I
1	Product Defects Database							
2	Workgroup	Group Leader	Defects	Units	% Defective		Descriptive Statistics	
3	A	Hammond	8	969	0.8%		Count	20
4	B	Brimson	4	815	0.5%		Mean	8.9
5	C	Reilly	14	1,625	0.9%		Median	8.5
6	D	Richardson	3	1,453	0.2%		Mode	8
7	E	Durbin	9	767	1.2%		Weighted Mean %	0.8%
8	F	O'Donoghue	10	1,023	1.0%		Maximum	19
9	G	Voyatzis	15	1,256	1.2%		Minimum	0
10	H	Granick	8	781	1.0%		2nd Largest	15
11	I	Aster	13	999	1.3%		3rd Smallest	4
12	J	Shore	9	1,172	0.8%			
13	K	Fox	0	936	0.0%			
14	L	Bolter	7	1,109	0.6%			
15	M	Renaud	8	1,021	0.8%			
16	N	Ibbitson	6	812	0.7%			
17	O	Harper	11	977	1.1%			
18	P	Ferry	5	1,182	0.4%			
19	Q	Richens	7	961	0.7%			
20	R	Munson	12	689	1.7%			
21	S	Little	10	1,104	0.9%			
22	T	Jones	19	1,308	1.5%			

Performing Calculations on the Bottom k Values

You can probably guess that performing calculations on the smallest k values is similar to performing calculations on the top k values. In fact, the only difference is that you substitute the SMALL() function for LARGE():

{=FUNCTION(SMALL(*range*, {1,2,3,...,*k*})))}

For example, the following array formula sums the smallest three defect values in the defects database:

{=SUM(SMALL(D3:D22,{1,2,3})))}

Calculating Measures of Variation

Descriptive statistics such as the mean, median, and mode fall under what statisticians call *measures of central tendency* (or sometimes *measures of location*). These numbers are designed to give you some idea of what constitutes a "typical" value in a data set.

This is in contrast to the so-called *measures of variation* (or sometimes *measures of dispersion*), which are designed to give you some idea of how the values in a data set vary with respect to one another. For example, a data set in which all the values are the same would have no variability; in contrast, a data set with wildly different values would have high variability. Just what is meant by "wildly different" is what the statistical techniques in this section are designed to help you calculate.

12

Calculating the Range

The simplest measure of variability is the *range* (also sometimes called the *spread*), which is defined as the difference between a data set's maximum and minimum values. Excel doesn't have a function that calculates the range directly. Instead, you first apply the MAX() and MIN() functions to the data set. Then, when you have these extreme values, you calculate the range by subtracting the minimum from the maximum.

For example, here's a formula that calculates the range for the defects database:

```
=MAX(D3:D22) - MIN(D3:D22)
```

In general, the range is a useful measure of variation only for small sample sizes. The larger the sample is, the more likely it becomes that an extreme maximum or minimum will occur, and the range will be skewed accordingly.

Calculating the Variance

When computing the variability of a set of values, one straightforward approach is to calculate how much each value deviates from the mean. You can then add those differences and divide by the number of values in the sample to get what might be called the *average difference*. The problem, however, is that, by definition of the arithmetic mean, adding the differences (some of which are positive and some of which are negative) gives the result 0. To solve this problem, you need to add the *absolute values* of the deviations and then divide by the sample size. This is what statisticians call the *average deviation*.

Unfortunately, this simple state of affairs is still problematic because (for highly technical reasons) mathematicians tend to shudder at equations that require absolute values. To get around this, they instead use the *square* of each deviation from the mean, which always results in a positive number. They sum these squares and divide by the number of values, and the result is then called the *variance*. This is a common measure of variation, although interpreting it is difficult because the result isn't in the units of the sample: It's in those units squared. What does it mean to speak of "defects squared," for example? This doesn't matter that much for our purposes because, as you'll see in the next section, the variance is used chiefly to get to the standard deviation.

> **NOTE** Keep in mind that this explanation of variance is simplified considerably. If you'd like to know more about this topic, you can consult an intermediate statistics book.

In any case, variance is usually a standard part of a descriptive statistics package, so that's why I'm covering it. Excel calculates the variance by using the VAR.P(), VAR.S(), and VAR() functions:

```
VAR.P(number1[,number2,...])
VAR.S(number1[,number2,...])
VAR(number1[,number2,...])
```

> `number1, number2,...`   A range, an array, or a list of values of which you want the variance

You use the `VAR.P()` function in Excel 2010 or later if your data set represents the entire population (as it does, for example, in the product defects case); you use the `VAR.S()` function in Excel 2010 or later if your data set represents only a sample from the entire population. If you need to maintain compatibility with Excel 2007 and earlier versions, use the `VAR()` function (which assumes that your data represents a sample from the entire population).

For example, to calculate the variance of the values in the defects database, you use the following formula:

```
=VAR.P(D3:D22)
```

> **NOTE**   If you need to determine the variance over a range or an array that includes text values or logical values, use the `VARPA()` and `VARA()` functions instead. These functions ignore text values and treat logical values as either 1 (for `TRUE`) or 0 (for `FALSE`).

Calculating the Standard Deviation

As I mentioned in the previous section, in real-world scenarios, the variance is really used only as an intermediate step for calculating the most important of the measures of variation: the *standard deviation*. This measure tells you how much the values in the data set vary with respect to the average (the arithmetic mean). What exactly this means won't become clear until you learn about frequency distributions in the next section. For now, however, it's enough to know that a low standard deviation means that the data values are clustered near the mean, and a high standard deviation means that the values are spread out from the mean.

The standard deviation is defined as the square root of the variance. This means that the resulting units will be the same as those used by the data. For example, the variance of the product defects is expressed in the meaningless *defects squared* units, but the standard deviation is expressed in *defects*.

You could calculate the standard deviation by taking the square root of the `VAR()` result, but Excel offers a more direct route:

```
STDEV.P(number1[,number2,...])
STDEV.S(number1[,number2,...])
STDEV(number1[,number2,...])
```

> `number1, number2,...`   A range, an array, or a list of values of which you want the standard deviation

You use the `STDEV.P()` function in Excel 2010 or later if your data set represents the entire population (as in the product defects case); you use the `STDEV.S()` function in Excel 2010 or later if your data set represents only a sample from the entire population. If you want to maintain compatibility with Excel 2007 and earlier versions, use the `STDEV()` function (which assumes that your data represents a sample from the entire population).

For example, to calculate the standard deviation of the values in the defects database, you use the following formula (see Figure 12.4):

```
=STDEV.P(D3:D22)
```

> **NOTE** If you need to determine the standard deviation over a range or an array that includes text values or logical values, use the `STDEVPA()` and `STDEVA()` functions instead. These functions ignore text values and treat logical values as either `1` (for `TRUE`) or `0` (for `FALSE`).

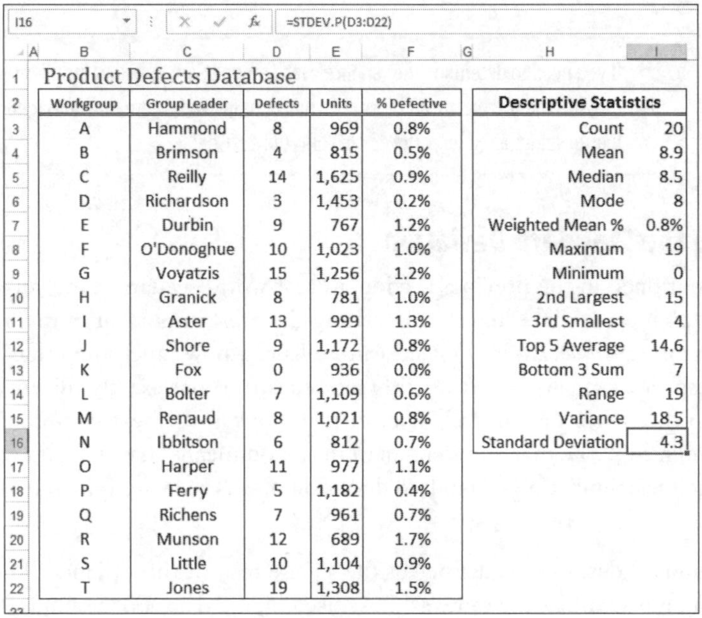

I16 =STDEV.P(D3:D22)

Product Defects Database

Workgroup	Group Leader	Defects	Units	% Defective
A	Hammond	8	969	0.8%
B	Brimson	4	815	0.5%
C	Reilly	14	1,625	0.9%
D	Richardson	3	1,453	0.2%
E	Durbin	9	767	1.2%
F	O'Donoghue	10	1,023	1.0%
G	Voyatzis	15	1,256	1.2%
H	Granick	8	781	1.0%
I	Aster	13	999	1.3%
J	Shore	9	1,172	0.8%
K	Fox	0	936	0.0%
L	Bolter	7	1,109	0.6%
M	Renaud	8	1,021	0.8%
N	Ibbitson	6	812	0.7%
O	Harper	11	977	1.1%
P	Ferry	5	1,182	0.4%
Q	Richens	7	961	0.7%
R	Munson	12	689	1.7%
S	Little	10	1,104	0.9%
T	Jones	19	1,308	1.5%

Descriptive Statistics	
Count	20
Mean	8.9
Median	8.5
Mode	8
Weighted Mean %	0.8%
Maximum	19
Minimum	0
2nd Largest	15
3rd Smallest	4
Top 5 Average	14.6
Bottom 3 Sum	7
Range	19
Variance	18.5
Standard Deviation	4.3

Figure 12.4
The product defects worksheet, showing the results of the `VAR.P()` and `STDEV.P()` functions.

Working with Frequency Distributions

A *frequency distribution* is a data table that groups data values into *bins*—ranges of values—and shows how many values fall into each bin. For example, here's a possible frequency distribution for the product defects data:

Bin (Defects)	Count
0–3	2
4–7	5
8–11	8
12–15	4
16+	1

The size of each bin is called the *bin interval*. How many bins should you use? The answer usually depends on the data. If you want to calculate the frequency distribution for a set of student grades, for example, you'd probably set up six bins: 0–49, 50–59, 60–69, 70–79, 80–89, and 90+. For poll results, you might group the data by age into four bins: 18–34, 35–49, 50–64, and 65+.

If your data has no obvious bin intervals, you can use the following rule:

> If n is the number of values in the data set, enclose n between two successive powers of 2 and take the higher exponent to be the number of bins.

For example, if n is 100, you'd use 7 bins because 100 lies between 2^6 (64) and 2^7 (128). For the product defects, n is 20, so the number of bins should be 5 because 20 falls between 2^4 (16) and 2^5 (32).

> **TIP**
>
> Here's a worksheet formula that implements the bin-calculation rule:
>
> ```
> =CEILING(LOG(COUNT(input_range), 2), 1)
> ```

The FREQUENCY() Function

To help you construct a frequency distribution, Excel offers the FREQUENCY() function:

FREQUENCY(*data_array*, *bins_array*)

data_array	A range or an array of data values
bins_array	A range or an array of numbers representing the upper bounds of each bin

Here are some things you need to know about this function:

- For the *bins_array*, you enter only the upper limit of each bin. If the last bin is open ended (such as 16+), you don't include it in the *bins_array*. For example, here's the *bins_array* for the product defects frequency distribution shown earlier: {3, 7, 11, 15}.

> **CAUTION**
>
> Make sure you enter your bin values in ascending order.

- The FREQUENCY() function returns an array (the number of values that fall within each bin) that is one greater than the number of elements in *bins_array*. For example, if the *bins_array* contains four elements, FREQUENCY() returns five elements. (The extra element is the number of values that fall in the open-ended bin.)
- Because FREQUENCY() returns an array, you must enter it as an array formula. To do this, select the range in which you want the function results to appear (again, make

this range one cell bigger than the *bins_array* range), type in the formula, and press Ctrl+Shift+Enter.

Figure 12.5 shows the product defects database with a frequency distribution added. The *bins_array* is the range K4:K7, and the FREQUENCY() results appear in the range L4:L8, with the following formula entered as an array in that range:

```
{=FREQUENCY(D3:D22, K4:K7)}
```

Figure 12.5
The product defects worksheet with the frequency distribution added.

	B	C	D	E	F	G	H	I	J	K	L
1	Product Defects Database										
2	Workgroup	Group Leader	Defects	Units	% Defective		Descriptive Statistics			Frequency Distribution	
3	A	Hammond	8	969	0.8%		Count	20		Bins	FREQUENCY()
4	B	Brimson	4	815	0.5%		Mean	8.9		3	2
5	C	Reilly	14	1,625	0.9%		Median	8.5		7	5
6	D	Richardson	3	1,453	0.2%		Mode	8		11	8
7	E	Durbin	9	767	1.2%		Weighted Mean %	0.8%		15	4
8	F	O'Donoghue	10	1,023	1.0%		Maximum	19			1
9	G	Voyatzis	15	1,256	1.2%		Minimum	0			
10	H	Granick	8	781	1.0%		2nd Largest	15			
11	I	Aster	13	999	1.3%		3rd Smallest	4			
12	J	Shore	9	1,172	0.8%		Top 5 Average	14.6			
13	K	Fox	0	936	0.0%		Bottom 3 Sum	7			
14	L	Bolter	7	1,109	0.6%		Range	19			
15	M	Renaud	8	1,021	0.8%		Variance	18.5			
16	N	Ibbitson	6	812	0.7%		Standard Deviation	4.3			
17	O	Harper	11	977	1.1%		Skewness	0.25			
18	P	Ferry	5	1,182	0.4%		Kurtosis	0.51			
19	Q	Richens	7	961	0.7%						
20	R	Munson	12	689	1.7%						
21	S	Little	10	1,104	0.9%						
22	T	Jones	19	1,308	1.5%						

Understanding the Normal Distribution and the NORMDIST() Function

The next few sections require some knowledge of perhaps the most famous object in the statistical world: the *normal distribution* (also called the *normal frequency curve*). This distribution refers to a set of values that are symmetrically clustered around a central mean, with the frequencies of each value highest near the mean and falling off as farther from the mean (either to the left or to the right).

Figure 12.6 shows a chart that displays a typical normal distribution. In fact, this particular example is called the *standard normal distribution*, and it's defined as having mean 0 and standard deviation 1. The distinctive bell shape of this distribution is why it's often called the *bell curve*.

To generate this normal distribution, I used Excel's NORM.DIST() function, which returns the probability that a given value exists within a population:

```
NORM.DIST(x, mean, standard_dev, cumulative)
NORMDIST(x, mean, standard_dev, cumulative)
```

x	The value you want to work with.
mean	The arithmetic mean of the distribution.
standard_dev	The standard deviation of the distribution.
cumulative	A logical value that determines how the function results are calculated. If *cumulative* is TRUE, the function returns the cumulative probabilities of the observations that occur at or below *x*; if *cumulative* is FALSE, the function returns the probability associated with *x*.

Figure 12.6
The standard normal distribution (mean 0 and standard deviation 1) generated by the NORMDIST() function.

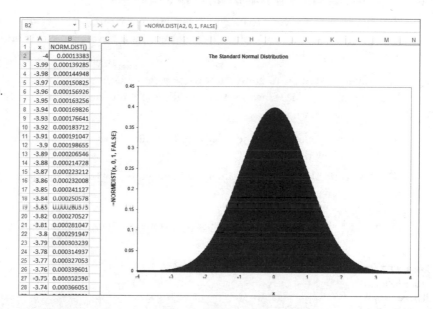

Use the NORM.DIST() function in Excel 2010 or later; use the NORMDIST() function if you need to maintain compatibility with Excel 2007 and earlier versions.

For example, consider the following example, which computes the standard normal distribution—mean 0 and standard deviation 1—for the value 0:

```
=NORM.DIST(0, 0, 1, TRUE)
```

With the *cumulative* argument set to TRUE, this formula returns 0.5, which makes intuitive sense because, in this distribution, half of the values fall below 0. In other words, the probabilities of all the values below 0 add up to 0.5.

Now consider the same function, but this time with the *cumulative* argument set to FALSE:

```
=NORM.DIST(0, 0, 1, FALSE)
```

This time, the result is 0.39894228. In other words, in this distribution, about 39.9% of all the values in the population are 0.

For our purposes, the key point about the normal distribution is that it has direct ties to the standard deviation:

- Approximately 68% of all the values fall within one standard deviation of the mean (that is, either one standard deviation above or one standard deviation below).
- Approximately 95% of all the values fall within two standard deviations of the mean.
- Approximately 99.7% of all the values fall within three standard deviations of the mean.

The Shape of the Curve I: The SKEW() Function

How do you know if your frequency distribution is at or close to a normal distribution? In other words, does the shape of your data's frequency curve mirror that of the normal distribution's bell curve?

One way to find out is to consider how the values cluster around the mean. For a normal distribution, the values cluster symmetrically about the mean. Other distributions are asymmetric in one of two ways:

- **Negatively skewed**—The values are bunched above the mean and drop off quickly in a "tail" below the mean.
- **Positively skewed**—The values are bunched below the mean and drop off quickly in a "tail" above the mean.

Figure 12.7 shows two charts that display examples of negative and positive skewness.

Figure 12.7
The distribution on the left is negatively skewed; the distribution on the right is positively skewed.

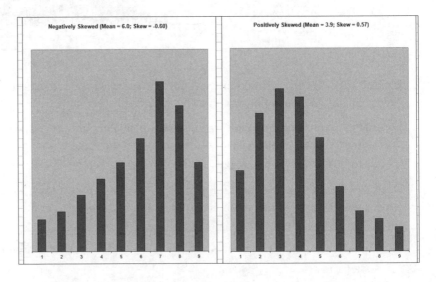

In Excel, you calculate the skewness of a data set by using the SKEW() function:

```
SKEW(number1[,number2,...])
```

> number1, number2, ...   A range, an array, or a list of values for which you want the
> skewness

For example, the following formula returns the skewness of the product defects:

```
=SKEW(D3:D22)
```

The closer the SKEW() result is to 0, the more symmetric the distribution is, so the more like the normal distribution it is.

The Shape of the Curve II: The KURT() Function

Another way to find out how close your frequency distribution is to a normal distribution is to consider the flatness of the curve:

- **Flat**—The values are distributed evenly across all or most of the bins.
- **Peaked**—The values are clustered around a narrow range of values.

Statisticians call the flatness of the frequency curve the *kurtosis*. A flat curve has a negative kurtosis, and a peaked curve has a positive kurtosis. The further these values are from 0, the less the frequency is like the normal distribution. Figure 12.8 shows two charts that display examples of negative and positive kurtosis.

Figure 12.8
The distribution on the left has a negative kurtosis; the distribution on the right has a positive kurtosis.

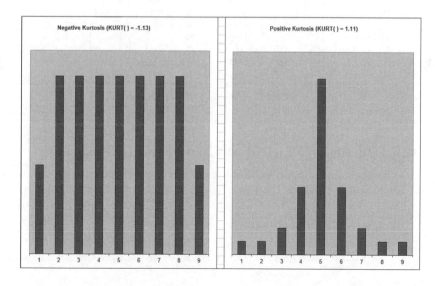

12

In Excel, you calculate the kurtosis of a data set by using the KURT() function:

```
KURT(number1[,number2,...])
```

> number1, number2,...   A range, an array, or a list of values for which you want the
> kurtosis

For example, the following formula returns the kurtosis of the product defects:

```
=KURT(D3:D22)
```

Figure 12.9 shows the final product defects worksheet, including values for the skewness and kurtosis.

Figure 12.9
The final product defects worksheet, showing the values for the distribution's skewness and kurtosis.

	I18			✕ ✓ fx	=KURT(D3:D22)				
◢	A	B	C	D	E	F	G	H	I
1		Product Defects Database							
2		Workgroup	Group Leader	Defects	Units	% Defective		Descriptive Statistics	
3		A	Hammond	8	969	0.8%		Count	20
4		B	Brimson	4	815	0.5%		Mean	8.9
5		C	Reilly	14	1,625	0.9%		Median	8.5
6		D	Richardson	3	1,453	0.2%		Mode	8
7		E	Durbin	9	767	1.2%		Weighted Mean %	0.8%
8		F	O'Donoghue	10	1,023	1.0%		Maximum	19
9		G	Voyatzis	15	1,256	1.2%		Minimum	0
10		H	Granick	8	781	1.0%		2nd Largest	15
11		I	Aster	13	999	1.3%		3rd Smallest	4
12		J	Shore	9	1,172	0.8%		Top 5 Average	14.6
13		K	Fox	0	936	0.0%		Bottom 3 Sum	7
14		L	Bolter	7	1,109	0.6%		Range	19
15		M	Renaud	8	1,021	0.8%		Variance	18.5
16		N	Ibbitson	6	812	0.7%		Standard Deviation	4.3
17		O	Harper	11	977	1.1%		Skewness	0.25
18		P	Ferry	5	1,182	0.4%		Kurtosis	0.51
19		Q	Richens	7	961	0.7%			
20		R	Munson	12	689	1.7%			
21		S	Little	10	1,104	0.9%			
22		T	Jones	19	1,308	1.5%			

Using the Analysis ToolPak Statistical Tools

When you load the Analysis ToolPak, the add-in inserts a new Data Analysis button in the Ribbon's Data tab. Click this button to display the Data Analysis dialog box shown in Figure 12.10. This dialog box gives you access to 19 new statistical tools that handle everything from an analysis of variance (anova) to a z-test.

→ To learn how to activate the Analysis ToolPak add-in, **see** "Loading the Analysis ToolPak," **p. 136**.

Here's a summary of what each statistical tool can do for your data:

■ **Anova: Single Factor**—Performs a simple (that is, single-factor) analysis of variance. An analysis of variance (anova) tests the hypothesis that the means from several samples are equal.

Figure 12.10
The Data Analysis dialog box contains 19 powerful statistical-analysis features.

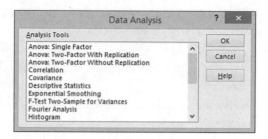

- **Anova: Two-Factor with Replication**—Performs a single-factor anova and includes more than one sample for each group of data.

- **Anova: Two-Factor Without Replication**—Performs a two-factor anova that doesn't include more than one sampling per group.

- **Correlation**—Returns the correlation coefficient: a measure of the relationship between two sets of data. This is also available via the following worksheet function:

  CORREL(*array1, array2*)

      array1   A reference, a range name, or an array of values for the first set of data.

      array2   A reference, a range name, or an array of values for the second set of data.

- **Covariance**—Returns the average of the products of deviations for each data point pair. Covariance is a measure of the relationship between two sets of data. This is also available via the following worksheet functions:

  COVARIANCE.P(*array1, array2*)
  COVARIANCE.S(*array1, array2*)
  COVAR(*array1, array2*)

      array1   A reference, a range name, or an array of values for the first set of data.

      array2   A reference, a range name, or an array of values for the second set of data.

- **Descriptive Statistics**—Generates a report showing various statistics (such as median, mode, and standard deviation) for a set of data.

- **Exponential Smoothing**—Returns a predicted value based on the forecast for the previous period, adjusted for the error in that period.

- **F-Test Two-Sample for Variances**—Performs a two-sample F-test to compare two population variances. This tool returns the one-tailed probability that the variances in the two sets aren't significantly different. This is also available via the following worksheet functions:

  F.TEST(*array1, array2*)
  FTEST(*array1, array2*)

      array1   A reference, a range name, or an array of values for the first set of data.

      array2   A reference, a range name, or an array of values for the second set of data.

12

■ **Fourier Analysis**—Performs a fast Fourier transform. You use Fourier analysis to solve problems in linear systems and to analyze periodic data.

■ **Histogram**—Calculates individual and cumulative frequencies for a range of data and a set of data bins. The FREQUENCY() function, discussed earlier in this chapter, is a simplified version of the Histogram tool.

■ **Moving Average**—Smoothes a data series by averaging the series values over a specified number of preceding periods.

■ **Random Number Generation**—Fills a range with independent random numbers.

■ **Rank and Percentile**—Creates a table containing the ordinal and percentage rank of each value in a set. These are also available via the following worksheet functions:

```
RANK.AVG(number,ref[,order])
RANK.EQ(number,ref[,order])
RANK(number,ref[,order])
```

number	The number for which you want to find the rank.
ref	A reference, a range name, or an array that corresponds to the set of values in which number will be ranked. (Note that ref must include number.)
order	An integer that specifies how number is ranked within the set. If order is 0 (this is the default), Excel treats the set as though it were ranked in descending order; if order is any nonzero value, Excel treats the set as though it were ranked in ascending order.

```
PERCENTILE.EXC(array, k)
PERCENTILE.INC(array, k)
PERCENTILE(array, k)
```

array	A reference, a range name, or an array of values for the set of data.
k	The percentile, expressed as a decimal value between 0 and 1.

■ **Regression**—Performs a linear regression analysis that fits a line through a set of values using the least squares method.

■ **Sampling**—Creates a sample from a population by treating the input range as a population.

■ **t-Test: Paired Two-Sample for Means**—Performs a paired two-sample Student's t-test to determine whether a sample's means are distinct. This is also available via the following worksheet functions (set type equal to 1):

```
T.TEST(array1, array2, tails, type)
TTEST(array1, array2, tails, type)
```

array1	A reference, a range name, or an array of values for the first set of data.
array2	A reference, a range name, or an array of values for the second set of data.
tails	The number of distribution tails.
type	The type of t-test you want to use: 1 = paired, 2 = two-sample equal variance (homoscedastic), 3 = two-sample unequal variance (heteroscedastic).

- **t-Test: Two-Sample Assuming Equal Variances**—Performs a paired two-sample Student's t-test, assuming that the variances of both data sets are equal. You can also use the TTEST() worksheet function with the *type* argument set to 2.

- **t-Test: Two-Sample Assuming Unequal Variances**—Performs a paired two-sample Student's t-test, assuming that the variances of both data sets are unequal. You can also use the TTEST() worksheet function with the *type* argument set to 3.

- **z-Test: Two-Sample for Means**—Performs a two-sample z-test for means with known variances. This is also available via the following worksheet functions:
  ```
  Z.TEST(array,x[,sigma])
  ZTEST(array,x[,sigma])
  ```

array	A reference, a range name, or an array of values for the data against which you want to test x.
x	The value you want to test.
sigma	The population (that is, the known) standard deviation. If you omit this argument, Excel uses the sample standard deviation.

The next few sections look at five of these tools in more depth: Descriptive Statistics, Correlation, Histogram, Random Number Generation, and Rank and Percentile.

Using the Descriptive Statistics Tool

You saw earlier in this chapter that Excel has separate statistical functions for calculating values such as the mean, maximum, minimum, and standard deviation values of a population or sample. If you need to derive all of these basic analysis stats, entering all those functions can be a pain. Instead, use the Analysis ToolPak's Descriptive Statistics tool. This tool automatically calculates 16 of the most common statistical functions and lays them all out in a table. Follow these steps to use this tool:

> **NOTE** Keep in mind that the Descriptive Statistics tool outputs only numbers, not formulas. Therefore, if your data changes, you'll have to repeat the following steps to run the tool again.

1. Select the range that includes the data you want to analyze (including the row and column headings, if any).

2. Select Data, Data Analysis to display the Data Analysis dialog box.

3. Select the Descriptive Statistics tool and click OK. Excel displays the Descriptive Statistics dialog box. Figure 12.11 shows the completed dialog box.

4. Use the Output Options group to select a location for the output. For each set of data included in the input range, Excel creates a table that is 2 columns wide and up to 18 rows high.

Figure 12.11
Use the Descriptive Statistics dialog box to select the options you want to use for the analysis.

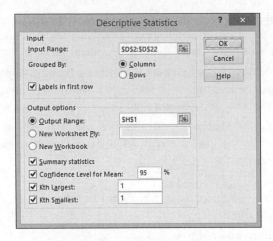

5. Select the statistics you want to include in the output:

- **Summary Statistics**—Select this option to include statistics such as the mean, median, mode, and standard deviation.

- **Confidence Level for Mean**—Select this option if your data set is a sample of a larger population and you want Excel to calculate the confidence interval for the population mean. A confidence level of 95% means that you can be 95% confident that the population mean will fall within the confidence interval. For example, if the sample mean is 10 and Excel calculates a confidence interval of 1.5, you can be 95% sure that the population mean will fall between 8.5 and 11.5.

- **Kth Largest**—Select this option to add a row to the output that specifies the kth largest value in the sample. The default value for k is 1 (that is, the largest value), but if you want to see any other number, enter a value for k in the text box.

- **Kth Smallest**—Select this option to include the sample's kth smallest value in the output. Again, if you want k to be something other than 1 (that is, the smallest value), enter a number in the text box.

6. Click OK. Excel calculates the various statistics and displays the output table. (See Figure 12.12 for an example.)

Determining the Correlation Between Data

Correlation is a measure of the relationship between two or more sets of data. For example, if you have monthly figures for advertising expenses and sales, you might wonder whether they're related. That is, do higher advertising expenses lead to more sales?

To determine this, you need to calculate the *correlation coefficient*. The coefficient is a number between –1 and 1 that has the following properties:

Figure 12.12

Use the Analysis ToolPak's Descriptive Statistics tool to generate the most common statistical measures for a sample.

	B	C	D	E	F		H		
1	Product Defects Database						*Defects*		
2	Workgroup	Group Leader	Defects	Units	% Defective				
3	A	Hammond	8	969	0.8%		Mean	8.9	
4	B	Brimson	4	816	0.5%		Standard Error	1	
5	C	Reilly	14	1,625	0.9%		Median	8.5	
6	D	Richardson	3	1,453	0.2%		Mode	8	
7	E	Durbin	9	767	1.2%		Standard Deviation	4.4	
8	F	O'Donoghue	10	1,024	1.0%		Sample Variance	19	
9	G	Voyatzis	15	1,256	1.2%		Kurtosis	0.5	
10	H	Granick	8	782	1.0%		Skewness	0.3	
11	I	Aster	13	999	1.3%		Range	19	
12	J	Shore	9	1,172	0.8%		Minimum	0	
13	K	Fox	0	936	0.0%		Maximum	19	
14	L	Bolter	7	1,109	0.6%		Sum	178	
15	M	Renaud	8	1,022	0.8%		Count	20	
16	N	Ibbitson	6	812	0.7%		Largest(1)	19	
17	O	Harper	11	978	1.1%		Smallest(1)	0	
18	P	Ferry	5	1,183	0.4%		Confidence Level(95.0%)	2.1	
19	Q	Richens	7	961	0.7%				
20	R	Munson	12	690	1.7%				
21	S	Little	10	1,105	0.9%				
22	T	Jones	19	1,309	1.5%				

Correlation Coefficient	Interpretation
1	The two sets of data are perfectly and positively correlated. For example, a 10% increase in advertising produces a 10% increase in sales.
Between 0 and 1	The two sets of data are positively correlated. For example, an increase in advertising leads to an increase in sales. The higher the number, the higher the correlation between the data.
0	There is no correlation between the data.
Between 0 and –1	The two sets of data are negatively correlated. For example, an increase in advertising leads to a *decrease* in sales. The lower the number is, the more negatively correlated the data is.
–1	The data sets have a perfect negative correlation. For example, a 10% increase in advertising leads to a 10% decrease in sales (and, presumably, a new advertising department).

To calculate the correlation between data sets, follow these steps:

1. Select Data, Data Analysis to display the Data Analysis dialog box.
2. Select the Correlation tool and then click OK. The Correlation dialog box, shown in Figure 12.13, appears.
3. Use the Input Range box to select the data range you want to analyze, including the row or column headings.
4. If you included labels in your range, select the Labels in First Row check box. (If your data is arranged in rows, this check box reads Labels in First Column.)

Figure 12.13
Use the Correlation dialog box to set up the correlation analysis.

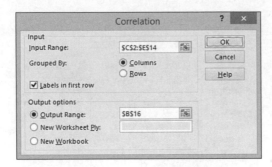

5. Because Excel displays the correlation coefficients in a table, use the Output Range box to enter a reference to the upper-left corner of the table. (If you're comparing two sets of data, the output range is three columns wide by three rows high.) You also can select a different sheet or workbook.

6. Click OK. Excel calculates the correlation and displays the table.

Figure 12.14 shows a worksheet that compares advertising expenses with sales. For a control, I've also included a column of random numbers (labeled Tea in China). The Correlation table lists the various correlation coefficients. In this case, the high correlation between advertising and sales (0.74) means that these two factors are strongly (and positively) correlated. As you can see, there is (as you might expect) almost no correlation among advertising, sales data, and the random numbers.

Figure 12.14
The correlation among advertising expenses, sales, and a set of randomly generated numbers.

	A	B	C	D	E
1	Correlation Between Advertising and Sales				
2			Advertising	Sales	Tea in China
3	Fiscal	1st Quarter	512,450	8,123,965	125,781
4	2014	2nd Quarter	447,840	7,750,500	499,772
5		3rd Quarter	500,125	7,860,405	735,374
6		4th Quarter	515,600	8,005,800	620,991
7	Fiscal	1st Quarter	482,754	8,136,444	894,312
8	2015	2nd Quarter	485,750	7,950,426	101,451
9		3rd Quarter	460,890	7,875,500	225,891
10		4th Quarter	490,400	7,952,600	823,969
11	Fiscal	1st Quarter	510,230	8,100,145	869,564
12	2016	2nd Quarter	515,471	8,034,125	495,102
13		3rd Quarter	525,850	8,350,450	119,939
14		4th Quarter	520,365	8,100,520	875,057
15					
16			Advertising	Sales	Tea in China
17		Advertising	1.00		
18		Sales	0.74	1.00	
19		Tea in China	0.07	-0.09	1.00
20					

NOTE The 1.00 values that run diagonally through the Correlation table signify that any set of data is always perfectly correlated to itself.

To calculate a correlation without going through the Correlation dialog box, use the `CORREL(array1, array2)` function. This function returns the correlation coefficient for the data in the two ranges given by `array1` and `array2`. (You can use references, range names, numbers, or an array for the function arguments.)

Working with Histograms

The Analysis ToolPak's Histogram tool calculates the frequency distribution of a range of data. It also calculates cumulative frequencies for your data and produces a bar chart that shows the distribution graphically.

Before you use the Histogram tool, you need to decide which groupings (or *bins*) you want Excel to use for the output. These bins are numeric ranges, and the Histogram tool works by counting the number of observations that fall into each bin. You enter the bins as a range of numbers, where each number defines a boundary of the bin.

For example, Figure 12.15 shows a worksheet with two ranges. One is a list of student grades. The second range is the bin range. For each number in the bin range, Histogram counts the number of observations that are greater than or equal to the bin value and less than (but *not* equal to) the next higher bin value. Therefore, in Figure 12.15, the six bin values correspond to the following ranges:

```
 0 <= Grade <  50
50 <= Grade <  60
60 <= Grade <  70
70 <= Grade <  80
80 <= Grade <  90
90 <= Grade < 100
```

> **CAUTION**
> For an accurate result, make sure you enter your bin values in ascending order.

Follow these steps to use the Histogram tool:

1. Select Data, Data Analysis to display the Data Analysis dialog box.
2. Select the Histogram tool and then click OK. Excel displays the Histogram dialog box. Figure 12.16 shows the dialog box already filled in.
3. Use the Input Range and Bin Range text boxes to enter the ranges holding your data and bin values, respectively.
4. Use the Output Options group to select a location for the output. The output range will be one row taller than the bin range, and it could be up to six columns wide (depending on which of the following options you select).

12

Figure 12.15
A worksheet set up to use the Histogram tool. Notice that you have to enter the bin range in ascending order.

	A	B	C	D	E
1		**Student Grades**			
2		**Student ID**	**Grade**		**Bin**
3		64947	82		50
4		69630	66		60
5		18324	52		70
6		89826	94		80
7		63600	40		90
8		25089	62		100
9		89923	88		
10		13000	75		
11		16895	67		
12		24918	62		
13		45107	71		
14		64090	53		
15		94395	74		
16		58749	65		
17		26916	66		
18		59033	67		
19		15450	68		
20		56415	69		
21		88069	69		

Figure 12.16
Use the Histogram dialog box to select the options you want to use for the histogram analysis.

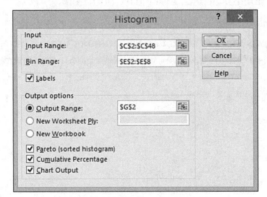

12

5. Select the other options you want to use for the frequency distribution:

- **Pareto**—If you select this check box, Excel displays a second output range with the bins sorted in order of descending frequency. (This is called a *Pareto distribution*.)

- **Cumulative Percentage**—If you select this option, Excel adds a new column to the output that tracks the cumulative percentage for each bin.

- **Chart Output**—If you select this option, Excel automatically generates a chart for the frequency distribution.

6. Click OK. Excel displays a histogram and its data, as shown in Figure 12.17.

Figure 12.17
The output of the
Histogram tool.

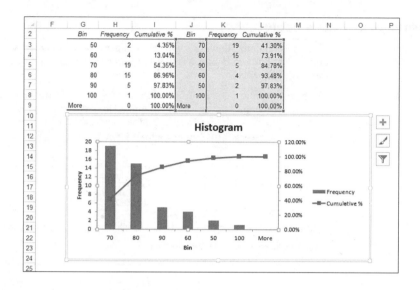

	Bin	Frequency	Cumulative %	Bin	Frequency	Cumulative %
2						
3	50	2	4.35%	70	19	41.30%
4	60	4	13.04%	80	15	73.91%
5	70	19	54.35%	90	5	84.78%
6	80	15	86.96%	60	4	93.48%
7	90	5	97.83%	50	2	97.83%
8	100	1	100.00%	100	1	100.00%
9	More	0	100.00%	More	0	100.00%

Using the Random Number Generation Tool

Unlike the RAND() function, which generates real numbers only between 0 and 1, the Analysis ToolPak's Random Number Generation tool can produce numbers in any range and can generate different distributions, depending on the application. Table 12.2 summarizes the seven available distribution types.

Table 12.2   The Distributions Available with the Random Number Generation Tool

Distribution	Description
Uniform	Generates numbers with equal probability from the range of values you provide. Using the range 0 to 1 produces the same distribution as the RAND() function.
Normal	Produces numbers in a bell curve (normal) distribution based on the mean and standard deviation you enter. This is good for generating samples of things such as test scores and the heights of people in a population.
Bernoulli	Generates a random series of 1s and 0s based on the probability of success on a single trial. A common example of a Bernoulli distribution is a coin toss (in which the probability of success is 50%; in this case, as in all other Bernoulli distributions, you would have to assign either heads or tails to be 1 or 0).
Binomial	Generates random numbers characterized by the probability of success over a number of trials. For example, you could use this type of distribution to model the number of responses received for a direct-mail campaign. The probability of success would be the average (or projected) response rate, and the number of trials would be the number of mailings in the campaign.
Poisson	Generates random numbers based on the probability of a designated number of events occurring in a time frame. The distribution is governed by a value, Lambda, that represents the mean number of events known to occur over the time frame.

12

Distribution	Description
Patterned	Generates random numbers according to a pattern that's characterized by a lower bound and an upper bound, a step value, and a repetition rate for each number and the entire sequence.
Discrete	Generates random numbers from a series of values and probabilities for these values (in which the sum of the probabilities equals 1). You could use this distribution to simulate the rolling of dice (where the values would be 1 through 6, each with a probability of 1/6; see the following example).

The following steps show how to use the Random Number Generation tool:

> **NOTE**
> If you'll be using a discrete distribution, be sure to enter the appropriate values and probabilities before starting the Random Number Generation tool.

1. Select Data, Data Analysis to display the Data Analysis dialog box.
2. Select the Random Number Generation tool and then click OK. The Random Number Generation dialog box appears, as shown in Figure 12.18.

Figure 12.18
Use the Random Number Generation dialog box to set up the options for your random numbers.

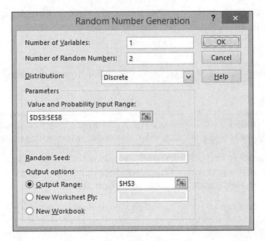

3. If you want to generate more than one set of random numbers, enter the number of sets (or variables) you need in the Number of Variables box. Excel enters each set in a separate column. If you leave this box blank, Excel uses the number of columns in the Output Range.
4. Use the Number of Random Numbers text box to enter how many random numbers you need. Excel enters each number in a separate row. If you leave this box blank, Excel fills the Output Range.

5. Use the Distribution drop-down list to select the distribution you want to use.

6. In the Parameters group, enter the parameters for the distribution you selected. (The options you see depend on the selected distribution.)

7. Use the Random Seed box to specify the value Excel should use to generate the random numbers. If you leave this box blank, Excel generates a different set each time. If you enter a value (which must be an integer between 1 and 32,767), you can reuse the value later to reproduce the same set of numbers.

8. Use the Output Options group to select a location for the output.

9. Click OK. Excel calculates the random numbers and displays them in the worksheet.

As an example, Figure 12.19 shows a worksheet that is set up to simulate rolling two dice. The Probabilities box shows the values (the numbers 1 through 6) and their probabilities (=1/6 for each). A discrete distribution is used to generate the two numbers in cells H3 and H4. The discrete distribution's Value and Probability Input Range parameter is the range $D$3:$E$8. Figure 12.20 shows the formulas used to display Die #1 and Die #2. (Notice that the formulas for Die #2 are similar to those for Die #1, except that $H$3 is replaced with $H$4.)

Figure 12.19
A worksheet that simulates the rolling of a pair of dice.

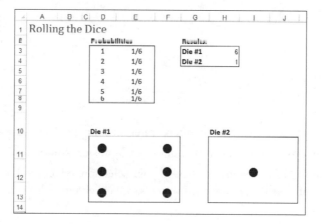

Figure 12.20
The formulas used to display Die #1 and Die #2.

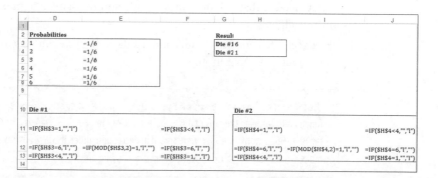

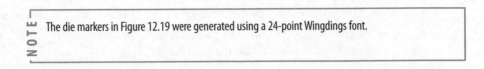

NOTE The die markers in Figure 12.19 were generated using a 24-point Wingdings font.

Working with Rank and Percentile

If you need to rank data, use the Analysis ToolPak's Rank and Percentile tool. This command not only ranks your data from first to last but also calculates the percentile—the percentage of items in the sample that are at the same level or a lower level than a given value. Follow these steps to use the Rank and Percentile tool:

1. Select Data, Data Analysis to display the Data Analysis dialog box.
2. Select the Rank and Percentile tool and then click OK. Excel displays the Rank and Percentile dialog box, shown in Figure 12.21.

Figure 12.21
Use the Rank and Percentile dialog box to select the options you want to use for the analysis.

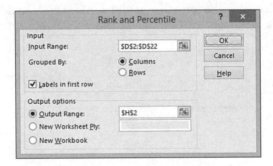

3. Use the Input Range text box to enter a reference for the data you want to rank.
4. Click the appropriate Grouped By option (Columns or Rows).
5. If you included row or column labels in your selection, select the Labels in First Row check box. (If your data is arranged in rows, the check box will read Labels in First Column.)
6. Use the Output Options group to select a location for the output. For each sample, Excel displays a table that is four columns wide and the same height as the number of values in the sample.
7. Click OK. Excel calculates the results and displays them in a table similar to the one shown in the range H2:K22 in Figure 12.22.

NOTE Use the RANK.AVG(*number*, *ref*[, *order*]) and RANK.EQ(*number*, *ref*[, *order*]) functions to calculate the rank of a *number* in the range *ref*. If *order* is 0 or is omitted, Excel ranks *number* as though *ref* were sorted in descending order. If *order* is any nonzero value, Excel ranks *number* as though *ref* were sorted in ascending order.

> For the percentile, use the `PERCENTRANK.EXC(range, x, significance)` or `PERCENTRANK.INC(range, x, significance)` function, where `range` is a range or an array of values, `x` is the value of which you want to know the percentile, and `significance` is the number of significant digits in the returned percentage. (The default is 3.)

Figure 12.22
Sample output from the Rank and Percentile tool.

Workgroup	Group Leader	Defects	Units	% Defective		Point	Defects	Rank	Percent
	Product Defects Database								
A	Hammond	8	969	0.8%		20	19	1	100.00%
B	Brimson	4	816	0.5%		7	15	2	94.70%
C	Reilly	14	1,625	0.9%		3	14	3	89.40%
D	Richardson	3	1,453	0.2%		9	13	4	84.20%
E	Durbin	9	767	1.2%		18	12	5	78.90%
F	O'Donoghue	10	1,024	1.0%		15	11	6	73.60%
G	Voyatzis	15	1,256	1.2%		6	10	7	63.10%
H	Granick	8	782	1.0%		19	10	7	63.10%
I	Aster	13	999	1.3%		5	9	9	52.60%
J	Shore	9	1,172	0.8%		10	9	9	52.60%
K	Fox	0	936	0.0%		1	8	11	36.80%
L	Bolter	7	1,109	0.6%		8	8	11	36.80%
M	Renaud	8	1,022	0.8%		13	8	11	36.80%
N	Ibbitson	6	812	0.7%		12	7	14	26.30%
O	Harper	11	978	1.1%		17	7	14	26.30%
P	Ferry	5	1,183	0.4%		14	6	16	21.00%
Q	Richens	7	961	0.7%		16	5	17	15.70%
R	Munson	12	690	1.7%		2	4	18	10.50%
S	Little	10	1,105	0.9%		4	3	19	5.20%
T	Jones	19	1,309	1.5%		11	0	20	0.00%

From Here

- Many of the descriptive statistics functions are also available in a list (or database) version that enables you to apply criteria. **See "Table Functions That Require a Criteria Range," p. 313.**

- Excel's AVERAGEIF() function calculates the mean of the items in a range that meet your specified criteria. **See "Using AVERAGEIF()," p. 315.**

- Excel's COUNTIF() function counts the number of items in a range that meet your specified criteria. **See "Using COUNTIF()," p. 313.**

- Regression analysis is an important statistical method for business. To read all about it, **see Chapter 16, "Using Regression to Track Trends and Make Forecasts," p. 371.**

12

Analyzing Data with Tables

Excel's forte is spreadsheet work, of course, but its row-and-column layout also makes it a natural flat-file database manager. In Excel, a *table* is a collection of related information with an organizational structure that makes it easy to find or extract data from its contents. (In legacy versions of Excel—that is, in versions prior to Excel 2007—a table was called a *list*.) Specifically, a table is a worksheet range that has the following properties:

- **Field**—A single type of information, such as a name, an address, or a phone number. In Excel tables, each column is a field.
- **Field name**—A unique name you assign to every table field. These names are always found in the first row of the table.
- **Field value**—A single item in a field. In an Excel table, the field values are the individual cells.
- **Record**—A collection of associated field values. In Excel tables, each row is a record.
- **Table range**—The worksheet range that includes all the records, fields, and field names of a table.

Planning an Excel Table

Suppose you want to set up an accounts receivable table. A simple system would include information such as the account name, account number, invoice number, invoice amount, due date, and date paid, as well as a calculation of the number of days overdue. Figure 13.1 shows how this system would be implemented as an Excel range.

Figure 13.1
Accounts receivable data in an Excel worksheet.

	A	B	C	D	E	F	G
1	**Current Date**	20-Feb-16					
2							
3	Account Name	Account Number	Invoice Number	Invoice Amount	Due Date	Date Paid	Days Overdue
4	Brimson Furniture	10-0009	117321	$2,144.55	19-Jan-16		32
5	Brimson Furniture	10-0009	117327	$1,847.25	1-Feb-16		19
6	Brimson Furniture	10-0009	.117339	$1,234.69	19-Feb-16	17-Feb-16	
7	Brimson Furniture	10-0009	117344	$875.50	5-Mar-16	28-Feb-16	
8	Brimson Furniture	10-0009	117353	$898.54	20-Mar-16	15-Mar-16	
9	Chimera Illusions	02-0200	117318	$3,005.14	14-Jan-16	19-Jan-16	
10	Chimera Illusions	02-0200	117334	$303.65	12-Feb-16	16-Feb-16	
11	Chimera Illusions	02-0200	117345	$588.88	6-Mar-16	6-Mar-16	
12	Chimera Illusions	02-0200	117350	$456.21	15-Mar-16	11-Mar-16	
13	Door Stoppers Ltd.	01-0045	117319	$78.85	16-Jan-16	16-Jan-16	
14	Door Stoppers Ltd.	01-0045	117324	$101.01	26-Jan-16		25
15	Door Stoppers Ltd.	01-0045	117328	$58.50	2-Feb-16		18
16	Door Stoppers Ltd.	01-0045	117333	$1,685.74	11-Feb-16	9-Feb-16	
17	Emily's Sports Palace	08-2255	117316	$1,584.20	12-Jan-16		39
18	Emily's Sports Palace	08-2255	117337	$4,347.21	18-Feb-16	17-Feb-16	
19	Emily's Sports Palace	08-2255	117349	$1,689.50	14-Mar-16		
20	Katy's Paper Products	12-1212	117322	$234.69	20-Jan-16		31
21	Katy's Paper Products	12-1212	117340	$1,157.58	21-Feb-16		

> **NOTE**
> You can download this chapter's sample workbook at www.mcfedries.com/books/
> book.php?title=excel-2016-formulas-and-functions.

Excel tables don't require elaborate planning, but you should follow a few guidelines for best results. Here are some pointers:

- Always use the top row of a table for the column labels.

- Field names must be unique, and they must be text or text formulas. If you need to use numbers, format them as text.

- Some Excel commands can automatically identify the size and shape of a table. To avoid confusing such commands, try to use only one table per worksheet. If you have multiple related tables, include them in other worksheets in the same workbook.

- If you have nontable data in the same worksheet, leave at least one blank row or column between the data and the table. This helps Excel identify the table automatically.

- Excel has a command that enables you to filter your table data to show only records that match certain criteria. (See "Filtering Table Data," later in this chapter, for details.) This command works by hiding rows of data. Therefore, if the same worksheet contains nontable data that you need to see or work with, don't place this data to the left or right of the table.

Converting a Range to a Table

Excel has a number of commands that enable you to work efficiently with table data. To take advantage of these commands, you must convert your data from a normal range to a table. Here are the steps to follow:

1. Click any cell within the range that you want to convert to a table.

2. You now have two choices:
   - To create a table with the default formatting, select Insert, Table (or press Ctrl+T).
   - To create a table with the formatting you specify, select Home, Format as Table and then click a table style in the gallery that appears.

   Excel displays the Create Table dialog box (or the Format as Table dialog box).

3. Ensure that the Where Is the Data for Your Table? box already shows the correct range coordinates. If it doesn't, enter the range coordinates or select the range directly on the worksheet.

4. If your range has column headers in the top row (as it should), make sure the My Table Has Headers check box is selected.

5. Click OK.

When you convert a range to a table, Excel makes three changes to the range, as shown in Figure 13.2:

- It formats the table cells.

- It adds drop-down arrows to each field header.

- In the Ribbon, you see a new Design tab under Table Tools whenever you select a cell within the table.

Figure 13.2
The accounts receivable data converted to a table.

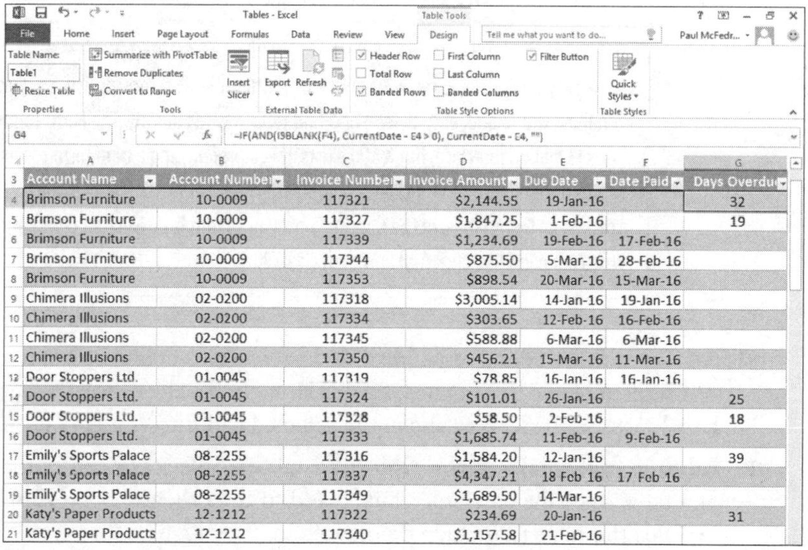

> **NOTE** If you ever need to change a table back to a range, select a cell within the table and select Design, Convert to Range.

Basic Table Operations

After you've converted a range to a table, you can start working with the data. Here's a quick look at some basic table operations:

- **Selecting a record**—Move the mouse pointer to the left edge of the leftmost column in the row you want to select (the pointer changes to a right-pointing arrow) and then click. You can also select any cell in the record and then press Shift+Spacebar.

- **Selecting a field**—Move the mouse pointer to the top edge of the column header. (The pointer changes to a downward-pointing arrow.) Click once to select just the field's data; click a second time to add the field's header to the selection. You can also select any cell in the field and then press Ctrl+Spacebar to select the field data; press Ctrl+Spacebar again to add the header to the selection.

- **Selecting an entire table**—Move the mouse pointer to the upper-left corner of a table (the pointer changes to an arrow pointing down and to the right) and then click. You can also select any cell in the table and press Ctrl+A.

- **Adding a new record at the bottom of a table**—Select any cell in the row below a table, type the data you want to add to the cell, and press Enter. Excel's AutoExpansion feature expands the table to include the new row. This also works if you select the last cell in the last row of the table and then press Tab.

> **NOTE** In legacy versions of Excel, you could work with table (list) records using a *data form*, a dialog box that enabled you to add, edit, delete, and find table records quickly. The Form command didn't make it into Excel's Ribbon interface, but it still exists. If you prefer using a data form to work with a table, add the Form command to the Quick Access Toolbar. Pull down the Customize Quick Access Toolbar menu and click More Commands. In the Choose Commands From list, select All Commands and then click Form in the command list. Click Add and then click OK.

- **Adding a new record anywhere in a table**—Select any cell in a record below which you want to add a new record. In the Home tab, select Insert, Insert Table Rows Above. Excel inserts a blank row above the selected cell into which you can enter the new data.

- **Adding a new field to the right of a table**—Select any cell in the column to the right of a table, type the data you want to add to the cell, and press Enter. AutoExpansion expands the table to include the new field.

- **Adding a new field anywhere in a table**—Select any cell in a column to the right of which you want to add a new field. In the Home tab, select Insert, Insert Table Columns to the Left. Excel inserts a blank field to the left of the selected cell.

- **Deleting a record**—Select any cell in a record you want to delete. In the Home tab, select Delete, Delete Table Rows.

- **Deleting a field**—Select any cell in a field you want to delete. In the Home tab, select Delete, Delete Table Columns.

- **Displaying table totals**—If you want to see totals for one or more fields, click inside a table, select the Design tab, and then click to select the Total Row check box. Excel adds a Total row at the bottom of the table. Each cell in the Total row has a drop-down list that enables you to select the function you want to use: Sum, Average, Count, Max, or Min, for example.

- **Formatting a table**—Excel comes with a number of built-in table styles you can apply with just a few mouse clicks. Click inside a table, select the Design tab, and then select a format from the Table Styles gallery. You can also use the check boxes in the Table Style Options group to toggle various table options, including Banded Rows and Banded Columns.

- **Resizing a table**—Resizing a table means adjusting the position of the lower-right corner of the table:

  - Move the corner down to add records.

  - Move the corner right to add fields.

  - Move the corner up to remove records from the table. (The data remains intact, however.)

  - Move the corner left to remove fields from the table. (Again, the data remains intact.)

  The easiest way to do this is to click-and-drag the resize handle that appears in the table's lower-right cell. You can also click inside the table and then click Design, Resize Table.

- **Renaming a table**—You'll see later in this chapter that Excel enables you to reference table elements directly (see "Referencing Tables in Formulas"). Most of the time these references include the table name, so you should consider giving your tables meaningful and unique names. To rename a table, click inside the table and then select the Design tab. In the Properties group, edit the Table Name text box.

13

Sorting a Table

One of the advantages of a table is that you can rearrange its records so that they're sorted alphabetically or numerically. This feature enables you to view the data in order by customer name, account number, part number, or any other field. You even can sort on multiple fields, which would enable you, for example, to sort a client table by state and then by name within each state.

For quick sorts on a single field, you have two choices to get started:

■ Click anywhere inside the field and then click the Data tab.

■ Pull down the field's drop-down arrow.

For an ascending sort, click Sort A to Z (or Sort Smallest to Largest for a numeric field or Sort Oldest to Newest for a date field); for a descending sort, click Sort Z to A (or Sort Largest to Smallest for a numeric field or Sort Newest to Oldest for a date field).

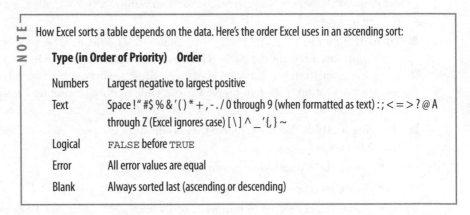

NOTE

How Excel sorts a table depends on the data. Here's the order Excel uses in an ascending sort:

Type (in Order of Priority)	Order
Numbers	Largest negative to largest positive
Text	Space ! " # $ % & ' ( ) * + , - . / 0 through 9 (when formatted as text) : ; < = > ? @ A through Z (Excel ignores case) [\ ] ^ _ ' { , } ~
Logical	FALSE before TRUE
Error	All error values are equal
Blank	Always sorted last (ascending or descending)

Performing a More Complex Sort

For more complex sorts on multiple fields, follow these steps:

1. Select a cell inside a table.
2. Select Data, Sort. Excel displays the Sort dialog box, shown in Figure 13.3.

Figure 13.3
Use the Sort dialog box to sort a table on one or more fields.

3. Use the Sort By list to select the field you want to use for the overall order for the sort.
4. Use the Order list to select either an ascending or descending sort.

5. (Optional) If you want to sort the data on more than one field, click Add Level, use the Then By list to click the field, and then select a sort order. Repeat for any other fields you want to include in the sort.

> **NOTE**
> You can specify up to 64 sorting levels.

> **CAUTION**
> Be careful when you sort table records that contain formulas. If the formulas use relative addresses that refer to cells outside their own record, the new sort order might change the references and produce erroneous results. If your table formulas must refer to cells outside the table, be sure to use absolute addresses.

6. (Optional) Click Options to specify one or more of the following sort controls:

   - **Case Sensitive**—Select this check box to have Excel differentiate between uppercase and lowercase during sorting. In an ascending sort, for example, lowercase letters are sorted before uppercase letters.
   - **Orientation**—Excel normally sorts table rows (the Sort Top to Bottom option) To sort table columns, select Sort Left to Right.

7. Click OK. Excel sorts the range.

Sorting a Table in Natural Order

It's often convenient to see the order in which records were entered into a table, or the *natural order* of the data. Normally, you can restore a table to its natural order by choosing Undo Sort in the Quick Access Toolbar immediately after a sort.

Unfortunately, after several sort operations, it's no longer possible to restore the natural order. The solution in this case is to create a new field, such as a field called Record, in which you assign consecutive numbers as you enter the data. The first record is 1, the second is 2, and so on. To restore the table to its natural order, you sort on the Record field.

13

> **CAUTION**
> The Record field works only if you add it either before you start inserting new records in the table or before you've irrevocably sorted the table. Therefore, when planning any table, you might consider always including a Record field just in case you need it.

Follow these steps to add a new field to a table:

1. Select a cell in the field to the right of where you want the new field inserted.
2. In the Home tab, select Insert, Table Columns to the Left. Excel inserts the column.
3. Rename the column header to the field name you want to use.

Figure 13.4 shows the accounts receivable table with a Record field added and the record numbers inserted.

Figure 13.4
The Record field tracks
the order in which records
are added to a table.

Record	Account Name	Account Number	Invoice Number	Invoice Amt	Due Date	Date Paid	rs O
	Current Date	20-Feb-16					
1	Brimson Furniture	10-0009	117321	$2,144.55	19-Jan-16		3
2	Brimson Furniture	10-0009	117327	$1,847.25	1-Feb-16		1
3	Brimson Furniture	10-0009	117339	$1,234.69	19-Feb-16	17-Feb-16	
4	Brimson Furniture	10-0009	117344	$875.50	5-Mar-16	28-Feb-16	
5	Brimson Furniture	10-0009	117353	$898.54	20-Mar-16	15-Mar-16	
6	Chimera Illusions	02-0200	117318	$3,005.14	14-Jan-16	19-Jan-16	
7	Chimera Illusions	02-0200	117334	$303.65	12-Feb-16	16-Feb-16	
8	Chimera Illusions	02-0200	117345	$588.88	6-Mar-16	6-Mar-16	
9	Chimera Illusions	02-0200	117350	$456.21	15-Mar-16	11-Mar-16	
10	Door Stoppers Ltd.	01-0045	117319	$78.85	16-Jan-16	16-Jan-16	
11	Door Stoppers Ltd.	01-0045	117324	$101.01	26-Jan-16		2
12	Door Stoppers Ltd.	01-0045	117328	$58.50	2-Feb-16		1
13	Door Stoppers Ltd.	01-0045	117333	$1,685.74	11-Feb-16	9-Feb-16	
14	Emily's Sports Palace	08-2255	117316	$1,584.20	12-Jan-16		3
15	Emily's Sports Palace	08-2255	117337	$4,347.21	18-Feb-16	17-Feb-16	
16	Emily's Sports Palace	08-2255	117349	$1,689.50	14-Mar-16		

> **TIP**
>
> If you're not sure how many records are in the table, and if the table isn't sorted in natural order, you might not know which record number to use next. To avoid guessing or searching through the entire Record field, you can generate the record numbers automatically by using the MAX () function. Click the formula bar and type (but don't confirm) the following:
>
> ```
> =MAX(Column:Column)
> ```
>
> Replace Column with the letter of the column that contains the record number (for example, MAX(A:A) for the table in Figure 13.4). Now select the formula and press F9. Excel displays the formula result, which will be the highest record number used so far. Therefore, your next record number will be one more than the calculated value.

Sorting on Part of a Field

Excel performs its sorting chores based on the entire contents of each cell in a field. This method is fine for most sorting tasks, but occasionally you need to sort on only part of a field. For example, your table might have a ContactName field that contains a first name and then a last name. Sorting on this field orders the table by each person's first name, which is probably not what you want. To sort on the last name, you need to create a new column that extracts the last name from the `ContactName` field. You can then use this new column for the sort.

Excel's text functions make it easy to extract substrings from a cell. In this case, assume that each cell in the `ContactName` field has a first name, followed by a space, followed by a last name. Your task is to extract everything after the space, and the following formula does the job (assuming that the name is in cell D4):

```
=RIGHT(D4, LEN(D4) - FIND(" ", D4))
```

➔ For an explanation of how this formula works, **see** "Extracting a First Name or Last Name," **p. 156**.

Figure 13.5 shows this formula in action. Column D contains the names, and column A contains the formula to extract the last name. I sorted on column A to order the table by last name.

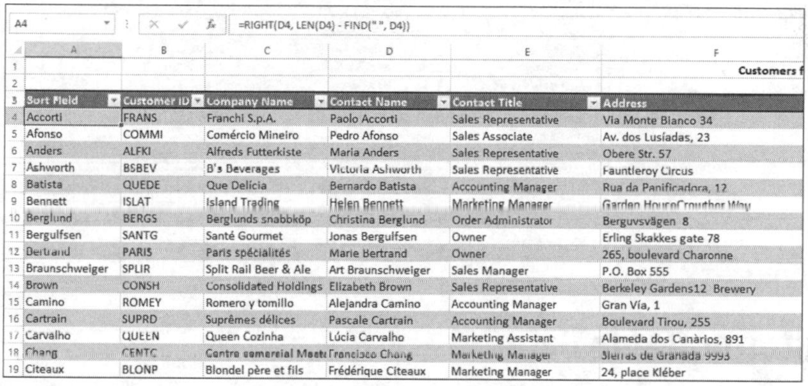

A4 =RIGHT(D4, LEN(D4) - FIND(" ", D4))

	A	B	C	D	E	F
1						Customers f
2						
3	Sort Field	Customer ID	Company Name	Contact Name	Contact Title	Address
4	Accorti	FRANS	Franchi S.p.A.	Paolo Accorti	Sales Representative	Via Monte Bianco 34
5	Afonso	COMMI	Comércio Mineiro	Pedro Afonso	Sales Associate	Av. dos Lusíadas, 23
6	Anders	ALFKI	Alfreds Futterkiste	Maria Anders	Sales Representative	Obere Str. 57
7	Ashworth	BSBEV	B's Beverages	Victoria Ashworth	Sales Representative	Fauntleroy Circus
8	Batista	QUEDE	Que Delícia	Bernardo Batista	Accounting Manager	Rua da Panificadora, 12
9	Bennett	ISLAT	Island Trading	Helen Bennett	Marketing Manager	Garden HouseCrowther Way
10	Berglund	BERGS	Berglunds snabbköp	Christina Berglund	Order Administrator	Berguvsvägen 8
11	Bergulfsen	SANTG	Santé Gourmet	Jonas Bergulfsen	Owner	Erling Skakkes gate 78
12	Bertrand	PARIS	Paris spécialités	Marie Bertrand	Owner	265, boulevard Charonne
13	Braunschweiger	SPLIR	Split Rail Beer & Ale	Art Braunschweiger	Sales Manager	P.O. Box 555
14	Brown	CONSH	Consolidated Holdings	Elizabeth Brown	Sales Representative	Berkeley Gardens12 Brewery
15	Camino	ROMEY	Romero y tomillo	Alejandra Camino	Accounting Manager	Gran Vía, 1
16	Cartrain	SUPRD	Suprêmes délices	Pascale Cartrain	Accounting Manager	Boulevard Tirou, 255
17	Carvalho	QUEEN	Queen Cozinha	Lúcia Carvalho	Marketing Assistant	Alameda dos Canàrios, 891
18	Chang	CENTC	Centro comercial Moctezuma	Francisco Chang	Marketing Manager	Sierras de Granada 9993
19	Citeaux	BLONP	Blondel père et fils	Frédérique Citeaux	Marketing Manager	24, place Kléber

Figure 13.5
To sort on part of a field, use Excel's text functions to extract the string you need for the sort.

> **TIP**
>
> If you'd rather not have the extra sort field (column A in Figure 13.5) cluttering the table, you can hide it by selecting a cell in the field and choosing Home, Format, Hide & Unhide, Hide Columns. Fortunately, you don't have to unhide the field to sort on it because Excel still includes the field in the Sort By table.

Sorting Without Articles

Tables that contain field values starting with articles (*A*, *An*, and *The*) can throw off your sorting. To fix this problem, you can borrow the technique from the preceding section and sort on a new field in which the leading articles have been removed. As before, you want to extract everything after the first space, but you can't just use the same formula because not all the titles have a leading article. You need to test for a leading article by using the following `OR()` function:

```
OR(LEFT(A2,2) = "A ", LEFT(A2,3) = "An ", LEFT(A2,4) = "The ")
```

Here, I'm assuming that the text being tested is in cell A2. If the left two characters are *A* followed by a space, or the left three characters are *An* followed by a space, or the left four characters are *The* followed by a space, this function returns `TRUE`. (That is, you're dealing with a title that has a leading article.)

Now you need to package this `OR()` function inside an `IF()` test. If the `OR()` function returns `TRUE`, the command should extract everything after the first space; otherwise, it should just return the entire title. Here it is:

```
=IF( OR(LEFT(A2,2) = "A ", LEFT(A2,3) = "An ", LEFT(A2,4) = "The "),
➥RIGHT(A2, LEN(A2) - FIND(" ", A2, 1)), A2)
```

Figure 13.6 shows this formula in action.

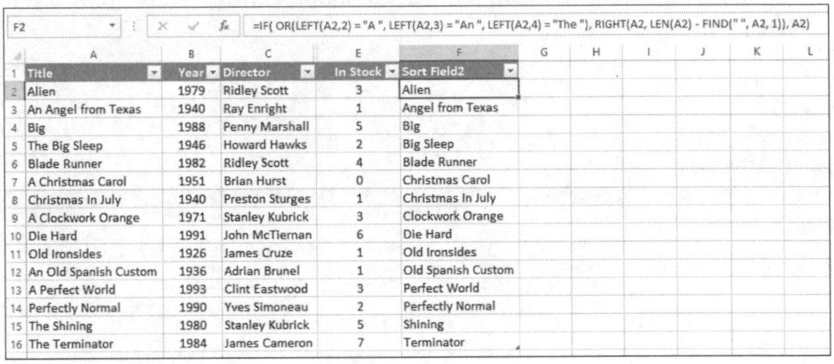

F2 | =IF(OR(LEFT(A2,2) = "A ", LEFT(A2,3) = "An ", LEFT(A2,4) = "The "), RIGHT(A2, LEN(A2) - FIND(" ", A2, 1)), A2)

	Title	Year	Director	In Stock	Sort Field2
2	Alien	1979	Ridley Scott	3	Alien
3	An Angel from Texas	1940	Ray Enright	1	Angel from Texas
4	Big	1988	Penny Marshall	5	Big
5	The Big Sleep	1946	Howard Hawks	2	Big Sleep
6	Blade Runner	1982	Ridley Scott	4	Blade Runner
7	A Christmas Carol	1951	Brian Hurst	0	Christmas Carol
8	Christmas In July	1940	Preston Sturges	1	Christmas In July
9	A Clockwork Orange	1971	Stanley Kubrick	3	Clockwork Orange
10	Die Hard	1991	John McTiernan	6	Die Hard
11	Old Ironsides	1926	James Cruze	1	Old Ironsides
12	An Old Spanish Custom	1936	Adrian Brunel	1	Old Spanish Custom
13	A Perfect World	1993	Clint Eastwood	3	Perfect World
14	Perfectly Normal	1990	Yves Simoneau	2	Perfectly Normal
15	The Shining	1980	Stanley Kubrick	5	Shining
16	The Terminator	1984	James Cameron	7	Terminator

Figure 13.6
A formula that removes leading articles for proper sorting.

Filtering Table Data

One of the biggest problems with large tables is that it's often hard to find and extract the data you need. Sorting can help, but in the end, you're still working with the entire table. What you need is a way to define the data that you want to work with and then have Excel display only those records onscreen. This is called *filtering* your data, and Excel offers several techniques that get the job done.

Using Filter Lists to Filter a Table

Excel's Filter feature makes filtering out subsets of your data as easy as selecting an option from a drop-down list. In fact, that's literally what happens. When you convert a range to a table, Excel automatically turns on the Filter feature, which is why you see drop-down arrows in the cells containing the table's column labels. (You can toggle Filter off and on by choosing Data, Filter.) Clicking one of these arrows displays a table of all the unique entries in the column. Figure 13.7 shows the drop-down table for the Account Name field in the accounts receivable table.

There are two basic techniques you can use in a Filter list:

Figure 13.7
For each table field, Filter adds drop-down lists that contain only the unique entries in the column.

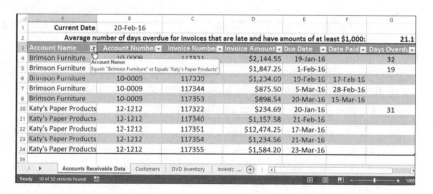

Account Name	Account Number	Invoice Number	Invoice Amount	Due Date	Date Paid	Days Overdue
		117321	$2,144.55	19-Jan-16		32
		117327	$1,847.25	1-Feb-16		19
		117339	$1,234.69	19-Feb-16	17-Feb-16	
		117344	$875.50	5-Mar-16	28-Feb-16	
		117353	$898.54	20-Mar-16	15-Mar-16	
		117318	$3,005.14	14-Jan-16	19-Jan-16	
		117334	$303.65	12-Feb-16	16-Feb-16	
		117345	$588.88	6-Mar-16	6-Mar-16	
		117350	$456.21	15-Mar-16	11-Mar-16	
		117319	$78.85	16-Jan-16	16-Jan-16	
		117324	$101.01	26-Jan-16		25
		117328	$58.50	2-Feb-16		18
		117333	$1,685.74	11-Feb-16	9-Feb-16	
		117316	$1,584.20	12-Jan-16		39
		117337	$4,347.21	18-Feb-16	17-Feb-16	
		117349	$1,689.50	14-Mar-16		
Katy's Paper Pro	12-1212	117322	$234.69	20-Jan-16		31

(Drop-down menu shown: Sort A to Z; Sort Z to A; Sort by Color; Clear Filter From "Account Name"; Filter by Color; Text Filters; Search; (Select All), Brimson Furniture, Chimera Illusions, Door Stoppers Ltd., Emily's Sports Palace, Katy's Paper Products, Lone Wolf Software, Meaghan Manufacturing, O'Donoghue Inc., Real Solemn Officials; OK / Cancel)

- ■ Deselect an item's check box to hide that item in the table.
- ■ Click to deselect the Select All item, which deselects all the check boxes, and then click to select the check box for each item you want to see in the table.

For example, Figure 13.8 shows the resulting records when I deselect all the check boxes and then select only the check boxes for Brimson Furniture and Katy's Paper Products. The other records are hidden and can be retrieved whenever needed. To continue filtering the data, you can select an item from one of the other tables. For example, you could select a month from the Due Date list to see only the invoices due within that month.

Figure 13.8
Clicking an item in a Filter drop-down list displays only records that include the item in the field.

	A	B	C	D	E	F	G
1	**Current Date**	20-Feb-16					
2	**Average number of days overdue for invoices that are late and have amounts of at least $1,000:**						21.1
3	Account Name	Account Number	Invoice Number	Invoice Amount	Due Date	Date Paid	Days Overdue
4	Brimson Furniture	10-0009	117321	$2,144.55	19-Jan-16		32
5	Brimson Furniture	10-0009	117327	$1,847.25	1-Feb-16		19
6	Brimson Furniture	10-0009	117339	$1,234.69	19-Feb-16	17-Feb-16	
7	Brimson Furniture	10-0009	117344	$875.50	5-Mar-16	28-Feb-16	
8	Brimson Furniture	10-0009	117353	$898.54	20-Mar-16	15-Mar-16	
20	Katy's Paper Products	12-1212	117322	$234.69	20-Jan-16		31
21	Katy's Paper Products	12-1212	117340	$1,157.58	21-Feb-16		
22	Katy's Paper Products	12-1212	117351	$12,474.25	17-Mar-16		
23	Katy's Paper Products	12-1212	117354	$1,234.56	21-Mar-16		
24	Katy's Paper Products	12-1212	117355	$1,584.20	23-Mar-16		
56							

(Tooltip: Account Name: Equals "Brimson Furniture" or Equals "Katy's Paper Products")

Sheet tabs: Accounts Receivable Data | Customers | DVD Inventory | Invento ...
Ready　10 of 52 records found

13

CAUTION

Because Excel hides the rows that don't meet the criteria, you shouldn't place any important data either to the left or to the right of the table.

Here are three things to notice about a filtered table:

- Excel reminds you that the table is filtered on a particular column by adding a funnel icon to the column's drop-down list button.
- You can see the exact filter by hovering the mouse over the filtered column's drop-down button. As you can see in Figure 13.8, Excel displays a banner that tells you the filter criteria.
- Excel also displays a message in the status bar telling you the number of records it filtered (again, refer to Figure 13.8).

Working with Quick Filters

The items you see in each drop-down table are called the *filter criteria*. Besides selecting specific criteria (such as an account name), Excel also offers a set of *quick filters* that enable you to apply specific criteria. The quick filters you see depend on the data type of the field, but in each case you access them by pulling down a field's Filter drop-down list:

- **Text Filters**—This command appears when you're working with a text field. It displays a submenu of filters that includes Equals, Does Not Equal, Begins With, Ends With, Contains, and Does Not Contain.
- **Number Filters**—This command appears when you're working with a numeric field. It displays a submenu of filters that includes Equals, Does Not Equal, Greater Than, Less Than, Between, Top 10, Above Average, and Below Average.
- **Date Filters**—This command appears when you're working with a date field. It displays a submenu of filters that includes Equals, Before, After, Between, Tomorrow, Today, Next Week, This Month, Last Year, and many others. Figure 13.9 shows the Date Filters menu that appears for the accounts receivable table.

Whichever quick filter you select (or if you click the Custom Filter command that appears at the bottom of each quick filter menu), Excel displays the Custom AutoFilter dialog box, an example of which is shown in Figure 13.10.

You use the two drop-down lists across the top to set up the first part of your criterion. The drop-down on the left contains a list of Excel's comparison operators (such as Equals and Is Greater Than). The combo box on the right enables you to select a unique item from the field or enter your own value. For example, if you want to display invoices with an amount less than $1,000, click the Is Less Than operator and enter **1000** in the text box.

For text fields, you also can use *wildcard characters* to substitute for one or more characters. Use the question mark (?) wildcard to substitute for a single character. For example, if you enter **sm?th**, Excel finds both Smith and Smyth. To substitute for groups of characters, use the asterisk (*). For example, if you enter ***carolina**, Excel finds all the entries that end with "carolina."

Figure 13.9
For a date field, the Date Filters command offers a wide range of quick filters that you can apply.

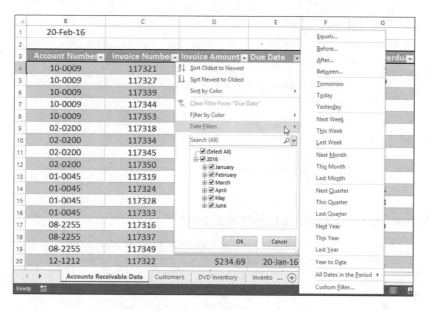

Figure 13.10
Use the Custom AutoFilter dialog box to specify your quick filter criteria or enter custom criteria.

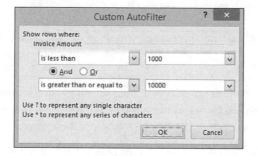

> **TIP** To include a wildcard as part of the criteria, precede the character with a tilde (~). For example, to find OVERDUE?, enter **OVERDUE~?**.

13

You can create *compound criteria* by clicking the And or Or button and then entering another criterion in the bottom two drop-down lists. Use And when you want to display records that meet both criteria; use Or when you want to display records that meet at least one of the two criteria.

For example, to display invoices with an amount less than $1,000 and greater than or equal to $10,000, you fill in the dialog box as shown in Figure 13.10.

Showing Filtered Records

When you need to redisplay records that have been filtered via Filter, use any of the following techniques:

- To display the entire table and remove the Filter feature's drop-down arrows, deselect the Data, Filter command.

- To display the entire table without removing the Filter drop-down arrows, select Data, Clear.

- To remove the filter on a single field, display that field's Filter drop-down list and select the Clear Filter from *Field* command, where *Field* is the name of the field.

Using Complex Criteria to Filter a Table

The Filter feature should take care of most of your filtering needs, but it's not designed for heavy-duty work. For example, Filter can't handle the following accounts receivable criteria:

- Invoice amounts greater than $100, less than $1,000, or greater than $10,000
- Account numbers that begin with 01, 05, or 12
- Days overdue greater than the value in cell J1

To work with these more sophisticated requests, you need to use *complex criteria*.

Setting Up a Criteria Range

Before you can work with complex criteria, you must set up a *criteria range*. A criteria range has some or all of the table field names in the top row, with at least one blank row directly underneath. You enter your criteria in the blank row below the appropriate field name, and Excel searches the table for records with field values that satisfy the criteria. This setup gives you two major advantages over Filter:

- By using either multiple rows or multiple columns for a single field, you can create compound criteria with as many terms as you like.

- Because you're entering your criteria in cells, you can use formulas to create *computed criteria*.

You can place the criteria range anywhere on the worksheet outside the table range. The most common position, however, is a couple of rows above the table range. Figure 13.11 shows the accounts receivable table with a criteria range (A2:G3). As you can see, the criteria are entered in the cell below the field name. In this case, the displayed criteria will find all Brimson Furniture invoices that are greater than or equal to $1,000 and that are overdue (that is, invoices that have a value greater than 0 in the Days Overdue field).

Figure 13.11
Set up a separate criteria range (A2:G3, in this case) to enter complex criteria.

	A	B	C	D	E	F	G
1	**Current Date**	20-Feb-16					
2	Account Name	Account Number	Invoice Number	Invoice Amount	Due Date	Date Paid	Days Overdue
3	Brimson Furniture			>=1000			>0
4							
5	Account Name	Account Number	Invoice Number	Invoice Amount	Due Date	Date Paid	Days Overdue
6	Brimson Furniture	10-0009	117321	$2,144.55	19-Jan-16		32
7	Brimson Furniture	10-0009	117327	$1,847.25	1-Feb-16		19
8	Brimson Furniture	10-0009	117339	$1,234.69	19-Feb-16	17-Feb-16	
9	Brimson Furniture	10-0009	117344	$875.50	5-Mar-16	28-Feb-16	
10	Brimson Furniture	10-0009	117353	$898.54	20-Mar-16	15-Mar-16	
11	Chimera Illusions	02-0200	117318	$3,005.14	14-Jan-16	19-Jan-16	
12	Chimera Illusions	02-0200	117334	$303.65	12-Feb-16	16-Feb-16	
13	Chimera Illusions	02-0200	117345	$588.88	6-Mar-16	6-Mar-16	
14	Chimera Illusions	02-0200	117350	$456.21	15-Mar-16	11-Mar-16	
15	Door Stoppers Ltd.	01-0045	117319	$78.85	16-Jan-16	16-Jan-16	
16	Door Stoppers Ltd.	01-0045	117324	$101.01	26-Jan-16		25
17	Door Stoppers Ltd.	01-0045	117328	$58.50	2-Feb-16		18
18	Door Stoppers Ltd.	01-0045	117333	$1,685.74	11-Feb-16	9-Feb-16	

Filtering a Table with a Criteria Range

After you've set up your criteria range, you can use it to filter the table. The following steps take you through the basic procedure:

1. Copy the table field names that you want to use for the criteria and paste them into the first row of the criteria range. If you'll be using different fields for different criteria, consider copying all your field names into the first row of the criteria range.

> **TIP**
> The only problem with copying the field names to the criteria range is that if you change a field name, you must change it in two places (that is, in the table and in the criteria). So, instead of just copying the names, you can make the field names in the criteria range dynamic by using a formula to set each criteria field name equal to its corresponding table field name. For example, you could enter =B5 in cell B2 of Figure 13.11.

2. Below each field name in the criteria range, enter the criteria you want to use.

3. Select a cell in the table and then select Data, Advanced. Excel displays the Advanced Filter dialog box, shown in Figure 13.12.

Figure 13.12
Use the Advanced Filter dialog box to select your table and criteria ranges.

4. Ensure that the List Range text box contains the table range (which it should if you selected a cell in the table beforehand). If it doesn't, select the text box and select the table (including the field names).

5. In the Criteria Range text box, select the criteria range (again, including the field names you copied).

6. To avoid including duplicate records in the filter, select the Unique Records Only check box.

7. Click OK. Excel filters the table to show only those records that match your criteria (see Figure 13.13).

Figure 13.13
The accounts receivable table filtered using the complex criteria specified in the criteria range.

	A	B	C	D	E	F	G
1	**Current Date**	20-Feb-16					
2	Account Name	Account Number	Invoice Number	Invoice Amount	Due Date	Date Paid	Days Overdue
3	Brimson Furniture			>=1000			>0
4							
5	Account Name	Account Number	Invoice Number	Invoice Amount	Due Date	Date Paid	Days Overdue
6	Brimson Furniture	10-0009	117321	$2,144.55	19-Jan-16		32
7	Brimson Furniture	10-0009	117327	$1,847.25	1-Feb-16		19

Entering Compound Criteria

To enter compound criteria in a criteria range, use the following guidelines:

- To find records that match all the criteria, enter the criteria on a single row.
- To find records that match one or more of the criteria, enter the criteria on separate rows.

Finding records that match all the criteria is equivalent to activating the And button in the Custom AutoFilter dialog box. The sample criteria shown in Figure 13.11 match records with the account name Brimson Furniture *and* an invoice amount greater than $1,000 *and* a positive number in the Days Overdue field. To narrow the displayed records, you can enter criteria for as many fields as you like.

> **TIP**
> You can use the same field name more than once in compound criteria. To do this, you include the appropriate field multiple times in the criteria range and enter the appropriate criteria below each label.

Finding records that match at least one of several criteria is equivalent to activating the Or button in the Custom AutoFilter dialog box. In this case, you need to enter each criterion on a separate row. For example, to display all invoices with amounts greater than or equal to $10,000 or that are more than 30 days overdue, you would set up your criteria as shown in Figure 13.14.

Figure 13.14
To display records that match one or more of the criteria, enter the criteria in separate rows.

	A	B	C	D	E	F	G
1	**Current Date**	20-Feb-16					
2	Account Name	Account Number	Invoice Number	Invoice Amount	Due Date	Date Paid	Days Overdue
3				>=10000			
4							>30
5							
6	Account Name	Account Number	Invoice Number	Invoice Amount	Due Date	Date Paid	Days Overdue
7	Brimson Furniture	10-0009	117321	$2,144.55	19-Jan-16		32
20	Emily's Sports Palace	08-2255	117316	$1,584.20	12-Jan-16		39
23	Katy's Paper Product:	12-1212	117322	$234.69	20-Jan-16		31
25	Katy's Paper Product:	12-1212	117351	$12,474.25	17-Mar-16		
30	Meaghan Manufactu	12-3456	117341	$11,585.23	25 Feb 16		
36	Refco Office Solution:	14-5741	117317	$303.65	13-Jan-16		38

> **CAUTION**
>
> Don't include any blank rows in your criteria range because blank rows throw off Excel when it tries to match the criteria.

Entering Computed Criteria

The fields in your criteria range aren't restricted to the table fields. You can create *computed criteria* that use a calculation to match records in the table. The calculation can refer to one or more table fields, or even to cells outside the table, and must return either TRUE or FALSE. Excel selects records that return TRUE.

To use computed criteria, add a column to the criteria range and enter the formula in the new field. Make sure that the name you give the criteria field is different from any field name in the table. When referencing the table cells in the formula, use the first data row of the table. For example, to select all records in which Date Paid is equal to Due Date in the accounts receivable table, enter the following formula:

```
=F6=E6
```

Note the use of relative addressing. If you want to reference cells outside the table, use absolute addressing.

> **TIP**
>
> Use Excel's AND, OR, and NOT functions to create compound computed criteria. For example, to select all records in which the Days Overdue value is less than 90 and greater than 31, type this:
>
> ```
> =AND(G6<90, G6>31)
> ```

Figure 13.15 shows a more complex example. The goal is to select all records whose invoices were paid after the due date. The new criterion—named Late Payers—contains the following formula:

```
=IF(ISBLANK(F6), FALSE(), F6 > E6)
```

13

Figure 13.15
Use a separate criteria range column for calculated criteria.

A3	▼	:	×	✓	fx	=IF(ISBLANK(F6), FALSE(), F6 > E6)		

	A	B	C	D	E	F	G
2	Late Payers						
3	FALSE						
4							
5	Account Name	Account Number	Invoice Number	Invoice Amount	Due Date	Date Paid	Days Overdue
11	Chimera Illusions	02-0200	117318	$3,005.14	14-Jan-16	19-Jan-16	
12	Chimera Illusions	02-0200	117334	$303.65	12-Feb-16	16-Feb-16	
34	Real Solemn Officials	14-1882	117342	$2,567.12	28-Feb-16	15-Mar-16	
38	Refco Office Solution:	14-5741	117361	$854.50	21-Apr-16	6-May-16	
39	Refco Office Solution:	14-5741	117363	$3,210.98	5-May-16	20-May-16	
45	Reston Solicitor Offic	07-4441	117357	$2,144.55	30-Mar-16	14-Apr-16	
46	Rooter Office Solvent	07-4441	117336	$78.85	15-Feb-16	2-Mar-16	
47	Rooter Office Solvent	16-9734	117348	$157.25	13-Mar-16	28-Mar-16	
48	Rooter Office Solvent	16-9734	117348	$157.25	13-Mar-16	28-Mar-16	

If the Date Paid field (column F) is blank, the invoice hasn't been paid, so the formula returns FALSE. Otherwise, the logical expression F6 > E6 is evaluated. If the Date Paid field (column F) is greater than the Due Date field (column E), the expression returns TRUE, and Excel selects the record. In Figure 13.15, the Late Payers cell (A3) displays FALSE because the formula evaluates to FALSE for the first row in the table.

Copying Filtered Data to a Different Range

If you want to work with the filtered data separately, you can copy it (or *extract* it) to a new location. Follow these steps:

1. Set up the criteria you want to use to filter the table.
2. If you want to copy only certain columns from the table, copy the appropriate field names to the range you'll be using for the copy.
3. Select Data, Advanced to display the Advanced Filter dialog box.
4. Select the Copy to Another Location option.
5. Enter your table and criteria ranges, if necessary.
6. Use the Copy To box to enter a reference for the copy location, using the following guidelines. (Note that, in each case, you must select the cell or range in the same worksheet that contains the table.)
   - To copy the entire filtered table, enter a single cell.
   - To copy only a specific number of rows, enter a range that contains the number of rows you want. If you have more data than fits in the range, Excel asks whether you want to paste the remaining data.
   - To copy only certain columns, select the column labels you copied in step 2.

┌─ CAUTION ───
If you select a single cell in which to paste the entire filtered table, make sure you won't be overwriting any data. Otherwise, Excel copies over the data without warning.
└───

7. Click OK. Excel filters the table and copies the selected records to the location you specified.

Figure 13.16 shows the results of an extract in the accounts receivable table.

Figure 13.16
This filter operation selects those records in which the Days Overdue field is greater than 0 and then copies the results to a range below the table.

	Days Overdue			
	>0			
	Account Name	Invoice Number	Invoice Amount	Days Overdue
60	Brimson Furniture	117321	$2,144.55	32
61	Brimson Furniture	117327	$1,847.25	19
62	Door Stoppers Ltd.	117324	$101.01	25
63	Door Stoppers Ltd.	117328	$58.50	18
64	Emily's Sports Palace	117316	$1,584.20	39
65	Katy's Paper Product:	117322	$234.69	31
66	O'Donoghue Inc.	117329	$1,234.56	17
67	O'Donoghue Inc.	117338	$2,144.55	2
68	Refco Office Solution:	117317	$303.65	38
69	Refco Office Solution:	117330	$456.78	17
70	Renaud & Son	117331	$565.77	12
71	Renaud & Son	117335	$3,005.14	7
72	Simpson's Ltd.	117332	$898.54	13
73	Voyatzis Designs	117325	$1,985.25	25

Referencing Tables in Formulas

In legacy versions of Excel, when you needed to reference part of a table in a formula, you usually just used a cell or range reference that pointed to the area within the table that you wanted to use in your calculation. That worked, but it suffered from the same problem caused by using cell and range references in regular worksheet formulas: The references often make the formulas difficult to read and understand. The solution with a regular worksheet formula is to replace cell and range references with defined names, but Excel offered no easy way to use defined names with tables.

That all changed beginning with Excel 2007 because the program now supports *structured referencing* of tables. This means that Excel offers a set of defined names—or *specifiers*, as Microsoft calls them—for various table elements (such as the data, the headers, and the entire table), as well as the automatic creation of names for the table fields. You can include these names in your table formulas to make your calculations much easier to read and maintain.

Using Table Specifiers

First, let's look at the predefined specifiers that Excel offers for tables. Table 13.1 lists the names you can use.

Table 13.1 Excel's Predefined Table Specifiers

Specifier	Refers To
#All	The entire table, including the column headers and total row.
#Data	The table data (that is, the entire table, not including the column headers and total row).
#Headers	The table's column headers.
#Totals	The table's total row.
@	The table row in which the formula appears. (This was #This Row in Excel 2007.)

Most table references start with the table name (as given by the Design, Table Name property). In the simplest case, you can just use the table name by itself. For example, the following formula counts the numeric values in a table named Table1:

```
=COUNT(Table1)
```

If you want to reference a specific part of the table, you must enclose that reference in square brackets after the table name. For example, the following formula calculates the maximum data value in a table named Sales:

```
=MAX(Sales[#Data])
```

> **TIP**
>
> You can also reference tables in other workbooks by using the following syntax:
>
> ```
> 'Workbook'!Table
> ```
>
> Here, replace *Workbook* with the workbook filename and replace *Table* with the table name.

> **NOTE**
>
> Using just the table name by itself is equivalent to using the #Data specifier. So, for example, the following two formulas produce the same result:
>
> ```
> =MAX(Sales[#Data])
> =MAX(Sales)
> ```

Excel also generates column specifiers based on the text in the column headers. Each column specifier references the data in the column, so it doesn't include the column's header or total. For example, suppose you have a table named Inventory, and you want to calculate the sum of the values in the field named Qty On Hand. The following formula does the trick:

```
=SUM(Inventory[Qty On Hand])
```

13

If you want to refer to a single value in a table field, you need to specify the row you want to work with. Here's the general syntax for this:

```
Table[[Row],[Field]]
```

Here, replace `Table` with the table name, `Row` with a row specifier, and `Field` with a field specifier. For the row specifier, you have only two choices: the current row and the totals row. The current row is the row in which the formula resides, and in Excel 2010 and later you use the @ specifier to designate the current row (in Excel 2007, this specifier was `#This Row`). In this case, however, you use @ followed by the name of the field in square brackets, like so:

```
@[Standard Cost]
```

For example, in a table named Inventory with a field named Standard Cost, the following formula multiplies the Standard Cost value in the current row by 1.25:

```
=Inventory[@[Standard Cost]] * 1.25
```

> **NOTE** If your formula needs to reference a cell in a row other than the current row or the totals row, you need to use a regular cell reference such as A3 or D6.

For a cell in the totals row, use the `#Totals` specifier, as in this example:

```
=Inventory[[#Totals],[Qty On Hand]] - Inventory[[#Totals],[Qty On Hold]]
```

Finally, you can also create ranges by using structured table referencing. As with regular cell references, you create a range by inserting a colon between two specifiers. For example, the following reference includes all the data cells in the Inventory table's Qty On Hold and Qty On Hand fields:

```
Inventory[[Qty On Hold]:[Qty On Hand]]
```

Entering Table Formulas

When you build a formula using structured referencing, Excel offers several tools that make it easy and accurate. First, note that table names are part of Excel's Formula AutoComplete feature. This means that after you type the first few letters of the table name, you'll see the formula name in the AutoComplete list, so you can then select the name and press Tab to add it to your formula. When you then type the opening square bracket ([), Excel displays a list of the table's available specifiers, as shown in Figure 13.17. The first few items are the field names, and the bottom five are the built-in specifiers. Select the specifier and press Tab to add it to your formula. Each time you type an opening square bracket, Excel displays the specifier list.

13

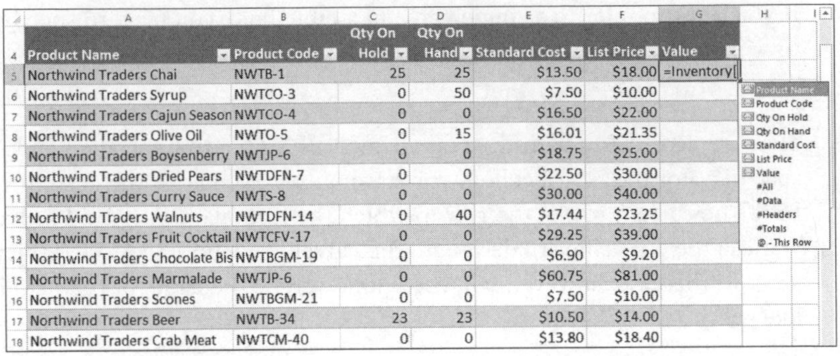

	A	B	C	D	E	F	G
4	Product Name	Product Code	Qty On Hold	Qty On Hand	Standard Cost	List Price	Value
5	Northwind Traders Chai	NWTB-1	25	25	$13.50	$18.00	=Inventory[
6	Northwind Traders Syrup	NWTCO-3	0	50	$7.50	$10.00	
7	Northwind Traders Cajun Season	NWTCO-4	0	0	$16.50	$22.00	
8	Northwind Traders Olive Oil	NWTO-5	0	15	$16.01	$21.35	
9	Northwind Traders Boysenberry	NWTJP-6	0	0	$18.75	$25.00	
10	Northwind Traders Dried Pears	NWTDFN-7	0	0	$22.50	$30.00	
11	Northwind Traders Curry Sauce	NWTS-8	0	0	$30.00	$40.00	
12	Northwind Traders Walnuts	NWTDFN-14	0	40	$17.44	$23.25	
13	Northwind Traders Fruit Cocktail	NWTCFV-17	0	0	$29.25	$39.00	
14	Northwind Traders Chocolate Bis	NWTBGM-19	0	0	$6.90	$9.20	
15	Northwind Traders Marmalade	NWTJP-6	0	0	$60.75	$81.00	
16	Northwind Traders Scones	NWTBGM-21	0	0	$7.50	$10.00	
17	Northwind Traders Beer	NWTB-34	23	23	$10.50	$14.00	
18	Northwind Traders Crab Meat	NWTCM-40	0	0	$13.80	$18.40	

Figure 13.17
Type a table name and the opening square bracket ([ ), and Excel displays a list of the table's specifiers.

One of my favorite Excel features is its support for automatic calculated columns. To demonstrate how this works, Figure 13.18 shows a full formula that I've typed into a table cell but haven't yet completed (by, say, pressing Enter). When I press Enter, Excel automatically fills the same formula down into the rest of the table's rows, as you can see in Figure 13.19. Excel also displays an AutoCorrect Options button, which enables you to reverse the calculated column, if desired.

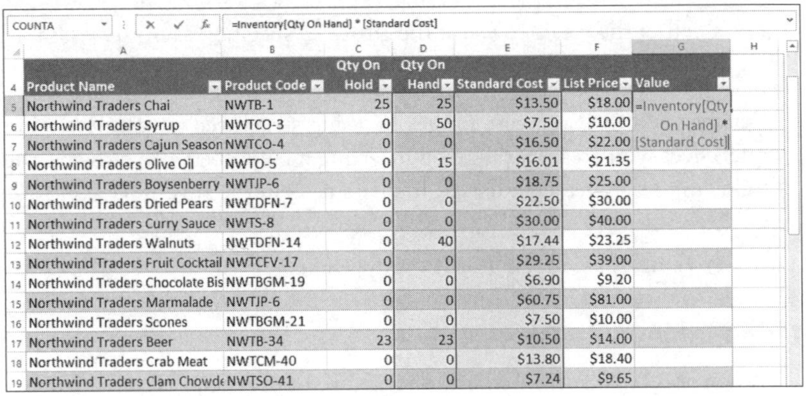

	A	B	C	D	E	F	G
4	Product Name	Product Code	Qty On Hold	Qty On Hand	Standard Cost	List Price	Value
5	Northwind Traders Chai	NWTB-1	25	25	$13.50	$18.00	=Inventory[Qty On Hand] * [Standard Cost]
6	Northwind Traders Syrup	NWTCO-3	0	50	$7.50	$10.00	
7	Northwind Traders Cajun Season	NWTCO-4	0	0	$16.50	$22.00	
8	Northwind Traders Olive Oil	NWTO-5	0	15	$16.01	$21.35	
9	Northwind Traders Boysenberry	NWTJP-6	0	0	$18.75	$25.00	
10	Northwind Traders Dried Pears	NWTDFN-7	0	0	$22.50	$30.00	
11	Northwind Traders Curry Sauce	NWTS-8	0	0	$30.00	$40.00	
12	Northwind Traders Walnuts	NWTDFN-14	0	40	$17.44	$23.25	
13	Northwind Traders Fruit Cocktail	NWTCFV-17	0	0	$29.25	$39.00	
14	Northwind Traders Chocolate Bis	NWTBGM-19	0	0	$6.90	$9.20	
15	Northwind Traders Marmalade	NWTJP-6	0	0	$60.75	$81.00	
16	Northwind Traders Scones	NWTBGM-21	0	0	$7.50	$10.00	
17	Northwind Traders Beer	NWTB-34	23	23	$10.50	$14.00	
18	Northwind Traders Crab Meat	NWTCM-40	0	0	$13.80	$18.40	
19	Northwind Traders Clam Chowde	NWTSO-41	0	0	$7.24	$9.65	

Figure 13.18
A new table formula, ready to be confirmed.

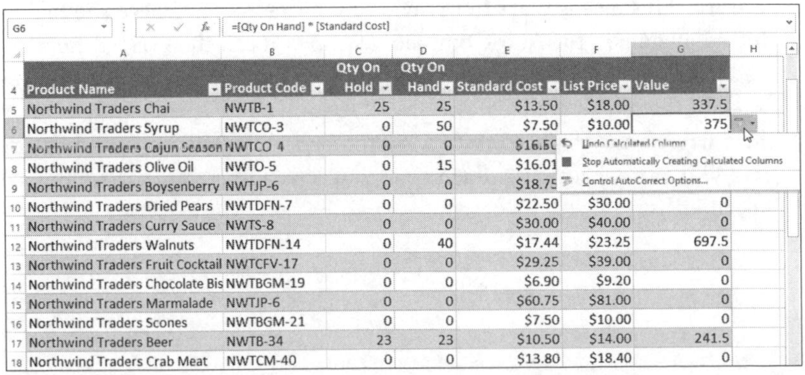

	A	B	C	D	E	F	G
4	Product Name	Product Code	Qty On Hold	Qty On Hand	Standard Cost	List Price	Value
5	Northwind Traders Chai	NWTB-1	25	25	$13.50	$18.00	337.5
6	Northwind Traders Syrup	NWTCO-3	0	50	$7.50	$10.00	375
7	Northwind Traders Cajun Season	NWTCO-4	0	0	$16.5		
8	Northwind Traders Olive Oil	NWTO-5	0	15	$16.01		
9	Northwind Traders Boysenberry	NWTJP-6	0	0	$18.7		
10	Northwind Traders Dried Pears	NWTDFN-7	0	0	$22.50	$30.00	0
11	Northwind Traders Curry Sauce	NWTS-8	0	0	$30.00	$40.00	0
12	Northwind Traders Walnuts	NWTDFN-14	0	40	$17.44	$23.25	697.5
13	Northwind Traders Fruit Cocktail	NWTCFV-17	0	0	$29.25	$39.00	0
14	Northwind Traders Chocolate Bis	NWTBGM-19	0	0	$6.90	$9.20	0
15	Northwind Traders Marmalade	NWTJP-6	0	0	$60.75	$81.00	0
16	Northwind Traders Scones	NWTBGM-21	0	0	$7.50	$10.00	0
17	Northwind Traders Beer	NWTB-34	23	23	$10.50	$14.00	241.5
18	Northwind Traders Crab Meat	NWTCM-40	0	0	$13.80	$18.40	0

Figure 13.19
When you confirm a new table formula, Excel automatically fills the formula down into the rest of the table.

13

In Figure 13.19, notice also that Excel simplified the table formula by removing the table names, which it considers redundant.

Excel's Table Functions

To take your table analysis to a higher level, you can use Excel's *table functions*, which give you the following advantages:

- You can enter the functions into any cell in the worksheet.
- You can specify the range the function uses to perform its calculations.
- You can enter criteria or reference a criteria range to perform calculations on subsets of the table.

About Table Functions

To illustrate the table functions, consider an example: If you want to calculate the sum of a table field, you can enter SUM(range), and Excel produces the result. If you want to sum only a subset of the field, you must specify as arguments the particular cells to use. For tables containing hundreds of records, however, this process is impractical.

The solution is to use DSUM(), which is the table equivalent of the SUM() function. The DSUM() function takes three arguments: a table range, field name, and criteria range. DSUM() looks at the specified field in the table and sums only records that match the criteria in the criteria range.

The table functions come in two varieties: those that don't require a criteria range and those that do.

Table Functions That Don't Require a Criteria Range

Excel has three table functions that enable you to specify the criteria as an argument rather than a range: COUNTIF(), SUMIF(), and AVERAGEIF().

Using COUNTIF()

The COUNTIF() function counts the number of cells in a range that meet a single criteria:

    COUNTIF(*range*, *criteria*)

range	The range of cells to use for the count.
criteria	The criteria, entered as text, that determines which cells to count. Excel applies the criteria to *range*.

For example, Figure 13.20 shows a COUNTIF() function that calculates the total number of products that have no stock (that is, where the Qty On Hand field equals zero).

Figure 13.20
Use COUNTIF() to count the cells that meet a criteria.

	G2	▼ : × ✓ fx	=COUNTIF(Inventory[Qty On Hand], "=0")				
	A	B	C	D	E	F	G
2					Products with no stock		29
3							
4	Product Name ▾	Product Code ▾	Qty On Hold ▾	Qty On Hand ▾	Standard Cost ▾	List Price ▾	Value ▾
5	Northwind Traders Chai	NWTB-1	25	25	$13.50	$18.00	$337.50
6	Northwind Traders Syrup	NWTCO-3	0	50	$7.50	$10.00	$375.00
7	Northwind Traders Cajun Seasoninç	NWTCO-4	0	0	$16.50	$22.00	$0.00
8	Northwind Traders Olive Oil	NWTO-5	0	15	$16.01	$21.35	$240.19
9	Northwind Traders Boysenberry Sp	NWTJP-6	0	0	$18.75	$25.00	$0.00
10	Northwind Traders Dried Pears	NWTDFN-7	0	0	$22.50	$30.00	$0.00
11	Northwind Traders Curry Sauce	NWTS-8	0	0	$30.00	$40.00	$0.00
12	Northwind Traders Walnuts	NWTDFN-14	0	40	$17.44	$23.25	$697.50
13	Northwind Traders Fruit Cocktail	NWTCFV-17	0	0	$29.25	$39.00	$0.00
14	Northwind Traders Chocolate Biscu	NWTBGM-19	0	0	$6.90	$9.20	$0.00
15	Northwind Traders Marmalade	NWTJP-6	0	0	$60.75	$81.00	$0.00
16	Northwind Traders Scones	NWTBGM-21	0	0	$7.50	$10.00	$0.00
17	Northwind Traders Beer	NWTB-34	23	23	$10.50	$14.00	$241.50
18	Northwind Traders Crab Meat	NWTCM-40	0	0	$13.80	$18.40	$0.00

Using SUMIF()

The SUMIF() function is similar to COUNTIF(), except that it sums the range cells that meet its criteria:

```
SUMIF(range, criteria[, sum_range])
```

range
: The range of cells to use for the criteria.

criteria
: The criteria, entered as text, that determines which cells to sum. Excel applies the criteria to range.

sum_range
: The range from which the sum values are taken. Excel sums only those cells in sum_range that correspond to the cells in range and meet the criteria. If you omit sum_range, Excel uses range for the sum.

Figure 13.21 shows a Parts table. The SUMIF() function in cell F16 sums the Total Cost field for the parts where the Division field is equal to 3.

Figure 13.21
Use SUMIF() to sum cells that meet a criteria.

	F16	▼ : × ✓ fx	=SUMIF(Parts[Division], "=3", Parts[Total Cost])					
	A	B	C	D	E	F	G	H
4								
5	Parts Database							
6	Division	Description	Number	Quantity	Cost	Total Cost	Retail	Gross Margin
7	4	Gangley Pliers	D-178	57	$10.47	$ 596.79	$17.95	71.4%
8	3	HCAB Washer	A-201	856	$ 0.12	$ 102.72	$ 0.25	108.3%
9	3	Finley Sprocket	C-098	357	$ 1.57	$ 560.49	$ 2.95	87.9%
10	2	6" Sonotube	B-111	86	$15.24	$1,310.64	$19.95	30.9%
11	4	Langstrom 7" Wrench	D-017	75	$18.69	$1,401.75	$27.95	49.5%
12	3	Thompson Socket	C-321	298	$ 3.11	$ 926.78	$ 5.95	91.3%
13	1	S-Joint	A-182	155	$ 6.85	$1,061.75	$ 9.95	45.3%
14	2	LAMF Valve	B-047	482	$ 4.01	$1,932.82	$ 6.95	73.3%
15								
16				Total cost of Division 3 parts:		$1,589.99		

Using `AVERAGEIF()`

The `AVERAGEIF()` function calculates the average of a range of cells that meet its criteria:

```
AVERAGEIF(range, criteria[, average_range])
```

range	The range of cells to use for the criteria.
criteria	The criteria, entered as text, that determines which cells to average. Excel applies the criteria to *range*.
average_range	The range from which the average values are taken. Excel sums only those cells in *average_range* that correspond to the cells in *range* and meet the criteria. If you omit *average_range*, Excel uses *range* for the average.

In Figure 13.22, the `AVERAGEIF()` function in cell F17 averages the Gross Margin field for the parts where the Cost field is less than 10.

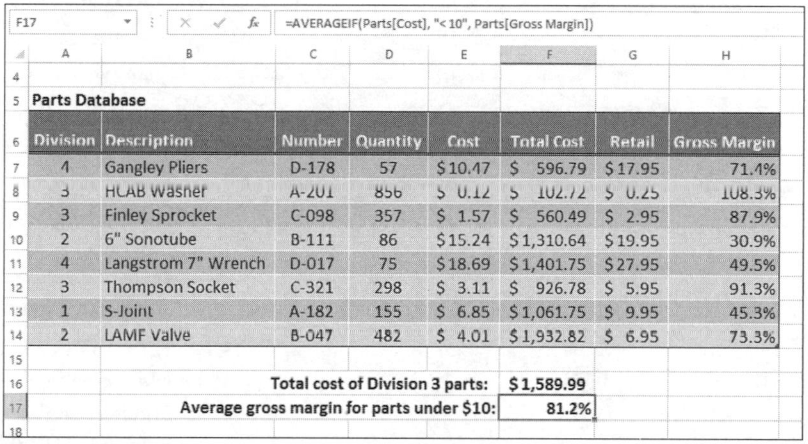

F17 =AVERAGEIF(Parts[Cost], "< 10", Parts[Gross Margin])

Parts Database

Division	Description	Number	Quantity	Cost	Total Cost	Retail	Gross Margin
4	Gangley Pliers	D-178	57	$10.47	$ 596.79	$17.95	71.4%
3	HCAB Washer	A-201	856	$ 0.12	$ 102.72	$ 0.25	108.3%
3	Finley Sprocket	C-098	357	$ 1.57	$ 560.49	$ 2.95	87.9%
2	6" Sonotube	B-111	86	$15.24	$1,310.64	$19.95	30.9%
4	Langstrom 7" Wrench	D-017	75	$18.69	$1,401.75	$27.95	49.5%
3	Thompson Socket	C-321	298	$ 3.11	$ 926.78	$ 5.95	91.3%
1	S-Joint	A-182	155	$ 6.85	$1,061.75	$ 9.95	45.3%
2	LAMF Valve	B-047	482	$ 4.01	$1,932.82	$ 6.95	73.3%

Total cost of Division 3 parts: $1,589.99

Average gross margin for parts under $10: 81.2%

Figure 13.22
Use `AVERAGEIF()` to sum cells that meet a criteria.

Using `AGGREGATE()`

The `AGGREGATE()` function is an all-purpose tool that can return a result for one of 19 summary functions—including `AVERAGE()`, `SUM()`, `COUNT()`, and the functions associated with variance and standard deviation—applied to the data in a numeric range. Here's the syntax:

```
AGGREGATE(function_num, options, ref1[, ref2,...])
```

function_num An integer value between 1 and 19 that specifies the summary function you want to apply:

function_num	Function
1	`AVERAGE()`
2	`COUNT()`
3	`COUNTA()`

4	`MAX()`
5	`MIN()`
6	`PRODUCT()`
7	`STDEV.S()`
8	`STDEV.P()`
9	`SUM()`
10	`VAR.S()`
11	`VAR.P()`
12	`MEDIAN()`
13	`MODE.SNGL()`
14	`LARGE()`
15	`SMALL()`
16	`PERCENTILE.INC()`
17	`QUARTILE.INC()`
18	`PERCENTILE.EXC()`
19	`QUARTILE.EXC()`

options   An integer between 0 and 7 that tells Excel which values to ignore when applying the summary function:

options	Ignores
0	Nested `SUBTOTAL()` and `AGGREGATE()` functions
1	Hidden rows and nested `SUBTOTAL()` and `AGGREGATE()` functions
2	Error values and nested `SUBTOTAL()` and `AGGREGATE()` functions
3	Hidden rows, error values, and nested `SUBTOTAL()` and `AGGREGATE()` functions
4	Nothing
5	Hidden rows
6	Error values
7	Hidden rows and error values

ref1, ref2, etc.   The range or ranges that contain the values to be summarized.

For example, the following formula calculates the largest value in the range A2:A100 while ignoring hidden rows and error values:

```
=AGGREGATE(14, 7, A2:A100)
```

Table Functions That Accept Multiple Criteria

In legacy versions of Excel, if you wanted to sum table values that satisfy two or more criteria, it was possible, but it usually required jumping through some serious formula hoops. For example, you could nest multiple IF() functions inside a SUM() function entered as an array formula. In other words, it was doable, but it wasn't for the faint of heart.

Beginning with Excel 2007, this was fixed, and Excel now offers three functions that enable you to specify multiple criteria: COUNTIFS(), SUMIFS(), and AVERAGEIFS(). Note that none of these functions requires a separate criteria range.

Using COUNTIFS()

The COUNTIFS() function counts the number of cells in one or more ranges that meet one or more criteria:

COUNTIFS(*range1, criteria1*[, *range2, criteria2, ...*])

range1	The first range of cells to use for the count.
criteria1	The first criteria, entered as text, that determines which cells to count. Excel applies the criteria to *range1*.
range2	The second range of cells to use for the count.
criteria2	The second criteria, entered as text, that determines which cells to count. Excel applies the criteria to *range2*.

You can enter up to 127 range/criteria pairs. For example, Figure 13.23 shows a COUNTIFS() function in cell H1 that returns the number of customers where the Country field equals USA and the Region field equals OR. (This is short for Oregon; don't confuse it with Excel's OR() function!)

Figure 13.23
Use COUNTIFS() to count the cells that meet one or more criteria.

Contact Title	Address	City	Region	PostalC	Country
Sales Representative	Via Monte Bianco 34	Torino		10100	Italy
Sales Associate	Av. dos Lusíadas, 23	São Paulo	SP	05432-043	Brazil
Sales Representative	Obere Str. 57	Berlin		12209	Germany
Sales Representative	Fauntleroy Circus	London		EC2 5NT	UK
Accounting Manager	Rua da Panificadora, 12	Rio de Janeirc	RJ	02389-673	Brazil
Marketing Manager	Garden HouseCrowther Way	Cowes	Isle of Wight	PO31 7PJ	UK
Order Administrator	Berguvsvägen 8	Luleå		S-958 22	Sweden
Owner	Erling Skakkes gate 78	Stavern		4110	Norway
Owner	265, boulevard Charonne	Paris		75012	France
Sales Manager	P.O. Box 555	Lander	WY	82520	USA
Sales Representative	Berkeley Gardens12 Brewery	London		WX1 6LT	UK
Accounting Manager	Gran Vía, 1	Madrid		28001	Spain
Accounting Manager	Boulevard Tirou, 255	Charleroi		B-6000	Belgium
Marketing Assistant	Alameda dos Canàrios, 891	São Paulo	SP	05487-020	Brazil

Formula bar: `=COUNTIFS(Customers[Country], "=USA", Customers[Region], "=OR")`

Customers from Oregon, USA: 4

Using `SUMIFS()`

The `SUMIFS()` function sums cells in one or more ranges that meet one or more criteria:

`SUMIFS(`*`sum_range, range1, criteria1[, range2, criteria2, ...]`*`)`

sum_range	The range from which the sum values are taken. Excel sums only those cells in *sum_range* that correspond to the cells that meet the criteria.
range1	The first range of cells to use for the sum criteria.
criteria1	The first criteria, entered as text, that determines which cells to sum. Excel applies the criteria to *range1*.
range2	The second range of cells to use for the sum criteria.
criteria2	The second criteria, entered as text, that determines which cells to sum. Excel applies the criteria to *range2*.

You can enter up to 127 range/criteria pairs. Figure 13.24 shows the Inventory table. The `SUMIFS()` function in cell G1 sums the Qty On Hand field for the products where the Product Name field includes Soup and the Qty On Hold field equals zero.

Figure 13.24
Use `SUMIFS()` to sum the cells that meet one or more criteria.

G1 =SUMIFS(Inventory[Qty On Hand], Inventory[Product Name], "*Soup*", Inventory[Qty On Hold], "=0")

	A	B	C	D	E	F	G
1		Products with "Soup" in the name and no stock on hold					55
2						Products with no stock	29
3							
4	Product Name	Product Code	Qty On Hold	Qty On Hand	Standard Cost	List Price	Value
5	Northwind Traders Chai	NWTB-1	25	25	$13.50	$18.00	$337.50
6	Northwind Traders Syrup	NWTCO-3	0	50	$7.50	$10.00	$375.00
7	Northwind Traders Cajun Seasoning	NWTCO-4	0	0	$16.50	$22.00	$0.00
8	Northwind Traders Olive Oil	NWTO-5	0	15	$16.01	$21.35	$240.19
9	Northwind Traders Boysenberry Sp	NWTJP-6	0	0	$18.75	$25.00	$0.00
10	Northwind Traders Dried Pears	NWTDFN-7	0	0	$22.50	$30.00	$0.00
11	Northwind Traders Curry Sauce	NWTS-8	0	0	$30.00	$40.00	$0.00
12	Northwind Traders Walnuts	NWTDFN-14	0	40	$17.44	$23.25	$697.50
13	Northwind Traders Fruit Cocktail	NWTCFV-17	0	0	$29.25	$39.00	$0.00
14	Northwind Traders Chocolate Biscu	NWTBGM-19	0	0	$6.90	$9.20	$0.00
15	Northwind Traders Marmalade	NWTJP-6	0	0	$60.75	$81.00	$0.00
16	Northwind Traders Scones	NWTBGM-21	0	0	$7.50	$10.00	$0.00

Using `AVERAGEIFS()`

The `AVERAGEIFS()` function averages cells in one or more ranges that meet one or more criteria:

`AVERAGEIFS(`*`average_range, range1, criteria1[, range2, criteria2, ...]`*`)`

average_range	The range from which the average values are taken. Excel averages only those cells in *average_range* that correspond to the cells that meet the criteria.
range1	The first range of cells to use for the average criteria.

criteria1	The first criteria, entered as text, that determines which cells to average. Excel applies the criteria to *range1*.
range2	The second range of cells to use for the average criteria.
criteria2	The second criteria, entered as text, that determines which cells to average. Excel applies the criteria to *range2*.

You can enter up to 127 range/criteria pairs. Figure 13.25 shows the accounts receivable table. The AVERAGEIFS() function in cell G2 averages the Days Overdue field for the invoices where the Days Overdue is greater than 0 and where the Invoice Amount field is greater than or equal to 1000.

Figure 13.25
Use AVERAGEIFS() to average the cells that meet one or more criteria.

Account Name	Account Number	Invoice Number	Invoice Amount	Due Date	Date Paid	Days Overdue
Current Date	20-Feb-16					
Average number of days overdue for invoices that are late and have amounts of at least $1,000:						20.1
Brimson Furniture	10-0009	117321	$2,144.55	19-Jan-16		32
Brimson Furniture	10-0009	117327	$1,847.25	1-Feb-16		19
Brimson Furniture	10-0009	117339	$1,234.69	19-Feb-16	17-Feb-16	
Brimson Furniture	10-0009	117344	$875.50	5-Mar-16	28-Feb-16	
Brimson Furniture	10-0009	117353	$898.54	20-Mar-16	15-Mar-16	
Chimera Illusions	02-0200	117318	$3,005.14	14-Jan-16	19-Jan-16	
Chimera Illusions	02-0200	117334	$303.65	12-Feb-16	16-Feb-16	
Chimera Illusions	02-0200	117345	$588.88	6-Mar-16	6-Mar-16	
Chimera Illusions	02-0200	117350	$456.21	15-Mar-16	11-Mar-16	
Door Stoppers Ltd.	01-0045	117319	$78.85	16-Jan-16	16-Jan-16	
Door Stoppers Ltd.	01-0045	117324	$101.01	26-Jan-16		25
Door Stoppers Ltd.	01-0045	117328	$58.50	2-Feb-16		18
Door Stoppers Ltd.	01-0045	117333	$1,685.74	11-Feb-16	9-Feb-16	
Emily's Sports Palace	08-2255	117316	$1,584.20	12-Jan-16		39

Table Functions That Require a Criteria Range

The remaining table functions require a criteria range. These functions take a little longer to set up, but the advantage is that you can enter compound and computed criteria.

All of these functions have the following format:

Dfunction(*database*, *field*, *criteria*)

Dfunction	The function name, such as DSUM or DAVERAGE.
database	The range of cells that make up the table you want to work with. You can use either a range name, if one is defined, or the range address.
field	The name of the field on which you want to perform the operation. You can use either the field name or the field number as the argument (in which the leftmost field is field number 1, the next field is field number 2, and so on). If you use the field name, enclose it in quotation marks (for example, "Total Cost").
criteria	The range of cells that hold the criteria you want to work with. You can use either a range name, if one is defined, or the range address.

13

TIP

To perform an operation on every record in a table, leave all the `criteria` fields blank. This causes Excel to select every record in the table.

Table 13.2 summarizes the table functions.

Table 13.2 Excel's Table Functions

Function	Description
DAVERAGE()	Returns the average of the matching records in a specified field.
DCOUNT()	Returns the count of the matching records.
DCOUNTA()	Returns the count of the nonblank matching records.
DGET()	Returns the value of a specified field for a single matching record.
DMAX()	Returns the maximum value of a specified field for the matching records.
DMIN()	Returns the minimum value of a specified field for the matching records.
DPRODUCT()	Returns the product of the values of a specified field for the matching records.
DSTDEV()	Returns the estimated standard deviation of the values in a specified field if the matching records are a sample of the population.
DSTDEVP()	Returns the standard deviation of the values of a specified field if the matching records are the entire population.
DSUM()	Returns the sum of the values of a specified field for the matching records.
DVAR()	Returns the estimated variance of the values of a specified field if the matching records are a sample of the population.
DVARP()	Returns the variance of the values of a specified field if the matching records are the entire population.

13

→ To learn about statistical operations such as standard deviation and variance, **see** Chapter 12, "Working with Statistical Functions," **p. 257**.

You enter table functions the same way you enter any other Excel function. You type an equal sign (=) and then enter the function—either by itself or combined with other Excel operators in a formula. The following examples show valid table functions:

```
=DSUM(A6:H14, "Total Cost", A1:H3)
=DSUM(Table, "Total Cost", Criteria)
=DSUM(AR_Table, 3, Criteria)
=DSUM(1993_Sales, "Sales", A1:H13)
```

The next two sections provide examples of the DAVERAGE() and DGET() table functions.

Using DAVERAGE()

The DAVERAGE() function calculates the average *field* value in the *database* records that match the *criteria*. In the Parts database, for example, suppose that you want to calculate the average gross margin for all parts assigned to Division 2. You set up a criteria range for the Division field and enter **2**, as shown in Figure 13.26. You then enter the following DAVERAGE() function (see cell H3):

```
=DAVERAGE(Parts[#All], "Gross Margin", A2:A3)
```

Figure 13.26
Use DAVERAGE() to calculate the field average in the matching records.

	A	B	C	D	E	F	G	H
	H3			fx	=DAVERAGE(Parts[#All], "Gross Margin", A2:A3)			
1	**Parts Criteria**							
2	**Division**							
3	2					Average Gross Margin for Division 2:		52.11%
4								
5	**Parts Database**							
6	**Division**	**Description**	**Number**	**Quantity**	**Cost**	**Total Cost**	**Retail**	**Gross Margin**
7	4	Gangley Pliers	D-178	57	$10.47	$ 596.79	$17.95	71.4%
8	3	HCAB Washer	A-201	856	$ 0.12	$ 102.72	$ 0.25	108.3%
9	3	Finley Sprocket	C-098	357	$ 1.57	$ 560.49	$ 2.95	87.9%
10	2	6" Sonotube	B-111	86	$15.24	$1,310.64	$19.95	30.9%
11	4	Langstrom 7" Wrench	D-017	75	$18.69	$1,401.75	$27.95	49.5%
12	3	Thompson Socket	C-321	298	$ 3.11	$ 926.78	$ 5.95	91.3%
13	1	S-Joint	A-182	155	$ 6.85	$1,061.75	$ 9.95	45.3%
14	2	LAMF Valve	B-047	482	$ 4.01	$1,932.82	$ 6.95	73.3%

Using DGET()

The DGET() function extracts the value of a single *field* in the *database* records that match the *criteria*. If there are no matching records, DGET() returns #VALUE!. If there's more than one matching record, DGET() returns #NUM!.

DGET() typically is used to query the table for a specific piece of information. For example, in the Parts table, you might want to know the cost of the Finley Sprocket. To extract this information, you would first set up a criteria range with the Description field and enter **Finley Sprocket**. You would then extract the information with the following formula (assuming that the table and criteria ranges are named Parts and Criteria, respectively):

```
=DGET(Parts[#All], "Cost", Criteria)
```

A more interesting application of this function would be to extract the name of a part that satisfies a certain condition. For example, you might want to know the name of the part that has the highest gross margin. Creating this model requires two steps:

1. Set up the criteria to match the highest value in the Gross Margin field.
2. Add a DGET() function to extract the description of the matching record.

13

Figure 13.27 shows how this is done. For the criteria, a new field called Highest Margin is created. As the text box shows, this field uses the following computed criteria:

```
=H7 = MAX(Parts2[Gross Margin])
```

Figure 13.27
A DGET() function that extracts the name of the part with the highest margin.

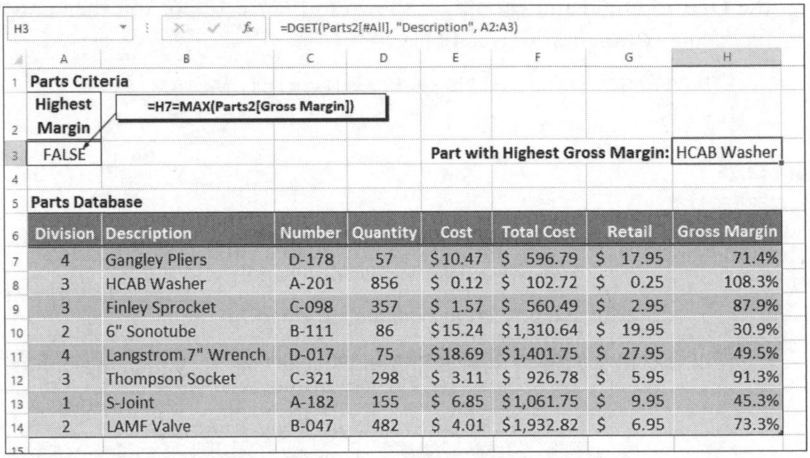

Excel matches only the record that has the highest gross margin. The DGET() function in cell H3 is straightforward:

```
=DGET(Parts2[#All], "Description", A2:A3)
```

This formula returns the description of the part that has the highest gross margin.

Case Study: Applying Statistical Table Functions to a Defects Database

Many table functions are most often used to analyze statistical populations. Figure 13.28 shows a table of defects found among 12 work groups in a manufacturing process. In this example, the table (B3:D15) is named Defects, and two criteria ranges are used—one for each of the group leaders, Johnson (G3:G4 is Criteria1) and Perkins (H3:H4 is Criteria2).

The table shows several calculations. First, DMAX() and DMIN() are calculated for each criteria. The range (a statistic that represents the difference between the largest and smallest numbers in the sample; it's a crude measure of the sample's variance) is then calculated using the following formula (Johnson's groups):

```
=DMAX(Defects[#All], "Defects", Criteria1) - DMIN(Defects[#All],
"Defects", Criteria1)
```

Of course, instead of using DMAX() and DMIN() explicitly, you can simply refer to the cells containing the DMAX() and DMIN() results.

Figure 13.28
Using statistical table functions to analyze a database of defects in a manufacturing process.

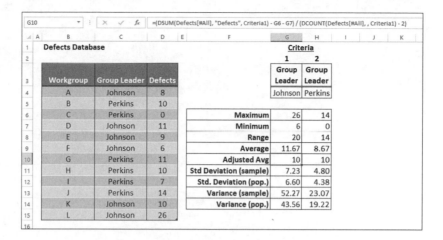

The next line uses DAVERAGE() to find the average number of defects for each group leader. Notice that the average for Johnson's groups (11.67) is significantly higher than that for Perkins's groups (8.67). However, Johnson's average is skewed higher by one anomalously large number (26), and Perkins's average is skewed lower by one anomalously small number (0).

To allow for this situation, the Adjusted Avg line uses DSUM(), DCOUNT(), and the DMAX() and DMIN() results to compute a new average without the largest and smallest number for each sample. As you can see, without the anomalies, the two leaders have the same average.

> **NOTE**
> As shown in cell G10 of Figure 13.28, if you don't include a field argument in the DCOUNT() function, it returns the total number of records in the table.

The rest of the calculations use the DSTDEV(), DSTDEVP(), DVAR(), and DVARP() functions.

From Here

13

- For coverage of the regular SUM() function, **see** "The SUM() Function," **p. 247.**
- For coverage of the regular COUNT() function, **see** "Counting Items with the COUNT() Function," **p. 261.**
- For coverage of the regular AVERAGE() function, **see** "The AVERAGE() Function," **p. 262.**
- For more detailed information on statistics such as standard deviation and variance, **see** Chapter 12, "Working with Statistical Functions," **p. 257.**

Analyzing Data with PivotTables

14

Tables and external databases can contain hundreds or even thousands of records. Analyzing that much data can be a nightmare without the right kinds of tools. To help you, Excel offers a powerful data analysis tool called a *PivotTable*. This tool enables you to summarize hundreds of records in a concise tabular format. You can then manipulate the layout of the table to see different views of your data. This chapter introduces you to PivotTables and shows you various ways to use them with your own data. Because this is a book about Excel formulas and functions, I don't go into tons of detail on building and customizing PivotTables. Instead, I focus on the extensive work you can do with built-in and custom PivotTable calculations.

What Are PivotTables?

To understand PivotTables, you need to see how they fit in with Excel's other database analysis features. Database analysis has several levels of complexity. The simplest level involves the basic lookup and retrieval of information. For example, if you have a database that lists the company sales reps and their territory sales, you could search for a specific rep to look up the sales in that rep's territory.

The next level of complexity involves more sophisticated lookup and retrieval systems, in which the criteria and extraction techniques discussed in Chapter 13, "Analyzing Data with Tables," are used. You can then apply subtotals and the table functions (also described in Chapter 13) to find answers to your questions. For example, suppose that each sales territory is part of a larger region, and you want to know the total sales in the East region. You could either subtotal by region or set up your criteria to match all territories in the East region and use the DSUM() function to get the total. To get more specific information, such as total East region sales in the second quarter, you just add the appropriate conditions to your criteria.

The next level of database analysis involves applying a single question to multiple variables. For example, if the company in the preceding example has four regions, you might want to see separate totals for each region, broken down by quarter. One solution would be to set up four different criteria and four different DSUM() functions. But what if there were a dozen regions? Or a hundred? Ideally, you need some way of summarizing the database information into a sales table that has a row for each region and a column for each quarter. This is exactly what PivotTables do and, as you'll see in this chapter, you can create your own PivotTables with just a few mouse clicks.

How PivotTables Work

In the simplest case, PivotTables work by summarizing the data in one field (called a *data field*) and breaking it down according to the data in another field. The unique values in the second field (called the *row field*) become the row headings. For example, Figure 14.1 shows a table of sales by sales representatives. With a PivotTable, you can summarize the numbers in the Sales field (the data field) and break them down by Region (the row field). Figure 14.2 shows the resulting PivotTable. Notice how Excel uses the four unique items in the Region field (East, Midwest, South, and West) as row headings.

Figure 14.1
A table of sales by sales representatives.

	A	B	C	D	E
1		Region	Quarter	Sales Rep	Sales
2		East	1st	Steven Buchanan	$192,345
3		West	1st	Michael Suyama	$210,880
4		East	1st	Margaret Peacock	$185,223
5		South	1st	Janet Leverling	$165,778
6		Midwest	1st	Anne Dodsworth	$155,557
7		South	1st	Nancy Davolio	$180,567
8		West	1st	Laura Callahan	$200,767
9		Midwest	1st	Andrew Fuller	$165,663
10		East	2nd	Steven Buchanan	$173,493
11		West	2nd	Michael Suyama	$200,203
12		East	2nd	Margaret Peacock	$170,213
13		South	2nd	Janet Leverling	$155,339
14		Midwest	2nd	Anne Dodsworth	$148,990
15		South	2nd	Nancy Davolio	$175,660
16		West	2nd	Laura Callahan	$190,290
17		Midwest	2nd	Andrew Fuller	$159,002
18		East	3rd	Steven Buchanan	$175,776
19		West	3rd	Michael Suyama	$205,534
20		East	3rd	Margaret Peacock	$192,345

NOTE You can download this chapter's sample workbooks at www.mcfedries.com/books/book.php?title=excel-2016-formulas-and-functions.

Figure 14.2
A PivotTable showing total sales by region.

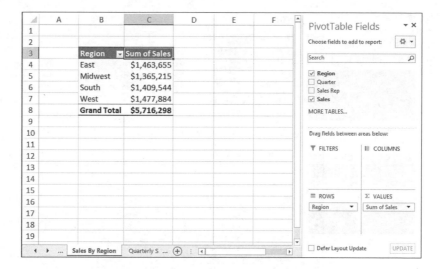

You can further break down your data by specifying a third field (called the *column field*) to use for column headings. Figure 14.3 shows the resulting PivotTable with the four unique items in the Quarter field (1st, 2nd, 3rd, and 4th) used to create the columns.

Figure 14.3
A PivotTable showing sales by region for each quarter.

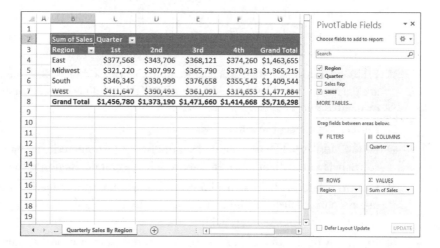

The big news with PivotTables is the pivoting feature. You can use it to see different views of your data. For example, you can drag the column field over to the row field area, as shown in Figure 14.4. As you can see, the result is that the table shows each region as the main row category, with the quarters as regional subcategories.

14

Figure 14.4
You can drag row or column fields to pivot the data and get a different view.

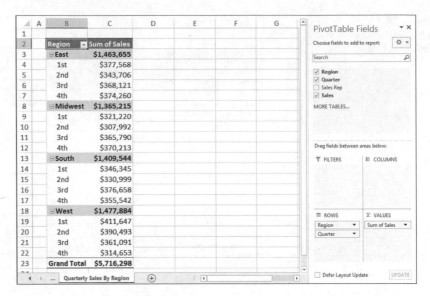

Some PivotTable Terms

PivotTables have their own terminology, so here's a quick glossary of some terms you need to become familiar with:

- **Data source**—The original data. You can use a range, a table, imported data, or an external data source.

- **Field**—A category of data, such as Region, Quarter, or Sales. Because most PivotTables are derived from tables or databases, a PivotTable field is directly analogous to a table or database field.

- **Label**—An element in a field.

- **Row field**—A field with a limited set of distinct text, numeric, or date values to use as row labels in the PivotTable. In the preceding example, Region is the row field.

- **Column field**—A field with a limited set of distinct text, numeric, or date values to use as column labels for the PivotTable. In the PivotTable shown in Figure 14.3, the Quarter field is the column field.

- **Filter**—A field with a limited set of distinct text, numeric, or date values that you use to filter the PivotTable view. For example, you could use the Sales Rep field as the filter. Selecting a different sales rep filters the table to show data only for that person.

- **PivotTable items**—The items from the source list used as row, column, and page labels.

- **Data field**—A field that contains the data you want to summarize in the table.

- **Data area**—The interior section of the table, in which the data summaries appear.

- **Layout**—The overall arrangement of fields and items in the PivotTable.

14

Building PivotTables

PivotTables look complex to build, but creating a basic PivotTable takes just a few steps. You can also build fancier PivotTables; Excel offers a wide range of options, styles, and features on the Ribbon.

Building a PivotTable from a Table or Range

The most common source for a PivotTable is an Excel table, although you can also use data that's set up as a regular range. You can use just about any table or range to build a Pivot-Table, but the best candidates for PivotTables exhibit two main characteristics:

- At least one of the fields contains *groupable* data. That is, the field contains data with a limited number of distinct text, numeric, or date values. In the Sales worksheet shown in Figure 14.1, the Region field is perfect for a PivotTable because, despite having dozens of items, it has only four distinct values: East, West, Midwest, and South.
- Each field in the list must have a heading.

Figure 14.5 shows a table that I'll use as an example to show you how to build a PivotTable. This is a list of orders placed in response to a three-month marketing campaign. Each record includes the following information:

- Date of the order
- Product ordered (there are four types: Printer stand, Glare filter, Mouse pad, and Copy holder)
- Quantity ordered
- Net dollars ordered
- Promotional offer selected by the customer (1 Free with 10 or Extra Discount)
- Advertisement to which the customer is responding (Direct mail, Magazine, or Newspaper)

Here are the steps to follow to summarize a table or range with a PivotTable:

1. Click a cell inside the table or range.
2. Determine how to proceed next, based on the type of data you want to summarize:
   - If you're working with a table, select Design, Summarize with PivotTable.
   - If you're working with a table or range, select Insert, PivotTable.
3. In the Create PivotTable dialog box that appears (see Figure 14.6), you should already see either the table name or the range address in the Select a Table or Range box. If not, enter or select the table name or range.

14

Figure 14.5
A table of orders to be summarized with a PivotTable.

	A	B	C	D	E	F	G
1		**SUMMER SALES PROMOTION - ORDERS**					
2		Date	Product	Quantity	Net $	Promotion	Advertisement
3		6/3/2015	Printer stand	11	$119.70	1 Free with 10	Direct mail
4		6/3/2015	Glare filter	6	$77.82	Extra Discount	Magazine
5		6/3/2015	Mouse pad	15	$100.95	Extra Discount	Newspaper
6		6/3/2015	Glare filter	11	$149.71	1 Free with 10	Magazine
7		6/4/2015	Mouse pad	22	$155.40	1 Free with 10	Magazine
8		6/4/2015	Mouse pad	3	$20.19	Extra Discount	Newspaper
9		6/4/2015	Copy holder	5	$33.65	Extra Discount	Direct mail
10		6/4/2015	Printer stand	22	$239.36	1 Free with 10	Newspaper
11		6/4/2015	Glare filter	10	$129.70	Extra Discount	Magazine
12		6/5/2015	Mouse pad	22	$155.40	1 Free with 10	Magazine
13		6/5/2015	Printer stand	8	$82.96	Extra Discount	Direct mail
14		6/5/2015	Printer stand	22	$239.40	1 Free with 10	Direct mail
15		6/5/2015	Copy holder	55	$388.50	1 Free with 10	Magazine
16		6/5/2015	Mouse pad	25	$168.25	Extra Discount	Newspaper
17		6/5/2015	Glare filter	22	$299.42	1 Free with 10	Magazine
18		6/6/2015	Mouse pad	33	$256.41	1 Free with 10	Magazine
19		6/6/2015	Printer stand	11	$119.70	1 Free with 10	Magazine
20		6/6/2015	Glare filter	22	$329.34	1 Free with 10	Magazine

Figure 14.6
Use the Create PivotTable dialog box to specify the table or range to use as the data source, as well as the location of the PivotTable.

4. Choose where you want the PivotTable report to appear:

   - **New Worksheet**—Click this option (it's selected by default) to have Excel create a new worksheet for the PivotTable.

   - **Existing Worksheet**—Click this option and then use the Location range box to type or select the cell where you want the PivotTable to appear. (The cell you specify will be the upper-left cell of the PivotTable.)

5. Click OK. Excel creates the PivotTable skeleton and displays the PivotTable Field List pane as well as two PivotTable Tools tabs: Analyze and Design (see Figure 14.7).

Figure 14.7
Excel starts off by creating
a barebones PivotTable
report.

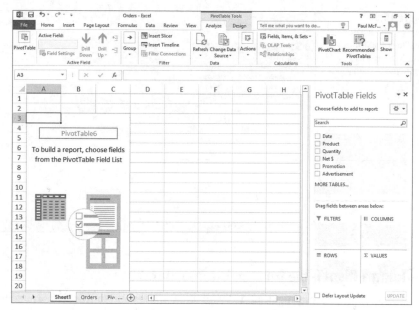

6. Add a field that you want to appear in the report. Excel gives you two ways to do this:

   - In the Choose Fields to Add to Report list, click to select the check box beside the field you want to add. If you select the check box of a numeric field, Excel adds it to the Values area; if you select the check box of a text field, Excel adds it to the Rows area.

   - Click-and-drag the field and drop it inside the area where you want the field to appear.

> **TIP**
> If you want to use a field in the PivotTable's column area, select its check box to add it to the Rows area, and then click-and-drag the field and drop it in the Columns area. You can also click-and-drag the field directly to the Columns area.

> **TIP**
> If you're using an exceptionally large data source, it may take Excel a long time to update the PivotTable as you add each field. In this case, click to select the Defer Layout Update check box, which tells Excel not to update the PivotTable as you add each field. When you're ready to see the current PivotTable layout, click Update.

7. Repeat step 6 to add all the fields you want included in the report. As you add each field, Excel updates the PivotTable report. For example, Figure 14.8 shows the report with the Quantity and Product fields added.

14

Figure 14.8
The PivotTable report with Product added to the Rows area and Quantity added to the Values area.

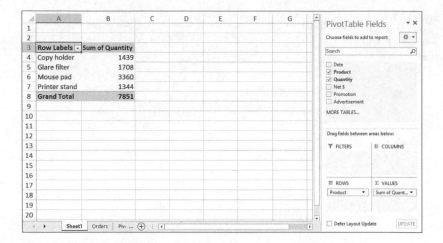

Building a PivotTable from an External Database

Excel can still put together a PivotTable even if your source data exists in an external database (for example, an Access or SQL Server database). If you have existing data connections on your system, you can use one of them as the data source. Otherwise, you can create a new connection on the fly. Here are the steps to follow:

1. Select Insert, PivotTable. Excel displays the Create PivotTable dialog box.
2. Select Use an External Data Source.
3. Click Choose Connection. Excel displays the Existing Connections dialog box.
4. If you see the connection you want to use, click it and skip to step 10. Otherwise, click Browse for More to open the Select Data Source dialog box.
5. Click New Source to launch the Data Connection Wizard.
6. Click the type of data source you want and then click Next.
7. Specify the data source. (How you do this depends on the type of data. For SQL Server, you specify the Server Name and Log On Credentials; for an ODBC data source, such as an Access database, you specify the database file.)
8. Select the database and table you want to use and then click Next.
9. Click Finish to complete the Data Connection Wizard.
10. To complete the PivotTable, follow steps 3 through 7 from the previous section.

> **NOTE**
> You can also create a PivotTable directly when you import data from an external source. In the Data tab's Get External Data group, select the type of data source you want to import and then follow the instructions on the screen. When you get to the Import Data dialog box, select the PivotTable Report option and then click OK.

Working with and Customizing a PivotTable

As I mentioned earlier, I'm going to concentrate in this chapter on PivotTable formulas and calculations. To that end, the list that follows takes you quickly through a few basic Pivot Table chores that you should know. Note that in almost all cases, you first need to click inside the PivotTable to enable the Analyze and Design tabs. Here's the list:

- **Selecting an entire PivotTable**—Select Analyze, Actions, Select, Entire PivotTable.
- **Selecting PivotTable items**—Select the entire PivotTable and then select Analyze, Actions, Select. In the list, click the PivotTable element you want to select: Labels and Values, Values, or Labels.
- **Formatting a PivotTable**—Select the Design tab and then click a style in the PivotTable Styles gallery.
- **Changing a PivotTable name**—Select the Analyze tab and then edit the PivotTable Name text box that appears in the PivotTable group.
- **Sorting a PivotTable**—Drop down the row or column header's filter button and then click either Sort A to Z or Sort Z to A. (If the field contains dates, click Sort Oldest to Newest or Sort Newest to Oldest, instead.)
- **Refreshing PivotTable data**—Select the Analyze tab and then click the top half of the Refresh button.
- **Filtering a PivotTable**—Click-and-drag a field to the Filters area, drop down the filter list, and then click an item in the list.
- **Grouping PivotTable data by date or numeric data**—Click the field, select Analyze, Group, Group Field to open the Grouping dialog box, and then click the grouping you want to use. For a date field, for example, you can group by months, quarters, or years.
- **Grouping PivotTable data by field items**—In the field, select each item you want to include in the group. Then select Analyze, Group, Group Selection.
- **Removing a field from a PivotTable**—Click-and-drag the field from the PivotTable Field List pane and drop it outside the pane.
- **Clearing a PivotTable**—Select Analyze, Actions, Clear, Clear All.

Working with PivotTable Subtotals

You've seen that Excel adds grand totals to a PivotTable for the row field and the column field. However, Excel also displays subtotals for the outer field of a PivotTable with multiple fields in the row or column area. For example, in Figure 14.9, you see two fields in the row area: Product (Copy holder, Glare filter, and so on) and Promotion (1 Free with 10 and Extra Discount). Product is the outer field, so Excel displays subtotals for that field.

The next few sections show you how to manipulate both the grand totals and the subtotals.

14

Figure 14.9
When you add multiple fields to the row or column area, Excel displays subtotals for the outer field.

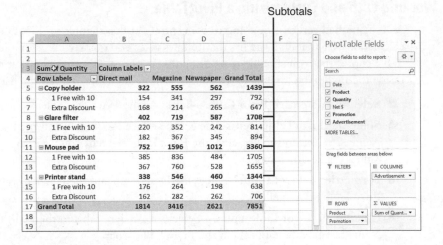

Hiding PivotTable Grand Totals

To remove grand totals from a PivotTable, follow these steps:

1. Select a cell inside the PivotTable.

2. Click the Design tab.

3. Select Grand Totals, Off for Rows and Columns. Excel removes the grand totals from the PivotTable.

Hiding PivotTable Subtotals

PivotTables with multiple row or column fields display subtotals for all fields except the innermost field (that is, the field closest to the data area). To remove these subtotals, follow these steps:

1. Select a cell in the field.

2. Click the Design tab.

3. Select Subtotals, Do Not Show Subtotals. Excel removes the subtotals from the PivotTable.

Customizing the Subtotal Calculation

The subtotal calculation that Excel applies to a field is the same calculation it uses for the data area. (See the next section for details on how to change the data field summary calculation.) You can, however, change this calculation, add extra calculations, and even add a subtotal for the innermost field. Click the field you want to work with, select Analyze, Active Field, Field Settings, and then use either of these methods:

■ To change the subtotal calculation, click Custom in the Subtotals group, click one of the calculation functions (Sum, Count, Average, and so on) in the Select One or More Functions list, and then click OK.

■ To add extra subtotal calculations, click Custom in the Subtotals group, use the Select One or More Functions list to click each calculation function you want to add, and then click OK.

Changing the Data Field Summary Calculation

By default, Excel uses a Sum function for calculating the data field summaries. Although Sum is the most common summary function used in PivotTables, it's by no means the only one. In fact, Excel offers 11 summary functions, as outlined in Table 14.1.

Table 14.1   Excel's Data Field Summary Calculations

Function	Description
Sum	Adds the values for the underlying data
Count	Displays the total number of values in the underlying data
Average	Calculates the average of the values for the underlying data
Max	Returns the largest value for the underlying data
Min	Returns the smallest value for the underlying data
Product	Calculates the product of the values for the underlying data
Count Numbers	Displays the total number of numeric values in the underlying data
StdDev	Calculates the standard deviation of the values for the underlying data, treated as a sample
StdDevp	Calculates the standard deviation of the values for the underlying data, treated as a population
Var	Calculates the variance of the values for the underlying data, treated as a sample
Varp	Calculates the variance of the values for the underlying data, treated as a population

Follow these steps to change the data field summary calculation:

1. Right-click any cell inside the data field.
2. Select Summarize Values By. Excel displays a partial list of the available summary calculations.
3. If you see the calculation you want, click it and skip the rest of these steps; otherwise, click More Options to open the Value Field Settings dialog box.
4. Select the summary calculation you want to use.
5. Click OK. Excel changes the data field calculation.

14

Using a Difference Summary Calculation

When you analyze business data, it's almost always useful to summarize the data as a whole: the sum of the units sold, the total number of orders, the average margin, and so on. For example, the PivotTable report shown in Figure 14.10 summarizes invoice data from a two-year period. For each customer in the row field, we see the total of all invoices broken down by the invoice date, which in this case has been grouped by year (2014 and 2015).

Figure 14.10
A PivotTable report showing customer invoice totals by year.

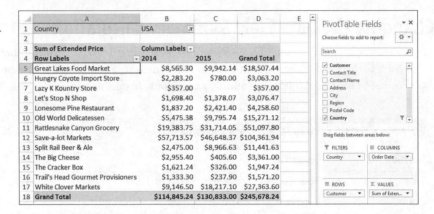

However, it's also useful to compare one part of the data with another. In the PivotTable shown in Figure 14.10, for example, it would be valuable to compare each customer's invoice totals in 2015 with those in 2014.

In Excel, you can perform this kind of analysis by using PivotTable *difference calculations*:

- **Difference From**—This difference calculation compares two numeric items and calculates the difference between them.

- **% Difference From**—This difference calculation compares two numeric items and calculates the percentage difference between them.

In each case, you must specify both a *base field* (the field in which you want Excel to perform the difference calculation) and the *base item* (the item in the base field that you want to use as the basis of the difference calculation). In the PivotTable shown in Figure 14.10, for example, Order Date would be the base field, and 2014 would be the base item.

Here are the steps to follow to set up a difference calculation:

1. Right-click any cell inside the data field.
2. Select Show Values As and then click either Difference From or % Difference From. Excel displays the Show Values As dialog box.
3. In the Base Field list, click the field you want to use as the base field.
4. In the Base Item list, click the item you want to use as the base item.
5. Click OK. Excel updates the PivotTable with the difference calculation.

Figure 14.11 shows both the completed Show Values As dialog box and the updated Pivot-Table with the Difference From calculation applied to the report from Figure 14.10.

Figure 14.11
The PivotTable report from Figure 14.10 with a Difference From calculation applied.

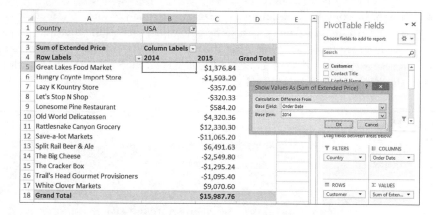

TOGGLING THE DIFFERENCE CALCULATION

Here's a VBA macro that toggles the PivotTable report in Figure 14.11 between a Difference From calculation and a % Difference From calculation:

```
Sub ToggleDifferenceCalculations()
    ' Work with the first data field
    With Selection.PivotTable.DataFields(1)
        ' Is the calculation currently Difference From?
        If .Calculation = xlDifferenceFrom Then
            ' If so, change it to % Difference From
            .Calculation = xlPercentDifferenceFrom
            .BaseField = "Order Date"
            .BaseItem = "2014"
            .NumberFormat = "0.00%"
        Else
            ' If not, change it to Difference From
            .Calculation = xlDifferenceFrom
            .BaseField = "Order Date"
            .BaseItem = "2014"
            .NumberFormat = "$#,##0.00"
        End If
    End With
End Sub
```

Using a Percentage Summary Calculation

When you need to compare the results that appear in a PivotTable report, just looking at the basic summary calculations isn't always useful. For example, consider the PivotTable report in Figure 14.12, which shows the total invoices put through by various sales reps,

14

broken down by quarter. In the fourth quarter, Margaret Peacock put through $64,429, whereas Robert King put through only $16,951. You can't say that the first rep is (roughly) four times as good a salesperson as the second rep because their territories or customers might be completely different. A better way to analyze these numbers would be to compare the fourth quarter figures with some base value, such as the first quarter total. The numbers are down in both cases, but again the raw differences won't tell you much. What you need to do is calculate the percentage differences and then compare them with the percentage difference in the Grand Total.

Figure 14.12
A PivotTable report showing sales rep invoice totals by quarter.

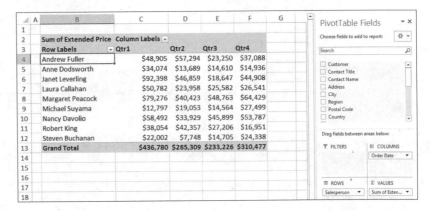

Similarly, knowing the raw invoice totals for each rep in a given quarter gives you only the most general idea of how the reps did with respect to each other. If you really want to compare them, you need to convert those totals into percentages of the quarterly grand total.

When you want to use percentages in your data analysis, you can use Excel's *percentage calculations* to view data items as a percentage of some other item or as a percentage of the total in the current row, column, or the entire PivotTable. Excel offers the following percentage calculations:

- **% Of**—This calculation returns the percentage of each value with respect to a selected base item. If you use this calculation, you must also select a base field and a base item upon which Excel will calculate the percentages.

- **% of Row Total**—This calculation returns the percentage that each value in a row represents with respect to the Grand Total for that row.

- **% of Column Total**—This calculation returns the percentage that each value in a column represents with respect to the Grand Total for that column.

- **% of Parent Row Total**—If you have multiple fields in the row area, this calculation returns the percentage that each value in an inner row represents with respect to the total of the parent item in the outer row. (This calculation also returns the percentage that each value in the outer row represents with respect to the Grand Total.)

14

- **% of Parent Column Total**—If you have multiple fields in the column area, this calculation returns the percentage that each value in an inner column represents with respect to the total of the parent item in the outer column. (This calculation also returns the percentage that each value in the outer column represents with respect to the Grand Total.)

- **% of Parent Total**—If you have multiple fields in the row or column area, this calculation returns the percentage of each value with respect to a selected base field in the outer row or column. If you use this calculation, you must also select a base field upon which Excel will calculate the percentages.

- **% of Grand Total**—This calculation returns the percentage that each value in the PivotTable represents with respect to the Grand Total of the entire PivotTable.

Here are the steps to follow to set up a difference calculation:

1. Right-click any cell inside the data field.

2. Select Show Values As and then click the percentage calculation you want to use. Excel displays the Show Values As dialog box.

3. If you chose either % Of or % of Parent Total, use the Base Field list to click the field you want to use as the base field.

4. If you clicked % Of, use the Base Item list to click the item you want to use as the base item.

5. Click OK. Excel updates the PivotTable with the percentage calculation.

Figure 14.13 shows both the completed Show Values As dialog box and the updated PivotTable with the % Of calculation applied to the report from Figure 14.12.

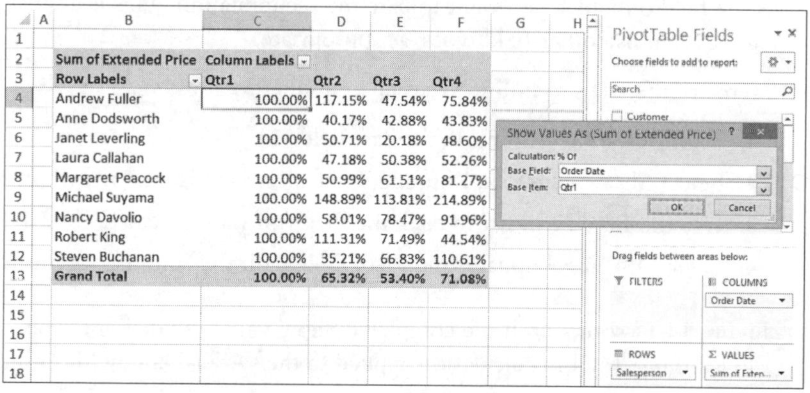

Figure 14.13
The PivotTable report from Figure 14.12 with a % Of calculation applied.

> **TIP**
>
> If you want to use a VBA macro to set the percentage calculation for a data field, set the `PivotField` object's `Calculation` property to one of the following constants:
>
> `xlPercentOf`, `xlPercentOfRow`, `xlPercentOfColumn`, or `xlPercentOfTotal`.
>
> When you switch back to Normal in the Show Values As list, Excel formats the data field as General, so you lose any numeric formatting you had applied. You can restore the numeric format by clicking inside the data field, choosing Analyze, Active Field, Field Settings, clicking Number Format, and then choosing the format in the Format Cells dialog box. Alternatively, you can use a macro that resets the `NumberFormat` property. Here's an example:
>
> ```
> Sub ReapplyCurrencyFormat()
>         With Selection.PivotTable.DataFields(1)
>             .NumberFormat = "$#,##0.00"
>         End With
>     End Sub
> ```

Using a Running Total Summary Calculation

When you set up a budget, it's common to have sales targets not only for each month but also cumulative targets as the fiscal year progresses. For example, you might have sales targets for the first month and the second month and also for the two-month total. You'd also have cumulative targets for three months, four months, and so on. Cumulative sums such as these are known as *running totals*, and they can be valuable in analysis. For example, if you find that you're running behind budget cumulatively at the six-month mark, you can make adjustments to process, marketing plans, customer incentives, and so on.

Excel PivotTable reports come with a Running Total summary calculation that you can use for this kind of analysis. Note that the running total is always applied to a base field, which is the field on which you want to base the accumulation. This is almost always a date field, but you can use other field types, as appropriate.

Here are the steps to follow to set up a running total calculation:

1. Right-click any cell inside the data field.
2. Select Show Values As, Running Total In. Excel displays the Show Values As dialog box.
3. Use the Base Field list to click the field you want to use as the base field.
4. Click OK. Excel updates the PivotTable with the running total calculation.

Figure 14.14 shows both the completed Show Values As dialog box and a PivotTable with the Running Total In calculation applied to the Order Date field (grouped by month).

Figure 14.14
The PivotTable report with a running total calculation.

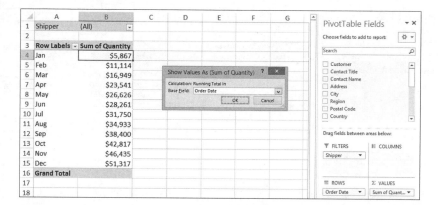

T I P

If you use many of these extra summary calculations, you might find yourself constantly returning the No Calculation value in the Show Values As menu. That requires a few mouse clicks, so it can be a hassle to repeat the procedure frequently. You can save time by creating a VBA macro that resets the PivotTable to Normal by setting the `Calculation` property to `xlNoAdditionalCalculation`. Here's an example:

```
Sub ResetCalculationToNormal()
    With Selection.PivotTable.DataFields(1)
        .Calculation = xlNoAdditionalCalculation
    End With
End Sub
```

Using an Index Summary Calculation

A PivotTable is great for reducing a large amount of relatively incomprehensible data into a compact, more easily grasped summary report. As you've seen in the past few sections, however, a standard summary calculation doesn't always provide you with the best analysis of the data.

Another good example of this is trying to determine the relative importance of the results in the data field. For example, consider the PivotTable report shown in Figure 14.15. This report shows the unit sales of four items (copy holder, glare filter, mouse pad, and printer stand), broken down by the type of advertisement the customer responded to (direct mail, magazine, and newspaper).

You can see, for example, that 1,012 mouse pads were sold via the newspaper ad (the second-highest number in the report), but only 562 copy holders were sold through the newspaper (one of the lower numbers in the report). Does this mean that you should only sell mouse pads in newspaper ads? That is, is the mouse pad/newspaper combination somehow more "important" than the copy holder/newspaper combination?

14

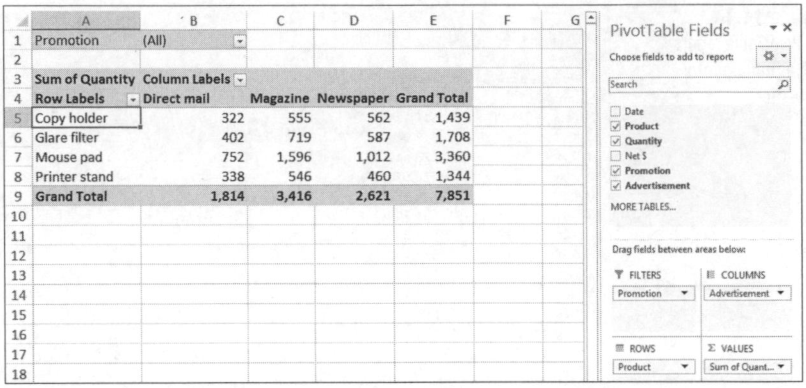

	A	B	C	D	E
1	Promotion	(All)			
2					
3	Sum of Quantity	Column Labels			
4	Row Labels	Direct mail	Magazine	Newspaper	Grand Total
5	Copy holder	322	555	562	1,439
6	Glare filter	402	719	587	1,708
7	Mouse pad	752	1,596	1,012	3,360
8	Printer stand	338	546	460	1,344
9	Grand Total	1,814	3,416	2,621	7,851

Figure 14.15
A PivotTable report showing unit sales of products broken down by advertisement.

You might think the answer is yes to both questions in the previous paragraph, but that's not necessarily the case. To get an accurate answer, you'd need to take into account the total number of mouse pads sold, the total number of copy holders sold, the total number of units sold through the newspaper, and the number of units overall. This is a complicated bit of business, to be sure, but each PivotTable report has an Index calculation that handles it for you automatically. The Index calculation returns the *weighted average* of each cell in the PivotTable data field, using the following formula:

```
(Cell Value) * (Grand Total) / (Row Total) * (Column Total)
```

In the Index calculation results, the higher the value, the more important the cell is in the overall results. Here are the steps to follow to set up an Index calculation:

1. Right-click any cell inside the data field.
2. Select Summarize Values By and then click the summary calculation you want to use.
3. Right-click any cell inside the data field.
4. Select Show Values As, Index. Excel updates the PivotTable with the index summary calculation.

Figure 14.16 shows the updated PivotTable with the Index applied to the report from Figure 14.15. As you can see, the mouse pad/newspaper combination scored an index of only 0.90 (the second-lowest value), whereas the copy holder/newspaper combination scored 1.17 (the highest value).

Creating Custom PivotTable Calculations

14

Excel's 11 built-in summary functions enable you to create powerful and useful PivotTable reports, but they don't cover every data analysis possibility. For example, suppose you have a PivotTable report that summarizes invoice totals by sales rep using the Sum function. That's useful, but you might also want to pay out a bonus to those reps whose total sales exceed some threshold. You could use the `GETPIVOTDATA()` function to create regular worksheet formulas to calculate whether bonuses should be paid and how much they should be (assuming each bonus is a percentage of the total sales).

→ For the details on the GETPIVOTDATA() function, **see** "Using PivotTable Results in a Worksheet Formula," **p. 347**.

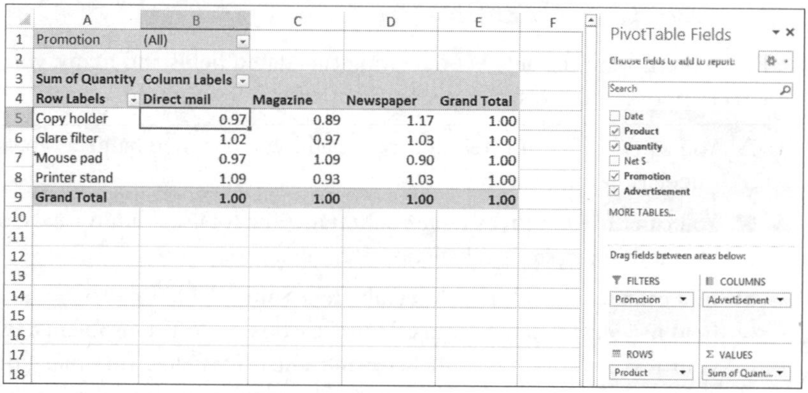

Figure 14.16
The PivotTable report from Figure 14.15 with an Index calculation applied.

However, this isn't very convenient. If you add sales reps, you need to add formulas; if you remove sales reps, existing formulas generate errors. And, in any case, one of the points of generating a PivotTable report is to perform *fewer* worksheet calculations, not more.

The solution in this case is to take advantage of Excel's *calculated field* feature. A calculated field is a new data field based on a custom formula. For example, if your invoice's Pivot-Table has an Extended Price field and you want to award a 5% bonus to those reps who did at least $75,000 worth of business, you'd create a calculated field based on the following formula:

```
=IF('Extended Price' >= 75000, 'Extended Price' * 0.05, 0)
```

> **NOTE**
> When you reference a field in your formula, Excel interprets this reference as the *sum* of that field's values. For example, if you include the logical expression 'Extended Price' >= 75000 in a calculated field formula, Excel interprets this as Sum of 'Extended Price' >= 75000. That is, it adds the Extended Price field and *then* compares it with 75000.

A slightly different PivotTable problem is when a field you're using for the row or column labels doesn't contain an item you need. For example, suppose your products are organized into various categories: Beverages, Condiments, Confections, Dairy Products, and so on. Suppose further that these categories are grouped into several divisions: Beverages and Condiments in Division A, Confections and Dairy Products in Division B, and so on. If the source data doesn't have a Division field, how do you see PivotTable results that apply to the divisions?

14

One solution is to create groups for each division. (That is, select the categories for one division, select Analyze, Group Selection, and repeat for the other divisions.) That works, but Excel gives you a second solution: Use calculated items. A *calculated item* is a new item in a row or column where the item's values are generated by a custom formula. For example, you could create a new item named Division A that is based on the following formula:

```
=Beverages + Condiments
```

Before getting to the details of creating calculated fields and items, you should know that Excel imposes a few restrictions on them. Here's a summary:

- You can't use a cell reference, range address, or range name as an operand in a custom calculation formula.

- You can't use the PivotTable's subtotals, row totals, column totals, or Grand Total as an operand in a custom calculation formula.

- In a calculated field, Excel defaults to a Sum calculation when you reference another field in your custom formula. However, this can cause problems. For example, suppose your invoice table has Unit Price and Quantity fields. You might think that you can create a calculated field that returns the invoice totals with the following formula:

```
=Unit Price * Quantity
```

  This won't work, however, because Excel treats the Unit Price operand as Sum of Unit Price, and it doesn't make sense to "add" the prices together.

- For a calculated item, the custom formula can't reference items from any field except the one in which the calculated item resides.

- You can't create a calculated item in a PivotTable that has at least one grouped field. You must ungroup all the PivotTable fields before you can create a calculated item.

- You can't use a calculated item as a filter.

- You can't insert a calculated item into a PivotTable in which a field has been used more than once.

- You can't insert a calculated item into a PivotTable that uses the Average, StdDev, StdDevp, Var, or Varp summary calculations.

Creating a Calculated Field

Here are the steps to follow to insert a calculated field into a PivotTable data area:

1. Click any cell in the PivotTable's data area.
2. Select Analyze, open the Fields, Items, & Sets list, and then select Calculated Field. Excel displays the Insert Calculated Field dialog box.
3. Use the Name text box to enter a name for the calculated field.
4. Use the Formula text box to enter the formula you want to use for the calculated field.

If you need to use a field name in the formula, position the cursor where you want the field name to appear, click the field name in the Fields list, and then click Insert Field.

5. Click Add.

6. Click OK. Excel inserts the calculated field into the PivotTable.

Figure 14.17 shows a completed version of the Insert Calculated Field dialog box, as well as the resulting Bonus field in the PivotTable. Here's the full formula that appears in the Formula text box:

```
=IF('Extended Price' >= 75000, 'Extended Price' * 0.05, 0)
```

Figure 14.17
A PivotTable report with a
Bonus calculated field.

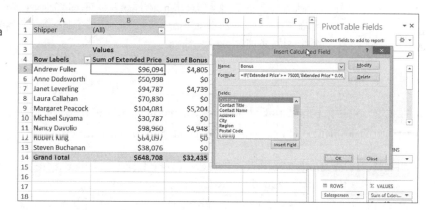

If you need to make changes to a calculated field, click any cell in the PivotTable's data area, select Analyze, open the Fields, Items, & Sets list, select Calculated Field, and then use the Name list to select the calculated field you want to work with. Make your changes to the formula, click Modify, and then click OK.

CAUTION

In Figure 14.17, notice that the Grand Total row also includes a total for the Bonus field. Notice, too, that the total displayed is incorrect! This is almost always the case with calculated fields. The problem is that Excel doesn't derive the calculated field's Grand Total by adding up the field's values. Instead, Excel applies the calculated field's formula to the Grand Total of whatever field you reference in the formula. For example, in the logical expression `'Extended Price' >= 75000`, Excel uses the Grand Total of the Extended Price field. Because this is definitely more than 75,000, Excel calculates the "bonus" of 5%, which is the value that appears in the Bonus field's Grand Total.

14

Creating a Calculated Item

Here are the steps to follow to insert a calculated item into a PivotTable's row or column area:

1. Click any cell in the row or column field to which you want to add the item.

2. Select Analyze, open the Fields, Items, & Sets list, and then select Calculated Item. Excel displays the Insert Calculated Item in "*Field*" dialog box (where *Field* is the name of the field you're working with).

3. Use the Name text box to enter a name for the calculated item.

4. Use the Formula text box to enter the formula you want to use for the calculated item.

> **NOTE** To add a field name to the formula, position the cursor where you want the field name to appear, click the field name in the Fields list, and then click Insert Field. To add a field item to the formula, position the cursor where you want the item name to appear, click the field in the Fields list, click the item in the Items list, and then click Insert Item.

5. Click Add.

6. Repeat steps 3–5 to add other calculated items to the field.

7. Click OK. Excel inserts the calculated item or items into the row or column field.

Figure 14.18 shows a completed version of the Insert Calculated Item in "*Field*" dialog box, as well as three items added to the Category row field:

```
Division A: =Beverage + Condiments
Division B: =Confections + 'Dairy Products'
Division C: ='Grains/Cereals' + 'Meat/Poultry' + Produce + Seafood
```

Figure 14.18
A PivotTable report with three calculated items added to the Category row field.

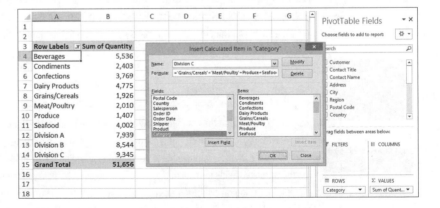

NOTE

To make changes to a calculated item, click any cell in the field that contains the item, select Analyze, open the Fields, Items, & Sets list, select Calculated Item, and then use the Name list to select the calculated item you want to work with. Make your changes to the formula, click Modify, and then click OK.

CAUTION

When you insert an item into a field, Excel remembers that item. (Technically, it becomes part of the data source's pivot cache.) If you then insert the same field into another PivotTable based on the same data source, Excel also includes the calculated items in the new PivotTable. If you don't want the calculated items to appear in the new PivotTable report, drop down the field's menu and deselect the check box beside each calculated item.

Using PivotTable Results in a Worksheet Formula

What do you do when you need to include a PivotTable result in a regular worksheet formula? At first, you might be tempted just to include a reference to the appropriate cell in the PivotTable's data area. However, that works only if your PivotTable is static and never changes. In the vast majority of cases, the reference won't work because the addresses of the report values change as you pivot, filter, group, and refresh the PivotTable.

If you want to include a PivotTable result in a formula and you want that result to remain accurate even as you manipulate the PivotTable, use Excel's `GETPIVOTDATA()` function. This function uses the data field, PivotTable location, and one or more (row or column) field/item pairs that specify the exact value you want to use. Here's the syntax:

```
GETPIVOTDATA(data_field, pivot_table[, field1, item1]...])
```

`data_field`	The name of the PivotTable data field that contains the data you want
`pivot_table`	The address of any cell or range within the PivotTable, or a named range within the PivotTable
`field1`	The name of the PivotTable row or column field that contains the data you want
`item1`	The name of the item within `field1` that specifies the data you want

Note that you always enter the `fieldn` and `itemn` arguments as a pair. If you don't include any field/item pairs, `GETPIVOTDATA()` returns the PivotTable Grand Total. You can enter up to 126 field/item pairs. This might make `GETPIVOTDATA()` seem like more work than it's worth, but the good news is that you'll rarely have to enter the `GETPIVOTDATA()` function by hand. By default, Excel is configured to generate the appropriate `GETPIVOTDATA()` syntax automatically. That is, you start your worksheet formula, and when you get to the part

14

where you need the PivotTable value, just click the value. Excel then inserts the GETPIVOTDATA() function with the syntax that returns the value you want.

For example, in Figure 14.19, you can see that I started a worksheet formula in cell F5 and then clicked cell B5 in the PivotTable. Excel generated the GETPIVOTDATA() function shown.

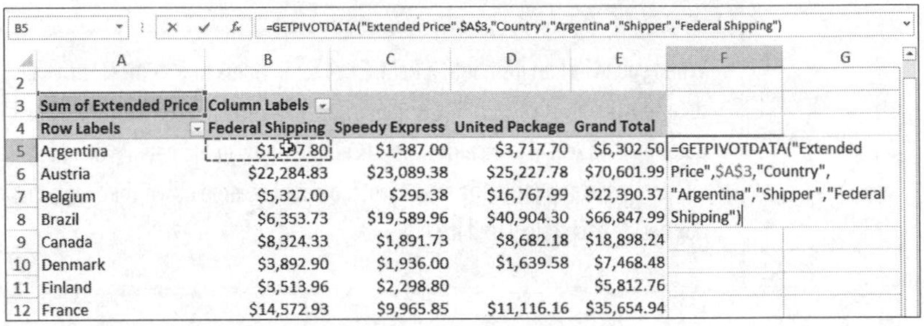

Figure 14.19
When you're entering a worksheet formula, click a cell in a PivotTable's data area, and Excel automatically generates the corresponding GETPIVOTDATA() function.

	A	B	C	D	E	F	G
	B5		fx	=GETPIVOTDATA("Extended Price",$A$3,"Country","Argentina","Shipper","Federal Shipping")			
2							
3	Sum of Extended Price	Column Labels					
4	Row Labels	Federal Shipping	Speedy Express	United Package	Grand Total		
5	Argentina	$1,597.80	$1,387.00	$3,717.70	$6,302.50	=GETPIVOTDATA("Extended	
6	Austria	$22,284.83	$23,089.38	$25,227.78	$70,601.99	Price",$A$3,"Country",	
7	Belgium	$5,327.00	$295.38	$16,767.99	$22,390.37	"Argentina","Shipper","Federal	
8	Brazil	$6,353.73	$19,589.96	$40,904.30	$66,847.99	Shipping")	
9	Canada	$8,324.33	$1,891.73	$8,682.18	$18,898.24		
10	Denmark	$3,892.90	$1,936.00	$1,639.58	$7,468.48		
11	Finland	$3,513.96	$2,298.80		$5,812.76		
12	France	$14,572.93	$9,965.85	$11,116.16	$35,654.94		

If Excel doesn't generate the GETPIVOTDATA() function automatically, that feature may be turned off. Follow these steps to turn it back on:

1. Select File, Options to open the Excel Options dialog box.
2. Click Formulas.
3. Click to select the Use GetPivotData Functions for PivotTable References check box.
4. Click OK.

> **TIP**
>
> You can also use a VBA procedure to toggle automatic GETPIVOTDATA() functions on and off. Set the Application.GenerateGetPivotData property to True or False, as in the following macro:
>
> ```
> Sub ToggleGenerateGetPivotData()
>     With Application
>         .GenerateGetPivotData = Not .GenerateGetPivotData
>     End With
> End Sub
> ```

From Here

- To learn more about the IF() function used in this chapter, **see** "Using the IF() Function," **p. 164**.
- For a complete look at Excel tables, **see** Chapter 13, "Analyzing Data with Tables."

Using Excel's Business Modeling Tools

At times, it's not enough to simply enter data into a worksheet, build a few formulas, and add a little formatting to make things presentable. In the business world, you're often called on to divine some inner meaning from the jumble of numbers and formula results that litter your workbooks. In other words, you need to *analyze* your data to see what nuggets of understanding you can unearth. In Excel, analyzing business data means using the program's business modeling tools. This chapter looks at a few of those tools and some analytic techniques that have many uses. You'll find out how to use Excel's numerous methods for what-if analysis, how to wield Excel's useful Goal Seek tool, and how to create scenarios.

Using What-If Analysis

What-if analysis is perhaps the most basic method for interrogating your worksheet data. With what-if analysis, you first calculate a formula, D, based on the input from variables A, B, and C. You then say, "What if I change variable A? Or B or C? What happens to the result?"

For example, Figure 15.1 shows a worksheet that calculates the future value of an investment based on five variables: the interest rate, period, annual deposit, initial deposit, and deposit type. Cell C9 shows the result of the FV() function. Now the questions begin:

- What if the interest rate is 7%?
- What if you deposit $8,000 per year? Or $12,000?
- What if you reduce the initial deposit?

Answering these questions is a straightforward matter of changing the appropriate variables and watching the effect on the result.

Figure 15.1
The simplest what-if analysis involves changing worksheet variables and watching the result.

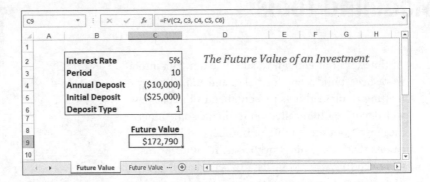

> **NOTE** You can download this chapter's sample workbook at www.mcfedries.com/books/ book.php?title=excel-2016-formulas-and-functions.

Setting Up a One-Input Data Table

The problem with modifying formula variables is that you see only a single result at one time. If you're interested in studying the effect a range of values has on a formula, you need to set up a *data table*. In the investment analysis worksheet, for example, suppose you want to see the future value of the investment with the annual deposit varying between $7,000 and $13,000. You could just enter these values in a row or column and then create the appropriate formulas. Setting up a data table, however, is much easier, as the following procedure shows:

1. Add to the worksheet the values you want to input into the formula. You have two choices for the placement of these values:

   - If you want to enter the values in a row, start the row one cell up and one cell to the right of the formula.

   - If you want to enter the values in a column, start the column one cell down and one cell to the left of the cell containing the formula, as shown in Figure 15.2.

2. Select the range that includes the input values and the formula. (In Figure 15.2, this is B9:C16.)

3. Select Data, What-If Analysis, Data Table. Excel displays the Data Table dialog box.

4. Fill in this dialog box based on how you set up your data table:

   - If you entered the input values in a row, use the Row Input Cell text box to enter the cell address of the input cell.

- If the input values are in a column, enter the input cell's address in the Column Input Cell text box. In the investment analysis example, you click cell **C4** and then $C$4 appears in the Column Input Cell text box, as shown in Figure 15.3.

Figure 15.2
Enter the values you want to input into the formula.

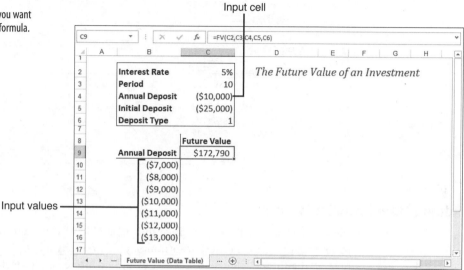

Figure 15.3
In the Data Table dialog box, enter the input cell where you want Excel to substitute the input values.

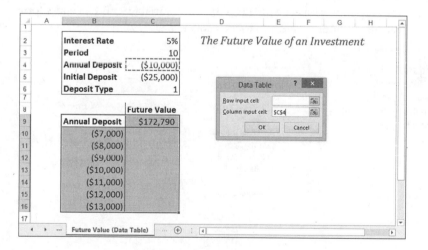

5. Click OK. Excel places each of the input values in the input cell; Excel then displays the results in the data table. Format the cells as necessary (see Figure 15.4).

Figure 15.4
Excel substitutes each input value into the input cell and displays the results in the data table.

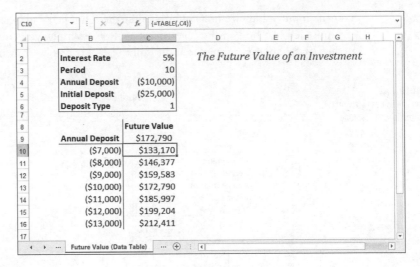

Adding More Formulas to the Input Table

You're not restricted to using just a single formula in a data table. If you want to see the effect of the various input values on different formulas, you can easily add them to the data table. For example, in the future value worksheet, it would be interesting to factor inflation into the calculations to see how the investment appears in today's dollars. Figure 15.5 shows the revised worksheet with a new Inflation variable (cell C7) and a formula that converts the calculated future value into today's dollars (cell D9).

Figure 15.5
To add a formula to a data table, enter the new formula next to the existing one.

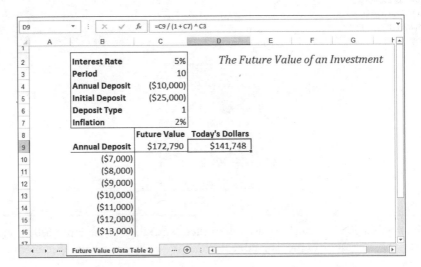

15

> **NOTE** This is the formula for converting a future value into today's dollars:
>
> `Future Value / (1 + Inflation Rate) ^ Period`
>
> Here, `Period` is the number of years from now that the future value exists.

To create the new data table, follow the steps outlined previously. However, make sure that the range you select in step 2 includes the input values and *both* formulas (that is, the range B9:D16 in Figure 15.5). Figure 15.6 shows the results.

Figure 15.6
The results of using multiple formulas in the data table.

	A	B	C	D	E	F	G
				`{=TABLE(,C4)}`			
2		Interest Rate	5%		*The Future Value of an Investment*		
3		Period	10				
4		Annual Deposit	($10,000)				
5		Initial Deposit	($25,000)				
6		Deposit Type	1				
7		Inflation	2%				
8			Future Value	Today's Dollars			
9		Annual Deposit	$172,790	$141,748			
10		($7,000)	$133,170	$109,246			
11		($8,000)	$146,377	$120,080			
12		($9,000)	$159,583	$130,914			
13		($10,000)	$172,790	$141,748			
14		($11,000)	$185,997	$152,582			
15		($12,000)	$199,204	$163,417			
16		($13,000)	$212,411	$174,251			

Future Value (Data Table 2)

> **NOTE** After you have a data table set up, you can do regular what-if analysis by adjusting the other worksheet variables. Each time you make a change, Excel recalculates every formula in the table.

Setting Up a Two-Input Data Table

You also can set up data tables that take two input variables. This option enables you to see the effect on an investment's future value when you enter different values—for example, the annual deposit and the interest rate. The following steps show you how to set up a two-input data table:

1. Enter one set of values in a column below the formula and the second set of values to the right of the formula in the same row, as shown in Figure 15.7.

2. Select the range that includes the input values and the formula (B8:G15 in Figure 15.7).

Figure 15.7
Enter the two sets of
values that you want to
input into the formula.

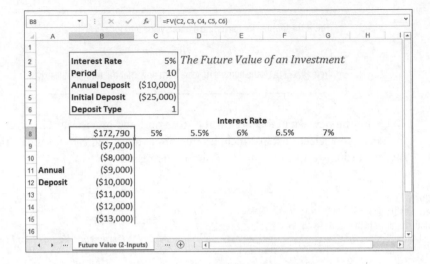

3. Select Data, What-If Analysis, Data Table to display the Data Table dialog box.

4. In the Row Input Cell text box, enter the cell address of the input cell that corresponds to the row values you entered (C2 in Figure 15.7—the Interest Rate variable).

5. In the Column Input Cell text box, enter the cell address of the input cell you want to use for the column values (C4 in Figure 15.7—the Annual Deposit variable).

6. Click OK. Excel runs through the various input combinations and then displays the results in the data table. Format the cells as necessary (see Figure 15.8).

Figure 15.8
Excel substitutes each
input value into the input
cell and displays the
results in the two-input
data table.

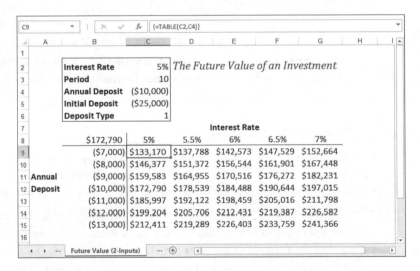

> **TIP**
>
> As mentioned earlier, if you make changes to any of the variables in a table formula, Excel recalculates the entire table. This isn't a problem in small tables, but large ones can take a very long time to calculate. If you prefer to control the table recalculation, select Formulas, Calculation, Calculation Options, Automatic Except for Data Tables. This tells Excel not to include data tables when it recalculates a worksheet. To recalculate your data tables, select Formulas, Calculation, Calculate Now (or press F9); to recalculate just the data tables in the current worksheet, select Formulas, Calculation, Calculate Sheet (or press Shift+F9).

Editing a Data Table

If you want to make changes to a data table, you can edit the formula (or formulas) as well as the input value. However, the data table results are a different matter. When you run the Data Table command, Excel enters an array formula in the interior of the data table. This formula is a TABLE() function (a special function available only by using the Data Table command) with the following syntax:

```
{=TABLE(row_input_ref, column_input_ref)}
```

Here, row_input_ref and $column\_input\_ref$ are the cell references you entered in the Data Table dialog box. The braces ({ }) indicate that this is an array, which means that you can't change or delete individual elements of the array. If you want to change the results, you need to select the entire data table and then run the Data Table command again. If you just want to delete the results, you must first select the entire array and then delete it.

→ To learn more about arrays, **see** "Working with Arrays," **p. 87**.

Working with Goal Seek

Here's a what-if question for you: What if you already know the result you want? For example, you might know that you want to have $50,000 saved to purchase new equipment five years from now or that you have to achieve a 30% gross margin in your next budget. If you need to manipulate only a single variable to achieve these results, you can use Excel's Goal Seek feature. You tell Goal Seek the final value you need and which variable to change, and it finds a solution for you (if one exists).

→ For more complicated scenarios with multiple variables and constraints, you need to use Excel's Solver feature. **See** Chapter 17, "Solving Complex Problems with Solver," **p. 411**.

How Does Goal Seek Work?

When you set up a worksheet to use Goal Seek, you usually have a formula in one cell and the formula's variable—with an initial value—in another. (Your formula can have multiple variables, but Goal Seek enables you to manipulate only one variable at a time.) Goal Seek operates by using an *iterative method* to find a solution. That is, Goal Seek first tries the variable's initial value to see whether that produces the result you want. If it doesn't, Goal Seek tries different values until it converges on a solution.

→ To learn more about iterative methods, **see** "Using Iteration and Circular References," **p. 93**.

Running Goal Seek

Before you run Goal Seek, you need to set up your worksheet in a particular way. This means doing three things:

1. Set up one cell as the *changing cell*. This is the value that Goal Seek will iteratively manipulate to attempt to reach the goal. Enter an initial value (such as 0) into the cell.

2. Set up the other input values for the formula and make them proper initial values.

3. Create a formula for Goal Seek to use to try to reach the goal.

For example, suppose you're a small-business owner looking to purchase new equipment worth $50,000 five years from now. Assuming your investments earn 5% annual interest, how much do you need to set aside every year to reach this goal? Figure 15.9 shows a worksheet set up to use Goal Seek:

■ Cell C6 is the changing cell: the annual deposit into the fund (with an initial value of 0).

■ The other cells (C4 and C5) are used as constants for the FV() function.

■ Cell C8 contains the FV() function that calculates the future value of the equipment fund. When Goal Seek is done, this cell's value should be $50,000.

Figure 15.9
A worksheet set up to use Goal Seek to find out how much to set aside each year to end up with a $50,000 equipment fund in five years.

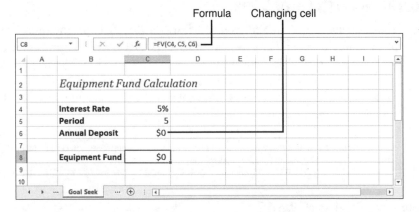

With your worksheet ready to go, follow these steps to use Goal Seek:

1. Select Data, What-If Analysis, Goal Seek. Excel displays the Goal Seek dialog box.

2. Use the Set Cell text box to enter a reference to the cell that contains the formula you want Goal Seek to manipulate (cell C8 in Figure 15.9).

3. Use the To Value text box to enter the final value you want for the goal cell (such as 50000).

4. Use the By Changing Cell text box to enter a reference to the changing cell. (This is cell C6 in Figure 15.9.) Figure 15.10 shows the completed Goal Seek dialog box.

Figure 15.10
The completed Goal Seek dialog box.

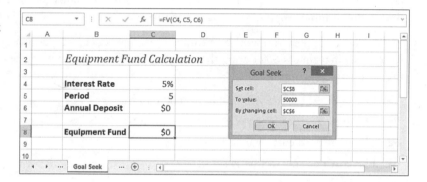

5. Click OK. Excel begins the iteration and displays the Goal Seek Status dialog box. When finished, the dialog box tells you whether Goal Seek found a solution (see Figure 15.11).

Figure 15.11
The Goal Seek Status dialog box shows you the solution (if one was found).

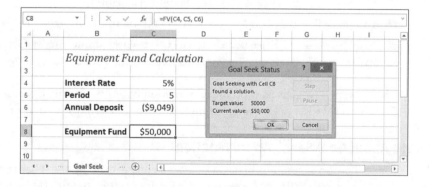

NOTE

Most of the time, Goal Seek finds a solution relatively quickly, and the Goal Seek Status dialog box displays the solution within a second or two. For longer operations, you can click Pause in the Goal Seek Status dialog box to stop Goal Seek. To walk through the process one iteration at a time, click Step. To resume Goal Seek, click Continue.

→ You can also calculate the required annual deposit using Excel's PMT ( ) function; **see** "Calculating the Required Regular Deposit," **p. 460**.

6. If Goal Seek found a solution, you can accept the solution by clicking OK. To ignore the solution, click Cancel.

Optimizing Product Margin

Many businesses use product margin as a measure of fiscal health. A strong margin usually means that expenses are under control and that the market is satisfied with your price points. Product margin depends on many factors, of course, but you can use Goal Seek to find the optimum margin based on a single variable.

For example, suppose you want to introduce a new product line, and you want the product to return a margin of 30% during the first year. Suppose, too, that you're operating under the following assumptions:

■ The sales during the year will be 100,000 units.

■ The average discount to your customers will be 40%.

■ The total fixed costs will be $750,000.

■ The cost per unit will be $12.63.

Given all this information, you want to know what price point will produce the 30% margin.

Figure 15.12 shows a worksheet set up to handle this situation. An initial value of $1.00 is entered into the Price per Unit cell (C4), and Goal Seek is set up in the following way:

■ The Set Cell reference is C14, the Margin calculation.

■ A value of 0.3 (the 30% Margin goal) is entered in the To Value text box.

■ A reference to the Price per Unit cell (C4) is entered into the By Changing Cell text box.

When you run Goal Seek, it produces a solution of $47.87 for the price, as shown in Figure 15.13. This solution can be rounded up to a more standard price point of $47.95.

A Note About Goal Seek's Approximations

Notice that the solution in Figure 15.13 is an approximate figure. That is, the margin value is 29.92%, not the 30% you were looking for. It's pretty close (it's off by only 0.0008), but it's not exact. Why didn't Goal Seek find the exact solution?

Figure 15.12
A worksheet set up to calculate a price point that will optimize gross margin.

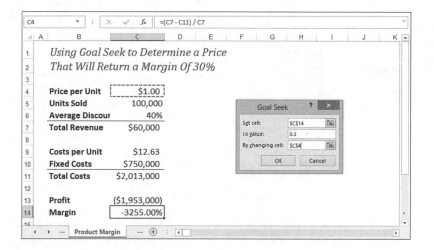

Figure 15.13
The result of Goal Seek's labors.

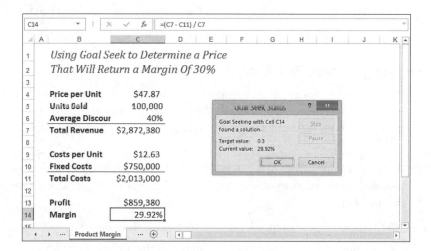

The answer lies in one of the options Excel uses to control iterative calculations. Some iterations can take an extremely long time to find an exact solution, so Excel compromises by setting certain limits on iterative processes. To see these limits, select File, Options and then click Formulas in the Excel Options dialog box that appears (see Figure 15.14). Two options control iterative processes:

■ **Maximum Iterations**—The value in this text box controls the maximum number of iterations. In Goal Seek, this represents the maximum number of values that Excel plugs into the changing cell.

■ **Maximum Change**—The value in this text box is the threshold that Excel uses to determine whether it has converged on a solution. If the difference between the current solution and the desired goal is less than or equal to this value, Excel stops iterating.

Figure 15.14
The Maximum Iterations and Maximum Change options place limits on iterative calculations.

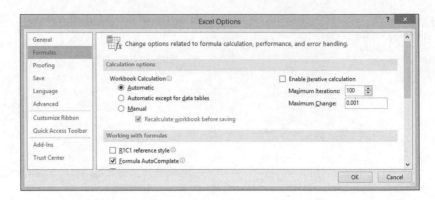

The Maximum Change value prevented us from getting an exact solution for the profit margin calculation. On a particular iteration, Goal Seek found the solution .2992, which put us within 0.0008 of our goal of 0.3. However, 0.0008 is less than the default value of 0.001 in the Maximum Change text box, so Excel called a halt to the procedure.

To get an exact solution, you would need to adjust the Maximum Change value to 0.0001.

Performing a Break-Even Analysis

In a *break-even analysis*, you determine the number of units you have to sell of a product so that your total profits are 0 (that is, the product revenue equals the product costs). Setting up a profit equation with a goal of 0 and varying the units sold is perfect for Goal Seek.

To try this, we'll extend the example used in the "Optimizing Product Margin" section. In this case, assume a unit price of $47.95 (the solution found to optimize product margin, rounded up to the nearest 95¢). Figure 15.15 shows the Goal Seek dialog box filled out as detailed here:

- The Set Cell reference is set to C12, the profit calculation.
- A value of 0 (the profit goal) is entered in the To Value text box.
- A reference to the Units Sold cell (C4) is entered into the By Changing Cell text box.

Figure 15.16 shows the solution: A total of 46,468 units must be sold to break even.

Solving Algebraic Equations

Algebraic equations don't come up all that often in a business context, but they do appear occasionally in complex models. Fortunately, Goal Seek also is useful for solving complex algebraic equations of one variable. For example, suppose you need to find the value of x to solve the rather nasty equation displayed in Figure 15.17. Although this equation is too complex for the quadratic formula, it can be easily rendered in Excel. The left side of the equation can be represented with the following formula:

```
=(((3 * A2 - 8) ^ 2) * (A2 - 1)) / (4 * A2 ^ 2 - 5)
```

Figure 15.15
A worksheet set up to calculate a price point that optimizes gross margin.

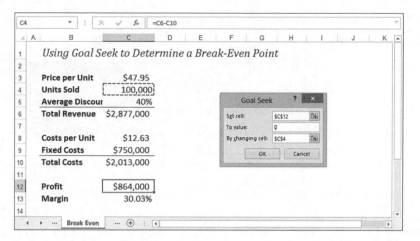

Figure 15.16
The break-even solution.

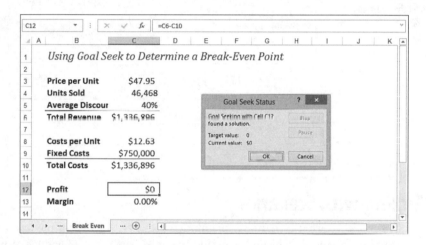

Cell A2 represents the variable *x*. You can solve this equation in Goal Seek by setting the goal for this equation to 1 (the right side of the equation) and by varying cell A2. Figure 15.17 shows a worksheet and the Goal Seek dialog box.

Figure 15.18 shows the result. The value in cell A2 is the solution (*x*) that satisfies the equation. Notice that the equation result (cell B2) is not quite 1. As mentioned earlier in this chapter, if you need higher accuracy, you must change Excel's convergence threshold. In this example, select File, Options, click Formulas, and type **0.000001** in the Maximum Change text box.

15

Figure 15.17
Solving an algebraic
equation with Goal Seek.

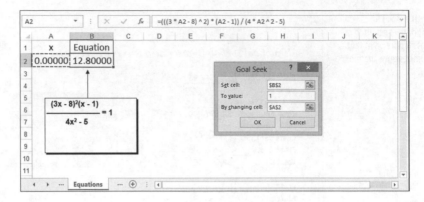

Figure 15.18
Cell A2 holds the solu-
tion for the equation in
cell B2.

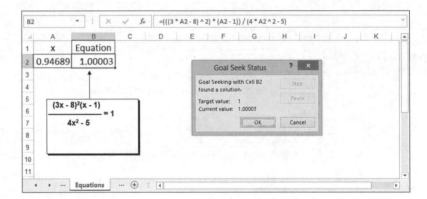

Working with Scenarios

By definition, what-if analysis is not an exact science. All what-if models make guesses and assumptions based on history, expected events, or some sort of voodoo. A particular set of guesses and assumptions that you plug into a model is called a *scenario*. Because most what-if worksheets can take a wide range of input values, you usually end up with a large number of scenarios to examine. Instead of going through the tedious chore of inserting all these values into the appropriate cells, Excel has a Scenario Manager feature that can handle the process for you. This section shows you how to wield this useful tool.

Understanding Scenarios

As you've seen in this chapter, Excel has powerful features that enable you to build sophisticated models that can answer complex questions. The problem, though, isn't in *answering* questions, but in *asking* them. For example, Figure 15.19 shows a worksheet model that analyzes a mortgage. You use this model to decide how much of a down payment to make, how long the term should be, and whether to include an extra principal paydown every month. The Results section compares the monthly payment and total paid for the regular mortgage and for the mortgage with a paydown. It also shows the savings and reduced term that result from the paydown.

→ The formula shown in Figure 15.19 uses the PMT () function, which is covered later in the book; **see** "Calculating a Loan Payment," **p. 435**.

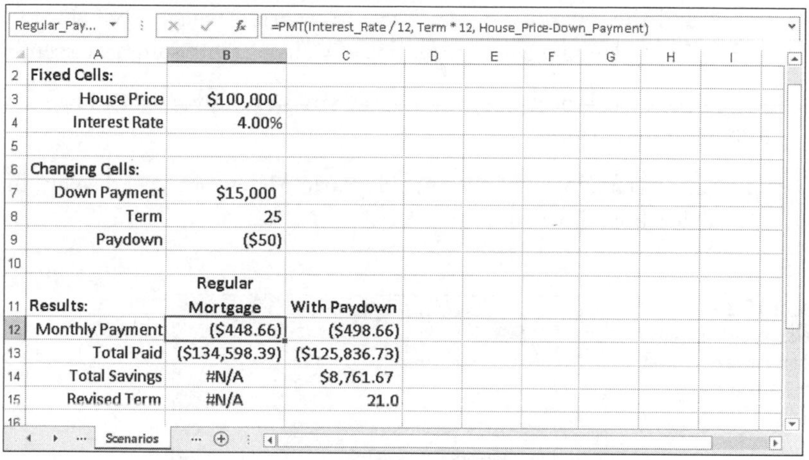

15

Figure 15.19
A mortgage analysis
worksheet.

Here are some possible questions to ask this model:

■ How much will I save over the term of the mortgage if I use a shorter term, make a larger down payment, and include a monthly paydown?

■ How much more will I end up paying if I extend the term, reduce the down payment, and forgo the paydown?

These are examples of *scenarios* that you would plug into the appropriate cells in the model. Excel's Scenario Manager helps by letting you define a scenario separately from the worksheet. You can save specific values for any or all of the model's input cells, give the scenario a name, and then recall the name (and all the input values it contains) from a list.

Setting Up Your Worksheet for Scenarios

Before creating a scenario, you need to decide which cells in your model will be the input cells. These will be the worksheet variables—the cells that, when you change them, change the results of the model. (Not surprisingly, Excel calls these the *changing cells*.) You can have as many as 32 changing cells in a scenario. For best results, follow these guidelines when setting up your worksheet for scenarios:

■ The changing cells should be constants. Formulas can be affected by other cells, and that can throw off the entire scenario.

- To make it easier to set up each scenario and to make your worksheet easier to understand, group the changing cells and label them (see Figure 15.19).
- For even greater clarity, assign a range name to each changing cell.

Adding a Scenario

To work with scenarios, you use Excel's Scenario Manager tool. This feature enables you to add, edit, display, and delete scenarios as well as create summary scenario reports.

When your worksheet is set up the way you want it, you can add a scenario to the sheet by following these steps:

1. Select Data, What-If Analysis, Scenario Manager. Excel displays the Scenario Manager dialog box, shown in Figure 15.20.

Figure 15.20
Excel's Scenario Manager enables you to create and work with worksheet scenarios.

2. Click Add. The Add Scenario dialog box appears. Figure 15.21 shows a completed version of this dialog box.

3. Use the Scenario Name text box to enter a name for the scenario.

4. Use the Changing Cells box to enter references to your worksheet's changing cells. You can type in the references (be sure to separate noncontiguous cells with commas) or select the cells directly on the worksheet.

5. Use the Comment box to enter a description for the scenario. This description appears in the Comment section of the Scenario Manager dialog box.

6. Click OK. Excel displays the Scenario Values dialog box, shown in Figure 15.22.

7. Use the text boxes to enter values for the changing cells.

Figure 15.21
Use the Add Scenario dialog box to define a scenario.

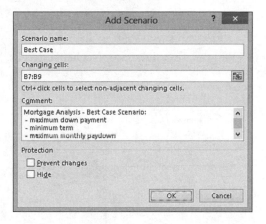

Figure 15.22
Use the Scenario Values dialog box to enter the values you want to use for the scenario's changing cells.

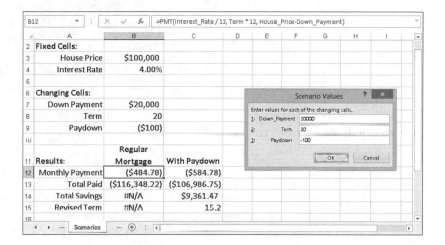

> **NOTE** Notice in Figure 15.22 that Excel displays the range name for each changing cell, which makes it easier to enter your numbers correctly. If your changing cells aren't named, Excel just displays the cell addresses instead.

8. To add more scenarios, click Add to return to the Add Scenario dialog box and repeat steps 3 through 7. Otherwise, click OK to return to the Scenario Manager dialog box.

9. Click Close to return to the worksheet.

Displaying a Scenario

After you define a scenario, you can enter its values into the changing cells by displaying the scenario from the Scenario Manager dialog box. The following steps give you the details:

15

1. Select Data, What-If Analysis, Scenario Manager.

2. In the Scenarios list, click the scenario you want to display.

3. Click Show. Excel enters the scenario values into the changing cells. Figure 15.23 shows an example.

Figure 15.23
When you click Show, Excel enters the values for the highlighted scenario into the changing cells.

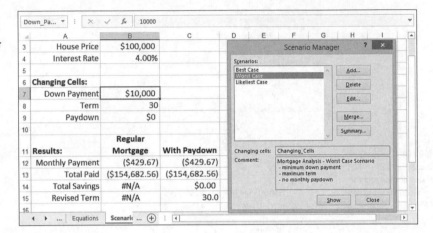

4. Repeat steps 2 and 3 to display other scenarios.

5. Click Close to return to the worksheet.

> **TIP**
> Displaying a scenario isn't hard, but it does require having the Scenario Manager onscreen. You can bypass the Scenario Manager by adding the Scenario list to the Quick Access Toolbar. Pull down the Customize Quick Access Toolbar menu and then click More Commands. In the Choose Commands From list, click All Commands. In the list of commands, click Scenario, click Add, and then click OK. (One caveat, though: If you select the same scenario twice in succession, Excel asks whether you want to redefine the scenario. Be sure to click No to keep the current scenario definition.)

Editing a Scenario

If you need to make changes to a scenario—whether to change the scenario's name, select different changing cells, or enter new values—follow these steps:

1. Select Data, What-If Analysis, Scenario Manager.

2. In the Scenarios list, click the scenario you want to edit.

3. Click Edit. Excel displays the Edit Scenario dialog box (which is identical to the Add Scenario dialog box, shown in Figure 15.21).

4. Make your changes, if necessary, and click OK. The Scenario Values dialog box appears (refer to Figure 15.22).

5. Enter the new values, if necessary, and then click OK to return to the Scenario Manager dialog box.

6. Repeat steps 2 through 5 to edit other scenarios.

7. Click Close to return to the worksheet.

Merging Scenarios

The scenarios you create are stored with each worksheet in a workbook. If you have similar models in different sheets (for example, budget models for different divisions), you can create separate scenarios for each sheet and then merge them later. Here are the steps to follow:

1. Select the worksheet in which you want to store the merged scenarios.

2. Select Data, What-If Analysis, Scenario Manager.

3. Click Merge. Excel displays the Merge Scenarios dialog box, shown in Figure 15.24.

Figure 15.24
Use the Merge Scenarios dialog box to select the scenarios you want to merge.

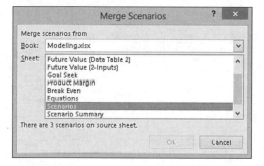

4. Use the Book drop-down list to click the workbook that contains the scenario sheet.

5. Use the Sheet list to click the worksheet that contains the scenario.

6. Click OK to return to the Scenario Manager.

7. Click Close to return to the worksheet.

Generating a Summary Report

You can create a summary report that shows the changing cells in each of your scenarios along with selected result cells. This is a handy way to compare different scenarios. You can try it by following these steps:

> **NOTE**
> When Excel sets up the scenario summary, it uses either the cell addresses or defined names of the individual changing cells and results cells, as well as the entire range of changing cells. Your reports will be more readable if you name the cells you'll be using before generating the summary.

1. Select Data, What-If Analysis, Scenario Manager.
2. Click Summary. Excel displays the Scenario Summary dialog box.
3. In the Report Type group, click either Scenario Summary or Scenario PivotTable Report.
4. In the Result Cells box, enter references to the result cells that you want to appear in the report (see Figure 15.25). You can select the cells directly on the sheet or type in the references. (Remember to separate noncontiguous cells with commas.)

Figure 15.25
Use the Scenario Summary dialog box to select the report type and result cells.

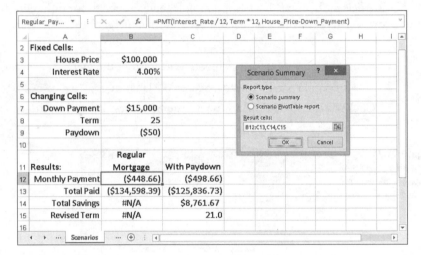

5. Click OK. Excel displays the report.

Figure 15.26 shows the Scenario Summary report for the Mortgage Analysis worksheet. The names shown in column C (Down_Payment, Term, and so on) are the names I assigned to each of the changing cells and result cells.

Figure 15.26
The Scenario Summary report for the Mortgage Analysis worksheet.

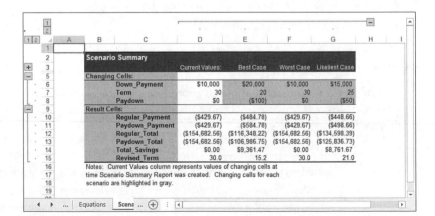

Figure 15.27 shows the Scenario PivotTable report for the Mortgage Analysis worksheet.

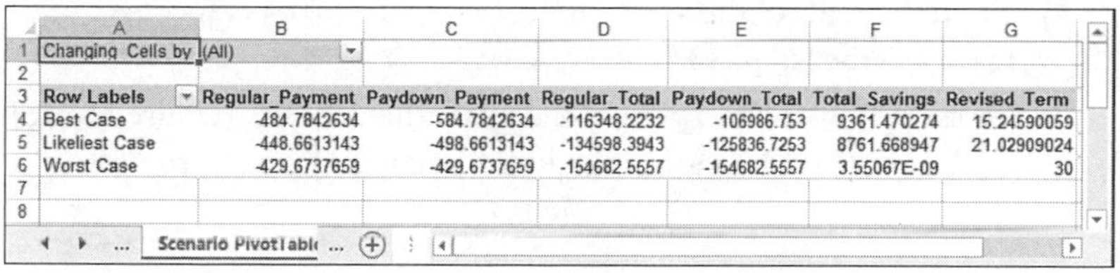

	A	B	C	D	E	F	G
1	Changing Cells by	(All)					
2							
3	Row Labels	Regular_Payment	Paydown_Payment	Regular_Total	Paydown_Total	Total_Savings	Revised_Term
4	Best Case	-484.7842634	-584.7842634	-116348.2232	-106986.753	9361.470274	15.24590059
5	Likeliest Case	-448.6613143	-498.6613143	-134598.3943	-125836.7253	8761.668947	21.02909024
6	Worst Case	-429.6737659	-429.6737659	-154682.5557	-154682.5557	3.55067E-09	30
7							
8							

Figure 15.27
The Scenario PivotTable report for the Mortgage Analysis worksheet.

> **NOTE**
> The PivotTable's page field—labeled Changing Cells By—enables you to switch between scenarios created by different users. If no other users have access to this workbook, you'll see only your name in this field's list.

Deleting a Scenario

If you have scenarios you no longer need, you can delete them by following these steps:

1. Select Data, What-If Analysis, Scenario Manager.
2. Use the Scenarios list to click the scenario you want to delete.

> **CAUTION**
> Excel doesn't ask you to confirm the deletion, and there's no way to retrieve a scenario that has been deleted accidentally (other than closing the workbook without saving changes or opening a previous version of the workbook), so be sure the scenario you highlighted is one you can live without.

3. Click Delete. Excel deletes the scenario.
4. Click Close to return to the worksheet.

From Here

- To understand and use iterative methods, **see** "Using Iteration and Circular References," **p. 93**.
- Consolidating data is useful for analyzing models that have similar data spread out over multiple sheets. To learn how this is done, **see** "Consolidating Multisheet Data," **p. 95**.
- Goal Seek's "big brother" is the Solver tool. **See** Chapter 17, "Solving Complex Problems with Solver," **p. 411**.

- Excel's Solver tool enables you to save its solutions as scenarios. **See** "Saving a Solution as a Scenario," **p. 418**.

- For the details of the PMT() function from a loan perspective, **see** "Calculating the Loan Payment," **p. 435**.

- To learn how to use PMT() to calculate the deposits required to reach an investment goal, **see** "Calculating the Required Regular Deposit," **p. 460**.

Using Regression to Track Trends and Make Forecasts

16

In these complex and uncertain times, forecasting business performance is increasingly important. Today, more than ever before, managers at all levels need to make intelligent predictions of future sales and profit trends as part of their overall business strategy. By forecasting sales six months, a year, or even three years down the road, managers can anticipate related needs such as employee acquisitions, warehouse space, and raw material requirements. Similarly, a profit forecast enables a company to plan for its future expansion.

Business forecasting has been around for many years, and various methods have been developed—some of them more successful than others. The most common forecasting method is the qualitative "seat of the pants" approach, in which a manager (or a group of managers) estimates future trends based on experience and knowledge of the market. This method, however, suffers from an inherent subjectivity and a short-term focus because many managers tend to extrapolate from recent experience and ignore the long-term trend. Other methods (such as averaging past results) are more objective but generally are useful for forecasting only a few months in advance.

This chapter presents a technique called *regression analysis*. Regression is a powerful statistical procedure that has become a popular business tool. In its general form, you use regression analysis to determine the relationship between one phenomenon and another. For example, car sales might be dependent on interest rates, and units sold might be dependent on the amount spent on advertising. The dependent phenomenon is called the *dependent variable*, or the *y-value*, and the phenomenon upon which it's dependent is called the *independent variable*, or the *x-value*. (Think of a chart or graph on which the independent variable is plotted along the horizontal [x] axis and the dependent variable is plotted along the vertical [y] axis.)

Given these variables, you can do two things with regression analysis:

- Determine the relationship between the known x- and y-values and use the results to calculate and visualize the overall trend of the data.

- Use the existing trend to forecast new y-values.

As you'll see in this chapter, Excel is well stocked with tools that enable you to both calculate the current trend and make forecasts no matter what type of data you're dealing with.

Choosing a Regression Method

Three methods of regression analysis are used most often in business:

- **Simple regression**—Use this type of regression when you're dealing with only one independent variable. For example, if the dependent variable is car sales, the independent variable might be interest rates. You also need to decide whether your data is linear or nonlinear:
  - *Linear* means that if you plot the data on a chart, the resulting data points resemble (roughly) a line.
  - *Nonlinear* means that if you plot the data on a chart, the resulting data points form a curve.

- **Polynomial regression**—Use this type of regression when you're dealing with only one independent variable, but the data fluctuates in such a way that the pattern in the data doesn't resemble either a straight line or a simple curve.

- **Multiple regression**—Use this type of regression when you're dealing with more than one independent variable. For example, if the dependent variable is car sales, the independent variables might be interest rates and disposable income.

You'll learn about all three methods in this chapter.

Using Simple Regression on Linear Data

With linear data, the dependent variable is related to the independent variable by some constant factor. For example, you might find that car sales (the dependent variable) increase by 1 million units whenever interest rates (the independent variable) decrease by 1%. Similarly, you might find that division revenue (the dependent variable) increases by $100,000 for every $10,000 you spend on advertising (the independent variable).

Analyzing Trends Using Best-Fit Lines

You make these sorts of determinations by examining the trend underlying the current data you have for the dependent variable. In linear regression, you analyze the current trend by calculating the *line of best fit*, or the *trendline*. This is a line through the data points for which the differences between the points above and below the line cancel each other out (more or less).

> **NOTE** Excel 2016 includes a new tool called Forecast Sheet that simplifies many of the tasks and calculations that I present in this chapter. To use it, select your data, click the Data tab, and then click Forecast Sheet. This opens the Create Forecast Worksheet dialog box, which shows a basic best-fit trendline. You can click Options and change the default settings to gain a bit more control over the result. Click Create to add the new forecasting worksheet.

16

Plotting a Best-Fit Trendline

The easiest way to see the best-fit line is to use a chart. Note, however, that this works only if your data is plotted using an XY (scatter) chart. For example, Figure 16.1 shows a worksheet with quarterly sales figures plotted on an XY chart. Here, the quarterly sales data is the dependent variable and the period is the independent variable. (In this example, the independent variable is just time, represented, in this case, by fiscal quarters.) You can add a trendline through the plotted points.

Figure 16.1
To see a trendline through your data, first make sure the data is plotted using an XY chart.

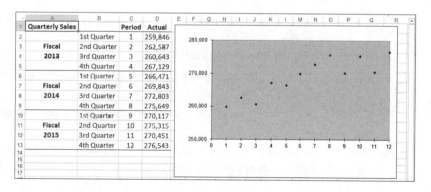

> **NOTE** You can download this chapter's sample workbooks at www.mcfedries.com/books/ book.php?title=excel-2016-formulas-and-functions.

The following steps show you how to add a trendline to a chart:

1. Select the chart and, if more than one data series are plotted, click the series you want to work with.

2. Select Design, Add Chart Element, Trendline, More Trendline Options. Excel displays the Format Trendline task pane, shown in Figure 16.2.

Figure 16.2
In the Format Trendline task pane, use the Trendline Options tab to select the type of trendline you want to see.

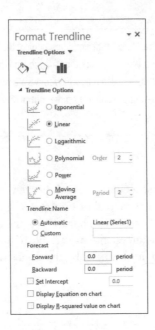

3. On the Trendline Options tab, click Linear.

4. Select the Display Equation on Chart check box. (See the next section, "Understanding the Regression Equation.")

5. Select the Display R-Squared Value on Chart check box. (See "Understanding R^2," later in this chapter.)

6. Click Close (X). Excel inserts the trendline. Note that you might need to drag the regression equation text box away from the trendline to read the values.

Figure 16.3 shows the best-fit trendline added to the chart.

Understanding the Regression Equation

In the steps outlined in the previous section, I instructed you to select the Display Equation on Chart check box. Doing this displays the *regression equation* on the chart, as pointed out in Figure 16.3. This equation is crucial to regression analysis because it gives you a specific formula for the relationship between the dependent variable and the independent variable.

Figure 16.3
The quarterly sales chart with a best-fit trendline added.

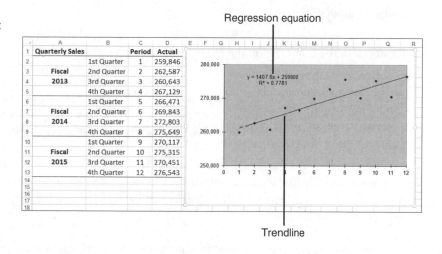

For linear regression, the best-fit trendline is a straight line with an equation that takes the following form:

$$y = mx + b$$

Here's how you can interpret this equation with respect to the quarterly sales data:

- **y**   This is the dependent variable, so it represents the trendline value (quarterly sales) for a specific period.

- **x**   This is the independent variable, which, in this example, is the period (quarter) you're working with.

- **m**   This is the slope of the trendline. In other words, it's the amount by which the sales increase per period, according to the trendline.

- **b**   This is the y-intercept, which means that it's the starting value for the trend.

Here's the regression equation for the example (refer to Figure 16.3):

$$y = 1407.6x + 259800$$

To determine the first point on the trendline, substitute 1 for x:

$$y = 1407.6 * 1 + 259800$$

The result is 261,207.6.

> **CAUTION**
>
> It's important not to view the trendline values as somehow trying to predict or estimate the actual y-values (sales). The trendline simply gives you an overall picture of how the y-values change when the x-values change.

Understanding R^2

When you click the Display R-Squared Value on Chart check box when adding a trendline, Excel places the following on the chart:

```
R² = n
```

Here, n is called the *coefficient of determination* (which statisticians abbreviate as r^2 and Excel abbreviates as R^2). This is actually the square of the correlation; as you learned in Chapter 12, "Working with Statistical Functions," the correlation tells you something about how well two things are related to each other. In this context, R^2 gives you some idea of how well the trendline fits the data. Roughly, it tells you the proportion of the variance in the dependent variable that is associated with the independent variable. Generally, the closer the result is to 1, the better the fit. Values below about 0.7 mean that the trendline is not a very good fit for the data.

→ To learn more about correlation, **see** "Determining the Correlation Between Data," **p. 280**.

> **TIP**
>
> If you don't get a good fit with a linear trendline, your data might not be linear. Try using a different trendline type to see if you can increase the value of R^2.

You'll see in the next section that it's possible to calculate values for the best-fit trendline. Having those values enables you to calculate the correlation between the known y-values and the generated trend values by using the CORREL() function:

```
CORREL(array1, array2)
```

Here, *array1* is a range reference to the dependent variable values that you know (such as the sales figures in D2:D13 in Figure 16.3), and *array2* is a range or an array containing the calculated trend points. Note that squaring the CORREL() result gives you the value of R^2.

Calculating Best-Fit Values Using TREND()

The problem with using a chart best-fit trendline is that you don't get actual values to work with. If you want to get some values on the worksheet, you can calculate individual trend-line values using the regression equation. However, what if the underlying data changes? For example, those values might be estimates, or they might change as more accurate data comes in. In that case, you need to delete the existing trendline, add a new one, and then recalculate the trend values based on the new equation.

If you need to work with worksheet trend values, you can avoid having to perform repeated trendline analyses by calculating the values using Excel's TREND() function:

```
TREND(known_y's[, known_x's][, new_x's][, const])
```

known_y's A range reference or an array of the known y-values—such as the historical values—from which you want to calculate the trend.

known_x's A range reference or an array of the x-values associated with the known y-values. If you omit this argument, the known_x's are assumed to be the array {1,2,3,...,n}, where n is the number of known_y's.

new_x's A range reference or an array of the new x-values for which you want corresponding y-values.

const A logical value that determines where Excel places the y-intercept. If you use FALSE, the y-intercept is placed at 0; if you use TRUE (this is the default), Excel calculates the y-intercept based on the known_y's.

To generate the best-fit trend values, you need to specify the known_y's argument and, optionally, the known_x's argument. In the quarterly sales example, the known y-values are the actual sales numbers, which lie in the range D2:D13. The known x-values are the period numbers in the range C2:C13. Therefore, to calculate the best-fit trend values, you select a range that is the same size as the known values and enter the following formula as an array:

```
{=TREND(D2:D13, C2:C13)}
```

Figure 16.4 shows the results of this TREND() array formula in column F. For comparison purposes, the sheet also includes the trend values (in column E) generated using the regression equation from the chart trendline shown in Figure 16.3. (Note that some of the values are slightly off. That's because the values for the slope and intercept shown in the regression equation have been rounded off for display in the chart.)

Figure 16.4
Best-fit trend values (F2:F13) created with the TREND() function.

	A	B	C	D	E	F
1	Quarterly Sales		Period	Actual	Trend (Equation)	TREND()
2		1st Quarter	1	259,846	261,208	261,208
3	Fiscal	2nd Quarter	2	262,587	262,615	262,615
4	2013	3rd Quarter	3	260,643	264,023	264,023
5		4th Quarter	4	267,129	265,430	265,431
6		1st Quarter	5	266,471	266,838	266,838
7	Fiscal	2nd Quarter	6	269,843	268,246	268,246
8	2014	3rd Quarter	7	272,803	269,653	269,654
9		4th Quarter	8	275,649	271,061	271,061
10		1st Quarter	9	270,117	272,468	272,469
11	Fiscal	2nd Quarter	10	275,315	273,876	273,876
12	2015	3rd Quarter	11	270,451	275,284	275,284
13		4th Quarter	12	276,543	276,691	276,692

F2 {=TREND(D2:D13, C2:C13)}

TIP In the previous section, I mentioned that you can determine the correlation between the known dependent values and the calculated trend values by using the CORREL() function. Here's an array formula that provides a shorthand method for returning the correlation:

```
{=CORREL(array1, TREND(known_y's, known_x's))}
```

Calculating Best-Fit Values Using `LINEST()`

Using `TREND()` is the most direct way to calculate trend values, but Excel offers a second method that calculates the trendline's slope and y-intercept. You can then plug these values into the general linear regression equation—$y = mx + b$—as m and b, respectively. You calculate the slope and y-intercept by using the `LINEST()` function:

```
LINEST(known_y's[, known_x's][, const][, stats])
```

`known_y's`   A range reference or an array of the known y-values from which you want to calculate the trend.

`known_x's`   A range reference or an array of the x-values associated with the known y-values. If you omit this argument, the `known_x's` are assumed to be the array {1,2,3,...,*n*}, where *n* is the number of `known_y's`.

`const`   A logical value that determines where Excel places the y-intercept. If you use `FALSE`, the y-intercept is placed at 0; if you use `TRUE` (this is the default), Excel calculates the y-intercept based on the `known_y's`.

`stats`   A logical value that determines whether `LINEST()` returns additional regression statistics besides the slope and intercept. The default is `FALSE`.

When you use `LINEST()` without the `stats` argument, the function returns a 1×2 array, where the value in the first column is the slope of the trendline and the value in the second column is the intercept. For example, the following formula, entered as a 1×2 array, returns the slope and intercept of the quarterly sales trendline:

```
{=LINEST(D2:D13, C2:C13)}
```

In Figure 16.5, the returned array values are shown in cells H2 and I2. This worksheet also uses these values to compute the trendline values by substituting $H$2 for *m* and $I$2 for *b* in the linear regression equation. For example, the following formula calculates the trend value for period 1:

```
=$H$2 * C2 + $I$2
```

If you set the `stats` argument to `TRUE`, the `LINEST()` function returns 10 regression statistics in a 5×2 array. The returned statistics are listed in Table 16.1, and Figure 16.6 shows an example of the returned array.

Table 16.1   Regression Statistics Returned by `LINEST()` When the `stats` Argument Is Set to `TRUE`

Array Location	Statistic	Description
Row 1, column 1	m	The slope of the trendline
Row 1, column 2	b	The y-intercept of the trendline
Row 2, column 1	se	The standard error value for *m*

Array Location	Statistic	Description
Row 2, column 2	seb	The standard error value for b
Row 3, column 1	R^2	The coefficient of determination
Row 3, column 2	sey	The standard error value for the y estimate
Row 4, column 1	F	The F statistic
Row 4, column 2	df	The degrees of freedom
Row 5, column 1	ssreg	The regression sum of squares
Row 5, column 2	ssresid	The residual sum of squares

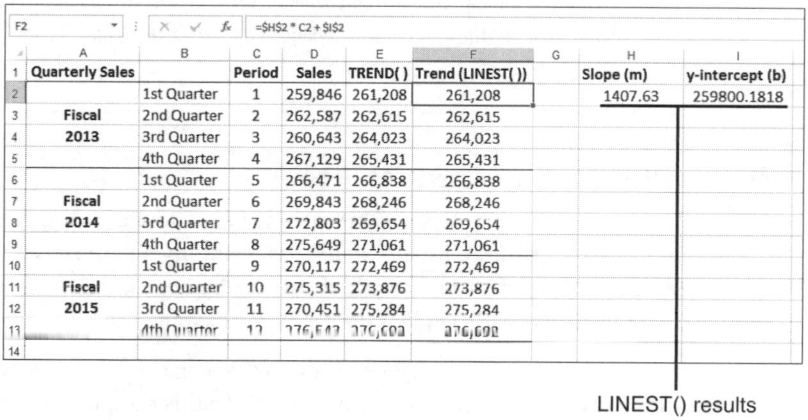

Figure 16.5
Best-fit trend values (F2:F13) created with the results of the LINEST() function (H2:I2) plugged into the linear regression equation.

LINEST() results

NOTE

These and other regression statistics are available via the Analysis ToolPak's Regression tool. Assuming that the Analysis ToolPak add-in is installed (see "Loading the Analysis ToolPak" in Chapter 6, "Understanding Functions"), select Data, Data Analysis, click Regression, and then click OK. Use the Regression dialog box to specify the ranges for the y-values and x-values and to select which statistics you want to see in the output.

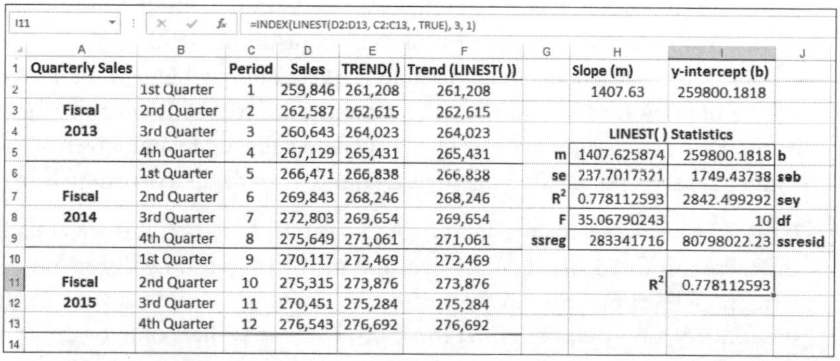

Figure 16.6
The range H5:I9 contains the array of regression statistics returned by LINEST() when its stats argument is set to TRUE.

Most of these values are beyond the scope of this book. However, notice that one of the returned values is R^2, the coefficient of determination, which tells how well the trendline fits the data. If you want just this value from the LINEST() array, use this formula (see cell I11 in Figure 16.6):

```
=INDEX(LINEST(known_y's, known_x's, , TRUE), 3, 1)
```

> **NOTE**
>
> You can also calculate the slope, intercept, and R^2 value directly by using the following functions:
>
> ```
> SLOPE(known_y's, known_x's)
> INTERCEPT(known_y's, known_x's)
> RSQ(known_y's, known_x's)
> ```
>
> The syntax for these functions is the same as that of the first two arguments of the TREND() function, except that the known_x's argument is required. Here's an example:
>
> ```
> =RSQ(D2:D13, C2:C13)
> ```

Analyzing the Sales Versus Advertising Trend

We tend to think of trend analysis as having a time component. That is, when we think about looking for a trend, we usually think about finding a pattern over a period of time. But regression analysis is more versatile than that. You can use it to compare any two phenomena, as long as one is dependent on the other in some way.

For example, it's reasonable to assume that there is some relationship between how much you spend on advertising and how much you sell. In this case, the advertising costs are the independent variable and the sales revenues are the dependent variable. You can apply regression analysis to investigate the exact nature of the relationship.

Figure 16.7 shows a worksheet that does this. The advertising costs are in A2:A13, and the sales revenues over the same period (these could be monthly numbers, quarterly numbers, and so on—the time period doesn't matter) are in B2:B13. The rest of the worksheet applies the same trend-analysis techniques that you've learned in the past few sections.

Making Forecasts

Knowing the overall trend exhibited by a data set is useful because it tells you the broad direction that sales or costs or employee acquisitions is going, and it gives you a good idea of how related the dependent variable is to the independent variable. But a trend is also useful for making forecasts in which you extend the trendline into the future (what will sales be in the first quarter of next year?) or calculate the trend value given some new independent value (if we spend $25,000 on advertising, what will the corresponding sales be?).

How accurate is such a prediction? A projection based on historical data assumes that the factors influencing the data over the historical period will remain constant. If this is a reasonable assumption in your case, the projection will be a reasonable one. Of course, the longer you extend the line, the more likely it is that some of the factors will change or that new ones will arise. As a result, best-fit extensions should be used only for short-term projections.

Figure 16.7
A trend analysis for advertising costs versus sales revenues.

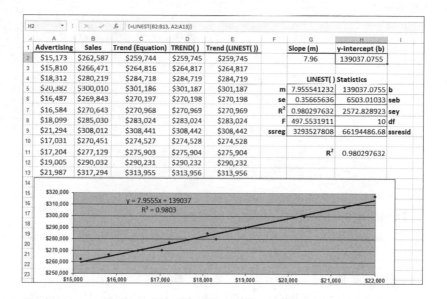

Plotting Forecasted Values

If you want just a visual idea of a forecasted trend, you can extend the chart trendline that you created earlier. The following steps show you how to add a forecasting trendline to a chart:

1. Select the chart and, if more than one data series are plotted, click the series you want to work with.

2. Select Design, Add Chart Element, Trendline, More Trendline Options to display the Format Trendline task pane.

3. On the Trendline Options tab, click Linear.

4. Select the Display Equation on Chart check box. (See "Understanding the Regression Equation," earlier in this chapter.)

5. Select the Display R-Squared Value on Chart check box. (See "Understanding R^2," earlier in this chapter.)

6. Use the Forward text box to select the number of units you want to project the trendline into the future. (For example, to extend the quarterly sales number into the next year, set Forward to 4 to extend the trendline by four quarters.)

7. Click Close (X). Excel inserts the trendline and extends it into the future.

Figure 16.8 shows the quarterly sales trendline extended by four quarters.

Figure 16.8
The trendline has been extended four quarters into the future.

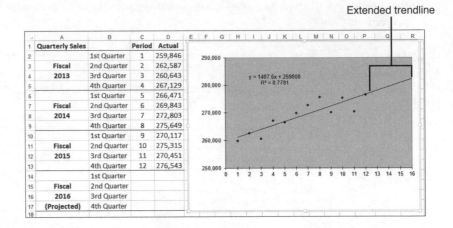

Extended trendline

Extending a Linear Trend with the Fill Handle

If you prefer to see exact data points in your forecast, you can use the fill handle to project a best-fit line into the future. Here are the steps to follow:

1. Select the historical data on the worksheet.

2. Click and drag the fill handle to extend the selection. Excel calculates the best-fit line from the existing data, projects this line into the new data, and calculates the appropriate values.

Figure 16.9 shows an example. Here, I've used the fill handle to project the period numbers and quarterly sales figures over the next fiscal year. The accompanying chart clearly shows the extended best-fit values.

Figure 16.9
When you use the fill handle to extend historical data into the future, Excel uses a linear projection to calculate the new values.

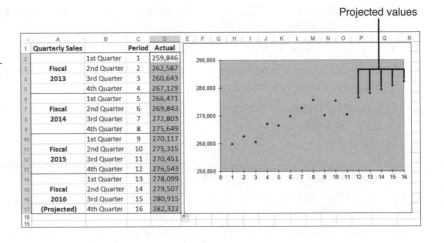

Projected values

Extending a Linear Trend Using the Series Command

You also can use the Series command to project a best-fit line. The following steps show you how it's done:

1. Select the range that includes both the historical data and the cells that will contain the projections (and ensure that the projection cells are blank).
2. Select Home, Fill, Series. Excel displays the Series dialog box.
3. Select AutoFill.
4. Click OK. Excel fills in the blank cells with the best-fit projection.

The Series command is also useful for producing the data that defines the full best-fit line so that you can see the actual trendline values. The following steps show you how it's done:

1. Copy the historical data into an adjacent row or column.
2. Select the range that includes both the copied historical data and the cells that will contain the projections. (Again, ensure that the projection cells are blank).
3. Select Home, Fill, Series. Excel displays the Series dialog box.
4. Select the Trend check box.
5. Click the Linear option.
6. Click OK. Excel replaces the copied historical data with the best-fit numbers and projects the trend onto the blank cells.

In Figure 16.10, the trend values created by the Series command are in E2:E13 and are plotted on the chart with the best-fit line on top of the historical data.

Figure 16.10
A best-fit trendline created with the Series command.

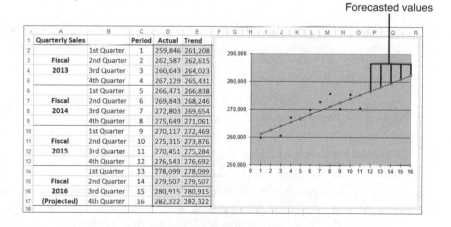

16

Forecasting with the Regression Equation

You can also forecast individual dependent values by using the regression equation that is returned when you add the chart trendline. (Remember that you must click the Display Equation on Chart check box when adding the trendline.) Recall the general regression equation for a linear model:

    y = mx + b

The regression equation displayed by the trendline feature gives you the *m* and *b* values, so to determine a new value for *y*, just plug in a new value for *x*.

For example, in the quarterly sales model, Excel calculated the following regression equation:

    y = 1407.6x + 259800

To find the trend value for the 13th period, you substitute 13 for *x*:

    y = 1407.6 * 13 + 259800

The result is 278,099, the projected sales for the 13th period (first quarter 2016).

Forecasting with TREND()

The TREND() function is also capable of forecasting new values. To extend a trend and generate new values, you need to add the *new_x's* argument to the TREND() function. Here's the basic procedure for setting this up on the worksheet:

1. Add the new x-values to the worksheet. For example, to extend the quarterly sales trend into the next fiscal year, you'd add the values 13 through 16 to the Period column.

2. Select a range large enough to hold all the new values. For example, if you're adding four new values, select four cells in a column or row, depending on the structure of your data.

3. Enter the TREND() function as an array formula, specifying the range of new x-values as the *new_x's* argument. Here's the formula for the quarterly sales example:

    {=TREND(D2:D13, C2:C13, C14:C17)}

Figure 16.11 shows the forecasted values in F14:F17. The values in column E were derived using the regression equation and are included for comparison.

Forecasting with LINEST()

Recall that the LINEST() function returns the slope and y-intercept of the trendline. When you know these numbers, forecasting new values is a straightforward matter of plugging them into the linear regression equation along with a new value of *x*. For example, if the slope is in cell H2, the intercept is in I2, and the new x-value is in C14, the following formula will return the forecasted value:

    =$H$2 * C14 + $I$2

Figure 16.11
The range F14:F17 contains the forecasted values calculated by the `TREND()` function.

F14 {=TREND(D2:D13, C2:C13, C14:C17)}

	A	B	C	D	E	F	G
1	**Quarterly Sales**		**Period**	**Actual**	**Trend (Equation)**	**TREND( )**	
2		1st Quarter	1	259,846	261,208	261,208	
3	**Fiscal**	2nd Quarter	2	262,587	262,615	262,615	
4	**2012**	3rd Quarter	3	260,643	264,023	264,023	
5		4th Quarter	4	267,129	265,430	265,431	
6		1st Quarter	5	266,471	266,838	266,838	
7	**Fiscal**	2nd Quarter	6	269,843	268,246	268,246	
8	**2014**	3rd Quarter	7	272,803	269,653	269,654	
9		4th Quarter	8	275,649	271,061	271,061	
10		1st Quarter	9	270,117	272,468	272,469	
11	**Fiscal**	2nd Quarter	10	275,315	273,876	273,876	
12	**2015**	3rd Quarter	11	270,451	275,284	275,284	
13		4th Quarter	12	276,543	276,691	276,692	
14		1st Quarter	13		278,099	278,099	
15	**Fiscal**	2nd Quarter	14		279,506	279,507	
16	**2016**	3rd Quarter	15		280,914	280,915	
17	**(Projected)**	4th Quarter	16		282,322	282,322	
18							

Forecasted values

Figure 16.12 shows a worksheet that uses this method to forecast the Fiscal 2016 sales figures.

Figure 16.12
The range F14:F17 contains the forecasted values calculated by the regression equation, using the slope (H2) and intercept (I2) returned by the `LINEST()` function.

F14 =$H$2 * C14 + $I$2

	A	B	C	D	E	F	G	H	I
1	**Quarterly Sales**		**Period**	**Sales**	**TREND( )**	**Trend (LINEST( ))**		**Slope (m)**	**y-intercept (b)**
2		1st Quarter	1	259,846	261,208	261,208		1407.63	259800.1818
3	**Fiscal**	2nd Quarter	2	262,587	262,615	262,615			
4	**2012**	3rd Quarter	3	260,643	264,023	264,023			
5		4th Quarter	4	267,129	265,431	265,431			
6		1st Quarter	5	266,471	266,838	266,838			
7	**Fiscal**	2nd Quarter	6	269,843	268,246	268,246			
8	**2014**	3rd Quarter	7	272,803	269,654	269,654			
9		4th Quarter	8	275,649	271,061	271,061			
10		1st Quarter	9	270,117	272,469	272,469			
11	**Fiscal**	2nd Quarter	10	275,315	273,876	273,876			
12	**2015**	3rd Quarter	11	270,451	275,284	275,284			
13		4th Quarter	12	276,543	276,692	276,692			
14		1st Quarter	13		278,099	278,099			
15	**Fiscal**	2nd Quarter	14		279,507	279,507			
16	**2016**	3rd Quarter	15		280,915	280,915			
17	**(Projected)**	4th Quarter	16		282,322	282,322			
18									

Forecasted values

NOTE

You can also calculate a forecasted value for *x* by using the `FORECAST()` function:

```
FORECAST(x, known_y's, known_x's)
```

Here, *x* is the new x-value that you want to work with, and *`known_y's`* and *`known_x's`* are the same as with the `TREND()` function (except that the *`known_x's`* argument is required). Here's an example:

```
=FORECAST(13, D2:D13, C2:C13)
```

16

Case Study: Trend Analysis and Forecasting for a Seasonal Sales Model

This case study applies some of the forecasting techniques from the previous sections to a more sophisticated sales model. The worksheets explore two different cases:

■ **Sales as a function of time**—Essentially, this case determines the trend over time of past sales and extrapolates the trend in a straight line to determine future sales.

■ **Sales as a function of the season (in a business sense)**—Many businesses are seasonal; that is, their sales are traditionally higher or lower during certain periods of the fiscal year. Retailers, for example, usually have higher sales in the fall, leading up to Christmas. If the sales for your business are a function of the season, you need to remove these seasonal biases to calculate the true underlying trend.

About the Forecast Workbook

The Forecast workbook includes the following worksheets:

■ **Monthly Data**—Use this worksheet to enter up to 10 years of monthly historical data. This worksheet also calculates the 12-month moving averages used by the Monthly Seasonal Index worksheet. Note that the data in column C—specifically, the range C2:C121—is a range named Actual.

■ **Monthly Seasonal Index**—Calculates the seasonal adjustment factors (the seasonal indexes) for the monthly data.

■ **Monthly Trend**—Calculates the trend of the monthly historical data. Both a normal trend and a seasonally adjusted trend are computed.

■ **Monthly Forecast**—Derives a three-year monthly forecast based on both the normal trend and the seasonally adjusted trend.

■ **Quarterly Data**—Consolidates the monthly actuals into quarterly data and calculates the four-quarter moving average (used by the Quarterly Seasonal Index worksheet).

■ **Quarterly Seasonal Index**—Calculates the seasonal indexes for the quarterly data.

■ **Quarterly Trend**—Calculates the trend of the quarterly historical data. Both a normal trend and a seasonally adjusted trend are computed.

■ **Quarterly Forecast**—Derives a three-year quarterly forecast based on both the normal trend and the seasonally adjusted trend.

> **TIP**
> The Forecast workbook contains dozens of formulas. You'll probably want to switch to manual calculation mode when working with this file.

The sales forecast workbook is driven entirely by the historical data entered into the Monthly Data worksheet, shown in Figure 16.13.

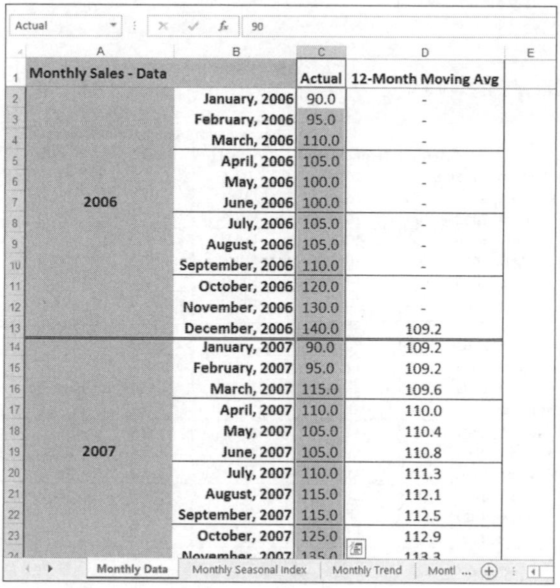

Figure 16.13
The Monthly Data
worksheet contains the
historical sales data.

Calculating a Normal Trend

As I mentioned earlier, you can calculate either a normal trend that treats all sales as a simple function of time or a deseasoned trend that takes seasonal factors into account. This section covers the normal trend.

All the trend calculations in the workbook use a variation of the TREND() function. Recall that the TREND() function's known_x's argument is optional; if you omit it, Excel uses the array {1,2,3,...,n}, where n is the number of values in the known_y's argument. When the independent variable is time related, you can usually get away with omitting the known_x's argument because the values are just the period numbers.

In this case study, the independent variable is in terms of months, so you can leave out the known_x's argument. The known_y's argument is the data in the Actual column, which, as I pointed out earlier, has been given the range name Actual. Therefore, the following array formula generates the best-fit trend values for the existing data:

```
{=TREND(Actual)}
```

This formula generates the values in the Normal Trend column of the Monthly Trend worksheet, shown in Figure 16.14.

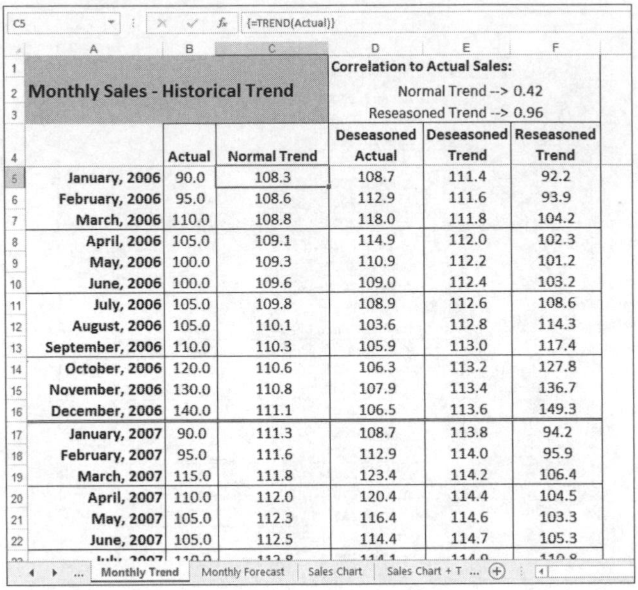

Figure 16.14
The Normal Trend column uses the TREND() function to return the best-fit trend values for the data in the Actual range.

			Correlation to Actual Sales:		
C5		fx {=TREND(Actual)}			
	A	B	C	D	E	F
1				Correlation to Actual Sales:		
2	Monthly Sales - Historical Trend				Normal Trend --> 0.42	
3					Reseasoned Trend --> 0.96	
4		Actual	Normal Trend	Deseasoned Actual	Deseasoned Trend	Reseasoned Trend
5	January, 2006	90.0	108.3	108.7	111.4	92.2
6	February, 2006	95.0	108.6	112.9	111.6	93.9
7	March, 2006	110.0	108.8	118.0	111.8	104.2
8	April, 2006	105.0	109.1	114.9	112.0	102.3
9	May, 2006	100.0	109.3	110.9	112.2	101.2
10	June, 2006	100.0	109.6	109.0	112.4	103.2
11	July, 2006	105.0	109.8	108.9	112.6	108.6
12	August, 2006	105.0	110.1	103.6	112.8	114.3
13	September, 2006	110.0	110.3	105.9	113.0	117.4
14	October, 2006	120.0	110.6	106.3	113.2	127.8
15	November, 2006	130.0	110.8	107.9	113.4	136.7
16	December, 2006	140.0	111.1	106.5	113.6	149.3
17	January, 2007	90.0	111.3	108.7	113.8	94.2
18	February, 2007	95.0	111.6	112.9	114.0	95.9
19	March, 2007	115.0	111.8	123.4	114.2	106.4
20	April, 2007	110.0	112.0	120.4	114.4	104.5
21	May, 2007	105.0	112.3	116.4	114.6	103.3
22	June, 2007	105.0	112.5	114.4	114.7	105.3

Monthly Trend | Monthly Forecast | Sales Chart | Sales Chart + T ...

> **NOTE** The values in column B of the Monthly Trend sheet are linked to the values in the Actual column of the Monthly Data worksheet. You use the values in the Monthly Data worksheet to calculate the trend, so technically you don't need the figures in column B. I included them, however, to make it easier to compare the trend and the actuals. Including the Actual values is also handy if you want to create a chart that includes these values.

To get some idea of whether the trend is close to your data, cell F2 calculates the correlation between the trend values and the actual sales figures:

```
{=CORREL(Actual, TREND(Actual))}
```

The correlation value of 0.42—and its corresponding value for R^2 of about 0.17—shows that the normal trend doesn't fit this data very well. You'll fix that later by taking into account the seasonal nature of the historical data.

Calculating the Forecast Trend

As you saw earlier in this chapter, to get a sales forecast, you extend the historical trendline into the future. This is the job of the Monthly Forecast worksheet, shown in Figure 16.15.

Calculating a forecast trend requires that you specify the *new_x's* argument for the TREND() function. In this case, the *new_x's* are the sales periods in the forecast interval. For example, suppose that you have a 10-year period of monthly data from January 2006 to December 2015. This involves 120 periods of data. Therefore, to calculate the trend for January 2016 (the 121st period), you use the following formula:

```
=TREND(Actual, , 121)
```

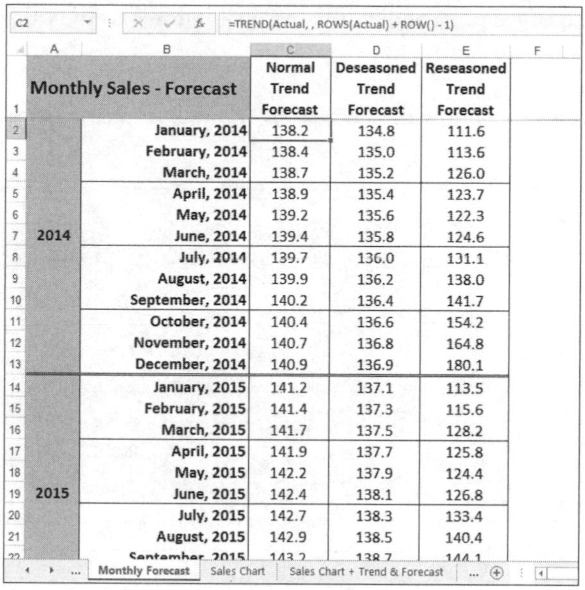

Figure 16.15
The Monthly Forecast worksheet calculates a sales forecast by extending the historical trend data.

C2			fx	=TREND(Actual, , ROWS(Actual) + ROW() - 1)		

	A	B	C	D	E	F
1		**Monthly Sales - Forecast**	Normal Trend Forecast	Deseasoned Trend Forecast	Reseasoned Trend Forecast	
2		January, 2014	138.2	134.8	111.6	
3		February, 2014	138.4	135.0	113.6	
4		March, 2014	138.7	135.2	126.0	
5		April, 2014	138.9	135.4	123.7	
6		May, 2014	139.2	135.6	122.3	
7	2014	June, 2014	139.4	135.8	124.6	
8		July, 2014	139.7	136.0	131.1	
9		August, 2014	139.9	136.2	138.0	
10		September, 2014	140.2	136.4	141.7	
11		October, 2014	140.4	136.6	154.2	
12		November, 2014	140.7	136.8	164.8	
13		December, 2014	140.9	136.9	180.1	
14		January, 2015	141.2	137.1	113.5	
15		February, 2015	141.4	137.3	115.6	
16		March, 2015	141.7	137.5	128.2	
17		April, 2015	141.9	137.7	125.8	
18		May, 2015	142.2	137.9	124.4	
19	2015	June, 2015	142.4	138.1	126.8	
20		July, 2015	142.7	138.3	133.4	
21		August, 2015	142.9	138.5	140.4	
22		September, 2015	143.2	138.7	144.1	

◀ ▶ ...	Monthly Forecast	Sales Chart	Sales Chart + Trend & Forecast	... ⊕

16

You use 122 as the *new_x's* argument for February 2016, 123 for March 2016, and so on.

The Monthly Forecast worksheet uses the following formula to calculate these *new_x's* values:

```
ROWS(Actual) + ROW() - 1
```

ROWS(Actual) returns the number of sales periods in the Actual range in the Monthly Data worksheet. ROW() - 1 is a trick that returns the number you need to add to get the forecast sales period. For example, the January 2016 forecast is in cell C2; therefore, ROW() - 1 returns 1.

Calculating the Seasonal Trend

Many businesses experience predictable fluctuations in sales throughout their fiscal year. Beach resort operators see most of their sales during the summer months; retailers look forward to the Christmas season for the revenue that will carry them through the rest of the year. Figure 16.16 shows a sales chart for a company that experiences a large increase in sales during the fall.

Because of the nature of the sales in companies that see seasonal fluctuations, the normal trend calculation doesn't give an accurate forecast. You need to include seasonal variations in your analysis, which involves four steps:

1. For each month (or quarter), calculate a *seasonal index* that identifies seasonal influences.
2. Use these indexes to calculate seasonally adjusted (or *deseasoned*) values for each month.
3. Calculate the trend based on these deseasoned values.

4. Compute the true trend by adding the seasonal indexes to the calculated trend (from step 3).

The next few sections show how the Forecast workbook implements each step.

Figure 16.16
A chart for a company showing seasonal sales variations.

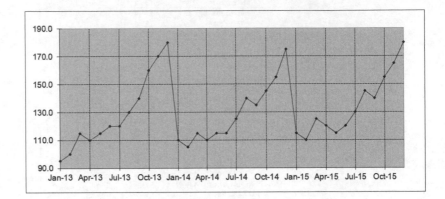

Computing the Monthly Seasonal Indexes

A *seasonal index* is a measure of how the average sales in a given month compare to a "normal" value. For example, if January has an index of 90, January's sales are (on average) only 90% of what they are in a normal month.

Therefore, you first must define what "normal" signifies. Because you're dealing with monthly data, you define normal as the 12-month moving average. (An *n*-month moving average is the average taken over the past *n* months.) The 12-Month Moving Avg column in the Monthly Data sheet (see column D in Figure 16.13) uses a formula named `TwelveMonthMovingAvg` to handle this calculation. This is a relative range name, so its definition changes with each cell in the column.

For example, here's the formula that's used in cell D13:

```
=AVERAGE(C2:C13)
```

In other words, this formula calculates the average for the range C2:C13, which is the preceding 12 months.

This moving average defines the "normal" value for any given month. The next step is to compare each month to the moving average. This is done by dividing each monthly sales figure by its corresponding moving-average calculation and multiplying by 100, which equals the sales *ratio* for the month. For example, the sales in December 2006 (cell C13) totaled 140.0, with a moving average of 109.2 (D13). Dividing C13 by D13 and multiplying by 100 returns a ratio of about 128. You can loosely interpret this to mean that sales in December were 28% higher than sales in a normal month.

To get an accurate seasonal index for December (or any other month), however, you must calculate ratios for every December for which you have historical data. Take an average of all these ratios to reach a true seasonal index (except for a slight adjustment, as you'll see).

The purpose of the Monthly Seasonal Index worksheet, shown in Figure 16.17, is to derive a seasonal index for each month. The worksheet's table calculates the ratios for every month over the span of the historical data. The Avg. Ratio column then calculates the average for each month. To get the final values for the seasonal indexes, however, you need to make a small adjustment. The indexes should add up to 1,200 (100 per month, on average) to be true percentages. As you can see in cell B15, however, the sum is 1,214.0. This means that you have to reduce each average by a factor of 1.0116 (1,214/1,200). The Seasonal Index column does that, thereby producing the true seasonal indexes for each month.

16

Figure 16.17
The Monthly Seasonal Index worksheet calculates the seasonal index for each month, based on monthly historical data.

D14			f_x	=IF('Monthly Data'!D13<>0,100*'Monthly Data'!C13/'Monthly Data'!D13,"")								
	A	B	C	D	E	F	G	H	I	J	K	L	M

Monthly Seasonal Index Calculations

	Avg. Ratio	Seasonal Index	2006 Ratios*	2007 Ratios	2008 Ratios	2009 Ratios	2010 Ratios	2011 Ratios	2012 Ratios	2013 Ratios	2014 Ratios	2015 Ratios
Jan	83.7	82.8	-	82.4	83.2	84.8	85.1	88.3	78.4	78.1	84.1	89.0
Feb	85.1	84.2	-	87.0	87.3	88.7	88.9	84.6	82.4	82.5	80.0	84.9
Mar	94.3	93.2	-	104.9	104.3	93.6	92.6	88.9	86.3	94.5	87.6	95.8
Apr	92.4	91.4	-	100.0	107.5	98.6	85.1	92.3	82.9	90.1	83.8	91.4
May	91.2	90.2	-	95.1	94.3	94.3	85.4	95.4	87.4	93.9	87.6	87.6
Jun	92.8	91.8	-	94.7	90.0	97.9	89.8	91.1	95.0	98.0	87.9	91.1
Jul	97.6	96.4	-	98.9	94.3	97.5	97.6	98.7	99.0	98.3	95.2	98.4
Aug	102.5	101.4	-	102.6	94.6	101.1	101.4	102.3	99.3	106.1	106.0	109.4
Sep	105.1	103.9	-	102.2	98.9	108.3	105.4	105.9	103.7	113.5	102.5	105.3
Oct	114.2	112.9	-	110.7	111.4	115.9	113.5	113.4	108.4	127.6	111.2	115.9
Nov	121.9	120.5	-	119.1	119.6	123.3	125.3	121.2	113.5	132.9	120.0	122.6
Dec	133.0	131.5	128.2	127.5	127.7	134.2	136.9	136.4	131.1	138.9	135.9	133.3
Total	1214.0	1200.0										
Adj	1.0116		*Each Ratio = Monthly Actual ÷ 12-Month Moving Average									

Calculating the Deseasoned Monthly Values

When you have the seasonal indexes, you need to put them to work to "level the playing field." Basically, you divide the actual sales figures for each month by the appropriate monthly index (and multiply them by 100 to keep the units the same). This effectively removes the seasonal factors from the data. (This process is called *deseasoning*, or *seasonally adjusting*, the data.)

The Deseasoned Actual column in the Monthly Trend worksheet performs these calculations (see Figure 16.18). Following is a typical formula (from cell D5):

```
=100 * B5 / INDEX(MonthlyIndexTable, MONTH(A5), 3)
```

B5 refers to the sales figure in the Actual column, and MonthlyIndexTable is the range A3:C14 in the Monthly Seasonal Index worksheet. The INDEX() function finds the appropriate seasonal index for the month (given by the MONTH(A5) function).

Figure 16.18
The Deseasoned Actual column calculates seasonally adjusted values for the actual data.

| D5 | ▼ | : | × | ✓ | fx | =100 * B5 / INDEX(MonthlyIndexTable, MONTH(A5), 3) |

	A	B	C	D	E	F	G
1				Correlation to Actual Sales:			
2	Monthly Sales - Historical Trend			Normal Trend --> 0.42			
3				Reseasoned Trend --> 0.96			
4		Actual	Normal Trend	Deseasoned Actual	Deseasoned Trend	Reseasoned Trend	
5	January, 2006	90.0	108.3	108.7	111.4	92.2	
6	February, 2006	95.0	108.6	112.9	111.6	93.9	
7	March, 2006	110.0	108.8	118.0	111.8	104.2	
8	April, 2006	105.0	109.1	114.9	112.0	102.3	
9	May, 2006	100.0	109.3	110.9	112.2	101.2	
10	June, 2006	100.0	109.6	109.0	112.4	103.2	
11	July, 2006	105.0	109.8	108.9	112.6	108.6	
12	August, 2006	105.0	110.1	103.6	112.8	114.3	
13	September, 2006	110.0	110.3	105.9	113.0	117.4	
14	October, 2006	120.0	110.6	106.3	113.2	127.8	
15	November, 2006	130.0	110.8	107.9	113.4	136.7	
16	December, 2006	140.0	111.1	106.5	113.6	149.3	
17	January, 2007	90.0	111.3	108.7	113.8	94.2	
18	February, 2007	95.0	111.6	112.9	114.0	95.9	
19	March, 2007	115.0	111.8	123.4	114.2	106.4	

Calculating the Deseasoned Trend

The next step is to calculate the historical trend based on the new deseasoned values. The Deseasoned Trend column uses the following array formula to accomplish this task:

```
{=TREND(DeseasonedActual)}
```

The name `DeseasonedActual` refers to the values in the Deseasoned Actual column (D5:D124).

Calculating the Reseasoned Trend

By itself, the deseasoned trend doesn't amount to much. To get the true historical trend, you need to add the seasonal factor back into the deseasoned trend. (This process is called *reseasoning* the data.) The Reseasoned Trend column does the job with a formula similar to the one used in the Deseasoned Actual column:

```
=E5 * INDEX(MonthlyIndexTable, MONTH(A5), 3) /100
```

Cell F3 uses CORREL() to determine the correlation between the Actual data and the Reseasoned Trend data:

```
=CORREL(Actual, ReseasonedTrend)
```

Here, `ReseasonedTrend` is the name applied to the data in the Reseasoned Trend column (F5:F124). As you can see, the correlation of 0.96 is extremely high, indicating that the new trend "line" is an excellent match for the historical data.

Calculating the Seasonal Forecast

To derive a forecast based on seasonal factors, combine the techniques you used to calculate a normal trend forecast and a reseasoned historical trend. In the Monthly Forecast worksheet (see Figure 16.15), the Deseasoned Trend Forecast column computes the forecast for the deseasoned trend:

```
=TREND(DeseasonedTrend, , ROWS(DeseasonedTrend) + ROW() - 1)
```

The Reseasoned Trend Forecast column adds the seasonal factors back into the deseasoned trend forecast:

```
=D2 * Index(MonthlyIndexTable, MONTH(B2), 3) / 100
```

D2 is the value from the Deseasoned Trend Forecast column, and B2 is the forecast month.

Figure 16.19 shows a chart comparing the actual sales and the reseasoned trend for the past three years of the sample data. The chart also shows two years of the reseasoned forecast.

Figure 16.19
A chart of the sample data, which compares actual sales, the reseasoned trend, and the reseasoned forecast.

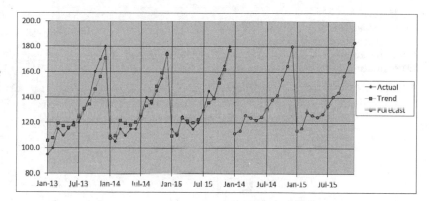

Working with Quarterly Data

If you prefer to work with quarterly data, the Quarterly Data, Quarterly Seasonal Index, Quarterly Trend, and Quarterly Forecast worksheets perform the same functions as their monthly counterparts. You don't have to reenter the data because the Quarterly Data worksheet consolidates the monthly numbers by quarter.

Using Simple Regression on Nonlinear Data

As you saw in the case study, the data you work with doesn't always fit a linear pattern. If the data shows seasonal variations, you can compute the trend and forecast values by working with seasonally adjusted numbers, as you also saw in the case study. But many business scenarios aren't either linear or seasonal. The data might look more like a curve, or it might fluctuate without any apparent pattern.

These nonlinear patterns might seem more complex, but Excel offers a number of useful tools for performing regression analysis on this type of data.

Working with an Exponential Trend

An *exponential* trend is a trend that rises or falls at an increasingly higher rate. Fads often exhibit this kind of behavior. A product might sell steadily but unspectacularly for a while, but then word starts getting around—perhaps because of a mention in the newspaper or on television—and sales start to rise. If these new customers enjoy the product, they tell their friends about it, and those people purchase the product, too. They tell *their* friends, the media notice that everyone's talking about this product, and a bona fide fad ensues.

This is called an exponential trend because, as a graph, it looks much like a number being raised to successively higher values of an exponent (for example, 10^1, 10^2, 10^3, and so on). This is often modeled using the constant e (approximately 2.71828), which is the base of the natural logarithm. Figure 16.20 shows a worksheet that uses the EXP() function in column B to return e raised to the successive powers in column A. The chart shows the results as a classic exponential curve.

Figure 16.20
Raising the constant e to successive powers produces a classic exponential trend pattern.

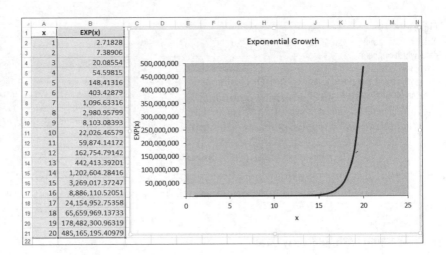

Figure 16.21 shows a worksheet that contains weekly data for the number of units sold of a product. As you can see, the unit sales hold steady for the first eight or nine weeks and then climb rapidly. As this chart illustrates, the sales curve is very much like an exponential growth curve. The next couple sections show you how to track the trend and make forecasts based on such a model.

Plotting an Exponential Trendline

The easiest way to see the trend and forecast is to add a trendline—specifically, an exponential trendline—to the chart. Here are the steps to follow:

1. Select the chart and, if more than one data series are plotted, click the series you want to work with.

2. Select Design, Add Chart Element, Trendline, More Trendline Options to display the Format Trendline task pane.

3. On the Trendline Options tab, click Exponential.

4. Click to select the Display Equation on Chart and Display R-Squared Value on Chart check boxes.

5. Click Close (X). Excel inserts the trendline.

Figure 16.21
The weekly unit sales show a definite exponential pattern.

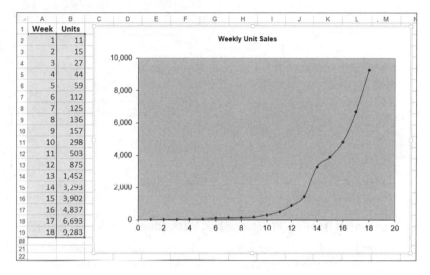

16

Figure 16.22 shows the exponential trendline added to the chart.

Calculating Exponential Trend and Forecast Values

In Figure 16.22, notice that the regression equation for an exponential trendline takes the following general form:

$$y = be^{mx}$$

Here, b and m are constants. So, knowing these values, given an independent value x, you can compute its corresponding point on the trendline using the following formula:

```
=b * EXP(m * x)
```

In the trendline of Figure 16.22, these constant values are `7.1875` and `0.4038`, respectively. So, the formula for trend values becomes this:

```
=7.1875 * EXP(0.4038 * x)
```

If x is a value between 1 and 18, you get a trend point for the existing data. To get a forecast, you use a value higher than 18. For example, using x equal to `19` gives a forecast value of 15,437 units:

```
-7.1875 * EXP(0.4038 * 19)
```

Figure 16.22

The weekly unit sales chart with an exponential trendline added.

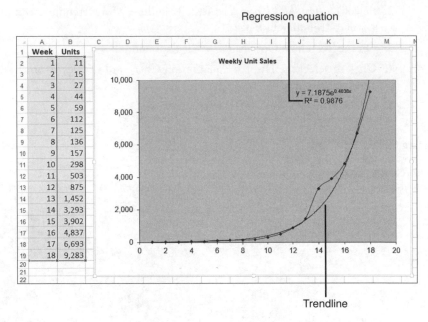

	A	B
1	**Week**	**Units**
2	1	11
3	2	15
4	3	27
5	4	44
6	5	59
7	6	112
8	7	125
9	8	136
10	9	157
11	10	298
12	11	503
13	12	875
14	13	1,452
15	14	3,293
16	15	3,902
17	16	4,837
18	17	6,693
19	18	9,283

Regression equation

$y = 7.1875e^{0.4038x}$
$R^2 = 0.9876$

Trendline

Exponential Trending and Forecasting Using the GROWTH() Function

As you learned with linear regression, it's often useful to work with actual trend values instead of just visualizing the trendline. With a linear model, you use the TREND() function to generate actual values. The exponential equivalent is the GROWTH() function:

```
GROWTH(known_y's[, known_x's][, new_x's][, const])
```

known_y's	A range reference or an array of the known y-values.
known_x's	A range reference or an array of the x-values associated with the known y-values. If you omit this argument, the *known_x's* are assumed to be the array {1,2,3,...,n}, where n is the number of *known_y's*.
new_x's	A range reference or an array of the new x-values for which you want corresponding y-values.
const	A logical value that determines the value of the b constant in the exponential regression equation. If you use FALSE, b is set to 1; if you use TRUE (which is the default), Excel calculates b based on the *known_y's*.

With the exception of a small difference in the *const* argument, the GROWTH() function syntax is identical to that of TREND(). You use the two functions in the same way as well. For example, to return the exponential trend values for the known values, you specify the *known_y's* argument and, optionally, the *known_x's* argument. Here's the formula for the weekly units example, which is entered as an array:

```
{=GROWTH(B2:B19, A2:A19)}
```

To forecast values using GROWTH(), add the *new_x's* argument. For example, to forecast the weekly sales for weeks 19 and 20, assuming that these x-values are in A20:A21, you use the following array formula:

    {=GROWTH(B2:B19, A2:A19, A20:A21)}

Figure 16.23 shows the GROWTH() formulas at work. The numbers in C2:C19 are the existing trend values, and the numbers in C20 and C21 are the forecast values.

Figure 16.23
The weekly unit sales with existing trend and forecast values calculated by the GROWTH() function.

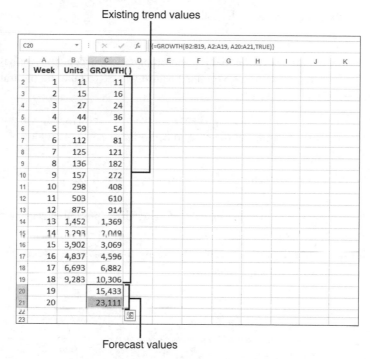

Existing trend values

Forecast values

What if you want to calculate the constants b and m? You can do that by using the exponential equivalent of LINEST(), which is LOGEST():

    LOGEST(known_y's[, known_x's][, const][, stats])

known_y's	A range reference or an array of the known y-values from which you want to calculate the trend.
known_x's	A range reference or an array of the x-values associated with the known y-values. If you omit this argument, the *known_x's* are assumed to be the array {1,2,3,...,n}, where *n* is the number of *known_y's*.
const	A logical value that determines the value of the b constant in the exponential regression equation. If you use FALSE, b is set to 1; if you use TRUE (this is the default), Excel calculates b based on the *known_y's*.

stats   A logical value that determines whether LOGEST() returns additional regression statistics besides b and m. The default is FALSE. If you use TRUE, LOGEST() returns the extra *stats*, which are (except for b and m) the same as those returned by LINEST().

Actually, LOGEST() doesn't return the value for m directly. That's because LOGEST() is designed for the following regression formula:

$$y = bm_1{}^x$$

However, this is equivalent to the following:

$$y = b * \text{EXP}(\text{LN}(m_1) * x)$$

This is the same as our exponential regression equation, except that we have LN(m_1) instead of just m. Therefore, to derive m, you need to use LN(m_1) to take the natural logarithm of the m_1 value returned by LOGEST().

As with LINEST(), if you set stats to FALSE, LOGEST() returns a 1×2 array, with m (actually m_1) in the first cell and b in the second cell. Figure 16.24 shows a worksheet that puts LOGEST() through its paces:

- The value of b is in cell H2. The value of m_1 is in cell G2, and cell I2 uses LN() to get the value of m.

- The values in column D are calculated using the exponential regression equation, with the values for b and m plugged in.

- The values in column E are calculated using the LOGEST() regression equation, with the values for b and m_1 plugged in.

Figure 16.24
The weekly unit sales with data generated by the LOGEST() function.

	A	B	C	D	E	F	G	H	I
							I2	f_x =LN(G2)	
1	Week	Units	GROWTH	y = b * EXP(m * x)	y = b * m1x		m1	b	m = LN(m1)
2	1	11	11	11	11		1.497483	7.187455976	0.403785747
3	2	15	16	16	16				
4	3	27	24	24	24			LOGEST( ) Statistics	
5	4	44	36	36	36	m1	1.497483072	7.187455976	b
6	5	59	54	54	54	se	0.011325276	0.122588809	seb
7	6	112	81	81	81	R2	0.987569651	0.249284732	sey
8	7	125	121	121	121	F	1271.172211	16	df
9	8	136	182	182	182	ssreg	78.99429927	0.994286043	ssresid
10	9	157	272	272	272				
11	10	298	408	408	408				
12	11	503	610	610	610				
13	12	875	914	914	914				
14	13	1,452	1,369	1,369	1,369				
15	14	3,293	2,049	2,049	2,049				
16	15	3,902	3,069	3,069	3,069				
17	16	4,837	4,596	4,596	4,596				
18	17	6,693	6,882	6,882	6,882				
19	18	9,283	10,306	10,306	10,306				
20	19		15,433	15,433	15,433				
21	20		23,111	23,111	23,111				
22									

Working with a Logarithmic Trend

A *logarithmic* trend is a trend that is the inverse of an exponential trend: The values rise (or fall) quickly in the beginning and then level off. This is a common pattern in business. For example, a new company hires many people up front, and then hiring slows over time. A new product often sells many units soon after it's launched, and then sales level off.

This pattern is described as logarithmic because it's typified by the shape of the curve made by the natural logarithm. Figure 16.25 shows a chart that plots the LN(x) function for various values of *x*.

16

Figure 16.25
The natural logarithm produces a classic logarithmic trend pattern.

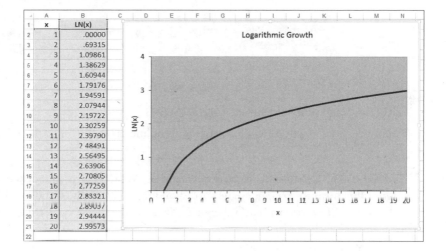

Plotting a Logarithmic Trendline

Plotting a Logarithmic Trendline

The easiest way to see the trend and forecast is to add a trendline—specifically, a logarithmic trendline—to the chart. Here are the steps to follow:

1. Select the chart and, if more than one data series are plotted, click the series you want to work with.
2. Select Design, Add Chart Element, Trendline, More Trendline Options to display the Format Trendline task pane.
3. On the Trendline Options tab, click Logarithmic.
4. Click to select the Display Equation on Chart and Display R-Squared Value on Chart check boxes.
5. Click Close (X). Excel inserts the trendline.

Figure 16.26 shows a worksheet that tracks the total number of employees at a new company. The chart shows the employee growth and a logarithmic trendline fitted to the data.

Figure 16.26
Total employee growth, with a logarithmic trendline added.

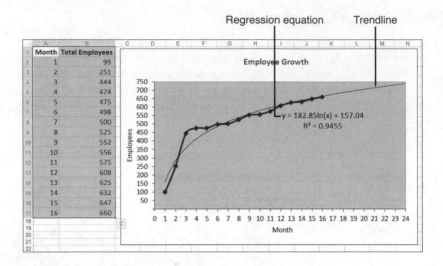

Calculating Logarithmic Trend and Forecast Values

The regression equation for a logarithmic trendline takes the following general form:

```
y = m * LN(x) + b
```

As usual, b and m are constants. So, knowing these values, given an independent value x, you can use this formula to compute its corresponding point on the trendline. In the trendline in Figure 16.26, these constant values are 182.85 and 157.04, respectively. So the formula for trend values becomes this:

```
=182.85 * LN(x) + 157.04
```

If x is a value between 1 and 16, you get a trend point for the existing data. To get a forecast, you use a value higher than 16. For example, using x equal to 17 gives a forecast value of 675 employees:

```
=182.85 * LN(17) + 157.04
```

Excel doesn't have a function that enables you to calculate the values of b and m yourself. However, it's possible to use the LINEST() function if you transform the pattern so that it becomes linear. When you have a logarithmic curve, you "straighten it out" by changing the scale of the x-axis to a logarithmic scale. Therefore, you can turn your logarithmic regression into a linear one by applying the LN() function to the *known_x's* argument:

```
=LINEST(known_y's, LN(known_x's))
```

For example, the following array formula returns the values of m and b for the Total Employees data:

```
{=LINEST(B2:B17, LN(A2:A17))}
```

Figure 16.27 shows a worksheet that calculates m (cell E2) and b (cell F2) and that uses the results to derive values for the current trend and the forecasts (column C).

Figure 16.27
The Total Employees worksheet, with existing trend and forecast values calculated by the logarithmic regression equation and values returned by the `LINEST()` function.

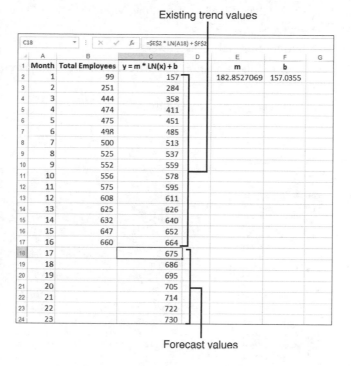

Existing trend values

Forecast values

Working with a Power Trend

The exponential and logarithmic trendlines are both "extreme" in the sense that they have radically different velocities at different parts of the curve. The exponential trendline begins slowly and then takes off at an ever-increasing pace; the logarithmic trendline shoots off the mark and then levels off.

Most measurable business scenarios don't exhibit such extreme behavior. Revenues, profits, margins, and employee head count often tend to increase steadily over time (in successful companies, anyway). If you're analyzing a dependent variable that increases (or decreases) steadily with respect to some independent variable, but the linear trendline doesn't give a good fit, you should try a *power* trendline. This is a pattern that curves steadily in one direction. To give you a flavor of a power curve, consider the graphs of the equations $y = x^2$ and $y = x^{-0.25}$ in Figure 16.28. The $y = x^2$ curve shows a steady increase, whereas the $y = x^{-0.25}$ curve shows a steady decrease.

Plotting a Power Trendline

If you think that your data fits the power pattern, you can quickly check by adding a power trendline to the chart. Here are the steps to follow:

1. Select the chart and, if more than one data series are plotted, click the series you want to work with.

2. Select Design, Add Chart Element, Trendline, More Trendline Options to display the Format Trendline task pane.

3. On the Trendline Options tab, click Power.

4. Click to select the Display Equation on Chart and Display R-Squared Value on Chart check boxes.

5. Click Close (X). Excel inserts the trendline.

Figure 16.28

Power curves are generated by raising x-values to some power.

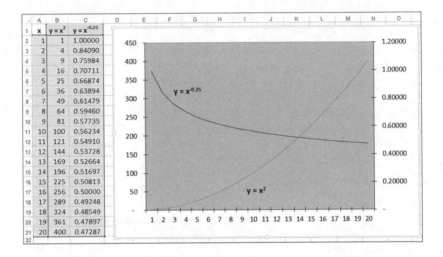

Figure 16.29 shows a worksheet that compares the list price of a product (the independent variable) with the number of units sold (the dependent variable). As the chart shows, this relationship plots as a steadily declining curve, so a power trendline has been added. Note, too, that the trendline has been extended back to the $5.99 price point and forward to the $15.99 price point.

Calculating Power Trend and Forecast Values

The regression equation for a power trendline takes the following general form:

$$y = mx^b$$

As usual, b and m are constants. Given these values and an independent value x, you can use this formula to compute its corresponding point on the trendline. In the trendline in Figure 16.29, these constant values are 423544 and -1.906, respectively. Plugging these into the general equation for a power trend gives the following:

```
=423544 * x ^ -1.906
```

If x is a value between 6.99 and 14.99, you get a trend point for the existing data. To get a forecast, you use a value lower than 6.99 or higher than 14.99. For example, using x equal to 16.99 gives a forecast value of 1,915 units sold:

```
=423544 * 16.99 ^ -1.906
```

Figure 16.29
A product's list price
versus unit sales, with a
power trendline added.

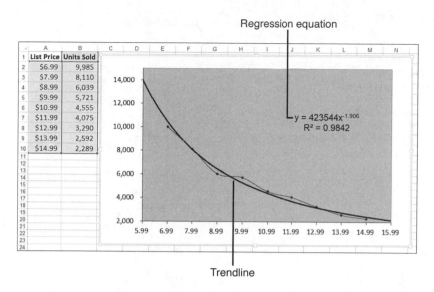

16

As with the logarithmic trend, Excel doesn't have functions that enable you to directly calculate the values of b and m. However, you can "straighten" a power curve by changing the scale of *both* the y-axis and the x-axis to a logarithmic scale. Therefore, you can transform the power regression into a linear regression by applying the natural logarithm—the LN() function—to both the *known_y's* and *known_x's* arguments:

    =LINEST(LN(known_y's), LN(known_x's))

Here's how the array formula looks for the list price versus units sold data:

    {=LINEST(LN(B2:B10, LN(A2:A10))}

The first cell of the array holds the value of b. Because it's used as an exponent in the regression equation, you don't need to "undo" the logarithmic transform. However, the second cell in the array—let's call it m_1—holds the value of m in its logarithmic form. Therefore, you need to "undo" the transform by applying the EXP() function to the result.

Figure 16.30 shows a worksheet performing these calculations. The LINEST() array is in E2:F2, and E2 holds the value of b (cell E2). To get m, cell G2 uses the formula =EXP(F2). The worksheet uses these results to derive values for the current trend and the forecasts (column C).

Using Polynomial Regression Analysis

The trendlines you've seen so far have been unidirectional. That's fine if the curve formed by the dependent variable values is also unidirectional, but that's often not the case in a business environment. Sales fluctuate, profits rise and fall, and costs move up and down, thanks to varying factors such as inflation, interest rates, exchange rates, and commodity prices. For these more complex curves, the trendlines covered so far might not give either a good fit or good forecasts.

Figure 16.30
The worksheet of list price versus units sold, with existing trend and forecast values calculated by the power regression equation and values returned by the LINEST() function.

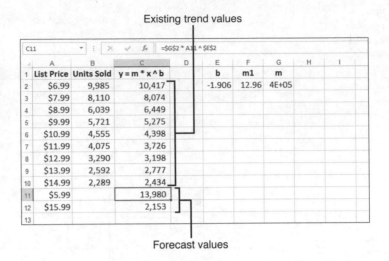

Existing trend values

Forecast values

If that's the case, you might need to turn to a *polynomial* trendline, which is a curve constructed out of an equation that uses multiple powers of *x*. For example, a *second-order* polynomial regression equation takes the following general form:

$$y = m_2 x^2 + m_1 x + b$$

The values m_2, m_1, and b are constants. Similarly, a *third-order* polynomial regression equation takes the following form:

$$y = m_3 x^3 + m_2 x^2 + m_1 x + b$$

These equations can go as high as a sixth-order polynomial.

Plotting a Polynomial Trendline

Here are the steps to follow to add a polynomial trendline to a chart:

1. Select the chart and, if more than one data series are plotted, click the series you want to work with.
2. Select Design, Add Chart Element, Trendline, More Trendline Options to display the Format Trendline task pane.
3. On the Trendline Options tab, click Polynomial.
4. Use the Order spin box to select the order of the polynomial equation you want.
5. Click to select the Display Equation on Chart and Display R-Squared Value on Chart check boxes.
6. Click Close (X). Excel inserts the trendline.

Figure 16.31 displays a simple worksheet that shows annual profits over 10 years, with accompanying charts showing two different polynomial trendlines.

Figure 16.31
Annual profits with two charts showing different polynomial trendlines.

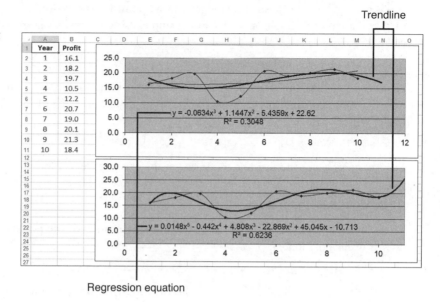

Regression equation

Generally, the higher the order you use, the tighter the curve will fit your existing data, but the more unpredictable will be your forecasted values. In Figure 16.31, the top chart shows a third-order polynomial trendline, and the bottom chart shows a fifth-order polynomial trendline. The fifth-order curve ($R^2 = 0.6236$) gives a better fit than the third-order curve ($R^2 = 0.3048$).

However, the forecasted profit for the 11th year seems more realistic in the third-order case (about 17) than in the fifth-order case (about 26).

In other words, you'll often have to try different polynomial orders to get a fit that you are comfortable with and forecasted values that seem realistic.

Calculating Polynomial Trend and Forecast Values

You've seen that the regression equation for an nth-order polynomial curve takes the following general form:

$$y = m_n x^n + \ldots + m_2 x^2 + m_1 x + b$$

So, as with the other regression equations, if you know the value of the constants, for any independent value x, you can use this formula to compute its corresponding point on the trendline. For example, the top trendline in Figure 16.31 is a third-order polynomial, so we need the values of m_3, m_2, and m_1, as well as b. From the regression equation displayed on the chart, we know that these values are, respectively, `-0.0634`, `1.1447`, `-5.4359`, and `22.62`. Plugging these into the general equation for a third-order polynomial trend gives the following:

```
=-0.0634 * x ^ 3 + 1.1447 * x ^ 2  + -5.4359 * x + 22.62
```

If x is a value between 1 and 10, you get a trend point for the existing data. To get a forecast, you use a value higher than 10. For example, using x equal to `11` gives a forecast profit value of 16.9:

```
=-0.0634 * 11 ^ 3 + 1.1447 * 11 ^ 2 + -5.4359 * 11 + 22.62
```

However, you don't need to put yourself through these intense calculations because the TREND() function can do it for you. The trick here is to raise each of the `known_x's` values to the powers from 1 to n for an nth-order polynomial:

```
{=TREND(known_y's, known_x's ^ {1,2,...,n})}
```

For example, here's the formula to use to get the existing trend values for a third-order polynomial using the year and profit ranges from the worksheet in Figure 16.31:

```
{=TREND(B2:B11, A2:A11 ^ {1,2,3})}
```

To get a forecast value, you raise each of the `new_x's` values to the powers from 1 to n for an nth-order polynomial:

```
{=TREND(known_y's, known_x's ^ {1,2,...,n}, new_x's ^ {1,2,...,n})}
```

For the profits forecast, if A12 contains 11, the following array formula returns the predicted value:

```
{=TREND(B2:B11, A2:A11 ^ {1,2,3}, A12 ^ {1,2,3})}
```

Figure 16.32 shows a worksheet that uses this TREND() technique to compute both the trend values for years 1 through 10 and a forecast value for year 11 for all the second-order through sixth-order polynomials.

Figure 16.32
The profits worksheet, with existing trend and forecast values calculated by the TREND() function.s

Existing trend values

D12   =TREND(B2:B11, A2:A11 ^ {1,2,3}, A12 ^ {1,2,3})

	A	B	C	D	E	F	G	H	I
1	Year	Profit	TREND( ) Order 2	TREND( ) Order 3	TREND( ) Order 4	TREND( ) Order 5	TREND( ) Order 6		
2	1	16.1	16.7	18.3	16.7	15.8	15.8		
3	2	18.2	16.4	15.8	17.7	19.8	20.1		
4	3	19.7	16.2	14.9	16.4	16.2	15.9		
5	4	10.5	16.3	15.1	14.9	13.3	13.1		
6	5	12.2	16.6	16.1	14.6	13.7	13.9		
7	6	20.7	17.1	17.5	16.0	16.9	17.1		
8	7	19.0	17.7	18.9	18.7	20.3	20.1		
9	8	20.1	18.6	19.9	21.4	21.5	21.2		
10	9	21.3	19.7	20.2	22.1	20.0	20.3		
11	10	18.4	20.9	19.3	17.8	18.7	18.6		
12	11		22.4	17.0	4.8	25.9	17.6		
13									
14	Order	m6	m5	m4	m3	m2	m1	b	
15	2					0.098863636	-0.612348485	17.18166667	
16	3				-0.06338384	1.14469697	-5.435858586	22.62	
17	4			-0.035533217	0.718346931	-4.576150932	10.1987568	10.425	
18	5		0.014782051	-0.442039627	4.808047786	-22.86893939	45.04497902	-10.71333333	
19	6	-0.001333333	0.058782051	-1.006282051	8.348047786	-34.07063636	61.46097902	-19.03333333	
20									

Forecast values

Note, too, that Figure 16.32 calculates the m_n values and b for each order of polynomial. This is done using LINEST() by again raising each of the *known_x's* values to the powers from 1 to n, for an nth-order polynomial:

```
{=LINEST(known_y's, known_x's ^ {1,2,...,n})}
```

The formula returns an n + 1×1 array in which the first n cells contain the constants m_n through m_1, and then the n+1st cell contains b. For example, the following formula returns a 3×1 array of the constant values for a third-order polynomial using the year and profit ranges:

```
{=LINEST(B2:B11, A2:A11 ^ {1,2,3})}
```

Using Multiple Regression Analysis

Focusing on a single independent variable is a useful exercise because it can tell you a great deal about the relationship between the independent variable and the dependent variable. However, in the real world of business, the variation that you see in most phenomena is a product of multiple influences. The movement of car sales isn't solely a function of interest rates; it's also affected by internal factors such as price, advertising, warranties, and factory-dealer incentives, as well as external factors such as total consumer disposable income and the employment rate.

The good news is that the linear regression techniques you learned earlier in this chapter are easily adapted to multiple independent variables.

As a simple example, let's consider a sales model in which the units sold—the dependent variable—is a function of two independent variables: advertising costs and list price. The worksheet in Figure 16.33 shows data for 10 products, each with its own advertising costs (column A) and list price (column B), as well as the corresponding unit sales (column C). The upper chart shows the relationship between units sold and list price, whereas the lower chart shows the relationship between units sold and advertising costs. As you can see, the individual trends look about right: Units sold goes down as the list price goes up; units sold goes up as the advertising costs go up.

However, the individual trends don't tell us much about how advertising and price *together* affect sales. Clearly, a low advertising budget combined with a high price will result in lower sales; conversely, a high advertising budget combined with a low price should increase sales. What we really want, of course, is to attach some hard numbers to these seat-of-the-pants speculations. You can get those numbers using that linear regression workhorse, the TREND() function.

To use TREND() when you have multiple independent variables, you expand the *known_x's* argument so that it includes the entire range of independent data. In Figure 16.33, for example, the independent data resides in the range A2:B11, so that's the reference you plug into the TREND() function. Here's the array formula for computing the existing trend values:

```
{=TREND(C2:C11, A2:B11)}
```

Figure 16.33
This worksheet shows raw data and trendlines for units sold versus advertising costs and list price.

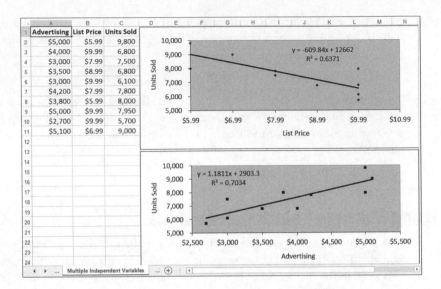

In multiple regression analysis, you're most often interested in what-if scenarios. What if you spend $6,000 in advertising on a $5.99 product? What if you spend $1,000 on a $9.99 product?

To answer these questions, you plug the values into the `new_x's` argument as an array. For example, the following formula returns the predicted number of units that will sell if you spend $6,000 in advertising on a $5.99 product:

```
{=TREND(C2:C11, A2:B11, {6000, 5.99})}
```

Figure 16.34 shows a worksheet that puts the multiple regression form of TREND() to work. The values in D2:D11 are for the existing trend, and values in D12:D13 are forecasts.

Figure 16.34
Trend and forecast values calculated by the multiple regression form of the TREND() function.

Existing trend values

	A	B	C	D	E	F	G	H
				fx	{=TREND(C2:C11, A2:B11, A12:B13)}			
1	**Advertising**	**List Price**	**Units Sold**	**TREND( )**			**LINEST( ) Statistics**	
2	$5,000	$5.99	9,800	9,463		-414.7637931	0.862275987	7636.123596
3	$4,000	$9.99	6,800	6,942		73.25497707	0.135032897	970.6746877
4	$3,000	$7.99	7,500	6,909	R^2	0.946836281	328.8879478	#N/A
5	$3,500	$8.99	6,800	6,925		62.33437113	7	#N/A
6	$3,000	$9.99	6,100	6,079		13485079.02	757170.9754	#N/A
7	$4,200	$7.99	7,800	7,944				
8	$3,800	$5.99	8,000	8,428				
9	$5,000	$9.99	7,950	7,804				
10	$2,700	$9.99	5,700	5,821				
11	$5,100	$6.99	9,000	9,135				
12	$6,000	$5.99		10,325				
13	$1,000	$9.99		4,355				
14								

Forecast values

Notice, too, that the worksheet in Figure 16.34 includes the statistics generated by the LIN-EST() function. The returned array is *three* columns wide because you're dealing with three variables (two independent and one dependent). Of particular interest is the value for R^2 (cell F4)—0.946836. It tells us that the fit between unit sales and the combination of advertising and price is an excellent one, which gives us some confidence about the validity of the predicted values.

From Here

- For detailed coverage of arrays, **see** "Working with Arrays," **p. 87**.

- You can use INDEX() to return results for the LINEST() and LOGEST() arrays directly. **See** "The MATCH() and INDEX() Functions," **p. 202**.

- To learn more about correlation, **see** "Determining the Correlation Between Data," **p. 280**

- For coverage of many of Excel's other statistical functions, **see** Chapter 12, "Working with Statistical Functions," **p. 257**.

16

Solving Complex Problems with Solver

17

In Chapter 15, "Using Excel's Business Modeling Tools," you learned how to use Goal Seek to find solutions to formulas by changing a single variable. Unfortunately, most problems in business aren't so easy. You'll usually face formulas with at least two and sometimes dozens of variables. Often, a problem will have more than one solution, and your challenge will be to find the *optimal* solution (that is, the one that maximizes profit, or minimizes costs, or matches other criteria). For these bigger challenges, you need a more muscular tool. Excel has just the answer: Solver. Solver is a sophisticated optimization program that enables you to find solutions to complex problems that would otherwise require high-level mathematical analysis. This chapter introduces you to Solver (a complete discussion would require a book in itself) and takes you through a few examples.

Some Background on Solver

Problems such as "What product mix will maximize profit?" and "What transportation routes will minimize shipping costs while meeting demand?" traditionally have been solved by using numerical methods such as *linear programming* and *nonlinear programming*. An entire mathematical field known as *operations research* has been developed to handle such problems, which are found in all kinds of disciplines. The drawback to linear and nonlinear programming is that solving even the simplest problem by hand is a complicated, arcane, and time-consuming business. In other words, it's a perfect job to hand off to a computer.

This is where Solver comes in. Solver incorporates many of the algorithms from operations research, but it keeps the sordid details in the background. All you do is fill out a dialog box or two, and Solver does the rest.

The Advantages of Solver

Solver, like Goal Seek, uses an iterative method to perform its magic. This means that Solver tries a solution, analyzes the results, tries another solution, and so on. However, this cyclic iteration isn't just guesswork on Solver's part. The program looks at how the results change with each new iteration and, through some sophisticated mathematical trickery, can tell (usually) in what direction it should head for the solution.

However, the fact that Goal Seek and Solver are both iterative doesn't make them equal. In fact, Solver brings a number of advantages to the table:

■ Solver enables you to specify multiple adjustable cells. You can use up to 200 adjustable cells in all.

■ Solver enables you to set up constraints on the adjustable cells. For example, you can tell Solver to find a solution that not only maximizes profit but also satisfies certain conditions, such as achieving a gross margin between 20% and 30%, or keeping expenses less than $100,000. These conditions are said to be *constraints* on the solution.

■ Solver seeks not only a desired result (the "goal" in Goal Seek), but also the optimal one. This means you can find a solution that is the maximum or minimum possible.

■ For complex problems, Solver can generate multiple solutions. You then can save these different solutions under different scenarios, as described later in this chapter.

When Do You Use Solver?

Solver is a powerful tool that most Excel users don't need. It would be overkill, for example, to use Solver to compute net profit given fixed revenue and cost figures. Many problems, however, require nothing less than the Solver approach. These problems cover many different fields and situations, but they all have the following characteristics in common:

■ They have a single *objective cell* (also called the *target cell*) that contains a formula you want to maximize, minimize, or set to a specific value. This formula could be a calculation, such as total transportation expenses or net profit.

■ The objective cell formula contains references to one or more *variable cells* (also called *unknowns* or *changing cells*). Solver adjusts these cells to find the optimal solution for the objective cell formula. These variable cells might include items such as units sold, shipping costs, or advertising expenses.

■ Optionally, there are one or more *constraint cells* that must satisfy certain criteria. For example, you might require that advertising be less than 10% of total expenses, or that the discount to customers be a number between 40% and 60%.

What types of problems exhibit these kinds of characteristics? A surprisingly broad range, as the following list shows:

- **The transportation problem**—This problem involves minimizing shipping costs from multiple manufacturing plants to multiple warehouses, while meeting demand.
- **The allocation problem**—This problem requires minimizing employee costs while maintaining appropriate staffing requirements.
- **The product mix problem**—This problem requires generating the maximum profit with a mix of products while still meeting customer requirements. You solve this problem when you sell multiple products with different cost structures, profit margins, and demand curves.
- **The blending problem**—This problem involves manipulating the materials used for one or more products to minimize production costs, meet consumer demand, and maintain a minimum level of quality.
- **Linear algebra**—This problem involves solving sets of linear equations.

Loading Solver

Solver is an add-in to Microsoft Excel, so you need to load Solver before you can use it. Follow these steps to load Solver:

1. Select File, Options to open the Excel Options dialog box.
2. Click Add-Ins.
3. Use the Manage list to click Excel Add-Ins and then click Go. Excel displays the Add-Ins dialog box.
4. In the Add-Ins Available list, click to select the Solver Add-In check box.
5. Click OK.
6. If Solver isn't installed, Excel displays a dialog box to let you know. Click Yes. Excel installs the add-in and adds a Solver button to the Data tab's Analyze group.

Using Solver

To help you get a feel for how Solver works, let's look at an example. In Chapter 15, you used Goal Seek to compute the break-even point for a new product. (Recall that the break-even point is the number of units that need to be sold to produce a profit of 0.) I'll extend this analysis by computing the break-even point for two products: a Finley sprocket and a Langstrom wrench. The goal is to compute the number of units to sell for both products so that the total profit is 0.

The most obvious way to proceed is to run Goal Seek twice to determine the break-even points for each product separately. Figure 17.1 shows the results.

Figure 17.1
The break-even points for two products (using separate Goal Seek calculations on the Product Profit cells).

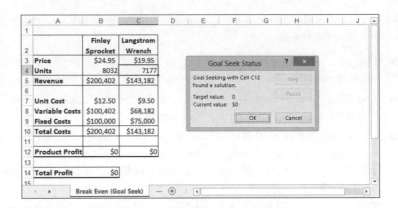

This method works, but the problem is that the two products don't exist in a vacuum. For example, there will be cost savings associated with each product because of joint advertising campaigns, combined shipments to customers (larger shipments usually mean better freight rates), and so on. To allow for this, you need to reduce the cost for each product by a factor related to the number of units sold of the other product. In practice, this would be difficult to estimate, but to keep things simple, I'll use the following assumption: The costs for each product are reduced by $1 for every unit sold of the other product. For instance, if the Langstrom wrench sells 10,000 units, the costs for the Finley sprocket are reduced by $10,000. I'll make this adjustment in the Variable Costs formula. For example, the formula that calculates variable costs for the Finley sprocket (cell B8) becomes the following:

```
=B4 * B7 - C4
```

Similarly, the formula that calculates variable costs for the Langstrom wrench (cell C8) becomes the following:

```
=C4 * C7 - B4
```

By making this change, you move out of Goal Seek's territory. The Variable Costs formulas now have two variables: the units sold for the Finley sprocket and the units sold for the Langstrom wrench. I've changed the problem from one of two single-variable formulas, which Goal Seek can easily handle (individually), to a single formula with two variables, which is the terrain of Solver.

To see how Solver handles such a problem, follow these steps:

1. Select Data, Solver. Excel displays the Solver Parameters dialog box.

2. In the Set Objective range box, enter a reference to the objective cell—that is, the cell with the formula you want to optimize. In the example, you enter **B14**. (Note that Solver converts your relative references to absolute references.)

3. In the To section, select the appropriate option button: Click Max to maximize the objective cell, click Min to minimize it, or click Value Of to solve for a particular value (in which case you also need to enter the value in the text box provided). In the example, you click Value Of and enter **0** in the text box.

4. Use the By Changing Variable Cells box to enter the cells you want Solver to change while it looks for a solution. In the example, you enter **B4,C4**. Figure 17.2 shows the completed Solver Parameters dialog box for this example. (Note that Solver changes all cell addresses to the absolute reference format.)

Figure 17.2
Use the Solver Parameters dialog box to set up the problem for Solver.

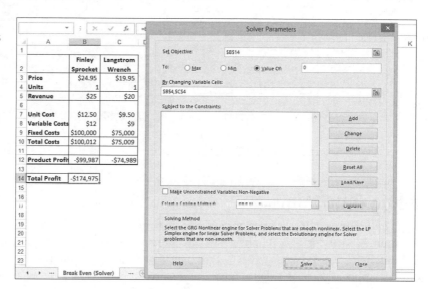

> **NOTE** You can enter a maximum of 200 cells in the By Changing Variable Cells text box.

5. Click Solve. (I discuss constraints and other Solver options in the next few sections.) As Solver works on the problem, you might see one or more Show Trial Solution dialog boxes. If so, click Continue in each one. Finally, Solver displays the Solver Results dialog box, which tells you whether it found a solution. (See the section "Making Sense of Solver's Messages," later in this chapter.)

6. If Solver found a solution you want to use, click the Keep Solver Solution option and then click OK. If you don't want to accept the new numbers, click Restore Original Values and click OK or just click Cancel. (To learn how to save a solution as a scenario, see the section "Saving a Solution as a Scenario," later in this chapter.)

Figure 17.3 shows the results for this example. As you can see, Solver has produced a total profit of 0 by running one product (the Langstrom wrench) at a slight loss and the other at a slight profit. Although this is certainly a solution, it's not really the one you want. Ideally, for a true break-even analysis, both products should end up with a product profit of 0. The problem is that you didn't tell Solver that was the way you wanted the problem solved. In other words, you didn't set up any *constraints*.

Figure 17.3
When Solver finishes its calculations, it displays the Solver Results dialog box and enters the solution (if it found one) into the worksheet cells.

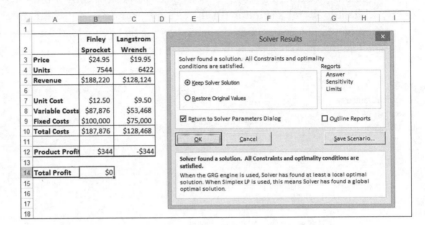

Adding Constraints

The real world puts restrictions and conditions on formulas. A factory might have a maximum capacity of 10,000 units a day, the number of employees in a company has to be a number greater than or equal to zero (negative employees would really reduce staff costs, but nobody has been able to figure out how to do it yet), and your advertising costs might be restricted to 10% of total expenses. These are examples of what Solver calls *constraints*. Adding constraints tells Solver to find a solution so that these conditions are not violated.

To find the best solution for the break-even analysis, you need to tell Solver to optimize both Product Profit formulas to 0. The following steps show you how to do this:

> **NOTE** If Solver's completion message is still onscreen from the last section, select Cancel to return to the worksheet without saving the solution.

1. Select Data, Solver to display the Solver Parameters dialog box. Solver reinstates the options you entered the last time you used Solver.
2. To add a constraint, click Add. Excel displays the Add Constraint dialog box.
3. In the Cell Reference box, enter the cell you want to constrain. In this case, enter cell **B12** (the Product Profit formula for the Finley sprocket).
4. Use the drop-down list in the middle of the dialog box to select the operator you want to use. The list contains several comparison operators for the constraint—less than or

equal to (<=), equal to (=), and greater than or equal to (>=)—as well as two other data type operators—integer (int) and binary (bin). In this case, select the equal to operator (=).

NOTE Use the int (integer) operator when you need a constraint, such as total employees, to be an integer value instead of a real number. Use the bin (binary) operator when you have a constraint that must be either TRUE or FALSE (or 1 or 0).

---

   5. If you chose a comparison operator in step 4, use the Constraint box to enter the value by which you want to restrict the cell. In this case, enter **0**. Figure 17.4 shows the completed dialog box for this example.

Figure 17.4
Use the Add Constraint dialog box to specify the constraints you want to place on the solution.

   6. If you want to enter more constraints, click Add and repeat steps 3 through 5. For the example, you also need to constrain cell C12 (the Product Profit formula for the Langstrom wrench) so that it, too, equals 0.

   7. When you're done, click OK to return to the Solver Parameters dialog box. Excel displays your constraints in the Subject to the Constraints list box.

NOTE You can add a maximum of 100 constraints. Also, if you need to make a change to a constraint before you begin solving, click the constraint in the Subject to the Constraints list box, click Change, and then make your adjustments in the Change Constraint dialog box that appears. If you want to delete a constraint that you no longer need, click it and then click Delete.

---

   8. Click Solve. Solver again tries to find a solution, but this time it uses your constraints as guidelines. Note that you might need to click Continue one or more times while Solver works on the solution.

Figure 17.5 shows the results of the break-even analysis after the constraints have been added. As you can see, Solver was able to find a solution in which both product margins are 0.

Figure 17.5
The solution to the break-even analysis after the constraints have been added.

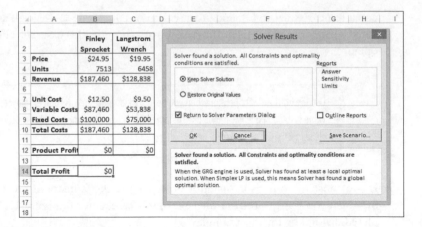

Saving a Solution as a Scenario

If Solver finds a solution, you can save the variable cells as a scenario that you can display at any time. Use the following steps to save a solution as a scenario:

1. Select Data, Solver to display the Solver Parameters dialog box.

2. Enter the appropriate objective cell, variable cells, and constraints, if necessary.

3. Click Solve to begin solving.

4. If Solver finds a solution, click Save Scenario in the Solver Results dialog box. Excel displays the Save Scenario dialog box.

5. Use the Scenario Name text box to enter a name for the scenario.

6. Click OK. Excel returns you to the Solver Results dialog box.

7. Keep or discard the solution, as appropriate.

→ To learn about scenarios, **see** "Working with Scenarios," **p. 362**.

Setting Other Solver Options

Most Solver problems should respond to the basic objective-cell/variable-cell/constraint-cell model you've looked at so far. However, for times when you're having trouble getting a solution for a particular model, Solver has a number of options that might help. Start Solver and, in the Solver Parameters dialog box, first note the check box named Make Unconstrained Variables Non-Negative. Select this check box to force Solver to assume that the cells listed in the By Changing Variable Cells list must have values greater than or equal to 0. This is the same as adding >=0 constraints for each of those cells, so it operates as a kind of implicit constraint on them. This is handy in models that use quite a few variable cells, none of which should have negative values.

Selecting the Method Solver Uses

Solver can use one of several solving methods—called *engines*—to perform its calculations. In the Solver Parameters dialog box, use the Select a Solving Method list to select one of the following engines:

- **Simplex LP**—Select this engine if your worksheet model is linear. In the simplest possible terms, a *linear* model is one in which the variables are not raised to any powers and none of the so-called transcendent functions—such as SIN() and COS()—is used. A linear model is so named because it can be charted as straight lines. If your formulas are linear, be sure to select Simplex LP because this will greatly speed up the solution process.

- **GRG Nonlinear**—Select this engine if your worksheet model is nonlinear and smooth. In general terms, a *smooth* model is one in which a graph of the equation used would show no sharp edges or breaks (called *discontinuities*).

- **Evolutionary**—Select this engine if your worksheet model is nonlinear and non-smooth. In practical terms, this usually means your worksheet model uses functions such as VLOOKUP(), HLOOKUP(), CHOOSE(), and IF() to calculate the values of the variable cells or constraint cells.

> **NOTE** If you're not sure which engine to use, start with Simplex LP. If it turns out that your model is nonlinear, Solver will recognize this and let you know. You can then try the GRG Nonlinear engine; if Solver can't seem to converge on a solution, you should try the Evolutionary engine.

Controlling How Solver Works

Solver has several options that you can set to determine how the tool performs its tasks. To see these options, open the Solver Parameters dialog box and click Options to display the Options dialog box, shown in Figure 17.6.

The following options in the All Methods tab control how Solver works no matter which method you use:

- **Constraint Precision**—This number determines how close a constraint cell must be to the constraint value you entered before Solver declares the constraint satisfied. The higher the precision (that is, the lower the number), the more accurate the solution but the longer it takes Solver to find it.

- **Use Automatic Scaling**—Select this check box if your model has variable cells that are significantly different in magnitude. For example, you might have a variable cell that controls customer discount (a number between 0 and 1) and sales (a number that might be in the millions).

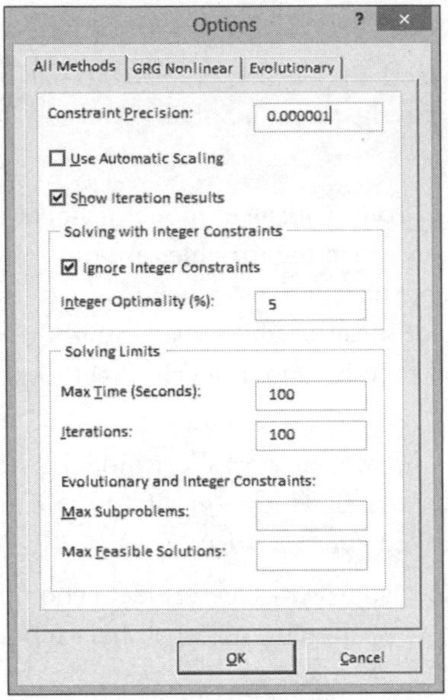

Figure 17.6
The Options dialog box controls how Solver solves a problem.

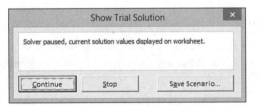

- **Show Iteration Results**—Leave this check box selected to have Solver pause and show you its trial solutions, as demonstrated in Figure 17.7. To resume, click Continue in the Show Trial Solution dialog box. If you find these intermediate results annoying, deselect the Show Iteration Results check box.

Figure 17.7
When the Show Iteration Results check box is selected, Solver displays the Show Trial Solution dialog box so that you can view each intermediate solution.

- **Ignore Integer Constraints**—Integer programming (in which you have integer constraints) can take a long time because of the complexity involved in finding solutions that satisfy exact integer constraints. If you find your models taking an abnormally long time to solve, select this check box. (Alternatively, increase the value in the Integer Optimality box, discussed next, to get an approximate solution.)

- **Integer Optimality**—If you have integer constraints, this box determines what percentage of the integer Solver has to be within before declaring the constraint satisfied. For example, if the integer tolerance is set to 5 (that is, 0.05%), Solver will declare a cell with the value 99.95 to be close enough to 100 to declare it an integer.

- **Max Time**—The amount of time Solver takes is a function of the size and complexity of the model, the number of variable cells and constraint cells, and the other Solver options you've chosen. If you find that Solver runs out of time before finding a solution, increase the number in this text box.

- **Iterations**—This box controls the number of iterations Solver tries before giving up on a problem. Increasing this number gives Solver more of a chance to solve the problem, but it takes correspondingly longer.

- **Max Subproblems**—If you use the Evolutionary engine or if you deselect the Ignore Integer Constraints check box, the value in the Max Subproblems box tells Solver the maximum number of subproblems it can investigate before it asks if you want to continue. A *subproblem* is an intermediate step that Solver uses to get closer to the final solution.

- **Max Feasible Solutions**—If you use the Evolutionary engine or if you deselect the Ignore Integer Constraints check box, the value in the Max Feasible Solutions box tells Solver the maximum number of feasible solutions that it can generate before it asks if you want to continue. A *feasible solution* is any solution (even a nonoptimal one) that satisfies all the constraints.

If you want to use the GRG Nonlinear engine, consider the following options in the GRG Nonlinear tab:

- **Convergence**—This number determines when Solver decides that it has reached (converged on) a solution. If the objective cell value changes by less than the Convergence value for five straight iterations, then Solver decides that a solution has been found, and it stops iterating. Enter a number between 0 and 1, keeping in mind that the smaller the number, the more accurate the solution will be but also the longer Solver will take to find a solution.

- **Derivatives**—Some models require Solver to calculate partial derivatives. The two Derivatives options specify the method Solver uses to do this. Forward differencing is the default method. The Central differencing method takes longer than forward differencing, but you might want to try it when Solver reports that it can't improve a solution. (See the section "Making Sense of Solver's Messages," later in this chapter.)

- **Use Multistart**—Select this check box to run the GRG Nonlinear engine using its Multistart feature. This means that Solver automatically runs the GRG Nonlinear engine from a number of different starting points, which Solver selects at random (although see the Require Bounds on Variables item, later in the list, for more information on this). Solver then gathers the points that produced locally optimal solutions and compares them to come up with a globally optimal solution. Use Multistart if the GRG Nonlinear engine is having trouble finding a solution to your model.

- **Population Size**—If you select the Use Multistart check box, use this text box to set the number of starting points that Solver uses. If Solver has trouble finding a globally optimal solution, try increasing the population size; if Solver takes a long time to find a globally optimal solution, try reducing the population size.

17

- **Random Seed**—If you select the Use Multistart check box, Solver generates random starting points for the GRG Nonlinear engine, and the random number generator is seeded with the current system clock value. This is almost always the best way to go. However, if you want to ensure that the GRG Nonlinear engine always uses the same starting points for consecutive runs, enter an integer (nonzero) value in the Random Seed text box.

- **Require Bounds on Variables**—Leave this check box selected to improve the likelihood that the GRG Nonlinear engine finds a solution when you use the Multistart method. This means that you must add constraints that specify both a lower bound and an upper bound for each cell in the By Changing Variable Cells range box. When Solver generates the random starting points for the GRG Nonlinear engine, it generates values that are within these lower and upper bounds, so it's more likely to find a solution (assuming that you enter realistic bounds for the variable cells). It's possible to use the GRG Nonlinear engine if you deselect the Require Bounds on Variables check box, but it means that Solver must select its random starting points from, essentially, an infinite supply of values, so it's less likely to find a globally optimal solution.

If you want to use the Evolutionary engine, you can configure the engine using the options in the Evolutionary tab. The Convergence, Population Size, Random Seed, and Require Bounds on Variables options are the same as those in the GRG Nonlinear tab, discussed earlier. The Evolutionary tab has the following unique options:

- **Mutation Rate**—The Evolutionary engine operates by randomly trying out certain values, usually within upper and lower bounds of the variable cells (assuming that you leave the Require Bounds on Variables check box selected), and if a trial solution is found to be "fit," that result becomes part of the *solution population*. It then mutates members of this population to see if it can find better solutions. The Mutation Rate value is the probability that a member of the solution population will be mutated. If you're having trouble getting good results from the Evolutionary engine, try increasing the mutation rate.

- **Maximum Time Without Improvement**—This is the maximum number of seconds the Evolutionary engine will take without finding a better solution before it asks if you want to stop the iteration. If you find that the Evolutionary engine runs out of time before finding a solution, increase the number in this text box.

Working with Solver Models

Excel attaches your most recent Solver parameters to the worksheet when you save it. If you want to save different sets of parameters, you can do so by following these steps:

1. Select Data, Solver to display the Solver Parameters dialog box.

2. Enter the parameters you want to save.

3. Click Options to display the Options dialog box.

4. Enter the options you want to save and then click OK to return to the Solver Parameters dialog box.

5. Click Load/Save. Solver displays the Load/Save Model dialog box to prompt you to enter a range in which to store the model.

6. Enter the range in the range box. Note that you don't need to specify the entire area— just the first cell. Keep in mind that Solver displays the data in a column, so pick a cell with enough empty space below it to hold all the data. You'll need one cell for the objective cell reference, one for the variable cells, one for each constraint, and one to hold the array of Solver options.

7. Click Save. Solver gathers the data, enters it into your selected range, and then returns you to the Solver Parameters dialog box.

Figure 17.8 shows an example of a saved model (the range F4:F8). I've changed the worksheet view to show formulas, and I've added some explanatory text so you can see exactly how Solver saves the model. Notice that the formula for the objective cell (F4) includes both the target (B14) and the target value (=0).

17

> **NOTE**
> To toggle formulas on and off in Excel, select Formulas, Show Formulas or press Ctrl+` (backquote).

Figure 17.8
A saved Solver model with formulas turned on so you can see what Solver saves to the sheet.

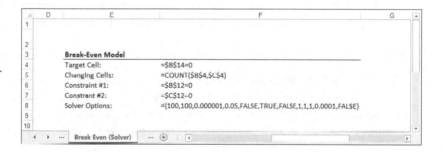

To use your saved settings, follow these steps:

1. Select Data, Solver to display the Solver Parameters dialog box.

2. Click Load/Save. Solver displays the Load/Save Model dialog box.

3. Select the entire range that contains the saved model.

4. Click Load. Excel asks if you want to replace the current model or merge the saved model with the current model.

5. Click Replace to use the saved model cells or click Merge to add the saved model to the current Solver model. Excel returns you to the Solver Parameters dialog box.

Making Sense of Solver's Messages

When Solver finishes its calculations, it displays the Solver Results dialog box and a message that tells you what happened. Some of these messages are straightforward, but others are more than a little cryptic. This section looks at the most common messages and gives their translations.

If Solver finds a solution successfully, you see one of the following messages:

- **Solver found a solution. All constraints and optimality conditions are satisfied—** This is the message you hope to see. It means that the value you wanted for the objective cell has been found, and Solver was able to find the solution while meeting your constraints within the precision and integer tolerance levels you set.

- **Solver has converged to the current solution. All constraints are satisfied—** Solver normally assumes that it has a solution if the value of the objective cell formula remains virtually unchanged during a few iterations. This is called *converging to a solution*. Such is the case with this message, but it doesn't necessarily mean that Solver has found a solution. The iterative process might just be taking a long time, or the initial values in the variable cells might have been set too far from the solution. You should try rerunning Solver with different values. You also can try using a higher precision setting (that is, entering a smaller number in the Constraint Precision text box).

- **Solver cannot improve the current solution. All constraints are satisfied—**This message tells you that Solver has found a solution, but it might not be the optimal one. Try setting the precision to a smaller number or, if you're using the GRG Nonlinear engine, try using the central differencing method for partial derivatives.

If Solver doesn't find a solution, you see one of the following messages telling you why:

- **The Set Cell values do not converge—**This means that the value of the objective cell formula has no finite limit. For example, if you're trying to maximize profit based on product price and unit costs, Solver won't find a solution; the reason is that continually higher prices and lower costs lead to higher profit. You need to add (or change) constraints in your model, such as setting a maximum price or minimum cost level (for example, the amount of fixed costs).

- **Solver could not find a feasible solution—**Solver couldn't find a solution that satisfied all your constraints. Check your constraints to make sure they're realistic and consistent.

- **Stop chosen when the maximum x limit was reached—**This message appears when Solver bumps up against either the maximum time limit or the maximum iteration limit. If it appears that Solver is heading toward a solution, click Keep Solver Solution and try again.

■ **The conditions for Assume Linear Model are not satisfied**—Solver based its iterative process on a linear model, but when the results are put into the worksheet, they
don't conform to the linear model. You need to select the GRG Nonlinear engine and
try again.

Case Study: Solving the Transportation Problem

The best way to learn how to use a complex tool such as Solver is to get your hands dirty
with some examples. Excel thoughtfully comes with several sample worksheets that use
simplified models to demonstrate the various problems Solver can handle. This case study
looks at one of these worksheets in detail.

The *transportation problem* is the classic model for solving linear programming problems.
The basic goal is to minimize the costs of shipping goods from several production plants to
various warehouses scattered around the country. Your constraints are as follows:

■ The amount shipped to each warehouse must meet the warehouse's demand for goods.

■ The amount shipped from each plant must be greater than or equal to 0.

■ The amount shipped from each plant can't exceed the plant's supply of goods.

Figure 17.9 shows the model for solving the transportation problem.

Figure 17.9
A worksheet for solv-
ing the transportation
problem.

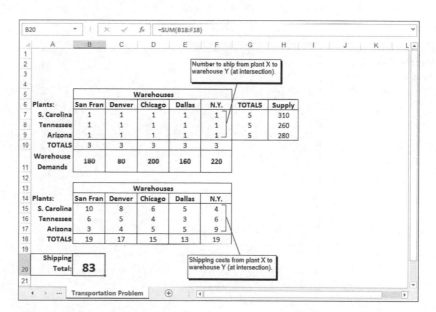

The top table (A6:F10) lists the three plants (A7:A9) and the five warehouses (B6:F6). This table holds the number of units shipped from each plant to each warehouse. In the Solver model, these are the variable cells. The total shipped to each warehouse (B10:F10) must match the warehouse demands (B11:F11) to satisfy constraint number 1. The amount shipped from each plant (B7:F9) must be greater than or equal to 0 to satisfy constraint number 2. The total shipped from each plant (G7:G9) must be less than or equal to the available supply for each plant (H7:H9) to satisfy constraint number 3.

> **NOTE**
> When you need to use a range of values in a constraint, you don't need to set up a separate constraint for each cell. Instead, you can compare entire ranges. For example, the constraint that the total shipped from each plant must be less than or equal to the plant supply can be entered as follows:
>
> ```
> G7:G9 <= H7:H9
> ```

The bottom table (A14:F18) holds the corresponding shipping costs from each plant to each warehouse. The total shipping cost (cell B20) is the objective cell you want to minimize.

Figure 17.10 shows the final Solver Parameters dialog box that you'll use to solve this problem. (Note also that I selected the Simplex LP engine in the Select a Solver Method list.) Figure 17.11 shows the solution that Solver found.

Figure 17.10
The Solver Parameters dialog box filled in for the transportation problem.

Figure 17.11
The optimal solution for the transportation problem.

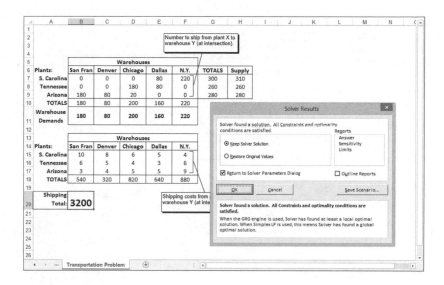

Displaying Solver's Reports

When Solver finds a solution, the Solver dialog box gives you the option of generating three reports: the Answer report, Sensitivity report, and Limits report. Click the reports you want to see in the Reports list box and then click OK. Excel displays each report on its own worksheet.

> **TIP**
> If you've named the cells in your model, Solver uses these names to make its reports easier to read. If you haven't already done so, you should define names for the objective cell, variable cells, and constraint cells before creating a report.

The Answer Report

The Answer report displays information about the model's objective cell, variable cells, and constraints. For the objective cell and variable cells, Solver shows the original and final values. For example, Figure 17.12 shows this portion of the answer report for the transportation problem solution.

For the constraints, the report shows the address and name for each cell, the final value, the formulas, and two values called the *status* and the *slack*. Figure 17.13 shows an example from the transportation problem. The status can be one of three values:

- **Binding**—The final value in the constraint cell equals the constraint value (or the constraint boundary, if the constraint is an inequality).
- **Not Binding**—The constraint cell value satisfied the constraint, but it doesn't equal the constraint boundary.
- **Not Satisfied**—The constraint was not satisfied.

Figure 17.12
The Objective Cell and Variable Cells sections of Solver's Answer report.

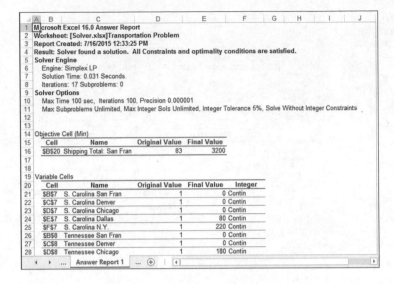

Figure 17.13
The Constraints section of Solver's Answer report.

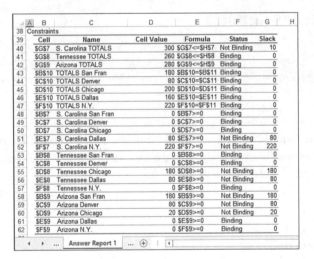

The slack is the difference between the final constraint cell value and the value of the original constraint (or its boundary). In the optimal solution for the transportation problem, for example, the total shipped from the South Carolina plant is 300, but the constraint on this total was 310 (the total supply). Therefore, the slack value is 10 (or close enough to it). If the status is binding, the slack value is always 0.

The Sensitivity Report

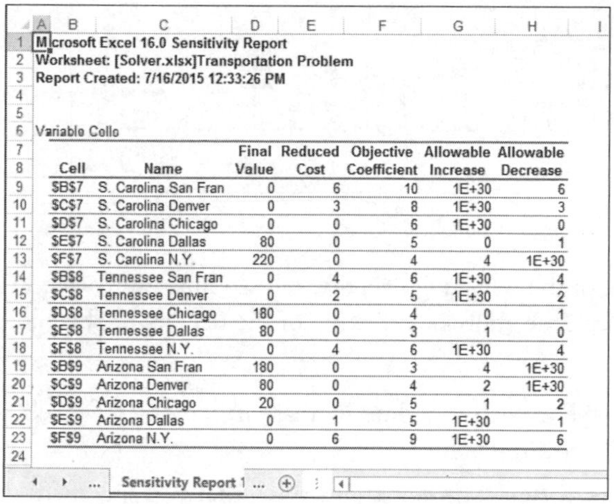

Microsoft Excel 16.0 Sensitivity Report
Worksheet: [Solver.xlsx]Transportation Problem
Report Created: 7/16/2015 12:33:26 PM

Variable Cells

Cell	Name	Final Value	Reduced Cost	Objective Coefficient	Allowable Increase	Allowable Decrease
$B$7	S. Carolina San Fran	0	6	10	1E+30	6
$C$7	S. Carolina Denver	0	3	8	1E+30	3
$D$7	S. Carolina Chicago	0	0	6	1E+30	0
$E$7	S. Carolina Dallas	80	0	5	0	1
$F$7	S. Carolina N.Y.	220	0	4	4	1E+30
$B$8	Tennessee San Fran	0	4	6	1E+30	4
$C$8	Tennessee Denver	0	2	5	1E+30	2
$D$8	Tennessee Chicago	180	0	4	0	1
$E$8	Tennessee Dallas	80	0	3	1	0
$F$8	Tennessee N.Y.	0	4	6	1E+30	4
$B$9	Arizona San Fran	180	0	3	4	1E+30
$C$9	Arizona Denver	80	0	4	2	1E+30
$D$9	Arizona Chicago	20	0	5	1	2
$E$9	Arizona Dallas	0	1	5	1E+30	1
$F$9	Arizona N.Y.	0	6	9	1E+30	6

Sensitivity Report 1

Figure 17.14
The Variable Cells section of Solver's Sensitivity report.

The Sensitivity report attempts to show how sensitive a solution is to changes in the model's formulas. The layout of the Sensitivity report depends on the type of model you're using. For a linear model (that is, a model in which you selected the Simplex LP engine), you see a report similar to the one shown in Figure 17.14.

This report is divided into two sections. The top section, called Variable Cells, shows for each cell the address and name of the cell, its final value, and the following measures:

- **Reduced Cost**—The corresponding increase in the objective cell, given a one-unit increase in the variable cell
- **Objective Coefficient**—The relative relationship between the variable cell and the objective cell
- **Allowable Increase**—The change in the objective coefficient before there would be an increase in the optimal value of the variable cell
- **Allowable Decrease**—The change in the objective coefficient before there would be a decrease in the optimal value of the variable cell

Figure 17.15
The Constraints section of
Solver's Sensitivity report.

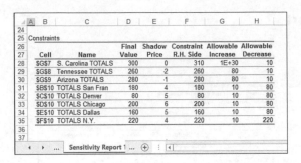

Cell	Name	Final Value	Shadow Price	Constraint R.H. Side	Allowable Increase	Allowable Decrease
$G$7	S. Carolina TOTALS	300	0	310	1E+30	10
$G$8	Tennessee TOTALS	260	-2	260	80	10
$G$9	Arizona TOTALS	280	-1	280	80	10
$B$10	TOTALS San Fran	180	4	180	10	80
$C$10	TOTALS Denver	80	5	80	10	80
$D$10	TOTALS Chicago	200	6	200	10	80
$E$10	TOTALS Dallas	160	5	160	10	80
$F$10	TOTALS N.Y.	220	4	220	10	220

The bottom section of the Sensitivity report, called Constraints (see Figure 17.15), shows for each constraint cell the address and name of the cell, its final value, and the following values:

- **Shadow Price**—The corresponding increase in the objective cell, given a one-unit increase in the constraint value

- **Constraint R.H. Side**—The constraint value that you specified (that is, the right-hand side of the constraint equation)

- **Allowable Increase**—The change in the constraint value before there would be an increase in the optimal value of the variable cell

- **Allowable Decrease**—The change in the constraint value before there would be a decrease in the optimal value of the variable cell.

The Sensitivity report for a nonlinear model shows the variable cells and the constraint cells. For each cell, the report displays the address, name, and final value. The Variable Cells section also shows the Reduced Gradient value, which measures the corresponding increase in the objective cell, given a one-unit increase in the variable cell (similar to the Reduced Cost measure for a linear model). The Constraints section also shows the Lagrange Multiplier value, which measures the corresponding increase in the objective cell, given a one-unit increase in the constraint value (similar to the Shadow Price in the linear report).

The Limits Report

The Limits report, shown in Figure 17.16, displays the objective cell and its value, as well as the variable cells and their addresses, names, values, and the following measures:

- **Lower Limit**—The minimum value that the variable cell can assume while keeping the other variable cells fixed and still satisfying the constraints

- **Upper Limit**—The maximum value that the variable cell can assume while keeping the other variable cells fixed and still satisfying the constraints

- **Objective Result**—The objective cell's value when the variable cell is at the lower limit or upper limit

Figure 17.16
Solver's Limits report.

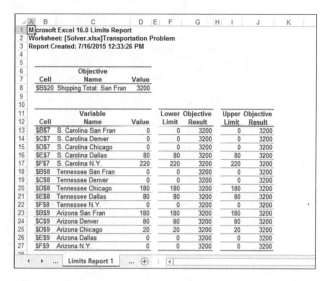

From Here

- To learn about using iteration to solve problems, **see** "Using Iteration and Circular References," **p. 93**.

- For simple models, the Goal Seek tool might be all you need. **See** "Working with Goal Seek," **p. 355**.

- To learn about scenarios, **see** "Working with Scenarios," **p. 362**.

Building Loan Formulas

18

Excel is loaded with financial features that give you powerful tools for building worksheets that manage both business and personal finances. You can use these functions to calculate such things as the monthly payment on a loan, the future value of an annuity, the internal rate of return of an investment, or the yearly depreciation of an asset. The final three chapters of this book cover these and many other uses for Excel's financial formulas.

This chapter covers formulas and functions related to loans and mortgages. You'll learn about the time value of money; how to calculate loan payments, loan periods, the principal and interest components of a payment, and the interest rate; and how to build an amortization schedule.

Understanding the Time Value of Money

The *time value of money* means that a dollar in hand now is worth more than a dollar promised at some future date. This seemingly simple idea underlies not only the concepts and techniques you learn in this chapter but also the investment formulas in Chapter 19, "Building Investment Formulas," and the discount formulas in Chapter 20, "Building Discount Formulas." A dollar now is worth more than a dollar promised in the future for two reasons:

- You can invest a dollar now. If you earn a positive return, the sum of the dollar and interest earned will be worth more than the future dollar.

■ You might never see the future dollar. Due to bankruptcy, cash-flow problems, or any number of other reasons, there's a risk that the company or person promising you the future dollar might not be able to deliver it.

These two factors—interest and risk—are at the heart of most financial formulas and models. More realistically, these factors really mean that you're mostly comparing the benefits of investing a dollar now versus getting a dollar in the future *plus* some *risk premium*—an amount that compensates for the risk you're taking in waiting for the dollar to be delivered.

You compare these by looking at the *present value* (the amount something is worth now) and the *future value* (the amount something is worth in the future). They're related as follows:

A. Future value = Present value + Interest

B. Present value = Future value − discount

Much financial analysis boils down to comparing these formulas. If the present value in A is greater than the present value in B, A is the better investment; conversely, if the future value in B is better than the future value in A, B is the better investment.

Most of the formulas you'll work with over the next three chapters involve these three factors—the present value, the future value, and the interest rate (or the discount rate)—plus two related factors: the *periods*, which are the number of payments or deposits over the term of the loan or investment, and the *payment*, which is the amount of money paid out or invested in each period.

When building your financial formulas, you need to ask yourself the following questions:

■ **Who or what is the subject of the formula?** On a mortgage analysis, for example, are you performing the analysis on behalf of yourself or the bank?

■ **Which way is the money flowing with respect to the subject?** For the present value, future value, and payment, enter money that the subject receives as a positive quantity and enter money that the subject pays out as a negative quantity. For example, if you're the subject of a mortgage analysis, the loan principal (the present value) is a positive number because it's money that you receive from the bank; the payment and the remaining principal (the future value) are negative because they're amounts that you pay to the bank.

■ **What is the time unit?** The underlying unit of both the interest rate and the period must be the same. For example, if you're working with the annual interest rate, you must express the period in years. Similarly, if you're working with monthly periods, you must use a monthly interest rate.

■ **When are the payments made?** Excel differentiates between payments made at the end of each period and those made at the beginning.

Calculating a Loan Payment

When negotiating a loan to purchase equipment or a mortgage for your house, the first concern that comes up is almost always the size of the payment you'll need to make each period. This is just basic cash-flow management because the monthly (or whatever) payment must fit within your budget.

To return the periodic payment for a loan, use the PMT() function:

```
PMT(rate, nper, pv[, fv][, type])
```

rate	The fixed rate of interest over the term of the loan.
nper	The number of payments over the term of the loan.
pv	The loan principal.
fv	The future value of the loan.
type	The type of payment. Use 0 (the default) for end-of-period payments; use 1 for beginning-of-period payments.

For example, the following formula returns the monthly payment of a $10,000 loan with an annual interest rate of 6% (0.5% per month) over five years (60 months):

```
=PMT(0.005, 60, 10000)
```

Loan Payment Analysis

Financial formulas rarely use hard-coded function arguments. Instead, you almost always are better off placing the argument values in separate cells and then referring to those cells in the formula. This enables you to do a rudimentary form of loan analysis by plugging in different argument values and seeing the effects they have on the formula result.

Figure 18.1 shows an example of a worksheet set up to perform such an analysis. The PMT() formula is in cell B7, and the function arguments are stored in B4 (rate), B5 (nper), and B6 (pv).

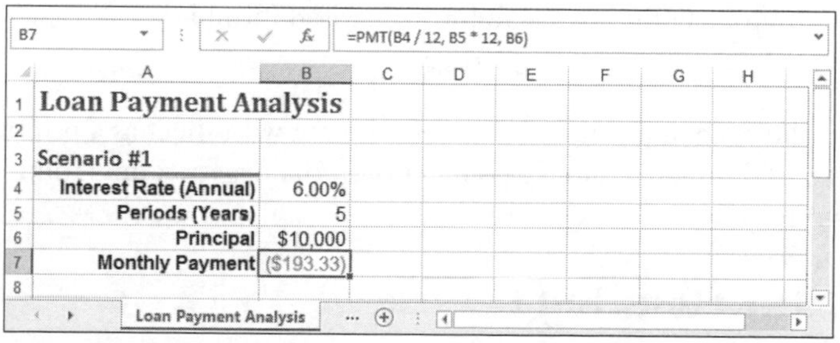

Figure 18.1
To perform a simple loan analysis, place the PMT() function arguments in separate cells and then change those cell values to see the effect on the formula.

You can download this chapter's sample workbook at www.mcfedries.com/books/book.php?title=excel-2016-formulas-and-functions.

Note two things about the formula and result in cell B7:

- The interest rate is an annual value, and the periods are expressed in years, so to get a monthly payment, you must convert these values to their monthly equivalents. This means that the interest rate is divided by 12 and the number of periods is multiplied by 12:

```
=PMT(B4 / 12, B5 * 12, B6)
```

- The PMT() function returns a negative value, which is correct because this worksheet is set up from the point of view of the person receiving the loan, and the payment is money that flows away from that person.

Working with a Balloon Loan

Many loans are set up so that the payments take care of only a portion of the principal, with the remainder due as an end-of-loan balloon payment. This balloon payment is the future value of the loan, so you need to factor it into the PMT() function as the fv argument.

You might think that the pv argument should be the partial principal—that is, the original loan principal minus the balloon amount. This seems right because the loan term is designed to pay off the partial principal. That's not the case, however. In a balloon loan, you also pay interest on the balloon part of the principal. That is, each payment in a balloon loan has three components:

- A paydown of the partial principal
- Interest on the partial principal
- Interest on the balloon portion of the principal

Therefore, the PMT() function's *pv* argument must be the entire principal, with the balloon portion as the (negative) *fv* argument.

For example, suppose that the loan from the previous section has a $3,000 balloon payment. Figure 18.2 shows a new worksheet that adds the balloon payment to the model and then calculates the payment using the following revised formula:

```
=PMT(B2 / 12, B3 * 12, B4, -B5)
```

Note that the balloon payment is entered into the worksheet as a positive value (because it represents, in this model, money going out), so the negation operation is used in the formula (-B5) to convert it to a negative value.

Calculating Interest Costs, Part 1

When you know the payment, you can calculate the total interest costs of a loan by first figuring the total of all the payments and then subtracting the principal. The remainder is the total interest paid over the life of the loan.

Figure 18.2
To allow for an end-of-loan balloon payment, add the *fv* argument to the PMT() function.

B6	▼	:	×	✓	*fx*	=PMT(B2 / 12, B3 * 12, B4, -B5)					

	A	B	C	D	E	F	G	H
1	Loan Payment Analysis							
2	Interest Rate (Annual)	6.00%						
3	Periods (Years)	5						
4	Principal	$10,000						
5	Balloon Payment	$3,000						
6	Monthly Payment	($150.33)						
7								

Balloon Loan

Figure 18.3 shows a worksheet that performs this calculation. In column B, cell B7 contains the total amount paid (the monthly payment multiplied by the number of months), and cell B8 takes the difference. Column C performs the same calculations on the loan with a balloon payment. As you can see, in the balloon payment scenario, the payment total is about $2,600 smaller, but the total interest is about $400 higher.

Figure 18.3
To calculate total interest paid out over the life of a loan, multiply the periodic payment by the number of periods and then subtract the principal paid.

B8	▼	:	×	✓	*fx*	=B4 + B7				

	A	B	C	D	E	F	G
1	Loan Payment Analysis						
2	Interest Rate (Annual)	6.00%	6.00%				
3	Periods (Years)	5	5				
4	Principal	$10,000	$10,000				
5	Balloon Payment	$0	$3,000				
6	Monthly Payment	($193.33)	($150.33)				
7	Total Payments	($11,599.68)	($9,019.78)				
8	Total Interest Costs	($1,599.68)	($2,019.78)				
9							

Interest Costs

Calculating the Principal and Interest

Any loan payment has two components: principal repayment and interest charges. Interest charges are almost always *front loaded*, which means that the interest component is highest at the beginning of the loan and gradually decreases with each payment. This means, conversely, that the principal component increases gradually with each payment.

To calculate the principal and interest components of a loan payment, use the PPMT() and IPMT() functions, respectively:

```
PPMT(rate, per, nper, pv[, fv][, type])
IPMT(rate, per, nper, pv[, fv][, type])
```

rate   The fixed rate of interest over the term of the loan.

per   The number of the payment period (where the first payment is 1 and the last payment is the same as *nper*).

nper   The number of payments over the term of the loan.

pv   The loan principal.

fv The future value of the loan (the default is `0`).

type The type of payment. Use `0` (the default) for end-of-period payments; use `1` for beginning-of-period payments.

Figure 18.4 shows a worksheet that applies these functions to the loan. The table shows the principal (column F) and interest (column G) components of the loan for the first 10 periods and for the final period. Note that with each period, the principal portion increases and the interest portion decreases. However, the total remains the same (as confirmed by the Total column), which is as it should be because the payment remains constant through the life of the loan.

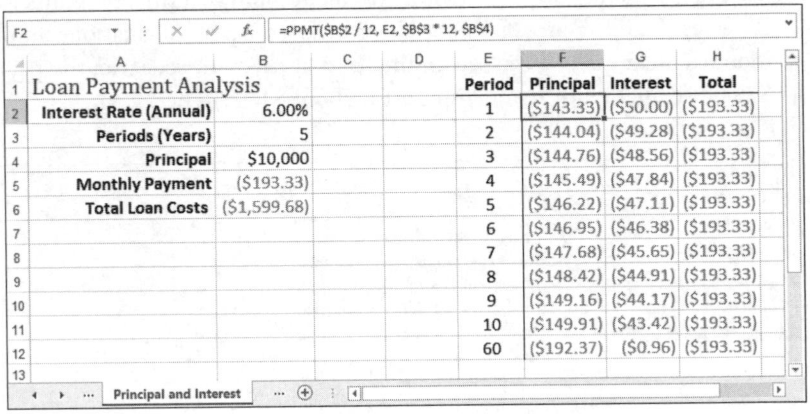
F2 =PPMT($B$2 / 12, E2, $B$3 * 12, $B$4)

	A	B	C	D	E	F	G	H
1	Loan Payment Analysis				Period	Principal	Interest	Total
2	Interest Rate (Annual)	6.00%			1	($143.33)	($50.00)	($193.33)
3	Periods (Years)	5			2	($144.04)	($49.28)	($193.33)
4	Principal	$10,000			3	($144.76)	($48.56)	($193.33)
5	Monthly Payment	($193.33)			4	($145.49)	($47.84)	($193.33)
6	Total Loan Costs	($1,599.68)			5	($146.22)	($47.11)	($193.33)
7					6	($146.95)	($46.38)	($193.33)
8					7	($147.68)	($45.65)	($193.33)
9					8	($148.42)	($44.91)	($193.33)
10					9	($149.16)	($44.17)	($193.33)
11					10	($149.91)	($43.42)	($193.33)
12					60	($192.37)	($0.96)	($193.33)
13								

Figure 18.4
This worksheet uses the `PPMT()` and `IPMT()` functions to break out the principal and interest components of a loan payment.

Calculating Interest Costs, Part 2

Another way to calculate the total interest paid on a loan is to sum the various `IPMT()` values over the life of the loan. You can do this by using an array formula that generates the values of the `IPMT()` function's *per* argument. Here's the general formula:

```
{=IPMT(rate, ROW(INDIRECT("A1:A" & nper)), nper, pv[, fv][, type])}
```

The array of *per* values is generated by the following expression:

```
ROW(INDIRECT("A1:A" & nper))
```

The `INDIRECT()` function converts a string range reference into an actual range reference, and then the `ROW()` function returns the row numbers from that range. By starting the range at A1, this expression generates integer values from `1` to *nper*, which covers the life of the loan.

For example, here's a formula that calculates the total interest cost of the loan model shown in Figure 18.4:

```
{=SUM(IPMT(B2 / 12, ROW(INDIRECT("A1:A" & B3 * 12)), B3 * 12, B4))}
```

Calculating Cumulative Principal and Interest

Knowing how much principal and interest you pay each period is useful, but it's usually handier to know how much principal or interest you've paid in total up to a given period. For example, if you sign up for a mortgage with a five-year term, how much principal will you have paid off by the end of the term? Similarly, a business might need to know the total interest payments a loan requires in the first year so that it can factor the result into its expense budgeting.

You could solve these kinds of problems by building a model that uses the PPMT() and IPMT() functions over the time frame you're dealing with and then summing the results. However, Excel has two functions that offer a more direct route:

```
CUMPRINC(rate, nper, pv, start_period, end_period, type)
CUMIPMT(rate, nper, pv, start_period, end_period, type)
```

rate	The fixed rate of interest over the term of the loan.
nper	The number of payments over the term of the loan.
pv	The loan principal.
start_period	The first period to include in the calculation.
end_period	The last period to include in the calculation.
type	The type of payment. Use 0 for end-of-period payments; use 1 for beginning-of-period payments.

The main difference between CUMPRINC() and CUMIPMT() and PPMT() and IPMT() is the *start_period* and *end_period* arguments. For example, to find the cumulative principal or interest in the first year of a loan, you set *start_period* to 1 and *end_period* to 12; for the second year, you set *start_period* to 13 and *end_period* to 24. Here are a couple of formulas that calculate these values for any year, assuming that the year value (1, 2, and so on) is in cell D2:

```
start_period: (D2 - 1) * 12 + 1
end_period: D2 * 12
```

Figure 18.5 shows a worksheet that returns the cumulative principal and interest paid in each year of a loan, as well as the total principal and interest for all five years.

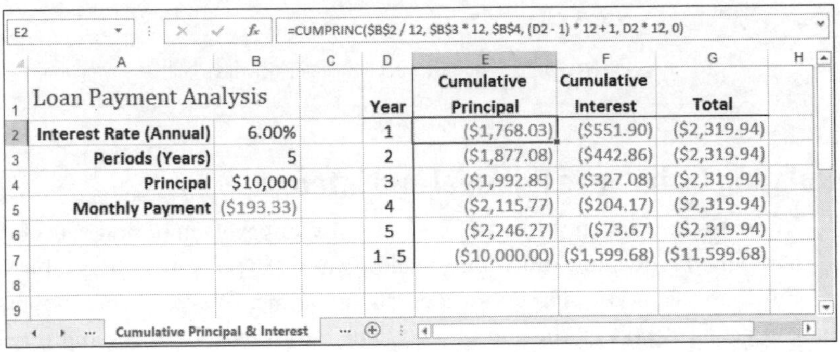

Figure 18.5
This worksheet uses the
CUMPRINC() and
CUMIPMT() functions
to return the cumulative
principal and interest for
each year of a loan.

	A	B	C	D	E	F	G	H
					Cumulative	Cumulative		
1	Loan Payment Analysis			Year	Principal	Interest	Total	
2	Interest Rate (Annual)	6.00%		1	($1,768.03)	($551.90)	($2,319.94)	
3	Periods (Years)	5		2	($1,877.08)	($442.86)	($2,319.94)	
4	Principal	$10,000		3	($1,992.85)	($327.08)	($2,319.94)	
5	Monthly Payment	($193.33)		4	($2,115.77)	($204.17)	($2,319.94)	
6				5	($2,246.27)	($73.67)	($2,319.94)	
7				1 - 5	($10,000.00)	($1,599.68)	($11,599.68)	
8								
9								

Formula bar: `=CUMPRINC($B$2 / 12, $B$3 * 12, $B$4, (D2 - 1) * 12 + 1, D2 * 12, 0)` (cell E2)

Sheet tab: Cumulative Principal & Interest

> **NOTE**
>
> Note that the CUMIPMT() function gives you an easier way to calculate the total interest costs for a loan. Just set *start_period* to 1 and *end_period* to the number of periods (the value of *nper*).

> **CAUTION**
>
> Although the CUMPRINC() function works as advertised if the loan includes a balloon payment, the CUMIPMT() function does not.

Building a Loan Amortization Schedule

A loan *amortization schedule* is a table that shows a sequence of calculations over the life of a loan. For each period, the schedule shows figures such as the payment, the principal and interest components of the payment, the cumulative principal and interest, and the remaining principal. The next few sections take you through various amortization schedules designed for different scenarios.

Building a Fixed-Rate Amortization Schedule

The simplest amortization schedule is just a straightforward application of three of the payment functions you've seen so far: PMT(), PPMT(), and IPMT(). Figure 18.6 shows the result, which has the following features:

■ The values for the four main arguments of the payment functions are stored in the range B2:B5.

■ The amortization schedule is shown in A9:G18. Column A contains the period, and subsequent columns calculate the payment (B), principal component (C), interest component (D), cumulative principal (E), and cumulative interest (F). The Remaining Principal column (G) shows the original principal amount (B4) minus the cumulative principal for each period.

Figure 18.6
This worksheet shows a basic amortization schedule for a fixed-rate loan.

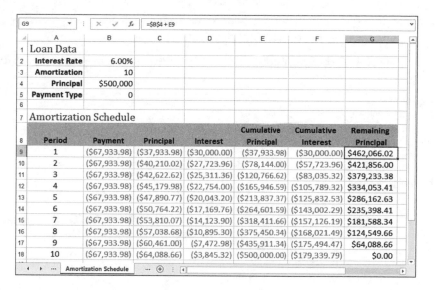

- The cumulative principal and interest values are calculated by adding the running totals of the principal and interest components. You need to do this because the CUMPRINC() and CUMIPMT() functions don't work with balloon payments. If you never use balloon payments, you can convert the worksheet to use these functions.
- This schedule uses a yearly time frame, so no adjustments are applied to the `rate` and `nper` arguments.

→ The amortization schedule in Figure 18.6 assumes that the interest rate remains fixed throughout the life of the loan. To learn how to build an amortization schedule for a variable-rate loan, **see** "Building a Variable-Rate Mortgage Amortization Schedule," **p. 447**.

Building a Dynamic Amortization Schedule

The problem with the amortization schedule in Figure 18.6 is that it's static. It works well if you change the interest rate or the principal, but it doesn't handle other types of changes very well:

- If you want to use a different time basis—for example, monthly instead of annual—you need to edit the initial formulas for payment, principal, interest, cumulative principal, and cumulative interest, and then refill the schedule.
- If you want to use a different number of periods, you need to either extend the schedule (for a longer term) or shorten the schedule and delete the extraneous periods (for a shorter term).

Both operations are tedious and time-consuming enough that they greatly reduce the value of the amortization schedule. To make the schedule truly useful, you need to reconfigure it so that the schedule formulas and the schedule itself adjust automatically to any change in the time basis or the length of the term.

Figure 18.7 shows a worksheet that implements such a dynamic amortization schedule.

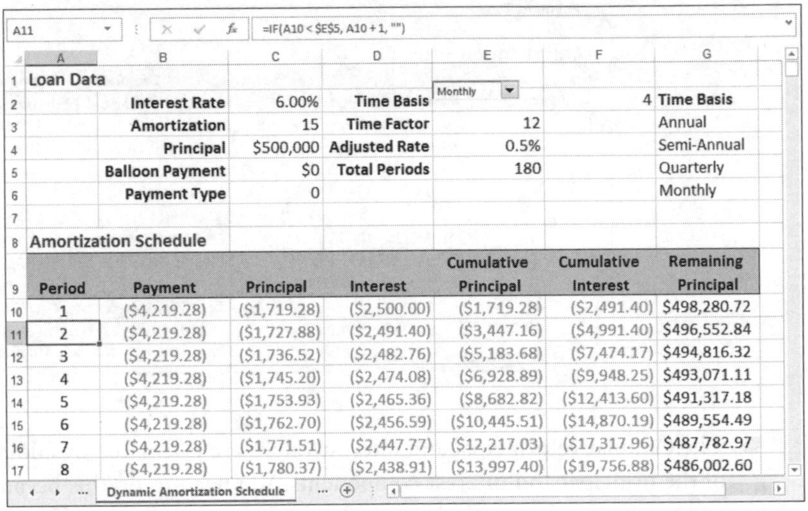
A11 =IF(A10 < $E$5, A10 + 1, "")

	A	B	C	D	E	F	G
1	Loan Data						
2		Interest Rate	6.00%	Time Basis	Monthly	4	Time Basis
3		Amortization	15	Time Factor	12		Annual
4		Principal	$500,000	Adjusted Rate	0.5%		Semi-Annual
5		Balloon Payment	$0	Total Periods	180		Quarterly
6		Payment Type	0				Monthly
7							
8	Amortization Schedule						
9	Period	Payment	Principal	Interest	Cumulative Principal	Cumulative Interest	Remaining Principal
10	1	($4,219.28)	($1,719.28)	($2,500.00)	($1,719.28)	($2,491.40)	$498,280.72
11	2	($4,219.28)	($1,727.88)	($2,491.40)	($3,447.16)	($4,991.40)	$496,552.84
12	3	($4,219.28)	($1,736.52)	($2,482.76)	($5,183.68)	($7,474.17)	$494,816.32
13	4	($4,219.28)	($1,745.20)	($2,474.08)	($6,928.89)	($9,948.25)	$493,071.11
14	5	($4,219.28)	($1,753.93)	($2,465.36)	($8,682.82)	($12,413.60)	$491,317.18
15	6	($4,219.28)	($1,762.70)	($2,456.59)	($10,445.51)	($14,870.19)	$489,554.49
16	7	($4,219.28)	($1,771.51)	($2,447.77)	($12,217.03)	($17,317.96)	$487,782.97
17	8	($4,219.28)	($1,780.37)	($2,438.91)	($13,997.40)	($19,756.88)	$486,002.60

Dynamic Amortization Schedule

Figure 18.7
This worksheet uses a dynamic amortization schedule that adjusts automatically to changing the time basis or the length of the term.

18

Here's a summary of the changes you make to create this schedule's dynamic behavior:

- To change the time basis, select a value—Annual, Semiannual, Quarterly, or Monthly—in the Time Basis drop-down list. These values come from the text literals in the range G3:G6. The number of the selected list item is stored in cell F2.

➔ To learn how to add a list box to a worksheet, **see** "Using Dialog Box Controls on a Worksheet," **p. 103**.

- The time basis determines the *time factor*, the amount by which you have to adjust the rate and the term. For example, if the time basis is Monthly, the time factor is 12. This means that you divide the annual interest rate (C2) by 12, and you multiply the term (C3) by 12. These new values are stored in the Adjusted Rate (E4) and Total Periods (E5) cells. The Time Factor cell (E3) uses the following formula:

```
=CHOOSE(F2, 1, 2, 4, 12)
```

- Given the adjusted rate (E4) and the total periods (E5), the schedule formulas can reference these cells directly and always return the correct value for any selected time basis. For example, here's the expression that calculates the payment:

```
PMT(E4, E5, C4, C5, C6)
```

- The schedule adjusts its size automatically, depending on the Total Periods value (E5). If Total Periods is 15, the schedule contains 15 rows (not including the headers); if Total Periods is 180, the schedule contains 180 rows.

■ Dynamically adjusting the size of the schedule is a function of the Total Periods value (E5). The first period (A10) is always 1; each subsequent period checks the previous value to see if it's less than Total Periods. Here's the formula in cell A11:

```
=IF(A10 < $E$5, A10 + 1, "")
```

If the period value of the cell above the current cell is less than Total Periods, the current cell is still within the schedule, so calculate the current period (the value from the cell above plus 1) and display the result; otherwise, you've gone past the end of the schedule, so display a blank.

■ The various payment columns check the period value. If it's not blank, calculate and display the result; otherwise, display a blank. Here's the formula for the Payment value in B11:

```
=IF(A11 <> "", PMT($E$4, $E$5, $C$4, $C$5, $C$6), "")
```

These changes result in a totally dynamic schedule that adjusts automatically as you change the time basis or the term.

> **NOTE** The formulas in the amortization schedule have been filled down to row 500, which should be enough room for just about any schedule (up to about 40 years, using the monthly basis). If you require a longer schedule, you'll have to fill in the schedule formulas past the last row that will appear in your schedule.

18

Calculating the Term of a Loan

In some loan scenarios, you need to borrow a certain amount at the current interest rates, but you can spend only so much on each payment. If the other loan factors are fixed, the only way to adjust the payment is to adjust the term of the loan: A longer term means smaller payments; a shorter term means larger payments.

You could figure out the term by adjusting the *nper* argument of the PMT() function until you get the payment you want. However, Excel offers a more direct solution in the form of the NPER() function, which returns the number of periods of a loan:

```
NPER(rate, pmt, pv[, fv][, type])
```

rate	The fixed rate of interest over the term of the loan.
pmt	The periodic payment.
pv	The loan principal.
fv	The future value of the loan. (The default is 0.)
type	The type of payment. Use 0 (the default) for end-of-period payments; use 1 for beginning-of-period payments.

For example, suppose that you want to borrow $10,000 at 6% interest with no balloon payment, and the most you can spend is $750 per month. What term should you get?

Figure 18.8 shows a worksheet that uses `NPER()` to calculate the answer: 13.8 months. Here are some things to note about this model:

- The interest rate is an annual value, so the `NPER()` function's *`rate`* argument divides the rate by 12.
- The payment is already a monthly number, so no adjustment is necessary for the *`pmt`* attribute.
- The payment is negative because it's money that you pay to the lender.

Figure 18.8
This worksheet uses `NPER()` to determine the number of months that a $10,000 loan should be taken out at 6% interest to ensure a monthly payment of $750.

B7 =NPER(B2 / 12, B3, B4, B5, B6)

	A	B	C	D	E	F	G
1	Loan Term Analysis						
2	Interest Rate (Annual)	6.00%					
3	Payment (Monthly)	($750)					
4	Principal	$10,000					
5	Balloon Payment	$0					
6	Type	0					
7	Term (Months)	13.8					
9	Ending the Loan After 13 Months				Ending the Loan After 14 Months		
10	Period	Principal	Cumulative Principal		Period	Principal	Cumulative Principal
11	1	($700.00)	($700.00)		1	($700.00)	($700.00)
12	2	($703.50)	($1,403.50)		2	($703.50)	($1,403.50)
13	3	($707.02)	($2,110.52)		3	($707.02)	($2,110.52)
14	4	($710.55)	($2,821.07)		4	($710.55)	($2,821.07)
15	5	($714.11)	($3,535.18)		5	($714.11)	($3,535.18)
16	6	($717.68)	($4,252.85)		6	($717.68)	($4,252.85)
17	7	($721.26)	($4,974.12)		7	($721.26)	($4,974.12)
18	8	($724.87)	($5,698.99)		8	($724.87)	($5,698.99)
19	9	($728.49)	($6,427.48)		9	($728.49)	($6,427.48)
20	10	($732.14)	($7,159.62)		10	($732.14)	($7,159.62)
21	11	($735.80)	($7,895.42)		11	($735.80)	($7,895.42)
22	12	($739.48)	($8,634.89)		12	($739.48)	($8,634.89)
23	13	($743.17)	($9,378.07)		13	($743.17)	($9,378.07)
24	Remaining Principal After 13 Months		($621.93)		14	($746.89)	($10,124.96)
25	Future Value After 13 Months		($621.93)		Overpayment Principal After 14 Months		$124.96
26						Future Value After 14 Months	$124.96

Loan Term Analysis

Of course, in the real world, although it's not unusual to have a noninteger term, the last payment must occur at the beginning or end of the last loan period. In the example, the bank uses the term 13.8 months to calculate the payment, principal, and interest, but it rightly insists that the last payment be made at either the 13th period or the 14th period. The tables after the `NPER()` formula in Figure 18.8 investigate both scenarios.

If you elect to end the loan after the 13th period, you'll still have a bit of principal left over. To see why, the amortization table shows the period (column A) as well as the principal paid each period (column B), as returned by the `PPMT()` function. The Cumulative Principal column (column C) shows a running total of the principal. As you can see, after 13 months, the total principal paid is only $9,378.07, which leaves $621.93 remaining (cell C24). Therefore, the 13th payment will be $1,371.93 (the usual $750 payment, plus the remaining $621.93 principal).

> **NOTE** The cumulative principal values are calculated using the SUM() function. You can't use the CUMPRINC() function in this case because CUMPRINC() truncates the *nper* argument to an integer value.

If you elect to end the loan after the 14th period instead, you'll end up overpaying the principal. To see why, the second amortization table shows the Period (column E), Principal (column F), and Cumulative Principal (column G) columns. After 14 months, the total principal paid is $10,124.96, which is $124.96 more than the original $10,000 principal. Therefore, the 14th payment will be $625.04 (the usual $750 payment minus the $124.96 principal overpayment).

> **NOTE** Another way to calculate the principal that is left over or overpaid is to use the FV() function, which returns the future value of a series of payments. For the 13-month scenario, you run FV() with the *nper* argument set to 13 (see cell C25 in Figure 18.8); for the 14-month scenario, you run FV() with the *nper* argument set to 14 (see cell G26). You'll learn about FV() in detail in Chapter 19.

Calculating the Interest Rate Required for a Loan

A slightly less common loan scenario arises when you know the loan term, payment, and principal, and you need to know what interest rate will satisfy these parameters. This is useful in a number of circumstances:

- You might want to wait until interest rates fall to the value you want.
- You might regard the calculated interest rate as a maximum rate that you can pay, knowing that anything less will enable you to reduce either the payment or the term.
- You could use the calculated interest rate as a negotiating tool with your lender by asking for that rate and walking away from the deal if you don't get it.

To determine the interest rate given the other loan factors, use the RATE() function:

```
RATE(nper, pmt, pv[, fv][, type][, guess])
```

nper	The number of payments over the term of the loan.
pmt	The periodic payment.
pv	The loan principal.
fv	The future value of the loan. (The default is 0.)
type	The type of payment. Use 0 (the default) for end-of-period payments; use 1 for beginning-of-period payments.
guess	A percentage value that Excel uses as a starting point for calculating the interest rate. (The default is 10%.)

18

→ The RATE() function's *guess* argument indicates that this function uses iteration to determine the answer. To learn more about iteration, **see** "Using Iteration and Circular References," **p. 93**.

For example, suppose you want to borrow $10,000 over five years with no balloon payment and a monthly payout of $200. What rate will satisfy these criteria? The worksheet in Figure 18.9 uses RATE() to derive the result: 7.4%. Here are some notes about this model:

- The term is in years, so the RATE() function's *nper* argument multiplies the term by 12.
- The payment is already a monthly number, so no adjustment is necessary for the *pmt* attribute.
- The payment is negative because it's money that you pay to the lender.
- The result of the RATE() function is multiplied by 12 to get the annual interest rate.

Figure 18.9
This worksheet uses RATE() to determine the interest rate required to pay a $10,000 loan over five years at $200 per month.

	A	B	C	D	E	F	G	H	I
	B8	▾	:	× ✓	*fx*	=RATE(B2 * 12, B3, B4, B5, B6, B7) * 12			
1	Loan Rate Analysis								
2	Term (Years)	5							
3	Payment (Monthly)	($200)							
4	Principal	$10,000							
5	Balloon Payment	$0							
6	Type	0							
7	Guess	5%							
8	Interest Rate (Annual)	7.4%							
9									
	◀ ▶ ⋯ Loan Rate Analysis ⋯ ⊕ : ◀								▶

Calculating How Much You Can Borrow

If you know the current interest rate your bank is offering for loans, when you want to have the loan paid off, and how much you can afford each month for the payments, you might then wonder what is the maximum amount you can borrow under those terms. To figure this out, you need to solve for the principal—that is, present value. You do this in Excel by using the PV() function:

```
PV(rate, nper, pmt[, fv][, type])
```

rate   The fixed rate of interest over the term of the loan.

nper   The number of payments over the term of the loan.

pmt   The periodic payment.

fv   The future value of the loan. (The default is 0.)

type   The type of payment. Use 0 (the default) for end-of-period payments; use 1 for beginning-of-period payments.

For example, suppose the current loan rate is 6%, you want the loan paid off in five years, and you can afford payments of $500 per month. Figure 18.10 shows a worksheet that calculates the maximum amount you can borrow—$25,862.78—using the following formula:

```
=PV(B2 / 12, B3 * 12, B4, B5, B6)
```

Figure 18.10
This worksheet uses
PV() to calculate the
maximum principal you
can borrow, given a fixed
interest rate, term, and
monthly payment.

	A	B	C	D	E	F	G	H
1	Loan Principal Analysis							
2	Interest Rate (Annual)	6.00%						
3	Term (Years)	5						
4	Payment (Monthly)	($500)						
5	Balloon Payment	$0						
6	Type	0						
7	Maximum Principal	$25,862.78						
8								

B7   =PV(B2 / 12, B3 * 12, B4, B5, B6)

Loan Principal Analysis

Case Study: Working with Mortgages

For both businesses and people, a mortgage is almost always the largest financial transaction. Whether it's millions of dollars for a new building or hundreds of thousands of dollars for a house, a mortgage is serious business. It pays to know exactly what you're getting into, both in terms of long-term cash flow and in terms of making good decisions up front about the type of mortgage so that you minimize your interest costs. This case study takes a look at mortgages from both points of view.

Building a Variable-Rate Mortgage Amortization Schedule

For simplicity's sake, it's possible to build a mortgage amortization schedule like the ones shown earlier in this chapter. However, these are not always realistic because a mortgage rarely uses the same interest rate over the full amortization period. Instead, you usually have a fixed rate over a specific *term* (usually one to five years), and you then renegotiate the mortgage for a new term. This renegotiation involves changing three things:

■ The interest rate over the coming term, which will reflect current market rates.

■ The amortization period, which will now be shorter by the length of the previous term. For example, a 25-year amortization will drop to a 20-year amortization after a 5-year term.

■ The present value of the mortgage, which will be the remaining principal at the end of the term.

Figure 18.11 shows an amortization schedule that takes these mortgage realities into account.

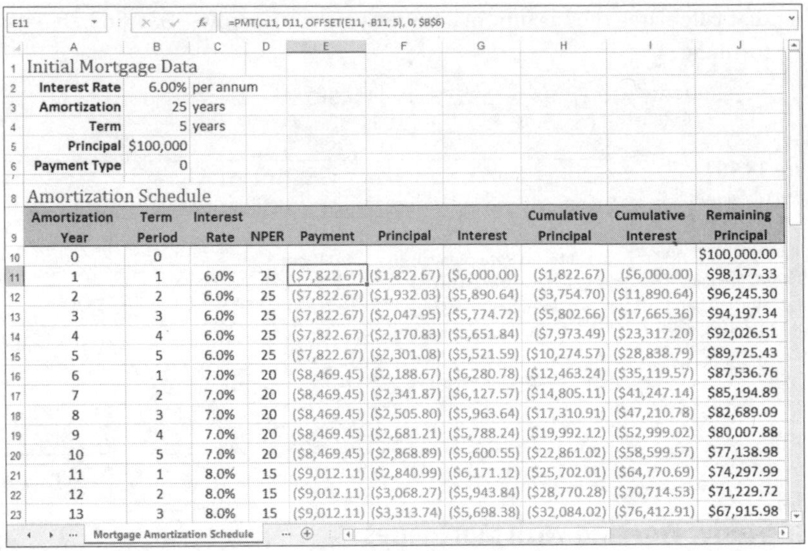

Initial Mortgage Data

Interest Rate	6.00%	per annum
Amortization	25	years
Term	5	years
Principal	$100,000	
Payment Type	0	

Amortization Schedule

Amortization Year	Term Period	Interest Rate	NPER	Payment	Principal	Interest	Cumulative Principal	Cumulative Interest	Remaining Principal
0	0								$100,000.00
1	1	6.0%	25	($7,822.67)	($1,822.67)	($6,000.00)	($1,822.67)	($6,000.00)	$98,177.33
2	2	6.0%	25	($7,822.67)	($1,932.03)	($5,890.64)	($3,754.70)	($11,890.64)	$96,245.30
3	3	6.0%	25	($7,822.67)	($2,047.95)	($5,774.72)	($5,802.66)	($17,665.36)	$94,197.34
4	4	6.0%	25	($7,822.67)	($2,170.83)	($5,651.84)	($7,973.49)	($23,317.20)	$92,026.51
5	5	6.0%	25	($7,822.67)	($2,301.08)	($5,521.59)	($10,274.57)	($28,838.79)	$89,725.43
6	1	7.0%	20	($8,469.45)	($2,188.67)	($6,280.78)	($12,463.24)	($35,119.57)	$87,536.76
7	2	7.0%	20	($8,469.45)	($2,341.87)	($6,127.57)	($14,805.11)	($41,247.14)	$85,194.89
8	3	7.0%	20	($8,469.45)	($2,505.80)	($5,963.64)	($17,310.91)	($47,210.78)	$82,689.09
9	4	7.0%	20	($8,469.45)	($2,681.21)	($5,788.24)	($19,992.12)	($52,999.02)	$80,007.88
10	5	7.0%	20	($8,469.45)	($2,868.89)	($5,600.55)	($22,861.02)	($58,599.57)	$77,138.98
11	1	8.0%	15	($9,012.11)	($2,840.99)	($6,171.12)	($25,702.01)	($64,770.69)	$74,297.99
12	2	8.0%	15	($9,012.11)	($3,068.27)	($5,943.84)	($28,770.28)	($70,714.53)	$71,229.72
13	3	8.0%	15	($9,012.11)	($3,313.74)	($5,698.38)	($32,084.02)	($76,412.91)	$67,915.98

Figure 18.11
A mortgage amortization schedule that reflects the changing interest rates, amortization periods, and present value at each new term.

18

Here's a summary of what's happening with each column in the amortization:

- **Amortization Year**—This column gives the year of the overall amortization. This is mainly used to help calculate the Term Period values. Note that the values in this column are generated automatically based on the value in the Amortization (Years) cell (B3).
- **Term Period**—This column gives the year of the current term. This is a calculated value (it uses the `MOD()` function) based on the value in the Amortization Year column and the value in the Term (Years) cell (B4).
- **Interest Rate**—This is the interest rate applied to each term. You enter these rates by hand.
- **NPER**—This is the amortization period applied to each term. It's used as the *`nper`* argument for the `PMT()`, `PPMT()`, and `IPMT()` functions. You enter these values by hand.
- **Payment**—This is the monthly payment for the current term. The `PMT()` function uses the Interest Rate column value for the *`rate`* argument and the NPER column value for the *`nper`* argument. For the *`pv`* argument, the function grabs the remaining balance at the end of the previous term by using the `OFFSET()` function in the following general form:

  ```
  OFFSET(current_cell, -Term_Period, 5)
  ```

  In this formula, *`current_cell`* is a reference to the cell containing the formula, and *`Term_Period`* is a reference to the corresponding cell in the Term Period column. For example, here's the formula in E11:

  ```
  OFFSET(E11, -B11, 5)
  ```

  Because the value in B11 is `1`, the function goes up one row and right five columns, which returns the value in J10 (in this case, the original principal).

- **Principal and Interest**—These columns calculate the principal and interest components of the payment, and they use the same techniques as the Payment column.

- **Cumulative Principal and Cumulative Interest**—These columns calculate the total principal and interest paid through the end of each year. Because the interest rate isn't constant over the life of the loan, you can't use `CUMPRINC()` and `CUMIPMT()`. Instead, these columns use running `SUM()` functions.

- **Remaining Principal**—This column calculates the principal left on the loan by subtracting the value in the Principal column for each year. At the end of each term, the Remaining Principal value is used as the *pv* argument in the `PMT()`, `PPMT()`, and `IPMT()` functions over the next term. In Figure 18.11, for example, at the end of the first five-year term, the remaining principal is $89,725.43, so that's the present value used throughout the second five-year term.

Allowing for Mortgage Principal Paydowns

Many mortgages today allow you to include in each payment an extra amount that goes directly to paying down the mortgage principal. Before you decide to take on the financial burden of these extra paydowns, you probably want two questions answered:

- How much more quickly will I pay off the mortgage?
- How much money will I save over the amortization period?

Both questions are easily answered using Excel's financial functions. Consider the mortgage-analysis model I've set up in Figure 18.12. The Initial Mortgage Data area shows the basic numbers needed for the calculations: the annual interest rate (cell B2), the amortization period (B3), the principal (B4), and the paydown that is to be added to each payment (B5; notice that this is a negative number because it represents a monetary outflow).

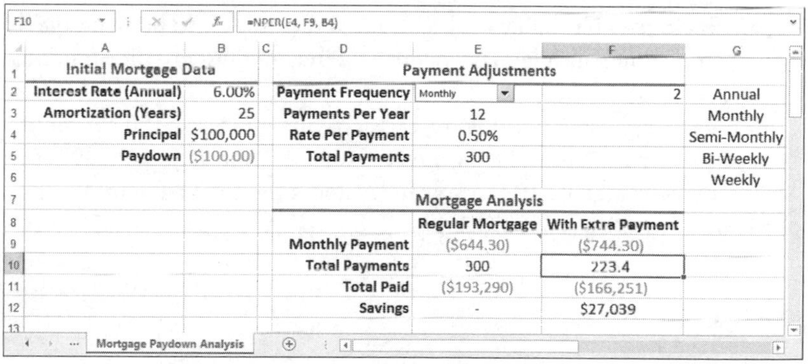

Figure 18.12
A mortgage-analysis worksheet that calculates the effect of making extra monthly paydowns toward the principal.

The Payment Adjustments area contains four values:

- **Payment Frequency**—Use this drop-down list to specify how often you make your mortgage payments. The available values—Annual, Monthly, Semi-Monthly,

Bi-Weekly, and Weekly—come from the range G2:G6; the number of the selected list item is stored in cell F2.

■ **Payments Per Year (E3)**—This is the number of payments per year, as given by the following formula:

```
=CHOOSE(F2, 1, 12, 24, 26, 52)
```

■ **Rate Per Payment**—This is the annual rate divided by the number of payments per year.

■ **Total Payments**—This is the amortization value multiplied by the number of payments per year.

The Mortgage Analysis area shows the results of various calculations:

■ **Frequency Payment (*Frequency* is the selected item in the drop-down list.)**—The Regular Mortgage payment (E9) is calculated using the PMT() function, where the *rate* argument is the Rate Per Payment value (E4) and the *nper* argument is the Total Payments value (E5):

```
=PMT(E4, E5, B4, 0, 0)
```

The With Extra Payment value (F9) is the sum of the Paydown (B5) and the Regular Mortgage payment (E9).

■ **Total Payments**—For the Regular Mortgage (E10), this is the same as the Total Payments value (E5). It's copied here to make it easy for you to compare this value with the With Extra Payment value (F10), which calculates the revised term with the extra paydown included. It does this with the NPER() function, where the *rate* argument is the Rate Per Payment value (E4) and the *pmt* argument is the payment in the With Extra Payment column (F9).

■ **Total Paid**—These values multiply the Payment value by the Total Payments value for each column.

■ **Savings**—This value (cell F12) takes the difference between the Total Paid values to show how much money you save by including the paydown in each payment.

In the example shown in Figure 18.12, paying an extra $100 per month toward the mortgage principal reduces the term on a $100,000 mortgage from 300 months (25 years) to 223.4 months (about 18.5 years) and reduces the total amount paid from $193,290 to $166,251, a savings of $27,039.

From Here

- To learn how to add a list box to a worksheet, **see** "Using Dialog Box Controls on a Worksheet," **p. 103**.

- The RATE() function uses iteration to calculate its value. To learn more about iteration, **see** "Using Iteration and Circular References," **p. 83**.

- Many of the functions you learned in this chapter—including PMT(), RATE(), and NPER()—can also be used with investment calculations. **See** Chapter 19, "Building Investment Formulas," **p. 453**.

- The PV() function is most often used in discount calculations. **See** "Calculating the Present Value," **p. 468**.

18

Building Investment Formulas

19

The time value of money concepts introduced in Chapter 18, "Building Loan Formulas," applies equally well to investments. The only difference is that you need to reverse the signs of the cash values. That's because loans generally involve receiving a principal amount (positive cash flow) and paying it back over time (negative cash flow). An investment, on the other hand, involves depositing money into the investment (negative cash flow) and then receiving interest payments (or whatever) in return (positive cash flow).

With this sign change in mind, this chapter takes you through some Excel tools for building investment formulas. You'll learn about the wonders of compound interest; how to convert between nominal and effective interest rates; how to calculate the future value of an investment; ways to work toward an investment goal by calculating the required interest rate, term, and deposits; and how to build an investment schedule.

Working with Interest Rates

As I mentioned in Chapter 18, the interest rate is the mechanism that transforms a present value into a future value. (Or, operating as a discount rate, it's what transforms a future value into a present value.) Therefore, when working with financial formulas, it's important to know how to work with interest rates and to be comfortable with certain terminology. You've already seen (again, in Chapter 18) that it's crucial for the interest rate, term, and payment to use the same time basis. The next sections show you a few other interest rate techniques you should know.

Understanding Compound Interest

An interest rate is described as *simple* if it pays the same amount each period. For example, if you have $1,000 in an investment that pays a simple interest rate of 10% per year, you'll receive $100 each year.

Suppose, however, that you were able to add the interest payments to the investment. At the end of the first year, you would have $1,100 in the account, which means you would earn $110 in interest (10% of $1,100) the second year. Being able to add interest earned to an investment is called *compounding*, and the total interest earned (the normal interest plus the extra interest on the reinvested interest—the extra $10, in the example) is called *compound interest*.

Nominal Versus Effective Interest

Interest can also be compounded within the year. For example, suppose that your $1,000 investment earns 10% compounded semiannually. At the end of the first six months, you receive $50 in interest (5% of the original investment). This $50 is reinvested, and for the second half of the year, you earn 5% of $1,050, or $52.50. Therefore, the total interest earned in the first year is $102.50. In other words, the interest rate appears to actually be 10.25%. So which is the correct interest rate, 10% or 10.25%?

To answer that question, you need to know about the two ways that most interest rates are most often quoted:

- **The nominal rate**—This is the annual rate before compounding (the 10% rate, in the example). The nominal rate is always quoted along with the compounding frequency—for example, 10% compounded semiannually.

> **NOTE**   The nominal annual interest rate is often shortened to APR, or the annual percentage rate.

- **The effective rate**—This is the annual rate that an investment actually earns in the year after the compounding is applied (the 10.25%, in the example).

In other words, both rates are "correct," except that, with the nominal rate, you also need to know the compounding frequency.

If you know the nominal rate and the number of compounding periods per year (for example, semiannually means 2 compounding periods per year, and monthly means 12 compounding periods per year), you get the effective rate per period by dividing the nominal rate by the number of periods:

```
=nominal_rate / npery
```

Here, `npery` is the number of compounding periods per year. To convert the nominal annual rate into the effective annual rate, you use the following formula:

```
=(1 + nominal_rate / npery) ^ npery - 1
```

Conversely, if you know the effective rate per period, you can derive the nominal rate by multiplying the effective rate by the number of periods:

```
=effective_rate * npery
```

To convert the effective annual rate to the nominal annual rate, you use the following formula:

```
=npery * (effective_rate + 1) ^ (1 / npery) - npery
```

Fortunately, the next section shows you two functions that can handle the conversion between the nominal and effective annual rates for you.

Converting Between the Nominal Rate and the Effective Rate

To convert a nominal annual interest rate to the effective annual rate, use the `EFFECT()` function:

```
EFFECT(nominal_rate, npery)
```

| `nominal_rate` | The nominal annual interest rate |
| `npery` | The number of compounding periods in the year |

For example, the following formula returns the effective annual interest rate for an investment with a nominal annual rate of 10% that compounds semiannually:

```
=EFFECT(0.1, 2)
```

Figure 19.1 shows a worksheet that applies the `EFFECT()` function to a 10% nominal annual rate using various compounding frequencies.

Figure 19.1
The formulas in column D use the `EFFECT()` function to convert the nominal rates in column C to effective rates based on the compounding periods in column B.

	A	B	C	D	E
	Compounding Frequency	Compounding Periods	Nominal Annual	Effective Annual	
2	Annually	1	10.0%	10.00%	
3	Semi-annually	2	10.0%	10.25%	
4	Quarterly	4	10.0%	10.38%	
5	Monthly	12	10.0%	10.47%	
6	Weekly	52	10.0%	10.51%	
7	Daily	365	10.0%	10.52%	

NOTE You can download the workbook that contains this chapter's examples at www.mcfedries.com/books/book.php?title=excel-2016-formulas-and-functions.

If you already know the effective annual interest rate and the number of compounding periods, you can convert the rate to the nominal annual interest rate by using the NOMINAL() function:

```
NOMINAL(effect_rate, npery)
```

   effect_rate   The effective annual interest rate

   npery   The number of compounding periods in the year

For example, the following formula returns the nominal annual interest rate for an investment with an effective annual rate of 10.52% that compounds daily:

```
=NOMINAL(0.1052, 365)
```

Calculating the Future Value

Just as the payment is usually the most important value for a loan calculation, the future value is usually the most important value for an investment calculation. After all, the purpose of an investment is to place a sum of money (the present value) in some instrument for a time, after which you end up with some new (and hopefully greater) amount: the future value.

To calculate the future value of an investment, Excel offers the FV() function:

```
FV(rate, nper[, pmt][, pv][, type])
```

   rate   The fixed rate of interest over the term of the investment.

   nper   The number of periods in the term of the investment.

   pmt   The amount deposited in the investment each period. (The default is 0.)

   pv   The initial deposit. (The default is 0.)

   type   The type of deposit. Use 0 (the default) for end-of-period deposits; use 1 for beginning-of-period deposits.

Because both the amount deposited per period (the *pmt* argument) and the initial deposit (the *pv* argument) are sums that you pay out, these must be entered as negative values in the FV() function.

The next few sections take you through various investment scenarios using the FV() function.

The Future Value of a Lump Sum

In the simplest future value scenario, you invest a lump sum and let it grow according to the specified interest rate and term, without adding any deposits along the way. In this case, you use the FV() function with the *pmt* argument set to 0:

```
FV(rate, nper, 0, pv, type)
```

For example, Figure 19.2 shows the future value of $10,000 invested at 5% over 10 years.

Figure 19.2
When calculating the future value of an initial lump sum deposit, set the FV () function's *pmt* argument to 0.

	A	B	C	D
B7		=FV(B2, B3, B4, B5, B6)		
1	The Future Value of a Lump Sum			
2	Interest Rate (Annual)	5.0%		
3	Term (Years)	10		
4	Deposit Per Period	$0		
5	Initial Deposit	($10,000)		
6	Deposit Type	0		
7	Future Value	$16,288.95		
8				

> **TIP**
>
> Excel's FV () function doesn't work with continuous compounding. Instead, you need to use a worksheet formula that takes the following general form (where e is the mathematical constant e):
>
> `=pv * e ^ (rate * nper)`
>
> For example, the following formula calculates the future value of $10,000 invested at 5% over 10 years compounded continuously (and it returns a value of $16,487.21):
>
> `=10000 * EXP(0.05 ^ 10)`

The Future Value of a Series of Deposits

Another common investment scenario is to make a series of deposits over the term of the investment, without depositing an initial sum. In this case, you use the FV () function with the *pv* argument set to 0:

`FV(rate, nper, pmt, 0, type)`

For example, Figure 19.3 shows the future value of $100 invested each month at 5% over 10 years. Notice that the interest rate and term are both converted to monthly amounts because the deposit occurs monthly.

Figure 19.3
When calculating the future value of a series of deposits, set the FV () function's *pv* argument to 0.

	A	B	C	D	E
B7		=FV(B2 / 12, B3 * 12, B4, B5, B6)			
1	The Future Value of a Series of Deposits				
2	Interest Rate (Annual)	5.0%			
3	Term (Years)	10			
4	Deposit Per Month	($100)			
5	Initial Deposit	$0			
6	Deposit Type	0			
7	Future Value	$15,528.23			
8					

19

The Future Value of a Lump Sum Plus Deposits

For best investment results, you should invest an initial amount and then add to it with regular deposits. In this scenario, you need to specify all the FV() function arguments (except *type*). For example, Figure 19.4 shows the future value of an investment with a $10,000 initial deposit and $100 monthly deposits at 5% over 10 years.

Figure 19.4
This worksheet uses the full FV() function syntax to calculate the future value of a lump sum plus a series of deposits.

	B7	▼	:	×	✓	*fx*	=FV(B2 / 12, B3 * 12, B4, B5, B6)		
◢	A		B	C	D	E	F	G	H
1	The Future Value of a Lump Sum Plus a Series of Deposits								
2	Interest Rate (Annual)		5.0%						
3	Term (Years)		10						
4	Deposit Per Month		($100)						
5	Initial Deposit		($10,000)						
6	Deposit Type		0						
7	Future Value		$31,998.32						
8									

Working Toward an Investment Goal

Instead of just seeing where an investment will end up, it's often desirable to have a specific monetary goal in mind and then ask yourself, "What will it take to get me there?"

Answering this question means solving for one of the four main future value parameters—interest rate, number of periods, regular deposit, and initial deposit—while holding the other parameters (and, of course, your future value goal) constant. The next four sections take you through this process.

Calculating the Required Interest Rate

Say that you know the future value that you want, when you want it, and the initial deposit and periodic deposits you can afford. What interest rate do you require to meet your goal? You answer this question by using the RATE() function, which you first encountered in Chapter 18. Here's the syntax for that function from the point of view of an investment:

```
RATE(nper, pmt, pv, fv[, type][, guess])
```

nper   The number of deposits over the term of the investment.

pmt   The amount invested with each deposit.

pv   The initial investment.

fv   The future value of the investment.

type   The type of deposit. Use 0 (the default) for end-of-period deposits; use 1 for beginning-of-period deposits.

guess   A percentage value that Excel uses as a starting point for calculating the interest rate. (The default is 10%.)

For example, if you need $100,000 10 years from now, you are starting with $10,000, and you can deposit $500 per month. What interest rate is required to meet your goal? Figure 19.5 shows a worksheet that comes up with the answer: 6%.

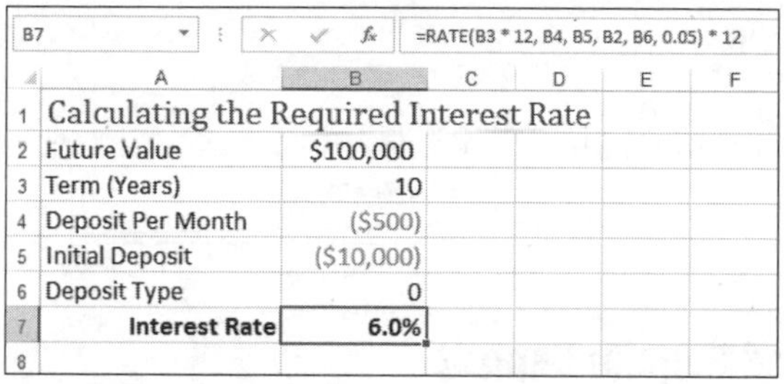

Figure 19.5
Use the RATE () function to work out the interest rate required to reach a future value, given a fixed term, a periodic deposit, and an initial deposit.

B7	▼	:	✕	✓	*fx*	=RATE(B3 * 12, B4, B5, B2, B6, 0.05) * 12

⁴	A	B	C	D	E	F
1	Calculating the Required Interest Rate					
2	Future Value	$100,000				
3	Term (Years)	10				
4	Deposit Per Month	($500)				
5	Initial Deposit	($10,000)				
6	Deposit Type	0				
7	Interest Rate	6.0%				
8						

➔ To work with the RATE () function in a loan context, **see** "Calculating the Interest Rate Required for a Loan," **p. 445**.

Calculating the Required Number of Periods

Given your investment goal, if you have an initial deposit and an amount that you can afford to deposit periodically, how long will it take to reach your goal at the prevailing market interest rate? You answer this question by using the NPER() function (which was introduced in Chapter 18). Here's the NPER() syntax from the point of view of an investment:

```
NPER(rate, pmt, pv, fv[, type])
```

rate   The fixed rate of interest over the term of the investment.

pmt   The amount invested with each deposit.

pv   The initial investment.

fv   The future value of the investment.

type   The type of deposit. Use 0 (the default) for end-of-period deposits; use 1 for beginning-of-period deposits.

For example, suppose that you want to retire with $1,000,000. You have $50,000 to invest, you can afford to deposit $1,000 per month, and you expect to earn 5% interest. How long will it take to reach your goal? The worksheet in Figure 19.6 answers this question: 349.4 months, or 29.1 years.

➔ To work with the **NPER()** function in a loan context, **see** "Calculating the Term of a Loan," **p. 443**.

19

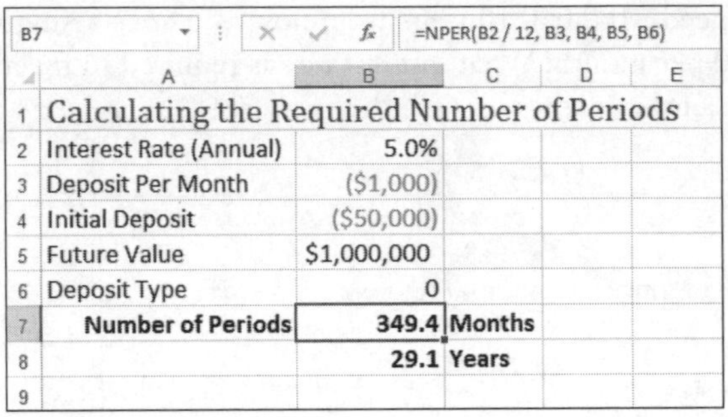

Figure 19.6
Use the NPER() func-
tion to calculate how
long it will take to reach a
future value, given a fixed
interest rate, a periodic
deposit, and an initial
deposit.

	A	B	C	D	E
	B7		fx =NPER(B2 / 12, B3, B4, B5, B6)		
1	Calculating the Required Number of Periods				
2	Interest Rate (Annual)	5.0%			
3	Deposit Per Month	($1,000)			
4	Initial Deposit	($50,000)			
5	Future Value	$1,000,000			
6	Deposit Type	0			
7	Number of Periods	349.4	Months		
8		29.1	Years		
9					

Calculating the Required Regular Deposit

Suppose that you want to reach your future value goal by a certain date and that you have an initial amount to invest. Given current interest rates, how much extra do you have to periodically deposit into the investment to achieve your goal? The answer here lies in the PMT() function from Chapter 18. Here are the PMT() function details from the point of view of an investment:

```
PMT(rate, nper, pv, fv[, type])
```

rate   The fixed rate of interest over the term of the investment.

nper   The number of deposits over the term of the investment.

pv   The initial investment.

fv   The future value of the investment.

type   The type of deposit. Use 0 (the default) for end-of-period deposits; use 1 for beginning-of-period deposits.

For example, suppose you want to end up with $50,000 in 15 years to finance your child's college education. If you have no initial deposit and you expect to get 7.5% interest over the term of the investment, how much do you need to deposit each month to reach your target? Figure 19.7 shows a worksheet that calculates the result using PMT(): $151.01 per month.

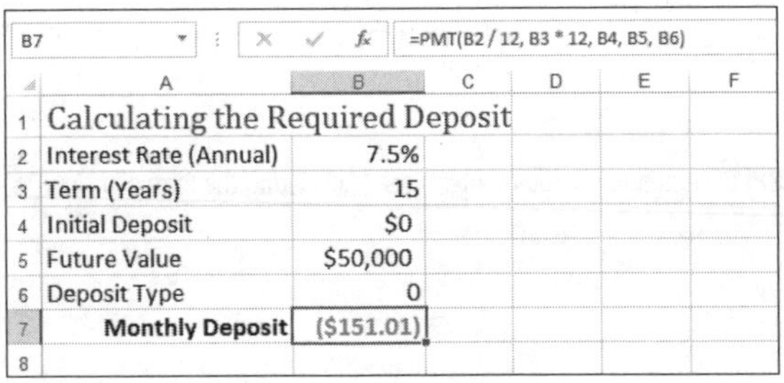

Figure 19.7
Use the PMT() func-
tion to derive how much
you need to deposit
periodically to reach a
future value, given a fixed
interest rate, a number
of deposits, and an initial
deposit.

	A	B	C	D	E	F
	B7		fx =PMT(B2 / 12, B3 * 12, B4, B5, B6)			
1	Calculating the Required Deposit					
2	Interest Rate (Annual)	7.5%				
3	Term (Years)	15				
4	Initial Deposit	$0				
5	Future Value	$50,000				
6	Deposit Type	0				
7	Monthly Deposit	($151.01)				
8						

→ To work with the PMT() function in a loan context, **see** "Calculating a Loan Payment," **p. 435**.

Calculating the Required Initial Deposit

For the final standard future value calculation, suppose that you know when you want to reach your goal, how much you can deposit each period, and how much the interest rate will be. What, then, do you need to deposit initially to achieve your future value target? To find the answer, you use the PV() function. Here are the PV() function details from the point of view of an investment:

```
PV(rate, nper, pmt, fv[, type])
```

rate   The fixed rate of interest over the term of the investment.

nper   The number of deposits over the term of the investment.

pmt   The amount invested with each deposit.

fv   The future value of the investment.

type   The type of deposit. Use 0 (the default) for end-of-period deposits; use 1 for beginning-of-period deposits.

For example, suppose your goal is to end up with $100,000 in three years to purchase new equipment. If you expect to earn 6% interest and can deposit $2,000 monthly, what does your initial deposit have to be to make your goal? The worksheet in Figure 19.8 uses PV() to calculate the answer: $17,822.46.

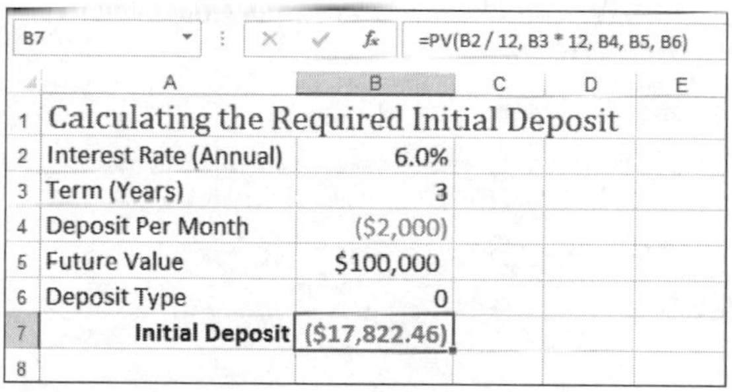

Figure 19.8
Use the PV() function to find out how much you need to deposit initially to reach a future value, given a fixed interest rate, number of deposits, and periodic deposit.

B7	▾	:	×	✓	*fx*	=PV(B2 / 12, B3 * 12, B4, B5, B6)

▲	A	B	C	D	E
1	Calculating the Required Initial Deposit				
2	Interest Rate (Annual)	6.0%			
3	Term (Years)	3			
4	Deposit Per Month	($2,000)			
5	Future Value	$100,000			
6	Deposit Type	0			
7	Initial Deposit	($17,822.46)			
8					

19

→ To work with the PV() function in a discount context, **see** "Calculating the Present Value," **p. 468**.

Calculating the Future Value with Varying Interest Rates

All the future value examples that you've worked with so far have assumed that the interest rate remained constant over the term of the investment. This will always be true for fixed-rate investments, but for other investments, such as mutual funds, stocks, and bonds, using a fixed rate of interest is, at best, a guess about what the average rate will be over the term.

For investments that offer a variable rate over the term, or when the rate fluctuates over the term, Excel offers the FVSCHEDULE() function, which returns the future value of some initial amount, given a schedule of interest rates:

FVSCHEDULE(*principal*, *schedule*)

principal The initial investment

schedule A range or an array containing the interest rates

For example, the following formula returns the future value of an initial $10,000 deposit that makes 5%, 6%, and 7% over three years:

```
=FVSCHEDULE(10000, {0.05, 0.06, 0.07})
```

Similarly, Figure 19.9 shows a worksheet that calculates the future value of an initial deposit of $100,000 into an investment that earns 5%, 5.5%, 6%, 7%, and 6% over five years.

NOTE If you want to know the average rate earned on the investment, use the RATE() function, where *nper* is the number of values in the interest rate schedule, *pmt* is 0, *pv* is the initial deposit, and *fv* is the negative of the FVSCHEDULE() result. Here's the general syntax:

```
RATE(ROWS(schedule), 0, principal, -FVSCHEDULE(principal,
schedule))
```

Figure 19.9
Use the
FVSCHEDULE() function to return the future value of an initial deposit in an investment that earns varying rates of interest.

B9		fx	=FVSCHEDULE(B2, B4:B8)				

	A	B	C	D	E	F	G	H	I
1	Calculating the Future Value with Varying Interest Rates								
2	Principal	$100,000							
3	Rates:								
4	2016	5.0%							
5	2017	5.5%							
6	2018	6.0%							
7	2019	7.0%							
8	2020	6.0%							
9	Future Value	$133,179.47							
10	Average Rate	5.9%							
11									

Case Study: Building an Investment Schedule

If you're planning future cash-flow requirements or future retirement needs, it's often not enough just to know how much money you'll have at the end of an investment. You might need to also know how much money is in the investment account or fund at each period throughout the life of the investment.

To do this, you need to build an *investment schedule*. This is similar to an amortization schedule, except that it shows the future value of an investment at each period in the term of the investment.

→ To learn about amortization schedules, **see** "Building a Loan Amortization Schedule," **p. 440**.

In a typical investment schedule, you need to take two things into account:

■ The periodic deposits put into the investment, particularly the amount deposited and the frequency of the deposits. The frequency of the deposits determines the total number of periods in the investment. For example, a 10-year investment with semiannual deposits has 20 periods.

■ The compounding frequency of the investment (annually, semiannually, and so on). Assuming that you know the APR (that is, nominal annual interest rate), you can use the compounding frequency to determine the effective rate.

Note, however, that you can't simply use the EFFECT() function to convert the known nominal rate into the effective rate. That's because you're going to calculate the future value at the end of each period, which might or might not correspond to the compounding frequency. (For example, if the investment compounds monthly and you deposit semiannually, there will be six months of compounding to factor into the future value at the end of each period.)

Getting the proper effective rate for each period requires three steps:

1. Use the EFFECT() function to convert the nominal annual rate into the effective annual rate, based on the compounding frequency.

2. Use the NOMINAL() function to convert the effective rate from step 1 into the nominal rate, based on the deposit frequency.

3. Divide the nominal rate from step 2 by the deposit frequency to get the effective rate per period. This is the value that you'll plug in to the FV() function.

Figure 19.10 shows a worksheet that implements an investment schedule using this technique.

Here's a summary of the items in the Investment Data portion of the worksheet:

■ **Nominal Rate (APR) (B2)**—This is the nominal annual rate of interest for the investment.

■ **Term (Years) (B3)**—This is the length of the investment, in years.

■ **Initial Deposit (B4)**—This is the amount deposited at the start of the investment. Enter this as a negative number (because it's money that you're paying out).

■ **Periodic Deposit (B5)**—This is the amount deposited at each period of the investment. (Again, this number must be negative.)

■ **Deposit Type (B6)**—This is the *type* argument of the FV() function.

■ **Deposit Frequency**—Use this drop-down list to specify how often the periodic deposits are made. The available values—Annually, Semi-Annually, Quarterly, Monthly, Weekly, and Daily—come from the range F2:F7; the number of the selected list item is stored in cell E2.

19

Figure 19.10
An investment schedule that takes into account deposit frequency and compounding frequency to return the future value of an investment at the end of each deposit period.

F11	▾ : × ✓ *fx*	=FV($D$6, A11, $B$5, $B$4, $B$6)			

	A	B	C	D	E	F
1	Investment Data					
2	Nominal Rate (APR)	6.00%	Deposit Frequency	Annually ▾	1	Annually
3	Term (Years)	10	Deposits Per Year	1		Semi-Annually
4	Initial Deposit	($100,000)	Compounding Frequency	Semi-Annually ▾	2	Quarterly
5	Periodic Deposit	($5,000)	Compounds Per Year	2		Monthly
6	Deposit Type	0	Effective Rate Per Period	6.09%		Weekly
7			Total Periods	10		Daily
8						
9	Investment Schedule					
10	Period	Interest Earned	Cumulative Interest	Cumulative Deposits	Total Increase	Future Value
11	1	$6,090.00	$6,090.00	$5,000.00	$11,090.00	$111,090.00
12	2	$6,765.38	$12,855.38	$10,000.00	$22,855.38	$122,855.38
13	3	$7,481.89	$20,337.27	$15,000.00	$35,337.27	$135,337.27
14	4	$8,242.04	$28,579.31	$20,000.00	$48,579.31	$148,579.31
15	5	$9,048.48	$37,627.79	$25,000.00	$62,627.79	$162,627.79
16	6	$9,904.03	$47,531.83	$30,000.00	$77,531.83	$177,531.83
17	7	$10,811.69	$58,343.51	$35,000.00	$93,343.51	$193,343.51
18	8	$11,774.62	$70,118.13	$40,000.00	$110,118.13	$210,118.13
19	9	$12,796.19	$82,914.33	$45,000.00	$127,914.33	$227,914.33
20	10	$13,879.98	$96,794.31	$50,000.00	$146,794.31	$246,794.31
21						

- **Deposits Per Year (D3)**—This is the number of periods per year, as given by the following formula:

  ```
  =CHOOSE(E2, 1, 2, 4, 12, 52, 365)
  ```

- **Compounding Frequency**—Use this drop-down list to specify how often the investment compounds. You get the same options as in the Deposit Frequency list. The number of the selected list item is stored in cell E4.

- **Compounds Per Year (D5)**—This is the number of compounding periods per year, as given by the following formula:

  ```
  =CHOOSE(E4, 1, 2, 4, 12, 52, 365)
  ```

- **Effective Rate Per Period (D6)**—This is the effective interest rate per period, as calculated using the three-step algorithm outlined earlier in this section. Here's the formula:

  ```
  =NOMINAL(EFFECT(B2, D5), D3) / D3
  ```

- **Total Periods (D7)**—This is the total number of deposit periods in the loan, which is just the term multiplied by the number of deposits per year.

Here's a summary of the columns in the Investment Schedule portion of the worksheet:

- **Period (column A)**—This is the period number of the investment. The Period values are generated automatically based on the Total Periods value (D7).

  → The dynamic features used in the investment schedule are similar to those used in the dynamic amortization schedule; see "Building a Dynamic Amortization Schedule," **p. 441**.

- **Interest Earned (column B)**—This is the interest earned during the period. It's calculated by multiplying the future value from the previous period by the Effective Rate Per Period (D6).

- **Cumulative Interest (column C)**—This is the total interest earned in the investment at the end of each period. It's calculated by using a running sum of the values in the Interest Earned column.

- **Cumulative Deposits (column D)**—This is the total amount of the deposits added to the investment at the end of each period. It's calculated by multiplying the Periodic Deposit (B5) by the current period number (column A).

- **Total Increase (column E)**—This is the total amount by which the investment has increased over the Initial Deposit at the end of each period. It's calculated by adding the Cumulative Interest and the Cumulative Deposits.

- **Future Value (column F)**—This is the value of the investment at the end of each period. Here's the FV() formula for cell F11:

```
=FV($D$6, A11, $B$5, $B$4, $B$6)
```

From Here

- To get the details on the concept of the time value of money, **see** "Understanding the Time Value of Money," **p. 433**.

- To work with the RATE() function in a loan context, **see** "Calculating the Interest Rate Required for a Loan," **p. 445**.

- To work with the NPER() function in a loan context, **see** "Calculating the Term of a Loan," **p. 443**.

- To work with the PMT() function in a loan context, **see** "Calculating a Loan Payment," **p. 435**.

- To learn about amortization schedules, **see** "Building a Loan Amortization Schedule," **p. 440**.

- To work with the PV() function in a discount context, **see** "Calculating the Present Value," **p. 468**.

19

Building Discount Formulas

20

In Chapter 19, "Building Investment Formulas," you saw that investment calculations largely use the same time-value-of-money concepts as the loan calculations that you learned about in Chapter 18, "Building Loan Formulas." The difference is the direction of the cash flows. For example, the present value of a loan is a positive cash flow because the money comes to you; the present value of an investment is a negative cash flow because the money goes out to the investment.

Discounting also fits into the time-value-of-money scheme, and you can see its relation to present value, future value, and interest earned in the following equations:

Future value = Present value + Interest

Present value = Future value – Discount

In Chapter 18, you learned about a form of discounting when you determined how much money you could borrow (the present value) when you know the current interest rate that your bank offers for loans, when you want to have the loan paid off, and how much you can afford each month for the payments.

→ **See** "Calculating How Much You Can Borrow," **p. 446**.

Similarly, in Chapter 19, you learned about another application of discounting when you calculated the initial deposit required (the present value) to reach a future goal, knowing how much you can deposit each period and how much the interest rate will be.

→ **See** "Calculating the Required Initial Deposit," **p. 461**.

This chapter takes a closer look at Excel's discounting tools, including present value and profitability as well as cash-flow analysis measures such as net present value and internal rate of return.

Calculating the Present Value

The time-value-of-money concept tells you that a dollar now is not the same as a dollar in the future. You can't compare them directly because it's like comparing the temporal equivalent of the proverbial apples and oranges. From a discounting perspective, the present value is important because it turns those future oranges into present apples. That is, it enables you to make a true comparison by restating the future value of an asset or investment in today's terms.

You know from Chapter 19 that calculating a future value relies on compounding. That is, a dollar today grows by applying interest on interest, like this:

Year 1: $1.00 × (1 + rate)

Year 2: $1.00 × (1 + rate) × (1 + rate)

Year 3: $1.00 × (1 + rate) × (1 + rate) × (1 + rate)

→ **See** "Understanding Compound Interest," **p. 454**.

More generally, given an interest rate and a period nper, the future value of a dollar today is calculated as follows:

```
=$1.00 * (1 + rate) ^ nper
```

Calculating the present value uses the reverse process. That is, given some discount rate, a future dollar is expressed in today's dollars by dividing instead of multiplying:

Year 1: $1.00 / (1 + rate)

Year 2: $1.00 / (1 + rate) / (1 + rate)

Year 3: $1.00 / (1 + rate) / (1 + rate) / (1 + rate)

In general, given a discount rate and a period nper, the present value of a future dollar is calculated as follows:

```
=$1.00 / (1 + rate) ^ nper
```

The result of this formula is called the *discount factor*, and multiplying it by any future value restates that value in today's dollars.

Taking Inflation into Account

The future value tells you how much money you'll end up with, but it doesn't tell you how much that money is *worth*. In other words, if an object costs $10,000 now and your investment's future value is $10,000, it's unlikely that you'll be able to use that future value to purchase the object because it will probably have gone up in price. That is, inflation erodes the purchasing power of any future value; to know what a future value is worth, you need to express it in today's dollars.

For example, suppose that you put $10,000 initially and $100 per month into an investment that pays 5% annual interest. After 10 years, the future value of that investment will be $31,998.32. Assuming that the inflation rate stays constant at 2% per year, what is the investment's future value worth in today's dollars?

Here, the discount rate is the inflation rate, so the discount factor is calculated as follows:

```
=1 / (1.02) ^ 10
```

This returns 0.82. Multiplying the future value by this discount factor gives the present value: $26,249.77.

Calculating Present Value Using PV()

You're probably wondering what happened to Excel's PV() function. I've held off on introducing it so that you could see how to calculate present value from first principles. Now that you know what's going on behind the scenes, you can make your life easier by calculating present values directly using the PV() function:

```
PV(rate, nper, pmt[, fv][, type])
```

rate   The fixed rate over the term of the asset or investment.

nper   The number of periods in the term of the asset or investment.

pmt   The amount earned by the asset or deposited into the investment with each deposit.

fv   The future value of the asset or investment.

type   When the *pmt* occurs. Use 0 (the default) for the end of each period; use 1 for the beginning of each period.

For example, to calculate the effect of inflation on a future value, you apply the PV() function to the future value, where the *rate* argument is the inflation rate:

```
PV(inflation rate, nper, 0, fv)
```

> **NOTE** When you set the PV() function's *pmt* argument to 0, you can ignore the *type* argument because it's meaningless without payments.

Figure 20.1 shows a worksheet that uses PV() to derive the answer of $26,249.77 using the following formula:

```
=PV(B9, B3, 0, -B7)
```

20

Note that this is the same result you derived using the discount factor, which is shown in Figure 20.1 in cell B10. (The table in D2:E13 shows the various discount factors for each year.)

NOTE You can download this chapter's sample workbook at www.mcfedries.com/books/ book.php?title=excel-2016-formulas-and-functions.

Figure 20.1
Use the PV ( ) function to calculate the effects of inflation on a future value.

B11	▼ : × ✓ *fx*	=PV(B9, B3, 0, -B7)				
⊿	A	B	C	D	E	F
1	Taking Inflation Into Account					
2	Interest Rate (Annual)	5.0%		Year	Discount Factor	
3	Term (Years)	10		0	1.00	
4	Deposit Per Month	($100)		1	0.98	
5	Initial Deposit	($10,000)		2	0.96	
6	Deposit Type	0		3	0.94	
7	Future Value	$31,998.32		4	0.92	
8				5	0.91	
9	Inflation Rate	2%		6	0.89	
10	Present Value (Discount Factor)	$26,249.77		7	0.87	
11	Present Value (PV() Function)	$26,249.77		8	0.85	
12				9	0.84	
13				10	0.82	
14						

The next few sections take you through some examples of using PV ( ) in discounting scenarios.

Income Investing Versus Purchasing a Rental Property

If you have some cash to invest, one common scenario is to wonder whether the cash is better invested in a straight income-producing security (such as a bond or certificate) or in a rental property.

One way to analyze this is to gather the following data:

■ On the fixed-income security side, find your best deal in the time frame you're looking at. For example, you might find that you can get a bond that matures in 10 years with a 5% yield.

■ On the rental property side, find out what the property produces in annual rental income. Also, estimate what the rental property will be worth at the same future date that the fixed-income security matures. For example, you might be looking at a rental property that generates $24,000 a year and is estimated to be worth $1 million in 10 years.

Given this data (and ignoring complicating factors such as rental property expenses), you want to know the maximum that you should pay for the property to realize a better yield than with the fixed-income security.

To solve this problem, use the PV() function as follows:

```
=PV(fixed income yield, nper, rental income, future property value)
```

Figure 20.2 shows a worksheet model that uses this formula. The result of the PV() function is $799,235. You interpret this to mean that if you pay less than that amount for the property, the property is a better deal than the fixed-income security; if you pay more, you're better off going the fixed-income route.

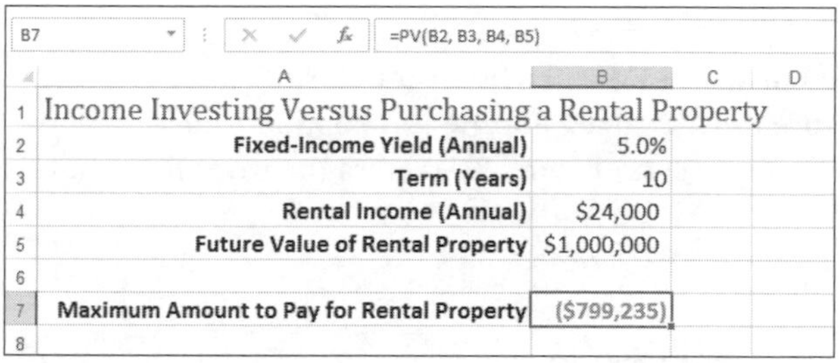

Figure 20.2

Use the PV() function to compare investing in a fixed-income security versus purchasing a rental property.

B7	▼	:	×	✓	*fx*	=PV(B2, B3, B4, B5)		

	A	B	C	D
1	Income Investing Versus Purchasing a Rental Property			
2	Fixed-Income Yield (Annual)	5.0%		
3	Term (Years)	10		
4	Rental Income (Annual)	$24,000		
5	Future Value of Rental Property	$1,000,000		
6				
7	Maximum Amount to Pay for Rental Property	($799,235)		
8				

Buying Versus Leasing

Another common business conundrum is whether to purchase equipment outright or to lease it. Again, you figure the present value of both sides to compare them, with the preferable option being the one that provides the lower present value. (This ignores complicating factors such as depreciation and taxes.)

Assume (for now) that the purchased equipment has no market value at the end of the term and that the leased equipment has no residual value at the end of the lease. In this case, the present value of the purchase option is simply the purchase price. For the lease option, you determine the present value using the following form of the PV() function:

```
-PV(discount rate, lease term, lease payment)
```

For the discount rate, you plug in a value that represents either a current investment rate or a current loan rate. For example, if you could invest the lease payment and get 6% per year, you would plug 6% into the function as the rate argument.

Suppose you can either purchase a piece of equipment for $5,000 now or lease the equipment for $240 a month over two years. Assuming a discount rate of 6%, what's the present value of the leasing option? Figure 20.3 shows a worksheet that calculates the answer: $5,415.09. This means that purchasing the equipment is the less costly choice.

What if the equipment has a future market value (on the purchase side) or a residual value (on the lease side)? This won't make much difference in terms of which option is better because the future value of the equipment raises the two present values by about the same amount. However, note how you calculate the present value for the purchase option:

```
=purchase price + PV(discount rate, term, 0, future value)
```

Figure 20.3
Use the PV () function
to compare buying versus
leasing equipment.

B7				f_x	=PV(B2 / 12, B3 * 12, B4, B5)		
	A			B	C	D	
1	Buying Versus Leasing						
2	Discount Rate			6.0%			
3	Term (Years)			2			
4	Lease Payment (Monthly)			($240)			
5	Future Value of Equipment			$0			
6	Purchase Price			$5,000			
7	Present Value of Leasing Option			$5,415.09			
8	Present Value of Buying Option			$5,000.00			
9							

That is, the present value of the purchase option is the price plus the present value of the equipment's future market value. (For the lease option, you include the residual value as the PV () function's *fv* argument.) Figure 20.4 shows the worksheet with a future value added.

Figure 20.4
Use the PV () function
to compare buying versus
leasing equipment that
has a future market or
residual value.

B8				f_x	=B6 + PV(B2 / 12, B3 * 12, 0, B5)		
	A			B	C	D	
1	Buying Versus Leasing						
2	Discount Rate			6.0%			
3	Term (Years)			2			
4	Lease Payment (Monthly)			($240)			
5	Future Value of Equipment			($1,000)			
6	Purchase Price			$5,000			
7	Present Value of Leasing Option			$6,302.27			
8	Present Value of Buying Option			$5,887.19			
9							

Discounting Cash Flows

One very common business scenario is to put some money into an asset or investment that generates income. By examining the cash flows—the negative cash flows for the original investment and any subsequent outlays required by the asset, and the positive cash flows for the income generated by the asset—you can figure out whether you've made a good investment.

For example, consider the situation discussed earlier in this chapter: You invest in a property that generates a regular cash flow of rental income. When analyzing this investment, you have three types of cash flow to consider:

- The initial purchase price (negative cash flow)
- The annual rental income (positive cash flow)
- The price you get by selling the property (positive cash flow)

Earlier you used the PV () function to calculate that an initial purchase price of $799,235 and an assumed sale price of $1 million gives you the same return as a 5% fixed-income security over 10 years. Let's verify this using a cash-flow analysis. Figure 20.5 shows a worksheet set up to show the cash flows for this investment. Row 3 shows the net cash flow each year. (In practice, this would be the rental income minus the costs incurred while maintaining and repairing the property.) Row 4 shows the cumulative net cash flows. Note that columns F through I (years 4 through 7) are hidden so that you can see the final cash flow: the rent in year 10 plus the sale price of the property.

Figure 20.5
The yearly and cumulative cash flows for a rental property.

	A	B	C	D	E	J	K	L
1	Year	0	1	2	3	8	9	10
2	CASH FLOW	Purchase						Sale
3	Net Cash Flow	($799,235)	$24,000	$24,000	$24,000	$24,000	$24,000	$1,024,000
4	Cumulative Net Cash Flow	($799,235)	($775,235)	($751,235)	($727,235)	($607,235)	($583,235)	$440,765
5								

Calculating the Net Present Value

The *net present value* is the sum of a series of net cash flows, each of which has been discounted to the present using a fixed discount rate. If all the cash flows are the same, you can use the PV() function to calculate the present value. But when you have a series of varying cash flows, as in the rental property example, you can apply the PV() function directly.

Excel has a direct route to calculating net present value, but let's take a second to examine a method that calculates this value from first principles. This will help you understand exactly what's happening in this kind of cash-flow analysis.

To get the net present value, you first have to discount each cash flow. You do that by multiplying the cash flow by the discount factor, which you calculate as described earlier in this chapter.

Figure 20.6 shows the rental property cash-flow worksheet with the discount factors (row 8) and the discounted cash flows (rows 9 and 10).

Figure 20.6
The discounted yearly and cumulative cash flows for a rental property.

C8 =1/(1+$B$7)^C1

	A	B	C	D	E	J	K	L
1	Year	0	1	2	3	8	9	10
2	CASH FLOW	Purchase						Sale
3	Net Cash Flow	($799,235)	$24,000	$24,000	$24,000	$24,000	$24,000	$1,024,000
4	Cumulative Net Cash Flow	($799,235)	($775,235)	($751,235)	($727,235)	($607,235)	($583,235)	$440,765
5								
6	DISCOUNTING							
7	Discount Rate	5%						
8	Discount Factor	1	0.95	0.91	0.86	0.68	0.64	0.61
9	Discounted Cash Flow	($799,235)	$22,857	$21,769	$20,732	$16,244	$15,471	$628,647
10	Discounted Cumulative Cash Flow	($799,235)	($776,378)	($754,609)	($733,877)	($644,118)	($628,647)	$0
11								

The key number to notice in Figure 20.6 is the final Discounted Cumulative Cash Flow value in cell L10, which is $0. This is the net present value, the sum of the cumulative discounted cash flows at the end of year 10. This result makes sense because you already know that the initial cash flow—the purchase price of $799,235—was the present value of the rental income with a discount rate of 5% and a sale price of $1 million.

In other words, purchasing the property for $799,235 enables you to break even—that is, the net present value is 0—when all the cash flows are discounted into today's dollars using the specified discount rate.

> **NOTE** The discount rate that returns a net present value of 0 is sometimes called the *hurdle rate*. In other words, it's the rate that you must surpass to make the asset or investment worthwhile.

The net present value can also tell you whether an investment is positive or negative:

- If the net present value is negative, this can generally be interpreted in two ways: Either you paid too much for the asset or the income from the asset is too low. For example, if you plug –$900,000 into the rental property model as the initial cash flow (that is, the purchase price), the net present value works out to –$100,765, which is the loss on the property in today's dollars.

- If the net present value is positive, this can generally be interpreted in two ways: Either you got a good deal for the asset or the income makes the asset profitable. For example, if you plug –$700,000 into the rental property model as the initial cash flow (that is, the purchase price), the net present value works out to $99,235, which is the profit on the property in today's dollars.

Calculating Net Present Value Using NPV()

The model built in the previous section was designed to show you the relationship between the present value and the net present value. Fortunately, you don't have to jump through all those worksheet hoops every time you need to calculate the net present value. Excel offers a much quicker method with the NPV() function:

```
NPV(rate, values)
```

rate	The discount rate over the term of the asset or investment
values	The cash flows over the term of the asset or investment

For example, to calculate the net present value of the cash flows in Figure 20.6, you use the following formula:

```
=NPV(B7, B3:L3)
```

That's markedly easier than figuring out discount factors and discounted cash flows. However, the NPV() function has one quirk that can seriously affect its results. NPV() assumes that the initial cash flow occurs at the end of the first period. However, in most cases, the initial cash flow—usually a negative cash flow, indicating the purchase of an asset or a deposit into an investment—occurs at the beginning of the term. This is usually designated as period 0. The first cash flow resulting from the asset or investment is designated as period 1.

The upshot of this NPV() quirk is that the function result is usually understated by a factor of the discount rate. For example, if the discount rate is 5%, the NPV() result must be increased by 5% to factor in the first period and get the true net present value. Here's the general formula:

```
net present value = NPV() * (1 + discount rate)
```

Figure 20.7 shows a new worksheet that contains the rental property's net cash flows (B3:L3) as well as the discount rate (B5). The net present value is calculated using the following formula:

```
=NPV(B5, B3:L3) * (1 + B5)
```

Figure 20.7
The net present value calculated using the NPV() function plus an adjustment.

B6			fx	=NPV(B5, B3:L3) * (1 + B5)								
	A	B	C	D	E	F	G	H	I	J	K	L
1	Year	0	1	2	3	4	5	6	7	8	9	10
2	CASH FLOW	Purchase										Sale
3	Net Cash Flow	($799,235)	$24,000	$24,000	$24,000	$24,000	$24,000	$24,000	$24,000	$24,000	$24,000	$1,024,000
4	DISCOUNTING											
5	Discount Rate	5%										
6	Net Present Value	$0.00										
7												

CAUTION

Make sure that you adjust the discount rate to reflect the frequency of the discounting periods. If the periods are annual, the discount rate must be an annual rate. If the periods are monthly, you need to divide the discount rate by 12 to get the monthly rate.

Net Present Value with Varying Cash Flows

The major advantage of using NPV() over PV() is that NPV() can easily accommodate varying cash flows. You can use PV() directly to calculate the break-even purchase price, assuming that the asset or investment generates a constant cash flow each period. Alternatively, you can use PV() to help calculate the net present value for different cash flows if you build a complicated discounted cash flow model such as the one shown for the rental property in Figure 20.6.

You don't need to worry about either of these scenarios if you use NPV(). That's because you can simply enter the cash flows as the NPV() function's *values* argument.

For example, suppose that you're thinking of investing in a new piece of equipment that will generate income, but you don't want to make the investment unless the machine will generate a return of at least 10% in today's dollars over the first five years. Your cash-flow projection looks like this:

Year 0: $50,000 (purchase price)

Year 1: –$5,000

Year 2: $15,000

Year 3: $20,000

Year 4: $21,000

Year 5: $22,000

Figure 20.8 shows a worksheet that models this scenario with the cash flows in B4:G4. Using the target return of 10% as the discount rate (B6), the NPV() function returns $881 (B7). This amount is positive, which means that the machine will make at least a 10% return in today's dollars over the first five years.

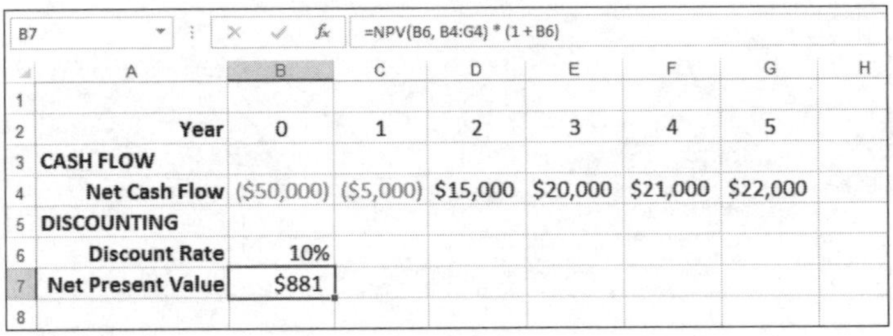

Figure 20.8
To see whether a series of cash flows meets a desired rate of return, use that rate as the discount rate in the NPV() function.

B7	▾ : × ✓ *fx*	=NPV(B6, B4:G4) * (1 + B6)						
⊿	A	B	C	D	E	F	G	H
1								
2	Year	0	1	2	3	4	5	
3	**CASH FLOW**							
4	Net Cash Flow	($50,000)	($5,000)	$15,000	$20,000	$21,000	$22,000	
5	**DISCOUNTING**							
6	Discount Rate	10%						
7	Net Present Value	$881						
8								

Net Present Value with Nonperiodic Cash Flows

The examples you've seen so far have assumed that the cash flows were periodic, meaning that they occur with the same frequency throughout the term (such as yearly or monthly). In some investments, however, the cash flows occur sporadically. In such a case, you can't use the NPV() function, which works only with periodic cash flows.

Happily, Excel offers the XNPV() function, which can handle nonperiodic cash flows:

```
XNPV(rate, values, dates)
```

rate   The annual discount rate over the term of the asset or investment.

values   The cash flows over the term of the asset or investment.

dates   The dates on which each of the cash flows occurs. Make sure the first value in dates is the date of the initial cash flow. All the other dates must be later than this initial date, but they can be listed in any order.

For example, Figure 20.9 shows a worksheet with a series of cash flows (B4:G4) and the dates on which they occur (B5:G5). Assuming a 10% discount rate (B7), the XNPV() function returns a value of $845, using the following formula (B8):

```
=XNPV(B7, B4:G5, B5:G5)
```

> **NOTE**
> Note that the XNPV() function doesn't have the missing-first-period quirk of the NPV() function. Therefore, you can use XNPV() straight up without adding a first-period factor.

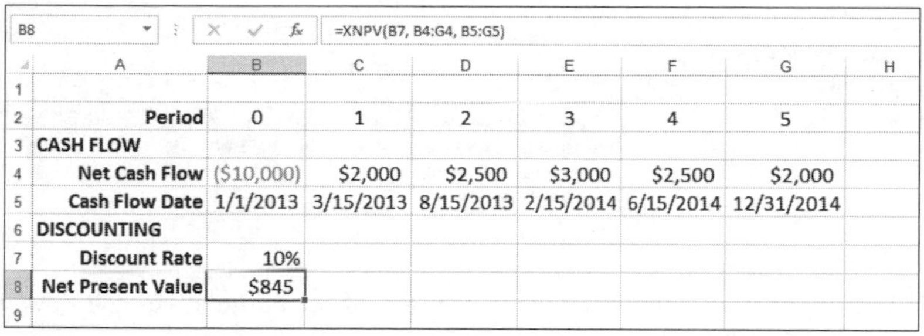

Figure 20.9
Use the XNPV () function to calculate the net present value for a series of nonperiodic cash flows.

	A	B	C	D	E	F	G	H
		B8		fx	=XNPV(B7, B4:G4, B5:G5)			
1								
2	Period	0	1	2	3	4	5	
3	CASH FLOW							
4	Net Cash Flow	($10,000)	$2,000	$2,500	$3,000	$2,500	$2,000	
5	Cash Flow Date	1/1/2013	3/15/2013	8/15/2013	2/15/2014	6/15/2014	12/31/2014	
6	DISCOUNTING							
7	Discount Rate	10%						
8	Net Present Value	$845						
9								

Calculating the Payback Period

If you purchase a store, a piece of equipment, or an investment, your hope always is to at least recoup your initial outlay through the positive cash flows generated by the asset. The point at which you recoup the initial outlay is called the *payback period*. When analyzing a business case, one of the most common concerns is when the payback period occurs: A short payback period is better than a long one.

Simple Undiscounted Payback Period

Finding the undiscounted payback period is a matter of calculating the cumulative cash flows and watching when they turn from negative to positive. The period that shows the first positive cumulative cash flow is the payback period.

For example, suppose you purchase a store for $500,000 and project the following cash flows:

Year	Net Cash Flow	Cumulative Net Cash Flow
0	–$500,000	–$500,000
1	$55,000	–$445,000
2	$75,000	–$370,000
3	$80,000	–$290,000
4	$95,000	–$195,000
5	$105,000	–$90,000
6	$120,000	$30,000

As you can see, the cumulative cash flow turns positive in year 6, so that's the payback period.

Instead of simply eyeballing the payback period, you can use a formula to calculate it. Figure 20.10 shows a worksheet that lists the cash flows and uses the following array formula to calculate the payback period (see cell B5):

```
{=SUM(IF(SIGN(C4:I4) <> SIGN(OFFSET(C4:I4, 0, -1)), C1:I1, 0))}
```

20

Figure 20.10
Use a formula to calculate
the payback period.

	A	B	C	D	E	F	G	H
B5		f_x {=SUM(IF(SIGN(C4:I4) <> SIGN(OFFSET(C4:I4,0,-1)), C1:I1, 0))}						
1	Year	0	1	2	3	4	5	6
2	CASH FLOW	Purchase						
3	Net Cash Flow	($500,000)	$55,000	$75,000	$80,000	$95,000	$105,000	$120,000
4	Cumulative Net Cash Flow	($500,000)	($445,000)	($370,000)	($290,000)	($195,000)	($90,000)	$30,000
5	Payback Period	6						
6	Exact Payback Period	5.75						

The payback period occurs when the sign of the cumulative cash flows turns from negative to positive. Therefore, this formula uses IF() to compare each cumulative cash flow (C4:I4; you can ignore the first cash flow for this) with the cumulative cash flow from the previous period, as given by OFFSET(C4:I4, 0, -1). IF() returns 0 for all cases in which the signs are the same, and it returns the year value from row 1 (C1:I1) for the case in which the sign changes. Summing these values returns the year in which the sign changed, which is the payback period.

Exact Undiscounted Payback Point

If the income generated by the asset is always received at the end of the period, your analysis of the payback period is done. However, many assets generate income through-out the period. In this case, the payback period tells you that sometime within the period, the cumulative cash flows reaches 0. It might be useful to calculate exactly when during the period the payback occurs. Assuming that the income is received at regular intervals throughout the period, you can find the exact payback point by comparing how much is required to reach the payback with how much was earned during the payback period.

For example, suppose that the cumulative cash flow value was –$50,000 at the end of the previous period and that the asset generates $100,000 during the payback period. Assuming regular cash flow throughout the period, this means that the first $50,000 brought the cumulative cash flow to 0. Because this is half the amount earned in the payback period, you can say that the exact payback point occurred halfway through the period.

More generally, you can use the following formula to calculate the exact payback point:

```
=Payback Period - Cumulative Cash Flow at Payback / Cash Flow at Payback
```

For example, suppose you know that the store's payback period occurs in year 6, that the cumulative cash flow after year 6 is $30,000, and that the cash flow for year 6 was $120,000. Here's the formula:

```
=6 - 30,000 / 120,000
```

The answer is 5.75, meaning that the exact payback point occurs three-quarters of the way through the sixth year.

To derive this in a worksheet, you first calculate the payback period and then use this num-ber in the INDEX() function to return the values for the payback period's cumulative cash flow and net cash flow. Here's the formula used in Figure 20.11:

```
=B5 - INDEX(B4:H4, B5 + 1) / INDEX(B3:H3, B5 + 1)
```

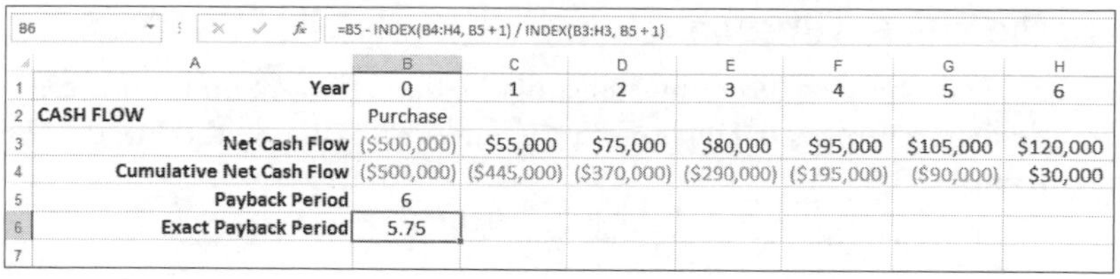

Figure 20.11
Use a formula to calculate
the exact payback point.

Discounted Payback Period

Of course, the undiscounted payback period tells you only so much. To get a true measure of the payback, you need to apply these payback methods to the discounted cash flows. This tells you when the investment is paid back in today's dollars.

To do this, you need to set up a schedule of discounted net cash flow and cumulative cash flow for each period and extend the periods until the cumulative discounted cash flow becomes positive. You can then use the formulas presented in the previous two sections (adjusted for the extra periods) to calculate the payback period and exact payback point (if applicable). Figure 20.12 shows the discounted payback values for the store's cash flows.

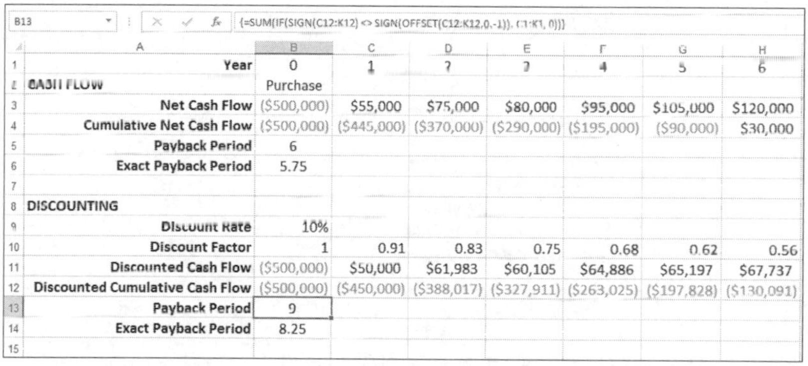

Figure 20.12
To derive the discounted payback values, create a schedule of discounted cash flows, extend the periods until the cumulative discounted cash flow turns positive, and then apply the payback formulas.

Calculating the Internal Rate of Return

In the earlier example with varying cash flows, the discount rate was set to 10% because that was the minimum return required in today's dollars over the first five years after purchasing the equipment. This rate of return of an investment based on today's dollars is called the *internal rate of return*. It's actually defined as the discount rate required to get a net present value of $0.

In the equipment example, using a discount rate of 10% produced a net present value of $881. This is a positive amount, which means that the equipment actually produced an internal rate of return higher than 10%. What, then, was the actual internal rate of return?

Using the IRR() Function

You could figure this out by adjusting the discount rate up (in this case) until the NPV() calculation returns 0. However, Excel offers an easier method in the form of the IRR() function:

```
IRR(values[, guess])
```

values   The cash flows over the term of the asset or investment.

guess   An initial estimate of the internal rate of return. (The default is 0.1.)

> **CAUTION**
>
> The IRR() function's *values* argument must contain at least one positive value and one negative value. If all the values have the same sign, the function returns the #NUM! error.

Figure 20.13 shows the cash flows generated by the equipment purchase and the resulting internal rate of return (cell B7) calculated by the IRR() function:

```
=IRR(B3:G3)
```

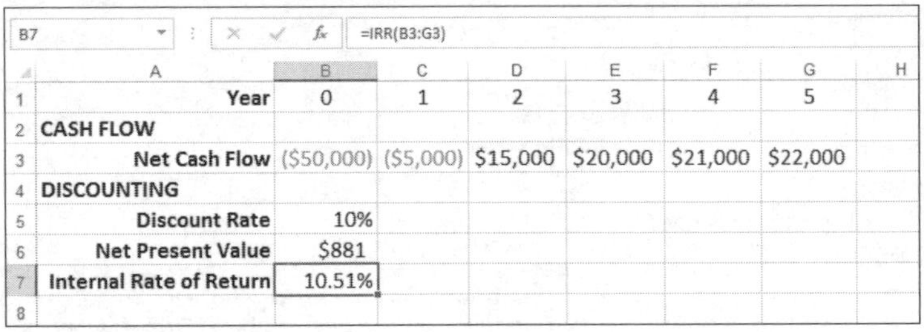

Figure 20.13
Use the IRR() function to calculate the internal rate of return for a series of periodic cash flows.

	A	B	C	D	E	F	G	H
1	Year	0	1	2	3	4	5	
2	CASH FLOW							
3	Net Cash Flow	($50,000)	($5,000)	$15,000	$20,000	$21,000	$22,000	
4	DISCOUNTING							
5	Discount Rate	10%						
6	Net Present Value	$881						
7	Internal Rate of Return	10.51%						
8								

The calculated value of 10.51% means that plugging this value into the NPV() function as the discount rate would return a net present value of 0.

> **NOTE** The IRR() function uses iteration to find a solution that is accurate to within 0.00001%. If it can't find a solution within 20 iterations, it returns the #NUM! error. If this happens, try using a different value for the guess argument.

Calculating the Internal Rate of Return for Nonperiodic Cash Flows

As with NPV(), the IRR() function works only with periodic cash flows. If your cash flows are nonperiodic, use the XIRR() function instead:

```
XIRR(values, dates[, guess])
```

values   The cash flows over the term of the asset or investment.

dates   The dates on which each of the cash flows occur. Make sure that the first value in dates is the date of the initial cash flow. All the other dates must be later than this initial date, but they can be listed in any order.

guess   An initial estimate of the internal rate of return. (The default is 0.1.)

Figure 20.14 shows a worksheet with nonperiodic cash flows and the resulting internal rate of return (cell B8) calculated using the XIRR() function:

```
=XIRR(B3:G3, B4:G4)
```

Figure 20.14
Use the XIRR() function to calculate the internal rate of return for a series of nonperiodic cash flows.

	A	B	C	D	E	F	G
1	Period	0	1	2	3	4	5
2	CASH FLOW						
3	Net Cash Flow	($10,000)	$2,000	$2,500	$3,000	$2,500	$2,000
4	Cash Flow Date	1/1/2016	3/15/2016	8/15/2016	2/15/2017	6/15/2017	12/31/2017
5	DISCOUNTING						
6	Discount Rate	10%					
7	Net Present Value	$842					
8	Internal Rate of Return	18.93%					
9							

B8 fx =XIRR(B3:G3, B4:G4)

Calculating Multiple Internal Rates of Return

Rarely does a business pay cash for major capital investments. Instead, some or all of the purchase price is usually borrowed from the bank. When calculating the internal rate of return, two assumptions are made:

- The discount for negative cash flows is money paid to the bank to service borrowed money.
- The discount for positive cash flows is money reinvested.

However, a third assumption also is at work when you use the IRR() function: The finance rate for negative cash flows and the reinvestment rate for positive cash flows are the same. In the real world, this is rarely true: Most banks charge interest for a loan that is 2 to 4 points higher than what you can usually get for an investment.

To handle the difference between the finance rate and the reinvestment rate, Excel enables you to calculate the *modified internal rate of return* using the MIRR() function:

```
MIRR(values, finance_rate, reinvest_rate)
```

values   The cash flows over the term of the asset or investment

finance_rate   The interest rate you pay for negative cash flows

reinvest_rate   The interest rate you get for positive cash flows that are reinvested

20

For example, suppose you're charged 8% for loans, and you can get 6% for investments. Figure 20.15 shows a worksheet that calculates the modified internal rate of return based on the cash flows in B3:G3 and these rates:

```
=MIRR(B3:G3, B5, B6)
```

Figure 20.15
Use the `MIRR()` function to calculate the modified internal rate of return when you're charged one rate for negative cash flows and a different rate for positive cash flows.

B7 =MIRR(B3:G3, B5, B6)

	A	B	C	D	E	F	G	H
1	Year	0	1	2	3	4	5	
2	CASH FLOW							
3	Net Cash Flow	($50,000)	($5,000)	$15,000	$20,000	$21,000	$22,000	
4	DISCOUNTING							
5	Finance Rate	8%						
6	Reinvestment Rate	6%						
7	Internal Rate of Return	9.14%						
8								

Case Study: Publishing a Book

Let's put some of this cash-flow analysis to work in an example that, although still simplified, is more realistically detailed than the ones you've seen so far in this chapter. Specifically, this case study looks at the business case of publishing a book, taking into account the costs involved (both up front and ongoing) and the positive cash flow generated by the book. The cash-flow analysis will calculate the book's payback period (undiscounted and discounted), as well as the yearly values for the net present value and the internal rate of return.

Per-Unit Constants

In publishing, many of the calculations involving both operating costs and sales are performed using per-unit (that is, per-book) constants. This case study uses the following six constants, as shown in Figure 20.16:

- **List Price**—The suggested retail price of the book
- **Average Customer Discount**—The amount taken off the retail price when selling the book to bookstores
- **PP&B**—The per-unit costs for paper, printing, and binding
- **Cost of Sales**—The per-unit costs of selling the book, including commissions, distribution, and so on
- **Author Royalty**—The percentage of the list price that the author receives
- **Margin**—The per-unit margin, which is the list price minus the customer discount, PP&B, cost of sales, and author royalty, divided by the list price

Figure 20.16
The per-unit constants used in the operating cost and sales calculations.

B7 =(B2 * (1 - B3) - B4 - B5 - (B2 * B6)) / B2

	A	B	C	D
1	PER-UNIT CONSTANTS			
2	List Price	$24.95		
3	Average Customer Discount	45%		
4	PP&B	$5.00		
5	Cost of Sales	$3.75		
6	Author Royalty	7.5%		
7	Margin	12.4%		
8				

Operating Costs and Sales

Figure 20.17 shows the annual operating costs and sales for the book over 10 years. For the references to cells B2 through B7 in the following list of costs and sales, see Figure 20.16:

- **Units Printed**—The number of books printed during the year.
- **Units Sold**—The number of units sold during the year.
- **New Title Costs**—Costs associated with producing the book, including acquiring, editing, indexing, and so on.
- **Total PP&B**—The total paper, printing, and binding costs during the year. This is the year's Units Printed value (from row 10) multiplied by the PP&B value (B4).
- **Marketing**—The marketing and publicity costs during the year.
- **Total Cost of Sales**—The total cost of sales during the year. This is the year's Units Sold value (from row 11) multiplied by the Cost of Sales value (B5).
- **Author Advance**—The advance on royalties paid to the author. The assumption is that this value is paid at the beginning of the project, so it's placed in year 0.
- **Author Royalties**—The royalties paid to the author during the year. This is generally the year's Units Sold value (from row 11) multiplied by the List Price (B2) and the Author Royalty (B6). However, the formula also takes into account the Author Advance, and it doesn't pay royalties until the advance has earned out.
- **$ Sales**—The total sales, in dollars, during the year. This is the year's Unit Sold value (from row 11) multiplied by the List Price (B2) minus the Average Customer Discount (B3).
- **Translation Rights**—Payments for translation rights sold during the year.
- **Book Club Rights**—Payments for book club rights sold during the year.

Cash Flow

With the operating costs and sales available, you can calculate the net cash flow for each year by subtracting the sum of the operating costs from the sum of the sales. Figure 20.18 shows the book's net cash flows in row 27, as well as its cumulative net cash flows (row 28). You also get the discounted net and cumulative cash flows using a discount rate of 12.4%. This is the same as the per-unit Margin value (B7 from Figure 20.16), and it is the target rate of return for the book.

Figure 20.17
The operating costs and sales for each year.

		C15	▼ : × ✓ ƒx	=C10 * $B$4					
	A	B	C	D	E	F	G	H	I	J
9	Year	0	1	2	3	4	5	6	7	8
10	Units Printed	0	50,000	0	0	0	0	0	0	
11	Units Sold	0	17,000	10,500	4,000	3,500	3,000	2,500	2,000	1,
12										
13	OPERATING COSTS									
14	New Title Costs	$0	$2,500	$0	$0	$0	$0	$0	$0	
15	Total PP&B	0	$250,000	$0	$0	$0	$0	$0	$0	
16	Marketing	0	$15,000	$5,000	$2,000	$2,000	$1,000	$1,000	$1,000	$1,
17	Total Cost of Sales	$0	$63,750	$39,375	$15,000	$13,125	$11,250	$9,375	$7,500	$5,
18	Author Advance	$25,000	$0	$0	$0	$0	$0	$0	$0	
19	Author Royalties	$0	$6,811	$19,648	$7,485	$6,549	$5,614	$4,678	$3,743	$2,
20										
21	SALES									
22	$ Sales	$0	$233,283	$144,086	$54,890	$48,029	$41,168	$34,306	$27,445	$20,
23	Translation Rights	$0	$5,000	$0	$0	$2,500	$0	$0	$0	
24	Book Club Rights	$0	$0	$1,000	$0	$0	$0	$1,000	$0	
25										
26	CASH FLOW									
27	Net	($25,000)	($99,779)	$81,063	$30,405	$28,854	$23,304	$20,253	$15,203	$11,
28	Cumulative	($25,000)	($124,779)	($43,716)	($13,311)	$15,544	$38,848	$59,101	$74,303	$85,

Figure 20.18
The yearly net and cumulative cash flows and their discounted versions.

		B27	▼ : × ✓ ƒx	=SUM(B22:B24) - SUM(B14:B19)					
	A	B	C	D	E	F	G	H	I	J
13	OPERATING COSTS									
14	New Title Costs	$0	$2,500	$0	$0	$0	$0	$0	$0	
15	Total PP&B	0	$250,000	$0	$0	$0	$0	$0	$0	
16	Marketing	0	$15,000	$5,000	$2,000	$2,000	$1,000	$1,000	$1,000	$1,
17	Total Cost of Sales	$0	$63,750	$39,375	$15,000	$13,125	$11,250	$9,375	$7,500	$5,
18	Author Advance	$25,000	$0	$0	$0	$0	$0	$0	$0	
19	Author Royalties	$0	$6,811	$19,648	$7,485	$6,549	$5,614	$4,678	$3,743	$2,
20										
21	SALES									
22	$ Sales	$0	$233,283	$144,086	$54,890	$48,029	$41,168	$34,306	$27,445	$20,
23	Translation Rights	$0	$5,000	$0	$0	$2,500	$0	$0	$0	
24	Book Club Rights	$0	$0	$1,000	$0	$0	$0	$1,000	$0	
25										
26	CASH FLOW									
27	Net	($25,000)	($99,779)	$81,063	$30,405	$28,854	$23,304	$20,253	$15,203	$11,
28	Cumulative	($25,000)	($124,779)	($43,716)	($13,311)	$15,544	$38,848	$59,101	$74,303	$85,
29	Discount Rate	12.4%								
30	Discount Factor	1.00	0.89	0.79	0.70	0.63	0.56	0.50	0.44	
31	Discounted Net	($25,000)	($88,748)	$64,130	$21,394	$18,059	$12,972	$10,028	$6,695	$4,
32	Discounted Cumulative	($25,000)	($113,748)	($49,618)	($28,223)	($10,165)	$2,808	$12,835	$19,530	$23,

Cash-Flow Analysis

Finally, you're ready to analyze the cash flow, as shown in Figure 20.19. There are six values:

- **Undiscounted Payback Period**—The year in which the book's undiscounted cumulative cash flows turn positive.

- **Undiscounted Payback Point**—The exact point in the payback period at which the book's undiscounted cumulative cash flows turn positive.

- **Discounted Payback Period**—The year in which the book's discounted cumulative cash flows turn positive.

- **Discounted Payback Point**—The exact point in the payback period at which the book's discounted cumulative cash flows turn positive.

- **Net Present Value**—The net present value calculation at the end of each year, as returned by the NPV() function (with the fudge factor added, as explained earlier; see "Calculating Net Present Value Using NPV()").

- **Internal Rate of Return**—The internal rate of return calculation at the end of each year, as returned by the IRR() function. Note that we don't start this calculation until year 2 because in year 1 there are nothing but negative cash flows.

Figure 20.19
The cash-flow analysis for the book example.

Formula bar: G39 =NPV($B$29, $B$27:G27) * (1 + $B$29)

	A	B	C	D	E	F	G	H	I	J
26	CASH FLOW									
27	Net	($25,000)	($99,779)	$81,063	$30,405	$28,854	$23,304	$20,253	$15,203	$11,
28	Cumulative	($25,000)	($124,779)	($43,716)	($13,311)	$15,544	$38,848	$59,101	$74,303	$85,
29	Discount Rate	12.4%								
30	Discount Factor	1.00	0.89	0.79	0.70	0.63	0.56	0.50	0.44	
31	Discounted Net	($25,000)	($88,748)	$64,130	$21,394	$18,059	$12,972	$10,028	$6,695	$4,
32	Discounted Cumulative	($25,000)	($113,748)	($49,618)	($28,223)	($10,165)	$2,808	$12,835	$19,530	$23,
33										
34	CASH FLOW ANALYSIS									
35	Undiscounted Payback Period	4								
36	Undiscounted Payback Point	3.5								
37	Discounted Payback Period	5								
38	Discounted Payback Point	4.8								
39	Net Present Value		($113,748)	($49,618)	($28,223)	($10,165)	$2,808	$12,835	$19,530	$23,
40	Internal Rate of Return			-30.77%	-7.36%	6.69%	13.78%	17.87%	20.02%	21.
41										

> **NOTE**
> To get the internal rate of return for year 2 (cell D40), I had to use -0.1 as the *guess* argument for the IRR() function:
>
> ```
> =IRR($B$27:D27, -0.1)
> ```
>
> Without this initial estimate, Excel can't complete the iteration, and it returns the #NUM! error.

From Here

- The IRR() and MIRR() functions use iteration to calculate results. To learn more about iteration, **see** "Using Iteration and Circular References," **p. 93**.

- To get the details on the time value of money, **see** "Understanding the Time Value of Money," **p. 433**.

- To use the PV() function in a loan context, **see** "Calculating How Much You Can Borrow," **p. 446**.

- To use the PV() function in an investment context, **see** "Calculating the Required Initial Deposit," **p. 461**.

- For the details on compound interest, **see** "Understanding Compound Interest," **p. 454**.

20

Index

Symbols & Numerics

A

M

N

Q

R

T